MONASTIC ESTATES IN LATE ANTIQUE AND EARLY ISLAMIC EGYPT

OSTRACA, PAPYRI, AND ESSAYS IN MEMORY OF SARAH CLACKSON

Sarah Clackson (1965-2003)

AMERICAN STUDIES IN PAPYROLOGY

Series Editor
Ann Ellis Hanson

VOLUME 46
MONASTIC ESTATES IN LATE ANTIQUE AND EARLY ISLAMIC EGYPT
OSTRACA, PAPYRI, AND ESSAYS IN MEMORY OF SARAH CLACKSON
(*P.Clackson*)

EDITED BY
ANNE BOUD'HORS, JAMES CLACKSON, CATHERINE LOUIS, AND PETRA SIJPESTEIJN

Monastic Estates in Late Antique and Early Islamic Egypt

Ostraca, Papyri, and Essays in Memory of
Sarah Clackson

(*P. Clackson*)

edited by

Anne Boud'hors, James Clackson, Catherine Louis,
and Petra Sijpesteijn

The American Society of Papyrologists
Cincinnati, Ohio

Monastic Estates in Late Antique and Early Islamic Egypt.
Ostraca, Papyri, and Essays in Memory of Sarah Clackson (*P.Clackson*)

Anne Boud'hors, James Clackson, Catherine Louis, and Petra Sijpesteijn

Library of Congress Cataloging-in-Publication Data

Monastic estates in late antique and early Islamic Egypt : ostraca, papyri, and studies in honour of Sarah Clackson / edited by Anne Boud'hors ...[et al.].
    p. cm. -- (American studies in papyrology ; v. 46)
 Includes bibliographical references and index.
 ISBN-13: 978-0-9700591-8-5 (alk. paper)
 ISBN-10: 0-9700591-8-3 (alk. paper)
 1. Coptic philology. 2. Ostraka--Egypt. 3. Coptic language--Papyri. I. Clackson, S. (Sarah) II. Bouvarel-Boud'hors, Anne.
 PJ2017.C58M66 2008
 493'.2--dc22

                         2008037186

Copyright © 2009 The American Society of Papyrologists

ISBN 10 0-9700591-8-3
ISBN 13 978-0-9700591-8-5

Contents

Editors' Preface	ix
Sarah Clackson and Coptic Papyrology—R.S. Bagnall	xi
Bibliography of Sarah Clackson	xv
Note on Editorial Procedure	xix
Table of Ostraca, Papyri, and Essays	xx
List of Plates	xxii
Ostraca (*O.Clackson* **1-34**)	1
Papyri (*P.Clackson* **35-50**)	52
Essays	129
Indices	245
Plates	251

PREFACE

During the last months of her life, Sarah commented several times on her remarkable luck in having been able to spend her working time doing what she liked doing best: reconstructing monastic archives and editing papyri. As yet another proof of her commitment to her research and the seriousness of purpose with which she approached her field, she had expressed the wish that a conference be organised in her memory at Oxford dedicated to the topic of her research. In her short but intensive career, Sarah had built up an extensive international scholarly network, and scholars from all over the world, many of them friends as well as Sarah's colleagues, came to Christ Church, Oxford, in September 2004 to participate in a two-day symposium entitled "The Administration of Monastic Estates in Late Antique and Early Islamic Egypt."

That this conference was possible we owe to the financial support and involvement of several individuals and institutions, and we thank them warmly for the conference's success. Christ Church was a most agreeable host and we would like to thank Dirk Obbink for facilitating the arrangements with the college. Without the generous funding of the British Academy, the Oriental Institute at Oxford, Christ's College Cambridge and the Griffith Institute, we would not have been able to sponsor the presence of so many eminent scholars from around the world. We are also very grateful for the moral support and kind help of Dorothy Thompson and John Baines.

This volume collects the papers presented at Sarah's conference with five additional ones: *O.Clackson* **34** (Terry Wilfong), *P.Clackson* **36-43** (Alain Delattre and Nikolaos Gonis), *P.Clackson* **46** (Nikolaos Gonis) and the essay by Martin Krause. The publication of the proceedings was made possible by generous support from the Sarah J. Clackson Coptic Fund, the Cambridge University Classics Faculty, and Christ's College, Cambridge. Catherine Louis did an enormous job of copy-editing the papers, and her many important corrections while doing so are much appreciated. We should also like to thank Alexander Schubert for his help in preparing the manuscript. We thank the anonymous readers who took the time to read the volume carefully and suggested many useful corrections and additions. The series editor, Ann Hanson, should also be mentioned.

Most of all, however, we would like to thank the presenters and participants at the conference who together provided the spirited academic discussion and congenial atmosphere that showed how valuable and alive Sarah's work continues to be. Sarah would have been proud.

13 April 2007   The Editors

Sarah donated her papers to the Griffith Institute in the University of Oxford, and a fund was established in her memory to support research in the fields to which these materials relate http://www.orinst.ox.ac.uk/general/grants.shtml#sccf. The fund provides travel and research grants to anyone undertaking work on Coptic manuscripts, especially those for which there is documentation in the Clackson bequest, including the viewing, preparation, and recording of material, but excluding conservation.

Donations to the fund should be sent to the Administrator, Oriental Institute, Pusey Lane, Oxford OX1 2LE, UK.

Sarah Clackson and Coptic Papyrology

Roger S. Bagnall

It is customary nowadays for events held in memory of an individual, whether a simple service, an elaborate set of recollections, or an entire conference, to be described as celebrations. It is generally hard to quarrel with the justice of the sentiment underlying this characterization without seeming churlish, because these occasions are opportunities to remember the gifts the person brought to life and work and to express our thankfulness that in some measure, large or small, we as individuals and as communities benefited from these gifts.

At the same time, however, it must be said that celebrations require a cheerfulness not easy to summon on demand in the face of great loss. We seem at times to be in danger of losing the ability to acknowledge grief and to mourn our losses—to absorb properly and in just measure what Roger Angell called "this accompanying trickle of rotten news" that goes along with even the most privileged and fortunate of lives. In the following remarks, I shall try to balance celebration and grief in offering a few words about Sarah Clackson as a figure in the history of Coptic papyrology. Our loss in the truncation of her passionate and brilliant scholarly career is very great, and it is essential in coming to terms with the magnitude of that loss that we see just how great it is.

As I began thinking about how to sketch the place that I see Sarah occupying in that history of scholarship, I had a moment of simultaneous panic and elation when the last volume of *BASP* (40 [2003]) arrived, bearing Terry Wilfong's eloquent evocation (pp. 7-10) of Sarah and her scholarship. Here my work was done for me—he says beautifully many things I had been thinking—but I could hardly just plagiarize it. I shall in fact quote from it here and there. But I shall begin with a bit of faintly quantitative reflection, perhaps a peculiarly personal form of comfort-seeking, one taking its starting-point from something Sarah contributed to the *Checklist of Editions*, the year-by-year list of editions of Coptic papyri and ostraka.

If one leaves out of account the volumes in which there are only a few Coptic documents annexed to a mass of something else, along with pure catalogues of literary manuscripts, the forty years before the publication of Sarah's volume of papyri from the Hermopolite monastery of Apollo saw exactly four volumes of Coptic papyri, along with seven of ostraka (some of them not very substantial).[1] Of the papyri, one is the slender volume of Florence texts published by Michael Browne, whose death last month was an unhappy loss to my generation of papyrologists, and another is the barely commented booklet of Yale papyri given in preliminary editions by Leslie MacCoull. In 2000, it had been 13 years since *CPR* XII and a third of a century since *BKU* III, the only volumes of Coptic papyri even remotely comparable to *P.Mon.Apollo*. That is a sobering thought.

The previous forty-year period was a bit richer. It was an era that knew Crum, Jernstedt, Kahle, Schiller, Till and Worrell. Even so, that period saw only five volumes of Coptic papyri and three of mixed papyri and ostraka, plus a few volumes of ostraka alone: about one for each undergraduate

---

[1] The ostraca are *O.Vind.Copt.*, *O.Mon.Phoib.*, *O.Deir el-Bahari* (just 19 texts), *O.Bawit*, *CPR* XX, *O.Ashm.Copt.*, *O.Brit.Mus.Copt.* II.

cohort or American presidential term.[2] And again, probably only one of the editions of papyri is of a scale and density comparable to *P.Mon.Apollo*. Editors of Coptic papyri have always been few, and Sarah filled a vast gap in our studies. Indeed, it is somewhat shocking to realize that, apart from the incomparable Crum, no editor of Coptic papyri in the last three-quarters of a century left a legacy of published documentary papyri larger than hers, when one takes into account the second volume that is still to come. Terry Wilfong's notice summons up Paul Kahle, Jr., as a comparable figure: in his words, "a brilliant Coptic papyrologist who was also a Lady Wallis Budge Fellow, author of a major monograph (a collection of texts from a single site that also addressed subjects of wider significance) and a series of important articles, a scholar whose untimely death was a severe loss to Coptic studies." That seems just right; it is in fact Balaizah that of the volumes of Coptic papyri published in the 80-year period I have surveyed is the most similar in all respects to *P.Mon.Apollo*.

What struck me from the very beginning of our acquaintance, however, was not simply scholarly productivity but Sarah's strong bent for mainstreaming Coptic papyrology, a field that even in some of its greatest practitioners—like Crum—remained stuck in editorial and presentational methods of a bygone era. Terry has spoken of "her intense desire to bring to Coptic papyrology the methods, principles and organization found in Greek papyrology, and indeed to help unite the various language-differentiated branches of papyrology into a unified scholarly endeavor." That is an accurate and insightful assessment. But there is room to be more specific. Many editions of Coptic papyri have been unrewarding reading for someone used to Greek papyrology, because they often lacked things that Hellenists take for granted—translations, for example, or dates, or line notes, or introductions, or all of these. These absences are not universal, and I think it is important to point to those who adopted more comprehensive approaches—Jernstedt, for example, although the use of Russian in his editions does not make them more accessible for most of us, Kahle himself, Michael Browne—a documentarist wishes he had edited more Coptic documents—, and Monika Hasitzka. But the deficiencies were widespread, and I think we may fairly judge that the extremely small population of the field contributed to preventing the development of a disciplinary consensus of the sort that Greek papyrology had developed for the most part by the time of the first world war. This is a point to which I shall return later.

Before leaving editorial practice, however, we must recognize that the achievement of *P.Mon.Apollo* is not only to provide a proper edition of the texts themselves with all of the presentational elements that a first-rate edition should have, but to historicize the texts. Here, again, the example of Kahle is important. And here we see how Sarah did not simply pick up standard practices from the edition of Greek papyri, but best practice. Even now, after all, the editors of many volumes of Greek papyri, even when their contents form some kind of unity, do little to tie the material together and exploit its contribution to understanding the society of ancient Egypt and of the Mediterranean world. But of course many of the best have done so, going back to magisterial examples like Wilcken's *Urkunden der Ptolemäerzeit*. It was this inspiring vision of what documents could be used for that Sarah adopted at an early stage of her work. It is worth adding, in passing, that although proper commentary on texts requires space, it also requires discipline, focus, and selection and is not to be

---

[2] Papyri: *P.HermitageCopt.*, *P.MoscowCopt.*, *CPR* IV, *P.Bal.*, *P.CLT*. Papyri and ostraca: *P.Sarga*, *P.Mon.Epiph.*, *P.Mich.Copt.* Ostraka: *O.CrumST*, *O.CrumVC*, *O.Medin.HabuCopt.*

confused with dumping onto paper everything one knows. The professionalism and maturity that Sarah's editorial work displayed from an early stage was essential to its character.

Closely and necessarily linked to this historical approach was the integration of scholarly work across the lines of language-based disciplinary boundaries. No one would claim novelty for stating the desirability of such a method, I think; it has been a staple of thinking about Hellenistic history and documents, for example, for a couple of generations now, and the more integrative approach to late antiquity prevalent in the last three decades has also favored such attitudes. But it is, as we all know, easier to praise integration than to practice it, and practice has tended to lag advice by about a generation. The ambivalence toward Greek displayed by Crum's *Coptic Dictionary* is perhaps emblematic of the historic state of affairs in the field of Coptic studies, even though Crum himself knew the relevant Greek papyri well. But is still worth saying that Sarah embodied to an unusual degree, at an operational level, the conviction that our Greek, Coptic, and eventually Arabic papyri are all the products of a single society, one that we can understand only by seeing it as the complex and multilingual matrix that it was. Her frame of reference, in a collegial sense as well as a documentary one, was broad.

It was also systematizing and pedagogical. This is another area in which time would have allowed her to do much more. Most of us, I imagine, know about her plan for a Coptic papyrological primer. She was keen on the development of databases, both of metadata and of text, again to help make Coptic papyrology a more normal field, one with the underpinnings that allow both research and teaching. Even after she knew that her chances of a normal life-span were no better than even, she kept her focus on the long-term development of her field. Her last project proposal, for the Humboldt-Stiftung, was for a Hermopolite database. The conceptualization of that database was, as always with Sarah's projects, based on a collegial view of the field, one in which one took account of what other people were doing and collaborated wherever possible. Her work on the *Checklist* was only the most fully realized of these cooperative ventures.

In pursuit of understanding, in search of documents, and in the development of collegial projects, Sarah traveled a great deal. Some of her visits to collections were focused on particular bodies of material she was seeking, especially connected with Apa Apollo. But one had the feeling that such aims were really as much justifications for travel grant requests as her actual motives. What she was really in search of was a comprehensive understanding of every possible collection containing Coptic papyri, to see how it had been formed and what its sources were. This museum papyrology, as I would call it, as a subset of the museum archaeology of which Terry speaks, was informed by the wider tendencies in archaeological circles today to try to reconstruct material assemblages scattered through museums and to resurrect material once excavated and buried in museum storerooms rather than being fully published. But her museum papyrology had a distinctive flavor related to the vagaries of the papyrological marketplace. It is, once again, Kahle and Crum of whom one is reminded in this aspect of Sarah's work. This, to my mind, is one of the greatest of our losses in her early departure from our midst. We might have had from her a proper reconstruction of the archaeology and history of the finds of Coptic papyri and ostraka, something that would have contributed enormously to our understanding of the social place of Coptic writing and reading and thus to the culture of the late antique society of Egypt. This remains a great desideratum. And even more broadly, I think that all of the pieces in the giant jigsaw puzzle would eventually have been put into their proper place, as far as it is humanly possible to do so. That could have come only at a late stage of this long-term task of seeing everything that there is to see. If we admire the reconstructive efforts Sarah carried out in her lifetime, we can only imagine what these long-term results might have been like. Last March, when in a storage area on the stairs leading up from the second floor of the Egyptian Museum in Cairo I found three wooden crates full of Coptic ostraka, returned a few months before the 1952 revolution by the Oriental Institute of Chicago and the Metropolitan Museum and untouched since, coming from the excavations at Medinet Habu and Deir el-Bahri respectively, it was no longer possible to have that information wind up in the hands I would have wished.

Terry, like all of us who encountered Sarah in the course of these travels, remembers the side of them that was not purely professional and the joy with which she explored the larger world. That is not at first sight part of my topic in these remarks. But in another way it was, because it was a form of community-building. I mentioned earlier my sense that Coptic documentary papyrology was on the whole a fairly lonely way of life in earlier generations, and perhaps even quite recently. There were few colleagues doing the same sort of work, and although of course all Coptic papyrologists read the publications of the others, it is often hard to find a sense that they cohered in any meaningful way. These scholars give the impression of doing things their own way and in a context formed by something other than the Coptic papyrologists of their day. Arthur Schiller, for example, although he knew the other Copticists of his period, was far more importantly shaped by Romanists, and his community of methods was with them, not with others who edited Coptic documents.

This state of affairs has not yet completely passed away. But it is on its way out. Our presence here at this conference in Sarah's memory is a testimony to the creation of a kind of community. This side of professional life is most commonly called "networking" today, and Sarah was a champion networker. But the term is too narrow to do her justice, because it tends to suggest a selfish professionalism aimed at enhancing one's own position. That is not what I am talking about. Sarah was much more community-oriented than that, and I think that community-building is a much more apt description of her activity. She was, I think, fortunate in her timing in this respect, particularly in the sense that many of those present here at this gathering have made their own contributions toward starting to shape Coptic papyrology into a coherent field, too. Sarah was only at the beginning of her work in helping to form this field and this community, and one can only imagine what several more decades might have meant for them. But the relative youth of this gathering gives me hope that Sarah's work will be carried on by others and that Coptic papyrology will become the field she sought to make it.

BIBLIOGRAPHY OF SARAH CLACKSON

BOOKS

1) *The Elephantine Papyri in English. Three Millennia of Cross-Cultural Continuity and Change* (= *Documenta et Monumenta Orientis Antiqui* 22). E. J. Brill, Leiden 1996 (with B. Porten, J. J. Farber, G. Vittmann, L. S. B. MacCoull, and contributions by S. Hopkins and R. Katzoff).

2) *Dictionary of Manichaean Texts.* Vol. 1. *Texts from the Roman Empire* (*Texts in Syriac, Greek, Coptic and Latin*) (= *Corpus Fontium Manichaeorum: Subsidia* II). Brepols, Turnhout 1998 (with E. Hunter and S. N. C. Lieu, in association with M. Vermes).

3) *Coptic and Greek Texts Relating to the Hermopolite Monastery of Apa Apollo* (= *Griffith Institute Monographs*), Oxford 2000.

4) *Checklist of Editions of Greek, Latin, Demotic and Coptic Papyri, Ostraca and Tablets.* 5th ed. (= *Bulletin of the American Society of Papyrologists, Supplement* 9). 2001 (with J. F. Oates, R. S. Bagnall, A. A. O'Brien, J. D. Sosin, T. G. Wilfong, K. A. Worp).

5) *It is Our Father Who Writes: Orders from the Monastery of Apollo at Bawit* (= *American Studies in Papyrology* 43). Oxford: Oxbow 2008.

ARTICLES AND CONTRIBUTIONS

1) (as Sarah J. Quinn) "A New Kingdom Stela in Girton College Showing Amenophis I Wearing the *hprs*," *Journal of Egyptian Archaeology* 77 (1991), pp. 169-175.

2) "The Michaelides Coptic Manuscript Collection in the Cambridge University Library and British Library," in D. W. Johnson, ed., *Acts of the Fifth International Congress of Coptic Studies, Washington, 12-15 August 1992.* Rome 1993. Vol. II, pp. 123-138.

3) "Jonathan Byrd 36.2: Another ⲡⲉⲛⲉⲓⲱⲧ ⲡⲉⲧⲥϩⲁⲓ Text," *Bulletin of the American Society of Papyrologists* 30 (1993), pp. 67-68.

4) "The Michaelides Manuscript Collection," *Zeitschrift für Papyrologie und Epigraphik* 100 (1994), pp. 223-226.

5) "Four Coptic Papyri from the Patermouthis Archive in the British Library," *Bulletin of the American Society of Papyrologists* 32 (1995), pp. 97-116.

6) Contribution to I. Gardner, ed., *Kellis Literary Texts.* Vol. I (= *Dakhleh Oasis Project* 4; *Oxbow Monograph* 69). Oxford 1996.

7) "An Unedited Coptic Leaf of *Genesis* in Cambridge University Library (P.Camb. UL Or. 1699 Π i)," *Bulletin of the American Society of Papyrologists* 35 (1998), pp. 135-144.

8) "Something Fishy in *CPR* XX," *Archiv für Papyrusforschung* 45 (1999), pp. 94-95.

9) "Ostraca and Graffiti Excavated at el-Amarna," in S. Emmel *et al.*, eds., *Akten des 6. Internationalen Koptologenkongresses, Münster, 20.-26. Juli 1996* (= *Sprachen und Kulturen des christlichen Orients, Coptic Series*, 2). Wiesbaden 1999. Vol. II, pp. 268-278.

10) "The Papyrus Collections of Cambridge," in W. Clarysse, H. Verreth, eds., *Papyrus Collections Worldwide, 9-10 March 2000 (Brussels/Leuven)*. Koninklijke Vlaamse Academie van België voor Wetenschappen en Kunsten. Brussels 2000, pp. 25-36.

11) "Reconstructing the Archives of the Monastery of Apollo at Bawit," in I. Andorlini, G. Bastianini, M. Manfredi and G. Menci, eds., *Atti del XXII Congresso Internazionale di Papirologia, Firenze, 23-29 agosto 1998*. Florence 2001. Vol. I, pp. 219-236.

12) "Fish and Chits: The *Synodontis schall*," *Zeitschrift für ägyptische Sprache und Altertumskunde* 129 (2002), pp. 6-11.

13) *Korr. Tyche* 484-489: 484. "P.Vindob. G 16802. 2 Lemlakati ('Man from Alexandria')—A New Anthroponym; 485. P.Vindob. K. 11375; 486. *MPER* XVIII 219 = *BKU* 1 57—ἐπι τῷ εροι; 487. *CPR* IV 198; 488. *P.Laur.* V 205, 23—ξυλοκόπιον; 489. *P.Bingen* 150—Another Apollo," *Tyche* 17 (2002), pp. 260-262.

14) "Nouvelles recherches sur les papyrus de Baouit," in C. Cannuyer, ed., *Études coptes VIII: Dixième journée d'études, Lille 14-16 juin 2001* (= *Cahiers de la bibliothèque copte* 13). Lille/Paris 2003, pp. 77-84.

15) "Appendix E: A Coptic Inscription from Sinai Copied by Linant de Bellefonds," *Syria* 80 (2003), p. 103.

16) "12. Mani's Imprisonment and Death," "14. Praise for the Martyred Mani," "15. The Sufferings of Mani Compared to Those of Other True Apostles," "16. The Institution of the *bema*," "19. Persecution of the Manichaean Church," "20. The Prayer and Martyrdom of Sisinnios (Mar Sisin)"; in I. Gardner and S. N. C. Lieu, eds., *Manichaean Texts from the Roman Empire*. Cambridge 2004, pp. 85-88, 89-94, 102-108.

17) "Papyrology and the Utilization of Coptic Sources," in P. M. Sijpesteijn and L. Sundelin, eds., *Papyrology and the History of Early Islamic Egypt*. Leiden/Boston 2004, pp. 21-44.

18) "Museum Archaeology and Coptic Papyrology: The Bawit Papyri," in M. Immerzeel and J. van der Vliet, eds., *Coptic Studies on the Threshold of a New Millennium. Proceedings of the Seventh*

International Congress of Coptic Studies. Leiden, 27 August -2 September 2000 (= *Orientalia Lovaniensia Analecta* 133). Leuven/Paris/Dudley MA 2004, pp. 477-490.

19) "Monasteries of Middle Egypt," in R. S. Bagnall and D. W. Rathbone, eds., *Egypt from Alexander to the Early Christians: An Archaeological and Historical Guide*. London/Los Angeles: The British Museum Press and The J. Paul Getty Museum, 2004, pp. 174-182.

20) "Greek and Coptic Medical Prescriptions from the Michaelides Collection in Cambridge University Library," in H. Harrauer and R. Pintaudi, eds., *Gedenkschrift Ulrike Horak (P.Horak)* (= *Papyrologica Florentina* 34). Florence 2004, Vol. I pp. 73-83.

21) "Coptic and Greek Ostraca from Kom el-Nana," in J. Faiers, *Late Roman Pottery at Amarna and Related Studies* (= *Egypt Exploration Society—Excavation Memoirs* 72). London 2005, pp. 245-262.

22) Translation and Commentary of Catalogue Numbers. 117, 118 and 119 in G. T. Martin, *Stelae from Egypt and Nubia in the Fitzwilliam Museum, Cambridge, c. 3000 BC-AD 1150*. Cambridge 2005, pp. 174-177.

23) "Archimandrites and *andrismos*: a Preliminary Survey of Taxation at Bawit," in B. Palme, ed., *Akten des 23. Internationalen Papyrologenkongresses. Wien 22.-28. Juli 2001* (= *Papyrologica Vindobonensia* 1). Vienna 2007, pp. 103-107.

24) "Coptic Oxyrhynchus," in A. K. Bowman, R. A. Coles, N. Gonis, D. Obbink and P. J. Parsons, eds., *Oxyrhynchus: A City and Its Texts* (= *Egypt Exploration Society—Graeco-Roman Memoirs* 93). London, 2007, pp. 332-341.

REVIEWS

1) K. Schüssler, ed., *Biblia Coptica. Die koptischen Bibeltexte. Bd. 1. Das sahidische Alte und Neue Testament* (Wiesbaden, 1995), *Bulletin of the American Society of Papyrologists* 35 (1998), pp. 229-234.

2) R. Cribiore, *Writing, Teachers, and Students in Graeco-Roman Egypt* (Atlanta, 1996), *Journal of Egyptian Archaeology* 86 (2000), pp. 22-29.

3) C. Cannuyer, *Coptic Egypt: The Christians of the Nile* (New York, 2001), *Egyptian Archaeology* 19 (2001), p. 43.

4) J. Clédat, *Le Monastère et la nécropole de Baouit* (= *MIFAO* 111, Cairo, 1999), *Bulletin of the American Society of Papyrologists* 39 (2002), pp. 189-204.

5) P. Bridel *et al.*, *Explorations aux Qouçour el-Izeila lors des campagnes 1981, 1982, 1984, 1985, 1986, 1989 et 1990.* (= EK 8184, tome III, Leuven, 1999), *Bibliotheca Orientalis* 60, 1/2 (2003), pp. 142-144.

NOTE ON EDITORIAL PROCEDURE

Abbreviations for Greek and Coptic documentary texts edited in monographic volumes are given according to the *Checklist of Editions of Greek, Latin, Demotic and Coptic Papyri, Ostraca and Tablets*, 5th ed., eds. J. F. Oates, R. S. Bagnal, S. J. Clackson, A. A. O'Brien, J. D. Sosin, T. G. Wlfong and K. A. Worp (*BASP Suppl.* 9, 2001). An updated electronic version of the Checklist may be consulted online at: http:scriptorium.lib.duke.edu/papyrus/texts/clist.html.

For Arabic documentary texts, abbreviations have been given according to the *Checklist of Arabic Papyri*, eds. J. F. Oates, P. M. Sijpesteijn and A. Kaplony (*BASP* 42 (2005) 127-166). An online, updated version of the Arabic Checklist can be consulted at: www.ori.uzh.ch/isap/isapchecklist.html.

Journals are abbreviated according to the 'Abréviations des périodiques et collections' published by the Institut français d'archéologie orientale and which can be consulted on the internet at: www.ifao.egnet.net.

Texts in this volume are presented according to the usual papyrological practices. The following signs have their usual senses:

( )	Resolution of abbreviation or symbol
[ ]	Lacuna in the papyrus
< >	Letters omitted by the scribe
´	Letters written, then deleted, by the scribe
{ }	Letters erroneously written by the scribe
$\underset{.}{\alpha}\underset{.}{\beta}\underset{.}{\gamma}$	Letters, the reading of which is uncertain or would be uncertain outside of the context
. . .	Letters of which part or all remain but which have not been read
[± 5]	Approximate number of letters lost in a lacuna and not restored
`αβγ´	Letters inserted by the scribe above the line

TABLE OF OSTRACA, PAPYRI, AND ESSAYS

O. CLACKSON **1-17**   1
Ostraca de Baouît conservés à l'Institut d'égyptologie d'Heidelberg
Anne Boud'hors (CNRS, Paris) and Sarah Clackson

O. CLACKSON **18-33**   23
Les ostraca etmoulon. Quelques aspects du transport du blé dans l'Égypte copte
Alain Delattre (Université Libre de Bruxelles)

O. CLACKSON **34**   49
A New Text from Frange in the Kelsey Museum of Archaeology
Terry G. Wilfong (University of Michigan, Ann Arbor)

P. CLACKSON **35**   52
A Greek-Coptic Glossary from the Beinecke Collection
James Clackson (University of Cambridge) and Sarah Clackson

P. CLACKSON **36-43**   61
Le dossier des reçus de taxe grecs du monastère d'Apa Apollô à Baouît
Alain Delattre and Nikolaos Gonis (University College, London)

P. CLACKSON **44**   72
"Essig und Öl." Heilung von Leib und Seele als Thema eines Briefes
Hans Förster (Österreichische Nationalbibliothek)

P. CLACKSON **45-46**   102
A Mid-Eighth-Century Trilingual Tax Demand Related to the Monastery of Apa Apollo at Bawit
Petra M. Sijpesteijn (CNRS, Paris/University of Leiden) and Sarah Clackson

Appendix
Nikolaos Gonis

P. CLACKSON **47**   122
A Fragment of a Coptic Document from the Monastery of Apa Apollo
Sofia Torallas Tovar (CSIC, Madrid)

P. CLACKSON **48-50**   124
Three Greek Montserrat Texts Related to the Monastery of Apa Apollo
Sofia Torallas Tovar and Klaas A. Worp (University of Leiden)

Essays

Property Ownership and Tax Payment in Fourth-Century Monasticism   129
Malcolm Choat (Macquarie University)

Conversion religieuse dans un graffito de Baouît? Révision de SB III 6042   141
Jean-Luc Fournet (École Pratique des Hautes Études, Paris)

Die anaphorische Interzession für die Verstorbenen nach den frühen   148
Zeugnissen koptischer Liturgie
Jutta Henner (Österreichische Bibelgesellschaft/Universität Wien)

Die koptischen Kaufurkunden von Klosterzellen des Apollo-Klosters von   159
Bawit aus abbasidischer Zeit
Martin Krause (Universität Münster)

The Monastic Rules of Shenoute   170
Bentley Layton (Yale University)

The Church, Clerics, Monks, and Credit in the Papyri   178
Tomasz Markiewicz (University of Warsaw)

The Cultivation of Monastic Estates in Late Antique and Early Islamic   205
Egypt. Some Evidence from Coptic Land Leases and Related Documents
Tonio Sebastian Richter (University of Leipzig)

Das Archiv des Archimandriten Apa Georgios. Texte aus P.Fay.Copt. *und*   216
P.Lond.Copt.
Georg Schmelz (Universität Heidelberg)

P.Oxy. LXIII 4397: *The Monastery Comes First or Pious Reasons before*   225
Earthly Securities
Jakub Urbanik (University of Warsaw)

Monks and Monastic Dwellings: P.Dubl. 32-34, P.KRU 105, *and* BL   236
MS.Or. 6201-6206 *Revisited*
Ewa Wipszycka (University of Warsaw)

LIST OF PLATES

Plate I
- 1 *SBKopt.* I 226 = Ägyptologisches Institut Heidelberg inv. 993
- 2 *SBKopt.* I 234 = Ägyptologisches Institut Heidelberg inv. 998

Plate II
- 3 *SBKopt.* I 233 = Ägyptologisches Institut Heidelberg inv. 994
- 4 *SBKopt.* I 230 = Ägyptologisches Institut Heidelberg inv. 987

Plate III
- 5 *SBKopt.* I 227 = Ägyptologisches Institut Heidelberg inv. 996
- 6 *SBKopt.* I 228 = Ägyptologisches Institut Heidelberg inv. 980

Plate IV
- 7 *SBKopt.* I 229 = Ägyptologisches Institut Heidelberg inv. 979
- 8 *SBKopt.* I 231 = Ägyptologisches Institut Heidelberg inv. 986

Plate V
- 9 *SBKopt.* I 232 = Ägyptologisches Institut Heidelberg inv. 981
- 10 Ägyptologisches Institut Heidelberg inv. 995

Plate VI
- 11 *SB* XVIII 13563 = Ägyptologisches Institut Heidelberg inv. 984
- 12 *SB* XVIII 13564 = Ägyptologisches Institut Heidelberg inv. 992

Plate VII
- 13 Ägyptologisches Institut Heidelberg inv. 988
- 14 Ägyptologisches Institut Heidelberg inv. 991

Plate VIII
- 15 Ägyptologisches Institut Heidelberg inv. 990
- 16 Ägyptologisches Institut Heidelberg inv. 983

Plate IX
- 17 Ägyptologisches Institut Heidelberg inv. 997

Plate X
- 18 O.Brit.Mus. inv. GR 1999.6-29.1, British Museum; photo Charles Ede, Ltd.
- 19 O.Berol. inv. 14705, Ägyptisches Museum u. Papyrussammlung SMB; photo Margarete Büsing

LIST OF PLATES   xxiii

Plate XI
- 25   *SBKopt.* I 151 = Kelsey Mus. inv. 25009, Courtesy of Kelsey Museum of Archaeology
- 26   O.Berol. inv. 14706, Ägyptisches Museum u. Papyrussammlung SMB; photo Margarete Büsing

Plate XII
- 29   *SBKopt.* I 167 = Kelsey Mus. inv. 25028, Courtesy of Kelsey Museum of Archaeology
- 31   O.Berol. inv. 14713, Ägyptisches Museum u. Papyrussammlung SMB; photo Margarete Büsing

Plate XIII
- 32   *SBKopt.* I 185 = Kelsey Mus. inv. 25041, Courtesy of Kelsey Museum of Archaeology
- 33   O.IFAO

Plate XIV
- 34   Kelsey Mus. inv. 25124, Courtesy of Kelsey Museum of Archaeology

Plate XV
- 36   P.Heid. inv. K. 308 verso
- 37   P.CtYBR inv. 1841 verso
- 38   P.Brux. inv. E. 9483 verso

Plate XVI
- 39   P.CtYBR inv. 1843 verso
- 40   P.Heid. inv. K. 308 recto

Plate XVII
- 41   P.CtYBR inv. 1841 recto
- 42   P.Brux. inv. E. 9483 recto
- 43   P.CtYBR inv. 1843 recto

Plate XVIII
- 44   P.Vindob. K. 4725 recto
- 44   P.Vindob. K. 4725 verso

Plate XIX
- 45   P.Camb.UL Michael. 807 recto

Plate XX
- 46   P.Camb.UL Michael. 807 verso

Plate XXI
- 47   P.Monts.Roca inv. 549 recto
- 47   P.Monts.Roca inv. 549 verso

Plate XXII
48 P.Monts.Roca inv. 516 recto
48 P.Monts.Roca inv. 516 verso

Plate XXIII
49 P.Monts.Roca inv. 619
50 P.Monts.Roca inv. 713

Plate XXIV
50 P.Monts.Roca inv. 713, seal [1]
50 P.Monts.Roca inv. 713, seal [2]

Ostraca, Papyri, and Essays

O.Clackson **1-17**

Ostraca de Baouit conserves a l'Institut d'Égyptologie d'Heidelberg

Anne Boud'hors et Sarah Clackson

Un apport remarquable de Sarah Clackson à nos disciplines aura été d'avoir ouvert la voie à la reconstruction des archives du monastère d'Apollo à Baouit, en Moyenne-Egypte. L'œuvre de pionnier qu'elle a menée dans ce domaine se trouve désormais à notre disposition et nous donne large matière à réflexion, alors même que les recherches se trouvent stimulées par la reprise des fouilles archéologiques sur le site, après presque un siècle d'interruption. Ainsi le chantier qu'elle avait en quelque sorte rouvert ne risque-t-il pas de se refermer avec sa disparition.[1]

Le sort de la documentation papyrologique de Baouit ressemble un peu à celui de la bibliothèque du monastère Blanc: l'histoire de la découverte du site et les circonstances de fouilles ont fait que, si une grande partie des pièces sont conservées au Louvre, beaucoup d'autres se trouvent dans des collections variées. Il y a une quinzaine d'années, nous n'avions pas idée de l'ampleur de cette dispersion. Nous connaissions (et encore, fort mal, puisque le travail est resté inédit) la thèse de Martin Krause, faite à partir des papyrus de la British Library,[2] et certaines éditions ponctuelles. L'hypothèse de travail de Sarah, selon laquelle il existait des formulaires caractéristiques du monastère de Baouit, s'est révélée extraordinairement féconde, et on en voit le beau résultat dans son ouvrage *P.Mon.Apollo*, ainsi que dans ses communications au congrès de papyrologie de Florence en 1998, au congrès d'études coptes à Leiden en 2000, aux journées d'études coptes de Lille en 2001.[3]

Pour ce qui est des ostraca, c'est évidemment le fonds du Louvre qui a fourni le point de départ, puisqu'on était assuré de savoir, grâce aux carnets de l'archéologue Jean Clédat,[4] quelles pièces avaient été trouvées au cours des fouilles, alors que le monastère d'Apollo est rarement nommé dans les textes eux-mêmes. Le repérage des formulaires caractéristiques permettait alors d'attribuer à Baouit des pièces parallèles, déjà publiées sans mention de provenance, ou inédites, conservées dans plusieurs collections publiques et privées.

Parmi ces collections, celle de l'Institut d'égyptologie d'Heidelberg méritait une attention particulière. En effet Friedrich Bilabel avait déjà publié une dizaine d'ostraca concernant des transports de blé, reproduisant un formulaire aujourd'hui bien connu, qui commence par l'expression ϣⲓⲛⲉ ⲛⲥⲁ- ("aller chercher, commander, réclamer," etc.).[5] La provenance de ces pièces était inconnue. Bilabel signalait que l'aspect de la poterie lui rappelait la céramique trouvée lors des fouilles de Qarâra. De fait, dans le registre d'inventaire, un des ostraca (*O.Clackson* **2**, Heid. inv. 998) porte la mention

---

[1] La synthèse la plus récente sur le site se trouve dans Delattre 2007. Cf. aussi, pour l'histoire des fouilles, Bénazeth 1995.

[2] Krause 1958.

[3] Clackson 2000, 2001, 2003, 2004.

[4] Voir la publication tardive de la dernière campagne de Clédat avec, en particulier, l'édition des ostraca, dans Clédat 1999. La référence aux ostraca sera faite par le sigle "*O.Bawit*."

[5] Bilabel 1933.

"Karâra." Dans le catalogue de la collection, aucune autre précision n'est donnée que "Oberägypten."[6] Il est possible que tout le lot d'ostraca (inv. 979-998)[7] ait été acheté à un marchand, éventuellement pendant les fouilles de Qarâra. La provenance de Baouit me semble assurée par le formulaire pour *O.Clackson* **1-16** (Heid. inv. nos. 979-981, 983-984, 986-996 et 998; *O.Clackson* **17** (Heid. inv. 997), également publié ici, est trop fragmentaire pour pouvoir faire une hypothèse. Quant aux deux ostraca inv. 982 et 985, ils ne font pas partie des documents de Baouit. Leur contenu et leur aspect permettent de les rattacher sans aucun doute aux "archives des huiliers d'Aphroditô,"[8] et ils feront l'objet d'une autre publication.

Les textes à formulaire ϣⲓⲛⲉ ⲛⲥⲁ-, importants pour l'étude de l'économie du monastère, présentaient un certain nombre de difficultés non résolues, et avaient été publiés sans photo. Sarah travailla sur ces ostraca en février 2002, lors d'un séjour d'étude qu'elle fit à Heidelberg dans le cadre d'une bourse du Deutscher Akademischer Austauschdienst. Au cours de ce séjour, elle identifia d'autres ostraca du même lot, inédits, et conçut le projet d'une nouvelle publication de l'ensemble de ces pièces. Elle l'aurait certainement terminée dans les meilleures conditions grâce à la bourse de la fondation Humboldt qu'elle avait obtenue pour l'année 2003-2004, pour travailler à l'Institut de Papyrologie d'Heidelberg.

Sarah m'envoya une copie de son travail en mars 2003, alors que je terminais le manuscrit de la publication des ostraca de Baouit conservés à l'Ifao du Caire, dont quelques-uns sont très proches de ceux d'Heidelberg. Nous n'eûmes pas le temps de rediscuter certaines difficultés d'interprétation communes aux textes de ces deux collections, ni de reparler de notre projet d'étude comparative systématique de tous les ostraca de type ϣⲓⲛⲉ ⲛⲥⲁ-. Sa publication des ostraca d'Heidelberg était néanmoins dans un état assez bien avancé, en particulier l'édition et la traduction des textes, et j'ai essayé de la respecter telle qu'elle était, en répondant si possible aux questions que Sarah m'y posait et en faisant les mises à jours nécessaires. L'utilisation de nos deux langues respectives (anglais et français) permet, je l'espère, de lire cette étude comme une vraie collaboration.

Il me reste à remercier tous ceux qui m'ont aidée à mener à terme cette publication. James Clackson m'a transmis tous les documents dont je pouvais avoir besoin. En février 2005, je suis allée travailler deux jours à l'Institut d'égyptologie d'Heidelberg, où madame Dina Faltings, conservateur de la collection, a tout fait pour me faciliter l'examen des originaux. Enfin, sur les conseils du professeur John Baines et grâce à la générosité de la fondation Sarah Clackson, j'ai pu effectuer un court séjour à Oxford en mars 2005, et consulter les archives de Sarah déposées au Griffith Institute.[9] J'ai bénéficié des apports importants de la thèse d'Alain Delattre, quand elle était en cours de publication, ainsi que de discussions avec lui. Et Jean-Luc Fournet, par ses interventions et ses suggestions lors du colloque, m'a permis de mettre au clair un certain nombre de points délicats.

---

[6] Cf. Feucht 1986.

[7] Le n° inv. 989 a été attribué par erreur à un ostracon qui porte déjà le n° inv. 981 (*O.Clackson* **9**). Quant au n° inv. 999, il est probablement en démotique. Comme l'avait remarqué Sarah, le registre d'inventaire n'est pas très fiable quant aux dates d'acquisition, puisque les pièces inv. 976-978 ont été achetées en 1934, un an après la publication des ostraca ϣⲓⲛⲉ ⲛⲥⲁ- par Bilabel: ces derniers ont pu être inventoriés tardivement.

[8] Cf. Gascou et Worp 1990.

[9] Que John Baines soit remercié pour son chaleureux accueil, ainsi que l'équipe des archives du Griffith Institute, Mesdames Elizabeth Fleming et Alison Hobby, Monsieur Jaromir Malek, grâce à qui j'ai pu travailler dans d'excellentes conditions.

1. LA QUESTION DES SIGLES

Les 94 ostraca coptes des fouilles de Clédat publiés dans le MIFAO 111 (Louvre et probablement Musée égyptien du Caire) sont désignés par *O.Bawit* 1-94, les 67 ostraca coptes des fouilles de J. Maspero (IFAO) par *O.BawitIFAO* 1-67.[10] Les ostraca d'Heidelberg portent déjà, outre leur numéro d'inventaire, un numéro dans le *SBKopt*.I. Sarah avait prévu de leur attribuer un n° "*O.Bawit*." Les éditeurs du volume ont préféré adopter le sigle *O.Clackson* **1-16**. Dix de ces textes, dont un encore inédit, suivent le formulaire bien connu qui commence par ϣⲓⲛⲉ ⲛⲥⲁ-, six autres se rattachent à des dossiers également déjà connus.

2. ABRÉVIATIONS PROBLÉMATIQUES DANS LES ORDRES DE TRANSPORT ϣⲓⲛⲉ ⲛⲥⲁ-

L'ensemble du formulaire a fait l'objet de discussions sur lesquelles je ne reviens pas.[11] Les abréviations problématiques sont signalées par l'astérisque.

1	ϣⲓⲛⲉ ⲛⲥⲁ X ϭⲟⲟⲩⲛⲉ ⲛⲥⲟⲩⲟ
2	ⲙⲛ X ϭⲟⲟⲩⲛⲉ ⲛⲁⲣⲁⲕⲉ
3 (ou 4)	ⲉⲣⲉ ⲥⲓ(ⲧⲟⲩ) ⲁⲣⲧ(ⲁⲃⲁⲓ) Y ⲁⲑⲉ(-)*/ ⲧ(ⲟⲩ)* ⲁ(-)* ϩⲓϣⲟⲩ
4 (ou 3)	ⲛⲧⲉ *NN (toponyme)*
5	ϩⲓⲧⲛ *NN (anthroponyme)*
6	γί(νεται) σί(του) θαλλία X ἀρτ(άβαι) Y ἀθε(-)* / τ(οῦ)* δ(-)*
7	*Date (mois, jour, année indictionnelle)*
8	N φορά

Il s'agit de "faire rentrer" une certaine quantité de sacs de blé (= 1) et de sacs d'arakos (= 2), dans lesquels il y a une certaine quantité d'artabes (qui font parfois l'objet d'une précision) (= 3 ou 4), provenant d'un domaine agricole (= 4 ou 3), par les soins d'un transporteur (= 5). Suit un résumé en grec des quantités de marchandises, constitué d'abréviations (= 6). Puis le document est daté (= 7) et se termine sur le numéro de la livraison (= 8). Dans les parties 3 et 6, les précisions concernant les artabes (suivies ici d'une astérisque) semblent facultatives et n'ont pas été définitivement élucidées. Or, aux quelques attestations des textes d'Heidelberg, les *O.BawitIFAO* ont apporté plusieurs occurrences supplémentaires de ces abréviations et ont permis d'assurer au moins leur lecture (αθ^ε et το δ) et de proposer des interprétations.[12] Puisque ces indications ne sont pas systématiquement présentes, elles sont probablement d'ordre secondaire. Ce caractère facultatif est confirmé par le fait que αθε est parfois ajouté au-dessus de la ligne (*O.BawitIFAO* 3 et *O.Clackson* **2**, l. 5 et 6), et ne semble pas toujours repris, non plus que το δ, dans le résumé en grec.

Pour αθ^ε, la proposition de Bilabel était ἀθε(τήσιμος), "à retrancher (du calcul)," qui n'aboutit pas à un sens réellement clair. Au moment de la publication des *O.BawitIFAO*, Dieter Hagedorn m'avait

---
[10] Cf. Boud'hors 2004.
[11] Cf. Tait 1994, *O.Bawit*: 247-248, *O.BawitIFAO*: 2-7.
[12] Cf. *O.BawitIFAO*: 6-7.

fait une proposition de lecture très séduisante: ἀθη(ναῖον) (μέτρον). La mesure "athénienne," ou "(du temple) d'Athéna" semble bien attestée en Moyenne-Egypte.[13] Cette hypothèse avait contre elle le fait qu'on a systématiquement un ε et non un η. Mais le papyrus de Baouit *P.Clackson* **47**, publié ici même par S. Torallas, donne l'expression suivante: ⲛⲧⲟⲓⲡⲉ ⲛⲧⲁⲑⲉⲛⲏⲥ, "de la mesure d'Athènes," qui désigne certainement la même chose. J'adopte donc cette interprétation, et je propose de rétablir cette lecture dans tous les *O.BawitIFAO* qui contiennent l'abréviation.

Pour το δ/, la lecture est désormais sûre. Bilabel lisait τὸ α, et proposait τ(οῦ) α(ὐτοῦ), mais son interprétation, possible pour les deux textes dans lesquels il la trouvait, ne tient pas dans les *O.BawitIFAO*. Ici encore deux propositions ont été faites: το(ῦ) δ(ικαίου), "du dikaion" (où l'expression aurait désigné une artabe définie par l'autorité juridique du monastère), ou τ(οῦ) δ(είγματος), "selon la norme," suggestion de Klaas Worp à laquelle je me suis rangée pour les *O.BawitIFAO*. Une lecture το(ῦ) δ(ημοσίου) est suggérée par Jean-Luc Fournet: artabes réservées au paiement de l'impôt, ou définies par le bureau fiscal? On pourrait encore penser à το(ῦ) δ(οχικοῦ) (μέτρου), "de la mesure officielle," indication qui est parfois associée à la mesure athénienne.[14] J'avoue ne pas pouvoir trancher.

Nous aurions donc dans la documentation des ostraca de Baouit des précisions contenant plusieurs sortes d'artabes:

- l'artabe, sans autre précision (standard?)
- l'artabe "selon la norme" (la même que la précédente?) Ou "de l'impôt"? Ou "officielle"?
- l'artabe "athénienne"
- la "petite" artabe (si la restitution ⲛⲧⲕⲟⲩⲓ ⲛ[ⲟⲓⲡⲉ], littéralement "de la petite mesure" de Bilabel dans *O.Clackson* **4** est correcte).

La différence entre toutes ces artabes est difficile à établir précisément. Et le rapport entre le nombre de sacs (ⲥⲟⲟⲩⲛⲉ/θαλλίον) et le nombre d'artabes n'est pas régulier.[15] Je ne vois donc pas pour le moment à quoi tendent ces distinctions.

3. Autres formulaires

Sarah propose la réédition de deux ostraca publiés par Brunsch[16] (*O.Clackson* **11** et **12**), ainsi que la publication de six textes inédits. Etant donné la proximité du formulaire de ces ostraca de Brunsch avec ceux de plusieurs *O.BawitIFAO*, il fait en effet peu de doute qu'il faut les rattacher à ce dossier (même si Sarah ne le dit pas explicitement pour chacun). Six de ces textes ont pour particularité d'être entièrement constitués d'abréviations de mots grecs. Ils reprennent une partie des indications données

---

[13] Cf. Clarysse 1985 et Förster 2001: 16. Il est à noter que les attestations coptes sont plutôt en faveur d'une interprétation "mesure d'Athéna" que "mesure athénienne." La discussion serait peut-être à reprendre.
[14] Cf. Clarysse 1985: 235.
[15] Cf. *O.BawitIFAO*: 8-9.
[16] Brunsch 1980: 21-22.

par les ostraca de type ϣⲓⲛⲉ ⲛⲥⲁ-, mais dans un ordre différent et de façon systématiquement abrégée.

TEXTES COMMENÇANT PAR LE NUMERO DE LIVRAISON: *O.Clackson* **11-15**: cf. *O.BawitIFAO* 17, 19(?), 20, 21 (avec peut-être le même personnage que dans *O.Clackson* **11** et **12**), 50(?). Les textes concernent probablement du blé, mais la présence des mots "artabe" et "blé" semble facultative (θαλλίον suffit). En revanche apparaît la mention des "chamelées" (charge d'un chameau) qui montre que ce genre de texte concerne plus directement le travail du chamelier. On remarquera que les quantités indiquées semblent généralement plus petites que dans les ostraca ϣⲓⲛⲉ ⲛⲥⲁ-. Il y avait probablement plusieurs chameliers par φορά. L'absence de la date semble être le cas le plus fréquent (sauf dans *O.Clackson* **15**). L'ostracon P 2025 du Naprstek Museum de Prague[17] est de même sorte (à l'exception du numéro de livraison, ses données sont exactement les mêmes que dans *O.Clackson* **14**) et provient donc très vraisemblablement de Baouit.[18] Il faut noter que son éditeur le date du 6e siècle (voir plus loin les questions de datation).

TOPONYME EN TETE: *O.Clackson* **16**: cf. *O.BawitIFAO* 36-40 et *O.Bawit* 42-47. Tous ces ostraca sont des transports de vin. La composition du toponyme est assez caractéristique de la documentation de Baouit (cf. *O.BawitIFAO* et P.Brux. inv. E.8155+8154, étudié dans *P.Brux.Bawit*, même si, sous sa forme abrégée, il n'est pas tout à fait explicite.

4. LA QUESTION DU BILINGUISME

Les textes de type ϣⲓⲛⲉ ⲛⲥⲁ- montrent un enchevêtrement de formules en copte et en grec. Il apparaît que les parties en grec sont en fait des segments figés et la plupart du temps abrégés, utilisés à des fins administratives. Le même phénomène se retrouve dans les nombreux ordres de paiement du monastère publiés dans *P.Brux.Bawit*. Dans l'édition des textes, j'utilise les caractères coptes pour transcrire tout ce qui se trouve dans une phrase de syntaxe copte, réservant la police grecque pour les segments entièrement constitués d'abréviations grecques. Dans l'apparat, seuls les caractères coptes sont utilisés, pour illustrer le fait que le scribe est le même.

5. QUESTIONS GÉNÉRALES SUR L'INTÉRÊT DE CES TEXTES

NOMBRE: en faisant un calcul grossier, on arrive à plus de 230 ostraca attribuables au monastère de Baouit, presque tous relatifs à des transports de marchandises, dont les plus importantes sont le blé et le vin.

DATATION: les ostraca de type ϣⲓⲛⲉ ⲛⲥⲁ- peuvent être datés du 8e siècle, grâce à certaines écritures très proches de celles des ordres de paiement sur papyrus qui sont souvent écrits au dos de documents

---

[17] Cf. Pintaudi 1993 (= *SB* 15280).

[18] Les ostraca P. 2014-2017 et P. 2019 du même musée sont de type ϣⲓⲛⲉ ⲛⲥⲁ-: cf. Oerter 2001.

en arabe (cf. *P.Brux.Bawit*). Grâce à la mention du jour de la semaine sur certains textes, K. Worp a pu proposer des dates précises dont nous retenons que c'est la première moitié du 8ᵉ siècle qui semble convenir le mieux.[19] On remarque que c'est le plus souvent en Thôth que se font les transports de vin, c'est-à-dire après les vendanges, en Pauni ou Epiphi que se font les transports de céréales (après la moisson). On a souvent affaire à des séries d'ostraca datant de la même année indictionnelle. J'aurais volontiers daté aussi du 8ᵉ siècle les *O.Clackson* **11-16** et tous ceux du même genre, étant donné les parentés des indications fournies avec celles des textes ϣⲓⲛⲉ ⲛⲥⲁ-. Cependant, Jean-Luc Fournet note que leur paléographie ferait pencher plutôt pour le 6ᵉ siècle, ce qui était avancé comme datation par R. Pintaudi pour l'ostracon de même type conservé à Prague.[20] J'avoue ne pas être très convaincue et préférer m'appuyer, plutôt que sur des considérations paléographiques qui sont d'autant moins fiables qu'on a affaire à des scribes coptes n'écrivant en grec que des formules figées, sur le fait que, lors des fouilles, les différents types d'ostraca (ϣⲓⲛⲉ ⲛⲥⲁ- et autres) ont été trouvés au même endroit et ont donc des chances d'être à peu près contemporains.

FONCTION: ces ostraca étaient-ils archivés ou bien jetés une fois devenus inutiles? La deuxième solution est sans doute plus plausible, car les ostraca fonctionnent plutôt comme des documents provisoires et les données qui y sont contenues semblent être reprises dans des comptes ou listes sur papyrus qui pouvaient, eux, être de véritables documents d'archives. Dans ces listes, les transports peuvent être classés par lieu de production, par numéro de convoi, par transporteur, par date. Ces "tris" devaient être facilités par le fait que les différentes données sont placées alternativement en tête dans les différents types de formulaires. Est-ce justement à cela, à faciliter l'archivage, que servaient ces ostraca? On peut essayer d'imaginer la situation suivante:

1) l'ostracon ϣⲓⲛⲉ ⲛⲥⲁ-, qui est le plus complet et le plus rédigé, est le document de base. Peut-être est-il confié au responsable du convoi (φορά), qui le rapporte.

2) A partir de ce document, l'économat rédige quelques aide-mémoire où sont portées, en grec et de manière abrégée, les indications principales concernant plus directement tel ou tel aspect de l'opération. Il devait y avoir des périodes d'activité assez intense, puisque les transports semblent souvent regroupés sur un mois au plus.

3) Les aide-mémoire vont servir à leur tour à fabriquer des listes récapitulatives, sur papyrus, qui permettront de payer les salaires et de tenir à jour les comptes. A ce moment-là, les ostraca deviennent inutiles et on peut les jeter.

Comme il a été dit, le grec semble rester la langue de référence pour cette gestion, ce qui ne reflète pas forcément une pratique encore courante de la langue dans le monastère à cette période.

PROSOPOGRAPHIE ET TOPONYMIE: il n'est pas besoin d'insister sur l'enrichissement que les ostraca apportent sur ce plan pour la connaissance, non pas tant du monastère lui-même, mais de toutes les unités agricoles qu'il possédait et de la population qui travaillait pour lui.

---

[19] Cf. Worp 2002.
[20] Cf. Pintaudi 1993.

Le chantier de Baouit est désormais largement ouvert et prometteur. Sur le plan archéologique, bien sûr, grâce à la reprise des fouilles, mais aussi sur le plan de ce que l'on appelle "Museum archaeology", un terme utilisé par Sarah elle-même dans sa communication au congrès de Leiden. Plusieurs lots ou collections, identifiés ou étudiés par elle, restent à exploiter, parmi lesquels les papyrus trouvés par Clédat et conservés au Louvre, ceux du musée d'Ismaïlia, et une partie d'un lot de papyrus de l'université de Louvain, documents détruits mais dont les microfilms ont été conservés. Je ne pense pas être moi-même en mesure, dans les années qui viennent, de poursuivre des recherches sur la documentation de Baouit. Mais Alain Delattre, déjà fin connaisseur de l'histoire du monastère, a accepté de prendre la relève pour une partie de ces dossiers. C'est une immense satisfaction, que Sarah, j'en suis sûre, aurait pleinement partagée.

O.Clackson 1

SBKopt. I 226   13,3 x 17 cm 8e siècle
Ägyptologisches Institut Heidelberg inv. 993
Plate I

Pottery: chunky red ware, heavily ribbed and pitched
Preservation: a complete text of 7 lines with ink partially faded, especially in the final line.
[Ecriture: peu cursive; cf. *O.BawitIFAO* 5; la partie en grec est plus rapide]
Bibliography: Bilabel 1933: 556-558, n°1; Feucht 1986: 214, n°642.

1   ✝ ϢⲒⲚⲈ ⲚⲤⲀ ϨⲘⲎ ⲘⲚ ⲞⲨⲈⲒ
2   ⲚϬⲞⲞⲨⲚⲈ ⲚⲤⲞⲨⲞ ⲚⲦⲈ ⲠⲘⲀⲚⲂⲒϪ
3   ⲈⲢⲈ ⲤⲒ(ⲦⲞⲨ) (ⲀⲢⲦⲀⲂⲀⲒ) Ⲙ ⲀⲐⲈ(ⲚⲀⲒⲞⲨ) ϨⲒⲰⲞⲨ ⲘⲚ ⲤⲒ(ⲦⲞⲨ) (ⲀⲢⲦⲀⲂⲀⲒ) ⲒϚ ⲦⲞ(Ⲩ) Ⲁ.(-)
4   ϨⲒⲦⲚ ⲈⲚⲰⲬ ⲠⲞⲨⲞⲈⲒⲈⲘⲀⲤⲈ
5   γί(νεται) θαλλί(α) μα σί(του) (ἀρτάβαι) μ (καὶ) το(ῦ) δ(-) ἀρτ(άβαι) ιϚ
6   Παῦν(ι) η ἰνδ(ικτίονος) ιβ ✝
7   α (καὶ) β φορά

3. ⲤⲒ⸍ ⲧ, Ⲁⲑᵉ⸍, ⲤⲒ⸍ ⲧ, ⲦⲞ Ⲁ⸍ || 5. γ⸍ θαλλ⸍, ⲤⲒ⸍ ⲧ, ς ⲦⲞ Ⲁ⸍ ἀρᵀ || 6. παυν⸍, ινδ⸍ || ς, φορᵃ⸍

1   ✝ Faire rentrer quarante et un
2   sacs de blé de Pmanbij
3   dans lesquels (il y a) 40 artabes athéniennes de blé, et 16 artabes de blé du δ(-),
4   par Enoch l'éleveur de veaux.
5   Total : 41 sacs, 40 artabes athéniennes de blé et 16 artabes du δ(-).
6   Le 7 (du mois de) Pauni, 12e (année de l')indiction.
7   1ère et 2e livraisons.

2. ⲡⲙⲁⲛⲃⲓⲭ: toponyme mentionné aussi dans un autre ostracon de type ϣⲓⲛⲉ ⲛⲥⲁ- (SBKopt. II, 1028).

4. ⲡⲟⲩⲟⲉⲓⲉⲙⲁⲥⲉ: "the rearer of young," Bilabel "Stierbauer," restored in SBKopt. I 230.4/5. A person with this title called Biktor also occurs in Naprstek P 2019.4. [Cf. aussi *O.BawitIFAO* 2 (même nom) et *O.Nancy* (Apollô). J'aligne ma traduction sur celle que donne *P.Brux.Bawit*, n° 28, pour le grec μοσχοτρόφος, qui doit désigner, comme il le dit, le même métier.]

6. Παυν/ η: Bilabel read Παυν/ κ "Payni 20."

7. Sauf erreur de ma part, c'est la seule occurrence de la mention de deux livraisons à la fois.

O.Clackson 2

SBKopt. I 234 11,8 x 15,5 cm 8ᵉ siècle
Ägyptologisches Institut Heidelberg inv. 998
Plate I

Pottery: thick, red ware. Surface very porous, partially abraded and pitted, obscuring the legibility of many letters. [Cf. *O.BawitIFAO* 4-6 (sorte de poterie qui comporte un noyau noir cerné de deux couches rouges).]
Preservation: 10 lines of text are poorly preserved, the left-hand side of ll. 5-10 have broken off; it may be that further lines are now missing from the ends of the text.
Bibliography: Bilabel 1933: 562, n°9.
[N.B. Pour cet ostracon, le registre d'inventaire de la collection porte la mention "Karâra" (voir introduction).]

```
 1                    ☩
 2    ☩ ϣⲓⲛⲉ ⲛⲥⲁ ⲧⲁⲓⲟⲩ ⲙⲛ ⲥⲟ ⲛϭⲟⲟⲩⲛⲉ
 3    ⲛⲥⲟⲩⲟ ⲉⲣⲉ ⲥⲓ(ⲧⲟⲩ) ⲁⲣⲧ(ⲁⲃⲁⲓ) ⲙⲃ ⲃ_γ ⲥⲓ(ⲧⲟⲩ) (ⲕⲁⲓ) ⲁⲣⲧ(ⲁⲃⲁⲓ) ⲙ ⲧⲟ(ⲩ) ⲁ̣.(-)
 4    ϩⲓϣⲟⲩ ⲙⲛ ⲙⲏⲧⲥⲛⲟⲟⲩⲥⲉ ⲛϭⲟⲟⲩⲛⲉ
 5    [ⲛ]ⲁⲣⲁⲕⲉ ⲉⲣⲉ ⲁⲣⲁⲕⲉ ⲁⲣⲧ(ⲁⲃⲁⲓ) ⲓⲁ `ⲁⲑⲉ(ⲛⲁⲓⲟⲩ)´ . [. .]ϭⲟⲟⲩⲛ̣ⲉ
 6    [    ]ⲟⲩ . . . ⲛ̣ . ⲧ̣ . [. . .] . ⲕⲣⲓⲑ(ⲏⲥ) ⲁⲣⲧ(ⲁⲃⲁⲓ) `ⲁⲑⲉ(ⲛⲁⲓⲟⲩ)´ . ⲁ\
 7    [         ] . . . ϛ σί(του) ἀρτ(άβαι) μβ β_γ
 8    [            ]δ ἀθε(ναίου) (καὶ) κριθ(ῆς)
 9    [            ] . . . . .
10    [                ] . .
```

3. ⲥⲓ/ ⲁⲣⲧ/, ʃ ⲥⲓ/ ⲁⲣⲧ/, ⲧⲟ ⲁ/ ‖ 5. ⲁⲣⲧ/ ⲁⲑᵉ/ ‖ 6. ⲕⲣⲓᵉ ⲁⲣⲧ/ ⲁⲑᵉ/ ‖ 7. ⲥⲓ/ ⲁⲣⲧ/ ‖ 8. ⲁⲑᵉ/ ʃ ⲕⲣⲓᵉ

1   †
2   † Faire rentrer cinquante-six sacs
3   de blé, dans lesquels (il y a) 42 artabes 2/3 de blé et 40 artabes de blé du δ(-),
4   ainsi que douze sacs
5   d'arakos dans [lesquels (il y a) 14 artabes athéniennes d'arakos […] sacs
6   […] ?4 ½ artabes athéniennes d'orge.
7   […]6, 42 ⅔ artabes de blé.
8   […]4 [artabes] athéniennes, et d'orge
9   […]
10   […].

Il y a peu à améliorer de la lecture de Bilabel, qui était d'une grande acuité, mais avec beaucoup d'incertitudes, excepté pour la lecture de "2/3" (l. 3 et 7, où il lisait ⅛), qui est assurée par des parallèles (*O.BawitIFAO* 1 et 2). Le formulaire semble très complexe et met en jeu plusieurs céréales. On remarquera qu'il manque les mentions de provenance, de transporteur, de date et de livraison. Celle de la provenance pouvait se trouver dans une lacune (l. 6 ou 7), les autres pouvaient venir après la ligne 10, dans une partie du tesson qui a disparu.

A partir de la ligne 6, la lecture et les reconstitutions de Sarah, partiellement conformes à celles de Bilabel, sont les suivantes:

5   [ⲛ]ⲁⲣⲁⲕⲉ ⲉⲣⲉ ⲁⲣⲁⲕⲉ ⲁⲣⲧ(ⲁⲃⲁⲓ) ⲓⲇ ⲁⲑⲉ(-) [ϥ] †[ⲉ ⲛ]ϭ[ⲟ]ⲟⲩⲛⲉ
6   [   ].ⲟⲩ [.]..ⲙⲟⲧ[..]ⲣ.ⲥ ⲕⲣⲓ(-) ⲁⲣⲧ(ⲁⲃⲁⲓ) ⲇ𐅵
7   [γι⸍] θαλ⸍ νϛ ϲι⸍ αρᵗ μβ β𐅷
8   [ϥ ϲι⸍ αρᵗ μ το α⸌ ϥ θαλ⸍ ιβ αρακᵉ⸍ ι]δ αθᵉ ϥ κριθ
9   [αρτ(αβαι) δ𐅵 ?   κρι]θ .. αραᵏ
10   [   ]..

O.Clackson 3

SBKopt. I 233   9,7 x 10,4 cm   8ᵉ siècle
Ägyptologisches Institut Heidelberg, inv. 994
Plate II

Pottery: red ware, ribbed (very shallow). Upper surface of the pot is flaking off in places.
Preservation: the right-hand side of the first 5 lines of text is preserved; it is possible that a sixth and final line is now broken off.
Bibliography: Bilabel 1933: 561, n° 8.

1   [† ϣⲓⲛⲉ ⲛⲥⲁ xx]ⲛϭⲟⲟⲩⲛⲉ
2   [ⲛⲥⲟⲩⲟ … ⲛ]ⲧⲉ ⲡⲟϩⲉ . .
3   [ⲉⲣⲉ ⲥⲓ(ⲧⲟⲩ) ⲁⲣⲧ(ⲁⲃⲁⲓ) ⲝⲃ] ϩⲓϣⲱⲟⲩ ϩⲓⲧⲟⲟⲧϥ

4   [N- NN ... Π]ṂⲀ̄Ṇ̄ⲔⲨⲢⲒⲤ ...
5   [γί(νεται) cί(του) θαλλί(α) xx ἀρτ(άβαι)] ξβ ἐγ(ρ)ά(φη) Ἐπὶφ ζ ἰνδ(ικτίονος) ιβ

5. ⲉⲅˣ, ⲓⲛˣ⸍

1   [✝ Faire rentrer xx] sacs
2   [de blé ...]de Pohe
3   dans lesquels (il y a) [62 artabes de blé] par
4   [NN ... P]mankuris ...
5   [Total: xx sacs de blé, artabes] 62. Ecrit le 7 (du mois d') Epiphi, 12ᵉ (année de l')indiction.

3. ϨⲒϢⲞⲨ: Bilabel read ϨⲘⲠϢⲞⲨ

4. Π]ⲘⲀ̄Ṇ̄ⲔⲨⲢⲒⲤ: Bilabel did not reconstruct Π]. Following this there may be two further letters, the second of which looks like part of a Ϭ, a Ⲭ or an Ⲟ.

5. Sarah proposait de lire, après la lacune, ξβ αθε(-), qu'elle restaurait aussi à la ligne 3, tout en remarquant: "Bilabel read [ ]ẋ ⲔⲀⲀᵉ⸍, interpreting ⲔⲀⲀᵉ⸍ as a form of κάδος. The alpha and theta in αθᵉ⸍, restored after SBKopt. I 226, 234, are curiously formed—is it correct?" En effet le tracé des lettres me paraît plus proche de ce qui est écrit dans *O.Clackson* 4, l.7, c'est pourquoi je préfère ἐγ(ρ)ά(φη).

O.Clackson 4

SBKopt. I 230   9,7 x 8,5 cm   8ᵉ siècle
Ägyptologisches Institut Heidelberg inv. 987
Plate II

Pottery: fine red ware, ribbed (very shallow).
Preservation: the upper left side of this text is preserved, with 9 lines. The ink has faded in places and the surface of the pottery is pitted, sometimes distorting the appearance of the letters in the photograph. [Cf. *O.BawitIFAO* 55].
[Ecriture: un peu penchée à droite, peu cursive sauf dans les parties en grec (cf. *O.BawitIFAO* 8).]
Bibliography: Bilabel 1933: 560, n° 5.

1   β[φ?   ]
2   ϢⲒⲚⲈ [ⲚⲤⲀ   xx   ⲚϬⲞⲞⲨⲚⲈ]
3   ⲚⲤⲞⲨⲞ ⲚⲦⲈ[
4   ⲚⲈṂⲞⲚⲦ ϨⲒ[ⲦⲚ   NN   ⲠⲞⲨⲞⲈⲒⲈ]
5   ⲚⲈⲘⲀⲤⲈ Ⲛ̇ⲪⲞⲒ̇[
6   cί(του) ἀρτ(άβαι) Ⲏ ⲚⲦⲔⲞⲨⲒⁿᵉ[Ⲛ[

7   Κῦροc ἔγρ(αψα) ✝ α[
8   θαλλ[

6. cι/ αρᵗ ‖ 7. εγρ/

1   2ᵉ [livraison ?].
2   Faire rentrer [*xx* sacs]
3   de blé de […]
4   *–nemont* par [… l'éleveur]
5   de veaux du champ-[…]
6   8 artabes de blé de la petite […].
7   Ecrit par Kuros ✝ […].
8   Sacs […].

1. β[φ: restored following *O.Bawit* 35, 36, 38, 41. See my note in review in *BASP* [Clackson 2002]: judging from the evidence of *O.Bawit* 36 reproduced in photo 276 (this part of the *O.Bawit* 35 is illegible in photo 275), it seems indisputable that the element at the beginning of these four ostraca should be interpreted as β φ(ορά), "delivery 2," as the editors themselves suggested on p. 269. [Cf. aussi *O.BawitIFAO* 6.]

Bilabel restored a line above the present line 1, with a central cross, but such an arrangement is not found in the comparable texts which begin with the delivery number (*O.Bawit* 35, 36, 38, 41).

4. ⲛⲉⲙⲟⲛⲧ: more likely than ⲛⲥⲙⲟⲛⲧ or ⲡⲥⲙⲟⲛⲧ.

5. ⲛⲉⲙⲁⲥⲉ: reconstruct [ⲉⲛⲱⲭ ⲡⲟⲩⲟⲉⲓⲉ] in l. 4 if linked with ⲉⲛⲱⲭ ⲡⲟⲩⲟⲉⲓⲉⲙⲁⲥⲉ who occurs in *SBKopt*. I 226.4 [= *O.Clackson* 1] and possibly in SBKopt. I 231.3-4 [*O.Clackson* 8.]

Bilabel restored ⲉⲣⲉ at the end of the lacuna. If ⲕⲩⲣⲟⲥ can be read in l. 7, reconstruct something like ⲛϥⲟⲓ[ⲙⲡⲕⲩⲣⲟⲥ?

6. cι/ η: Bilabel thought that the oblique stroke at the end of the cί(του) abbreviation was uncertain and read the amount of wheat as κ "20."

ⲛ[ ]: Bilabel restored ⲕⲟⲩⲓ ⲛ[ⲟⲓⲡⲉ ⲛ?] "small measure," see Crum Dict. ⲟⲓⲡⲉ [256a.]

7. Κῦροc: a reading of Κιροc is also possible. Possibly part of a longer name such as Apakyros [cf. Ἀπακιρε *O.BawitIFAO* 21 (?), *O.Clackson* 11 et 12.]

εγρ/ ✝: the rho looks certain, but is a reading of cιρ/ likely, followed by θ instead the cross? Bilabel read κ.ρ.. γι/ θα[λ/], and suggested reading the initial letters ⲕⲁⲣⲧ✝ or ⲕⲁⲣⲡⲉ. [Je crois que la lecture de Sarah est la bonne. On peut hésiter entre ἔγρ(αψα) et ἐγρ(άφη).]

8. θαλλ[: Bilabel read ⲑⲁⲗⲓ[and conjectured whether this was to be interpreted as ⲑⲁⲗ(ⲁⲓⲁ) or as ⲑⲁⲗ(ⲗ)ⲓ(ⲁ).

O.Clackson 5

SBKopt. I 227   11,8 x 14,5 cm   8ᵉ siècle
Ägyptologisches Institut Heidelberg inv. 996
Plate III

Pottery: thick brown ware, ribbed.
[Ecriture: probablement la même main que celle de *O.Nancy* (cf. *O.BawitIFAO*, p. 99).]
Preservation: the outer surface records 5 lines of complete text, with a further 2 lines on the inner surface which, before conservation, were mostly obscured with the thick layer of a mud-like substance which coated the inner surface of the pot.
Bibliography: Bilabel 1933: 558, n° 2; Feucht 1986: 214, n° 646.

      Face externe
1   ϯ ϣⲓⲛⲉ ⲛⲥⲁ ⲧⲁ`ⲓⲟⲩ´ ⲛⲥⲟⲟⲩ-
2   ⲛⲉ ⲛⲥⲟⲩⲟ ⲛⲧⲉⲡⲙⲁ ⲛ̄ⲁⲡⲁϫⲱⲓ̈
3   ⲉⲣⲉ (ⲥⲓ)ⲧⲟⲩ (ⲁⲣⲧⲁⲃⲁⲓ) ⲝⲁ ϩⲓⲧⲟⲩ ϩⲓⲧⲉⲛ ⲡⲉⲧⲣⲟⲥ
4   ⲡⲡⲓⲥⲧⲓⲕⲟ(ⲥ) γί(νεται) θαλλ(ί)α ν ⲥⲓ́(του) (ἀρτάβαι) ξα
5   Ἐπὶφ ιγ ἰνδ(ικτίονος) ιβ β φορά
      Face interne
6?
7?

1. ⲧⲁⁱᵒʸ ‖ 3. ⲥⲓ⁄ ⸚ ‖ 4. ⲡⲓⲥⲧⲓⲕᵒ ɣ⁄ θλλᵃ, ⲥⲓ⁄ ⸚ ‖ 5. ⲓⲛⲇ⁄ φορᵃ⁄

1   ϯ Faire rentrer cinquante sacs
2   de blé du domaine d'Apa Jôi
3   dans lesquels (il y a) 61 artabes de blé, par Petros
4   le *pistikos*. Total : 50 sacs, 61 artabes de blé.
5   Le 13 (du mois d') Epiphi, 12ᵉ (année de l')indiction. 2ᵉ livraison.
6?
7?

1. ⲧⲁⲓⲟⲩ: the first two letters were changed to ⲧⲁ-, possibly from ⲥⲉ, and ⲓⲟⲩ is written above them. [Cette correction a aussi été effectuée à la l.4, où le ν a été réécrit sur un ξ. La main du correcteur ne semble pas être celle du scribe. Comment interpréter cette correction, qui ne porte que sur le nombre de sacs ("60" corrigé en "50"), et non d'artabes?]

2. ⲛ̄ⲁⲡⲁϫⲱⲓ̈: only the left-hand dot of the trema is preserved.

3. Bilabel read ϩⲓⲧⲛ. [Noter que la graphie est la même que dans *O.Nancy*, ce qui confirme l'identité des mains.]

4. Pour le titre de *pistikos*, qui désigne un homme de confiance ou un intendant, voir aussi *O.Bawit* 63 et 64, *O.BawitIFAO* 1, 3, 4, 9, 11.

5. ιβ: written with open beta; Bilabel read ια.

6-7. From what can still be seen, the hand of the text of the inner surface appears to be the same as on the outer, although some of the strokes are written with a somewhat finer nib. If this is indeed the docket, it possibly records the date (restore Επιφ ιγ ινδ/ ιβ in l. 7?), and the amount of wheat. The two characters clearly discernible at the end of this line look like ru written upside down. [De fait on n'est même pas sûr du sens de lecture de ces lignes. On peut aussi se demander si elles ont un rapport avec l'erreur corrigée dans le nombre de sacs.]

O.Clackson 6

SBKopt. I 228 9,5 x 11,5 cm 8ᵉ siècle
Ägyptologisches Institut Heidelberg inv. 980
Plate III

Pottery: red ware, ribbed and pitched.
Preservation: the outer surface records 8 lines of complete text.
[Ecriture: un peu du même genre que celle de *O.Clackson* 1, en moins exercée.]
Bibliography: Bilabel 1933: 559, n°3; Feucht 1986: 214, n° 644.

1 ☦ ϢΙΝΕ ΝⲤΑ
2 ΤΑΪΟΥ ΝⲤΟΟΥΝΕ
3 ΝⲤΟΥΟ ΝΤΕ ΠΜΑ ΝΑΠΑ
4 ϪⲰΙ ΕΡΕ ⲤΙ(ΤΟΥ) (ΑΡΤΑΒΑΙ) ξ\ ϨΙⲰΟΥ
5 ϨΙΤΝ ΠΑⲤΟΝ ΠΕΤΡΕ
6 γί(νεται) θαλλί(α) ν cί(του) (ἀρτάβαι) ξ\ Ἐπὶφ
7   ιζ ἰνδ(ικτίονος) ιβ
8   γ φο(ρά)

4. ci/ ÷ ‖ 6. ΓΙ/ ΘΑΛΛΙ/, ci/ ÷ ‖ 7. ΙΝΑ/ ‖ 8. φο?

1 ☦ Faire rentrer
2 cinquante sacs
3 de blé du domaine d'Apa
4 Jôi, dans lesquels (il y a) 60 ½ artabes de blé,
5 par le frère Petre.
6 Total: 50 sacs, 60 ½ artabes de blé. (Mois d') Epiphi
7 le 17, 12ᵉ (année de l')indiction.
8 3ᵉ livraison.

Il y a beaucoup de similarités entre le contenu de cet ostracon et celui de *O.Clackson* **5**, alors qu'ils n'ont pas été écrits par la même main.

O.Clackson 7

SBKopt. I 229   7,5 x 8,5 cm   8ᵉ siècle
Ägyptologisches Institut Heidelberg inv. 979
Plate IV

Pottery: fine red ware with yellowish slip, ribbed (very shallow).
Preservation: the outer surface records 8 lines of complete text.
[Ecriture: proche de celles de *O.Nancy* et de *O.BawitIFAO* 1.]
Bibliography: Bilabel 1933: 559-560, n° 4; Feucht 1986: 214, n° 643.

```
1              ┼
2      ┼ ϢΙΝЄ ΝⲤⲀ ϢΜΟΥΝЄ
3      ΝϬΟΟΥΝЄ ΝⲤΟΥΟ ЄΡЄ
4      ⲤΙ(ΤΟΥ) ΑΡΤ(ΑΒΑΙ) ΙΑ∫ ϨΙϢΟΥ ΝΤЄ ΦΟΪ-
5      ΠΑΤΑΠЄ ϨΙΤΝ ΑΠΟΛΛѠ ΠΜΑΝ-
6      ϬΑΜΟΥΛ γί(νεται) ⲤΙ(του) Θαλλία η
7      ⲤΙ(του) ἀρτ(άβαι) ιαϚ μ(ηνὶ) Ἐπὶ(φ) δ ἰνδ(ικτίονος)
8           ιβ γ φ(ορά)
```

4. ⲤΙ⸍ ΑΡᵀ || 6. Γι⸍ ⲤΙ⸍ || 7. ⲤΙ⸍ ΑΡᵀ, Μ´, ΙΝᴬ⸍ || 8. φ?

```
1              ┼
2      ┼ Faire rentrer huit
3      sacs de blé dans
4      lesquels (il y a) 11 ½ artabes de blé, du champ-
5      -(de)-Patape, par Apollo le cha-
6      -melier. Total: 8 sacs de blé,
7      11 ½ artabes de blé. Le 4 du mois d'Epiphi, (année de l') indiction
8      12. 3ᵉ livraison.
```

5. Patape est un anthroponyme.

7. L'abréviation de μ(ηνὶ) est écrite de la même façon que sur certains ordres de paiement de Baouit, avec un trait au-dessus du μ qui redescend, presque comme un accent circonflexe: Cf. *P.Brux.Bawit*, en part. n° 3.

8. The most obvious reading is γ φ "delivery 3," but the letter following γ looks more like an alpha than a phi. Bilabel read ΥΛ, and suggested that "etwa in Υ· der Rest einer Subskription zu erkennen und dahinter λ [ΦΟΡᴬ⸍] zu ergänzen ist, vermag ich nicht zu entscheiden." No parallels for the delivery

details recorded in this way in *O.Bawit*. [La lecture de Sarah est juste. Je pense qu'il n'y a rien après le φ, et cette manière d'écrire est la même que celle de *O.Clackson* **4**, l.1.]

O.Clackson **8**

SBKopt. I 231   6,5 x 7,8 cm   8ᵉ siècle
Ägyptologisches Institut Heidelberg inv. 986
Plate IV

Pottery: red ware, pitched [couche interne noire, couche externe rouge.]
Preservation: the right hand side of what appears to be a 5-line text is preserved.
[Ecriture: un peu penchée; cf. *O.BawitIFAO* 5 et 11.]
Bibliography: Bilabel 1933: 560-561, n° 6.

```
1   [† ϢINE NCA] ϪΟΥϢΤΕ NϬΟΟΥΝΕ
2   [NCΟΥΟ NTEΦ]ΟΙ NΚΛΑΥΔΕ
3   [ΕΡΕ CI(TOY) (APTABAI) xx 2I]ϢΟΥ 2ITN ENWX
4   [ΠΟΥΟΙΕΜΑCΕ γί(νεται) cί(του) θαλλί(α) κ
5   [                    ] α φορ(ά)
```

4. θαλλι ‖ 5. φορ⸌

1   [Faire rentrer] vingt sacs
2   [de blé du ch]amp de Klaude,
3   dans lesquels (il y a) [xx artabes de blé], par Enoch
4   [l'éleveur de veaux. Total:] 20 sacs [de blé]
5   [...]. 1ᵉʳᵉ livraison.

1. ϪΟΥϢΤΕ: Bilabel read ϪΟΥϢΤ.

2. Φ]ΟΙ NΚΛΑΥΔΕ: Bilabel did not restore Φ]ΟΙ.

4. [ΠΟΥΟΙΕΜΑCΕ: this restoration follows ENWX ΠΟΥΟΕΙΕΜΑCΕ in *SBKopt.* I 226.4 [= *O.Clackson* **1**. Mais il faut rester prudent, car Enôch est un nom très fréquent, et on connaît au moins un Enôch chamelier dans *O.Clackson* **15** et *O.BawitIFAO* 31.]

5. α φορ⸌: Bilabel read β φορ⸌.

O.Clackson **9**

SBKopt. I 232   5,7 x 4,1 cm   8ᵉ siècle
Ägyptologisches Institut Heidelberg inv. 981
Plate V

Pottery: red ware, with a heavily pitted surface, distorting the legibility of some letters; [poterie poreuse, avec noyau noir et couches externes rouges.]
Preservation: the left-hand side of the first 5 lines of text is preserved. [L'écriture et la poterie rappellent celles d'*O.BawitIFAO* 6.]
Bibliography: Bilabel 1933: 561, n° 7. Note that this ostracon was accessioned twice in error, the second time as inv. n° "989".

1   † ϢΙΝΕ[ΝΣΑ ?]
2   ΣΕ ΝϬΟΟΥ[ΝΕ]
3   ΝΣΟΥΟ Ν[ΤΕ ?]
4   ΛΟ ΕΡΕ[ΣΙ(ΤΟΥ) (ΑΡΤΑΒΑΙ) *xx*]
5   ΖΙϢΟΥ [ΖΙΤΝ ΝΝ]

1   † Faire [rentrer]
2   ??? sacs
3   de blé d[e …]
4   -lo, dans lesquels (il y a) [xx artabes de blé,
5   par NN] …

1-2. [ΝΣΑ?]ΣΕ: it may be that "sixty" should be read, or that some further text is missing at the end of l. 1, in which case [ΜΝΤΑ]ΣΕ "sixteen," [ϪΟΥΤΑΣΕ] "twenty-six," [ΜΜΑΒΤΑΣΕ] "thirty-six," and so on, may have been intended. Bilabel read [ϤΤ]ΟΕ "four" and suggested that [Σ]ΟΕ "six" might also be reconstructed.

O.Clackson 10

11,5 x 12,7 cm   8ᵉ siècle

Ägyptologisches Institut Heidelberg inv. 995
Plate V

Pottery: red ware. [Surface noircie par la poussière.]
Preservation: all 7 lines of text may be preserved.
[Ecriture: penchée un peu inhabituelle.]
Bibliography: this ostracon was not published by Bilabel along with the other shine nsa-formula texts.

1   † ϢΪΝΕ ΝΣΑ
2   ΣΕ ΝϬΟΥΝΕ ΝΣΟΥΟ [ΝΤΕ]
3   ΦΟΙ ΝΜΑΚΑΡΕ ΕΡ[Ε]
4   ΣΙ(ΤΟΥ) ΑΡΤ(ΑΒΑΙ) ΟΓ\ ΖΙϢΟΥ [?]
5   ΠΡϢΤ(Η) Α ΦϤ(ΡΑ) ΖΙΤΝ ΠΑΣΟΝ

6   ϊⲱⲁⲛⲏⲥ ⲡⲉⲡⲓⲥⲧⲓⲕⲟⲥ
7   γί(νεται) θαλλί(α) ξ Μεσορ(ὴ) ιε
Broken off presumably?

4. ⲥι/ ⲁⲣᵀ ‖ 5. ⲡⲣⲱᵀ ⲫⲱ/ ‖ 7. ⲅι/ ⲑⲁⲗⲗι/, ⲙⲉⲥⲟⲣ/

1   ☧ Faire rentrer
2   soixante sacs de blé du
3   champ de Makare, dans
4   lesquels (il y a) 73 ½ artabes de blé [?]
5   Première, 1ᵉʳᵉ, livraison, par frère
6   Iôanês le pistikos.
7   Total: 60 sacs. Le 15 du (mois de) Mesorê. (?)

5. C'est la première occurrence d'un numéro de livraison en toutes lettres. Cette façon d'écrire est peut-être à mettre en relation avec la main, non familière, qui a écrit ce texte.

O.Clackson 11

SB XVIII 13563   5,3 x 5,4 cm   8ᵉ siècle (?)
Ägyptologisches Institut Heidelberg inv. 984
Plate VI

[Poterie: brune, légèrement côtelée.]
Bibliography: Brunsch 1980: 21-22, n° 9 (pl. 10-11).

1   ☧ θ φορὰ δ(ιὰ)' Ἀπα-
2   κιρε καμ(ή)λ(ια) β
3   θαλλ(ί)α η

1. φορᵅ/ δ/ ‖ 2. καμᵛ ‖ 3. θαλλᵅ

1   ☧ 9ᵉ livraison. Par Apa-
2   -kire. 2 chamelées,
3   8 sacs.

1-2. δ/: omitted by Brunsch.
[Le nom du personnage se retrouve dans les deux ostraca suivants. Dans *O.BawitIFAO* 21, on a dans la même position: Κῖρε. Il faut donc peut-être lire ἀπα Κῖρε.]
[καμᵛ ou καμᵑ]

O.Clackson 12

SB XVIII 13564 8,2 x 6,7 cm 8ᵉ siècle (?)
Ägyptologisches Institut Heidelberg, inv. 992
Plate VI

[Poterie: brune et côtelée, enduite.]
Bibliography: Brunsch 1980: 21-22, n° 10 (pl. 10-11).

   1 ✝ ιε φορὰ δ(ιὰ)
   2 Ἀπακιρε καμ(ή)λ(ια) β
   3 θαλλ(ί)α η

   1. φορᵅ╱ δ╱ ‖ 2. καμᵞ ‖ 3. θαλλᵅ

   1 15ᵉ livraison. Par
   2 Apakire. 2 chamelées,
   3 8 sacs.

1. δ╱: omitted by Brunsch
2. καμᵞ β: omitted by Brunsch
3. Brunsch read θαλλιᵒᵛ λ "30 sacks"

O.Clackson 13

       8,1 x 7,3 cm   8ᵉ siècle (?)
Ägyptologisches Institut Heidelberg, inv. 988
Plate VII

Pottery: brown ware, ribbed and pitched. Uses rim and neck of pot as well as part of the body.
Inédit.

   1 ✝ ϛ φορὰ δ(ιὰ) Ἀπακι-
   2 ρε καμ(ή)λ(ια) γ
   3 θαλλ(ία) η ἀρτ(άβαι) θ γ´

   1. φορᵅ╱ δ╱ ‖ 2. καμᵞ ‖ 3. θαλλ, αρᵗ

   1 ✝ 6ᵉ livraison. Par Apaki-
   2 -re. 3 chamelées,
   3 8 sacs, 9 artabes ⅓.

On distingue des traces d'encre entre les lignes 2 et 3, elles sont peut-être dues à la présence du rebord de l'assiette.

O.Clackson 14

6,2 x 7,5 cm   8ᵉ siècle (?)

Ägyptologisches Institut Heidelberg inv. 991
Plate VII

Pottery: brown ware, pitched.
Inédit.

1   † ιζ φορὰ δ(ιὰ) Βίκ(τωρ)
2   καμ(ή)λ(ια) β θαλλ(ία) ϛ

1. φορᵅ⸌ δ⸌ βικ⸌ ‖ 2. καμᵞ, θαλλ

1   17ᵉ livraison. Par Biktôr.
2   2 chamelées, 6 sacs.

Compare with Naprstek Museum, Prague, ostracon P 2025 (Pintaudi 1993), which records a transport by Victor of two camels with 6 sacks for the 11th delivery. No provenance, and suggested date = 6ᵗʰ c. [Cf. introduction.]

O.Clackson 15

6,2 x 7 cm   8ᵉ siècle (?)

Ägyptologisches Institut Heidelberg inv. 990
Plate VIII

Pottery: red ware with a lighter slip, pitched.
Inédit.

1   † η φο(ρὰ) δ(ιὰ)' Ενῶχ
2   καμ(η)λ(ίτης) cί(του) θαλλ(ία) ϊ
3   μ(ηνὶ) Φ(α)ῶ(φι) ια ἰ(ν)δ(ικτίονος) ι †

1. φᵒ⸌ δ⸌ ‖ 2. καμᵞ cι⸌ θαλλ ‖ 3. μ́ φᵂ⸌, ιᵟ

1   † 8ᵉ livraison. Par Enoch
2   (le) chamelier. 10 sacs de blé.

3   Mois de Phaôphi, le 11, 10ᵉ (année de l')indiction.

1. Or delivery κ "20."
2. Date très proche de celle de *O.BawitIFAO* 25.

O.Clackson **16**

Ägyptologisches Institut Heidelberg inv. 983
Plate VIII

6,3 x 5,2 cm   8ᵉ siècle (?)

Pottery: brown ware, ribbed and pitched.
[Ecriture: cf. *O.BawitIFAO* 40, qui est probablement de la même main.]
Preservation: all 5 lines of text may be preserved?
Inédit.

1   † τόπου νοτ(αρίου)
2   δ(ιὰ) Ταυρῖνε
3   οἴ(νου) παλαιοῦ μ(-)γ(-) ο
4   ἑξήκ(οντα) Θώ(θ) κα
5   ἰνδ(ικτίονος) ιβ † ε φο(ρά)

1. νοτ ‖ 2. δ⸍ ‖ 3. οι⸍ παλαιου μγ ‖ 4. εξηκ⸍ θω⸍ ‖ 5. ινδ, φο⸍

1   † Du domaine du *notarios*,
2   par Taurine,
3   70 m(-)g(-) de vin vieux,
4   soixante. (Mois de) Thôth, le 21,
5   12ᵉ (année de l')indiction † 5ᵉ livraison.

1. L'interprétation proposée par Sarah pour le toponyme (νοτ(αρίου), "from the *topos* of the *notarios*") est parfaitement convaincante. Ce toponyme est en effet attesté en copte dans le *SBKopt*. I, 291, l. 3-4: ⲡⲙⲁ ⲙ̄ⲡⲛⲟⲧⲁⲣⲓⲥ. Or ce texte est un ordre émis par le supérieur du monastère, de type ⲡⲉⲛⲉⲓⲱⲧ ⲡⲉⲧⲥϩⲁⲓ, formule que Sarah a identifiée comme caractéristique du monastère de Baouit et dont elle a (re)publié toutes les attestations dans un livre à paraître (Clackson 2008, dont j'ai pu consulter la version définitive, grâce à la gentillesse de James Clackson). Qui plus est, dans ce document, l'intermédiaire est un certain ⲧⲁⲩⲣⲓⲛⲉ ⲡⲁⲡⲙⲁⲛⲁⲉ, qui est probablement le même personnage qu'ici. S'il n'y avait pas ce parallèle, la proposition de J.-L. Fournet, τόπου νοτ(ίνου), "le domaine du sud," serait tout aussi vraisemblable: on connaît par exemple une νοτίνη ἐκκλησία dans *P.Lond.Copt.* 1077 et on peut également invoquer le toponyme ⲡⲉⲙϩⲓⲧ ⲛ̄ⲡⲙⲟⲟⲩ ("le nord de l'eau") attesté dans *P.Brux.Bawit*, n° 12.

3. Sarah lisait "100 metra of old wine." Je pense que la mesure est plutôt le μέγα ou le μαγαρικόν (cf. la discussion à ce sujet dans *O.BawitIFAO*, p. 62). Quant au chiffre, il me semble bien lire un o (70). Il y a évidemment une distorsion avec la lecture ἑξήκ(οντα), "soixante," de la ligne suivante, qui semble pourtant quasi certaine elle aussi (voir le formulaire parallèle de *O.BawitIFAO* 40): faut-il supposer une erreur d'une dizaine de la part du scribe?

[*O.Clackson* 17?]

11 x 10,3 cm   8ᵉ siècle (?)
Ägyptologisches Institut Heidelberg inv. 997
Plate IX

Poterie: lisse
Préservation: seulement la partie droite, avec quelques lettres.
Inédit. Rien n'indique, en dehors de l'appartenance au même lot que les autres, que cet ostracon vienne de Baouit.

1   ]ⲙⲛ̄ⲧⲁ ??
2   ]. ⲟⲥⲉ̣
3   ] . . ⁻
4   ]ⲁⲯⲁⲛⲉ ⁻ ⲁ

3, 4. il me semble reconnaître le sigle des artabes: ⁻
4. Peut-être "30 artabes de légumes" (ⲗⲁⲭⲁⲛⲉ = λάχανον), mais on pourrait aussi lire ⲗ]ⲁⲯⲁⲛⲉ = λαμψάνη.]

BIBLIOGRAPHIE

Bénazeth, D. (1995). "Histoire des fouilles de Baouît," in: Rosenstiehl, J.-M. (ed.) *CBC 8: Etudes coptes IV*. Louvain: Peeters, 53-62.

Bilabel, F. (1933). "Aegyptiaca II," *Aegyptus* 13, 555-562.

Boud'hors, A. (2004). *Ostraca grecs et coptes de Baouit*. Le Caire: Institut français d'archéologie orientale (= *O.BawitIFAO*).

Brunsch, W. (1980). "10 Ostraka aus Heidelberg," *Enchoria* X, 15-22.

Clackson S. J. (2001). "Reconstructing the Archives of the Monastery of Apollo at Bawit," in: Andorlini, I., Bastianini, G., Manfredi, M. et Menci, G. (eds.) *Atti del XXII Congresso*

Internazionale di papirologia (Firenze, 23-29 agosto 1998). Florence: Istituto papirologico "G. Vitelli," 219-236.

Clackson, S. J. (2003). "Nouvelles recherches sur les papyrus de Baouit," in: Cannuyer, C. (ed.) *CBC 13: Etudes coptes VIII*. Lille/Paris: Association francophone de Coptologie, 77-84.

Clackson, S. J. (2002). "Review of Clédat, J. (1999)," *BASP* 39, 189-204.

Clackson, S. J. (2004). "Museum Archaeology and Coptic Papyrology: the Bawit Papyri," in: Immerzeel, M. et Vliet, J. van der (eds.) *OLA 135: Coptic Studies on the Threshold of a New Millenium I. Proceedings of the Seventh International Congress of Coptic Studies*, Leiden 2000. Leuven: Peeters, 477-490.

Clackson, S. J. (2008). *It is Our Father Who Writes: Orders from the Monastery of Apollo at Bawit* (= *American Studies in Papyrology* 43). Oxford: Oxbow.

Clarysse, W. (1985). "The athenian Measure at Hermopolis," *ZPE* 60, 232-236.

Clédat, J. (1999). Bénazeth, D. et Rutschowscaya, M.-H. (eds.) *MIFAO* 111: *Le monastère et la nécropole de Baouit*. Le Caire: Institut français d'archéologie orientale.

Feucht, E. et alii. (1986). *Vom Nil zum Neckar, Kunstschätze Ägyptens aus pharaonischer und koptischer Zeit an der Universität Heidelberg*. Berlin/Heidelberg: Springer-Verlag.

Förster, H. (2002). *Wörterbuch der griechischen Wörter in den koptischen dokumentarischen Texten*. Berlin: De Gruyter.

Gascou, J. et Worp, K. A. (1990). "Un dossier d'ostraca du VIe siècle. Les archives des huiliers d'Aphroditô," in: Capasso, M., Messeri Savorelli, G. et Pintaudi, R. (eds.) *PapFlor XIX: Miscellanea Papyrologica in occasione del bicentenario dell'edizione della Charta Borgiana*. Florence: Gonnelli, 217-244 (vol.1) and pl. XXII-XXVIII (vol.2).

Krause, M. (1958). *Das Apa-Apollon-Kloster zu Bawit: Untersuchungen unveröffentlichter Urkunden als Beitrag zur Geschichte des ägyptischen Mönchtums*. University of Leipzig. Dissertation.

Oerter, W. 2001. "Recherchen zum koptischen Schrifttum in Prager Museen und Sammlungen (Stand August 1998)," in: Andorlini, I., Bastianini, G., Manfredi, M. et Menci, G. (eds.) *Atti del XXII Congresso Internazionale di papirologia (Firenze, 23-29 agosto 1998)*. Florence: Istituo papirologico "G. Vitelli," 1051-1056.

Pintaudi, R. (1993). "Ricevuta di trasporto," *AnPap* V, 143-144.

Tait, W. J. (1994). "A Coptic 'Enquiry' about a Delivery of Wheat," in: Eyre, C., Leahy, A. et Leahy, E. M. (eds.) *The Unbroken Reed: Studies in the Culture and Heritage of Ancient Egypt in Honour of A. F. Shore*. London, 337-42.

Worp, K. A. (2002). "The Date of *O.Crum VC* 111 and *O.Bawit* 56-58 & 62," *ZPE* 138, 121-122.

O. Clackson **18-33**

Les ostraca *etmoulon*. Quelques aspects du transport du ble dans l'Egypte copte

Alain Delattre

Le dossier des ostraca *etmoulon* se compose de 171 textes publiés,[1] pour la plupart apparus sur le marché des antiquités dans les années 1920[2] et dispersés ensuite, essentiellement entre 1924 et 1937, entre diverses collections, dont le Musée du Caire ou celui de Berlin et les Universités de Munich et du Michigan.[3] Tous ces textes enregistrent des livraisons de blé et proviennent sans doute d'un grand domaine ou d'un monastère. Les documents présentent tous un même formulaire (qui comprend la mention ⲉⲧⲙⲟⲩⲗⲟⲛ "au moulin") et forment donc un lot cohérent, qui date de la même époque et provient du même lieu.[4]

Les premiers documents ont été publiés par A. Mallon à la fin des années 1920, mais les études les plus complètes et les plus approfondies sont celles de W. Hengstenberg en 1931. Il faut encore mentionner les travaux de H.C. Youtie et W.H. Worrell en 1942 et celui de J. Shelton en 1990.[5] Je propose ici une étude de ces documents, notamment à la lumière de plusieurs ostraca inédits: un texte dont S. Clackson avait entamé l'édition (*O.Clackson* **18**), un ostracon de l'IFAO (*O.Clackson* **33**) et 12 ostraca conservés à Berlin (*O.Clackson* **19-23, 26-28, 30** et **31**).

1. La provenance

Différentes provenances ont été proposées par les éditeurs. A. Mallon pensait à la région thébaine, plus particulièrement Karnak, là où il a acheté ses ostraca.[6] W. Hengstenberg estimait plutôt que les textes proviennent de Moyenne-Égypte. En effet, un des vendeurs d'antiquités lui avait affirmé que les ostraca venaient d'ed-Deir (près d'Assiout).[7] W. Hengstenberg considérait cependant, sur base de quelques arguments linguistiques, qu'ils venaient plus probablement de la région d'Hermoupolis.[8] Par ailleurs, W. Hengstenberg mentionne aussi l'affirmation d'un autre marchand selon laquelle les textes

---

* Cet article est la version amplifiée de la communication présentée à la réunion. Il a été tenu compte pour la version écrite de l'apport des textes de Berlin.

[1] À une exception près, Jakobielsky 1960: 36, tous ont été repris dans le Sammelbuch copte (*SBKopt.* I 54-223).—On trouvera en annexe un tableau reprenant tous les ostraca *etmoulon*; la numérotation utilisée ici pour renvoyer aux textes est celle du tableau, sauf pour les textes édités ou réédités ici (*O.Clackson* **1** à **16**).

[2] Exception faite du texte n° 13, cf. *infra*.

[3] On en trouve aussi dans les Universités de Macquarie, de Munich, de Yale, de Trèves et de Varsovie, au Kelsey Museum ainsi qu'à l'IFAO et dans des collections privées.

[4] Par ailleurs, plusieurs mains de scribes sont identifiables.

[5] Cf. la bibliographie en fin d'article.

[6] Cf. Mallon 1927: 152.

[7] Cf. Hengstenberg 1931b: 122.

[8] Cf. Hengstenberg 1931b: 136

proviendraient d'un site copte à l'extrême ouest du Fayoum, sans autre précision.[9] D'autres provenances ont encore été proposées.[10]

Un élément permet cependant de trancher: un des textes (13) a été trouvé lors de fouilles archéologiques en Moyenne-Égypte, dans les environs de Manqabad plus précisément. La première hypothèse de Hengstenberg se révèle donc juste: les ostraca *etmoulon* proviennent de Moyenne-Égypte.

2. LA DATE

Diverses dates ont également été proposées (entre le IVe et le VIIe siècle). Les datations se basent sur des critères paléographiques, assez difficiles à manier. Il existe un certain nombre de mains identifiables (apparemment moins de dix[11]). Certaines mains sont pratiquement livresques, d'autres sont nettement plus cursives (comme la "main 1"[12]). Je pense, à la suite de plusieurs auteurs, que ces textes datent probablement du VIIe siècle, sans que l'on puisse exclure le VIe siècle.

3. LA STRUCTURE DES TEXTES

Dans le cadre de ce travail, j'ai étudié tous les textes publiés ainsi que les inédits dont j'avais connaissance. Un tableau récapitulatif des différents éléments du formulaire est présenté en annexe. Quatre éléments sont indispensables:

1. La date (jour, mois et année de l'indiction). Les éléments de la date peuvent apparaître dans des ordres différents.

2. Un toponyme. Il s'agit du domaine producteur d'où vient le blé.

3. L'objet du transport, c'est-à-dire le blé. La plupart du temps le blé est mis dans des sacs et transporté en chariots. Chaque sac contient 3 artabes de blé et chaque chariot est chargé avec 5 sacs. Il y a des exceptions cependant.

4. La mention ⲉⲧⲙⲟⲩⲗⲟⲛ "au moulin." Il s'agit de la destination du blé.

D'autres éléments sont facultatifs:

5. La mention ⲥⲉⲛⲉ.

6. On trouve parfois aussi d'autres mentions, comme le numéro du convoi.

---

[9] Cf. Hengstenberg 1931b: 137. Mais ces textes ne présentent pas de trace de fayoumismes, cf. Youtie et Worrell 1942: 256.

[10] Jakobielsky pense que l'ostracon a été trouvé à Edfou; l'hypothèse de K. Galling n'est pas fondée, cf. Bagnall 1979: 6-7.

[11] Cf. Youtie et Worell 1942: 256-257.

[12] Cf. Youtie et Worell 1942: 257.

3.1 *La date*

La date se compose du jour, du mois et de l'année. Les textes sont datés entre la 3e et la 11e année d'un cycle indictionnel.[13] Certaines années sont mieux représentées que d'autres: 2 documents datent de la 3e année; 30 de la 6e; 56 de la 7e; 14 de la 8e; 46 de la 9e; 1 de la 10e[14] et 16 de la 11e. L'indication de l'année est perdue dans 22 ostraca.

Les livraisons de blé au moulin se répartissent entre le 13 Pachôn et le 2 Mésôré, soit entre 8 mai et le 26 juillet. La grande majorité des textes sont datés des mois de Pauni et d'Épeiph (Pauni dans 99 documents et Épeiph dans 65), soit la période qui suit la moisson. Onze textes sont datés des mois adjacents (Pachôn dans 9 documents[15] et Mésôrè dans 2[16]). Un texte cependant est daté du 15 Athyr (11/12 novembre; texte n° 150), mais ce texte présente d'autres particularités. Dans 11 documents, la mention du mois est perdue.

3.2 *Les lieux de production*

Le corpus des ostraca *etmoulon* a conservé les noms d'une trentaine de toponymes producteurs de blé, qui appartiennent selon toute vraisemblance à un "Large estate," un grand domaine, ou à un monastère. La plupart sont construit sur (п)мл N-, littéralement "le lieu de...," suivi d'un nom propre; mais on trouve aussi d'autres formulations, notamment en пгот N- "le champ de..." et плго N- "le grenier de..."

Voici la liste des toponymes classés par ordre d'importance des attestations:[17] Manapollô (33),[18] Manhatré (23),[19] Manpaterné (15), Manariôn (13),[20] Mannepèrgos (12), Manpabinaios (10),[21] (Man)paiomtioué (9), Phoimprès (8),[22] Pialo (6), Manadam (5), Manpag'au (5), Manpéhrétôr (5), Mangou(n)thé (4), Manabraham (3), Tehrèfé (3), Manadôra (2), Manapalaure(n)té (2), Manatôré (= Manadôra?; 2), Mangéôrgé (2), Mantasa (2), Nsouopalen (2),[23] Pnog'eniôhé (2), Tbasilikè (2), Mangé...o... (1), Mapéhrèten (=Manpéhrétôr?; 1), Nemhoté (1), Nmozekièl (1), Pahoensékeina (1),

---

[13] La grande homogénéité du matériel ainsi que certaines mains de scribes qui ont été mises en évidence permettent de proposer que tous ces textes datent d'un même cycle. Cependant, il est tout à fait possible que les textes de la 3e année datent du cycle suivant. J'ai choisi la disposition chronologique la plus économique.

[14] Texte n° 149; cette occurrence n'est pas certaine, cf. Youtie et Worrell 1942: 258, n. 6.

[15] Ce sont les textes n°s 33, 34, 103, 104, 105, 106, 166, 167 et 168.

[16] Ce sont les textes n°s 102 et 165.

[17] J'ai indiqué entre parenthèses le nombre d'attestations. Dans la transcription française des toponymes, j'écris tout à la suite (man+nom propre).—Certains toponymes, pourtant grands producteurs, sont rarement attestés. C'est le cas notamment du Manadôra, attesté deux fois seulement dans la documentation, mais pour des convois de 15 chariots à chaque fois. Peut-être ce domaine était-il assez éloignés du moulin, et les transports s'y effectuaient-ils moins souvent et pour de plus grandes quantités?

[18] Y compris le мл ндпоλоγ (106).

[19] Je joins ici aussi le пмл ндпд гдтре (151).

[20] Y compris le "мднлрιω)N" (86 et 115).

[21] Y compris мд NПдвлNOC (14).

[22] Dans toutes les orthographes attestées.

[23] Il n'est pas clair s'il s'agit d'un toponyme.

Pahontmoue (1), Pahozékièl (1), Phoik...? (1), Phoinapa (1), ?Tmoue paremjotp (1). Dans 8 ostraca, le toponyme n'est pas conservé. Aucun de ces toponymes n'est sûrement attesté ailleurs.[24] Il faut noter aussi que quelques documents mentionnent deux toponymes différents, c'est-à-dire deux lieux de production différents (n°s 102, 106 et 165?).

Le plus gros producteur de blé est le Manapollô, sans doute le domaine le plus important, du moins dans l'état actuel de la documentation. En une année, la 6e du cycle indictionnel, 73 chariots répartis en 17 chargements ont transporté plus de 1000 artabes de blé du Manapollô. Sur l'ensemble des attestations, près de 200 chariots remplis de blé sont partis de ce lieu et ont été envoyés au moulin, ce qui correspond à environ 3000 artabes de blé.

Ces indications de quantités permettent en effet de se faire une petite idée de la taille de ce domaine. Sachant que le rendement moyen d'une aroure équivaut à 10 artabes[25] et en se basant sur les chiffres de la 6e année du cycle indictionnel, on peut estimer que le Manapollô devait avoir une superficie minimale (car nous n'avons pas tous les textes) de 100 aroures (soit 24 hectares). On obtient des approximations équivalentes pour le Manhatré.[26]

3.3 *Les produits et les quantités*

Dans les ostraca de la série *etmoulon*, le blé est normalement transporté dans des sacs (σάκκοι), placés sur des chariots (ἅμαξαι). De manière générale, chaque chariot est chargé de 5 sacs remplis de 3 artabes. Les exceptions sont nombreuses: presque un chargement sur quatre ne suit pas cette règle (voir *infra*).

Souvent plusieurs chariots sont envoyés ensemble, en convoi (φορά), chercher le blé au domaine producteur (cf. *infra*). Chaque convoi peut compter entre 1[27] et 30[28] chariots. Chaque jour, plusieurs convois sont envoyés dans différents lieux de production (le plus grand nombre de convois différents envoyés le même jour est de 7[29]). Deux convois peuvent être envoyés deux jours consécutifs au même endroit ou plusieurs convois peuvent être envoyés au même lieu un même jour.

Mais les chariots ne constituent pas le seul moyen de transport du blé: quelques textes enregistrent des transports par chameaux. Il faut remarquer à ce propos que le texte n° 106 mentionne les deux moyens de transport: l'ostracon note deux livraisons, l'une de 45 artabes de blé du Manhatré, réparties sur 3 chariots, et l'autre de 34 artabes de blé du Manapolou,[30] transportées par chameaux dans 17 *thallia*.

---

[24] Ces toponymes se situent sans doute en Moyenne-Égypte, puisque nous avons vu plus haut que ce groupe d'ostraca provient de cette région.

[25] Cf. Rathbone 1991: 243, mais les rendements sont parfois supérieurs.

[26] 2250 artabes de blé, transportées en 150 chariots, proviennent du Manhatré. Viennent ensuite le Manpaterné, avec 86 chariots (transportant environ 1290 artabes de blé), le Manariôn, avec 71 chariots (transportant environ 1065 artabes de blé) et le Mannépèrgos avec 46 chariots (transportant environ 700 artabes de blé)...

[27] Cf. les textes n°s 96, 103, 114, 122, 128, 130, 139. La quantité minimale de blé transporté mentionnée dans les ostraca *etmoulon* est de 4 artabes (n° 174), mais dans ce cas le transport est effectué par chameau.

[28] Cf. le texte n° 84.

[29] Cf. les textes n°s 5-11; voir aussi les textes n°s 127-131 (cinq chargements différents datés du même jour, totalisant 18 chariots).

[30] Ce toponyme ne fait sans doute qu'un avec le Manapollôn.

Le transport du blé par chameaux est attesté clairement dans cinq textes (textes n°s 104, 106, 150, 164 et 165).[31] L'examen des attestations montre que ces livraisons sont essentiellement réalisées en dehors des mois de Pauni et d'Épeiph (la grande période de transport): soit un peu avant[32] ou un peu après,[33] ou encore tout à fait en dehors.[34] On peut donc imaginer que le transport par chameaux est marginal et utilisé au début ou à la fin de la saison du transport, lorsque le transport par chariots n'est pas ou plus opérationnel. Les chameaux sont apparemment également requis pour le transport de quantités peu importantes de blé, c'est-à-dire inférieures au chargement normal d'un chariot (soit 15 artabes).[35]

Le blé transporté sur les chariots est usuellement placé dans des sacs[36] d'une capacité de 3 artabes, tandis que les chameaux le transportent en *thallia* de 2 artabes. On trouve cependant dans quelques textes des chariots chargés de sacs et de *thallia* (textes n°s 87, 139 et 151). Dans un texte (n° 168), on a ajouté au chargement du chariot deux ⲕⲓⲣ "paniers."

La qualité du blé est rarement indiquée. Deux fois le blé est peut-être qualifié de "vieux": ⲥⲟⲩⲟ (ⲛ)ⲡⲁⲗⲉⲛ "vieux blé" (textes n°s 164 et 165). Il faut cependant noter que l'interprétation de ces textes est difficile. Dans le texte n° 164, il n'y a pas de toponyme indiqué et dans le n° 165, on peut se demander ce que désigne ⲡⲁⲣⲉⲙϩⲟⲧⲉⲡ. Il faut remarquer aussi que les deux textes datent de la fin de la "saison" (27 Épeiph et 2 Mésôré) et que dans les deux cas le transport s'est effectué par chameaux.

3.4 *Le rapport chariot/sacs/artabes*

Le rapport régulier est de 1:5:15, c'est-à-dire qu'un chariot est normalement chargé avec 5 sacs contenant 15 artabes (soit 3 artabes par sac). Diverses irrégularités apparaissent cependant dans les rapports chariot/sacs/artabes. Les variations où le rapport est inférieur ne posent pas de problème. On conçoit aisément que les chariots aient pu ne pas être toujours chargés au maximum de leur capacité. La plupart des exceptions sont de faible ampleur (chariots un peu sous- ou surchargés). On remarque en outre que souvent les irrégularités apparaissent à plusieurs niveaux, c'est-à-dire que des ajustements ont été réalisés. Par exemple, s'il manquait un sac, on pouvait remplir les autres un peu plus pour que les chariots soient remplis avec un nombre suffisant d'artabes, comme dans le texte n° 88 où 9 chariots assurent le transport de 44 sacs seulement (1 sac manque), mais qui contiennent 134 artabes (soit deux en trop par rapport aux sacs), ce qui fait que l'écart au lieu d'être de 3 artabes puisqu'il manque un sac, n'est que d'une artabe.

Les chariots ne sont apparemment jamais chargés de plus de 17 artabes.

Je présente ici les principales irrégularités constatées:

– Le nombre de sacs par chariot est supérieur à 5. Dans un certain nombre de cas, les chariots transportent des quantités plus importantes, comme dans les textes n°s 73 (4:21:63), 97 (3:16:48),

---

[31] Probablement aussi dans le texte 28, daté du 28 Pachôn, et qui enregistre le transport de 23 artabes de blé.
[32] Cf. les textes n°s 104, daté du 13 Pachôn, et 106, daté du 30 Pachôn.
[33] Cf. les textes n°s 165, daté du 2 Mésôrè, et aussi 164, daté du 27 Épeiph, soit la fin de la «saison».
[34] Cf. le texte n° 150, daté du 15 Athyr.
[35] Cf. les textes n°s 43 (10 artabes), 144 (1 + 13 artabes?) et 174 (4 artabes).
[36] Sur les sacs, cf. Mayerson 1998.

147 (2:11:33) et 182 (4:22:66). Il faut remarquer toutefois que l'excédent est minime: une artabe à une artabe et demi en plus par chariot.

Cependant, il arrive aussi que, même s'il y a trop de sacs par chariot, le total d'artabes par chariot est de 15 (ou inférieur), parce que le nombre d'artabes par sac est inférieur à 3 (ce qui fait que le rapport chariot/artabes est "correct" ou légèrement inférieur); c'est le cas dans les textes n°s 20 (15:77:224), 92 (4:23:59), 102 (8:45:75+45); 140 (21; 106; 312) et 155 (6:35:90).

– Le nombre de sacs par chariot est inférieur à 5. Le chariot n'est donc pas tout à fait rempli, comme dans les textes n°s 55 (7:32:96), 82 (3:12:36), 131 (5:24:60(+?)+12) et 156 (2:8:24). Il peut aussi arriver que le chariot soit rempli de sacs et de *thallia*, comme dans le texte n° 151 (4:19 sacs et 1 *thallion*:59). Il arrive également que le nombre d'artabes par sac soit aussi divergent: il peut être inférieur à 3 comme dans les textes n°s 42 (5:23:68), 79 (13:64:174+16) et 80 (7:33:81+15); ou supérieur à 3 comme dans les textes n°s 88 (9:44:134) et 141 (12:55:168). Dans le texte n° 120 (4:1…:55) on ne peut déterminer si le rapport entre artabes et sacs est inférieur ou supérieur à 3. Dans le document n° 149 (10:45:135), on peut se demander si un chariot n'est pas simplement revenu vide.[37] De manière générale, les écarts avec la norme sont donc assez modérés.

– Le nombre d'artabes par sac est supérieur à 3.[38] Les sacs sont parfois surchargés, comme dans les textes n°s 23 (3:15:47+…), 27 (9:45:141), 34 (7:35:105+11),[39] 94 (11:55:166) et 95 (9:45:124+12). Dans tous les cas, les chariots ne sont pas chargés à plus de 17 artabes, soit deux de plus que la normale.

– Le nombre d'artabes par sac est inférieur à 3.[40] Il arrive très souvent que les sacs ne soient pas assez remplis. Cela s'explique aisément: si le nombre d'artabes disponibles dans le domaine n'est pas divisible par le nombre de sacs, ces derniers, ou une partie d'entre eux, ne sont pas remplis au maximum de leurs capacités (3 artabes).[41] Cela arrive dans les textes n°s 25 (7:35:90), 35 (2:15:30), 72 (2:10:27), 129 (4:20:44+13) et 142 (11:66:162).

Dans quelques cas, on peut soupçonner que les irrégularités du texte sont le fait d'une erreur du scribe ou d'une mauvaise lecture de l'éditeur, comme dans les textes n°s 121 et 163, où le nombre de sacs n'est pas indiqué; le texte n° 118 (50:50:105), où il faut sans doute corriger le nombre de chariots en "10"; le texte n° 137 (19:45:135), où il doit n'y avoir que 9 chariots; le texte n° 180 où la séquence ⲡⲛⲓⲉ doit signifier 165. Les graves irrégularités qui apparaissent dans les textes n°s 162 (6:28:160) et 184 (4:50:161+18) ne sont pas explicables, peut-être dans ces cas aussi les lectures sont-elles à revoir. Dans quelques cas enfin, l'état fragmentaire du texte ne permet pas de déterminer exactement où se situe l'irrégularité (textes n°s 74, 123, 183).

---

[37] À moins qu'il ne s'agisse d'une faute du scribe, qui aurait écrit 10 pour 9, cf. Youtie et Worell (1942): 258, n. 6.

[38] Je n'ai pas tenu compte ici des textes où le nombre de sacs par chariot est lui aussi anormal (textes n°s 88 et 141); ces cas particuliers sont traités dans les paragraphes précédents.

[39] On peut se demander dans ce cas si les 11 artabes de blé "séné" ne sont pas incluses dans les 105 artabes.

[40] Je n'ai pas tenu compte ici des textes où le nombre de sacs par chariot est lui aussi anormal (textes n°s 20, 42, 79, 80, 92, 102, 124, 141); ces cas particuliers sont traités dans les paragraphes précédents.

[41] À moins que ces sacs n'aient une capacité différente, mais cela semble peu probable.

3.5 La destination du blé

Les ostraca se terminent usuellement par la mention de la destination du blé (ⲉⲧⲙⲟⲩⲗⲟⲛ ou ⲉⲡⲙⲁⲛⲟⲩϩⲉ).

Depuis les travaux de W. Hengstenberg, on reconnaît dans la séquence ⲉⲧⲙⲟⲩⲗⲟⲛ[42] le mot grec μυλών "Moulin."[43] Normalement les textes de la série se terminent par cette mention, mais il arrive dans quelques documents que la séquence se trouve au milieu du texte (textes n°s 1, 166, 168).

Dans quelques textes cependant, le lieu de destination du blé n'est pas le moulin mais le ⲡⲙⲁⲛⲟⲩϩⲉ. Les sept documents[44] où cette variante apparaît datent de la 11e année de l'indiction. Dans l'un d'entre eux, le blé est destiné à la fois au moulin et au grenier du ⲡⲙⲁⲛⲟⲩϩⲉ (texte n° 159).

La signification exacte du terme est problématique et encore discutée. W. Hengstenberg a pensé à rapprocher le mot du copte ⲛⲟⲩϩⲉ "séparer" (ⲡⲙⲁ ⲛⲛⲟⲩϩⲉ); dans ce cas il s'agirait d'un lieu où on sépare le blé (peut-être entre le blé destiné à la consommation et le blé aux semailles de l'année suivante). Youtie et Worell[45] rapprochent l'élément ⲛⲟⲩϩⲉ du verbe ⲟⲩⲱϩ "placer," le ⲡⲙⲁ ⲛⲟⲩϩⲉ/ⲛⲟⲩⲱϩ serait une sorte de magasin, d'entrepôt.

3.6 La mention ⲥⲉⲛⲉ

Le mot ⲥⲉⲛⲉ apparaît dans une vingtaine de textes. Le plus souvent, une certaine quantité transportée est dite ⲥⲉⲛⲉ, et l'autre pas.

Diverses hypothèses ont été proposées pour comprendre ce mot:

– ⲥⲉⲛⲉ pour ⲧⲥⲁⲛⲟ "ajuste!" (c'est l'hypothèse d'Hengstenberg, revue par Worrell et Youtie). Il s'agirait donc d'une quantité de blé à ajouter pour remplir les chariots (pour faire correspondre le nombre d'artabes à la capacité des chariots). Mais il serait assez étrange d'avoir un verbe à cet endroit.

– ⲥⲉⲛⲉ = ⲥⲏⲛⲉ "grenier." Il s'agirait dans ce cas de la destination du blé; mais cette solution est peu probable, car la préposition ⲉ- manque.

– ⲥⲉⲛⲉ = "Wagenkasten." Selon K. Galling le mot ⲥⲉⲛⲉ renvoie à un mode de transport.[46] Il rapproche le mot de ⲥⲏⲛⲉ "grenier" et estime que l'expression désignerait donc du grain déposé directement, en vrac, dans le chariot.

– ⲥⲉⲛⲉ comme description de la qualité du blé. C'est l'hypothèse de L. Saint-Paul Girard.[47] Cette hypothèse se base sur une variante que l'on trouve dans un texte où, à la place de ⲥⲉⲛⲉ, on

---

[42] On trouve une fois l'orthographe ⲉⲧⲙⲩⲗⲟⲛ (n° 157) et une fois ⲉⲧⲙⲟⲩⲗⲱⲛ (n° 106).

[43] Μυλών désigne le local où l'on moud le blé. Le terme est attesté dans les papyrus grecs du IVe au VIe siècle, cf. Battaglia 1989: 157 et 160.

[44] Cf. textes n°s 158, 159, 161, 162, 163, 178 et 183.

[45] Cf. Youtie et Worrell 1942: 259-260.

[46] Cf. Galling 1966: 48-49, n. 19: "es muß sich bei eine besondere Transportart handeln."

[47] Cf. Saint-Paul Girard 1929: 101.

trouve le mot grec ⲥⲁⲡⲣⲟⲛ "pourri" (texte n° 168). Le contexte est le même; ⲥⲉⲛⲉ décrirait donc une qualité particulière du blé. Comme il y a des textes qui mentionnent uniquement une quantité séné, il est peu probable que ⲥⲉⲛⲉ soit la traduction de σαπρόν: on voit mal pourquoi on prendrait la peine de transporter du blé pourri, à moins que le blé n'ait été gâté durant le transport.

La question de la signification exacte du mot reste ouverte.

3.7 *Autres éléments*

Parfois, les textes mentionnent le numéro du convoi (*phora*). Dans quelques ostraca, la mention indique clairement qu'il s'agit d'un convoi (n°s 150, 165, 167, 168); dans les autres, la formulation est ambiguë et le mot *phora* (ou son abréviation) est absent: on trouve à la place ⲁ/ ou ⲁⲓ/ suivi d'un chiffre, ce qui a été interprété comme l'abréviation de δι(ὰ) x (φορᾶς), cf. les textes 87, 92, 97, 139, 156, 159, 174).

Dans un cas au moins on peut douter de cette résolution: le texte 168 pose problème parce qu'il mentionne deux livraisons différentes (l. 1 ⲉ ⲫⲟⲣ et l. 5 ⲁ ⲃ). Il semble plutôt que la séquence ⲁ ⲃ que l'on trouve dans le résumé corresponde aux deux paniers (ⲃⲓⲣ ⲃ) de la l. 4.

Donc, les mentions ⲁ/ ou ⲁⲓ/ suivi d'un chiffre représentent peut-être la mention du convoi, mais peut-être aussi une indication sur les contenants et les quantités transportées, mais je ne vois pas de quelle abréviation il pourrait s'agir dans ce cas.

S'il s'agit bien chaque fois d'un convoi, sont attestés des transports durant le premier convoi (textes n°s 139, 150, 156, 165 et 174), le deuxième (textes n°s 159 et 167), le troisième (textes n°s 92 et 97), le quatrième (texte n° 87) et le cinquième (texte n° 168). Rappelons que le nombre maximum de convois attestés en une journée est de 7.

Enfin, on trouve dans un texte le nom du transporteur (n° 33: ϩⲓⲧⲉⲛ ⲙⲱⲥⲏⲥ) et un autre contient une note adressée au transporteur (n° 111).

4. *O.CLACKSON* **18-33**
(ÉDITION D'OSTRACA *ETMOULON* INÉDITS)

Je présente ici l'édition de 16 ostraca *etmoulon* inédits. Le premier texte, maintenant conservé au British Museum, avait été repéré par S. Clackson sur le marché des antiquités (*O.Clackson* **18**).[48]

On trouvera ensuite l'édition de documents inédits des Staatliche Museen de Berlin.[49] Ces textes, mentionnés par W. Beltz,[50] font partie d'un lot, offert aux Staatliche Museen en 1931 (inv. 14705-

---

[48] Le British Museum a acheté ce texte auprès de l'antiquaire Charles Ede. Une photographie et une brève description du texte ont été publiés dans un catalogue de vente en 1999 (*Writing and Lettering in Antiquity* 18). — Je remercie M. D. Williams, conservateur de la section des antiquités grecques et romaines du British Museum, de m'avoir autorisé à publier ce texte. Je remercie également M. James Ede pour toutes les informations qu'il a bien voulu me faire parvenir sur cet ostracon.

[49] Je remercie Mme I. Müller, conservatrice au Staatliche Museen zu Berlin, de m'avoir autorisé à publier ces documents.

14718).⁵¹ La présence au sein du lot berlinois de textes exactement identiques m'a amené à ventiler les éditions en trois "sous-dossiers":—textes datés du 9 Pauni de la 6ᵉ année de l'indiction (*O.Clackson* **19-25**);—textes datés du 5 Pauni de la 7ᵉ année de l'indiction (*O.Clackson* **26-29**);—textes datés du 28 Pauni de la 7ᵉ année de l'indiction (*O.Clackson* **30-32**). J'y ai ajouté la réédition de quelques textes identiques conservés au Kelsey Museum (*O.Clackson* **24, 25, 29** et **32**).⁵² Il est probable que ces textes ont été découverts ensemble et qu'ils ont été vendus séparément par le marchand d'antiquités.

Il faut noter aussi que ces trois "sous-dossiers" de textes constituent une exception dans le corpus. On ne trouve pas d'autre exemple de textes datés du même jour et enregistrant des livraisons de blé identiques, provenant du même toponyme.⁵³

Enfin, je joins l'édition d'un ostracon *etmoulon* de l'IFAO (*O.Clackson* **33**).⁵⁴

O.Clackson **18**

O.Brit.Mus. inv. GR 1999.6-29.1   18,8 x 12,2 cm   VIᵉ-VIIᵉ siècles
Plate X   Moyenne-Égypte

Cependant les trois premières lignes posent quelques problèmes: il n'y a apparemment pas de mention du lieu de production. On peut donc se demander si le texte est bien du même type que les autres (sans même évoquer la note des lignes 4-9).

        1   ⲡⲁⲩⲛ/ ⲏ ⲑ ⲓ//
        2   ⲕ ⲏⲙⲉⲣ/ ⲉⲧⲙⲟⲩⲗⲟⲛ
        3   ⲁⲙⲁϩ ⲏ ⲥⲁⲕⲕ/ ⲙ ⲥⲓ — ⲣⲕ̄

        4   ⲁⲩⲱ ⲁⲓ̈ϫⲟⲟⲩ ⲧⲁϭⲟⲗⲧⲉ ⲛ̄ϩⲓⲣⲟⲩϩⲉ
        5   ⲛ̄ⲧⲁⲓ̈ⲥϩⲁⲓ̈ⲥ ⲉⲧⲃⲉⲁϫⲉ ⲡⲁⲣⲁ
        6   ⲙⲉⲣⲟⲥ ⲧⲟⲩⲧ ⲉⲥⲧⲓⲛ ϣⲁⲕϣⲓⲛⲉ
        7   ⲛ̄ⲥⲁ ϯⲧⲉ ⲛⲁϭⲟⲗⲧⲉ
        8   ⲙ̄ⲡⲟⲟⲩ †

        1   Pauni, le 8; 9ᵉ année de l'indiction.
        2   2ᵉ jour (?). Au moulin.

---

⁵⁰ Cf. Beltz 1980.

⁵¹ Deux textes du lot, qui sont aussi probablement des textes du corpus, ne sont pas édités ici en raison de leur mauvais état de conservation. Ce sont O.Berol. inv. 14709 (7 x 8,4 cm), où l'on lit à la dernière ligne [ⲉⲧ]ⲙⲟⲩⲗⲟⲛ, et O.Berol. inv. 14711 (7,3 x 7,9 cm), totalement illisible.

⁵² Je remercie M. R. Meador-Woodruff du Kelsey Museum of Archeology de m'avoir aimablement fourni des images digitales de ces ostraca.

⁵³ On peut se demander si ce ne sont pas des copies, mais il semble peu vraisemblable de faire 7 copies du même texte. L'hypothèse de falsifications a également été envisagée, mais semble très peu probable.

⁵⁴ Je remercie M. Chr. de Beauvais, administrateur provisoire de l'IFAO, de m'avoir autorisé à publier ce document.

3	Chariots: 8; sacs 40; artabes de blé: 120.
4	Et j'ai envoyé le chariot le soir
5	où je l'ai écrit sur l'ostracon ...,
6	ce qui veut dire que tu dois aller chercher
7	neuf chariots
8	aujourd'hui. †

2. ⲕ ⲏⲙⲉⲣ/ À cette place, on s'attend à un toponyme. Il est pourtant peu probable que ce soit le cas ici en raison de l'abréviation, même si l'indication du lieu de production est normalement obligatoire. Un seul autre texte ne mentionne pas de toponyme: ce document est daté du 7 Pauni de la 9ᵉ année de l'indication, soit un jour avant ce texte-ci. La séquence ⲕⲏⲙⲉⲣ/ pourrait aussi être comprises comme β ἡμέρ(αι/ῶν/ας) "2 jours ou 2ᵉ jour." Comme il est question de "hier soir" et de "aujourd'hui" dans la note en dessous du texte, l'interprétation 2ᵉ jour semble possible.

2. ⲉⲧⲙⲟⲩⲗⲟⲛ La séquence ⲉⲧⲙⲟⲩⲗⲟⲛ se trouve au milieu du texte (cf. p. ex. textes nᵒˢ 166 et 168).

4-9. La note des l. 4-9 nous laisse entrevoir le fonctionnement général du transport dont les ostraca *etmoulon* sont les témoins. Le transporteur devait s'occuper de huit chariots (cf. l. 3), et la note lui indique qu'il y a un chariot supplémentaire à prendre en charge, donc il devra s'occuper de neuf chariots.

5-6. ⲡⲁⲣⲁ | ⲙⲉⲣⲟⲥ Le sens de cette expression pose problème. Les traduction usuelles, "à tour de rôle" ou "en partie," ne donnent pas un sens satisfaisant.

O.Clackson 19-25
(Sept textes datés du 9 Pauni de la 6ᵉ année de l'indication)

Je donne ici l'édition de cinq ostraca de Berlin apparemment identiques, dont voici la traduction: "† Pauni, le 9; 6ᵉ année de l'indication. Manapollô. Chariots: 2; sacs: 10; artabes de blé: 30. Au moulin." J'y ai ajouté la réédition de *SBKopt.* I 150 et 151 (Kelsey Museum, inv. 25009 et 25006), qui présentent le même texte.

L'envoi en un seul jour de sept convois différents semble étonnant au regard du reste de la documentation. L'explication la plus plausible est d'imaginer qu'il s'agit dans chaque texte des deux mêmes chariots, qui auraient fait sept fois l'aller-retour entre le Manapollô et le moulin le même jour.

O.Clackson 19

O.Berol. inv. 14705　　　　　　　　　6,6 x 6,9 cm　　　　　　　　　VIᵉ-VIIᵉ siècles
Plate X　　　　　　　　　　　　　　　　　　　　　　　　　　　　Moyenne-Égypte

1　　+ ⲡⲁⲩ/ : ⲑ : ⲁⲓⲛⲕ/ ⲋ :

2   ḅịN : ṃḁ Nαπολⲱⲛ
3   αμα⳽/ : ⲃ ⲥακ : ι
4   ⲥι ⸗ λ
5   ⲉⲧⲙⲟⲩλⲟⲛ

2. ḁịN : Le scribe a sans doute voulu écrire une nouvelle fois l'abréviation de ἰνδικτίων. Il s'agit donc sans doute d'une dittographie.

O.Clackson 20

O.Berol. inv. 14707　　　　　　　6 x 7,3 cm　　　　　　　VIᵉ-VIIᵉ siècles
No plate　　　　　　　　　　　　　　　　　　　　　　　　Moyenne-Égypte

1   + παυ ⲑ αινκ : ⳽ :
2   μα ṇαπολⲱⲛ -
3   αμα⳽/ : ⲃ ⲥακ/ : ι
4   ⲥι ⸗ λ
5   ⲉⲧⲙⲟⲩλⲟⲛ

O.Clackson 21

O.Berol. inv. 14712　　　　　　　9,5 x 7 cm　　　　　　　VIᵉ-VIIᵉ siècles
No plate　　　　　　　　　　　　　　　　　　　　　　　　Moyenne-Égypte

1   + παυ ⲑ
2   ḁịṇḁκ/ : ⳽ :
3   μα ⲛαπολⲱⲛ
4   αμα⳽/ ⲃ : ⲥακ ị
5   ⲥι ⸗ . λ
6   ⲉⲧⲙⲟⲩλⲟⲛ

2. ḁịṇḁκ/ L'abréviation ḁịṇḁκ/ est attestée une fois: *SBKopt.* I 151 (également daté du 9 Pauni de la 6ᵉ année de l'indiction).
5. ⲥι ⸗ . λ On retrouve exactement le même trait dans O.Mich. inv. 25009.

O.Clackson 22

O.Berol. inv. 14715   6,5 x 7,2 cm   VIe-VIIe siècles
No plate   Moyenne-Égypte

```
1    + ΠΑΥ/ Θ Α.ΙΝ-
2    Κ · Ϛ : ΜΑ ΝΑΠ-
3    Ο . Α ΛΛΦ
4    ΑΜΑΞ/ : Β : ϹΑΚ Ι
5          ϹΙ ÷ Λ
6    ΕΤΜΟΥΛΟΝ
```

2-3. ΜΑ ΝΑΠ|Ο . Α ΛΛΦ Il faut sans doute reconnaître dans cette séquence le toponyme Manapollô (avec une faute au milieu du mot).

O.Clackson 23

O.Berol. inv. 14716   8,7 x 7,3 cm   VIe-VIIe siècles
No plate   Moyenne-Égypte

```
1    + ΠΑΥ/ · Θ : Α.ΙΝΚ : Ϛ : -
2    ΜΑ ΝΑΠΟΛΦΝ : -
3    ΑΜΑΞ/ : Β : ϹΑΚ : Ι -
4          ϹΙ ÷ Λ
5    ΕΤΜΟΥΛΟΝ
```

O.Clackson 24

SBKopt. I 150 = Kelsey Museum inv. 25006 10,2 x 7 cm   VIe-VIIe siècles
No plate   Moyenne-Égypte

```
1    + ΠΑΥ/ · Θ
2    Α.ΙΝΚ/ : Ϛ :
3    ΜΑ ΝΑΠΟΛΦΝ
4    ΑΜΑΞ/ : Β : ϹΑΚ : Ι
5          ϹΙ ÷ : Λ :
6    ΕΤΜΟΥΛΟΝ
```

O.Clackson 25

SBKopt. I 151 = Kelsey Museum inv. 25009 13,2 x 7 cm   VIe-VIIe siècles
Plate XI   Moyenne-Égypte

    1   + ΠΑΥ · Θ
    2   ΑΙΝΑΚ/ : Ϛ :
    3   ΜΑ ΝΑΠΟΛΩΝ
    4   ΑΜΑΞ/ : Β : ϹΑΚ/ : Ι
    5   ϹΙ ÷ . Λ
    6   ΕΤΜΟΥΛΟΝ

5. ϹΙ ÷ . Λ On retrouve exactement le même trait dans O.Berol. inv. 14712.

O.Clackson 26-29
(Quatre textes datés du 5 Pauni de la 7e année de l'indiction)

Je donne ici l'édition de trois textes de Berlin apparemment identiques, dont voici la traduction: "† 7e année de l'indiction; Pauni, le 5. Mannépèrgos. Chariots: 3; sacs: 15; artabes de blé: 45. Au moulin." J'y ai ajouté la réédition de *SBKopt.* I 167 (O.Mich. inv. 25028), qui présente le même texte.

O.Clackson 26

O.Berol. inv. 14706   4,5 x 8,9 cm   VIe-VIIe siècles
Plate XI   Moyenne-Égypte

    1   + ΙΝΑΚ/ : Ζ : ΠΑΥ : Ε ΜΑ Ν-
    2   ΝΕΠΗΡΓΟϹ : - ΑΜΑΞ:
    3   Γ : ϹΑΚ : ΙΕ -
    4   ϹΙ ÷ ΜΕ
    5   [ΕΤΜΟΥΛΟ]Ν

O.Clackson 27

O.Berol. inv. 14708   7,1 x 8,7 cm   VIe-VIIe siècles
No plate   Moyenne-Égypte

    1   + ΙΝΑΙΚ/ : Ζ :-

2   ⲡⲁⲩ : ⲉ : ⲙⲁ ⲛ-
3   ⲛⲉⲣⲡⲏⲣⲅⲟⲥ =
4   ⲁⲙⲁⳉ ⲅ : ⲥⲁⲕ
5   : ⲓⲉ
6   ⲥⲓ ⲻ ⲙⲉ
7   [ⲉⲧⲙⲟⲩⲗⲟⲛ]

1. ⲍ Le ⲍ est écrit couché (comme un ⲛ).

O.Clackson 28

O.Berol. inv. 14714   6,8 x 6 cm   VIᵉ-VIIᵉ siècles
No plate   Moyenne-Égypte

1   [+ ⲓⲛⲁ(ⲓ)ⲕ/ : ⲍ :]
2   ⲡⲁⲩ : ⲉ : ⲙⲁ ⲛ
3   ⲛⲉⲡⲏⲣⲅⲟⲥ =
4   ⲁⲙⲁⳉ : ⲅ : ⲥⲁⲕ
5   . ⲓⲉ
6   ⲥⲓ ⲻ . .
7   ⲉⲧⲙⲟⲩⲗⲟ[ⲛ]

6. ⲥⲓ ⲻ . . La lecture du chiffre est très difficile. Les traces évoquent un ⲗ, mais les parallèles et le nombre de chariots et de sacs indiquent qu'il doit s'agir de ⲙⲉ (45).

O.Clackson 29

SBKopt. I 167 = O.Mich. inv. 25028   7,8 x 6,7 cm   VIᵉ-VIIᵉ siècles
Plate XII   Moyenne-Égypte

1   + ⲓⲛⲁⲕ/ : ⲍ :
2   ⲡⲁⲩ/ : ⲉ : ⲙⲁ ⲛ-
3   ⲛⲉⲡⲏⲣⲅⲟⲥ =
4   ⲁⲙⲁⳉ/ : ⲅ : ⲥ-
5   ⲁⲕ : ⲓⲉ : -
6   ⲥⲓ ⲻ ⲙⲉ
7   [. . .] . [. .]

O.Clackson 30-32
(Trois textes datés du 28 Pauni de la 7ᵉ année de l'indiction)

Je donne ici l'édition de trois textes de Berlin apparemment identiques, dont voici la traduction: "† 7ᵉ année de l'indiction; Pauni, le 28. Manpabinéos. Chariots: 8; sacs: 40; artabes de blé 120. Au moulin." J'y ai ajouté la réédition de *SBKopt.* I 185 (O.Mich. inv. 25041), qui présente le même texte.

O.Clackson 30

O.Berol. inv. 14710   5,8 x 8,5 cm   VIᵉ-VIIᵉ siècles
No plate   Moyenne-Égypte

1   + ιν.α.κ/ : z : παυ : κη :
2   μα ν:παβινεος :
3   αμαξ : η : cακ : ν̣ :
4   cι ⸗ ρκ :
5   ετμογλον

O.Clackson 31

O.Berol. inv. 14713   8,4 x 10,7 cm   VIᵉ-VIIᵉ siècles
Plate XII   Moyenne-Égypte

1   + ιν.α.κ/ · z : παυ : κη : μα ν-
2   παβινεος : αμαξ/ : η : cακ
3   : μ : : cι ⸗ ρκ =
4   ετμογλον

O.Clackson 32

SBKopt. I 185 = Kelsey Museum inv. 25041 10,7 x 14 cm   VIᵉ-VIIᵉ siècles
Plate XIII   Moyenne-Égypte

1   + ιν.α.κ/ : z : παυ/ : κη : μα ν-
2   παβϊνεος : αμαξ/ : η : cακ/ :
3   : μ :
4   : cι ⸗ ρκ =
5   ετμογλον

O.Clackson **33**
(Un ostracon *etmoulon* de l'IFAO)

O.IFAO   10,5 x 8,5 cm   VIe-VIIe siècles
Plate XIII   Moyenne-Égypte

1 + ⲓⲛⲁⲕ/ : ⲍ : ⲡⲁⲩ/
2 : ⲍ : ⲙⲁ ⲛⲁⲣⲓⲱⲛ :
3 ⲁⲙⲁⲝ/ : ⲉ : ⲥⲁⲕ/ ⲕⲉ
4   ⲥⲓ — : ⲟⲉ =
5 ⲉⲧⲙⲟⲩⲗⲟⲛ

1 † 7e année de l'indiction; Pauni,
2 le 7. Manariôn.
3 Chariots: 5; sacs: 25;
4 artabes de blé 45.
5 Au moulin.

5. Synthese

Selon l'hypothèse de W. Hengstenberg, les ostraca *etmoulon* sont des "lettres de voiture" (Frachtbrief en allemand; waybill en anglais).[55] Le transporteur aurait été chargé d'aller chercher une certaine quantité de blé dans un domaine producteur et de l'amener au moulin.

Cependant, on peut s'interroger dans ce cas sur le pourquoi des anomalies dans les quantités: il n'y a pas de raison pour que l'on ait envoyé des chariots chercher du blé sans être chargés au maximum de leur capacité. De plus, le texte n° 168 mentionne du blé pourri: il serait étrange d'envoyer quelqu'un chercher du blé impropre à la consommation. Il est donc probable que les ostraca *etmoulon* ont été écrits après coup, une fois que le grain est arrivé.

En tenant compte de ces différents éléments, je propose de reconstituer le cheminement du blé du domaine producteur au moulin ainsi:[56]

1) Le responsable de l'acheminement, c'est-à-dire le transporteur, va chercher, avec les chariots, du blé dans un domaine producteur, conformément aux ordres du bureau central.

---

[55] La seule remise en question de cette hypothèse est celle de Wenger, qui a proposé d'y voir des notes de comptabilité. Mais *O.Clackson* **18** montre qu'il y a un destinataire au document et qu'il est chargé du transport des chariots. Ce n'est donc pas une note de comptabilité.

[56] Il s'agit d'une reconstitution hypothétique, mais qui permet, il me semble, de mieux rendre compte des textes du dossier, y compris de la note adressée au tranporteur dans *O.Clackson* **18**. Le responsable du secrétariat du grand domaine ou du monastère indique peut-être par cette note qu'il a envoyé un chariot au moulin le soir du 7 Pauni. Le 8 Pauni (le lendemain, soit le 2e jour par rapport au 7 Pauni?), il envoie huit chariots au moulin. Mais, pour une raison ou une autre, le chariot envoyé la veille est resté au moulin et donc le transporteur doit amener huit chariots au moulin et revenir avec neuf.

2) Ensuite, au bureau central du "Large Estate" ou du monastère, la quantité de blé est comptée: le blé séné est séparé, de même que les grains pourris. Le blé est ensuite expédié au moulin. Et c'est à ce moment que l'on rédige l'ostracon *etmoulon* que l'on remet sans doute au transporteur, comme un mémento ou une lettre de voiture.

3) Le transporteur amène le blé au moulin et montre sans doute l'ostracon *etmoulon* pour que le responsable du moulin puisse vérifier la marchandise.

BIBLIOGRAPHIE

Ahmed Bay Kamal, M. (1915). "Rapport sur les fouilles éxécutées dans le zone comprise entre Déîrout, au nord et Déîr-el-Ganadlah, au sud," *ASAE* 177-206.

Bagnall, R. S. (1979). "Ostraca from the Yale Collection," *BASP* 16, 3-11.

Battaglia, E. (1989). *"Artos." Il lessico della panificazione nei papiri greci*. Milan: Vita e Pensiero.

Beltz, W. (1980). "Katalog der koptischen Handschriften der Papyrus-Sammlung der Staatlichen Museen zu Berlin (Teil II)," *APF* 27, 121-222.

Galling, K. (1966). "Datum und Sinn der graeco-koptischen Mühlenostraca im Licht neuer Belege aus Jerusalem," *ZDPV* 82, 46-56.

Hengstenberg, W (1931a). "Die griechisch-koptischen ⲘⲞⲨⲖⲞⲚ-Ostraka," *ZÄS* 66, 51-68.

Hengstenberg, W. (1931b). "Nachtrag zu 'Die griechisch-koptischen ⲘⲞⲨⲖⲞⲚ-Ostraka'," *ZÄS* 66, 122-138.

Jakobielsky, S. (1960). "Rekopisy koptyskie," in: *Katalog Rekopisow egipskich, koptyjskich i etiopskich*. Varsovie: Panstwowe Wydawnictwo Naukowe, 26-39.

Mallon, A. (1927). "Quelques ostraca coptes de Thèbes," *REgA* 1, 152-154.

Mallon, A. (1928). "Nouvelle série d'ostraca ⲈⲦⲘⲞⲨⲖⲞⲚ," *REgA* 2, 88-96.

Mallon, A. (1929). "Les ostraca coptes de Thèbes contenant des comptes de récolte," *REgA* 3, 78-80.

Mayerson, Ph. (1998). "The Sack (Σάκκος) is the Artaba Writ Large," *ZPE* 122, 189-194.

Rathbone, D. (1991). *Economic Rationalism and Rural Society in Third-Century A.D. Egypt. The Heroninos Archive and the Appianus Estate*. Cambridge: Cambridge University Press.

Saint-Paul Girard, L. (1929). "Adversaria coptica. 2 La formule ⲘⲞⲨⲖⲞⲚ," *BIFAO* 28, 99-102.

Shelton, J. (1991). "An etmoulon Ostracon at Trier," *Enchoria* 17, 109-114.

Wenger, L. (1932). "Juristische Literaturübersicht III (1914-1931)," *APF* 10, 98-176.

Wessely, C. (1928). "Über vier Ostraka aus Luxor," *Philologische Wochenschrift* 1928, 509.

ANNEXE: TABLEAU RECAPITULATIF DES OSTRACA *ETMOULON*

Je présente ici un tableau récapitulatif des différents éléments du formulaire des ostraca *etmoulon*. Le classement proposé est chronologique. Dans la colonne "mois et jour," l'astérisque (*) indique que la mention du mois et du jour suit celle de l'année de l'indiction. Dans les colonnes "sacs" et "artabes de blé," les données surprenantes ou les chiffres qui ne correspondent pas au nombre des chariots suivant le rapport usuel (1:5:15) sont signalés par un point d'exclamation (!).

	Sigle	Collection	Mois et jour	Indiction	Lieu	Chariots	Sacs	Artabes	Autres
1	*SBKopt.* I 146	O.Mich. inv. 25037	Pauni 14	3ᵉ (ⲓⲛⲁ/)	Manariôn (ⲁ̄)			105	
2	*SBKopt.* I 147	O.Mich. inv. 25001	Pauni 16	3ᵉ (ⲓⲛⲁ/)	Manapolôn (ⲁ̄)	...	...	...	
3	*SBKopt.* I 93	O.Cair.	Pauni 1	6ᵉ (ⲁⲓⲛⲕ/)	Manapolôn	6	30	90	
4	*SBKopt.* I 149	O.Mich. inv. 25027	Pauni 8	6ᵉ (ⲁⲓⲛⲕ/)	Manapolôn	[5]	25	75	
5	*O.Clackson* 24	*SBKopt.* I 150 = O.Mich. inv. 25006	Pauni 9	6ᵉ (ⲁⲓⲛⲕ/)	Manapolôn	2	10	30	
6	*O.Clackson* 25	*SBKopt.* I 151 = O.Mich. inv. 25009	Pauni 9	6ᵉ (ⲁⲓⲛⲁ̣ⲕ/)	Manapolôn	2	10	30	
7	*O.Clackson* 19	O.Berol. inv. 14705	Pauni 9	6ᵉ (ⲁⲓⲛⲕ/)	Manapolôn	2	10	30	
8	*O.Clackson* 20	O.Berol. inv. 14707	Pauni 9?	6ᵉ (ⲁⲓⲛⲕ/)?	Manapolôn	2	10	30	
9	*O.Clackson* 21	O.Berol. inv. 14712	Pauni 9	6ᵉ (ⲁⲓⲛⲁ̣ⲕ/)?	Manapolôn	2	10?	30?	
10	*O.Clackson* 22	O.Berol. inv. 14715	Pauni 9	6ᵉ (ⲁ̣ⲓ̣ⲛ̣ⲕ/)	Manapolôn?	2	10	30	
11	*O.Clackson* 23	O.Berol. inv. 14716	Pauni 9	6ᵉ (ⲁⲓⲛⲕ/)	Manapolôn	2	10	30	
12	*SBKopt.* I 152	O.Mich. inv. 25016+25040	Pauni 10	6ᵉ (ⲁⲓⲛⲕ/)	Phoimprès	7	35	105	
13	*SBKopt.* I 223	O.Assiout	Pauni 12	6ᵉ (ⲁⲓⲛⲕ/?)	Manapollôn (ⲁ̄)	7	35	105	
14	*SBKopt.* I 153	O.Mich. inv. 25191	Pauni 15	6ᵉ (ⲁⲓⲛⲕ/)	Manpabanos	5	25	75	
15	*SBKopt.* I 54	O.München 17	Pauni 20	6ᵉ (ⲁⲓⲛⲕ/)	Manapolôn	7	35	105	
16	*SBKopt.* I 154	O.Mich. inv. 25008	Pauni 24	6ᵉ (ⲁⲓⲛⲕ/)	Manapolôn	7	35	105	
17	*SBKopt.* I 155	O.Mich. inv. 25036	Pauni 24	6ᵉ (ⲁⲓⲛⲕ/)	Manariôn	7	35	105	

18	*SBKopt.* I 148	O.Mich. inv. 25192	Pauni ...1	6ᵉ (ⲁⲓⲛⲕ/)	Manpaterné	3	15	45	
19	*SBKopt.* I 55	O.München 14	Épeiph 3	6ᵉ (ⲁⲓⲛⲕ/)	Manariôn	7	35	105	
20	*SBKopt.* I 56	O.München 10	Épeiph 5?	6ᵉ (ⲁⲓⲛⲕ/)	Manadôra	15	77	224!	
21	*SBKopt.* I 57	O.München 19	Épeiph 6	6ᵉ (ⲁⲓⲛⲕ/)	Manapolôn	4	20	60	
22	*SBKopt.* I 94	O.Cair.	Épeiph 6	6ᵉ (ⲁⲓⲛⲕ/)	Manpag'au	7	35	105	
23	*SBKopt.* I 156	O.Mich. inv. 25007	Épeiph 8	6ᵉ (ⲁⲓⲛⲕ/)	Manapolô	3	15	47! séné..	
24	*SBKopt.* I 95	O.Cair.	Épeiph 12	6ᵉ (ⲁⲓⲛⲕ/)	Manpaterné	7	35	105	
25	*SBKopt.* I 58	O.München 18	Épeiph 13	6ᵉ (ⲁⲓⲛⲕ/)	Manpaterné	7	35	90!	
26	*SBKopt.* I 157	O.Mich. inv. 25005	Épeiph 15	6ᵉ (ⲁⲓⲛⲕ/)	Manpaiomtioué	3	15	45	
27	*SBKopt.* I 158	O.Mich. inv. 25018	Épeiph 15	6ᵉ (ⲁⲓⲛⲕ/)	Piaalô	9	45	141!	
28	*SBKopt.* I 159	O.Mich. inv. 25011	Épeiph 17	6ᵉ (ⲁⲓⲛⲕ/)	Manhatré	4	20	60	
29	*SBKopt.* I 160	O.Mich. inv. 25032	Épeiph 17	6ᵉ (ⲁⲓⲛⲕ/)	Pialô	3	15	45! (s)éné …	
30	*SBKopt.* I 161	O.Mich. inv. 25002	Épeiph ...	6ᵉ (ⲁⲓⲛⲕ/)	Manapolôn	7	35	105	
31	*SBKopt.* I 162	O.Mich. inv. 25024	Épeiph ...	6ᵉ (ⲁⲓⲛⲕ/)	Manapolôn	7	35	105	
32	*SBKopt.* I 163	O.Mich. inv. 25039	Épeiph ...	6ᵉ (ⲁⲓⲛⲕ/)	Manapollôn	6	30	90	
33	*SBKopt.* I 59	O.München 20	Pachôn 28 *	7ᵉ (ⲛⲓⲁⲕ/)	Manadam			23!	
34	*SBKopt.* I 165	O.Mich. inv. 4183	Pachôn 28 *	7ᵉ (ⲛⲓⲁⲕ/)	Mantasa	7	35	105 séné 11	
35	*SBKopt.* I 166	O.Mich. inv. 25004	Pauni 1 *	7ᵉ (ⲛⲓⲁⲕ/)	Phoimprès	2	15!	30	
36	*SBKopt.* I 60	O.München 15	Pauni 4 *	7ᵉ (ⲛⲓⲁⲕ/)	Manpaterné	2	10	30	
37	*O.Clackson* 29	*SBKopt.* I 167 = O.Mich. inv. 25028	Pauni 5 *	7ᵉ (ⲓⲛⲁⲕ/)	Manépèrgos	3	15	45	
38	*O.Clackson* 26	O.Berol. inv. 14706	Pauni 5*	7ᵉ (ⲓⲛⲁⲕ/)	Mannépèrgos	3	15	45	
39	*O.Clackson* 27	O.Berol. inv. 14708	Pauni 5*	7ᵉ (ⲓⲛⲁⲓⲕ/)	Mannépèrgos	3	15	45	
40	*O.Clackson* 28	O.Berol. inv. 14714	Pauni 5*	7ᵉ (...)?	Mannépèrgos	3	15	45	
41	*SBKopt.* I 168	O.Mich. inv. 25048	Pauni 5 *	7ᵉ (ⲓⲛⲁⲕ/)	Manhatré	3	15	45	

42	*SBKopt.* I 169	O.Mich. inv. 4172	Pauni 6 *	7ᵉ (ⲓⲛⲁⲕ/)	Manpag'au	5	23!	68!
43	*SBKopt.* I 61	O.München 6	Pauni 7 *	7ᵉ (ⲓⲛⲁⲕ/)	Tbasilikè			séné 10!
44	*SBKopt.* I 62	O.München 12	Pauni 7 *	7ᵉ (ⲓⲁⲛⲕ/)	Manhatré	8	40	120
45	*SBKopt.* I 170	O.Mich. inv. 25044	Pauni 7 *	7ᵉ (ⲓⲛⲁⲕ/)	Mangéôrgé	8	40	120
46	*O.Clackson* 33	O.IFAO	Pauni 7 *	7e (ⲓⲛⲁⲕ/)	Manariôn	5	25	75
47	*SBKopt.* I 171	O.Mich. inv. 25031	Pauni 9 *	7ᵉ (ⲓⲛⲁⲕ/)	Manépèrgos	3	15	45
48	*SBKopt.* I 172	O.Mich. inv. 25047	Pauni 9 *	7ᵉ (ⲓⲛⲁⲕ/)	Phoiémpèé?	5	25	75
49	*SBKopt.* I 63	O.München 13	Pauni 10 *	7ᵉ (ⲓⲛⲁⲕ/)	Manariôn	2	10	30
50	*SBKopt.* I 64		Pauni 10 *	7ᵉ (ⲓⲛⲁⲕ/)	Mannépèrgos	5	25	75
51	*SBKopt.* I 173	O.Mich. inv. 9665	Pauni 11 *	7ᵉ (ⲓⲛⲁⲕ/)	Manapollôn	9	45	135
52	*SBKopt.* I 174	O.Mich. inv. 4173	Pauni 12 *	7ᵉ (ⲓⲛⲁⲕ/)	Mannépèrgos	9	45	135
53	*SBKopt.* I 175	O.Mich. inv. 4175	Pauni 12 *	7ᵉ (ⲓⲛⲁⲕ/)	Manhatré	9	45	135
54	*SBKopt.* I 176	O.Mich. inv. 25019	Pauni 12 *	7ᵉ (ⲓⲛⲁⲕ/)	Phoiempès	9	45	135
55	*SBKopt.* I 65	O.München 5	Pauni 14 *	7ᵉ (ⲓⲛⲁⲕ/)	Manpaiomtioué	7	32	96!
56	*SBKopt.* I 66	O.München 3	Pauni 18 *	7ᵉ (ⲓⲁⲛⲕ/)	Manpaiomtioué	9	45	135
57	*SBKopt.* I 177	O.Mich. inv. 4181	Pauni 19 *	7ᵉ (ⲓⲛⲁⲕ/)	Manariôn	7	35	105
58	*SBKopt.* I 67	O.München 16	Pauni 20 *	7ᵉ (ⲓⲛⲁⲕ/)	Manapollôn	7	35	105
59	*SBKopt.* I 68	O.München 1	Pauni 21 *	7ᵉ (ⲓⲛⲁⲕ/)	Manapollôn	9	45	135
60	*SBKopt.* I 178	O.Mich. inv. 25012	Pauni 21 *	7ᵉ (ⲓⲛⲁⲕ/)	Manpaterné	6	30	90
61	*SBKopt.* I 179	O.Mich. inv. 4178	Pauni 22 *	7ᵉ (ⲓⲛⲁⲕ/)	Manpaiomtioué	9	45	135
62	*SBKopt.* I 69		Pauni 23 *	7ᵉ (ⲓⲛⲁⲕ/)	Manapollôn	8	40	120
63	*SBKopt.* I 180	O.Mich. inv. 4180	Pauni 23 *	7ᵉ (ⲓⲛⲁⲕ/)	Manpaterné	9	45	135
64	*SBKopt.* I 181	O.Mich. inv. 4182	Pauni 23 *	7ᵉ (ⲓⲛⲁⲕ/)	Manhatré	9	45	135
65	*SBKopt.* I 70	O.München 8	Pauni 26 *	7ᵉ (ⲓⲛⲁⲕ/)	Manpaterné	9	45	135
66	*SBKopt.* I 182	O.Mich. inv. 9663	Pauni 27 *	7ᵉ (ⲓⲛⲁⲓⲕ/)	Mapaiomtioué (ⲋⲗ)	9	45	135
67	*SBKopt.* I 183	O.Mich. inv. 4179	Pauni 27 *	7ᵉ (ⲓⲛⲁⲕ/)	Manhatré	8	40	120
68	*SBKopt.* I 184	O.Mich. inv. 4174	Pauni 28 *	7ᵉ (ⲓⲛⲁⲕ/)	Manhatré	8	40	120

69	O.Clackson 32	SBKopt. I 185 = O.Mich. inv. 25041	Pauni 28 *	7ᵉ (ⲓⲛⲁⲕ/)	Manpabinéos	8	40	120	
70	O.Clackson 30	O.Berol. inv. 14710	Pauni 28*	7ᵉ (ⲓⲛⲁⲕ/)	Manpabinéos	8	40	120	
71	O.Clackson 31	O.Berol. inv. 14713	Pauni 28*	7ᵉ (ⲓⲛⲁⲕ/)	Manpabinéos	8	40	120	
72	SBKopt. I 186	O.Mich. inv. 4177	Pauni 29 *	7ᵉ (ⲓⲛⲁⲕ/)	Manpaterné	2	10	séné 27!	
73	SBKopt. I 71	O.München 21	Pauni 29 *	7ᵉ (ⲓⲛⲁⲓⲕ/)	Manapolôn (ⲥⲁ)	4	21	63!	
74	SBKopt. I 187	O.Mich. inv. 25025	Pauni... *	7ᵉ (ⲓⲛⲁⲕ/)	Manpag'au	6	...	108!	
75	SBKopt. I 73	O.München 7	Pauni... *	7ᵉ (...ⲁⲕ/)	Mannépèrgos	9	45	135	
76	SBKopt. I 72	O.München 11	Pauni... *	7ᵉ (...ⲕ/)	Manapollôn	8	40	120	
77	SBKopt. I 164	O.Mich. inv. 25030	Pauni ... *	7ᵉ (ⲓⲁⲛⲕ/)	Manapolôn	8	40	120	
78	SBKopt. I 188	O.Mich. inv. 25045	Épeiph 2 *	7ᵉ (ⲓⲛⲁⲓⲕ/)	Piiahalô (ⲥⲁ)	14	70	210	
79	SBKopt. I 74	O.München 4	Épeiph 2 *	7ᵉ (ⲓⲛⲁⲕ/)	Mangouthé	13	64	174! séné 16	
80	SBKopt. I 76	O.München 9	Épeiph 7 *	7ᵉ (ⲓⲛⲁⲕ/)	Manapalaurété	7	33	81! séné 15	
81	SBKopt. I 75		Épeiph 7 *	7ᵉ (ⲓⲛⲁⲓⲕ/)	Manatôré (ⲥⲁ)	4	20	60	
82	SBKopt. I 189	O.Mich. inv. 25033	Épeiph 8 *	7ᵉ (ⲓⲛⲁⲕ/)	Térèfé	3	12!	36	
83	SBKopt. I 190	O.Mich. inv. 25035	Épeiph 8 *	7ᵉ (ⲓⲛⲁⲓⲕ/)	Phoiprès	5	25	séné 75!	
84	SBKopt. I 191	O.Mich. inv. 25021	Épeiph 9 *	7ᵉ (ⲓⲛⲁⲓⲕ/)	Pmanatôré (ⲥⲁ)	30	150	450	
85	SBKopt. I 192	O.Mich. inv. 9664	Épeiph 13 *	7ᵉ (ⲓⲛⲁⲓⲕ/)	Pnog'niôhé (ⲥⲁ)	15	75	225	
86	SBKopt. I 77		Épeiph 14 *	7ᵉ (ⲓⲛⲁⲕ/)	Manarishn (ô?)	7	35	75! séné 30	
87	SBKopt. I 193	O.Mich. inv. 25042	Épeiph 14 *	7ᵉ (ⲓⲛⲁⲓⲕ/)	Pmanhatré (ⲥⲁ)	12	60 + 1 thal.	60 séné 121	di 4
88	SBKopt. I 142	O.Yale 4	Épeiph 17 *	7ᵉ (ⲓⲛⲁⲓⲕ//)	Mapéhrèten (ⲥⲁ)	9	44!	134!	
89	SBKopt. I 195	O.Mich. inv. 9679	Pauni 8 *	8ᵉ (ⲛⲓⲁⲕ/)	Mannépègos	7	35	105	
90	SBKopt. I 196	O.Mich. inv. 9667	Pauni 9 *	8ᵉ (ⲓⲛⲁⲓⲕ/)	Phoinprès (ⲥⲁ)	6	30	90	

91	*SBKopt.* I 197	O.Mich. inv. 9673	Pauni 10 *	8ᵉ (ⲛⲓⲁ.ⲕ/)	Manhatré	7	35	105	
92	*SBKopt.* I 198	O.Mich. inv. 9676	Pauni 18 *	8ᵉ (ⲛⲓ.ⲁ.ⲕ/)	Manadam	4	23	59 d/ 3	
93	*SBKopt.* I 199	O.Mich. inv. 9672	Pauni 28 *	8ᵉ (ⲛⲓⲁ.ⲕ/)	Manapolôn	20	100	300	
94	*SBKopt.* I 200	O.Mich. inv. 9681	Pauni 30 *	8ᵉ (ⲓⲛ.ⲁ.ⲓⲕ/)	Piahalô (ⳉⲗ)	11	55	166!	
95	*SBKopt.* I 194	O.Mich. inv. 9671	Pauni? *	8ᵉ (ⲛⲓⲁ.ⲕ/)	Mantasa	9	45	124 séné 12!	
96	*SBKopt.* I 201	O.Mich. inv. 9670	Épeiph 16 *	8ᵉ (ⲛⲓⲁ.ⲕ/)	Paiomtioué	1	5	séné 15!	
97	*SBKopt.* I 202	O.Mich. inv. 9666	Épeiph 18 *	8ᵉ (ⲛⲓⲁ.ⲕ/)	Manpaiomtioué	3	16	48	d/ 3
98	*SBKopt.* I 203	O.Mich. inv. 9669	Épeiph 23 *	8ᵉ (ⲛⲓⲁ.ⲕ/)	Mangouthé	3	15	30 séné 14!	
99	*SBKopt.* I 204	O.Mich. inv. 9674	Épeiph 25 *	8ᵉ (ⲓⲛ.ⲁ.ⲓⲕ/)	Manapalaurenté (ⳉⲗ)	20	...	...	
100	*SBKopt.* I 205	O.Mich. inv. 9680	Épeiph 28 *	8ᵉ (ⲛⲓⲁ.ⲕ/)	Phoinapa	24	120	360	
101	*SBKopt.* I 206	O.Mich. inv. 9668	Épeiph 30 *	8ᵉ (ⲛⲓⲁ.ⲕ/)	Manpérètôr	24	120	360	
102	*SBKopt.* I 207	O.Mich. inv. 9678a+b+9675	Mésôrè 2 *	8ᵉ (ⲛⲓⲁ.ⲕ/)	Manpéhrètôr; Pialô et Manphrètôr	8	45!	75! séné 45!	
103	*SBKopt.* I 96	O.Cair.	Pachôn 13 *	9ᵉ (ⲓⲛ.ⲁ.ⲓⲕ/)	Téhrèfé	1	5	15	
104	*SBKopt.* I 78		Pachôn 13 *	9ᵉ (ⲁ.ⲓⲛⲕ/)	Man...		5 + 7 *thal.*	...	
105	*SBKopt.* I 208	O.Mich. inv. 25046	Pachôn 22 *	9ᵉ (ⲁ.ⲓⲛⲕ/)	Manapolôn	4	20	60	
106	*SBKopt.* I 79	O.München 22	Pachôn 30	9ᵉ (ⲓⲁ./⁄)	Manhatré (ⳉⲗ) Manapolou (ⳉⲗ)	3!	15 + 17 *thal.*	45 34	
107	*SBKopt.* I 80	O.München 2	Pauni 1 *	9ᵉ (ⲁ.ⲓⲛⲕ/)	Manpabinos	3	15	45	
108	Jakobielsky (1960)	O.Vars. Mus. 139907	Pauni 4 *	9ᵉ (ⲁ.ⲓⲛⲕ/)	Manhatré	3	15	45	
109	*SBKopt.* I 136	O.Cair.	Pauni 7	9ᵉ (ⲕ...?)	...?	9	-	...	
110	*SBKopt.* I 97	O.Cair.	Pauni 7	9ᵉ (ⲓ[ⲛⲕ/)		9	45	135	
111	*O.Clackson* **18**	O.Brit.Mus. inv. GR 1999. 6-29.1	Pauni 8	9ᵉ (ⲓ/⁄)		8	40	120	note
112	*SBKopt.* I 209	O.Mich. inv. 25190	Pauni 15 *	9ᵉ (ⲁ.ⲓⲛⲕ/)	Manpaterné	7	35	105	
113	*SBKopt.* I 98	O.Cair.	Pauni 16 *	9ᵉ (ⲁ.ⲓⲛⲕ/)	Manpabinéos	6	30	90	

114	*SBKopt.* I 99	O.Cair.	Pauni 16 *	9ᵉ (ⲀⲒⲚⲔ/)	Manariôn	1	5	15	
115	*SBKopt.* I 81		Pauni 21	9ᵉ (ⲒⲚⲀⲒⲔ/)	Manarishn (ô?) (ⳉⲀ)	7	35	105	
116	*SBKopt.* I 100	O.Cair.	Pauni 23 *	9ᵉ (ⲀⲒⲚⲔ/)	Manpabinéos	7	35	105	
117	*SBKopt.* I 101	O.Cair.	Pauni 24 *	9ᵉ (ⲀⲒⲚⲔ/)	Manhatré	7	35	105	
118	*SBKopt.* I 82		Pauni 25 *	9ᵉ (ⲀⲒⲚⲔ/)	Manpaterné	50!	50	105	
119	*SBKopt.* I 102	O.Cair.	Pauni 26 *	9ᵉ (ⲀⲒⲚⲔ/)	Manhatré	10	50	150	
120	*SBKopt.* I 145	(coll. K. Galling)	Pauni 27	9ᵉ (ⲒⲚⲀⲒⲔ/)	Mampaiomtioué (ⳉⲀ)	4	1...	55!	
121	*SBKopt.* I 103	O.Cair.	Pauni 27 *	9ᵉ (ⲀⲒⲚⲔ/)	Manariôn	8	?	120	
122	*SBKopt.* I 143	O.Trier inv. OL 1988.17	Pauni ...3 *	9ᵉ (ⲀⲒⲚⲔ/)	Manpabinnaios	1	5	15	
123	*SBKopt.* I 83		P... *	9ᵉ (ⲀⲒⲔ/)	Manapolôn ([Man])	2	...	1...!	
124	*P.MacquarieCopt.*[57]	O.Macquarie inv. 2152	Pauni ...*	9e (ⲒⲚⲀⲔ/)	Manabaraham	4	19	29 séné 26	d/ 2
125	*SBKopt.* I 84		Épeiph 1 *	9ᵉ (ⲀⲒⲚⲔ/)	Manhatré	10	50	150	
126	*SB Kopt.* I 104	O.Cair.	Épeiph 1	9ᵉ (ⲚⲀⲒⲔ/)	Pmanapolôn (ⳉⲀ)	10	50	150	
127	*SBKopt.* I 105	O.Cair.	Épeiph 5	9ᵉ (ⲀⲒⲚⲔ/)	Manhatré	7	35	105	
128	*SBKopt.* I 85		Épeiph 5	9ᵉ (ⲚⲒⲀⲔ/)	Manpaterné	1	5	15	
129	*SBKopt.* I 106	O.Cair.	Épeiph 5	9ᵉ (ⲚⲀⲒⲔ/)	Manpabinéos	4	20	44 séné 13	
130	*SBKopt.* I 144	Collection K. Galling	Épeiph 5	9ᵉ (ⲚⲒⲀⲔ/)	Manariôn	1	5	15	
131	*O.Köln*[58]	Université de Cologne	Épeiph 5	9ᵉ (ⲚⲒⲀⲔ/)	Mangéôrgé	5	24!	60(+?) séné 12	
132	*SBKopt.* I 107	O.Cair.	Épeiph 6	9ᵉ (ⲚⲒⲀⲔ/)	Manpag'au	4	20	60	
133	*SBKopt.* I 108	O.Cair.	Épeiph 8	9ᵉ (ⲚⲒⲀⲔ/)	Manpaterné	6	30	90	
134	*SBKopt.* I 109	O.Cair.	Épeiph 8	9ᵉ (ⲚⲒⲀⲔ/)	Manpaterné	2	10	30	
135	*SBKopt.* I 110	O.Cair.	Épeiph 9	9ᵉ (ⲚⲒⲀⲔ/)	Manadam	4	20	60	
136	*SBKopt.* I 86		Épeiph 10	9ᵉ (ⲚⲀⲒⲔ/)	Manpaterné	5	25	75	
137	*SBKopt.* I 87		Épeiph 10	9ᵉ (ⲚⲒⲀⲔ/)	Phoimprès	9 (ou 19?)	45	135	
138	*SBKopt.* I 111	O.Cair.	Épeiph 11	9ᵉ (ⲚⲒⲀⲔ/)	Manhatré	2	10	30	

---

[57] Le texte sera bientôt publié dans *P.MacquarieCopt.* (éd. M. Choat et I. Gardner). Je remercie M. Choat de m'avoir aimablement fourni une transcription de ce texte et de m'avoir autorisé à le citer avant sa publication.

[58] Cet ostracon, maintenant conservé à l'Université de Cologne, a été publié dans le catalogue de vente *Text, Manuscripts and Documents 2200 B.C. to 1600 A.D.*, Sam Fogg, Londres, 1995: 22-23 (n° 16).

139	*SBKopt.* I 112	O.Cair.	Épeiph 17	9ᵉ (ⲛⲓⲁⲕ/)	Manpéhrètôr	1	5 + ... *thal.*?	16 séné..	d/ 1
140	*SBKopt.* I 113	O.Cair.	Épeiph 18	9ᵉ (ⲛⲓⲕ/)	Mangounthé	21	106	312!	
141	*SBKopt.* I 88		Épeiph 19	9ᵉ (ⲛⲓⲁⲕ/)	Pnog'eniôhé	12	55!	168!	
142	*SBKopt.* I 114	O.Cair.	Épeiph 19	9ᵉ (ⲛⲓⲁⲕ/)	Mangounthé	11	66	162!	
143	*SBKopt.* I 115	O.Cair.	Épeiph 20	9ᵉ (...ⲁⲕ/)	Phoik...?	?	?	? séné	
144	*SBKopt.* I 89		Épeiph 21	9ᵉ (ⲛⲓⲕ/)	Manpag'au			1? séné 13	
145	*SBKopt.* I 116	O.Cair.	Épeiph 21	9ᵉ (ⲛⲓⲁⲕ/)	Manhatré	[2]	10	30	
146	*SBKopt.* I 137	O.Cair.	Épeiph 24	9ᵉ (ⲓ...)	Pahontmoue	...	...	...	
147	*SBKopt.* I 90		Épeiph	9ᵉ (ⲛⲓⲁⲕ/)	Mannépèrgos	2	11	33!	
148	*SBKopt.* I 138	O.Cair.	... *	9ᵉ (ⲓⲛⲕ/)	...fé (Téhrèfé?)	5	25	75	
149	*SBKopt.* I 210	O.Mich. inv. 25010	Pauni 10 *	10ᵉ (ⲓⲛⲁⲕ/)	Manpaterné	10	45!	135!	
150	*SBKopt.* I 211	O.Mich. inv. 25026	Athyr 15	11ᵉ (ⲁⲓ//)	Nemhoté (ⲉⲁ)	di/ kam/ 16	40 *thal.*	76	1ᵉ phora
151	*SBKopt.* I 118	O.München 25	Pauni 5	11ᵉ (ⲓⲛⲁⲓⲕ/)	Manapahatré (ⲉⲁ)	4	19 + 1 *thal.*	59	
152	*SBKopt.* I 135		Pauni 8	11ᵉ (ⲛ̄ⲁⲓⲕ/)	Manpurgos	...	...	...	
153	*SBKopt.* I 119	O.München 26	Pauni 12	11ᵉ (ⲛ̄ⲁⲓⲕ/)	Manhatré	7	35	105	
154	*SBKopt.* I 120	O.München 27	Pauni 13	11ᵉ (ⲛ̄ⲁⲓⲕ/)	Manariôn	7	35	105	
155	*SBKopt.* I 121	O.München 28	Pauni 15	11ᵉ (ⲓⲛⲁⲓⲕ//)	Manadam (ⲉⲁ)	6	35!	90!	
156	*SBKopt.* I 122	O.München 29	Pauni 17	11ᵉ (ⲛ̄ⲁⲓⲕ/)	Manadam	2	8	24!	di/ 1
157	*SBKopt.* I 212	O.Mich. inv. 25330	Pauni 22	11ᵉ (ⲁⲕ/)	Manpabinnéos	7	35	105	
158	*SBKopt.* I 123	O.München 30	Pauni 23	11ᵉ (ⲁⲓⲕ/)	Manhatré	6	30	90	epma-nouhé
159	*SBKopt.* I 124	O.München 31	Pauni 29	11ᵉ (ⲓⲛⲁⲓⲕ/)	Manabraham (ⲉⲁ)	3	15	30 omoi séné 15	di /b epaho npma-nouhé
160	*SBKopt.* I 126	O.München 33	Épeiph 6	11ᵉ (...)	...	...	...	...	
161	*SBKopt.* I 127	O.München 34	Épeiph 7	11ᵉ (ⲁⲓⲕ/)	Manhatré	8	40	120	epma-nouhé

162	SBKopt. I 128	O.München 35	Épeiph 7	11ᵉ (ⲁ.ⲓⲕ/)	Manpurgos	6	28!	120	epma-nouhé
163	SBKopt. I 125	O.München 32	Épeiph 12	11ᵉ (ⲁ.ⲓⲕ/)	Manapollôn	18		250	epma-nouhé
164	SBKopt. I 129	O.München 36	Épeiph 27	11ᵉ (ⲁ.ⲓⲕ/)	Nsouopalen? (ⲅⲗ)		16 thal.	32	
165	SBKopt. I 130	O.München 37	Mésôrè 2	11ᵉ (ⲓⲁ.ⲓ/)	Tmoue paremjotp souonpalen?	7 chameaux?	26 thal.	52	1ᵉ phora
166	SBKopt. I 91	O.Berl. 14703	Pachôn 27		Pahoensékeina	6	30	90	
167	SBKopt. I 139	O.Cair.	Pachôn 25		Nmozekièl	8	40	120	2ᵉ phora
168	SBKopt. I 92		Pachôn 28		Pahozékièl	3	15! + 2 bir	34! (d 2) "sap-ron" 11!	5ᵉ phora
169	SBKopt. I 213	O.Mich. inv. 25022	Pauni 21	...ᵉ (ⲁ.ⲓⲛⲕ/)	Phoiempès	14	70	210	
170	SBKopt. I 214	O.Mich. inv. 9677	Pauni 23 *	...ᵉ (ⲛⲓⲁ.ⲕ/)	Manariôn	10	50	150	
171	SBKopt. I 215	O.Mich. inv. 25034	Pauni ... *	...ᵉ (ⲁ.ⲓⲛⲕ/)	Manapolôn	6	30	90	
172	SBKopt. I 131	O.München 38	Pauni ...	...ᵉ (n̄ⲁ.ⲓⲕ/)	Tbasi[likè]	...	...	...	
173	SBKopt. I 216	O.Mich. inv. 25013	Épeiph 6	...	Manhatré	7	35	105	
174	SBKopt. I 140	O.Cair.	Épeiph 22 *	...	Manpaiomtioué			4 séné	aa (d/a?)
175	SBKopt. I 141	O.Cair.	Épeiph...	...	Manp[èrgos?]			lzd/	
176	SBKopt. I 218	O.Mich. inv. 25017	Épeiph ...	...	Manadôra	15	75	225	
177	SBKopt. I 217	O.Mich. inv. 25014	Épeiph ...	...	Manhatré	6	30	90	
178	SBKopt. I 132	O.München 39	Épeiph ...	...ᵉ (n̄ⲁ.ⲓⲕ/)	Piah...	...	...	...	epma-nouhé?
179	SBKopt. I 219	O.Mich. inv. 25043	... 26	...ᵉ (ⲁ.ⲓⲛⲕ/)	Manapolôn	7	35	105	
180	SBKopt. I 117	O.Cair.	...	...ᵉ (ⲁ.ⲓ̄ⲛⲕ/)	Mangé...o...	11	[55]	165?!	
181	SBKopt. I 220	O.Mich. inv. 25023	... *	...ᵉ (ⲓⲛⲁ.ⲓⲕ/)	Ma... (ⲅⲗ)	...	...	4...	
182	SBKopt. I 133	O.München 40	...	...	...	4	22!	66!	

183	*SBKopt.* I 134	O.München 41	...	...	...	...	...	27!	epma-nouhé
184	*SBKopt.* I 221	O.Mich. inv. 4176	...	...	...aham	4	50	161 séné 18!	
185	*SBKopt.* I 222	O.Mich. inv. 25029	...	...	Manphrètôr? (ⲁⲗ)	3	15	45	
186	O.Berol. inv. 14709	O.Berol. inv. 14709	...	...	...	...	...	...	
187	O.Berol. inv. 14711	O.Berol. inv. 14711	...	...	...	...	...	...	

O. Clackson **34**

A New Text from Frange in the Kelsey Museum of Archaeology[1]

Terry G. Wilfong

Among the unpublished Coptic ostraca in the Kelsey Museum of Archaeology is a letter by the well-known Theban monk Frange. This ostracon was acquired for the University of Michigan by Professor Carl Schmidt in Cairo as part of a large group of Coptic ostraca that came to the Kelsey Museum in 1937.[2] I offer this small addition to the dossier of published Frange texts in memory of Sarah Clackson, with whom I had discussed so many Coptic texts over the years.[3]

The text is written on one side of a piece of limestone; most of the ostraca written by Frange are on limestone (as opposed to pottery), which is not surprising given the fact that limestone is the more common medium for monastics living in the west Theban hills where Frange seems to have spent much of his life. The text is very nearly complete, in that ink traces of almost all of the letters survive, but the whole of the ostracon is very badly abraded, especially on the right side where the ends of lines are difficult to read. The hand is typical of that of Frange's less formal correspondence—a bold uncial hand with very distinctive letter forms (his more formal correspondence, to which he sometimes signed his name as "Phrangas," is written in a more standard semi-cursive hand).

Kelsey Museum of Archaeology	9,9 x 11,4 x 1,7 cm	Late VII/early VIII century[4]
inv. 25124		Western Thebes[5]
Plate XIV		

---

[1] This ostracon is published courtesy of the Kelsey Museum of Archaeology, University of Michigan; I would like to thank the Kelsey Museum registrars Robin Meador-Woodruff and Sebastián Encina for facilitating access to and photography of this artifact.

[2] For more information on the unpublished Kelsey Museum Coptic ostraca, and a summary description of the ostracon published below, see Wilfong 2004, especially 545-546 for the collection and 550-551 for the Frange ostracon.

[3] Although I would have preferred that my tribute to Sarah be more substantial, I think she would have appreciated this small bit of "museum archaeology," an ostracon that I was able to show her when she visited Ann Arbor in 2001.

[4] Frange's dates are a problem. Traditionally he was assumed to have been a witness to the Sassanian domination of Egypt in the early seventh century, but as far as I have been able to determine, this is only due to the proposed identification of his name as Persian in origin. If the "Efranke" of *P.KRU* 38 is the same as our Frange, then he would have been alive (with a deceased biological father named David) in 738; but this identification is far from certain. I have tended to propose a later date for Frange than is usual (discussion conveniently summarized in Heurtel 2004: 84) on the basis of his possible relation to the Koloje archive; the presence of Frange documents in the Monastery of Epiphanius texts might support an earlier date (although the traditional date for the abandonment of this monastery may itself be subject to revision). But the many new Frange texts now coming to light may well change my ideas; in any case, one hopes that they will provide more secure information about Frange's dates of activity.

[5] Except for the well-known *etmoulon* ostraca (*O.Mich.Copt.Etmoulon* = *SBKopt.* I 146-222), most if not all of the Michigan Coptic ostraca acquired by Schmidt appear to come from western Thebes. Frange is attested in excavated ostraca from the west Theban Monasteries of Phoibammon and Epiphanius, the town of Jeme (Medinet Habu) and by the recent finds in Theban Tomb 29.

Limestone.

1	☦ ⲁⲛⲟⲕ
2	ϥⲣⲁⲛⲅⲉ ⲉⲓ-
3	ⲥϩⲁⲓ̈ ⲙⲡⲁⲉⲓⲱⲧ
4	ⲓⲉⲍⲉⲕⲓⲏⲗ ⲁⲕ̣-
5	ϫⲓ ⲛ̄ⲟⲉⲓⲕ ⲛⲁⲛ̣
6	ⲙ̄ⲡ̄ⲣ̄ ⲥⲧⲟϥ
7	ⲙ̣ⲙⲟϥ ⲉⲃⲟⲗ
8	ϣ̣ⲗⲏⲗ ⲉϫⲱⲓ̈
9	ⲟⲩϫⲁⲓ̈ ϩ︤ⲙ︥
10	ⲡϫⲟⲉⲓⲥ ... ☦

+ It is I, Frange, who write to my father Ezekiel. You (5) received the bread from us. Do not reject it. Pray for me. Farewell in (10) the lord. +

1-2: Published documents written by Frange include *O.Crum* 394, 396, Ad. 63, *O.CrumST* 18, 267, *O.CrumVC* 81 (= *O.Ashm.Copt.* 19), *O.Brit.Mus.Copt.* 14239 (= *O.Rain.UnterrichtCopt.* 153), 27427, *O.Medin.HabuCopt.* 138-140, *SBKopt.* II 840 (= *O.Cairo JdE 46977*) (on limestone) and *O.CrumST* 320, *O.Mon.Epiph.* 119, 247, 351, 376, 412, *SBKopt.* II 860 (= *BKU* II 263) and 863 (= *BKU* I 162). It is probably not a coincidence that most of Frange's more formal correspondence was written on pottery sherds with a pen. Letters written to Frange include *O.Brit.Mus.Copt.* 14246, *O.Medin.HabuCopt* 137, *SBKopt.* II 858;[6] note that Frange's correspondents sometimes seem to be imitating his handwriting, as is very clear in *O.Medin.HabuCopt.* 137. There are a number of other texts, published and unpublished, that relate to Frange with varying degrees of certainty (the witness statement in *P.KRU* 38, for example), and a substantial body of new texts from archaeological excavations; see Boud'hors and Heurtel 2002, Heurtel 2002 and 2003 for details of the find at TT29 and preliminary descriptions of the texts.

3-4: In *O.Crum* 396 (vso 1-3), Frange asks his correspondent to greet "my father Ezekiel, the elder, in my name." Although the term of address in the Michigan ostracon is highly abraded, "father" fits the traces much better than ⲥⲟⲛ "brother," and it is possible that these two ostraca are in reference to the same Ezekiel; the name is common enough, though, that it is difficult to be certain. In support of the identification of the Ezekiel in the Michigan text with that of *O.Crum* 396, these two ostraca are the only published ones that Frange ends with the phrase "pray for me" before the standard closing formula. In any case, the term "father" here is likely to be spiritual rather than biological.

6-7: The verb here begins ⲥⲧ- and the omicron following is clear. Although there are various verbs beginning in ⲥⲧⲟ- (including ⲥⲧⲟⲓ "to smell," and ⲥⲧⲟⲓⲭⲉ "to attest to," clearly not appropriate

---

[6] This latter text described as "Turin: inv. Unbekannt" in *SBKopt.* II, but the facsimile in the publication in Stern 1878: 12-13 designates it as "Berlin 2160."

here), the only verb that both suits the traces and makes sense in the context is (ⲧ)ⲥⲧⲟ (Crum, *Dict.* 436a-437a), which, with the following ⲉⲃⲟⲗ, means "to reject, to turn back." In prepersonal form, the verb is (ⲧ)ⲥⲧⲟ⸗ in Sahidic; traces following that could be read as pronominal object ϥ, although this is reconstructed as much from logic as from the traces themselves, followed by ⲙ̄ⲙⲟϥ acting either as a redundant "dummy" object or, less likely, prepositional phrase "from him" in reference to the otherwise unspecified deliverer of the bread.

9-10: Frange closes with the standard "farewell in the lord" and a crossed rho; between these two elements there is a short flourish or space-filler that appears to be decorative, as is found in various other Frange letters (although not otherwise in this specific position).

BIBLIOGRAPHY

Boud'hors, A. and Heurtel, C. (2002). "The Coptic Ostraca from the Tomb of Amenemope," *EgArch* 22, 7-9.

Heurtel, C. (2002). "Nouveaux aperçus de la vie anachorétique dans la montagne thébaine: Les ostraca coptes de la tombe TT29," *BSFE* 154, 29-45.

Heurtel, C. (2003). "Que fait Frange dans la cour de la tombe TT 29? Fouilles dans la cour de la tombe TT 29," in : Cannuyer, C. (ed.) *Etudes Coptes VIII. Dixième Journée d'études Lille 14-16 juin 2001.* (*CBC* 13). Louvain: Peeters, 177-204.

Heurtel, C. (2004). *Les inscriptions coptes et grecques du temple d'Hathor à Deir el-Médîna suivies de la publications des notes manuscrites de François Daumas (1946-1947).* (*BEC* 16). Le Caire: Institut français d'archéologie orientale.

Stern, L. (1878). "Sahidische Inschriften," *ZÄS* 16, 9-28.

Wilfong, T. G. (2004). "New Texts in Familiar Hands: Unpublished Michigan Coptic Ostraca by Known Scribes" in: Immerzeel, M. and Vliet, J. van der (eds.) *Coptic Studies on the Threshold of a New Millennium: Proceedings of the Seventh International Congress of Coptic Studies.* (*OLA* 133). Leuven: Peeters, I: 551-557.

A Greek-Coptic Glossary from the Beinecke Collection

James Clackson and Sarah Clackson

Sarah Clackson was H. P. Kraus fellow in early books and manuscripts at the Beinecke Rare Book and Manuscript Library in Yale in 2001, during which time she viewed and transcribed many texts. This text she left for me to publish, having provided a full transcription before her death. Full details of the papyrus, information on its acquisition, and an image of the text can be found on the online catalogue of the Yale Papyrus Collection.[1]

The text itself contains a list of Greek words with their Coptic equivalents, written in two columns of over 30 lines each. It is one of a growing number of bilingual glossaries known from the ancient world. The Greek-Latin glossaries have in general been well studied[2] but fewer Greek-Coptic examples have been published and in general they have been less well studied. Ten glossaries are published or republished as texts 256-266 in *P.Rain.UnterrichtKopt.*[3] including the lengthy word-list of Dioscorus of Aphrodito.[4]

In Kramer 2001: 5[5] a distinction is drawn between "popular glossaries" (*Gebrauchsglossare, glossari popolari*) and "school glossaries" (*Schulglossare, glossari eruditi*). The former are texts drawn up by individuals for their own use in understanding every-day conversations or useful words in a language in which they have no competence; the latter are part of a more structured framework of scholarship or education, and they share certain characteristic features with the so-called *hermeneumata* which survive in manuscript form. The *hermeneumata*[6] include Greek-Latin word-lists arranged alphabetically and by subject (so called *capitula* glossaries) and short conversations given in both languages. Kramer argues that the *hermeneumata* and the papyrus glossaries all probably reflect selections from larger language "manuals" which might have included *capitula* glossaries, alphabetic glossaries, conversations, conjugations, and word by word glosses on selected text.

It is not always easy to assign the existing Greek-Coptic glossaries to the popular or school glossary category. Take, for example, the most extensive papyrus glossary currently known, that of Dioscorus. The original editors, Bell and Crum, thought that "[Dioscorus'] principal object was to extend his knowledge of the Greek language,"[7] but more recently Jean-Luc Fournet has emphasized that the text should be located in "une ambiance scolaire."[8] Comparison with the Greek-Latin examples published by Kramer support the view that Dioscorus' glossary is indeed a school glossary. It contains not just

---

[1] http://highway49.library.yale.edu/papyrus/oneSET.asp?pid=4501%20qua (January, 2008).

[2] See Kramer 1983 and 2001 for recent editions of the most complete examples.

[3] Hasitzka 1990.

[4] Pack² 354, republished as *P.Rain.UnterrichtKopt.* 256; in what follows I shall use the text numbers as in *P.Rain.UnterrichtKopt.*

[5] Following Kramer 1996.

[6] Published by Goetz 1892.

[7] Bell and Crum 1925: 181.

[8] Fournet 1999: 689.

word-lists, but also some *sententiae*, and these may also have featured in other language manuals and schoolbooks. Not all Coptic glossaries are school glossaries, however—*P.Rain.UnterrichtKopt.* 263 features words for birds and animals and verb forms in Greek and Coptic and does not show the thematic grouping of vocabulary or the arrangement of the material of the school glossaries. *P.Clackson* 35 shows many important similarities with the Greek-Coptc glossaries of the school type, including the following:

– Greek words are given without the article but Coptic words with, as in *P.Rain.UnterrichtKopt.* 256 (in part), 260, 262 and 264;

– Greek words and their Coptic equivalents are separated by the punctuation mark (:) in column II, the same sign is used in *P.Rain.UnterrichtKopt.* 256, 257a, 260 and 264;

– Greek words are cited in the nominative, apart from words which denote uncountable objects, such as "wheat," "barley" and "water" which are given in the genitive; the fragmentary glossary *P.Rain.UnterrichtKopt.* 257 also cites the word for "oil" in the genitive.

Most importantly, the grouping of vocabulary items in *P.Clackson* 35 largely mirrors *capitula* glossaries found in the manuscript *hermeneumata* and in other papyrus examples of school glossaries. I have included in the table also parallels from BNF 332Arm, a monolingual text with Greek written in Armenian letters which clearly contains analogous material including *capitula*, *sententiae* and *chreiae*.[9]

P.Clackson 35	Items listed	Title	Parallels in *hermeneumata* and papyrus texts
Col. I 1-8	pig, wheat, barley, vegetable seed	*de agricultura / de rusticatione*	Goetz 1892: 26-7; 199-200 260-2; 356-8. *P.Rain.UnterrichtKopt.* 256: 385-400.
Col. I 13-24	ass, bull, heifer, sheep, goat, lion	*de quadrupedibus*	Goetz 1892: 188-9; 258-9. *P.Rain.UnterrichtKopt.* 256: 65-108; 262: 16-30. Kramer 1983 no.9.
Col. I 25-30	crocodile, Nile fish	**de bestiis in Nilo*	*P.Rain.UnterrichtKopt.* 256: 401-12
Col. I 31-2, 35-8	pot, mortar, shell	*de fictilibus*	Goetz 1892: 24; 193-4; 270-1; 326; 369. *P.Rain.UnterrichtKopt.* 256: 360-5.
Col. II 1-3	horse, brood-mare, camel	*de iumentis*	Goetz 1892: 431-2. *P.Rain.UnterrichtKopt.* 262: 16-22.
Col. II 1-3	bird, goose	*de auibus*	Goetz 1892: 17-8; 89-90; 187-8; 387-8. Kramer 1983 no.13.
Col. II 17-19	tunic, linen, cloak	*de uestimentis*	Goetz 1892: 21-2; 92; 322-3; 369-70. BNF 332Arm A 32-3
Col. II 25, 28-30, 33-5	house, cistern, well, door, ladder, cell	*de habitatione*	Goetz 1892: 190-1; 268-9; 312-3; 364-5. *P.Rain.UnterrichtKopt.* 256: 187-8.

Unparalleled in surviving texts are the grouping of objects relating to wood and forestry (wood, tree, axe, staff) at Col. II 6-9; and items made from woven or plaited work (rope, basket, sieve, reed) at Col. II 10-13, although the *hermeneumata* do contain analogous lists of items connected with a certain

---

[9] Published in Clackson 2000.

trade, such as medicine or sea-faring, and items constructed from similar material, as the lists of objects made from iron or from leather. In Dioscorus' glossary words which probably refer to palm leaf baskets and basket making occur at lines 368-373, although the text here is damaged. Note also that a selection of words which relate to plaited items—tent, rope, reed—also occurs at BNF 332Arm B. 17.

However, there are also aspects of *P.Clackson* **35** which may encourage a different view of the nature of the text. The arrangement of the words is less systematic than other school glossaries, with Greek words written above the Coptic words in Column I but alongside them in Column II. In Column I there seems to be the inclusion of the beginnings of a conjugation, with "I know" and "I do not know" interrupting the *capitula* glossaries. And the *capitula* sections start to break down in Column II, as shown by the sequences "year," "month," "dog," "house" (ll. 22-5) and "well," "natron," "egg," "door" (ll. 30-33). Similar phenomena can also be found in other papyrus texts: in BNF 332Arm there is a very noticeable mixing of material from different sections of the putative original "language manual" and in Dioscorus' glossary a list of body parts, corresponding to the *de membris* section of the *hermeneumata*, is interrupted between lines 180 and 275 with extraneous material. One might be tempted to explain these oddities through assuming that the text is compiled through dictation, but there are relatively few spelling "mistakes" in the Greek. Compare the spelling of the word for "goat," αιγιδιν in *P.Clackson* **35** but εκιτν in *P.Rain.UnterrichtKopt.* 262.1; in the latter the writer appears to have been a Greekless Copt who took down the Greek words by ear. If *P.Clackson* **35** was composed in this way one would expect far more errors of this type. The Coptic also gives no reason to doubt the writer's competence in the language. Despite the peculiarities of this text, it would seem best to place it in a school milieu, and I am inclined to think that it represents a late stage in the tradition of glossaries when the coherence of the original lists had begun to be lost.[10]

In the edition of the text I am very grateful to Dr Jacques van der Vliet, who has made a number of helpful suggestions on the transcription and commentary. He also adds the following observations:

"It might be not uninteresting to say something about the kind of Coptic that is used here. Quite a number of entries show forms that are not standard Sahidic (if such a thing exists) but are instead classified by Crum as A (Akhmimic) or F (Fayyumic). Examples in question are the general preference for /a/ over Sah. /o/ (e.g. ⲥⲁⲗⲉϥ, ⲍⲁⲥⲉⲙ, etc.), the avoidance of double vowels (ⲉⲥⲁⲩ, ⲑⲏⲃⲉ), and forms like ⲙⲉⲥⲉ (Sah. normally ⲙⲁⲥⲉ), ⲛⲅⲉ for ⲛⲅⲓ (if so correct) or ϭⲁⲣⲱⲙ (Sah. normally ϭⲉⲣⲱⲃ). ... On the whole it looks as if this glossary came into existence somewhere in Middle Egypt."

---

[10] See also the commentary on line 1 for another possible example of an error which may have come through the transmission of this word-list.

P.Clackson 35

P.CtYBR inv. 4501 qua　　　　　32,9 x 14,7 cm　　　　　VII-VIII century
No plate

In the original Column I is written alongside Column II, here they are given separately.

→

		Col. I	
1		χοιρος	pig
2		ⲡⲣⲓⲣ	pig
3		σιτου	wheat
4		ⲡⲉⲥⲟⲩⲟ	wheat
5		κριθης	barley
6		ⲡⲓⲱⲧ	barley
7		λαχανοσπερμον	vegetable seed
8		ϯⲉⲙⲉⲥⲓⲙ	-radish
9		οιδα	I know
10		ⲗⲉⲓ̈ⲙⲉ	I know
11		ουκ οιδα	I do not know
12		ⲡⲉⲓ̈ⲙⲉ	I do not know
13		ονοθηλια	she-ass
14		ⲧⲉⲱ	she-ass
15		ταυρος	bull
16		ⲡⲙⲉⲥⲉ	bull
17		δαμαλιν	heifer
18		ⲕⲉϩⲥⲉ̣	heifer
19		προβατα	sheep
20		ⲡⲉⲥⲁⲩ	sheep
21		αιγιδιν	goat
22		ⲧⲃⲁⲙⲡⲉ	goat
	]ⲁⲁⲩ		
23		λεον	lion
	..		
24		ⲡⲙⲟⲩⲓ̈	lion
	]ⲱⲕ		
25		κορκοδιλλος	crocodile
26		ⲡⲉⲙⲥⲁϩ	crocodile
27		λαδιτιν	'Nile perch'
28		ⲡⲗⲁⲧⲟⲥ	'Nile perch'
29		σιμαριν	Nile fish
30		ⲥⲓⲙⲟⲩⲥ	Nile fish

31	κυθρα	pot
32	ⲡϭⲁⲗⲉϩⲧ	pot
33	μαχαιριν	knife
34	ⲥⲧⲟⲣⲧⲉ	knife
35	θυϊα	mortar
36	ⲧⲉⲙⲭⲁ̄ϩⲧ	mortar
37	μυϊα	fly (?)
38	ⲡⲭⲉⲕ	shell
39	δακτυλος	finger
40	ⲡⲧⲏⲃⲉ	finger

1 χοῖρος ‖ 3 σίτου ‖ 5 κριθῆς ‖ 7 λαχανόσπερμον ‖ 9 οἶδα ‖ 11 οὐκ οἶδα ‖ 13 ὀνοθήλεια ‖ 15 ταῦρος ‖ 17 δαμάλιον ‖ 19 πρόβατα ‖ 21 αἰγίδιον ‖ 23 λέων ‖ 25 κροκόδιλος ‖ 27 λατίδιον ‖ 29 σιμάριον ‖ 31 κύθρα ‖ 33 μαχαιρίον ‖ 35 θυία ‖ 39 δάκτυλος

Col. II

1	[ι]ππος : ⲡⲉϩⲧⲟ̣	horse
2	[φ]ορα̣δαριν : ⲧⲉϩⲧⲟ̣ⲣ̣	brood-mare
3	[κ]αμηλος : ⲡϭⲁⲙⲟⲩⲗ	camel
4	ορνι[θ]ιν : ⲡⲧⲁⲡⲟⲓ	bird
5	χηναριν : ⲡⲱⲃⲉ̣ⲧ	goose
6	ξηλον : ⲡϣⲉ	wood
7	πελεκιν : ⲡⲕⲉⲗ[ⲉⲃⲓⲛ]	axe
8	δενδρον : ⲡϣ[ⲏⲛ]	tree
9	[ρ]αβδος : ⲡϭⲁⲣⲱⲙ	staff
10	σχοινιν : ⲛ̄ϭⲉϩⲑⲟⲧ	rope, cord
11	σφυριδιν : ⲡⲃⲓⲣ	basket
12	κοσκινον : ⲡϣⲁⲗⲉϥ	sieve
13	καλαμος : ⲡⲕⲁϣ	reed
14	διορυξ : ⲡⲓⲟⲣ	canal
15	οδος : ⲫⲁⲩ̄ⲧⲛ̄	road
16	υδατος : ⲡⲙⲟⲟⲩ	water
17	στιχαριν : ⲧⲉϣⲧⲏ[ⲛ]	tunic
18	οθονιν : ⲧⲉⲛⲓ̈ⲁⲩ	linen-cloth
19	μαφοριν : ⲡⲡⲁⲗⲗⲓⲛ	cloak
20	συκα : ⲡⲕⲉⲛⲧⲉ	fig
21	κοριαξους : ⲧⲣⲁⲙⲉ	tilapia fish
22	ενιαυτ[ος :]ⲧⲉ̣ⲣⲟⲙⲡⲉ̣	year
23	μην.. : ⲡⲉ̣ⲃ̣ⲟⲧ	month
24	κυνος : ⲡⲟ̣[ⲩϩ]ⲟ̣ⲣ	dog
25	οικος : ⲡⲏ̣ⲉⲓ̈	house

26	ελαιουργος : ⲡϭⲁⲗ..		oil-manufacturer
27	ελαιου : ⲡⲛⲉϩ		oil
28	λουτρο. : [±3].ⲣⲉⲛ		bath
29	λακκος : ⲡⲁϭⲁⲛ :		cistern
30	φρεαρ : ⲧϣϥⲧⲉ		well
31	νιτρον : ϥⲁⲥⲉⲙ		natron
32	ωα : ⲧⲥⲁⲩϩⲉ		egg
33	θυρα : ⲡⲣⲟ		door
34	πεσσω : ⲡⲧⲟⲧⲉⲣ		staircase
35	κελλιν : ⲧⲣⲉⲓ		cell

1 ἵππος ‖ 2 φοραδάριον ‖ 3 κάμηλος ‖ 4 ὀρνίθιον ‖ 5 χηνάριον ‖ 6 ξύλον ‖ 7 πελέκιον ‖ 8 δένδρον ‖ 9 ῥάβδος ‖ 10 σχοίνιον ‖ 11 σφυρίδιον ‖ 12 κόσκινον ‖ 13 κάλαμος ‖ 14 διῶρυξ ‖ 15 ὁδός ‖ 16 ὕδατος ‖ 17 στιχάριον ‖ 18 ὀθόνιον ‖ 19 μαφόριον ‖ 20 σῦκα ‖ 21 κοριαξός ‖ 22 ἐνιαυτός ‖ 23 μήν ‖ 24 κυνός ‖ 25 οἶκος ‖ 26 ἐλαιοῦργος ‖ 27 ἐλαίου ‖ 29 λάκκος ‖ 30 φρέαρ ‖ 31 νίτρον ‖ 32 ὧον ‖ 33 θύρα ‖ 34 πέσσος ‖ 35 κελλίον

Col. I.

1. The word for "pig" is not included with the quadrupeds, later in the glossary, but with the agricultural terms. In Dioscorus' glossary exactly the same phenomena is found, with "pig" (ὗς) given after terms describing the plough and its parts and before words for "wheat" and "barley."[11] The Coptic gloss given there describes part of a wagon, so the original editors understood the Greek term to be descriptive of part of a plough.[12] Here however the Greek term is glossed by a Coptic word for "pig." It is possible that the word in this position did originally refer to a part of a plough, but that over time the true meaning of the Greek word was lost and it was reanalyzed as "pig" and replaced by χοῖρος.

8. The first part of ϯⲉⲙⲉⲥⲓⲙ is obscure, but ⲥⲓⲙ is a Coptic word for fodder, grass or radish,[13] which does occur as the second element of compounds (as Jacques van der Vliet points out to me (personal communication)) as for example ⲃⲉⲣⲥⲓⲙ.[14]

13-14. The same equivalence between Greek ὀνοθήλεια and Coptic ⲉⲓⲱ is found in *P.Rain. UnterrichtKopt.* 262.20. Dioscorus gives the same Coptic word for Greek ὄνος,[15] as does *P.Rain. UnterrichtKopt.* 263:3.

15-16. In *P.Rain.UnterrichtKopt.* 256.65 ταῦρος is glossed by Coptic ⲃⲁⲓⲧ but this text and *P.Rain.UnterrichtKopt.* 262.24 use the form ⲙⲓⲥⲉ (here spelt ⲙⲉⲥⲉ) for which see Crum 186a s.v.

---

[11] *P.Rain.UnterrichtKopt.* 256.392.
[12] Bell and Crum 1925: 217.
[13] Crum 1934: 334.
[14] Crum 1934: 43b.
[15] *P.Rain.UnterrichtKopt.* 256.100.

17. The Coptic word given as equivalent to Greek δαμάλιον has been read by Jacques van der Vliet, who notes that it is "the normal translation of the Greek word (see Crum 48a, s.v. ⲃⲁϨⲥⲉ)."

19-20. The Greek and Coptic words for "sheep" also occur in *P.Rain.UnterrichtKopt.* 256.89, 262.29 and 263.2.

21-22. *P.Rain.UnterrichtKopt.* 256.96, 262.30 and 263.1 again share this equivalence. Note that the words for "bull," "sheep" and "goat" occur in the same order in all three Greek-Coptic glossaries. The significance of the letters at the margin of this line and the next two is not clear.

23-24. The same Greek and Coptic words for "lion" are given by Dioscorus *P.Rain.UnterrichtKopt.* 256.83.

25-26. Again, this gloss is also found in Dioscorus' glossary (*P.Rain.UnterrichtKopt.* 256.404); Dioscorus gives the Greek form as κορκόδειλος, showing the same initial sequence κορκ-.

27. The Greek word here represents λατίδιον, a diminutive of λάτος, the word which provides the Coptic gloss.

29-30. Again the Greek word σιμάριον, attested in papyri as a word for a fish, is a diminutive of σῖμος, the word given as the Coptic equivalent.

34. ϭⲧⲟⲣⲧⲉ is metathesized for ⲧϭⲟⲣⲧⲉ.[16]

38. Sarah Clackson suggested that this word was the Coptic equivalent for "fly" related to ϫⲱⲕⲉ "prick sting goad",[17] or ϫⲁⲕ "clap,"[18] but ϫⲉⲕ is attested as the Coptic word for "shell,"[19] and it is possible here that the Greek in the line above stands not for μυῖα "fly" but μύαξ "mussel, shell." The inclusion of a word for "shell" is perhaps more likely in the context of pots and knives than "fly."

39-40. The same pair of words occurs at *P.Rain.UnterrichtKopt.* 256.296.

Col II.

1. The same pair occurs in Dioscorus' glossary, *P.Rain.UnterrichtKopt.* 256.76, and in *P.Rain.UnterrichtKopt.* 263.3-4. *P.Rain.UnterrichtKopt.* 262 has a different gloss for "horse."

2. In Dioscorus' glossary the Coptic word for "mare," written Ϩⲧⲟⲱⲣⲉ glosses Greek φοράς (*P.Rain.UnterrichtKopt.* 256.81).

3. The same gloss is given by Dioscorus, *P.Rain.UnterrichtKopt.* 256.71.

4. ⲡⲧⲁⲡⲟⲓ is metathesized for ⲧⲡⲁⲡⲟⲓ. This gloss is also found at *P.Rain.UnterrichtKopt.* 260.11 and 263.1. Jacques van der Vliet notes that in this text and *P.Rain.UnterrichtKopt.* 260 the word is given in the feminine, although the masculine form is the one usually recorded in modern dictionaries.

10. ⲛ̄ϭⲉϨⲟⲟⲧ uniquely in this text the article is not written but instead the morpheme ⲛ̄ϭⲓ which normally is attached to postponed subject nouns. Ϩⲟⲟⲧ I take to be somehow connected with ϣⲟⲱⲧ "rope of palm fibre"[20] with interchange of Ϩ for ϣ. Jacques van der Vliet suggests that the form Ϩⲟⲟⲧ

---

[16] Crum 1934: 829b.
[17] Crum 1934: 763a.
[18] Crum 1934: 760b.
[19] Crum 1934: 761a.
[20] Crum 1934: 555a.

may result from a metathesis of a hypothetical T-ϩTOT to ϩTϩOT (T-ϩTOT represents the article with *ϩTOT, the expected counterpart to Bohairic ϣⲑⲱⲧ).

12. Jacques van der Vliet points out that the initial ⲡ- of ⲡϯ·ⲁⲗⲉϥ (for ⲥⲟⲗϥ "sieve"[21]) is redundant, as ϯ represents the article ⲡ- with the initial ⲥ- of the lexeme.

19. The Coptic word glossing Greek μαφόριον is itself a loanword from Greek πάλλιον.[22]

21. The same equation between Greek κοριαξός and Coptic ⲧⲣⲁⲙⲉ is found in Dioscorus' glossary.[23]

23. After the final -ν of μήν there appears to be a second ν in the original text.

24. The word for "dog," ⲟⲩϩⲟⲣ, can be restored here by comparison with *P.Rain.UnterrichtKopt.* 262.27 and 263.3.

26. There is no Coptic word beginning ϭⲁⲗ- meaning "oil-manufacturer." Jacques van der Vliet suggests that the word may "be a composite with ⲅⲁⲗ- (pc. of ⲅⲱⲗ, 'to collect,' see Crum 806b-807a). Then, *ⲡⲅⲁⲗⲛⲉϩ ('oil-gatherer,' unattested, but at least possible) would seem logical."

28. The Coptic word for "bath" intended here may be the Greek loan-word ⲗⲟⲩⲧⲏⲣⲓⲛ or ⲗⲱⲧⲏⲣⲓⲛ.[24]

29. λάκκος and φρέαρ also appear in consecutive lines in *P.Rain.UnterrichtKopt.* 256.187-8 but there λάκκος is glosssed by ϣⲛⲓ, the normal Coptic word for "cistern." ⲡⲁϭⲁⲛ is Coptic ⲗⲁϭⲟⲛ or ⲗⲁϭⲁⲛ "a vessel or tank of metal."[25]

34. Greek πεσσω must represent the word πεσσός, attested as the word for a staircase in the papyri.[26] The Coptic equivalent ⲡⲧⲟⲧⲉⲣ means staircase or ladder.[27]

---

[21] Crum 1934: 333a.
[22] Förster 2002: 603.
[23] *P.Rain.UnterrichtKopt.* 256: 421-422.
[24] See Förster 2002: 484.
[25] Crum 1934: 26b.
[26] See Husson 1983: 226-229.
[27] Crum 1934: 431b s.v. ⲧⲱⲣⲧ.

BIBLIOGRAPHY

Bell, H. I. and Crum, W. E. (1925). "A Greek-Coptic Glossary," *Aegyptus* 6, 177-226.

Clackson, J. (2000). "A Greek Papyrus in Armenian Script," *ZPE* 129, 223-258.

Crum, W. E. (1934). *A Coptic Dictionary*. Oxford: Clarendon Press.

Fournet, J.-L. (1999). *Hellénisme dans l'Égypte du VIe siècle: la bibliothèque et l'oeuvre de Dioscore d'Aphrodité*. Cairo: Institut français d'archéologie orientale.

Förster, H. (2002). *Wörterbuch der griechischen Wörter in den koptischen dokumentarischen Texten*. Berlin: De Gruyter.

Goetz, G. (1892). *Corpus Glossariorum Latinorum III: hermeneumata Pseudodositheana*. Leipzig: Teubner.

Hasitzka, M. (1990). *Neue Texte und Dokumentation zum Koptisch-Unterricht (Mitteilungen aus der Papyrussammlung der Österreichischen Nationalbibliothek in Wien n.s. XVIII)*. Vienna: Hollinek.

Husson, G. (1983). *OIKIA. Le vocabulaire de la maison privée en Egypte d'après les papyrus grecs*. Paris: Sorbonne.

Kramer, J. (1983). *Glossaria bilinguia in papyris et membranis reperta*. Bonn: Habelt.

Kramer, J. (1996). "I glossari tardo-antichi di tradizione papiracea," in J. Hamesse (ed.) *Les manuscrits des lexiques et glossaires de l'antiquité tardive à la fin du moyen âge: actes du colloque international organisé par le "Ettore Marjorana Centre for Scientific Culture" (Erice, 23-30 septembre 1994)*. (*Textes et études du moyen âge*, 4) Louvain-la neuve: Fédération Internationale des Instituts d'Études Mediévales. 23-55.

Kramer, J. (2001). *Glossaria bilinguia altera (C. Gloss. Biling. II)*. Archiv für Papyrusforschung und verwandte Gebiete, Beiheft 8. München/Leipzig : K.G. Saur München.

P.CLACKSON 36-43

LE DOSSIER DES REÇUS DE TAXE GRECS DU MONASTERE D'APA APOLLO A BAOUIT[1]

ALAIN DELATTRE ET NIKOLAOS GONIS

Il y a quelques années, à l'occasion de la publication de P.Duk. inv. 498, N. Gonis a mis en évidence un petit dossier de reçus de taxe de capitation (*andrismos*) qui proviennent du monastère d'apa Apollô à Baouît.[2] Ces documents présentent une structure identique et sont signés par Biktôr (*P.Lond.* V 1747, *P.Lond.* V 1748, *SB* XIV 11332,[3] *SB* XXVI 16646,[4] *SB* XXVI 16788[5]). On peut ajouter à la série deux autres pièces, signées par des responsables différents: *P.Amst.* I 63[6] et *P.Lugd.Bat.* XIX 24.[7] Nous proposons ici une synthèse sur ce dossier et l'édition de quatre nouvelles pièces: *P.Clackson* 36 (= P.Heid. inv. 308v), *P.Clackson* 37 (= P.CtYBR inv. 1841v), *P.Clackson* 38 (= P.Brux. inv. 9483v) et *P.Clackson* 39 (= P.CtYBR inv. 1843v).[8] L'édition des textes au verso desquels les reçus de taxe sont notés est jointe en annexe (*P.Clackson* 40-43).

Sur le plan matériel, les documents se présentent sous la forme de petits coupons de papyrus de forme rectangulaire,[9] longs d'à peu près 10-15 cm, sur 5-8 cm de haut.[10] L'orientation des fibres est indifférente.[11] La structure des textes se conforme à un formulaire strict:

---

[1] Les deux auteurs avaient chacun préparé une édition de textes inédits. Il nous a semblé opportun de réunir ici nos travaux. *P.Clackson* 36 et 37 ont été édités par N. Gonis; l'édition des textes *P.Clackson* 38 et 39, ainsi que l'introduction et l'annexe (*P.Clackson* 40-43), sont dus à A. Delattre.

[2] Cf. Gonis 2000.

[3] Cf. Packman 1975, n° 2.

[4] = P.Louvre E 27615v, cf. Boud'hors 1995.

[5] = P.Duk. inv. 498v, cf. Gonis 2000.

[6] Cf. aussi Sijpesteijn 1972, n° 1. Seule la partie gauche du papyrus est conservée. Le texte peut être édité ainsi (réédition à partir de la photographie fournie dans l'édition, pl. 63): † Ἔσχο(ν) παρὰ σοῦ Μηνᾶ μο[νάζ(ον)τ(ος) - - -] | χρυσοῦ νομισμ(α)τ(ίου) δρίτον γί(νεται) ν[ο(μισματίου) - - -] | 2ᵉ m. Μοῦι στοιχε(ῖ) † "J'ai reçu de toi, Mèna le moine... un tiers de sou d'or, total 1/3 de sou d'or... Moui marque son accord †" (*ed. pr.*: † Ἔσχο(ν) παρὰ σοῦ Μηνᾶ μο[ναχοῦ | χρυσοῦ νομισμ(α)τ(ίου) τρίτον, γί(νεται) ν[ο(μισματίου) | Πκοῦι στοιχ(εῖ) †). La ressemblance paléographique avec les textes de la série (notamment avec la main de Pinoutiôn, cf. texte 1, n. 4) permet d'exclure la datation proposée par les éditeurs (VIᵉ siècle). La formule ἔσχο(ν) παρὰ σοῦ en tête de document est attestée dans 19 documents, dont 6 appartiennent au dossier dont il est question ici. Les autres éléments du formulaire, le format et le fait que le contributeur est un moine, permettent de proposer que *P.Amst.* I 63 appartient à cette série de reçus de taxe de Baouît. Il faut noter par ailleurs que le papyrus (n° d'inv. 30) appartient au même lot, acquis en 1969, que deux textes qui proviennent aussi du monastère de Baouît: *P.Amst.* I 47 et 48 (n° d'inv. 76 et 77).

[7] N. Gonis avait déjà émis l'hypothèse, sur base du formulaire, de l'appartenance de ce texte au dossier (cf. Gonis 2000, 151). L'hypothèse est maintenant confirmée, puisque le responsable qui a signé le document, Germanos, a également signé deux textes à *incipit* ⲡⲉⲛⲉⲓⲱⲧ ⲡⲉⲧⲥϩⲁⲓ (un inédit de la collection de Bruxelles: P.Brux. inv. E 9146v et le papyrus BM EA inv. 75330v, publiés dans Clackson 2008, n° 21).

[8] Nous remercions les professeurs R. Babcock et D. Hagedorn de nous avoir autorisés à publier les papyrus des collections de Yale et Heidelberg; ces textes ont été étudiés à partir de photographies digitales.

[9] Sauf *SB* XXVI 16788 qui a la forme d'un carré d'environ 7,5 cm de côté.

– † ἔσχον παρὰ σοῦ/ὑμῶν + nom du (des) contribuable(s), avec éventuellement son (leur) titre;

– ἀπὸ ἀνδρισμοῦ + année de l'indiction;

– le montant payé, p. ex. χρυσοῦ ἀρίθμια, souvent suivi d'un total: γίνεται ἀρίθμια;

– la date (jour, mois et année de l'indiction);

(– le nom du scribe;)

– la signature du (des) responsable(s).

Les reçus sont adressés à un ou plusieurs contribuable(s). Il s'agit le plus souvent de moine(s).

Tous les reçus mentionnent des paiements pour l'*andrismos*. Il faut noter par ailleurs que le monastère produisait sans doute aussi d'autres reçus en grec pour d'autres taxes. *P.Lugd.Bat.* XXV 78, par exemple, porte apparemment le texte d'un reçu de taxe écrit en grec.[12] Ce document provient du monastère de Baouît, puisqu'il est signé par Danièl, un supérieur de ce monastère, comme le montre la comparaison des signatures entre les reçus de taxe et les ordres à *incipit* ⲡⲉⲛⲉⲓⲱⲧ ⲡⲉⲧⲥϩⲁⲓ du même personnage.[13]

Les montants sont compris entre ⅓ et 2 sous d'or. Apparemment, l'impôt ne dépasse pas un sou par personne. Dans *P.Lugd.Bat.* XIX 24, 2, les éditeurs ont lu γ "3," mais l'examen de la planche montre qu'il faut lire γ' "⅓."

Les documents sont tous datés de manière relative (année de l'indiction). La paléographie et les rapprochements prosopographiques permettent de les dater de la première moitié du VIIIe siècle.

Trois scribes différents apparaissent dans le dossier: Mousaios, Pinouti(os) et Phib. Ce dernier est attesté dans un seul document (*P.Clackson* 37). Mousaios est attesté dans d'autres documents, encore inédits, du monastère (P.Duk. inv. 1053v; P.Iand. inv. 19). Sa période d'activité couvre au moins six ans (2e à 8e année d'une indiction). Pinoutiôn lui a probablement succédé. L'examen du dossier des reçus de taxe montre en effet que Mousaios est actif dans les 5e, 6e et 8e années d'un cycle indictionnel (*P.Clackson* 38; *P.Lond.* V 1748; *P.Clackson* 39) et que Pinoutiôn est actif pendant la 1e, la 8e et la 9e année d'un cycle (*P.Clackson* 36; *P.Lond.* V 1747; *SB* XIV 11332; *SB* XXVI 16646; et sans doute aussi *SB* XXVI 16788). Le fait que le responsable Biktôr est attesté dans des textes écrits par Mousaios (*P.Lond.* V 1748 et *P.Clackson* 39) et dans un autre de la main de Pinoutiôn (*P.Lond.* V 1747) rend la proximité chronologique des deux scribes, et le remplacement du premier par le second, très probable. Dans ce cadre, on peut placer la fin de l'activité de Mousaios entre le 20 Athyr de la 8e année d'un cycle indictionnel (*P.Clackson* 39, écrit par Mousaios) et le 3 Mécheir de la même 8e année (*SB* XXVI 16646, rédigé par Pinoutiôn). *P.Clackson* 36, signé par Pinoutiôn et daté de la 1e année de l'indiction,

---

[10] La longueur varie entre 9,8 et 17 cm (toujours sans tenir compte de *SB* XXVI 16788); la hauteur mesure entre 4 et 8,9 cm.

[11] Dans un certain nombre de cas, le reçu de taxe est écrit au dos d'un autre document (cf. *infra*), ce qui limite le choix de l'orientation. Mais même quand le verso est vierge, le document est écrit tantôt perpendiculairement (*P.Amst.* I 63, *SB* XIV 11332), tantôt parallèlement aux fibres (*P.Lugd.Bat.* XIX 24).

[12] Cf. Gonis 1999.

[13] Cf. p. ex. *BKU* III 367. Les textes signés par Daniel (y compris deux inédits) sont publiés dans Clackson 2008., n°s 14-17.

est dans le cadre de cette hypothèse, postérieur (cycle suivant) à *P.Lond.* V 1747; *SB* XXVI 16646; *SB* XIV 11332, datés des 8ᵉ et 9ᵉ année d'un cycle.

Plusieurs responsables différents apparaissent dans les textes: Apollô, Biktôr, Germanos, Hèlias, Johannès le *kathègètès*, Sernè, Mèna et Moui. Biktôr est le plus souvent attesté, régulièrement avec un ou plusieurs autre(s) responsables (Biktôr et Apollô dans *SB* XIV 11332 et *SB* XXVI 16646, Sernè, Èlias et Biktôr dans *P.Lond.* V 1748 ou de Biktôr et Mèna dans *P.Clackson* **39**).[14]

Seul un personnage est muni d'un titre: Johannès, le *kathègètès*. La fonction des autres responsables est difficile à préciser. *P.Lugd.Bat.* XIX 24 apporte peut-être un début de réponse: le document est signé par Germanos, qui est aussi connu comme supérieur du monastère (cf. note 7, *supra*). Il n'est donc pas impossible que ce soit le supérieur du monastère de Baouît, accompagné éventuellement d'autres responsables, qui signe les reçus de taxe de ce dossier.[15]

Bibliographie

Boud'hors, A. (1995). "Papyrus de Clédat au Musée du Louvre," in: *Divitiae Aegypti. Koptologische und verwandte Studien zu Ehren von Martin Krause*. Wiesbaden : L. Reichert Verlag, 29-35.

Clackson, S. J. (2008). *It is Our Father Who Writes: Orders from the Monastery of Apollo at Bawit* (= *American Studies in Papyrology* 43). Oxford: Oxbow.

Gonis, N. (1999). "Korr. Tyche 328," *Tyche* 14, 329-330.

Gonis, N. (2000). "Two Poll-Tax Receipts from Early Islamic Egypt," *ZPE* 131, 150-154.

Packman, Z. M. (1975). "Two Receipts from the Yale Collection," *BASP* 12, 13-18.

Sijpesteijn, P. J. (1972). "Some Byzantine Papyri from the Amsterdam Collection," *Studia Byzantina et Neohellenica Neerlandica = Byzantina Neerlandica* 3, 1-8.

---

[14] Cette pratique de double signature n'est pas sans rappeler *P.Lugd.Bat.* XXV 78, signé par l'archimandrite Danièl et par un certain Makaré.

[15] Il est aussi possible que Germanos exerçait une autre fonction lorsqu'il a signé le document.

Tableau des reçus de taxe de Baouit

	Contribuable(s)	Montant	Date	Responsable	Scribe
1. *P.Clackson* **36**	Saias, le moine	⅓ de nom.	6 Choiach 1ère ind.	Biktôr; Iôannès le kathègètès	Pinoutiôn
2. *P.Clackson* **37**	... Géôrgé... moine(s)	½ nom.	(2e ind.)	(Phib) Biktôr	Phib
3. *P.Lugd.Bat.* XIX 24	Kuriakos le chantre et moine	⅓ de nom.	12 Phaôphi 3e ind.	Germanos	...
4. *P.Lond.* V 1748	Apollô le chantre et son fils, les moines	2 nom.	17 Phaôphi 5e ind.	Sernè; Hèlias; Biktôr	Mousaios
5. *P.Clackson* **38**	... moine(s)	...	30 Phaôphi 6°ind.	Biktôr?	Mousaios
6. *P.Clackson* **39**	...	2 nom.	20 Hathyr 8e ind.	Biktôr; Mèna	Mousaios
7. *SB* XXVI 16646	Bètsch, le moine	½ nom.	3 Mécheir 8e ind.	Biktôr et Apollô	Pinoutiôn
8. *P.Lond.* V 1747	Pamoun, fils d'Onnophrios	1 nom.	14 Phaôphi 9e ind.	Biktôr	Pinoutiôn
9. *SB* XIV 11332	Môysès, celui de Pkaukès	1 nom.	7 Hathyr 9e ind.	Biktôr et Apollô	Pinoutiôn
10. *SB* XXVI 16788	Biktôr, fils de Psouros, le moine	1 nom.	25 Choiach 9e ind.	Biktôr	Pinoutiôn?
11. *P.Amst.* I 63?	Mèna, le moine	⅓ de nom.	...	Moui	...

P.Clackson 36

P.Heid. inv. K.308v 7,5 x 16,5 cm VIII century
Plate XV

1   + ἔσχον παρὰ σοῦ Σαιας μονάζ(ον)τ(ος)
2   ἀπὸ ἀνδ(ρισμοῦ) α ἰνδ(ικτίωνος) χρυσοῦ νομίσμ(α)τ(ος) τρίτον,
3   γί(νεται) ἀρ(ι)θ(μίου) γ΄. Χοιακ ϛ, ἰνδ(ικτίωνος) α. + Πιν(ου)τ(ίων) ἔγρα(ψα). +
4   (*m.*2)   Βίκτωρ στοιχεῖ. †
5   (*m.*3)   † Ἰωά(ννης) ⲡⲕⲁⲑ(ⲏⲅⲏⲧⲏⲥ) στηχεῖ. †

5. στοιχεῖ

1   I have received from you, Saias, monk,
2   from (the) *andrismos* of the 1st indiction, one-third of a *nomisma* of gold,
3   total ⅓ *arithmion*. Choiak 6, indiction 1. I, Pinoution, wrote.
4   (2nd hand) Victor agrees.
5   (3rd hand) Ioannes, the teacher, agrees.

1-4. The same structure is attested in *P.Lugd.Bat.* XIX 24, *P.Lond.* V 1747, *SB* XII 11332, XXVI 16646 (= P.Louvre E 27615), and 16788 (= P.Duk. inv. 498). See also above, introd. and n. 5.

1. Σαιας: A rare name, attested otherwise only in the fiscal codex from the Hermopolite village of Skar, published in *CPR* V.

μονάζ(ον)τ(ος): Cf. *P.Lugd.Bat.* XIX 24.1, *P.Lond.* V 1748.1, *SB* 16788.2, *P.Clackson* **37**.2, **38**.1.

2. ἀπὸ ἀνδ(ρισμοῦ): On this construction see *ZPE* 131 (2000), 152 (note to ll. 3-4).

νομίσμ(α)τ(ος): The same abbreviation occurs in *P.Amst.* 63.2 (see above, n. 5), *P.Lond.* V 1747.2, *SB* 11332.2 (followed by ἕν), 16646.2. All these texts are written by Pinoution (see below, 4 n.).

3. Choiak 6, indiction 1 = 2/3 December 702, 717, 732, etc.

Πιν(ου)τ(ίων) ἔγρα(ψα): Cf. *P.Lond.* V 1747.3, *SB* 11332.2, 16646.2. The same signature is probably to be recognised in *SB* 16788.6, though it is unclear how the name was abbreviated there. Pinoution used two types of handwriting: one is exemplified by *SB* 16788 and **1**; the other is found in *P.Lond.* V 1747, *SB* 11332, 16646, and probably *P.Amst.* 63, and has a deceptively early look (Bell assigned *P.Lond.* V 1747 to the sixth/seventh century).

5. ⲡⲕⲁⲑ(ⲏⲅⲏⲧⲏⲥ): On this term, "'teacher' in a religious sphere," see *P.Mon.Apollo* p. 26 with n. 134. Förster's *Wörterbuch* lists three inscriptions from the monastery of Apa Ieremias at Saqqara which attest the term, but there are a few more from Bawit: *MIFAO* 12, p. 108, 8, 3, *MIFAO* 39, p. 21, and *MIFAO* 59, pp. 118-19, 390, 2, all three referring to the same person, and *MIFAO* 59, p. 126, 434, 1f ⲃⲓⲕⲧⲱⲣ ⲕⲟⲩⲓ̈ ⲡϣⲁⲗ̣ⲗ̣ⲓ̣ⲟⲩ ⲡϣⲉ ⲛⲡϣ[ⲁⲗ]ⲗⲓⲟⲩ [ⲡⲉ]ⲕⲁⲧ?ⲅⲕⲏⲧⲏⲥ ⲙⲡⲁⲩⲏⲧ. This latter text is of some interest, since it refers to another "teacher" who had a role in the fiscal administration of the monastery.

P.Clackson 37

P.CtYBR inv. 1841v   11,7 x 7 cm   VIII century
Plate XV

```
1    + c.4 ἔσ]χ[ο(ν)] δ(ιὰ) Γεωργε κρ- traces of up to 8 letters
2    μονάζ(ον)τ(ος) (ὑπὲρ) ἀνδ(ρισμοῦ) δευτέρας ἰνδ(ικτίωνος) χρυ(σοῦ)
3    ἀρ(ι)θ(μίου) /, γί(νεται) ἀρ(ι)θ(μίου) ἥμεσει. + Φιβ ἔγρα(ψα) στοιχ(εῖ).
4    (m.2)    Βίκτωρ στηχε †
```

3. ἥμισυ ‖ 4. στοιχεῖ

1   ... I have received through George ...,
2   monk, for (the) *andrismos* of the second indiction, one-half
3   of an *arithmion* of gold, total ½ *arithmion*. I, Phib, wrote and agree.
4   (2nd hand) Victor agrees.

1. The break at the start of the line probably took away the date, not indicated elsewhere in the

document. See also next note.

ἔσ]χ[ο(ν)] δ(ιὰ) Γεωργε: The construction ἔσχον δ(ιὰ) + *name* has not occurred in any other text in this series, but is common enough in tax receipts of this period, especially from Hermopolis: see *P.Lond.* V 1739v.1, 1743.1, 1744.1, 1745.1, 1749.1, 1751.1, 1752.1, 1864.1, *P.Prag.* I 79.1, *P.Princ.* II 92.1, etc. In most of these texts, ἔσχον is preceded by a date.

2. Indiction 2 = 703/4, 718/19, 733/4, etc.

3. ἔγρα(ψα) στοιχ(εῖ): The same collocation (but without καί) occurs in *SPP* X 169.4.

4. στηχε: For the spelling cf. *P.Lond.* V 1747.4.

P.Clackson 38

P.Brux. inv. E. 9483v   4,6 x 5,2 cm   VIIIe siècle
Plate XV

Le fragment de papyrus de couleur brun rouge est très endommagé. On y lit en grec une date et le nom du scribe Mousaios. Il semble qu'on puisse y reconnaître les éléments du formulaire des reçus de taxe pour l'*andrismos* émis par le monastère.

On voit en bas du papyrus une *kollèsis* (bien visible au verso). Les trois lignes sont parallèles aux fibres. Les marges inférieure et supérieure sont conservées. L'écriture est très cursive et présente de nombreuses ligatures.

Le texte est écrit au verso d'un document qui a été découpé (cf. l'édition en annexe).

1   [† Ἔσχο(ν) παρά ... μ]οναζ(ον)τ( ) . . . . [   ]
2   [χρυσοῦ ...   ] Φ(α)ῶ(φι) λ ἰ(ν)δ(ικτίωνος) ϛ Μουσαίου ἔγρ(αψα) †
3   2e m.   [...   σ]τοιχεῖ

1. μοναζον^τ pap. ‖ 2. Φ^ω/ ι^δ/ Μουσαι^{ου} pap.

1   † J'ai reçu de toi/vous...) le(s) moine(s) ... (pour l'*andrismos* de la ...^e année de l'indiction... 2   nomisma... Total... nomisma). Phaôphi, le 30; 6e année de l'indiction. Mousaios j'ai écrit †

3   (Biktôr?) marque son accord.

1. [μ]οναζ(ον)τ( ): Le(s) contribuable(s) est (sont) désigné(s) comme moine(s). La lacune ne permet pas de déterminer s'il faut résoudre l'abréviation au singulier ou au pluriel.

. . . . [   ]: Les traces ne sont pas identifiables. Il faut sans doute lire et restituer ἀπο; ἀνδ(ρισμοῦ) ... (sans doute ϛ) ἰνδ(ικτίονος).

2. Μουσαί^{ου} Le scribe Mousaios a écrit de nombreux documents du monastère d'apa Apollô, en particulier des reçus de taxe (cf. *supra*).

3. [σ]τοιχεῖ: Le nom (ou les noms) du (ou des) responsable(s) n'est (ne sont) pas conservé(s). Plusieurs responsables sont attestés dans les reçus de taxe de l'*andrismos* du monastère: Apollô et Biktôr (*SB* XIV 11332 et *SB* XXVI 16646); Biktôr seul (*SB* XXVI 16788; *P.Lond.* V 1747 et 1748);

Germanos (*P.Lugd.Bat.* XIX, 24). La comparaison paléographique tend à suggèrer qu'il pourrait s'agir de Biktôr seul.

P.Clackson 39

P.CtYBR inv. 1843v 4,9 x 9,8 cm VIIIe siècle
Plate XVI

Le coupon de papyrus est de forme rectangulaire et de couleur brun-beige. Le texte est très bien conservé et presque complet: seule la première ligne manque.
Le papyrus porte le texte d'un reçu de taxe en grec, vraisemblablement pour l'*andrismos* (cf. les textes parallèles). Le document est écrit par le scribe Mousaios et signé par le responsable Biktôr, puis contresigné par un certain Mèna.
Les quatre lignes d'écriture sont parallèles aux fibres. Les marges de gauche, de droite et inférieure sont conservées. L'écriture de la première main est cursive et présente de nombreuses ligatures. La deuxième main est celle du responsable Biktôr. L'écriture en est lente et appliquée, mais on y trouve quelques ligatures. La troisième main est tout à fait maladroite.
Le texte est écrit au verso d'une lettre fragmentaire, découpée pour servir de support au reçu de taxe (cf. l'édition en annexe).

1 [† Ἔσχο(ν) παρὰ σοῦ/ὑμῶν ... μονάζ(ον)τ( ) ἀπὸ ἀνδ(ρισμοῦ)]
2 ὀγδόης ἰ(ν)[δ](ικτίωνος) χρυ(σοῦ) ἀρ(ί)θ(μια) δύο γί/(νεται) ἀρ(ί)θ(μια) β δύο
3 Ἀθὺ(ρ) κ ἰ(ν)δ(ικτίωνος) η Μουσαίου ἔγρ(αψα) †
4 2e m.   † Βίκτωρ στοιχε(ῖ) †
5 3e m.   † Μηνᾶ στοιχε(ῖ) †

1. μονάζ(ον)τ(ος) ou μοναζ(όν)τ(ων) ‖ 2. χρ^υ αρθ pap. ‖ 3. αθ^υ ι^δ pap.

1 († J'ai reçu de toi/vous... le(s) moine(s) ... pour l'*andrismos*)
2 de la huitième année de l'indiction deux *arithmia* d'or. Total: *arithmia* 2, deux.
3 Hathyr 20; 8e année de l'indiction. Mousaios j'ai écrit †
4 Biktôr marque son accord. †
5 † Mèna marque son accord †».

2. ὀγδόης: Les textes signés par Mousaios sont datés des 5e, 6e et 8e années d'un cycle indictionnel (probablement le même).

χρυ(σοῦ) ἀρ(ί)θ(μια) δύο: Généralement le montant exigé est d'un sou d'or par personne. Il est donc possible que le reçu soit adressé à deux contributeurs, peut-être un père et son fils, comme dans *P.Lond.* V 1748.

3. Μουσαίου: Mousaios est le scribe de nombreux textes du monastère, en particulier des reçus de taxes (cf. *supra*); son nom est toujours écrit au génitif.

4. Βίκτωρ: Le responsable Biktôr est attesté dans d'autres reçus d'*andrismos* (cf. *supra*).

P.Clackson **40-43**
(Annexe. Édition des rectos)

La plupart des reçus de taxe du dossier ont été écrits au verso d'un document plus ancien, découpé pour servir de support à un nouveau texte. On trouve ainsi aux rectos un protocole byzantin (10), un contrat (5 et 7?), une liste ou un compte (1 et 8), une lettre (2, 4 et 6?). Seuls trois papyrus ont le verso vierge (3, 9 et 11). Je propose ici l'édition des rectos des quatre reçus édités ici.

P.Clackson **40**

P.Heid. inv. K. 308r   16,5 x 7,5cm   VIIIe siècle
Plate XVI

Il s'agit apparemment une liste de noms, mais le texte est très difficile dans le détail.
Les onze lignes d'écriture sont perpendiculaires aux fibres. Aucune marge n'est conservée. L'écriture est bilinéaire.
Le verso a été réutilisé pour un reçu de taxe rédigé en grec (édité ici sous *P.Clackson* **36**).

             [- - -]
1   [ ]ακα̣   1   ...
2   [ ] αβραϩαμ   2   ... Abraham,
3   [ ] . πνο^{τ} 3   ... le notaire (?)
4   [ ] ṇ̄ϥсνηγ   4   ... ses frères
5   [ ]α πϥсον μν̄ πικ' ργ^{μ} [ ]   5   ... son frère et Pik...
6   [ ]γε πϥсον μ . . . . [ ]   6   ... -gé son frère et (?)
7   [ ]'ργ μηνα μν' τπελ[ ]   7   ... Mèna et ...
8   [ ]cεϣτ μη̣ρ τηρϥ̄ [ ]   8   ... tailleur(s) ...
9   [ ] πϊκογϫε ντιμε̣ [ ]   9   ... village ...
10 [ν]ιογοειε   10 ... les paysans ...
11 [ ]θε μν . . εϭογ πρωογ[ ]   11 ... et ... Prôou.
             [- - -]

1.]ακα̣: À ma connaissance, il n'y a qu'un seul nom terminant par ακα: τακα (*MIFAO* 111, p. 118, n° VII, l. 4).

5. πικ: Le nom propre πικ est attesté dans *BKU* III 335 et dans une inscription de Baouît (*MIFAO* 39, p. 30, n° XI: + ανακ πικ : φ[.]ε[.]νκεριακε). C'est probablement une variante du nom grec Πικῶς.

5. ⲣⲩᴹ: On pourrait interpréter la séquence ⲣⲩᴹ comme l'abréviation du mot grec ῥύμη "la rue," qui est attesté plusieurs fois en copte (cf. Förster 2002 : 712).

7.]ⲣⲩ: On pourrait interpréter cette séquence comme la fin d'un nom propre (cf. p ex. ⲡⲉⲧⲣⲩ dans *P.Bal.* 225). Mais on peut aussi envisager qu'il s'agisse, comme à la l. 5, d'une "adresse" avec la mention d'une rue.

8. ⲥⲉϣⲧ: Ce mot est attesté dans une inscription de Baouît (*MIFAO* 12, p. 80: + ⲡⲉⲛⲓⲱⲧ ⲁⲡⲁ ⲓⲁⲕⲱⲃ ⲡⲥⲉϣⲧ "† Notre père apa Jakôb, le tailleur").

ⲙⲏⲣ: Le mot ⲙⲏⲣ "rive" n'est attesté qu'une fois en sahidique (cf. Crum, *Dict.* 180a); il pourrait aussi s'agir d'un toponyme. On peut également penser au mot ⲙⲏⲣ "lien, corde..." (cf. Crum, *Dict.* 182a).

9. ⲡⲓⲕⲟⲩϫⲉ: Faut-il y voir un nom propre ou bien une forme de ⲕⲟⲩⲓ ("le petit village")?

P.Clackson 41

P.CtYBR inv. 1841r   7 x 11,7 cm   VIIIᵉ siècle
Plate XVII

Le morceau de papyrus est de couleur beige. On y déchiffre les restes très mutilés d'un texte copte, sans doute une lettre.
Les cinq lignes d'écriture sont perpendiculaires aux fibres. Aucune marge n'est conservée. L'écriture est bilinéaire.
Le verso a été réutilisé pour un reçu de taxe rédigé en grec (édité ici sous *P.Clackson* 37).

```
         [- - -]
1  [          ] . [                          ]
2  [      ]ⲡⲁϣⲏⲣⲉ ⲉⲛⲥⲛⲟⲩϥ . [                ]
3  [      ]ⲕ ⲛⲁϥ ϩⲛ ⲡ . . ⲉⲣ ⲟⲩⲣⲟⲙⲡⲉ ⲛ̣[    ]
4  [      ]ⲁⲣⲉϥ ⲉⲛⲛ . [ . . ] ⲩϥ [ . ] ⲛⲃⲉ . [ . ] ⲛϥⲉⲓⲛ[  ]
5  [            ] . . . ⲁⲣ . 'ⲡⲁ . . ⲙⲁ̣' . . ⲡⲉⲓⲡ . [  ]
```

"... mon fils, l'année dernière... à lui dans ... une année... et qu'il ..."

4.]ⲁⲣⲉϥ: On peut penser à un optatif (ⲙⲁⲣⲉϥ-).

5. . . . ⲁⲣ . 'ⲡⲁ . . ⲙⲁ̣' Il faut peut-être lire et interpréter cette séquence en ⲙ̣ⲁ̣ⲕⲁⲣⲉ̣ ⲡⲁⲣⲭⲙⲁ "Makaré, l'archimandrite."

P.Clackson 42
(Contrat)

P.Brux. inv. E. 9483r   4,6 x 5,2 cm   VIIIe siècle
Plate XVII

Le fragment de papyrus de couleur brune rouge est très endommagé. On y déchiffre la mention en copte des différents témoins qui apportent leur caution à un document.
On aperçoit au milieu du fragment une *kollèsis*. Les trois lignes d'écriture sont perpendiculaires aux fibres. L'encre de couleur noire est fortement effacée. La marge inférieure est conservée. L'écriture est bilinéaire et cursive.
Le verso a été réutilisé pour un reçu de taxe rédigé en grec (édité ici sous *P.Clackson* 38).

```
           [- - -]
       [    ] . † . . . ṃ . [            ]
       [    ] ṭịọ ⲙⲛⲧⲣⲉ † ⲁⲛ[ⲟⲕ         ]
       [    ] . ⲧⲓⲟ ⲙⲛⲧⲣⲉ [              ]
```

"... je suis témoin † Moi... je suis témoin..."

1. † . . . ṃ . : La lecture de ce passage est assez difficile. On peut envisager d'y lire en grec une date: + ἐγράφη μ(ηνὶ) Φ(α)[...] "† Écrit au mois de Pha..." (Phaôphi, Phamenôth ou Pharmouthi).

2. ṭịọ ⲙⲛⲧⲣⲉ: Il ne semble pas y avoir de différence de main entre l'indication de ce témoin et celle qui suit (l. 2-3). Il est donc probable que le scribe du document ait également écrit cette partie du texte.

P.Clackson 43

P.CtYBR inv. 1843r   4,9 x 9,8 cm   VIIIe siècle
Plate XVII

Le fragment de papyrus est de couleur brune beige. On y déchiffre les restes d'une lettre copte.
Les cinq lignes d'écriture sont perpendiculaires aux fibres. La marge de droite est conservée. L'écriture est bilinéaire.
La lettre a été découpée pour servir de support au reçu de taxe (édité ici sous *P.Clackson* 39).

```
          [- - -]
1    [    ]ⲛⲉⲕⲥϩⲁⲓ ⲛⲃⲧⲉϥ ⲡⲟⲟⲩ ⲁⲓⲕⲱ
2    [    ⲇⲓⲁ]ⲕⲟⲛⲓⲁ ⲙⲁⲗⲗⲟⲛ ⲁⲩⲉⲓ ⲛⲏⲧⲛ ⲁⲧⲛⲉϭⲱⲡ
3    [    ϩⲁ]ⲣⲉϩ ⲉⲣⲟⲕ ⲟⲩⲉⲛ ⲗⲟⲅⲓⲥⲙⲟⲥ ⲛ̣ⲙⲟⲕ
4    [    ⲉϣ]ⲱⲡⲉ ⲕⲟⲩⲱϣ ⲉⲓⲉⲕⲁ ⲡⲣⲱⲙⲉ ⲉⲃⲟⲗ
```

5   [   ]ⲕⲟⲥ ⲡϩⲟⲥⲓⲱᵀ ⲛⲉ . . . . [. . . .] ⲉ̣ . . . .
    [- - -]

1   ... ta lettre... aujourd'hui, j'ai laissé
2   ... *diakonia*, plutôt ils sont venus à vous, vous les avez pris
3   ... te garder et t'accorder la raison
4   ... si tu veux, je renverrai l'homme
5   ... la sainteté...

1. ⲛⲕⲧⲉϥ: Cette séquence est problématique. On pourrait y voir une forme de conjonctif ⲛⲕ- pour ⲛϥ, avec peut-être une forme du verbe ϯ "donner."

3. ϩⲁ]ⲣⲉϩ: Il faut sans doute restituer ⲡⲛⲟⲩⲧⲉ ou ⲡϫⲟⲉⲓⲥ ϩⲁ]ⲣⲉϩ ⲉⲣⲟⲕ (cf. p. ex. *O.Crum* 340).

ⲟⲩⲉⲛ ⲗⲟⲅⲓⲥⲙⲟⲥ ⲛ̅ⲙⲟ̣ⲕ̣: Je comprends cette séquence comme ⲟⲩⲛ̅ ⲗⲟⲅⲓⲥⲙⲟⲥ ⲛ̅ⲙⲟⲕ "qu'il y ait une raison pour toi...; que la raison te soit accordée..."

5. ⲡϩⲟⲥⲓⲱᵀ ⲛⲉ . . ⲕ̣ .: Plusieurs hypothèses de restitution sont envisageables: ⲛⲉⲓⲱⲧ "père," ⲛ̅ϫⲟⲉⲓⲥ "seigneur," ⲛ̅ⲥⲟⲛ "frère," ⲛⲉⲡⲓⲥⲕ° "évêque." Cette dernière solution semble la plus probable en raison des traces conservées.

P.CLACKSON 44

"ESSIG UND ÖL"
HEILUNG VON LEIB UND SEELE ALS THEMA EINES BRIEFES[*]

HANS FÖRSTER

P.Vindob. K. 4725	18,8 x 13,3 cm	VI. Jh.
Plate XVIII		

Vom mittelbraunen Papyrus guter Qualität sind der rechte, der linke und der untere Rand erhalten, der obere Rand fehlt. Der Papyrus ist beidseitig mit Karbontinte beschrieben. Der Schriftträger weist einige Fehlstellen mechanischer Art auf. Ein Riß verläuft in vertikaler Richtung durch das Fragment, an dessen Rändern Ausbrüche feststellbar sind. In der Mitte des Fragments und entlang des rechten Blattrandes finden sich größere Fehlstellen. Glättung und Festigung erfolgten mit 1%iger Klucel L Lösung in 50%igem Äthanol. Zur Sicherung der gefährdeten Teile wurden Japanpapierstreifchen mit 3%iger Klucel G Lösung in Äthanol angebracht.[1]

Aufgrund des erhaltenen Textes darf man vermuten, daß vom oberen Rand nicht zu viel fehlt. Die Bitte, gewürdigt zu werden einer Mitteilung über Gesundheit und Wohlergehen des Empfängers des Briefes findet sich meist nach einigen höflichen und einleitenden Zeilen. Hier ist diese Bitte in Zeile 5f belegt. Allerdings könnte man anführen, daß es trotz des fragmentarischen Charakters der ersten Zeilen fast sicher ist, daß in diesem Bereich bereits Text zu finden ist, der sonst zum eigentlichen Briefkorpus gehört. Dies scheint darauf hinzuweisen, daß sich der Verfasser nicht strikt an den Aufbau koptischer Briefe gehalten hat, und macht eine Aussage über den verlorenen Textumfang sehr schwierig.

```
1↓   ΚΑΤΑ ΟΥΜΝΤΑΘΗΤ . [ ] Ν[
2    ΕΡΕΠΕΚΣѠΜΑ ΜΤΟΝ . [                              †]
3    ϨΗΥ Ν̄ϨΟΥΟ ΠΛΗΝ ΕΡΕΠ[                    ΤΝ̄ΠΑΡΑΚΑΛΕΙ]
4    Ν̄ΝΟΥΤΕ ΕϤΕΧΑΡΙΖΕ Μ[ΜΟΚ] ΑΥѠ ΝΑ[† ΝΑ]Κ̣ Ν̄Μ̄ΠΤΑΛϬΟ Μ̄
5    ΠΕΚΣѠΜΑ ΜΝ̄ ΠΟΥΧΑΪ [Ν̄Τ]Ε̣Κψ̣ΥΧΗ [ΜΑΡΕΚΑ]ΑΝ Ν̄Μ̄Πϣ̄Α Ν̄ΣѠ
6    ΤΜ̄ Η ΝΑΥ ΕΠΕΚΟΥΧ[ΑΙ – ]ΟΥϬΟΜ[ – ]ΑΪ Ν̄ΤΑΤΚ̄ΜΝ̄Τ
```

---

[*] Sarah Clackson, die leider viel zu früh von uns gegangen ist, kämpfte lange gegen eine heimtückische Krankheit. Insofern liegt es nahe, ihr einen Text zu widmen, der mit dem Themenkomplex "Krankheit" verbunden ist. Der Beitrag entstand im Rahmen eines APART-Stipendiums (Austrian Programme for Advanced Research and Technology) der Österreichischen Akademie der Wissenschaften. Herrn Prof. Dr. Hermann Harrauer, dem Leiter der Papyrussammlung der Österreichischen Nationalbibliothek, danke ich für die gewährte Publikationserlaubnis. Jean-Luc Fournet danke ich für den Hinweis auf seinen Artikel über den hier verwendeten Frauennamen, eine Diskussion mit Sebastian Richter gab den Anstoß zur Auseinandersetzung mit der Konstruktion in Z. 10f., Cornelia Römer riet, der Frage nach der Person des "Apa Severus" noch genauer nachzugehen. Besonders möchte ich auch Anne Boud'hors für zahlreiche Hinweise und kritische Rückfragen im Rahmen der Endredaktion des Textes danken.

[1] Für die Überlassung des Restaurierberichtes danke ich der Restauratorin der Papyrussammlung, Frau Andrea Donau, welche die konservatorische Behandlung des *P.Clackson* 44 durchgeführt hat.

7   ⲙⲁⲓⲛⲟⲩⲧⲉ ⲧⲛ̄ⲟ̣ⲟ̣ⲩⲥ̣[–] . ⲡⲁⲅⲁⲑⲟⲛ ⲁⲛϫⲓⲧⲟⲩ ⲉⲩ . . [ⲁⲛ]
8   ϫⲏⲩ ⲙⲛ ⲛⲉⲕⲥⲙⲟⲩ ⲧⲏⲣ[ⲟ]ⲩ· ⲁⲛⲉⲩⲭⲁⲣⲓⲥⲧⲁ ⲛⲁⲕ ⲧⲟⲛ̣ⲉ̣
9   ϩⲓⲧⲛ̄ ⲧⲛⲟϭ ⲙ̄ⲡⲣⲟⲥⲫⲟⲣ[ⲁ] ⲉⲙⲛ̄ϭⲟⲙ ⲙⲟⲛ ⲉⲧⲟⲩⲉⲓⲟ ⲛⲁⲕ
10 ϩⲁⲣⲟⲥ ⲁⲗⲗⲁ ⲡⲉⲛⲧⲁⲕ[ⲧ]ⲛ̣ⲟⲟⲩⲥ ⲛⲁϥ ⲟⲩϩⲓⲕⲁⲛⲟⲥ ⲡⲉ ⲉⲑⲉ
11 ⲣⲁⲡⲉⲩⲉ ⲛ̄ⲧⲕ̄ⲯⲩⲭⲏ ⲙⲛ̄ⲡⲉ̣ⲕⲥⲱⲙⲁ ⲟⲩⲧⲉ ⲅⲁⲣ ⲧⲛ̄ⲙⲡϣ[ⲁ]
12 ⲁⲛ ⲛ̄ⲟⲓⲕⲟⲛⲟⲙⲓⲁ ⲛ̄ϯⲙⲓ̣[ⲛⲉ –] ⲕⲁⲧⲁ ⲑⲉ ⲛ̄ⲧⲁⲕⲕⲉⲗⲉⲩⲉ ϫⲉ
13 ⲧⲛⲟⲟⲩ ⲡⲛⲉϩ ⲙⲡⲑⲩⲥⲓⲁⲥⲧⲏⲣⲓⲟⲛ ⲉⲧⲟⲩⲁⲃ ⲛⲁⲓ ⲙⲛ̄ ⲟⲩ
14 ϣⲏⲙ ⲙⲟⲟⲩ· ⲉⲓⲥ ϩⲏⲧⲉ ⲁⲓⲧⲛⲟⲟⲩⲥⲉ ⲁⲩⲱ ⲁⲓⲧⲛⲟⲟⲩ ⲟⲩ
15 ⲕⲟⲩⲓ̈ ⲛ̄ⲕⲟⲟϩ ϩⲛ̄ ⲑⲟⲓ̈ⲧⲉ ⲛⲁⲡⲁ ⲥⲉⲩⲏⲣⲟⲥ ⲉⲓ̈ⲙⲉⲉⲩⲉ ϫⲉ ⲁⲕⲕⲁ
16 ⲧⲱⲕ ϩⲛ̄ⲧⲡⲟⲗⲓⲥ ϩⲁⲣⲉϩ ⲉⲣⲟⲥ ⲉⲙⲁⲧⲉ· ⲛⲁⲓ ⲉⲓ̈ⲥϩⲁⲓ ⲙⲟⲟⲩ ✝
17 ⲁⲥⲡⲁⲍⲉ ϫⲓⲛ ⲧⲉⲕⲁⲡⲉ ϣⲁϩⲁ ⲛⲉⲕⲟⲩⲉⲣⲏⲧⲉ· ⲁⲩⲱ ϯϣⲓⲛⲉ ⲉⲧⲁ
18 ⲙⲉⲣⲓⲧ ⲛ̄ϣⲉⲉⲣⲉ ⲕⲩⲣⲁⲕⲁ̣ⲗ̣ⲏ̣ ⲧⲟⲛ̣ⲉ̣ ⲙⲛ̄ ⲛⲁⲡⲉⲥϩⲓ̈ ⲧⲏⲣⲟ̣ⲩ̣
19 ⲧⲁⲙⲛ̄ⲧⲣⲉϥⲣ̄ⲛⲟⲃⲉ ϣⲗⲏⲗ ⲉⲧⲣⲉⲡⲛⲟⲩⲧⲉ ⲥⲙⲟⲩ ⲉⲣⲟⲥ
20 ⲙⲛ̄ⲡⲉⲥϩⲓ̈ ⲧⲏⲣϥ̄· ⲉⲓ̣[ⲥ] ⲛ̄ⲕⲟⲩⲓ̈ ⲛ̄ⲥⲧⲁⲩⲣⲟⲥ ⲁⲓ̈ϫⲟⲟⲩⲥⲉ
21 ⲛ̄ⲛⲉⲥϣⲏⲣⲉ·

Recto

22 ⲟⲩϫⲁⲓ̈ ⲟⲩϫⲁⲓ̈ ⲟⲩϫⲁⲓ̈ ϩ[ⲛ]ⲧⲉⲭⲁⲣⲓⲥ ⲛ̄ⲧⲉⲧⲣⲓⲁⲥ ⲉⲧⲟⲩ
23 ⲁⲁⲃ ⲛ̄ϩⲟⲙⲟⲟⲩⲥⲓⲟⲛ· ϫⲓⲛⲧⲁⲓ̈ⲥϩⲁⲓ ⲧⲓⲉⲡⲓⲥ
24 ⲧⲟⲗⲏ ⲁⲛⲉⲥⲛⲏⲩ ⲡⲁⲣⲁⲕⲁⲗⲉⲓ̣ ⲙⲟⲓ̈ ϫⲉ ⲕⲱⲣϣ̄
25 ⲉⲧⲉⲕⲙⲛ̄ⲧⲙⲁⲓ̈ⲛⲟⲩⲧⲉ ϫⲉ ⲉ̣ϣⲱⲡⲉ ⲟⲩⲛ̄ ⲟⲩϣⲏⲙ
26 ⲛ̄ϩⲙ̄ϫ ⲙⲟⲧⲛ̄ ⲉⲣⲱⲧⲛ̣ ⲁⲣⲓ ⲧⲁⲅⲁⲡⲏ ⲛⲙ̄ⲙⲁⲛ ⲕⲁⲛ
27 ⲉϣϫⲉ ⲟⲩⲃⲁⲣⲟⲥ ⲡⲉ ⲟⲩⲁϩ ⲡⲓⲕⲉⲁⲅⲁⲑⲟⲛ ⲉϫⲛ̄
28 ⲛⲉⲕⲕⲉⲁⲣⲉⲧⲏ̣ ⲧⲏⲣⲟ̣ⲩ

3. Die Ergänzung mit παρακαλέω scheint im Kontext aufgrund der grammatischen Konstruktion sinnvoll, auch wenn dieses Verbum normalerweise im Zusammenhang einer konkreten Bitte an reale Personen und nicht im religiösen Kontext der Bitte an eine höhere Macht Verwendung findet; ϣⲗⲏⲗ wie auch ⲕⲱⲣϣ, die der Schreiber des Briefes beide selbst verwendet (19; 24), werden mit nachfolgendem ⲉ- konstruiert; vgl. auch Westendorf, Handwörterbuch, *s.v.*; der von Crum, Dictionary, *s.v.* ϣⲗⲏⲗ belegte Gebrauch dieses Wortes mit nachfolgendem ⲛ-/ⲛⲁ= spricht ebenfalls gegen die Ergänzung, da die Person, für die gebeten wird, in dieser Form angefügt wird. ‖ 4. Auffällig ist auch, daß ⲛⲟⲩⲧⲉ ohne den bestimmten Artikel konstruiert wird. ‖ 5. Trotz der vergleichsweise kleinen Lakuna scheint eine Ergänzung mit dem kausativen Imperativ den Parallelen und dem Sinn der Stelle am ehesten zu entsprechen. ‖ 10. Zur Ergänzung der Lakuna vgl. den Abschnitt zu Schrift und Sprache.

1   gemäß (κατά) einer Herzlosigkeit
2   Während dein Körper (σῶμα) ruht
3   mehr nutzen. Jedoch (πλήν) während[… wir bitten (παρακαλέω)]
4   Gott, daß er dich beschenken (χαρίζω) möge und dir gebe mit der Gesundung
5   deines Körpers (σῶμα) auch das Heil deiner Seele (ψυχή)… mögest du uns würdigen, zu hören

6 oder (ἤ) zu sehen dein Heil… eine Macht… und deine Frömmigkeit
7 hat es (?) geschickt… gut (ἀγαθός). Wir haben sie erhalten und [wir haben]
8 auch deine ganzen Wohltaten erhalten. Wir danken (εὐχαριστέω) dir
9 durch das große Opfer (προσφορά), und wir können dich nicht dafür
10 entschädigen. Sondern (ἀλλά) der, dem du es geschickt hast, ist fähig (ἱκανός),
11 deine Seele (ψυχή) und deinen Körper (σῶμα) zu heilen (θεραπεύω). Auch sind wir nämlich (γάρ) nicht (οὔτε) wert
12 eines derartigen Austauschs (οἰκονομία)… in (κατά) der Art, in der du es befohlen (κελεύω) hast:
13 Sende das Öl des heiligen Altares (θυσιαστήριον) mir mit etwas
14 Wasser. Siehe, wir haben sie geschickt, und ich habe ein kleines Stück
15 aus dem Gewand des Apa (ἄπα) Severus gesandt. Ich denke du hast
16 das deine in der Stadt (πόλις) gelassen. Hüte es sehr. Das habe ich dir geschrieben.
17 Ich grüße (ἀσπάζω) <dich> von deinem Haupt bis zu deinen Füßen. Und ich frage sehr nach
18 meiner geliebten Tochter Kyrakale und nach ihrem ganzen Haus.
19 Ich armer Sünder[2] bete, daß Gott sie segnen möge
20 mit ihrem ganzen Haus. Siehe, die kleinen Kreuze (σταυρός), ich habe sie
21 ihren Kindern geschickt.

Recto
22 Lebe wohl. Lebe wohl. Lebe wohl in der Gnade (χάρις) der heiligen
23 wesenseinen (ὁμοούσιος) Dreiheit (τριάς). Seit ich diesen Brief (ἐπιστολή) geschrieben habe
24 haben die Brüder mich gebeten (παρακαλέω), daß ich eure Frömmigkeit[3]
25 bestürme: Wenn etwas
26 Essig leicht für euch ist, sei so gut (ἀγαπή) mit uns.[4] Und wenn (κἄν)
27 es etwas Schweres (βάρος) ist, lege auch noch diese gute Tat (ἀγαθός) auf
28 alle deine anderen Tugenden (ἀρετή).

Einleitung

Die Handschrift des *P.Clackson* **44** weist eine sehr auffällige Ähnlichkeit mit der Handschrift von K. 4730 (= *P.Harrauer* 57)[5] auf. Dieser Umstand macht eine ausführliche paläographische Datierung

---

[2] Wörtlich ist diese koptische Konstruktion wohl nicht übersetzbar, es handelt sich um die Bildung eines abstrakten Begriffes aus einem *Nomen agentis*, das aus dem im Koptischen üblichen Begriff für Sünde und dem Präfix ⲣⲉϥ- gebildet ist.

[3] Wörtl.: "Gottliebendheit."

[4] Wörtl.: "Tue die Liebe mit uns."

[5] Für die Edition vgl. Förster 2001.

überflüssig, vielmehr sei hierfür auf die Publikation von P.Vindob. K. 4730 verwiesen. Ferner muß die örtliche Nähe der beiden Texte innerhalb des Aufbewahrungsortes in der Österreichischen Nationalbibliothek erwähnt werden, beide gehören zu den Texten, die in Wien dem sogenannten Schenutearchiv zugeordnet wurden.[6] Es handelt sich hierbei um die Objekte mit den Signaturen P.Vindob. K. 4701-4812.[7] Bei diesen Texten handelt es sich um die Geschäftsbriefe eines gewissen Schenute, der vorwiegend mit Fragen der Verwaltung befaßt ist. Aufgrund des Inhaltes von *P.Clackson* 44 wird man wohl auch diesen Text—dies war auch bei der Veröffentlichung von P.Vindob. K. 4730 geschehen—ebenfalls aus dem Schenutearchiv ausschließen müssen.[8] Einerseits ist der Name des Verwalters, der dem Archiv seinen Namen gegeben hat und der ein wichtiges Kriterium für die Zusammenfassung der Texte war, in diesem Text nicht zu finden, andererseits ist der Verfasser des Textes hauptsächlich mit Fragen des religiösen Lebens beschäftigt und scheint selbst in einem monastischen Kontext zu leben. Insofern scheint es sinnvoll, auch *P.Clackson* 44 nicht mehr den "Schenute-Texten" zuzurechnen.

Bereits im Rahmen der Einleitung scheint es nötig, auf eine Textergänzung hinzuweisen, die einen Subjektwechsel voraussetzt. In Z. 4f geht es darum, daß Gott dem Empfänger des Briefes Heilung schenken möge. In Z. 5 stellt sich nun die Frage, wie die Fehlstelle zu ergänzen ist. Grundsätzlich ist es selbstverständlich nicht ausgeschlossen, daß an dieser Stelle weiterhin Gott das Subjekt ist, daß also Gott selbst es möglich macht, daß der Verfasser des Briefes von dem Gesundheitszustand des Empfängers erfährt (in diesem Fall wäre [ⲙⲁⲣⲉϥⲁ]ⲁⲛ zu ergänzen). Gegen diese Ergänzungsmöglichkeit sprechen zwei Gründe: Als erstes scheint es nötig, aufgrund der bereits erwähnten Nähe zu *P.Harrauer* 57 der Ergänzung mit [ⲙⲁⲣⲉⲕⲁ]ⲁⲛ den Vorzug zu geben, wird doch mit einer sehr ähnlichen Formulierung dort der Empfang eines Briefes bestätigt (vgl. Z. 5): ϩⲙⲡⲧⲣⲁⲙⲡⲱϣⲁ ⲛⲛⲉⲕⲥϩⲁⲓ̈. Ausgehend von der Annahme, daß es sich bei beiden Briefen um denselben Schreiber handelt, scheint diese Ergänzung gerechtfertigt und dem Kontext angemessen. In diesem Falle wäre dann eine Möglichkeit, das „Würdigen des Sehens" dahingehend zu verstehen, daß der Empfänger dem Verfasser einen Besuch abstattet. Dies setzt zusätzlich voraus, daß der Verfasser des Briefes von seinem derzeitigen Ort unabkömmlich ist. Allerdings scheinen auch im Koptischen Briefe teilweise als Ersatz einer persönlichen Begegnung aufgefaßt worden zu sein. Insofern ist eine persönliche Begegnung trotz der Verwendung des koptischen Begriffs ⲛⲁⲩ nicht zwingend vorausgesetzt[9]. Im Falle einer Ergänzung mit [ⲙⲁⲣⲉϥⲁ]ⲁⲛ würde es aus theologischer Sicht als Gnade aufgefasst, wenn die beiden sich treffen bzw. der Verfasser des Briefes von dem Empfänger eine Nachricht erhielte. Und hier ist die zweite Einwendung gegen diese Ergänzungsmöglichkeit vorzubringen: Auch wenn in damaliger Zeit nicht alle Briefe ihr Ziel erreichten, so scheint die Vorstellung doch selbst für die ägyptische Frömmigkeit übertrieben, daß es göttliche Gnade ist, wenn ein Brief seinen Sender erreicht. Hierfür sprechen auch die Entschuldigungsformeln—unter gleichzeitiger Berücksichtigung der Gelegenheitsformeln—der koptischen Briefe: Diese zeigen doch

---

[6] Nach dem handschriftlichen Kapselkatalog von Wessely ist dieser Papyrus aufgrund der Korrespondenz des Schenute datierbar.

[7] Vgl. hierzu Till 1941: 196.

[8] Insgesamt scheinen einige interessante Briefe diesem Archiv zugeordnet worden zu sein, die keine Beziehung zu dem besagten Verwalter Schenute haben.

[9] Siehe hierzu Biedenkopf-Ziehner 1996.

sehr deutlich, daß es menschliche Schwäche bzw. das Fehlen von Schreibmaterial ist—und daß hierfür um Entschuldigung gebeten wird, schließt höhere Gewalt aus[10]—, wenn ein Brief nicht geschrieben wird[11], und dies ist somit nach den typischen Wendungen in den koptischen Briefen auch der Hauptgrund dafür, daß man keine Nachrichten von der betreffenden Person erhält, nicht jedoch der fehlende göttliche Schutz bei der Beförderung der Post. Diese Überlegungen zwingen bei der Ergänzung zum Wechsel der Person.

1. Schrift und Sprache[12]

Das Schriftbild ist regelmäßig und ordentlich. Es läßt auf einen geübten Schreiber schließen. Der von ihm verfaßte Text ragt sprachlich weit über den Durchschnitt der dokumentarischen Texte hinaus. Viele koptische Briefe zeichnen sich durch einfache und kurze Sätze aus, häufig finden sich Verschreibungen und andere Fehler, dialektale Einflüsse sind oftmals Zeugen davon, daß diese Briefe von Menschen in alltäglichen Lebenssituationen verfaßt wurden. Von derartigen Texten unterscheidet sich *P.Clackson* **44**. Ein gebildeter Mann, der offensichtlich auch in der Theologie nicht nur oberflächlich bewandert ist—und die theologische Ausbildung war damals ja auch für geistliche Amtsträger nicht mit einem Studium, sondern vor allem mit einer Schriftkenntnis und dem Auswendiglernen einzelner biblischer Bücher verbunden—, schreibt ein gehobenes Sahidisch. Auffällig ist zum Beispiel eine Formulierung in Zeile 4, die eine gewisse Ähnlichkeit zu Formulierungen in Rechtsurkunden aus späterer Zeit aufweist.[13] In diesem Zusammenhang ist festzuhalten, daß eigentlich der bestimmte Artikel vor ⲚⲞⲨⲦⲈ in dieser Zeile zu erwarten wäre. Der für Zeile 5 erschlossene kausative Konjunktiv mag ebenso wie die Einleitung eines Konditionalis durch ⲈϢⲰⲠⲈ noch als relativ häufig in Briefen an einer vergleichbaren Stelle angesehen werden, doch sowohl das energetische Futur in Zeile 4 wie auch der Relativsatz des Perfekt (vgl. Zeile 6 u. 12) und die Verwendung des kausativen Infinitivs (19) zeigen sehr gut die weit überdurchschnittliche Beherrschung der koptischen Sprache und sind somit ein Hinweis auf die Bildung des Verfassers.

Interessant ist die Formulierung der Zeilen 10f. Bei ⲞⲨϨⲒⲔⲀⲚⲞⲤ ⲠⲈ[14] handelt es sich um den binären Kern eines Nominalsatzes. Es scheint nun, daß der Schreiber einen Relativsatz als erweitertes

---

[10] Vgl. auch nur die von Biedenkopf-Ziehner 1983: 66 zitierte Aufforderung: ⲀⲨⲰ ⲘⲠⲢ̅ⲢϢ ⲈϪⲞⲞⲨ ⲠⲎⲦⲚⲞⲨⲰ ⲚⲀⲒ̈, "Und wollt nicht versäumen (wörtl.: ablassen), mir eure Nachricht zu senden."

[11] Biedenkopf-Ziehner 1983: 28-31 u. 61-66.

[12] Es scheint bei der Edition dieses Briefes sinnvoll, von der üblichen Struktur eines Kommentars zu einem Papyrus, der formal ein Zeilenkommentar ist, abzuweichen. Die verschiedenen, interessanten Bereiche, die in dem Text berührt werden, lassen sich eher thematisch zusammenfassen.

[13] Vgl. hierfür in Zeile 4f die Wendung: ⲈϤⲈⲬⲀⲢⲒⲌⲈ Ⲙ̅[ⲘⲞⲔ] ⲀⲨⲰ ⲚⲀ[ϤϮ ⲚⲀ]Ⲕ Ⲛ̅ⲘⲠⲦⲀⲖϬⲞ Ⲙ̅ⲠⲈⲔⲤⲰⲘⲀ Ⲙ̅Ⲛ̅ ⲠⲞⲨϪⲀⲒ̈ [Ⲛ̅Ⲧ]ⲈⲔ̣ⲮⲨⲬⲎ̣. An der Stelle des hier Verwendung findenden energetischen Futurs ist in den Rechtsurkunden—ihrem juristischen Charakter entsprechend—meist entweder ein Konditionalis oder ein affirmatives Perfekt gebraucht. Auch ist die hier zu findende Wendung länger als die in den Urkunden anzutreffende; vgl. Förster 2002, *s.v.* χαρίζω.

[14] Für ἱκανός mit nachfolgendem Infinitiv (dort kausativer Infinitiv) vgl. Mk 1,7: ⲈⲀⲚⲄ̅ⲞⲨϨⲒⲔⲀⲚⲞⲤ ⲀⲚ ⲈⲦⲢⲀⲠⲀϨⲦ̅.

Subjekt dieses Nominalsatzes konstruiert.[15] Man wird als Verbum des Relativsatzes, das aufgrund der Lakuna des Papyrus nur teilweise erhalten ist, ϫοογ, ⲧⲛⲟογ bzw. ⲧⲛⲛⲟογ mit nachfolgendem Personalsuffix der 3. Pers. sg. fem. annehmen dürfen ([ⲧ]ⲛⲟογⲥ scheint aufgrund der erhaltenen Buchstabenreste am wahrscheinlichsten), das sich—wie auch schon ϩⲁⲣⲟⲥ in dieser Zeile—auf προσφορά bezieht. Der Sinn der Konstruktion ist offenkundig: Im vorangehenden Satz betonte der Verfasser, daß er nicht in der Lage sei, den Geber für die Gabe zu entschädigen. Dann findet offensichtlich ein Subjektwechsel statt: Der, dem der Empfänger des Briefes die Gabe gegeben hat, ist in der Lage, ihn zu heilen. Diese Aussage nach dem vorangehenden Text läßt nur einen Schluß zu: Die fromme Gabe, die dem Kloster übergeben wurde, wird in den größeren Zusammenhang gestellt, nicht das Kloster, sondern Gott ist letztlich der Empfänger dieser Gabe, die Klosterinsassen haben nur stellvertretend für diesen die Gabe angenommen.

2. Brüder, Töchter und Väter

Für diese Vermutung, daß *P.Clackson* 44 nicht von dem Verwalter Schenute verfaßt ist bzw. daß dieser Brief nicht mit seiner Tätigkeit in Verbindung gebracht werden kann, spricht neben den vorwiegend praktischen Fragen des religiösen Lebens, die diesen Brief auszeichnen, auch die in Zeile 24 zu findende Erwähnung der "Brüder," die den Verfasser nach Abschluß des eigentlichen Briefes mit der Bitte bestürmt hatten, um die Sendung von Essig (so dieser vorrätig sei) anzusuchen. Bei diesen Brüdern dürfte es sich nicht um leibliche Brüder—hier würde man statt ⲛⲉⲥⲛⲏⲩ wohl eher eine Formulierung erwarten, in der das persönliche Possessivpronomen das Verhältnis zu den Brüdern ausdrückt: ⲛⲁⲥⲛⲏⲩ ("meine Brüder")—, sondern um die Mitglieder einer religiösen Gemeinschaft handeln.[16] Handschrift, Aufbewahrungsort und Inhalt legen es nahe, daß es sich bei dem Verfasser dieses Briefes um den "niedrigsten Apollo" handeln dürfte, der auch den bereits erwähnten Brief geschrieben hat. Die Erwähnung der Brüder, die offensichtlich mit ihm in enger Gemeinschaft leben, macht es wahrscheinlich, daß der Verfasser des Briefes in einem Kloster lebte. Die offensichtliche Führungsposition, die er innehat—er kann um die Zusendung verschiedener Dinge bitten, ohne gleich erwähnen zu müssen, daß man ihren "gerechten Preis" zahlen wird—scheint darauf hinzuweisen, daß es sich bei dem Verfasser um einen Klostervorstand handeln dürfte, daß also der geistliche Vater der

---

[15] Ein Relativsatz kann grundsätzlich als Subjekt eines Satzes verwendet werden; vgl. hierzu Plisch 1999: 86, dort als Subjekt eines Verbalsatzes; eine der hier vorliegenden Satzkonstruktion vergleichbare Wendung findet sich Mk 14,44: ⲡⲉⲧ︤ⲛⲁ︦ϯ︦ⲡⲓ ⲉⲣⲱϥ ⲛ̄ⲧⲟϥ ⲡⲉ; zur gesamten Struktur vgl. Layton 2000: § 272.

[16] Siehe zu dieser Problematik auch Wilfong. 2002, 70: "Patterned on forms of address found in the Coptic translation of the New Testament, 'father,' 'mother,' 'son,' 'daughter,' and especially 'brother' and 'sister' were used freely in letters to describe nonbiological relationships 'in Christ.' These terms expressed religious relationships on levels similar to the family position—respected seniors were addressed as parents, juniors and inferiors as children, and relative equals as siblings—but do not necessarily reflect actual familial relationships. Without other evidence it is impossible to know for certain whether the writers of letters are using these terms to describe family relationships, religious relationships, or both." Siehe hierzu auch Bagnall 1993, 205: "'Brothers' and 'sisters' turn up in great numbers in letters as well; and many are addressed to them, and still more mention them for greeting. It has long been known that Egyptians used these terms not only for siblings but also for their spouses, and to some extent for more distant relatives or for close friends as well."

Brüder diesen Brief schreibt.[17] Hierfür spricht auch die in seiner Sprache zum Ausdruck kommende hohe Bildung. Die bei der Veröffentlichung von P.Vindob. K. 4730 (= *P.Harrauer* 57) in Erwägung gezogene Möglichkeit, daß der Verfasser ein Bischof sein könnte, scheint durch die aus *P.Clackson* **44** zu gewinnende zusätzliche Information über diese Person weiterhin nicht ausgeschlossen.[18]

Der Absender bezeichnet eine gewisse Kyrakale[19] als seine Tochter (vgl. Z. 18). Zwei mögliche Interpretationen legen sich nahe, es kann sich entweder um ein geistliches Verhältnis zwischen ihm und dieser Frau handeln—in ähnlicher Weise bezeichnen Geistliche ja auch junge Kleriker als ihre Söhne[20] und Leiterinnen von Frauengemeinschaften die ihnen untergebenen Nonnen als Kinder.[21] Dann wäre "ihr Haus," dem ebenfalls Segen vom Briefschreiber zugedacht ist, als Kloster zu interpretieren.[22] Die andere Möglichkeit wäre, daß es sich um die leibliche Tochter handelt. Hierfür würde sprechen, daß der Verfasser des Briefes diese Frau als seine "geliebte Tochter" bezeichnet, daß er also ein besonderes persönliches Naheverhältnis zum Ausdruck bringt. Daß eine Person nach einem ehelichen Leben, dem Kinder entsprungen sind, in ein Kloster eintritt, ist durch dokumentarische Texte belegt.[23] Insofern scheint es naheliegender, ein physisches und nicht nur ein geistliches Verwandtschaftsverhältnis aus der Erwähnung der "geliebten Tochter" abzuleiten, da sonst die Bezeichnung wohl beim Empfänger des Briefes Anstoß erregt hätte. Dies wird dadurch bestätigt, daß besagte Kyrakale selbst Söhne hat.[24] In diesem Zusammenhang muß auch auf die strikte Trennung

---

[17] Zur Verwendung des Titels πατήρ im monastischen Kontext bereits Anfang des 4. Jahrhunderts vgl. Holl 1928: 297: "Wenn schon im Jahr 334 der πατήρ, die προεστῶτες und die οἰκονόμοι bei den Melitianern sich finden und offenbar als etwas bereits Eingebürgertes sich finden, dann muß Pachomius diese Grundzüge seiner Klosterverfassung bereits in den 20er Jahren festgelegt haben."

[18] Vgl. hierzu unten den Abschnitt "5. Priester oder Bischof."

[19] Zu diesem Frauennamen vgl. Fournet und Gascou 2001: 146-147.

[20] Es sei auch nur auf *O.Vind.Copt.* 287 verwiesen, in dem ein Apa Dios vom Briefschreiber als Sohn bezeichnet wird. Der Zusammenhang läßt darauf schließen, daß es sich um eine geistliche, nicht jedoch leibliche Sohnschaft handelt.

[21] Vgl. Jördens 2004: 144. Allerdings bestand für Nonnen im schenutianischen Mönchtum ein Verbot, männliche Personen zu besuchen, auch wenn diese Verwandte waren; vgl. Krawiec 2002: 34: "The initial visits by Shenoute also led to another crisis over whether the women should be allowed to go to the men's community. Some of the women, as it turns out, had 'children' (or 'sons'), 'brethren,' 'menfolk,' and 'relatives' in the men's community. Although Shenoute's predecessors had not allowed the women to see their male relatives, the women were now doing so." Auch dies spricht eindeutig gegen einen monastischen Kontext als Lebenssituation der Kyrakale.

[22] Eine derartige Bedeutung des koptischen Begriffes ⲏⲓ findet sich auch in P.Vindob. K. 4728; vgl. hierzu Förster 2003. In diesem Text bezeichnet eine Nonne ihren Wohnort einfach als "Haus" (ⲏⲓ).

[23] Vgl. *CPR* IV, 152; in diesem Text vertritt der Sohn einer Nonne diese bei einem Rechtsgeschäft, das die Vermietung eines Haus betrifft; es ist offensichtlich, daß diese Frau—wie wohl auch der Verfasser des vorliegenden Briefes—erst nach dem Tod ihres Gatten und der Mündigkeit ihres Kindes in ein Kloster eingetreten ist.

[24] Auch wenn in Berichten aus dem christlichen Ägypten weibliche Asketen in Männerkleidern belegt sind, die eine geistliche Führungsrolle übernehmen und dabei auch junge Mönche ausbilden, so wird ihr Geschlecht normalerweise erst nach ihrem Tod erkannt; dies ist also keine Möglichkeit, die Söhne der Kyrakale als "geistliche Söhne" zu erklären. Insofern wird man annehmen müssen, daß Kyrakale die leibliche Tochter des Briefschreibers ist; vgl. u.a. Synek 1994: 200-201: "So heißt es von einer der zahlreichen Heiligen namens Theodora (genannt Theodoros), sie sei eine verheiratete Frau gewesen, habe aber die Familie verlassen und sei in ein Männerkloster eingetreten, wo sie als Mönch verkleidet ein asketisches Leben führte. Nach dem arabischen Synaxar soll Theodoros/a ihre Rolle so gut gespielt haben, daß sie sogar eine Verehrerin fand, die den vermeintlichen Mönch verführen wollte. Es wird erzählt, wie die von Theodoros/a zurückgewiesene Frau, als sie von einem anderen Mann schwanger wurde, die Heilige als Vater anzeigte. Theodoros/a, so die vita, wurde hierauf mit ihrem vermeintlichen Sohn in die Verbannung geschickt. Nach sieben Jahren durfte sie ins

zwischen Männern und Frauen im Mönchtum hingewiesen werden. Auch diese spricht gegen eine geistliche Mutterschaft der Kyrakale.[25]

3. GESUNDHEIT UND KRANKHEIT

In Zeile 4f wird erwähnt, daß sich offensichtlich der Empfänger der Zeilen nicht der vollen Gesundheit erfreut. Davor findet sich in Zeile 3 ein fragmentarischer Text, der sich mit etwas beschäftigt, das mehr Nutzen bringt. Auch ist in Zeile 2 von der "Ruhe des Körpers"—gewöhnlich ein Euphemismus für den Tod, jedoch an dieser Stelle sicherlich nicht so zu verstehen—die Rede. Die in Zeile 4f zu findende Bemerkung über den Gesundheitszustand ist gleichzeitig ein Segenswunsch: Gott möge dem Empfänger dieser Zeilen Gesundheit des Leibes und Heil der Seele schenken.

Grundsätzlich ist der Zusammenhang zwischen körperlicher Gesundheit und Seelenheil in der koptischen Kultur sehr eng. Krankheit, die ja vor allem erst einmal als physische Einschränkung oder sogar lebensbedrohlicher Einbruch eines Übels in das alltägliche Leben erlebt wird, wird häufig als Strafe Gottes oder als das Wirken böser Mächte auf den Menschen interpretiert.[26] Anhaltspunkte für diese Sicht finden sich bereits in den biblischen Texten.[27] Deswegen wird häufig angenommen, daß zur körperlichen Heilung die Abkehr vom sündigen Lebenswandel notwendig ist. Dies kann natürlich auch zu Krisen des spirituellen Lebens führen, wenn Menschen, deren Lebenswandel eigentlich unproblematisch oder sogar—wie im Falle eines Mönchs—offensichtlich herausragend war, in Krankheit verfallen.[28] Die enge Verbindung zwischen der jenseitigen Welt und der Gesundheit der

---

Kloster zurückkehren, wo sie bis zu ihrem Lebensende unerkannt blieb." Siehe hierzu auch Behlmer 2001; vgl. ferner auch Anson 1974, sowie Papaconstantinou 2004.

[25] Vgl. hierzu Krawiec 2002: 117: "The women were not only forbidden contact with anyone from the secular world, but also, as we have seen, from their male monastic brethren, relatives and nonrelatives alike. The women were banned from attending the funerals of their female companions since male monks would also be present; excepted were the female elder, and senior female monks, who were permitted to follow the male monks at a distance." Man wird überlegen müssen, ob nicht dieses Kontaktverbot den Ausschluß von Nonnen von den Beerdigungen ihrer Mitschwestern begründet. Für eine andere Hypothese vgl. jedoch Krause 1998: 107-108: "Die Anordnung, die Begräbnisse der Nonnen nur von Mönchen durchführen zu lassen, geht wohl, wie schon J. Quasten bemerkt hat, auf die Beobachtung zurück, daß die Frauen mehr als die Männer an den alten Bräuchen hingen."

[26] Siehe hierzu Vorgrimler 1990: 664: "Die biblischen Texte bezeugen die Zuwendung Jesu und der frühchristlichen Gemeinden zu den Kranken und das zugrundeliegende religiös-theologische Verständnis von Krankheit, die, wenigstens zum großen Teil, im Alten wie im Neuen Testament auf die Menschen zerstörende Wirkung der Sünde zurückgeführt wird. Krankheit wie Sünde gelten auch als Folgen des Einwirkens böser, überindividueller Kräfte auf den Menschen." Vgl. ferner Ebner 2001.

[27] Vgl. Scharbert 1990: 682: "In der Umwelt des Alten Testaments gilt Krankheit als ein Schicksal, das dämonische Mächte oder die Gottheit verhängt haben, wobei die Babylonier Krankheit auch als Strafe für Sünde und die Hethiter Pest als Folge von Vergehen eines Königs (Pestgebete des Murschilisch) verstehen. Auch im Alten Testament gilt Krankheit vielfach als nach dem Tat-Ergehenszusammenhang eintretende oder von Gott als Strafe verhängte Folge von Sünden... Krankheit zeigt den Zorn Gottes an... Darum kann sich die Meinung verbreiten, ein Kranker müsse ein Sünder sein, der Gottes Strafe erfahre." Siehe auch Eibach 1997: 427: "K(rankheit) ist Ausdruck dessen, daß das Verhältnis zw(ischen) Schöpfer u(nd) Geschöpf gestört ist (Gen 3,1ff.). Der Gläubige erlebt K(rankheit) nicht nur als Schmerz u(nd) Bedrohung des Lebens, sondern auch als Infragestellung des Gottesverhältnisses (Pss 22; 42; 77; 88 u.a.) u(nd) desh(alb) auch als Strafe Gottes, u(nd) zwar zunächst im gesamtmenschl(ichen) Sinn." Dieser altorientalische Kontext scheint das Denken und den Glauben der Kopten noch im 6. nachchristlichen Jahrhundert beeinflußt zu haben.

[28] Vgl. hierzu Förster 2001: 207-222.

Menschen zeigt sich auch auf der sprachlichen Ebene. Bereits das Gebet des Herrn kann von einem Kopten als Bitte darum verstanden werden, daß Gott es nicht zulassen möge, daß man krank werde, auch wenn eine derartige Übersetzung des bekannten Textes ungewohnt klingt: "Und führe uns nicht in Krankheit, sondern errette uns von dem Bösen."[29] Gleichzeitig kommt jedoch in dieser Übersetzung die enge Beziehung, die für einen Kopten der damaligen Zeit zwischen der körperlichen Beeinträchtigung durch eine Krankheit und dem Wirken böser Mächte gesehen wurde, sehr gut zum Ausdruck. Damit soll natürlich nicht behauptet werden, daß alle Kopten dieses Gebet nur so verstehen konnten, der Bedeutungsgehalt des Wortes πειρασμός macht es jedoch möglich, daß es so verstanden werden konnte. Ein derartiger Zusammenhang von körperlicher Unversehrtheit und dem Seelenheil eines Menschen wird auch in der Wendung, die sich in Zeile 5 des vorliegenden Briefes findet, vorausgesetzt.

Auf diesem Hintergrund wundert es nicht, daß Krankheit oftmals Anlaß für eigenes Gebet war, häufig pflegte man auch, andere um ihr Gebet zu bitten.[30] Die Bitte um ein derartiges fürbittendes Gebet eines Gläubigen kann sich ebenfalls auf biblische Wurzeln stützen. Im Jakobusbrief, der in einem Atemzug Sünde und Krankheit nennt, der also wenn schon keinen Kausalzusammenhang doch ein Näheverhältnis der spirituellen zur körperlichen Gesundheit anzunehmen scheint, heißt es: "Bekennt also einander eure Sünden und betet füreinander, daß ihr gesund werdet. Des Gerechten Gebet vermag viel, wenn es ernstlich ist."[31] Wichtige Adressaten dieser Bitte sind natürlich Geistliche, deren Gebeten, wie aus dem vorangegangenen Zitat deutlich wird, größere Wirksamkeit zugesprochen wird.[32]

Was genau die Krankheit war, an welcher der Empfänger litt, geht aus dem Zusammenhang nicht hervor. Die "Ruhe deines Körpers," von der in Zeile 2 die Rede ist, stellt in diesem Zusammenhang ganz offensichtlich keinen Euphemismus für das Sterben dar.[33] Insofern kann man die Vermutung anstellen, daß der Körper des Betreffenden tatsächlich in irgendeiner Weise "unruhig" war. Dann könnte man vermuten, daß es sich um Krämpfe oder epileptische Anfälle gehandelt haben könnte. Eine andere Möglichkeit wäre, daß die Ruhe im übertragenen Sinn gemeint ist als "Ruhe vor dem Leiden" und deshalb keine Schlußfolgerungen aus diesem Begriff gezogen werden dürfen.

---

[29] Vgl. Mt 6,13a: ⲚⲦⲘ̄ϪⲒⲦⲚ̄ ⲈϨⲞⲨⲚ ⲈⲠⲈⲒⲢⲀⲤⲘⲞⲤ. ⲀⲖⲖⲀ Ⲛ̄ⲄⲚⲀϨⲘⲈⲚ ⲈⲂⲞⲖ ϨⲒⲦⲞⲞⲦϤ̄ Ⲙ̄ⲠⲠⲞⲚⲎⲢⲞⲤ. In den dokumentarischen Texten finden sich zahlreiche Belege für die Bedeutung von πειρασμός als "Krankheit;" vgl. hierzu Förster 2002 s.v. Man kann natürlich die Vermutung äußern, daß auch eine aus dem Zusammenhang gerissene Interpretation der Aufforderung Jesu am Ölberg, daß die Jünger wachsam sein sollen, auf die körperliche Gesundheit bezogen werden kann (Mt 26,41), auch wenn es sich grundsätzlich um das Wachen in der Nacht handelt, auf das sich die Schwäche des Fleisches bezieht: ⲢⲞⲈⲒⲤ ϬⲈ Ⲛ̄ⲦⲈⲦⲚ̄ϢⲖⲎⲖ. ϪⲈⲔⲀⲤ Ⲛ̄ⲚⲈⲦⲚ̄ⲂⲰⲔ ⲈϨⲞⲨⲚ ⲈⲠⲈⲒⲢⲀⲤⲘⲞⲤ. ⲠⲈⲠⲚ̄Ⲁ ⲘⲈⲚ ⲢⲞⲞⲨⲦ Ⲧ̄ⲤⲀⲢⲜ ⲆⲈ ⲞⲨⲀⲤⲐⲈⲚⲎⲤ ⲦⲈ. "Wachet freilich und betet, damit ihr nicht in Versuchung geratet. Der Geist nämlich ist willig, das Fleisch aber schwach."

[30] So findet sich eine Bitte um Gebet in O.Vind.Copt. 363: "Betet [für mich], denn meine [Füße (?)] sind sehr krank." ϢⲖⲎⲖ ⲈⲖ̣[ϪⲰⲒ] | Ⲙ̄ⲘⲞⲚ ⲚⲀⲞⲨ[ⲈⲢⲎⲦⲈ (?)] | ϢⲰⲚⲈ ⲈⲘⲀⲦⲈ. In P.Kellis 19, 68, findet sich die Mitteilung, daß der Verfasser des Briefes für das "Heil" der Empfänger des Briefes betet: ⲈⲒϢⲖⲎⲖ ϨⲀ ⲠⲈⲦⲚ̄ⲞⲨϪⲈⲒ.

[31] Vgl. Jak. 5,16: "ἐξομολογεῖσθε οὖν ἀλλήλοις τὰς ἁμαρτίας καὶ εὔχεσθε ὑπὲρ ἀλλήλων, ὅπως ἰαθῆτε. Πολὺ ἰσχύει δέησις δικαίου ἐνεργουμένη."

[32] Vgl. hierzu auch P.Mon.Epiph. 144, 15; der Empfänger—ein Geistlicher—wird aufgefordert, für den Schreiber des Briefes zu beten: Ⲛ̄ⲄϢⲖⲎⲖ ⲈϪⲚ̄ⲠⲀⲎⲒ Ⲛ̄ⲀⲄⲀⲠⲎ Ⲙ̄ⲘⲞⲚ ⲚⲀϢⲎⲢⲈ ϢⲰⲚⲈ—"Bete für mein Haus in Liebe, denn meine Kinder sind krank." Für ein Stück mit ähnlichem Inhalt siehe auch P.Mon.Epiph. 359, 7ff.

[33] Für diesen Euphemismus vgl. Förster 2002, s.v. σῶμα.

4. ÖL UND ESSIG

In diesem Zusammenhang des Gebetes für Kranke spielt auch geweihtes Öl sehr häufig eine Rolle—im weiteren Verlauf des an dieser Stelle veröffentlichten Briefes wird dann auch ein "Öl des heiligen Altares" erwähnt, das an den Verfasser des Briefes geschickt werden soll. Dies erinnert an den Jakobusbrief, wo es heißt: "Ist jemand unter euch krank, der rufe zu sich die Ältesten der Gemeinde,[34] daß sie über ihm beten und ihn salben mit Öl[35] in dem Namen des Herrn. Und das Gebet des Glaubens wird dem Kranken helfen, und der Herr wird ihn aufrichten; und wenn er Sünden getan hat, wird ihm vergeben werden."[36] Auch das Matthäusevangelium berichtet von der Heilung von Kranken, die von einer Salbung mit Öl begleitet ist: "Und sie zogen aus und predigten, man solle Buße tun, und trieben viele böse Geister aus und salbten viele Kranke mit Öl und machten sie gesund."[37] Aus diesen beiden Stellen entwickelte sich das Sakrament der Krankensalbung. Als ältestes koptisches Zeugnis eines Gebetes über Öl, das für eine Salbung von Kranken verwendet wurde, gilt ein Zusatz zur Didache (10,8), der nur auf Koptisch erhalten ist: "Für das Salböl aber sagt folgendermaßen Dank: Wir danken dir, Vater, für den Wohlgeruch des Salböls, welches du uns kundgemacht hast durch Jesus, deinen Knecht.[38] Dir (sei/ist) die Herrlichkeit bis in Ewigkeit. Amen."[39]

---

[34] Vgl. hierzu auch Vorgrimler 1990: 665: "Die Ältesten sind entsprechend dem judenchristlichen Kolorit des Briefes die Gemeindevorsteher, denen die Fürbitte für den Kranken in der Gemeinde obliegt; davon verspricht der Glaube Rettung, Aufrichtung und, wenn nötig, Sündenvergebung, und zwar ohne Einschränkung. Von der Symbolhandlung der Ölsalbung wird das ganzheitlich gesehene Heil des Menschen erhofft. Die Erhörung der Fürbitte steht bei Gott allein; im Text gibt es keine Anhaltspunkte, das Ganze als Wunderheilung zu verstehen." Siehe hierzu auch Roetzer 1930: 195-196: "Daß übrigens geweihtes Öl schon früher in der afrikanischen Kirche zu Heilzwecken verwendet wurde, zeigt Tertullians Notiz, der Christ Prokulus habe Severus, den Vater des Kaisers Antoninus, mit Öl wiederhergestellt. Häretischen Frauen wirft er vor, daß sie sich in gleicher Weise mit Krankenheilungen abgeben, wie sie andere kirchliche Übungen wie Lehren, Taufen, Beschwörungen sich anmaßten."

[35] Vgl. Hofmeister 1948: 25: "Mit gutem Grund dürfen wir annehmen, daß die Christen hierzu einerseits reines Öl nahmen, andererseits aber auch ein Öl, das im Orient verhältnismäßig leicht zu bekommen und nicht zu teuer war, das ist das Olivenöl... Von irgendeiner Beimischung von Spezereien hören wir zunächst bei den Vätern nichts." Zum Ölpreis vgl. Morelli 1996: 139-152. Siehe hierzu auch Till 1951: 80: "Unter ⲛⲉϩ ohne Beiwort hat man wohl gewöhnliches Olivenöl zu verstehen (ἔλαιον κοινόν BD 56) oder Öl im allgemeinen, wobei es auf die Art und Beschaffenheit nicht weiter ankommt." Zum Öl allgemein siehe auch Sandy 1989; siehe auch Mayerson 2002. Zu den modernen Ritualen bei der Ölweihe und der damit verbundenen Krankensalbung vgl. Suttner 1975; zur Verwendung in der koptischen Kirche vgl. Suttner 1975: 371: "Als Empfänger gilt, wer von einer Krankheit betroffen ist. Man verwahrt sich dagegen, dass nur Todgeweihte das Sakrament empfangen dürfen, und betont, dass jede Krankheit berechtigt, die heilige Ölung zu erbitten. Auch Gesunden könne sie gespendet werden, hatte C. Kopp von koptischen Christen erfahren." Vgl. ferner Staubli 2003.

[36] Vgl. Jak 5, 14f.: ἀσθενεῖ τις ἐν ὑμῖν; προσκαλεσάσθω τοὺς πρεσβυτέρους τῆς ἐκκλησίας, καὶ προσευξάσθωσαν ἐπ' αὐτὸν ἀλείψαντες ἐλαίῳ ἐν τῷ ὀνόματι [τοῦ] κυρίου· καὶ ἡ εὐχὴ τῆς πίστεως σώσει τὸν κάμνοντα, καὶ ἐγερεῖ αὐτὸν ὁ κύριος· κἂν ἁμαρτίας ᾖ πεποιηκώς, ἀφεθήσεται αὐτῷ.

[37] Vgl. Mt 6,12-13: Καὶ ἐξελθόντες ἐκήρυξαν ἵνα μετανοῶσιν, καὶ δαιμόνια πολλὰ ἐξέβαλλον, καὶ ἤλειφον ἐλαίῳ πολλοὺς ἀρρώστους καὶ ἐθεράπευον.

[38] Hier sollte man vielleicht doch eher mit " Sohn" übersetzen.

[39] Vgl. für die Übersetzung Funk, Bihlmeyer und Witthaker 1992: 15; für den koptischen Text vgl. Schmidt 1925: 84-86 (Kol. Iʳ15-20): ⲉⲧⲃⲉ ⲡⲥⲉⲭⲓ ⲛ̄ⲁⲉ ⲛⲙⲡⲉ[ⲥⲧ]ⲓⲛⲟⲩϥⲓ ϣⲉⲡϩⲙⲁⲧ ⲛ̄ⲧⲉⲓ̈ϩⲏ ⲉⲧⲉⲧⲛ̄ⲭⲱ ⲙⲁⲥ ϫⲉ [ⲧⲉ]ⲛϣⲉⲡϩⲙⲁⲧ ⲛ̄ⲧⲁⲁⲧⲕ ⲡⲓⲱⲧ ⲉⲧⲃⲉ ⲡⲉⲥϯⲛ[ⲟⲩ]ϥⲓ ⲉⲧⲉϩⲁⲕ ⲧⲁⲙⲁⲛ ⲉⲗⲁϥ ⲉⲃⲁⲗ [ϩⲓ]ⲧⲉⲛ ⲓ̅ⲏ̅ⲥ̅ ⲡⲉⲕϣ[ⲏ]ⲣⲓ ⲡⲱⲕ ⲡ[ⲉ ⲡ]ⲁⲟⲩ ⲛ̄ϣⲁⲉⲛⲉϩ ⲁⲙⲉⲛ.

Die Verwendung von Öl in zeichenhaften kirchlichen Ritualen ist naheliegend. "Öl war in der Antike ein wesentliches Element der mediterranen Wirtschaft und kultivierten Lebensführung. Es fand Verwendung beim Kochen, bei der heilenden Salbung, als Heilmittel, im Badewesen, zu kosmetischen Zwecken und als Brennstoff für Lampen. Es gab Palm-, Kokos- und Muskatöl, doch am höchsten geschätzt und am schwierigsten zu gewinnen war das Olivenöl. Die goldfarbene, aus schwarzen Oliven gepreßte Flüssigkeit galt als Sinnbild für Güte, Gesundheit und Schönheit."[40] Die Tatsache, daß Öl auch grundsätzlich als Heilmittel bei Wunden eine Bedeutung hatte, ist sicher mit ausschlaggebend dafür, daß es auch bei Riten verwendet wird, in deren Rahmen um die Heilung von Krankheiten gebetet wird.[41] Und so ist es nicht verwunderlich, daß zur Heilung (oder wenigstens Linderung) der Leiden Gebetsöl angefordert und um das Gebet der "heiligen Brüder" gebeten wird, wie dies ein Mönch, ein Mensch des religiösen Lebens, in einem Brief tut, der auf einem Wiener Ostrakon erhalten ist: "Daß du ein wenig Gebetsöl schickst vom Altar der Heiligen (pl.) und die hl. Brüder bittest, daß sie sich für mich niederwerfen (und) Gott bitten für meine Sündhaftigkeit, denn mir geht es sehr schlecht. Seit dem 29. Hathor bin ich krank."[42] Das Martyrium des Schenufe berichtet davon, daß dieser mit seinen Brüdern über Öl betet, das dann die bereits elf Tage dauernden Wehen der einzigen Tochter des Gefängniswächters durch die Geburt eines gesunden Sohnes zu beenden vermag, nachdem vorher eine Vielzahl von Ärzten und Exorzisten nicht zu helfen vermocht hatten. Sehr schön zeigt sich in diesem Bericht der Ritus, der mit der Segnung des „Gebetsöls" verbunden war: „Es sprach der Heilige zu ihm: Bring mir ein wenig Öl, damit ich darüber bete, damit sich die Herrlichkeit Jesu Christi offenbare. Und sofort brachte man ihm etwas Öl. Der Heilige nahm es, bezeichnete es mit dem Kreuzzeichen, betete darüber, ging hinein zu seinen Brüdern, damit auch diese es (d.i. das Öl) mit dem Kreuzzeichen bezeichneten. Er[43] nahm es in dieser Stunde, er salbte seine Tochter damit. Und in dieser Stunde gebar sie einen Sohn (wörtl. männliches Kind) und nannte ihn Schenufe nach dem Namen des Heiligen."[44] Im weiteren Verlauf der Erzählung wird im Rahmen einer weiteren Heilung, bei der ebenfalls Öl Verwendung findet, auch das Gebet des Heiligen wiedergegeben, das dieser bei einer Salbung mit Öl verwendete: "Möge mein Herr Jesus Christus, von dem die Heilung und das Leben ausgeht, der den

---

[40] Dudlei 1998: 714; zu Öl, seiner Herstellung und Verwendung vgl. auch Brun 2003, siehe ferner Kaszynski 2001.

[41] Vgl. hierzu z. B. die Erzählung vom barmherzigen Samariter; Lk 10,34: καὶ προσελθὼν κατέδησεν τὰ τραύματα αὐτοῦ ἐπιχέων ἔλαιον καὶ οἶνον, ἐπιβιβάσας δὲ αὐτὸν ἐπὶ τὸ ἴδιον κτῆνος ἤγαγεν αὐτὸν εἰς πανδοχεῖον καὶ ἐπεμελήθη αὐτοῦ. "Und er ging zu ihm, goß Öl und Wein auf seine Wunden und verband sie ihm, hob ihn auf sein Tier und brachte ihn in eine Herberge und pflegte ihn." Die Verwendung von Wundöl ist alt- und neutestamentlich belegt; vgl. hierzu auch Hamp 1962. Von dieser Erzählung dürfte sich die im Orient teilweise bezeugte Sitte ableiten, dem Krankenöl Wein beizumischen; vgl. Hofmeister 1948: 32 u. 34. Zur medizinischen Verwendung von Öl siehe auch Till 1951: 80-82, der eine Vielzahl von vor allem äußerlichen Anwendungsbereichen für Öl in der koptischen Medizin anführt. Siehe hierzu auch Pease 1937.

[42] Vgl. *O.Vind.Copt.* 261, 4ff.: ⲉⲧⲣⲉⲕⲧⲛⲛⲟⲟⲩ ⲟⲩⲕⲟⲩⲓ̈ ⲛⲛⲉϩ ⲛϣⲗⲏⲗ ϩⲙ ⲡⲉⲑⲩⲥⲓⲁⲥⲧⲏⲣ/ | ⲛⲛⲉⲧⲟⲩⲁⲃ ⲁⲩⲱ ⲛⲅⲧⲃϩ ⲛⲉⲥⲛⲏⲩ ⲉⲧⲟⲩⲁⲁⲃ ⲉⲧⲣⲉⲩⲡⲁϩⲧⲟⲩ ϩⲁⲣⲟⲓ̈ ⲛⲥⲉⲧⲃϩ ⲡ|ⲛⲟⲩⲧⲉ ⲉϫⲛ ⲧⲁⲙⲛⲧⲣⲉϥⲣⲛⲟⲃⲉ ⲙⲙⲟⲛ ϯϩⲟⲣϣ ⲉⲙⲁⲧⲉ ϯϣⲱⲛⲉ ⲇⲉ | ϫⲛⲛ ⲥⲟⲩ ϫⲟⲩⲧⲯⲓⲥ ⲛⲁⲑⲱⲣ.

[43] Wie auch die Herausgeber bemerken, ist an dieser Stelle ein schlecht eingeführter Subjektwechsel zu finden, offensichtlich ist es nicht der Heilige, sondern der Vater, der seine eigene Tochter salbt.

[44] Schenufe, Martyrium 115,v,ii,26-116,r,i,15 (Reymond/Barns, Martyrdoms, 98): ⲡⲉϫⲉⲡϩⲁⲅⲓⲟⲥ ⲛⲁϥ ϫⲉ ⲁⲛⲉⲓⲛⲉ ⲛⲁⲓ̈ ⲛⲟⲩⲕⲟⲩⲓ̈ ⲛⲛⲉϩ, ⲧⲁϣⲗⲏⲗ ⲉϫⲱϥ, ⲁϥⲙⲟⲟϣⲉ ⲉϩⲟⲩⲛ ⲉⲛⲉϥⲥⲛⲏⲩ, ⲁϥⲧⲣⲟⲩⲥⲫⲣⲁⲅⲓⲍⲉ ⲙⲙⲟϥ ϩⲱⲱϥ· ⲁϥϫⲓⲧϥ ⲛⲧⲉⲩⲛⲟⲩ, ⲁϥⲧⲱϩⲥ ⲛⲧⲉϥϣⲉⲉⲣⲉ ⲛϩⲏⲧϥ· ⲁⲩⲱ ⲛⲧⲉⲩⲛⲟⲩ ⲁⲥⲙⲓⲥⲉ ⲛⲟⲩϣⲏⲣⲉ ⲛϩⲟⲟⲩⲧ, ⲁⲥⲙⲟⲩⲧⲉ ⲉⲣⲟϥ ϫⲉ ϣⲛⲟⲩϥⲉ ⲕⲁⲧⲁⲡⲣⲁⲛ ⲙⲡϩⲁⲅⲓⲟⲥ.

Blinden die Augen öffnet, der die Stummen reden macht, der die Tauben hören läßt, die Aussätzigen rein macht, der die Lahmen laufen läßt, der die Verkrümmten gerade richtet, mögest du heilen deinen Diener Julios, dieser, der trägt Sorge für deine Märtyrer. Denn du bist es, aus dem das Heil und das Leben hervorgehen. Und in diesem Augenblick salbte der Heilige den Körper des Julios; und es ließen nach die Schmerzen des Leidens, das in seinem Körper war."[45] Das aus diesen Berichten abzuleitende Ritual setzt sich offensichtlich aus einem verbalen Teil und einer dazugehörigen Gestik zusammen, über dem Öl wird gebetet und das Zeichen des Kreuzes[46] gemacht.[47]

Das Gebet des Schenufe richtet sich an Gott, der das Heil zu schenken vermag; das Öl, das bei der Salbung verwendet wird, findet in diesem Gebet keine Erwähnung. Dies muß betont werden, zeigt sich doch hierin eine klare Distanz zu magischen Praktiken. Wenn man die beiden Heilungen vergleicht, so fällt auf, daß der Wachmann im Auftrag des Schenufe seine Tochter salbt, während Schenufe selbst den kranken Julios salbt.[48] In diesem Zusammenhang spielt jedoch wohl nicht so sehr die magische Kraft des Öls eine Rolle, das bereits durch die reine Anwendung seine heilende Kraft und übernatürliche Wirksamkeit entfaltet. Vielmehr scheint es sich um das Problem zu handeln, daß ein Heiliger nicht ohne Probleme eine fremde Frau berühren kann—man denke nur an die sehr strikten Hinweise zum Umgang von Mönchen mit Frauen, die sich in verschiedenen Klosterregeln finden. Diese Trennung war so strikt, daß selbst nach dem Tod die örtliche Trennung von Mönchen und Frauen auf den Friedhöfen vorgesehen war.[49] Dies muß natürlich dazu führen, daß Schenufe die Tochter des Wächters nicht selbst salben kann. Gleichzeitig ist die Salbung durch Laien gut belegt.[50] In

---

[45] Schenufe, Martyrium 117,r,ii,3-29 (Reymond/Barns, Martyrdoms, 100): ⲉⲣⲉⲡⲁϫⲟⲉⲓⲥ ⲓ̅ⲥ̅ ⲡⲉⲭ̅ⲥ̅ ⲡⲉⲧⲉⲣⲉⲡⲧⲁⲗϭⲟ ⲙ̅ⲡⲱⲛ̅ϩ̅ ϣⲟⲟⲡ ⲉⲃⲟⲗ ϩⲓⲧⲟⲟⲧϥ̅, ⲡⲉⲛⲧⲁϥⲟⲩⲱⲛ ⲛ̅ⲛ̅ⲃⲁⲗ ⲛ̅ⲛ̅ⲃⲗ̅ⲗⲉ, ⲁϥⲧⲣⲉⲛⲉⲉⲙⲡⲟ ϣⲁϫⲉ, ⲁϥⲧⲣⲉⲛ̅ⲕⲟⲩⲣ ⲥⲱⲧⲙ̅, ⲛⲉⲧⲕⲏⲕ ⲉⲡⲥⲱⲃϩ̅ ⲁϥⲧⲃ̅ⲃⲟⲟⲩ, ⲁϥⲧⲣⲉⲛ̅ϭⲁⲗⲉ ⲙⲟⲟϣⲉ, ⲛⲉⲧϭⲏϭ ⲁϥⲥⲟⲟⲩⲧ̅ⲛ̅, ⲉⲕⲉⲣⲡⲁϩⲣⲉ ϩⲱⲱϥ ⲉⲡⲉⲕϩⲙ̅ϩⲁⲗ ⲓ̈ⲟⲩⲗⲓⲟⲥ, ⲡⲁⲓ̈ ⲉⲧϥⲓ ⲙ̅ⲡⲣⲟⲟⲩϣ ⲛ̅ⲛⲉⲕϩⲙ̅ϩⲁⲗ ⲙ̅ⲙⲁⲣⲧⲩⲣⲟⲥ· ϫⲉ ⲛ̅ⲧⲟⲕ ⲡⲉⲧⲉⲣⲉⲡⲧⲁⲗϭⲟ ⲙⲛ̅ⲡⲱⲛϩ̅ ϣⲟⲟⲡ ⲉⲃⲟⲗ ϩⲓⲧⲟⲟⲧⲕ̅. ⲛ̅ⲧⲉⲩⲛⲟⲩ ⲁⲡϩⲁⲅⲓⲟⲥ ⲧⲱϩⲥ̅ ⲙ̅ⲡⲥⲱⲙⲁ ⲛ̅ⲉⲓⲟⲩⲗⲓⲟⲥ, ⲁⲩⲃⲱϣ ⲛ̅ϭⲓ ⲙ̅ⲙⲟⲕϩⲥ̅ ⲙ̅ⲡⲧⲓⲧⲕⲁⲥ ⲉⲧϩⲙ̅ⲡⲉϥⲥⲱⲙⲁ.

[46] Zum Kreuzzeichen vgl. auch Schöllgen, Geerlings 1991: 204f: "Das Kreuzzeichen hat sowohl bekenntnishaften als auch apotropäischen Charakter. In der TA spricht Hippolyt an mehreren Stellen vom Bekreuzigen bzw. vom Kreuzzeichen... In einem eigenen Kapitel (TA 42) beschäftigt sich Hippolyt ausdrücklich mit dem Kreuzzeichen. Einleitend betont die TA die Schutzfunktion des Kreuzzeichens in der Versuchung. Es soll dargeboten werden «wie ein Schild». Die Heraushebung, mit Frömmigkeit solle die Stirn bezeichnet werden, ist ein Hinweis darauf, daß äußerer Ausdruck und innere Haltung zusammengehören."

[47] Auch Augustinus berichtet von einem derartigen Ritual—verbunden aus Gebet und Kreuzzeichen—bei der Weihe des Salböls für die Täuflinge. Falls das Kreuzzeichen dabei unterlassen wird, gilt die Weihe des Salböls nach Augustinus als nichtig; vgl. hierzu Roetzer 1930: 166-167. Für ein Gebet über dem Öl vgl. auch den Exorzismus über das Öl aus der Anàfora de Barcelona, 4, 6-25 u. 5, 1-10 (vgl Roca-Puig 1999: 104-111). Für die erwartete Wirkung bei Erkrankungen vgl. 4, 23-24: καὶ θεραπεύῃς ἀπὸ πάσης νόσου καὶ πάσης μαλακίας.

[48] Hofmeister 1948: 31: "Über die Bestandteile des Krankenöls in alter Zeit sind wir nicht ganz im klaren."

[49] Vgl. Schmitz 1930: 4 Anm. 1: "Dieser Wunsch nach Trennung der Geschlechter selbst im Tode ist geradezu zu einem literarischen Motiv geworden. So erzählt Johannes Moschus im Pratum Spirituale von dem Wunder, das der tote Abt Thomas zustande brachte, der nachts solange eine über ihm beigesetzte Frau aus dem Grabe wieder herausdrückte, bis man begriffen hatte, daß er nicht mit dieser Frau zusammen bestattet sein wollte."

[50] Vgl. Vorgrimler 1990: 665: "Ungebrochen ist der Brauch, daß Christen (d.h. auch Laien) sich selber und ihre Angehörigen salben können, unter Gebet um Gesundheit des Leibes und Nachlaß der Sünden; unbestritten ist, daß die Salbung keineswegs Todkranken vorbehalten war."

der koptischen Kirche scheint dieses Öl teilweise auch vorbeugend gegen Krankheit angewendet worden zu sein.[51]

Das in Zeile 13 erwähnte "Öl des Altars" (ⲡⲛⲉϩ ⲙⲡⲑⲩⲥⲓⲁⲥⲧⲏⲣⲓⲟⲛ ⲉⲧⲟⲩⲁⲁⲃ), dessen bereits erfolgte Sendung (es war auch "etwas Wasser" zusätzlich mitgeschickt worden—dabei könnte es sich um geweihtes Taufwasser[52] oder in anderer Weise mit Heiligem in Berührung gekommenes Wasser[53] gehandelt haben) der Verfasser des Briefes bestätigt, wurde offensichtlich durch eine kirchliche Feier gesegnet bzw. geweiht. Dies dürfte die Bezeichnung besser erklären als die Annahme, daß das Öl bereits durch die Berührung mit dem Altar geheiligt wurde.[54] Eine weitere Bezeichnung dieses Öls, das bereits von Cyprian bezeugt wird,[55] war "Öl der Danksagung."[56] Es ist zu vermuten, daß dieses Öl mit dem Gebetsöl,[57] das ja bereits erwähnt wurde, identisch ist, wird es doch nach der *vita* Pachoms auch

---

[51] Vorgrimler 1978: 226: "Nach einer nicht offiziell gebilligten Auffassung können in manchen Kirchen (so bei den Kopten) sogar Gesunde in der Fastenzeit die Salbung als Vorbeugung gegen Krankheit empfangen."

[52] Möglicherweise hat es sich um Wasser gehandelt, das bei der feierlichen Segnung des Wassers an Epiphanias dem entsprechenden Taufbecken oder Fluß entnommen worden war; vgl. hierzu Kranemann 2001.

[53] Für die Bedeutung und Heilwirkung von Wasser im Zusammenhang mit ägyptischen Märtyrern vgl. allgemein Baumeister 1972: 65-67, 118, 143; siehe hierzu auch Frankfurter 1994: 31.

[54] Vgl. Dölger 1974: 189 (unter Bezugnahme auf die *Canones* des Basilius): "Man erachtete es demnach für wichtig, daß das Öl mit dem Altare in Berührung kam und so seine Weihe erhielt. Das mag beachtet werden für die starke Hervorhebung Cyprians, daß «derjenige das Öl nicht heiligen könne, der keinen Altar habe». Jedenfalls hat man schon damals die Berührung des Öles (mindestens durch das Stellen des Ölgefäßes auf den Altar) für wichtig erachtet zur Segnung und Weihung des Öles." Falls es sich um eine reine Heiligung aufgrund einer Berührung des Altars handeln sollte, wäre natürlich zusätzlich zu fragen, warum dann die Bitte um Zusendung des Öls überhaupt nötig war, gab es doch sehr wahrscheinlich auch in direkter Nähe des Empfängers des vorliegenden Briefes einen Altar, auf den man das betreffende Öl kurz hätte stellen können. Auch zeigt das bereits zitierte Wiener Ostrakon (vgl. oben die Anm. 42), daß Gebetsöl beim Altar aufgehoben werden konnte. Von hier scheint es dann nur ein sehr kleiner—und im gewissen Sinn einleuchtender Schritt—, daß diesem Öl auch der Aufbewahrungsort seinen Namen gegeben haben könnte.

[55] Vgl. Cyprian Ep. 70,2 (Hartel, CSEL III,2,768 Z. 13-20).

[56] Dölger 1974: 188: "Den inneren Zusammenhang von Danksagung und dem Namen des Öls = ἔλαιον εὐχαριστίας bietet dagegen der Kopte, der damit sicher das Richtige getroffen hat." Zu diesem Öl vgl. auch Mitchell 1966: 2, 3, 6, 58 u. 92.

[57] Dies findet sich auch *O.Crum* Ad 48: ⲙⲁⲣⲉⲧⲉⲕⲙⲛⲧϣⲏⲣⲉ ⲃⲱⲕ ⲉϩⲟⲩⲛ ⲉⲡⲑⲩⲥⲓⲁⲥⲧⲏⲣⲓⲟⲛ ⲛⲅⲕⲁⲁϥ ⲉⲡϣⲟⲩⲱⲧ ⲙⲡⲛⲉϩ ⲛϣⲗⲏⲗ ⲛⲅϫⲟⲟⲩ ⲡⲕϫⲟⲩⲣ ⲙⲡⲁⲣⲭⲏⲇⲓⲁⲕ/ ⲛⲁϥ. ⲡⲛⲟⲩⲧⲉ ⲥⲟⲟⲩⲛ ϫⲉ ⲉⲕⲧⲙϫⲓ ⲡⲁⲅⲅⲏⲛ ⲁⲩⲱ ϫⲉ ⲉⲛⲉⲕⲧⲁⲁⲩⲉ ⲛⲁⲩ ⲕϩⲓⲃⲟⲗ ⲙⲡϣⲁ. Crum 1902: 35, bemerkt zu diesem Text: "Letter from an ecclesiastical superior. Recipient is asked to go into the sanctuary (θυσιαστήριον) and, from the cupboard of the 'oil of prayer,' to send the archdeacons key to him. 'God knows, if thou take not the jar (ἀγγεῖον) and do not …, thou art excluded from the feast'." Die Übersetzung scheint schwierig. Es muß die Frage gestellt werden, ob der Schlüssel tatsächlich vom "Brett des Gebetsöles" genommen wird. Die beiden Konjunktive setzen den kausativen Imperativ des ersten Satzes fort. Insofern scheint zu übersetzen: "Möge deine Sohnschaft zum Altar hineingehen und es legen auf das «Brett des Gebetsöls», und sende den Schlüssel des Erzdiakons ihm. Gott weiß, wenn du das Gefäß nicht nimmst und es ihnen nicht bringst, dann bist du vom Fest ausgeschlossen." Ganz offensichtlich soll etwas auf dieses Brett gelegt werden, auf dem sich üblicherweise das Gebetsöl in dieser Kirche befindet. Dieses Etwas kann wohl am ehesten als ein solches Gebetsöl angesehen werden, das in dem Gefäß ist, das der angeredete Kleriker unter keinen Umständen nicht bringen darf. Für diese Interpretation muß eigentlich nur das ⲧⲁⲟⲩⲟ in einer etwas breiteren Interpretation der Wortbedeutung als „bringen" angesehen werden, die parallele Konstruktion der beiden Konjunktive scheint gegen die Ansicht Crum's zu sprechen, daß sich der Schlüssel auf diesem Brett befindet; hierfür würde man eine Formulierung erwarten wie: ⲛⲅϫⲓ ⲡⲕⲥⲟⲩⲣ ⲉⲧ ϩⲙⲡϣⲟⲩⲱⲧ ⲙⲡⲛⲉϩ ⲛϣⲗⲏⲗ ⲛⲅϫⲟⲟⲩϥ ⲙⲡⲁⲣⲭⲏⲇⲓⲁⲕ/. Auch bleibt bei Crum's Interpretation unklar, was mit dem Gefäß gemeint ist, das doch dem Objekt zu entsprechen scheint, das auf das Brett gestellt werden soll, auf dem üblicherweise das Gebetsöl steht.

für Heilungen verwendet.⁵⁸ Gleichzeitig ist zu beachten, daß nur Bischöfe zur Weihe des Myron berechtigt waren,⁵⁹ daß aber das Verhältnis dieses Öls, das für sakramentale Salbungen verwendet wurde, zum Gebetsöl nicht immer völlig geklärt ist.⁶⁰

In diesem Zusammenhang muß man die Frage stellen, ob das Öl hier nicht aufgrund seines Aufbewahrungsortes—dies wäre dann in direkter Nähe des Altars—als "Öl des Altars" bezeichnet wurde—wobei nicht bestritten werden soll, daß selbstverständlich genügend Belege für durch Berührung mit dem Altar geheiligte Öle existieren.⁶¹ Insofern könnte man die Anspielung auf mögliche Berührungsreliquien in den folgenden Zeilen auch dahingehend interpretieren, daß das Öl durch die Berührung des Altars eines besonderen Ortes geheiligt worden war. Belegt ist die Warnung, dieses offenbar eher schwierig zu besorgende Öl nicht von Wahrsagern und Zauberern zu erbitten.⁶² Aber nicht nur das gesegnete oder geweihte Öl, sondern auch in besonderer Weise die Eucharistie war nach damaliger Auffassung in der Lage, neben dem Seelenheil auch physische Gesundung zu vermitteln.⁶³ Beides konnte am Bett aufbewahrt werden, um dem dort Ruhenden Segen und Schutz zu

---

⁵⁸ Vgl. hierfür den Bericht aus der Vita Pachoms (Amélineau 1888: 528): ⲁⲩⲱ ⲛⲧⲉⲓϩⲉ ⲁϥϣⲗⲏⲗ ⲉϫⲛ ⲟⲩⲛⲉϩ ⲁϥϫⲟⲟⲩϥ ⲛⲁⲥ ⲉⲃⲟⲗ ⲁⲩⲱ ⲛⲧⲉⲣⲉⲥⲧⲁϩⲥ ⲙⲙⲟϥ ϩⲛ ⲟⲩⲡⲓⲥⲧⲓⲥ ⲁⲥⲗⲟ ϩⲙⲡⲣⲁⲛ ⲙⲡϫⲟⲉⲓⲥ. "Und in dieser Art sprach er ein Gebet über ein Öl und sandte es ihr. Und nachdem sie es gläubig (wört.: in einem Glauben) eingerieben hatte, wurde sie gesund im Namen des Herrn." An dieser Heilung ist einerseits auffällig, daß Pachom ein Öl nimmt, das gerade zur Hand ist. Im Gegensatz hierzu sind die liturgischen Öle mit Spezereien versetzt. Zum anderen muß der Zusammenhang zwischen dem Glauben der geheilten Frau und der Wirkung des Öles gesehen werden, die Differenz zu einer magisch verstandenen Wirkung ist deutlich.

⁵⁹ In diesem Zusammenhang sollte allerdings berücksichtigt werden, daß bereits für das dritte Jahrhundert eine Ölweihe durch einen Bischof in der *Traditio apostolica* 5 des Hippolyt bezeugt ist; die Gebete bringen zum Ausdruck, daß das Öl die Kraft empfängt, Stärkung und Gesundheit zu vermitteln; vgl. hierzu u. a. Greshake 1997; vgl. hierzu auch Vorgrimler 1978: 218; für die *Traditio Apostolica* siehe Schöllgen, Geerlings 1991: 228-229.

⁶⁰ Vgl. hierzu Heiler 1937: 248: "Das *Myron* besteht aus feinstem Olivenöl, das, gleich dem Salböl des Alten Bundes (2. Mos. 30,20ff.) mit einer hohen Zahl von aromatischen Stoffen vermischt wird (die orthodoxen Ritualien schwanken zwischen 13 und 57; die russische Kirche verwendet jetzt 30). Die vielen Substanzen symbolisieren 'Die Mannigfaltigkeit der Gaben des heiligen Geistes,' zugleich auch den Wohlgeruch seiner Heiligkeit. Nach den Kanones der Konzile von Karthago, welche auch in der orthodoxen Kirche gültig sind, hat jeder Bischof die Vollmacht zur Myron-Weihe." Hofmeister 1948: 27, zählt als mögliche Bestandteile des Chrisam im 18. und 19. Jh. in Konstantinopel auf: "Als Ingredienzien sind zu nennen: Rosenwasser, Mastixharz, Amomum, Barbados-Aloe, langer Pfeffer, Muskatnüsse, Zimtrinde, Kassin, Storaxbalsam, Myrrhenöl, Kalmus, Narde usw.; als Essenzen Ceylon-Zimtkassienöl, Nelkenöl, Mekkabalsam, Zitronenöl usw." Für den Koptischen Ritus erwähnt er (27) u. a. "Myrrhe, Aloeholz, Kassiazimt, Gewürznelke. Im Gegensatz zum griechischen Ritus werden aber hier Balsam und die andern Substanzen nicht sofort dem Öl beigemischt, sondern erst nachdem das Öl zum vierten Male gekocht wurde." Leider ist aufgrund der Quellen nicht ganz ersichtlich, welche Bedingungen für die Weihe des Gebetsöls galten und ob diese möglicherweise ähnlich strikt waren wie bei Myron bzw. Chrisam.

⁶¹ Hofmeister 1948: 23: "Zum Salben verwendete man im Osten aber auch das Öl aus den Lampen, die in der Kirche brannten, und Öl, das man unter den Altar oder an die Gräber der Märtyrer stellte oder das mit deren Reliquien in Berührung kam. Ersteres bezeugen Johannes Chrysostomus sowie der Pilger Antonin von Piacenza, der im 6. Jahrhundert nach Jerusalem kam und hier bei der Aussetzung der Kreuzreliquie mit Öl gefüllte Gefäße vorfand, die zum Zweck der Segnung mit dem heiligen Holze in Berührung gebracht wurden, wobei ihr Inhalt wunderbar aufwallte. Letzteres bezeugt Jakob von Edessa."

⁶² Vgl. Vorgrimler 1990: 665.

⁶³ Vgl. Dölger 1975a: 240: "Wir haben also hier die Ausspendung der Eucharistie in die Hand—und damit die Möglichkeit, sie irgendwie mit nach Hause zu nehmen. Die Eucharistie konnte dann zu Hause zum ordnungsgemäßen Genuß gebraucht werden, aber die unkontrollierte Freiheit, sie auch anderweitig zu verwenden, war damit ebenfalls möglich geworden. Wir wissen ja auch, daß man die eucharistische Speise als Vorbeugemittel gegen etwaige Vergiftungen

spenden.⁶⁴ Teilweise gab es auch Pilgerampullen, die an den Pilgerstätten mit derartigem Öl gefüllt wurden.⁶⁵ In Ägypten besonders beliebt waren dabei Ampullen des heiligen Menas.⁶⁶ Die Form dieser Flaschen variierte nur sehr wenig.⁶⁷

Es war bereits erwähnt worden, daß oftmals dieses Öl mit verschiedenen wohlriechenden Essenzen und Zutaten versetzt wurde.⁶⁸ Neben dem sicherlich vorhandenen medizinischen Aspekt scheint auch eine Rolle zu spielen, daß der Einbruch des Jenseits in das Diesseits oftmals nicht nur von Licht und Geräusch, sondern auch von olfaktorischen Reizen begleitet wurde. So wird oftmals berichtet, daß von den Leichen verstorbener Heiliger ein besonderer Duft ausgeht.⁶⁹ Während die himmlischen Boten von Licht und Wohlgeruch begleitet sind, ist der Gedanke an die Unterwelt verbunden mit Dunkelheit und Gestank.⁷⁰ Insofern ist nicht verwunderlich, daß der Duft von Salbölen, die im religiösen Bereich Verwendung finden, ebenfalls religiös als Einbruch der jenseitigen Welt gedeutet werden kann.⁷¹

---

vor der Mahlzeit genoß, daß sie sogar als Medizin gebraucht wurde usw." Im Koptischen wird diese Auffassung auch sprachlich deutlich, wenn das Austeilen bzw. der Empfang des Brotes der Eucharistie als ϯ bzw. ϫⲓ ⲥⲙⲟⲩ—"Segen" austeilen bzw. empfangen—bezeichnet wird; vgl. hierzu Crum, Dict. *s.v.*

⁶⁴ Dölger 1975a: 244-245: "Nach den Ausführungen über das «Gesundheitsbrot» und das Opferteilchen als Heilmittel werden wir diese Kapsel mit Opferkuchen wohl nicht anders zu bewerten haben als eine Art Schutzmittel genau so wie Satyrus das eucharistische Brot am Halse trägt, oder wie in der christlichen Zeit des vierten Jahrhunderts die Evangelien-Kapseln, die man in Nachahmung antiker Sitte ebenfalls als Schutzmittel an das Bett band, oder das Fläschchen mit Segensöl vom Marytrergrab, das sogar ein Bischof wie *Theodoret von Cyrus* an seinem Bette aufhing." Engemann 1973: 12: "Außerdem wurde angenomen, daß bereits der bloße Besitz solchen Öls segensreiche und übelabwehrende Wirkung habe, so daß man Ölbehälter im Hause am Bett hängen hatte oder ständig wie ein Amulett am Halse trug."

⁶⁵ Vgl. hierzu Engemann 1973: 11f. Er führt als mögliche Herstellungsmethoden derartiger Öle an: Es konnte Öl von den Lampen verwendet werden, die an den heiligen Stätten brannten; es konnte Öl, das mit den Reliquien in Berührung gebracht worden war, oder auch Öl, das angeblich aus den Reliquien herausgetropft sein soll, in die Ampullen eingefüllt werden.

⁶⁶ Zu den Menasampullen vgl. Witt 2000.

⁶⁷ Vgl. auch Davies 1998: 304: "The form of these ampullae deviates relatively little. The body of the flasks are circular (or occasionally slightly oval) and flat, originally molded in two halves and then joined together. The neck of the flask and its two handles were added later by hand." Vgl. für außerägyptische Pilgerampullen auch Grabar 1958.

⁶⁸ Vgl. hierzu auch Grossmann 1998: 285: "According to a chemical analysis of remains in this underground vessel this oil contained a high percentage of suspended incense."

⁶⁹ Vgl. hierzu auch Albert 1993: 225: "Les parfums mystérieux et suaves qui accompagnent la mort des saints, émanant de leur dépouille mortelle, de leurs reliques ou plus rarement de leur corps vivant, sont parmi les signes de sainteté les plus cités dans les légendes hagiographiques."

⁷⁰ Vgl. Zandee 1960: 324 u. 341; siehe auch Kügler 2000: 19f: "Im Zentrum steht auch nicht die vielfältige Verwendung von Duftstoffen im alltäglichen Leben und in der Festgestaltung, sondern die spezifisch religiösen Bedeutungen, die Gerüchen zugeschrieben werden. In vielen antiken Kulturen ist der Wohlgeruch nämlich nicht nur eine angenehme Begleiterscheinung des Lebens, sondern ein Medium der Gotteserfahrung. Im Duft offenbart sich die Nähe des Göttlichen... Daß heilige Menschen einen besonderen Wohlgeruch verströmen, ist ein verbreiteter Topos in Heiligenlegenden. Solche Menschen stehen 'im Ruch der Heiligkeit,' wie umgekehrt mit dem Teufel und seiner Welt ein besonders widerwärtiger Gestank verbunden ist."

⁷¹ Vgl. Bechmann 2000: 47: "*Zusammenfassend* läßt sich also feststellen, daß sich die Symbolik des Duftgebrauchs bei der rituellen Versorgung des Toten nicht wesentlich von der schon beschriebenen unterscheidet. Die verwendeten Balsamierungsstoffe werden als Produkte der Götter selbst gedeutet. Ihr Duft ist also der Eigengeruch der Götter, in dem deren göttliche Kraft präsent ist. Wird dieser Duft auf den Toten übertragen, so wird auch die göttliche Lebenskraft auf ihn übertragen. Er wird duftmäßig in die Gemeinschaft der Götter aufgenommen und nimmt so teil an ihrem ewigen Leben." Die gilt analog natürlich auch für die Salbung kranker und geschwächter Personen.

Interessant ist, daß in dem Zusammenhang von Heilung und Gesundheit das griechische Adjektiv ἱκανός Verwendung findet, das in koptischen Texten nur selten belegt ist. Eigentlich scheint dieser Begriff vor allem die handwerkliche Fähigkeit einer Person, die für eine bestimmte Tätigkeit geeignet ist, zu beschreiben. An dieser Stelle des Briefes scheint jedoch Gott gemeint zu sein, der dem Empfänger des Briefes Heil und Segen zu schenken vermag.

Auch das "bißchen Essig," das am Ende des Briefes (vgl. Zeile 27) erwähnt wird und das im Gegenzug an den Verfasser des Briefes geschickt werden soll, falls es vorhanden ist, kann in Zusammenhang mit dem Themenkomplex von Krankheit und Heilung gesehen werden, der den Brief prägt. Essig war in der Antike meist als Weinessig (ὄξος) zu finden; er entsteht durch Gärung alkoholischer Flüssigkeit. Der ägyptische Essig wurde dabei von den Griechen und Römern sehr geschätzt.[72] Essig wurde als Zusatz zu Getränken und sogar zu Wein verwendet. In der Bezeichnung ὀξύκρατον und ὀξύκραμμα ist ein derartiges Mischgetränk aus Wasser und Essig im Griechischen belegt, die dem Lateinischen entnommene Bezeichnung *posca* ist in koptischen Texten zu finden und zeigt, daß dieses Getränk offensichtlich auch in Ägypten verwendet wurde.[73] Teilweise wird dieses Mischgetränk auch einfach als "Essig" bezeichnet.[74] Die gleiche Bezeichnung kann auch für schlechten—d.i. dann eben sauren—Wein gebraucht werden. Neben der Verwendung als Würzmittel von Speisen und als Konservierungsmittel—Essig kann Fäulnis verhindern—wurde Essig auch als Reinigungsmittel verwendet. Auch in der Heilkunst spielt der Essig eine vielfältige Rolle, so bei Augenleiden, Magen- und Darmerkrankungen, auch bei Gicht, Prellungen und zur Stillung von Blutungen wurde Essig verwendet.[75] Die in diesem Brief angeforderte kleine Menge scheint eher auf eine geplante medizinische Verwendung schließen zu lassen als auf eine der vielen anderen Verwendungsmöglichkeiten dieser ältesten, den Menschen zugänglichen Säure.

Selbstverständlich ist hierbei jedoch eine Frage aufgrund der höchst ungenauen Mengenangaben für den Essig nicht mehr zu lösen: Was verstand ein Kirchenmann dieser Zeit unter "wenig" bei Mengenangaben? Bekannt ist, daß teilweise erstaunlich große Mengen von Gütern durch kirchliche Hände liefen. So berichtet der bisher unveröffentlichte koptische Papyrus mit der Inventarnummer 98 aus der Papyrussammlung in Heidelberg[76] von einer Lieferung von 100 Artaben Weizen, die zu Brot verbacken werden sollen. Daß bereits 8 Artaben Weizen—oder besser gesagt vier Säcke, auch wenn erwähnt werden muß, daß nicht in allen Fällen ein Sack zwei Artaben entspricht[77]—der Kopfsteuer

---

[72] Vgl. Colin 1964: 636.

[73] Vgl. hierzu Förster 2002, *s.v.* φοῦσκα; das Wort ist zwei koptischen Texte belegt, und zwar als ⲥⲁⲛⲫⲟⲩⲥⲕⲁ, als "Händler von Erfrischungsgetränken."

[74] Vgl. Preisigke, *WB*, *s.v.* ὄξος.

[75] Zur Verwendung des Essigs vgl. Colin 1964: 635-646, sowie Stadler 1907; vgl. auch Till 1951: 54-55, der dort die verschiedenen in koptischen Texten belegten Verwendungen von Essig anführt. Im Koptischen wird teilweise zwischen Essig und "scharfem (ϫⲏϥ) Essig" unterschieden, auch alter und gekochter Essig haben besondere Anwendungsgebiete.

[76] Die Veröffentlichung von P. Heidelberg Kopt. inv. 98 wird durch den Verfasser des vorliegenden Beitrages vorbereitet.

[77] Vgl. Crum / Bell 1922: 20: "As pointed out in the introduction to 205, it is in these texts and apparently elsewhere frequently used along with artabae of corn in a way suggesting that 1 θαλλίον = 2 artabae, though there are difficulties in this view."

einer Person für ein halbes Jahr in arabischer Zeit entsprechen, ist bekannt.[78] Von Kirchen konnten allerdings noch weit größere Mengen an Getreide verteilt werden.[79] Auf dem Hintergrund dieser Mengenangaben ist "ein Wenig" tatsächlich sehr relativ. Auffällig ist sicherlich, daß in diesem Zusammenhang kein Gefäß erwähnt wird, daß also nicht einfach "eine Flasche" angefordert wird—hierfür wäre λάγυνος oder κόλλαθον zu erwarten.[80] Dies spricht dafür, daß keine genaue Menge angefordert bzw. erbeten wird. Letztlich scheint es der Verfasser des Briefes dem Empfänger überlassen zu haben, wie viel Essig geschickt wurde und ob es sich dabei um ein oder mehrere Gefäße handelt—und wahrscheinlich hat dann auch die erhaltene Menge die Verwendung mitbestimmt. Daß aber selbst Wein in aus heutiger Sicht eher geringen Mengen genossen wurde, ist ebenfalls bekannt.[81] Insofern kann natürlich auch eine eher geringe Menge Essig bereits für den täglichen Verzehr gedacht sein.

5. Priester oder Bischof

Falls es, wie oben als Möglichkeit diskutiert worden war, stimmen sollte, daß nicht jeder Geistliche berechtigt war, dieses "Öl des Gebetes" zu weihen,[82] könnte dies natürlich erklären, warum der Verfasser des Briefes vom Empfänger um die Zusendung des Öls gebeten worden war. Der Empfänger des Briefes wäre dann selbst nicht in der Lage gewesen, ein derartiges Öl in seiner Nähe herstellen zu lassen, weil es dafür keinen geeigneten Geistlichen gab, und sah sich deswegen genötigt, brieflich um die Zusendung der heilbringenden Flüssigkeit zu bitten. Bezüglich des Verfassers von *P.Clackson* **44**, von dem bereits erwähnt worden war, daß es aufgrund der Handschrift als wahrscheinlich gelten darf, daß er mit dem Verfasser des Briefes P.Vindob. K. 4730 (= *P.Harrauer* 57) identisch war, und von

---

[78] Siehe hierzu auch Clackson 2007: 104: "Poll-tax contributions could be collected from the monks in kind: in one text, a rug is assessed to be worth one solidus and accepted as a monk's poll-tax contribution in lieu of a monetary payment. In another text, four sacks are reckoned to be worth a poll-tax contribution of half a solidus. As well as the handiwork produced by the monks themselves, tax contributions might also be made in commodities such as wine: in P.Mich. inv. 1520, a wine payment is received as the andrismos payment of monks from another institution—the Monastery of Jeremias of Pmanbête."

[79] Zu *SPP* III 302 (=*SPP* XX 215) vgl. auch Schmelz 2002: 168: "Mit dem zweiten Text quittiert der Diakon und οἰκονόμος Zacharias seinem Adressaten den Erhalt von 715 1/2 Artaben Weizen für 'die kleinen Kirchen', denen der προνοητής Paulos vorsteht. Zacharias ist demnach Verwalter einer übergeordneten Institution, etwa der Bischofskirche, er nimmt das Getreide in Empfang und leitet es an Paulus weiter, dem mehrere Kirchen, wohl auf Dörfern, untergeordnet sind."

[80] Für diese Gefäße und ihre Belegstellen in koptischen Texten vgl. Förster, *Wörterbuch*, *s.v.*

[81] Vgl. Mitthof 2006: 27: "Nichtsdestotrotz bleibt festzuhalten, daß die unteren, grundbesitzlosen Schichten der Bevölkerung des griechisch-römischen Ägypten — und dies war der große Teil der Population — weitgehend unabhängig von Tätigkeit, Geschlecht und Alter eine monotone Diät pflegten, die hauptsächlich aus einer kräftigen Portion Brot bzw. Getreidebrei bestand (ca. 1 kg), verfeinert mit einem Schuß Öl (ca. 2cl) und gelegentlich ergänzt durch eine handvoll Hülsenfrüchte (ca. 100-150 g). Hinzu kam ein Becher einfachen und vermutlich recht säuerlichen Weines (ca. 2 dl)."

[82] Man mag natürlich auf die oben angeführte Erzählung über den heiligen Schenufe verweisen, daß auch andere Personen über einem derartigen Öl beteten; allerdings sei in Erinnerung gerufen, daß Heilige in derartigen Fragen nicht unter das gewöhnliche Kirchenrecht fallen.

dem bereits dort aufgrund seiner vergleichsweise hohen Bildung,[83] die in seiner Sprache und Orthographie zum Ausdruck kommt (dies gilt auch für *P.Clackson* 44), angenommen wurde, daß es sich um einen höhergestellten Geistlichen handeln dürfte, kann man also zusätzlich festhalten, daß er in der Lage war, ein derartiges Öl zu segnen. Daraus könnte man folgern, daß es sich bei dem Apollô, der in P.Vindob. K. 4730 als Absender erwähnt ist, wahrscheinlich um den Vorsteher eines bedeutenden Klosters, wenn nicht sogar um einen Bischof handelt.[84]

Der Schreiber bezeichnet sich selbst als "armen Sünder" (Zeile 19 ⲧⲁⲙⲛ̄ⲧⲣⲉϥⲉⲣⲛⲟⲃⲉ). Diese Selbstbezeichnung gehört in den Bereich der Bescheidenheitsprädikate, die im religiösen Kontext üblich sind—so bezeichnet sich Apollô in P.Vindob. K. 4730 als "niedrigsten,"[85] ohne seinen genauen geistlichen Rang zu erwähnen, auch wenn seine aus Schrift, Wortwahl und Sprache abzuleitende Bildung ganz offensichtlich weit über den Bildungsgrad hinausragte, den ein durchschnittlicher Geistlicher in Ägypten hatte.

6. Gottlieb

In diesem Zusammenhang muß allerdings bedacht werden, daß der Empfänger des Öls dem Verfasser des Briefes "befohlen" hatte, "das Öl des Altars und das Wasser" zu schicken (Zeile 12-13). Der Empfänger des Briefes war also offensichtlich in der Lage, dem Verfasser Befehle zu erteilen—der verwendete Begriff stellt eine sehr klare Anordnung dar, die letztlich keinen Widerspruch duldet bzw. die im Falle eines Widerspruchs zu Konsequenzen für den Befehlsempfänger führen kann.[86] Daraus kann man schließen, daß es sich bei dem Empfänger des Öls um eine einflußreiche und wohlhabende Person handelt, die sich in der Lage sieht, einem Geistlichen Befehle zu erteilen. Aus der Stellung des Geistlichen wäre jedoch in diesem Fall abzuleiten, daß er in einer gewissen Abhängigkeit zu dieser

---

[83] Diese Bildung war wohl bei weitem größer, als dies für den Durchschnitt der ägyptischen Kleriker zu erwarten war; vgl. hierzu Schmelz 2002: 55: "Des Weiteren verpflichten sich die neuen Kleriker, ein Evangelium innerhalb von zwei Monaten auswendig zu lernen und es vor dem Bischof aufzusagen. Kenntnis des Kirchenrechts und ausgewählter biblischer Schriften war demnach die theologische Bildung, die ein Kandidat für das Diakonen- oder Priesteramt in der Diözese Hermonthis mitbringen musste. Diese Anforderung entspricht dem Grundbestand des Klerikerwissens in der Alten Kirche. In der Vita des Bischofs Aphou von Oxyrhynchos wird berichtet, er habe von einem Diakon verlangt, 25 Psalmen, zwei Paulusbriefe und Teile eines Evangeliums auswendig zu wissen, von einem Priester, Teile des Deuteronomium, einige Proverbien und einige Stücke aus Jesaja. Can. 2 des Konzils von Nicäa (787) verlangt von einem Bischofskandidaten gute Kenntnis der Schrift und der Kanones; in einer Prüfung vor dem Metropoliten soll dies nachgewiesen werden." Ganz offensichtlich erfüllt der Verfasser von K. 4730 mehr als diese Mindestanforderungen für die Aufnahme in ein geistliches Amt.

[84] Vgl. auch Hofmeister 1948: 23: "Daß das Krankenöl in den ersten Jahrhunderten auch im Abendland für nichtsakramentale Salbungen verwendet wurde, dafür ist der beste Zeuge Papst Innozenz I., der in seinem Brief an Bischof Dezentius von Gubbio schreibt, daß es nicht nur den Priestern, sondern auch allen Christen erlaubt sei, das vom Bischof geweihte Krankenöl in ihren oder ihrer Angehörigen Nöten zur Salbung zu verwenden." Auch bei den Syrern ist die Weihe des Krankenöls den Bischöfen vorbehalten; vgl. Vries 1940: 217. In der griechisch-orthodoxen Kirche ist nach Vorgrimler jeder Priester zur Weihe des Krankenöls berechtigt; Vorgrimler 1978: 226: "Nach der Lehre der griechischen und russischen Orthodoxie hat die (jederzeit wiederholbare) Krankensalbung heilenden Charakter auch bei leichteren Krankheiten. Das Öl wird im allgemeinen vom Priester erst bei der Salbung geweiht."

[85] Vgl. für die häufige Verwendung dieses Bescheidenheitsprädikates auch Förster 2002, *s.v.* ἐλάχιστος.

[86] Vgl. Förster 2002, *s.v.* Unter anderem werden die Anordnungen bzw. Gebote Gottes als die inhaltliche Bestimmung eines Befehlens gesehen, das mit diesem Wort zum Ausdruck gebracht wird.

Person stand. Dies könnte ebenfalls, wie auch die anderen bereits erwähnten in diesem Brief zu findenden Indizien, darauf hinweisen, daß es sich um den Vorsteher eines Klosters und nicht um einen Bischof handelt.

Der Verfasser des Briefes drückt auch in der Art des Umgangs mit dem Empfänger aus, daß er für ihn eine besondere Hochachtung hegt. Er bezeichnet ihn als "Gottlieb."[87] Diese Anrede gehört grundsätzlich in den Bereich der byzantinischen Briefformeln, in denen sich eine Fülle ehrender Anreden findet,[88] die auch den koptischen Briefstil prägen.[89] Es handelt sich dabei um das koptische Äquivalent des griechischen θεόφιλος. Grundsätzlich scheint die ehrende Anrede "Gottlieb" (ⲙⲁⲓⲛⲟⲩⲧⲉ bzw. ⲙⲛⲧⲙⲁⲓⲛⲟⲩⲧⲉ) fast ausschließlich als Anrede für Geistliche Verwendung zu finden.[90] Insofern wird der Empfänger des Briefes wahrscheinlich selbst ein wohlhabender Geistlicher gewesen sein. Andernfalls müßte man annehmen, daß der Verfasser des Briefes durch diese Anrede seine besondere Wertschätzung zum Ausdruck bringen möchte und die herausragende Frömmigkeit des Briefempfängers—die sich möglicherweise in der außergewöhnlich großzügigen Zuwendung zum Kloster des Briefschreibers ausgedrückt hat—durch diese ehrende Anrede betonen. Am Rande sei bemerkt, daß auch das Lukasevangelium für einen "Theophilos" geschrieben ist.[91] Es muß fraglich bleiben, ob es sich dabei um eine reale Person oder eine rhetorisch gestaltete Einleitung des Evangeliums handelt, die jeden Leser als von Gott geliebte Person ansieht. Sicherlich denkbar ist, daß auch das die Beliebtheit des Gebrauchs dieser Anrede beeinflußt hat.

7. Geben und Nehmen

Der Eindruck, daß es sich beim Empfänger des Briefes um einen wohlhabenden Mitbürger gehandelt hat, wird bestätigt durch die Erwähnung des "großen Opfers" (Zeile 9), durch welches der Empfänger des Briefes dem Stifter dankt. Mit dem Begriff "Opfer"[92] wird meist eine fromme Stiftung für ein Kloster bezeichnet. Dies scheint auch hier der Fall zu sein.[93] Hierfür spricht auch, daß einige der

---

[87] Im Deutschen ist es nicht möglich, die durch das Präfix ⲙⲛⲧ- gebildete abstrakte Form dieser Bezeichnung auszudrücken.

[88] Vgl. auch *P.Harrauer* 57: 19 (dort jedoch ohne die Abstraktbildung mit Hilfe des Präfix ⲙⲛⲧ-): ⲧⲁⲁⲥ ⲙ̄ⲡⲙⲁⲓⲛⲟⲩⲧⲉ ϩⲛ ⲟⲩⲙⲉ. "Gib es dem in Wahrheit Gott liebenden…"

[89] Für die zahlreichen Belege in den dokumentarischen Texten vgl. Förster 2002, *s.v.* θεοφιλέστατος. Dieser Ehrentitel scheint meist für Geistliche Verwendung zu finden. Grundsätzlich wäre die Frage zu stellen, ob die im Koptischen zu findenden Substantivierung (ⲙⲛⲧⲙⲁⲓⲛⲟⲩⲧⲉ) als Versuch zu verstehen ist, den Superlativ des griechischen Adjektivs nachzubilden.

[90] Vgl. hierzu auch die Belege in *SBKopt.* I (Nr. 43,2 [Priester]; 49,2 [Priester; zu diesem Text vgl. auch die Korrekturen von Krause, *ZÄS* 112 (1985) 143-153]; 292,3 [Geistlicher]; 302,4 [wahrscheinlich Mönch]; 328,5 [Mönch]; 330,12 [wahrscheinlich Mönch]; 340,5 [Mönch]; 341,3 [Diakon]; 343,2 [Diakon]; 346,2 [Mönch]; 349,2 [Diakon]; 492.4 [Diakon]; 494,4 [Mönch]).

[91] Vgl. Lk 1,3.

[92] Vgl. Förster 2002, *s.v.* προσφορά.

[93] Für Schenkungen an Klöster vgl. Schiller 1932: 293: "Sehr häufig sind Schenkungen von unbeweglichem Vermögen, im allgemeinen von Land, wobei die Schenknehmer oft Klöster sind. Solche Schenkungen an Klöster sind auch in später verfaßten Kaufurkunden erwähnt." Siehe ferner Bruck 1954: 126-127: "Das byzantinische Recht begünstigte Geschenke und Vermächtnisse an die Kirche. Die praktische Bedeutung dieser rechtlichen Begünstigung der *piae causae* tritt zu Tage

Gaben, welche die Gemeinschaft um den Briefschreiber erhalten hat, als "Segen" bezeichnet werden (vgl. Zeile 8).[94] Auffällig ist allerdings, daß diese Zuwendung ausdrücklich als "groß" bezeichnet wird. Dies erweckt den Eindruck, daß es sich um eine vergleichsweise bedeutende Zuwendung handelt. Dies wird auch durch den Nachsatz zum Ausdruck gebracht. Der Schreiber sieht sich außer Standes, den frommen Geber zu entschädigen (Zeile 9f). Beim dem sich an diese Wendung anschließenden Satz findet ein Subjektwechsel statt. Zwar dankt der Empfänger im Namen der ganzen Gemeinschaft für die Zuwendung,[95] eine einzelne Person hat jedoch die Zuwendung, für welche die Gemeinschaft dankt, letztendlich erhalten und ist infolge in der Lage, den großzügigen Spender zu heilen.[96] Mit der dritten Person Singular scheint Gott gemeint zu sein, der aufgrund der frommen Zuwendung die Gesundheit schenkt.[97] Diese Interpretation wird auch bestätigt durch den vorangehenden Teil des Briefes, in dem von dem Gebet der Mönche zu Gott die Rede ist (Zeile 3f), "der dir Gnade erweisen möge und dir mit der Heilung deines Leibes und auch die Rettung deiner Seele gewähren möge." Auffällig ist sicherlich die Verwendung des griechischen Wortes heilen (θεραπεύω) in Zeile 10f. Dieser Begriff bezeichnet im Neuen Testament einerseits den Dienst an der Gottheit, andererseits die ärztliche Behandlung und wird im biblischen Kontext nur ganz vereinzelt von Gott verwendet.[98] In der patristischen Literatur kann er dann stärker auch von Gott gebraucht werden,[99] in den koptischen dokumentarischen Texten ist es vergleichsweise selten belegt und bezieht sich auf ärztliche Behandlung.[100] Man wird aufgrund der Verwendung dieses griechischen Begriffes wohl vermuten dürfen, daß der großzügige Spender ein sehr konkretes Ergebnis bei der Besserung seiner Gesundheit erwartet hat.

Im Zusammenhang mit den bereits eingetroffenen Zuwendungen an das Kloster fällt auch die vorsichtige Formulierung auf, mit welcher der Verfasser des Briefes um den Essig bittet. Wenn es ihm leicht fällt, dann soll ihm der Empfänger des Briefes diesen Gefallen tun. Und wenn es ihm Mühe macht, dann soll er diese Wohltat zu seinen anderen Tugenden hinzufügen. Fast hat man den Eindruck,

---

in den archäologischen Funden in den Gebieten des damaligen byzantinischen Reichs. In Syrien, Kappadozien und in Konstantinopel selbst beweist die Fülle der Ruinen von Klöstern und Kirchen eindeutig den ungeheuren Umfang der Schenkungen zu Gunsten der Kirche."

[94] Der koptische Begriff ⲥⲙⲟⲩ ist vieldeutig, er dürfte hier wohl als "Wohltat" bzw. "fromme Schenkung" zu verstehen sein, wobei sich die Frage stellt, ob es sich dabei um einen in irgendeiner Form geweihten Gegenstand gehandelt haben dürfte; vgl. für diese Bedeutung Crum, Dict., s.v.

[95] Zeile 7-10: ⲁⲛⲭⲓⲧⲟⲩ ⲉⲩ . . [ⲁⲛ]ⲭⲏⲩ ⲙⲛ ⲛⲉⲕⲥⲙⲟⲩ ⲧⲏⲣ[ⲟ]ⲩ· ⲁⲛⲉⲩⲭⲁⲣⲓⲥⲧⲁ ⲛⲁⲕ ⲧⲟⲛⲉ ϩⲓⲧⲛ ⲧⲛⲟϭ ⲙⲡⲣⲟⲥⲫⲟⲣ[ⲁ] ⲉⲙⲛϭⲟⲙ ⲙⲟⲛ ⲉⲧⲟⲩⲉⲓⲟ ⲛⲁⲕ ϩⲁⲣⲟⲥ "Wir haben sie erhalten und [wir haben] auch deine ganzen Wohltaten erhalten. Wir danken dir durch das große Opfer, und wir können dich nicht dafür entschädigen."

[96] Zeile 10-11: ⲁⲗⲗⲁ ⲡⲉⲛⲧⲁⲕ[ⲧⲛ]ⲛⲟⲟⲩⲥ ⲛⲁϥ ⲟⲩϩⲓⲕⲁⲛⲟⲥ ⲡⲉ ⲉⲑⲉⲣⲁⲡⲉⲩⲉ ⲛⲧⲕⲯⲩⲭⲏ ⲙⲛⲡⲉⲕⲥⲱⲙⲁ. "Sondern nachdem du es ihm geschickt hast, ist er fähig, deine Seele und deinen Körper zu heilen."

[97] Vgl. in diesem Zusammenhang auch Förster 2001: 217: "Wohl am eindrücklichsten—und auch sicher am erschütterndsten—ist der Zusammenhang zwischen Krankheit und 'Wirken Gottes' in den sogenannten 'Kinderschenkungsurkunden.' Ein Kind fällt in schwere Krankheit. Der Erziehungsberechtigte schwört, im Falle der Gesundung dieses Kind einem bestimmten Kloster zu schenken... Kinderschenkungen können auch für «die eigenen Sünden» vorgenommen werden. Eintretende Krankheit kann dann als Strafe für den Versuch, dieses Versprechen rückgängig zu machen, gewertet werden."

[98] Vgl. Aland und Aland 1988: s.v.

[99] Lampe 1961: s.v.

[100] Auch die Tatsache, daß der Verfasser von P.Harrauer 57 ebenfalls dieses Wort verwendet, darf als weiteres Indiz dafür gesehen werden, daß beide Texte von einem Verfasser stammen.

als wolle der Verfasser des Briefes den Wohltäter des Klosters nicht noch mit dieser Lapalie belästigen, während es gleichzeitig für ihn sehr wichtig ist, den Essig zu bekommen.

Die Tatsache, daß auch ein Stück Gewand des "Apa Severus" mitgeschickt wurde, wirft die Frage auf, ob das Kloster in einer besonderen Weise mit diesem offensichtlich als heilig verehrten Mann verbunden war.[101] Was die Person dieses Apa Severus angeht, kann und muß man selbstverständlich in Erwägung ziehen, daß es sich um Severus von Antiochia handelt, dessen enge Beziehungen zu Ägypten bekannt sind und der um 538 dort verstarb.[102] Der Kult dieses Heiligen ist in Ägypten gut belegt.[103] Eine weitere Frage in diesem Zusammenhang ist natürlich, ob das "Öl des Altars" seine besondere Weihe durch die Reliquien das Heiligen, die an diesem Ort aufbewahrt wurden, empfing.[104] ⲔⲀⲦⲰⲔ wird man wohl am besten als Verbindung des Status nominalis von ⲔⲰ mit dem Possessivpronomen fem. sg. (ⲦⲰⲔ) auffassen müssen. Offensichtlich besaß der Empfänger bereits ein Stück des Gewandes (ϩⲞⲒⲦⲈ ist ein fem. Nomen) als persönliches Eigentum, das er in der Stadt gelassen hat. Dieses wurde dort dann aller Wahrscheinlichkeit nach öffentlich verehrt.[105] Ganz offensichtlich wird man dabei an die Errichtung eines Reliquienschreines mit der entsprechenden kultischen Verehrung denken müssen.[106] Der Verfasser schränkt mit Hilfe des vorangestellten Circumstantialis ein, daß es sich zumindest nach seiner Auffassung so verhält. Für die Interpretation, daß es sich bei der Sendung des Gewandstücks um die Stiftung eines Reliquiars für eine Kirche gehandelt hat, könnte man auch anführen, daß der Verfasser des Briefes den Empfänger auffordert, darüber zu wachen. Die Frömmigkeit, die zur Reliquienverehrung gehört, kann sich auf altkirchliche Quellen[107] und großkirchliche Förderung berufen, auch wenn diese Frömmigkeit dem modernen Menschen oftmals sehr fremd anmutet.[108] Reliquien, die oftmals künstlerisch ausgestalteten und aus

---

[101] Vgl. Baus und Ewig 1985: 336: "Altar und Martyrergrab wurden also schon damals ideell und real in jene enge Verbindung miteinander gebracht, die später nach liturgischem Recht überall geschaffen werden sollte, wo es christliche Altäre gab. Dieses Anliegen ließ sich jedoch nur verwirklichen, wenn man Teile von Martyrerleibern an jene Gemeinden und Kirchen abgab, die nicht über so kostbaren Besitz verfügten, man mußte also zur Multiplikation der Martyrerreliquien durch Aufteilung in kleine und kleinste Teile schreiten." Siehe auch Angenendt 1994.

[102] Vgl. Knezevich 1991; Böhm 2000; Torrance 2000; Bruns 2002.

[103] Vgl. hierzu Papaconstantinou 2001: 188-190.

[104] Hierfür könnte man auch heidnische Prallelen anführen; vgl. Dölger 1975a: 243: "Dies setzt voraus, daß in der volkstümlichen Heilmethode die Verwendung von Opferstückchen eine besondere Rolle spielte. Die auf den Altar niedergelegten und damit in den Besitz der Gottheit übergegangene Gabe war durch das Opfer und die Berührung mit dem Altar geweiht und galt im Volksglauben als wirkungskräftig. So benutzte man sie als Heilmittel und als übelabwehrendes Schutzmittel." Siehe auch Angenendt 1998: 70: "Ein Grunddatum setzte Ambrosius, als er am 17. Juni 386 erstmals im Westen Märtyrergräber öffnete und die Gebeine an den Altar einer Kirche übertrug. Bewußt stellte er eine himmlisch-irdische Entsprechung her: Wie die Seelen der Märtyrer «unter dem himmlischen Altar» ihren Aufenthalt hatten (Apk 6,9), so die Leiber unter dem Irdischen. Die Verbindung von Reliquiengrab und Altar wurde essentiell."

[105] Vgl. auch Frankfurter 1998: 3: "And as the above text explains (fairly typically to the genre), the saints' power enters the human world through rather simple means: Christ assures the preservation of the martyrs' bones, the erection of a shrine to house them, and the angelic expertise to maintain effective healing there."

[106] Vgl. hierzu u.a. Angenendt 1999.

[107] Angenendt 1997: 149: "Die allgemeine Wertschätzung des Leibes steigerte sich bei den Heiligen zum Reliquienkult. Erstmals von Polykarp, über dessen auf das Jahr 156 oder vielleicht erst 167 zu datierenden Flammentod wir den ältesten Märtyrerbericht besitzen, wird erwähnt, daß man die Überbleibsel wie Edelsteine gesammelt habe."

[108] Baus und Ewig 1985: 337: "Die Martyrerverehrung als altchristliche Frömmigkeitsform wurde nicht etwa in der Hauptsache von der Laienwelt oder vom Mönchtum getragen, sondern in ihren wesentlichen Zügen auch von der Kirche und ihren Theologen mitbestimmt, gerechtfertigt und gefördert."

wertvollen Materialien gefertigten Reliquiare und ihre segenspendende Wirksamkeit waren verständlicherweise Objekte der Begehrlichkeit[109] und gegebenenfalls auch der (gewaltsamen oder heimtückischen[110]) Entwendung.[111] Allerdings konnte ein Gewand eines Heiligen auch direkt als "geistliches Heilmittel" eingesetzt werden, wie ein auf Papyrus erhaltener Brief zeigt, der in den Kontext des schenutianischen Mönchtums gehört und aus dem 6./7. Jh. stammt.[112]

Bei den "kleinen Kreuzen," die in Zeile 20f erwähnt werden, wird man vermuten müssen, daß sie wohl Anhänger[113] waren, die damals gerne getragen wurden (diese Sitte ist bis in die heutige Zeit nicht ausgestorben[114]). Für die Annahmen, daß es sich bei den mitgeschickten "kleinen Kreuzen"[115] um ein Amulett bzw. ein Phylakterion[116] gehandelt haben dürfte,[117] spricht auch die Tatsache, daß ein

---

[109] Baus und Ewig 1985: 336: "Parallel zu der von der Kirche noch einigermaßen kontrollierten Reliquienaufteilung lief das intensive Bemühen privater Kreise, in den Besitz solch kostbarer Phylakterien zu gelangen, das schon früh zu den bedenklichsten Auswüchsen eines weitverbreiteten Reliquienhandels führte, die von kirchlichen und staatlichen Stellen zwar mißbilligt wurden, aber nie restlos beseitigt werden konnten."

[110] Vgl. Engemann 1973: 11: "Begehrtestes Andenken für christliche Pilger war aus Palästina verständlicherweise ein Splitter des Holzes, das als Teil des Kreuzes Christi verehrt wurde, während Besucher von Heiligengräbern sich den Besitz einer Körperreliquie wünschten. Doch waren dem Wunsch nach Mitnahme dieser Andenken natürliche Grenzen gesetzt, so daß beispielsweise bei der Kreuzverehrung in Jerusalem von den Diakonen scharf aufgepaßt wurde, daß kein Pilger in das Holz biß, um einen Splitter zu erlangen."

[111] Angenendt 1997: 162-163: "Anstößig auch wirkten, damals wie heute, die 'heiligen Diebstähle,' die listige oder gar gewaltsamen Entwendung von Reliquien." Siehe auch Knöpf 2004: 418: "Der verehrungsvolle Umgang mit R., aber auch manche nach heutigem Empfinden pietätlose Handlungen an ihnen beruhen auf der Überzeugung von ihrem außerordentlichen immateriellen Wert, die wiederum aus der Vorstellung folgt, durch Kontakt mit R. an der in ihnen vorhandenen Kraft teilhaben zu können."

[112] Jördens 2004: 145-146: "Neu scheint zudem auch die Nachricht, daß man die Kleider des Heiligen als Reliquien aufbewahrte und in Notfällen als geistliches Heilmittel einsetzte. Dies paßt allerdings ausgezeichnet zu der Nachricht, daß Schenute selbst in seinem sogenannten Testament die Aufbewahrung seiner Gewänder angeordnet haben soll."

[113] Für entsprechende Anhänger vgl. u. a. Horak 1999: Nummern 59f. u. 66-70.

[114] Vgl. Dölger 1975: 86: "Das Kreuzzeichen war als gezeichnete Figur und als Segensgestus das große Wunderzeichen der Christen geworden, das jeden Zauber überwindet. Damit war es verständlich, daß man auch das plastisch geformte Kreuzchen in dem Sinne eines übel- und dämonenabwehrenden Zeichens trug. Wir sehen die Grundlagen dafür besonders klar in dem Kampf der Kirchenschriftsteller gegen das heidnische Amulett zutage treten. Man mußte danach trachten, für die oft recht merkwürdigen Anhängsel der Antike einen Ersatz zu bieten. Er bot sich ganz ungezwungen in dem kreuzförmigen Schmuck, in dem Kreuz-Phylakterion."

[115] Vgl. Dölger 1975: 93: "Das Kreuzchen soll im Sinne seines Trägers das drohende Unheil fernhalten, wie das Christusmonogramm am Helme Konstantins des Großen und das Kreuz am Helme der christlichen Soldaten. Das Kreuz galt ja immer im christlichen Altertum als das Siegeszeichen Jesu über die Feinde."

[116] Wobei kirchlicherseits das Bestreben offenkundig ist, magische Praktiken im Zusammenhang mit derartigen Phylakterien zu verhindern; vgl. auch nur die pseudonizänische koptische Glaubensauslegung, die von Haase 1920 übersetzt wurde (S. 36): "Erlaube (πείθειν) niemandem, in einer Krankheit oder (ἤ) in einem Schmerz (πάθος) oder (ἤ) in einem Kummer (λύπη) oder (ἤ) nach einem Schlangenbiß an den Ort eines Beschwörers zu gehen oder (οὔτε) eines solchen, der Phylakterien (φυλακτήριον) anlegt; tue dies niemals und laß nicht zu, daß jemand dir dies tut."

[117] Vgl. Dölger 1975: 88: "Die Mahnung der Prediger, die antik-heidnischen Amulette durch die Anhängekreuzchen zu ersetzen, war ideal gemeint. Aber andererseits war nun die Gefahr vorhanden, daß das Volk aus seiner heidnischen Überlieferung heraus recht stofflich dachte und der Kreuzfigur als solcher eine unmittelbar wirkende Kraft zuschreiben wollte. Die Gefahr bestand, daß schließlich das Anhängekreuzchen behandelt wurde wie ein antikes Amulett. Dies war dann der Fall, wenn man auf das Anhängekreuzchen unverständliche, sinnlose Zauberformeln schrieb, wie sie im Heidentum der Antike üblich waren."

Geistlicher sie schickt.[118] Dies scheint die theoretisch denkbare Möglichkeit, daß es sich um ein Kinderspielzeug gehandelt haben könnte, auszuschließen. Grundsätzlich wird man jedoch diese Amulette[119] eher in den Bereich der Volksfrömmigkeit[120] als in den Bereich der Magie bzw. Zauberei rücken müssen,[121] da zwischen beiden Bereichen zwar fließende Übergänge bestehen,[122] da aber nicht angegeben ist, ob überhaupt ein Text auf diesen Kreuzen zu finden war.

Bei der Vielzahl der offensichtlich religiös bedeutsamen und göttlichen Segen vermittelnden Objekte wird die Reise des Boten hoffentlich glatt und ohne Schwierigkeiten oder Beeinträchtigungen verlaufen sein. Zumindest ist dies unter diesen Voraussetzungen für einen Menschen der damaligen Zeit zu erwarten.[123]

8. Gruß und Kuß

Das Ende des Briefes wird durch die Betonung, daß der Verfasser "dies alles geschrieben habe," eingeleitet. Der Verfasser verwendet, um dies auszurücken, einen Circumstantialis. Dieser betont in besonderer Weise das, was geschrieben wurde.[124] Der darauffolgende Gruß zeichnet sich durch seine bei aller Formelhaftigkeit des Briefes doch spürbare Herzlichkeit aus. Das griechische Wort "Küssen" findet in einer Vielzahl koptischer Briefe Verwendung und hat dort die Bedeutung eines herzlichen Grußes.[125] Wenn die "Füße" im Rahmen des Grußes erwähnt werden, so wird diese Formel oftmals durch die Verwendung von distanzierenden Erweiterungen wie die "Spur der Füße," den "Boden" bzw.

---

[118] Für ein von Schenute selbst verfertigtes Kreuz, das Schutz und Hilfe bieten soll, vgl. auch Behlmer 1998: 350.

[119] Zur Definition des Amulettes vgl. Pfister 1917: 375: "A(mulett) ist ein kleinerer, krafterfüllter (orendistischer) Gegenstand, dessen Kraft sich dort wirksam zeigt, wo er angehängt oder befestigt wird."

[120] Vgl. Ruppert 1991: 702: "Ein magischer Mißbrauch im Sinne abergläubischer Verhaftungen kann sich mit allem verbinden, was mit Religion und christlichem Glauben zu tun hat."

[121] Darauf scheinen auch die Beschriftungen einiger derartiger Kreuzanhänger zu verweisen; vgl. Dölger 1975: 95-96: "Der Träger des Kreuzchens mit der *IXΘYΣ*-Formel wollte sich also dem Schutze seines Heilandes anvertrauen… Mit dem Texte vereint wird das getragene Kreuzchen zum immerwährenden stillen Gebet, daß Gott dem Träger Hilfe und Schutz gewähren möge in aller drohenden Gefahr. Wie das Anhängekreuzchen des Britischen Museums mit dem schönen Text aus Gal 6,14 bezeugt, ist der nicht ausgesprochene, aber mitgedachte Gedanke der: ich trage das Kreuz, das Wappenzeichen Jesu Christi, ihm diene ich furchtlos und treu. Die Folgerung ist: er ist mein Herr, er sei mein Schutz und mein Schirm. So gedacht ist 'das Phylakterion des Kreuzes' völlig im Geiste des Christentums."

[122] Vgl. auch Gerlitz 1993: 568-569: "Unklar bleiben auch die Funktionen, v(on) denen aus sich das Wesen des A(mulettes) eindeutig bestimmen u(nd) v(on) ähnl(ichen) mag(ischen) Objekten abgrenzen ließe… Die Grenzen sind vielmehr fließend, u(nd) man wird sagen müssen, daß es nahezu keinen Gegenstand gibt, der nicht zu irgendeiner Zeit als A(mulett) gebraucht worden wäre; darum kann man den Glauben an die mag(ischen) Kräfte, die dem A(mulett) innewohnen, nur mit der mag(ischen) Einstellung z(ur) Welt insg(esamt) erklären." Siehe auch Eckstein und Wazink: 1950, siehe ferner Beltz 1998.

[123] Vgl. hierzu auch Dölger 1975a: Satyrus hatte sich, als er noch nicht getauft war, bei einem Schiffbruch das Brot der Eucharistie um den Hals gebunden und war aus den Wellen errettet worden; aus dieser Begebenheit wird offensichtlich, daß einerseits selbst die Eucharistie von den Gläubigen nachhause oder auf Reisen mitgenommen wurde und daß man sich von diesem Sakrament auf der Reise Schutz und Rettung erhoffte. Man darf annehmen, daß dies natürlich auch für andere heilbringende und geweihte Gegenstände galt.

[124] Eine andere, in Briefen ebenfalls anzutreffende Formulierung, die das Perfekt I benützt, wäre z.B. ⲁⲓⲥϩⲁⲓ ⲛⲁⲓ ⲧⲏⲣⲟⲩ ⲛⲁⲕ; vgl. hierzu Förster 1999.

[125] Förster 2002, *s.v.*

den "Schemel unter den Füßen" oder auch den "Staub der Füße" erweitert.[126] Der Empfänger wird jedoch gegrüßt von Kopf bis zu den Füßen, der Gruß bezieht sich also auf die ganze Person. Man wird daraus also zumindest eine gewisse Gleichberechtigung der beiden Parteien ableiten können. Auch wenn der Empfänger des Briefes in der Lage war, dem Schreiber Befehle zu erteilen, so wäre bei einer tatsächlichen hierarchischen Abhängigkeit wohl eine größere Unterwürfigkeit im Rahmen dieses Grußes zu erwarten. Der mit ἀσπάζω eingeleitete Gruß findet sich sowohl am Anfang wie auch am Schluß koptischer Briefe.[127]

9. Am Ende das Heil

Schlußformeln koptischer Briefe verwenden in vielfältiger Ausformung einen Segensgruß, der den Wunsch einer guten Gesundheit des Briefempfängers zum Ausdruck bringt. Dieser Gruß wird am Beginn des Verso gleich dreimal wiederholt—normalerweise findet sich nur einmal das koptische ⲟⲩϫⲁⲓ. Diese seltene Häufung des Wunsches drückt möglicherweise die Sorge des Schreibers um die angegriffene Gesundheit des Empfängers des Briefes aus und möchte ihn wohl mit dieser Formulierung der Nachdrücklichkeit der Gebete für ihn versichern, die im Kloster für ihn gesprochen werden. "Diese Gruppe von Formeln findet sich fast ausschließlich am Ende eines Briefes. Die Formeln stellen eine Art Abschiedsgruß dar, sind also in gewisser Weise mit den Grußformeln verwandt. Der Aussage nach stehen sie jedoch in enger Beziehung zu den… Gesundheitsformeln, denn sie beschäftigen sich—wie jene—mit dem Wohlbefinden des Adressaten."[128] Die Stellung der Schlußformel bestätigt die Richtigkeit der Angabe, daß erst nach Abschluß des Briefes die Brüder den Schreiber gebeten haben, noch um die Zusendung von etwas Essig zu bitten.

Bemerkenswert ist in diesem Zusammenhang, daß die trinitarische Formel[129] um den Zusatz "wesensein" erweitert wird, der infolge der arianischen Wirren auf dem ersten Konzil von Konstantinopel definiert worden war. Diese dogmatisch ausführlichere Bestimmung der Dreifaltigkeit findet sich meist in der griechischen Einleitungsformel koptischer Urkunden,[130] sie ist für Briefe jedoch zumindest ungewöhnlich.

---

[126] Biedenkopf-Ziehner 1983: 100.

[127] Biedenkopf-Ziehner 1983: 79: "Die Grußformeln stehen normalerweise im Präskript der Briefe, finden sich aber auch nicht selten am Briefende."

[128] Biedenkopf-Ziehner 1983: 104.

[129] Für verschiedene Schlußformeln von Briefen, in denen die (heilige) Trinität erwähnt wird, vgl. Biedenkopf-Ziehner 1983: 106-107; unter den von ihr aufgeführten fünf Varianten, welche die "heilige Dreieinigkeit" enthalten, findet sich die in diesem Brief belegte Formel nicht.

[130] Für Belege vgl. Förster, Wörterbuch, *s.v.*; dort ist auch ein Beleg in einem Brief verzeichnet.

BIBLIOGRAPHIE

LACL: Döpp, S. und Geerlings, W. (eds.) (2002). *Lexikon der antiken christlichen Literatur*. Freiburg etc: Herder.

LThK: *Lexikon für Theologie und Kirche*. Freiburg etc: Herder.

RAC: *Reallexikon für Antike und Christentum*. Stuttgart: Hiersemann.

RE: *Paulys Realencyclopädie der classischen Altertumswissenschaft*. Stuttgart: Alfred Druckenmüller.

RGG: Religion in Geschichte und Gegenwart. Tübingen: Mohr Siebeck.

TRE: Theologische Realenzyklopädie. Berlin/New York: De Gruyter

Aland, K. und Aland, B. (eds.) (1988). *Griechisch-deutsches Wörterbuch zu den Schriften des Neuen Testaments und der frühchristlichen Literatur* (6th edn.). Berlin/New York: De Gruyter.

Albert, J.-P. (1993). "Le parfum et le sang," *Apocrypha* 4, 225-243.

Amélineau, E. (1888). "Fragments des vies de Pakhôme et de Théodore," in: Grébaut, E. (ed.). *MMAF*. Bd. 4. Paris: Ernest Leroux, 521-632.

Angenendt, A. (1994). "Zur Ehre der Altäre erhoben. Zugleich ein Beitrag zur Reliquienteilung," *RQCA* 89, 221-244.

Angenendt, A. (1997). *Heilige und Reliquien. Die Geschichte ihres Kultes vom frühen Christentum bis zur Gegenwart* (2nd edn.). München: Beck.

Angenendt, A. (1998). "Reliquien. II. Im Christentum," in: *TRE* 29, 69-74.

Angenendt, A. (1999). "Reliquien, II. Historisch-theologisch," in: *LThK* Bd. 8 (3rd edn.), 1091-1093.

Anson, J. (1974). "The Female Transvestite in Early Monasticism: The Origin and Development of a Motif," *Viator* 5, 1-32.

Bagnall, R. (1993). *Egypt in Late Antiquity*. Princeton: Princeton University Press.

Baumeister, Th. (1972). *Martyr Invictus. Der Martyrer als Sinnbild der Erlösung in der Legende und im Kult der frühen koptischen Kirche. Zur Kontinuität ägyptischen Denkens*. Münster: Regensberg (*Forschungen zur Volkskunde* 46).

Baus K. und Ewig E. (1985). *Die Kirche von Nikaia bis Chalkedon*. (= Nachdruck 1999). Freiburg etc: Herder. (= Jedin, H. (ed.), *Handbuch der Kirchengeschichte* II. 1. Halbband: *Die Reichskirche nach Konstantin dem Großen*).

Bechmann, U. (2000). "Die religiöse Bedeutung des Dufts im Alten Ägypten," in: Kügler, J. (ed.) *Die Macht der Nase. Zur religiösen Bedeutung des Duftes. Religionsgeschichte—Bibel—Liturgie*. Stuttgart: Bibelwerk (= *Stuttgarter Bibelstudien* 187), 25-47.

Behlmer, H. (1998). "Visitors to Shenoute's Monastery," in: Frankfurter, D. (ed.) *Pilgrimage and Holy Space in Late Antique Egypt*. Leiden: Brill (= *Religions in the Graeco-Roman World* 134), 341-371.

Behlmer, H. (2001). "Weibliche Körper im Mönchsgewand," in: Franz, C. und Schwibbe, G. (eds.) *Geschlecht weiblich: Körpererfahrungen—Körperkonzepte*. Berlin: Edition Ebersbach, 12-34.

Beltz, W. (1998). "Amulett. I. Religionsgeschichtlich," in: *RGG* 2 (4th edn.), 442-443.

Biedenkopf-Ziehner, A. (1983). *Untersuchungen zum koptischen Briefformular unter Berücksichtigung ägyptischer und griechischer Parallelen*. Würzburg: Harrassowitz (= *Koptische Studien* 1).

Biedenkopf-Ziehner, A. (1996). "Motive einiger Formeln und Topoi aus ägyptischen Briefen paganer und christlicher Zeit," *Enchoria* 23, 8-31.

Böhm, Th. (2000). "Severos v. Antiochien," in: *LThK* Bd. 9 (3rd edn.), 502-504.

Bruck, E. F. (1954). *Über römisches Recht im Rahmen der Kulturgeschichte*. Berlin: Springer.

Brun, J.-P. (2003). *Le vin et l'huile dans la méditerranée antique. Viticulture, oléiculture et procédés de transformation*. Paris: Editions Errance.

Bruns, P. (2002). "Severus von Antiochien," in: *LACL* (3rd edn.) 636-637.

Clackson, S. J. (2007). "Archimandrites and Andrismos: a Preliminary Survey of Taxation at Bawit," in: Palme, B. (Hg.), *Akten des 23. Internationalen Papyrologenkongresses: Wien, 22.-28. Juli 2001*, Wien: Österreichische Akademie der Wissenschaften (= *Papyrologica Vindobonensia* 1), 103-107.

Colin, J. (1964). "Essig," in: *RAC* 6, 635-646.

Crum, W. E. (1939). *A Coptic Dictionary* (= 2000). Oxford: Clarendon Press.

Crum, W. E. (1902). *Coptic Ostraca from the Collections of the Egypt Exploration Fund, the Cairo Museum and Others*. London: Egypt Exploration Fund.

Davis, S. J. (1998). "Pilgrimage and the cult of saint Thekla in late antique Egypt," in: Frankfurter, D. (ed.) *Pilgrimage and holy space in late antique Egypt*. Leiden etc: Brill (= *Religions in the Graeco-Roman World* 134), 303-339.

Dölger, F. J. (1974). "'Öl der Eucharistie.' Zum Schreiben der Synode von Karthago im Frühjahre 255," in: *AntChr* 2 (2nd edn.), 184-189.

Dölger, F. J. (1975). "Das Anhängekreuzchen der hl. Makrina und ihr Ring mit der Kreuzpartikel. Ein Beitrag zur religiösen Volkskunde des 4. Jahrhunderts nach der *Vita Macrinae* des Gregor von Nyssa," in: *AntChr* (2nd edn.), 81-116.

Dölger, F. J. (1975a). "Die Eucharistie als Reiseschutz. Die Eucharistie in den Händen der Laien. Volkskundliches aus der Rede des hl. Ambrosius auf den Tod seines Bruders Satyrus," in: *AntChr* 5 (2nd edn.), 232-247.

Dudlei, M. (1998). "Salbung IV. Kirchengeschichtlich und praktisch-theologisch," in: *TRE* 29, 714-717.

Ebner, M. (2001). "Krankheit und Heilung. III. Biblisch," in: *RGG* 4 (4th edn.), 1730-1731.

Eckstein, F. und Wazink, J. H. (1950). "Amulett," in: *RAC* 1, 397-411.

Eibach, U. (1997). "Krankheit," in: *LThK* 6 (3rd edn.), 426-430.

Engemann, J. (1973). "Palästinensische Pilgerampullen im F. J. Dölger-Institut in Bonn (mit 7 Abbildungen im Text und 16 Tafeln)," *JAC* 16, 5-27.

Förster, H. (1999). "Korr. Tyche 340. ἀκτ(ου)άριος oder ⲛⲁⲕ ⲧⲁⲣⲉ?," *Tyche* 14, 332-333.

Förster, H. (2001). "Christlicher Trostbrief (*P.Harrauer* 57)," in: Palme, B. (ed.) *Wiener Papyri als Festgabe zum 60. Geburtstag von Hermann Harrauer (P.Harrauer)*. Wien: Holzhausen, 207-222.

Förster, H. (2002). *Wörterbuch der griechischen Wörter in den koptischen dokumentarischen Texten*. Berlin: De Gruyter (= *TU* 148).

Förster, H. (2003). "'Es ist die Sitte der Schwestern...' Edition von P.Vindob. K. 4728," *Mitteilungen zur christlichen Archäologie* 9, 80-89.

Frankfurter, D. (1994). "The Cult of the Martyrs in Egypt before Constantine: The Evidence of the Coptic *Apocalypse of Elijah*," *VigChr* 48, 25-47.

Frankfurter, D. (1998). "Introduction: Approaches to Coptic Pilgrimage," in: Frankfurter, D. (ed.) *Pilgrimage and Holy Space in Late Antique Egypt*. Leiden: Brill (= *Religions in the Graeco-Roman World* 134), 3-48.

Fournet, J.-L. and Gascou, J. (2001). "À propos de *PSI* IX 1061 descr.: Le nom du daunier et une formation méconnue d'anthroponymes féminins," *ZPE* 135, 139-149.

Funk, F. X., Bihlmeyer, K. und Witthaker, M. (1992). *Die apostolischen Väter. Neu übersetzt und herausgegeben von A. Lindenmann u. H. Paulsen*. Tübingen: Mohr.

Gerlitz, P., (1993). "Amulett. I. Religionswissenschaftlich," in: *LThK* 1 (3rd edn.), 568-569.

Grabar, A. (1958). *Ampoules de terre sainte*. Paris: Klincksieck.

Greshake, G. (1997). "Krankensalbung II. Historisch-theologisch," in: *LThK* 6 (3rd edn.), 419-422.

Grossmann, P. (1998). "The Pilgrimage Center of Abû Mînâ," in: Frankfurter, D. (ed.) *Pilgrimage and Holy Space in Late Antique Egypt*. Leiden etc: Brill (= *Religions in the Graeco-Roman World* 134), 281-302.

Haase, F. (1920). *Die koptischen Quellen zum Konzil von Nicäa*. Paderborn: Schöningh (*SGKA* X/4).

Hamp, V. (1962). "Ölbaum, Öl," in: *LThK* 7 (2nd edn.), 1138-1139.

Hartel, W. (1965). *S. Thasci Caecili Cypriani Opera omnia*. New York etc: Johnson (*CSEL* 3).

Heiler, F. (1937). *Urkirche und Ostkirche*. München: Reinhardt.

Hofmeister, P. (1948). *Die heiligen Öle in der morgen- und abendländischen Kirche*, Würzburg: Augustinus-Verlag (= *Das östliche Christentum* NF 6/7).

Holl, K. (1928). "Die Bedeutung der neuveröffentlichten melitianischen Urkunden für die Kirchengeschichte," in: Holl, K. (ed.) *Gesammelte Aufsätze zur Kirchengeschichte. II. Der Osten*. Tübingen: Mohr, 283-297.

Horak, U. (1999). "Schmuck," in: Henner, J., Förster, H. und Horak, U. (eds.) *Christliches mit Feder und Faden. Christliches in Texten, Textilien und Alltagsgegenständen aus Ägypten. Katalog zur Sonderausstellung im Papyrusmuseum der Österreichischen Nationalbibliothek aus Anlaß des 14. Internationalen Kongresses für Christliche Archäologie*. Wien: Österreichische Verlagsgesellschaft (= *Nilus* 3), 71-81.

Jördens, A. (2004). "Reliquien des Schenute im Frauenkonvent," in: Cowey, J. M. und Kramer, B. (eds.) *Paramone. Editionen und Aufsätze von Mitgliedern des Heidelberger Instituts für Papyrologie zwischen 1982 und 2004*. München: K.G. Saur (= *APF.B* 16), 142-156.

Kaszynski, R. (2001). "Krankensalbung. I. Katholizismus," in: *RGG* 4 (4th edn.), 1725-1726.

Knezevich, L. (1991). "Severus of Antioch," in: *The Coptic Encyclopedia* Bd. 7, 2123-2125.

Köpf, U. (2004). "Reliquien, Reliquienverehrung. 2. Alte Kirche bis Reformation," in: *RGG* 7 (4th edn.), 418-421.

Kranemann, B. (2001). "Wasser III. Liturgisch," in: *LThK* Bd. 10 (3rd edn.), 986-988.

Krause, M. (1998). "Heidentum, Gnosis und Manichäismus, ägyptische Survivals," in: Krause, M. (ed.) *Ägypten in spätantik-christlicher Zeit. Einführung in die koptische Kultur*. Wiesbaden: Reichert (= *Sprachen und Kulturen des christlichen Orients* 4), 81-116.

Krawiec, R. (2002). *Shenoute and the Women of the White Monastery. Egyptian Monasticism in Late Antiquity*, Oxford: Oxford university press.

Kügler, J. (2000). "Die Macht der Nase: Duftdeutungen und ihre psychophysiologischen Grundlagen," in: Kügler, J. (ed.), *Die Macht der Nase. Zur religiösen Bedeutung des Duftes. Religionsgeschichte—Bibel—Liturgie*. Stuttgart: Katholisches Bibelwerk (= *SBS* 187), 11-24.

Lampe, G. W. H. (1961). *A Patristic Greek Lexicon* (= 2000). Oxford: Oxford university press.

Layton, B. (2000). *A Coptic Grammar. With Chrestomathy and Glossary. Sahidic Dialect*. Wiesbaden: Harrassowitz (= *PLO* 20).

Mayerson, P. (2002). "Qualitative Distinctions for ἔλαιον (Oil) and ψωμίον (Bread)," *BASP* 39, 101-109.

Mitchell, L. L. (1966). *Baptismal Anointing*. London: S.P.C.K. (= *Alcuin Club Collections* 48).

Mitthof, F. (2006). "Das Lebensnotwendige: Grundnahrungsmittel, Rationen, Preise", in: Froschauer, H. und Römer, C. (Hgg.), *Mit den Griechen zu Tisch in Ägypten*, Wien: Phoibos (= *Nilus* 12), 21-28.

Morelli, F. (1996). *Olio e retribuzioni nell'Egitto tardo (V-VIII d. C.)*. Firenze: Istituto Papirologico "G. Vitelli."

Papaconstantinou, A. (2001). *Le culte des saints en Égypte des Byzantines aux Abbassides. L'apport des inscriptions et des papyrus grecs et coptes*. Paris: CNRS.

Papaconstantinou, A. (2004). "'Je suis noire, mais belle': Le double langage de la *vie de Théodora d'Alexandrie, alias* Abba Thédore," in: *Lalies* 24, 63-86.

Pease, A. S. (1937). "Ölbaum IX. Medizinische Verwendung," in: *RE* 17/2, 2013-2014.

Pfister, (1917). "Amulett," in: Hoffmann-Krayer, E. und Bächtold-Stäubli, H. (eds.) *Handwörterbuch des deutschen Aberglaubens*. Bd. 1, 374-384.

Plisch, U. K. (1999). *Einführung in die koptische Sprache. Sahidischer Dialekt*. Wiesbaden: Reichert (*Sprachen und Kulturen des christlichen Orients* 5).

Reymond, E. A. E. und Barns, J. W. B. (1973). *Four Martyrdoms from the Pierpont Morgan Coptic Codices*. Oxford: Clarendon Press.

Roca-Puig, R. (1999). *Anàfora de Barcelona. I Altres pregàries (Missa del segle IV)*. Barcelona: Roca-Puig.

Roetzer, W. (1930). *Des heiligen Augustinus Schriften als liturgie-geschichtliche Quelle. Eine liturgie-geschichtliche Studie*. München: Huber.

Ruppert, H. J. (1991). "Magie IV. Praktisch-theologisch," in: *TRE* Bd. 21, 701-703.

Sandy, D. B. (1989). *The Production and Use of Vegetable Oils in Ptolemaic Egypt*. Atlanta: Scholars Press (= *BASP Suppl.* 6).

Scharbert, J. (1990). "Krankheit II. Altes Testament," in: *TRE* Bd. 19, 680-683.

Schiller, A. (1932). "Koptisches Recht. Eine Studie auf Grund der Quellen und Abhandlungen", *Kritische Vierteljahresschrift für Gesetzgebung und Rechtswissenschaft* 3. Folge Bd. 25 (= 61 der ganzen Reihe), 250-296.

Schmelz, G. (2002). *Kirchliche Amtsträger im spätantiken Ägypten nach den Aussagen der griechischen und koptischen Papyri und Ostraka*. München/Leipzig: K.G. Saur (= *APF*.B 13).

Schmidt, C. (1925). "Das koptische Didache-Fragment des British Museum," *ZNTW* 24, 81-99.

Schmitz, A. L. (1930). "Das Totenwesen der Kopten. Kritische Übersicht über die literarischen und monumentalen Quellen," *ZÄS* 65, 1-25.

Schöllgen, G. und Geerlings, W. (1991). *Zwölf-Apostel-Lehre. Apostolische Überlieferung. Lateinisch, Griechisch, Deutsch*. Freiburg etc: Herder (= *Fontes Christiani* 1).

Stadler (1907). "Essig," in: *RE* 11/1, 689-692.

Staubli, T. (2003). "Öl/Ölbaum," in: *RGG* 6 (4th edn.), 541.

Suttner, E.Chr. (1975). "Die Krankensalbung, 'das Öl des Gebetes' in den altorientalischen Kirchen," *Ephemerides liturgicae* 89, 371-396.

Synek, E.M. (1994). *Heilige Frauen der frühen Christenheit. Zu den Frauenbildern in hagiographischen Texten des christlichen Ostens*. Würzburg: Augustinus-Verlag (= *ÖC* 43).

Till, W. C. (1941). "Die Coptica der Wiener Papyrussammlung," *ZDMG* 95, 195-218.

Till, W. C. (1951). *Die Arzneikunde der Kopten*, Berlin: Akademie-Verlag.

Torrance, I. R. (2000). "Severus von Antiochien," in: *TRE* 31, 184-186.

Vorgrimler, H. (1978). *Handbuch der Dogmengeschichte IV/3: Buße und Krankensalbung*. Freiburg etc: Herder.

Vorgrimler, H. (1990). "Krankensalbung," in: *TRE* Bd. 19, 664-669.

Vries, W.de (1940). *Sakramententheologie bei den syrischen Monophysiten*. Rom: Pont. Institutum Orientalium studiorum (= *OCA* 125).

Wilfong, T. (2002). *Women of Jeme. Lives in a Coptic Town in Late Antique Egypt*, Ann Arbor: University of Michigan Press, (*New Texts from Ancient Cultures*).

Witt, J. (2000). *Werke der Alltagskultur. Teil 1: Menasampullen,* Staatliche Museen zu Berlin — Preußischer Kulturbesitz Skulpturensammlung und Museum für Byzantinische Kunst Bestandskataloge 2, Wiesbaden (*Spätantike—Frühes Christentum—Byzanz. Kunst im ersten Jahrtausend Reihe A: Grundlagen und Monumente Bd. 2.1*).

Zandee, J. (1960). *Death as an Enemy According to Ancient Egyptian Conceptions*. Leiden: Brill (= *SHR* 5).

P.CLACKSON 45-46

A MID-EIGHTH-CENTURY TRILINGUAL TAX DEMAND RELATED TO THE MONASTERY OF APA APOLLO AT BAWIT

PETRA M. SIJPESTEIJN AND SARAH CLACKSON[1]

The papyrus document that is the focus of this paper has a special place in the administrative history of Egypt's early Islamic period, illustrating the close parallelism that marked the usage of Egypt's three languages at this time, as well as the social and political interdependence that this parallelism reflects. Through it we see how the spread of Arabic was negotiated in the face of deeply embedded pre-existing linguistic traditions and the role played by innovations in administrative policy—and the tax structure in particular—in guiding this negotiation.

I am especially pleased to present it here in Sarah's memory as it was during my first visit to Cambridge more than ten years ago, when I first met Sarah, that she took me to the University Library to read it together.

1. *P.CLACKSON* 45 (P.CAMB.UL MICHAEL. 807)[2]

In Jumādā II 136/December 753, the Arab pagarch of the Upper Ashmūn (Hermopolite nome), Hishām b. Ziyād, issued an *entagion*, or tax demand-note, to one Ioannes son of Isidoros (Yuḥannis b. Isīdūr) of the monastery of Apa Apollo at Bawīṭ.[3] The *entagion* was written, strikingly, in two languages: Arabic and Coptic—the only example extant of a bilingual *entagion*. A Greek note was added to the top, probably referring to the payment having been made, adding a third language to the document. The note informs Ioannes that he has to pay two gold coins (l. 6 *dīnārayn?*; l. 16 *nomismata* 2) as his poll-tax assessment (l. 5 *jizyat raʾsika*) for the *hijra* year 136 (753 C.E.) (ll. 5-6, 16; l. 16 indiction 8). Ioannes is instructed to pay his tax to the local tax-collector (l. 6 *qubbāl qaryatika*; l. 17 *pboethos npektime*) in six instalments (l. 7 *sittat aṭbāl*; l. 17 *nco kataboule*). In conclusion the pagarch recommends that Ioannes obtain a receipt from the tax-collector (ll. 7, 18) and not pay more than the amount stated in his *entagion*. If the collector deviates from these prescriptions, Ioannes is not to pay him anything, but is to come to the pagarch (ll. 9-11; 21-22). Although the text follows the structure

---

[1] The information in this paper relies heavily on Sarah's notes and the edition and paper she prepared for the first International Society for Arabic Papyrology conference in Cairo in March 2001. I have in general refrained from indicating which individual phrases are based on Sarah's work and which on my own, except in the edition of the Greek and Coptic part of the text, which was prepared by Sarah, where I have indicated (in the commentary) at which points I deviated from her reading or translation. I should also like to thank Nikolaos Gonis for his comments on a draft of this article.

[2] *P.Clackson* 45 (P.Camb. UL Michael. 807) was among the papyri purchased by the University Library of Cambridge University in May and October 1977 from the manuscript collection of George Michaelides (Bierbier 1995: 286) together with a large collection of texts written in Hieratic, Demotic, Coptic, Greek, Latin, Arabic, Persian and Turkish. Texts from this collection are now also in the collections of the British Library and in the Palau-Ribes Collection (Clackson 1993 and 1994).

[3] For this monastery and the documents related to it, see *P.Mon.Apollo* and *P.Brux.Bawit*.

and uses the formulae of contemporary tax demand-notes, it also displays some extraordinary features which require comment. The verso of this papyrus was used for a later Greek tax-receipt whose edition appears as *P.Clackson* **46**.

P.Clackson **45**'s most salient feature, and the one which immediately marks it as highly unusual, is the three languages used. Bilingual Greek-Arabic tax demand-notes and other tax-related documents issued to village communities are attested from the time of the Arab conquest of Egypt. One of the first Arabic papyri, dated 22/643, was written in Greek and Arabic. It is a receipt for the delivery of sixty-five sheep to an Arab army unit by the Heracleopolite nome.[4] At this early time, when Arabic-speakers were few and far between in the Egyptian countryside, the use of both the conquerors' language and that of their indigenous administrators was necessary if both parties were to understand the transaction, and this practice continued in the central chancellery into the early eighth century as the documents from the archive of Basilios, the pagarch of Aphrodito, indicate.[5] Tax demand-notes for individual tax-payers, on the other hand, were written in the pagarchies for local consumption only and these were written entirely in Greek or Coptic.[6] Similarly, eighth-century tax demand-notes issued to other members of the Apa Apollo monastery were all written in Coptic only.[7]

This is not to say that the Arabic and Coptic of our text are exact translations of one another. A first difference is that of the name of the pagarch issuing the *entagion*. While the official is named Hishām b. Ziyād in the Arabic part of the text, the official seems to be described by his only partially read, *kunya*, in the Coptic part of the text, followed by the same patronymic. In the first five to six lines the differences between the two texts are minimal and largely attributable to the two different scribal traditions, each imposing the use of its own technical formulae. In the final part of the text, however, the deviations become more striking, even though the sense of the text remains the same. In the Arabic Ioannes is told to come to the pagarch if he does not manage to obtain a receipt from the collector; the Coptic, on the other hand, says that he should do so if the collector demands from him more than that stipulated in his *entagion*. Other lines (ll. 11, 19) also appear in one of the two texts only. Finally, only the Arabic mentions the name of the scribe and date the document was written, while the Coptic ends with the formula that the current *entagion* was written up as evidence for Ioannes.

P.Clackson **45**'s second remarkable feature is its sheer length, and especially the pagarch's extensive recommendations to safeguard Ioannes the tax-payer from abuse by the *boethos/qubbāl*. First of all, not only is Ioannes told to obtain a receipt for his payment sealed by the *boethos* and instructed not to pay more than the *entagion* demands, but the Arabic goes on to say that if the *qubbāl* refuses to give Ioannes a receipt, he should withhold payment altogether and come to the pagarch so that he might deal with the matter. The Coptic, on the other hand, states that if the *boethos* asks for anything more than what is required by the *entagion*, Ioannes should similarly approach the pagarch. The Coptic ends by saying that the *entagion* is written to inform Ioannes of these things. These benevolent admonitions of the pagarch's reflect a relatively well-established formulaic practice, and appear either singly or severally in ten eighth-century documents and all together in one Greek and one Coptic poll-

---

[4] *SB* VI 9576. The other Arabic papyrus, also dated 22/643, is the end of a tax demand-note for money taxes to be paid in *dīnārs* (unpublished; cf. Grohmann 1966: Tafel II) which might very well have been preceded by a Greek part.

[5] E.g. *P.Lond.* IV; *P.Heid.Arab.* I; Becker 1906.

[6] The first Arabic tax demand-note for an individual Christian tax-payer is dated 134/752, two years before our papyrus (*P.Cair.Arab.* III 169).

[7] *P.Mon.Apollo*, p. 42.

tax demand-note, the former written two years earlier in the Heracleopolite nome.[8] One Arabic tax demand-note also written two years earlier in Ashmūnayn uses three of the formulae with very close linguistic parallelism to our text.[9]

At first sight there does not seem to be any internal reason for the use of two languages, nor for such extensive instructions. So let us consider the external factors—Egypt's mid-eighth-century economic situation—to see whether it can help us explain the form of the papyrus.

2. The Early Muslim Fiscal Context

Immediately following the Muslim conquest of Egypt in 642 C.E. the fiscal and administrative system remained virtually unchanged, staffed in many cases by the same officials who had served under the Byzantines. Only at the highest levels in Fusṭāṭ did Arabs enter the administration, and even here an extensive community of Byzantine-trained scribes and officials continued to perform the basic functions of government. Further down the administrative hierarchy, pagarchs and *duces* continued to be chosen from among the land-owning indigenous élite,[10] and the system of imposts and tax collections continued more or less unchanged.

Acting on a mixture of financial and ideological motivations, the caliph 'Abd al-Malik (r. 65-86/685-705) instituted significant adjustments to the administrative organisation of the Islamic Empire. His governor 'Abd al-'Azīz (in office 65-86/685-705) was responsible for implementing these changes in Egypt. Starting at the end of the eighth century C.E. a series of administrative reforms took place which resulted in greater Arab participation at the lower levels of the administration and closer scrutiny of Egyptian tax-payers. It is around this time that Arabs start to replace Christian pagarchs and *duces*.[11] The Muslim pagarchs seem to have deviated in one important respect from their predecessors: no longer belonging to the traditional land-based Egyptian élite, they were not tied to the land they governed through private estates, but instead moved through different regional posts during their administrative careers.[12]

These reforms resulted in improved registration and supervision of tax-payers and their dues. The first land surveys and censuses took place under 'Ubayd Allāh b. al-Ḥabḥāb (in office 107-16/725-34).[13] Safe-conduct guarantees, neck seals and other measures tracked tax-payers and limited their movements,[14] while forced land assignments[15] and land development programs increased the agricultural acreage available.[16] Perhaps not surprisingly, the first Coptic revolts and signs of economic

---

[8] *CPR* XXII 7; *BKU* III 340.

[9] *P.Cair.Arab.* III 169. See below note 80.

[10] For administrative changes taking place in the first fifty years of Muslim rule, see Sijpesteijn 2007a and idem 2007b.

[11] Kindī, *Wulāt*: 69.

[12] Sijpesteijn 2004: 64-65.

[13] Abbott 1965; *CPR* XXII 3 introduction; Maqrīzī, *Khiṭaṭ*: I 201, 266; *History of the Patriarchs*: 74-75.

[14] Robinson 2005; Rāghib 1997.

[15] Morelli 2000.

[16] See for example Qurra b. Sharīk's draining of Birkat al-Ḥabash (Maqrīzī, *Khiṭaṭ*: II 49, 86).

stress in the papyri date to the end of the seventh century[17] and fugitive peasants start to appear in the papyri in large numbers in early eighth-century documents.[18]

It is in this period too that monks were taxed for the first time, the governor 'Abd al-'Azīz' son and financial director, al-Asbagh (in office 74-86/693-4-705), having allegedly removed the tax-exempt status from the monasteries, which had been in place in Egypt since Justinian's ruling.[19] Papyrus documents from the eighth century show monasteries and monks being subject to the same impositions recorded in the same kind of documents as other Egyptian tax-payers. In an unpublished Arabic papyrus letter someone is asked for "the names of the inhabitants of the monastery of Suyūṭ in the Fayyūm" in relation to the fiscal records in Fusṭāṭ,[20] and tax demand-notes and tax receipts for monks are preserved in large numbers.[21] This development coincided with the replacement of Christian pagarchs by Muslim ones, and while this change did not take place everywhere at the same pace, all surviving tax demand-notes for monasteries and individuals associated with monasteries were issued in the name of Muslim pagarchs.[22]

Monasteries were treated as tax collectivities at the same level as village communities. This meant that the pagarch sent tax demand-notes for the total taxes due to each monastery as a fiscal unity. The monastery then divided the total among the individuals under its responsibility, and the collection and delivery of these payments to the Muslim authorities were administered by the monastery.

These reforms, however, were enacted against the backdrop of the political turmoil of the late Umayyad period, and as tensions between those sympathetic to the old regime and those supporting the Abbasid revolutionaries escalated, Egypt began to feel the pressure of the conflict. When, in a last desperate attempt to withstand the Abbasid armies, the Umayyad caliph Marwān II (r. 127-32/744-50) tried to take control of Egypt after fleeing Damascus, the fighting came to Egypt proper, with Copts and Arabs rising in revolt against the Umayyads.[23] After the Abbasid victory in 132/750, resulting in the Umayyads' ejection and the relocation of the caliphal seat from Damascus to Baghdad, Abbasid troops took control of Egypt and the last Umayyad caliph was killed together with many of his supporters in the Upper Egyptian village of Buṣīr.[24] How these events influenced the daily life of Egyptian tax-payers is difficult to determine, but the Abbasid takeover, interestingly, has left no direct traces in the papyri. Egypt's governors continued to be appointed from outside Egypt, the only difference now being that their loyalties were owed to—just as their backgrounds lay with—the Abbasid court in Baghdad. Lower Muslim officials in Fusṭāṭ, on the other hand, continued to be chosen from among the local Muslim élite.[25]

---

[17] *SB* III 7240, dated 697; provenance Thebes (for the date, see Gascou and Worp 1982); Kindī, *Wulāt*: 74; *History of the Patriarchs*: 76.

[18] But already appearing earlier as in *P.Apoll*. 13 (676 or 661. For the date, see Gascou and Worp 1982). For eighth-century evidence, see *P.Lond*. IV 1332; 1333 (both 708); 1338, 1339; 1343 (all 709); *CPR* XXII 35 (750-69?); 36 (8th century); Diem 1984, text 10 (2nd/8th century).

[19] *History of the Patriarchs*: 50-1; Morimoto 1981: 114-115.

[20] P.Vindob. A 546 (8th century).

[21] *P.Bal*.; *P.Mon.Apollo*; *P.Mon.Epiph*. I, 177; *P.Lond*. IV, p. xvi.

[22] E.g. *P.Mon.Apollo* 28; *P.Bal*. 130.

[23] Kindī, *Wulāt*: 94, 95, 96; *History of the Patriarchs*: 156-157, 159-60, 162.

[24] Ṭabarī, *Ta'rīkh*: III 49-50; Kindī, *Wulāt*: 94-7; *History of the Patriarchs*: 134, 150-187.

[25] Kennedy 1998: 76-77. The pagarch Yaḥyā b. Hilāl continued to be in office after the Abbasid take-over (Gonis 2004b: 189-92).

The new governors continued the reforming policy of their predecessors. The late seventh and early eighth-century reforms in the administration and taxation system as described above and their by-products continued to affect Egyptian society into the second half of the eighth century. Fugitives continued to roam the Egyptian countryside,[26] and while the last safe-conduct guarantee was issued in 133/751-2, other kinds of documents took their place to track tax-payers throughout the country (see below). Coptic tax revolts protesting the increased rigor and effectiveness of Muslim taxation continued to erupt throughout the late Umayyad period—for example in 121/738 in Upper Egypt[27] and in 132/749 in Lower Egypt[28]—and into the Abbasid period in 135/752,[29] 150/767 and 156/772.[30]

The revolts immediately following the Abbasid takeover suggest that the new Abbasid governors implemented reforms in the taxation structure that resulted in heightened pressure on the indigenous population. The *History of the Patriarchs* reports that the Abbasid governor Abū 'Awn 'Abd Al-Malik b. Yazīd (in office 133-6/751-3 and 137-41/755-8), the governor mentioned in **45**, was forced to redesign the fiscal system in Egypt after the Umayyads had burnt all records at their defeat. His "doubling of the taxes" and introduction of new levies can also be taken as evidence of the Abbasid reform programme.[31]

No discussion of the specifics of these reforms appears in the literary sources, but the papyri do bear witness to some changes having taken place, although it remains difficult to determine the exact moment at which these took place, what caused them and the extent at which they were applied throughout Egypt. First, collective fiscal responsibility, in which villages and other communities received a demand-note for their total taxes due and were responsible for parcelling out liability to their members, began to be abandoned in favour of a system in which (some) individual tax-payers became directly responsible to the Muslim authorities for their tax payments, receiving their tax demand-notes and receipts directly from representatives of the Muslim authorities. Tax demand-notes in the name of pagarchs addressed to individual tax-payers, such as our papyrus, were all issued by *Muslim* pagarchs;[32] the first dated (Greek) tax receipt made out to an individual in the name of a

---

[26] *CPR* XXI, pp. 40-8. See also on the development of tax-farming in late-eighth-century Egypt which coincided with the disappearance of fugitives from the sources, Sijpesteijn 2001.

[27] Kindī, *Wulāt:* 81; *History of the Patriarchs:* 94-95.

[28] Kindī, *Wulāt:* 94.

[29] Kindī, *Wulāt:* 102.

[30] Kindī: 116-117, 119—all in Lower Egypt.

[31] *History of the Patriarchs:* 187, 190. See also Morimoto 1981: 172-173.

[32] E.g. Greek and Coptic receipts issued by Yazīd b. 'Abd al-Raḥmān *P.Ryl.Copt.* 117; *BKU* III 418; Yazīd b. Sa'īd *P.Ryl.Copt.* 118; fulān b. 'Abd al-Raḥmān *P.Ryl.Copt.* 119; Rāshid b. Khālid *BKU* III 339, 417; Nājid b. Muslim *CPR* XXII 8-10; 'Abd al-Malik b. Yazīd *CPR* XXII 7; Ibrāhīm b. Yaḥyā *CPR* XXII 13. I know of only two examples of *entagia* for individual tax-payers issued in the name of a Christian pagarch. Bell knew of only one non-Arab (pagarch), namely a certain *Paulos huios ...* writing an *entagion* to an individual tax-payer (*SPP* VIII 1180, dating from the eighth century, provenance Ihnās/Heracleopolite nome) (1945, 536). The second *entagion* (*SPP* VIII 1082) was sent to one or two tax-payers also in the Heracleopolite nome. It was re-edited by Gonis and Morelli (2000, the other *entagia* issued by Christian pagarchs they mention at the bottom of page 194 are irrelevant as these are not *entagia* for individual tax-payers). Rémondon mentions a third one written by the pagarch Petterios in the Arsinoite but this one was not for a single tax-payer (*SPP* VIII 1190. 1952, 260).

Muslim official is dated 714[33] and the first Arabic one dates from 148/765.[34] How these Muslim officials, and their responsibilities, related to the Coptic village headmen remains, however, to be determined.

Another change seems to be related to the introduction of the direct fiscal responsibility and communication between the pagarch and individual tax-payers. Some Abbasid tax receipts (*bara'āt*) contain formulae allowing their holders to travel freely, phrases which before that time appeared in safe-conduct guarantees.[35] With the tax receipts issued directly by the pagarchs rather than by local indigenous tax-collectors, the writing of separate safe-conducts in the pagarch's chancellery had become redundant. The emphasis on obtaining a receipt in our papyrus might be related to this change.

Let us then return to **45** to see how this system worked at Bawīṭ and how these changes are represented in our text.

3. RECONSTRUCTION

Ioannes was taxed for his yearly poll-tax as a member of the Apa Apollo monastery, but for some reason he received an individual tax demand-note directly from the Muslim pagarch. There is no reason to assume that Ioannes was not also liable for his taxes to the monastery, which remained responsible for the tax collection and the transfer of the accumulated taxes in one lump sum to the Muslim authorities, while probably also standing guarantor for the total amount of taxes for which the monastery was liable. Whether all individual tax-payers received their own tax demand-notes in the name of the pagarch is doubtful; there are simply not enough of such individual tax demand-notes preserved to support this. The monastery's responsibility extended beyond its own community and included nearby villages and other areas, as can be concluded from the tax payments made to the monastery.[36] While Ioannes was clearly associated with the monastery, he was not necessarily a monk, and might have been living in any one of the villages or estates falling under the monastery's financial control.

The function of the monastery as an intermediary between the tax-payers and the Muslim authorities streamlined tax payments in several ways. The monastery provided loans to individuals to pay their taxes[37] and exempted certain members from tax payments,[38] or allowed them to defer payments.[39] Several tax receipts for individual tax-payers show that the monastery also functioned as a goods-for-money exchange, accepting material goods and services in lieu of payments in coin.[40] The monastery

---

[33] Gonis 2001b: 226-7. For later examples see *CPR* XXI, p. 64. An undated seventh century Greek tax-receipt was made out in the name of Sulaymān and is the first tax-receipt made out by a representative of the Muslim administration at the village level (Gonis 2001b: 228).

[34] *P.Cair.Arab.* III 197.

[35] Rāghib 1997: 147 n. 39.

[36] Clackson 2008: introduction.

[37] *P.Mon.Apollo*, p. 26; text 38.

[38] Clackson 2008: texts 3, 5, 9, 10.

[39] Clackson 2008: texts 11.

[40] Clackson 2008: texts 1, 4, 12, 14, 15; Husselman 1951: 337-338.

was probably also responsible for issuing individual tax demand-notes in the name of the pagarch for the different yearly tax instalments.[41]

Papyri related to the monastery of Apa Apollo contain more specific information about the monks responsible for the collection of the poll-tax. The so-called "brothers of the poll-tax" (ⲚⲈⲤⲚⲎⲨ ⲘⲠⲀⲚⲀⲢⲒⲤⲘⲞⲤ), who appear in many of these documents, seem to have been responsible for the assignment and collection of the poll-tax in the communities that fell under the monastery's financial jurisdiction and for related record-keeping.[42] These "brothers of the poll-tax" committed themselves to collect and deliver the taxes for a certain village or area to the monastery.[43] "The collector of your village" mentioned in the Arabic and Coptic of our papyrus was obviously responsible for the actual collection of the taxes imposed on individual tax-payers by the monastery and probably worked for the monastery, perhaps as one of the "brothers of the poll-tax."[44] Contemporary tax receipts for tax payments made by monasteries mention *boethoi* and other financial officials associated with the monastery,[45] and tax receipts from Bawīṭ for individuals were given out by such monastery officials.[46] The Arabic papyri show that a similar pattern was in place in the southern Fayyūm at this time, with members of the local élite being responsible for the tax collection *and* standing guarantor for the total amount of taxes due in specific villages.[47] This system with local intermediaries who were responsible for the collection of taxes and the delivery of the total tax liability to the authorities continued into the eighth century, as can be concluded from the absence of any individual tax receipt issued by a Muslim official securely datable before the first quarter of the eighth century.[48]

What do the extensive formulae instructing Ioannes how to protect himself from abuse by the tax-collector tell us about the relationship between tax-payers and collectors at this time? Some of the same formulae—urging the tax payer (1) to obtain a receipt for his payment, (2) not to pay any more than that required of him in the demand-note, and (3) to come to the pagarch if he encounters any problems from the local tax-collector—appear in three Greek, six Coptic and one Arabic mid- and late-eighth-century tax demand-notes. Seven of these notes were for the poll-tax (*andrismos/diagraphon/jizya*),[49] combined in three cases with the *dapane*,[50] and in one with the *dapane*

---

[41] These tax demand-notes, although written in the name of the pagarch and produced at the pagarchy's chancellery, seem to have been completed with the names of individual tax-payers and the amounts due at the village level (Bell 1945). See also Gonis (forthcoming), text 13.

[42] Clackson 2008: texts 1, 4, 5, 9, 11, 14, 25.

[43] Clackson 2008.

[44] See also Patermoute who was *meizōn and hypodektes* of the *epoikion* of Apa Pinoution in C.E. 708 or 709 (*P.Lond.* IV 1570.1, 9) and Johannes and Mena who signed tax-receipts as priest *and boethos* at Bala'izah (*P.Bal.* 136; 133; 145).

[45] *Boethoi* e.g. in *P.Bal.* 135; 136; 146; 147; 149; 151. Other officials e.g. in *P.Ryl.Copt.* 125.

[46] Keri, who seems to have headed the monastery of Apa Apollo for two years, orders the 'brothers of the poll-tax' to give poll-tax receipts to individual tax-payers (Clackson 2008: texts 1, 4, 6 and I.11).

[47] Sijpesteijn 2004. Between the pagarch and the individual tax-payers stood a Muslim administrator whose responsibility extended over an area in the southern Fayyūm encompassing several villages. This official informed individual tax-payers of their dues, arranged for members of the local élite to stand guarantor and be responsible for the tax collection, and supervised Muslim tax-collectors who recorded the delivery of taxes at the central collection posts.

[48] See above notes 33 and 34. But the Muslim Maymūn b. Rāshid still paid his taxes to the Christian *māzūt* Shenūda in 156/772 (David-Weill 1971: text XVI).

[49] *BKU* III 340; *CPR* XXII 7 (134/751-2); *P.Cair.Arab.* III 169 (134/752).

[50] *P.Bal.* 130 Appendix (105/723-4, from Jeme); *P.Ryl.Copt.* 119.

and *embole* taxes.[51] Two further papyri demand a *demosion* payment, which might have included the poll-tax.[52] And finally, a Greek demand-note for an individual tax-payer of the Heracleopolite *nome* is for the wheat taxes.[53] Where specified, the taxes are to be paid to a tax-collector called a (*chryso*)*hypodektes* in the Greek documents, *boethos* in the Coptic, and *qubbāl* in the Arabic.

The closest parallels to **45** come from a Coptic poll-tax demand-note of unknown origin and date, an Arabic tax demand-note issued in the same Upper Ashmūn pagarchy and a Greek tax demand-note issued in the Heracleopolite pagarchy, both dated to two years earlier than our document.[54] The Arabic document is a poll-tax demand-note for the entire year; the Greek and the Coptic ones are also only for the poll-tax (*diagraphon*). This suggests that, rather than indicating that Ioannes in particular was in need of special protection, the formulae used at the end of our document were technical expressions used especially in tax demand-notes that informed tax-payers of their total of the yearly tax burden and issued in the pagarchy's chancellery, for which the first evidence is dated two years after the Abbasid revolution. This is exactly the year that the Abbasid governor Abū al-'Awn is said to have started his tax reforms, two years after a period of relative light tax-burdens for the indigenous population under the first Abbasid governor Ṣāliḥ b. 'Alī (in office 132-3/750-1).[55] Shorter, smaller tax demand-notes for separate instalments, which were not written in the pagarch's chancellery, but occasionally issued in his name, contained only some or none of the formulae. These formulae, introduced around the same time that individual tax-payers were made directly responsibility to the Muslim authorities for their tax payments, might well have been expressions of the same desire to check and diminish the role of regional middle-men, who, as members of the local élite, had hitherto been responsible for the collection of taxes in the countryside. On the other hand attestations of conflicts between local tax-payers and Muslim tax-collectors increase in this period, suggesting that there might in general have been a need to protect individual tax-payers against abuse from tax-collectors once the buffer between individual tax-payers and the fisc, in the form of Christian Egyptian middlemen, had disappeared. As mentioned above, these changes did not take place everywhere at the same time, nor where they applied uniformally in all of Egypt. But the more frequent appearance of tax-receipts issued by Muslim officials to individual tax-payers,[56] coincides with the first appearance of the more extensive tax-demandnotes in the 720's.

Another source informs us of other ways of redress open to Egyptian tax-payers in Upper Egypt. The only other known trilingual Coptic-Greek-Arabic papyrus was written in the Upper Egyptian town of Akhmīm (Panopolis) a few years after our papyrus between 137/754 and 140/757.[57] It records the statement made by some seventy men from the pagarchy of Akhmīm on the order of the Muslim pagarch. The men testify to having withdrawn a complaint against a Muslim tax-collector and his staff, affirming that they were not treated unjustly by him and agreeing that should any of them raise a complaint against the tax-collector in the future he will be liable to a fine.[58]

---

[51] *P.Bal.* 130 = Gonis 2004a (105/723-4?).

[52] *P.Mon.Apollo* 29, 30 (both mid-8th century).

[53] *SPP* VIII 1195 (104/723).

[54] *CPR* XXII 7; *P.Cair.Arab.* III 169.

[55] Kindī, *Wulāt*: 101; *History of the Patriarchs*: 188-9; Morimoto 1981: 148-149.

[56] See above, n. 33.

[57] *P.Cair.Arab.* III 167. For the date see *P.Cair.Arab.* IV p. 251 and Guest 1923.

[58] For other examples, see Sijpesteijn (forthcoming).

No revolts are reported in Upper Egypt between 135/752 and 150/767, and in general **45** was written in what seems to have been a relatively calm period. This might suggest that these measures to protect tax-payers against collectors were effective. Papyri from other areas in Egypt confirm that this period was one of administrative reforms leading to increased Muslim penetration of the administrative and economic organisation of the province. The Muslim state increased its presence in the administration by concentrating power in the hands of the Muslim pagarchs at the expense of local notables.

The use of Arabic in **45** can similarly be explained as an expression of administrative changes, namely the increased use of Arabic at lower levels in the administration over time. The Arab conquest in 642 C.E. brought not only a new religious but also a new linguistic rule to Egypt. Where Arabs interacted with Egyptians Arabic or partially Arabic documents appear. The first bilingual Arabic-Greek and Arabic papyri, written in the year of the conquest of Egypt, indicate that Arabic was used both in *ad hoc* communications with the conquered population as well as in documents related to the regularly collected taxes. In general, however, in the eighth century the presence of Arabs in the countryside was minimal and the papyri show in fact a remarkable continuity of daily life for individual Egyptians and little direct interaction with Muslim authorities. Arabic was used by the central chancellery in Fusṭāṭ to communicate with lower administrative officials, which explains the presence of Arabic papyri found in Upper Egyptian archives such as that of Basilios in Aphrodito/Ishqaw.

The pre-Islamic languages of Egypt, Coptic and Greek, continued of course to be used after the conquest. There was no mass exodus of Egyptians, including those who spoke Greek, forced to leave or emigrating on their own account. Greek continued to exist as a written and spoken language throughout Egypt, but the majority of Egyptians used Coptic as their main or only language of communication and, generally speaking, Greek had made less of an impact in Upper Egypt than in the areas closer to the administrative centre in the Delta and other areas of Lower Egypt. Greek continued to be a living part of the Muslim administration at the higher levels of the administration and in those areas where Greek had become widespread in the pre-Islamic period into the eighth century C.E.

As in the pre-Islamic period Coptic was most important in the administration at the village level, but in the Islamic period Coptic started to be used also for some documents at the level of the pagarchy, where Greek would have generally been used in the pre-Islamic period. When Greek lost its status as the language of Egypt's rulers, it was not Arabic, but Coptic, that benefited at the lower level of the society, extending from private use into that of the lower administration. This effect was more prominent in Upper Egypt where Greek had not made such a lasting impact and where Arabic had not yet made much of an impression either.

P.Clackson **45** primarily written in Arabic and Coptic fits these general observations well. Slowly, but surely the use of Arabic increased in the administration of the pagarchy with the arrival of Muslim pagarchs. The report preserved in literary sources that the governor 'Abd Allāh b. 'Abd al-Malik changed the language of the *dīwān* in Egypt from Greek or Coptic into Arabic in 87/705-6 signifies less an absolute change rather than the beginning of a move towards increased use of Arabic.[59] The text of **45** was written in both Arabic and Coptic. The Arabic is the first and thereby the most prominent part representing the presence of a new ruling power in Egypt that communicated in a new language. The Coptic text was still an essential part of the document. In fact, while a similar document

---

[59] Kindī, *Wulāt* 58-59; Ibn 'Abd al-Ḥakam *Futūḥ Miṣr*, 122.

from the pagarchy's chancellery would probably have been written in Greek in the pre-Islamic period, it was now written in Coptic. Coptic had been the most important language of administration in Upper Egyptian monastic and village communities, and its use extended in the Islamic period into the pagarchy's chancellery. From the same pagarchy where our papyrus originated, however, comes the first entirely Arabic tax demand-note for an individual Christian tax-payer, dated only a couple of years before **45**.

As with so many seemingly insignificant everyday documents, Ioannes' tax demand-note, from its very personal, small-scale vantage point, nevertheless offers some valuable insights into important transformations in the early Abbasid fiscal administration of Egypt. With the coming of Muslim pagarchs at the beginning of the eighth century C.E., not only the language, but the structure of the financial administration changed drastically. This new cadre of Muslim pagarchs, coming from non-landed backgrounds, were now professional bureaucrats, sent out by the central authorities to bring the administrative system under more direct Muslim control. At least initially, however, they remained dependent on the network of indigenous, local notables who continued to be responsible for the collection and delivery of taxes, overseeing the collection process itself and standing guarantor for its full payment. But as the government's push to deal directly with its tax-payers gathered momentum in the early Abbasid period, even this role was diminished. *P.Clackson* **45** shows all these processes in action.

P.Camb.UL Michael. 807 (A)   26 x 18 cm   Jumādā II 136/December 753
Plate XIX   Provenance unknown

A light brown papyrus with some worm holes and abrasions where upper-layer fibres have been worn away. A complete document is preserved on side (A) of the papyrus, although the left-hand side of the text is illegible in places. The text consists of 22 lines in three different languages: Greek 1 line (l. 1), Arabic 11 lines (ll. 2-12), and Coptic 10 lines (ll. 13-22); they are written with black ink perpendicular to the fibres. Side (B) was reused for a Greek receipt dated three years later, which is edited in an appendix.[60]

The Arabic has few diacritical dots, and *hamza* is absent following documentary practice. *Sīn* is written with three teeth. Some letters show characteristics of early script, such as *dāl* with a rightward bend at the top (l. 5 *dayr*) and *'ayn* with an extended horizontal line to the right (l. 5 *a'lā*; l. 9 *ghayruhu*, *'anka*; l. 11 *'indahu*, *'alā*). There is little space between letters and words.

1   ± 4 . μ( ) αν^υ ἰνδ(ικτίονος)?

2   بسم الله الرحمن الرحيم

3   هذا كتا[ب] من هشام بن ز[ياد] عامل [الا]مير [عب]ـد الملك بن يزيد على [اعلى] اشمون

4   ليحنس ابن [ا]سدور.(vac.)

5   من اهل دير ابو ابلوا من اعلى اشمون انه اصابك من جزية [ر]اسك لسنـ[ـة]

---

[60] The Coptic of this text was originally edited by Sarah Clackson; I have added the Arabic and Greek. I would like to thank Nick Gonis for his help in reading the Greek characters.

6 ست وثلثين وماية دنير[ين عددا فا]دفع ذلك [الى] قبل قريتك فى

7 ستة اطبل فا[ن] يكتتب [لك براءة] منها [...] بخاتم[ه] و[لا] تد[فع] اليه

8 شيا سوا ذلك الكم.. لان وحـ.. مى تكتبن ان خذ [....] فى قريت[لك

9 بجزية بعثت او غيره فان اخذ عنك حقا [..]ر اليها[فان] يكر[ه

10 ان يكتبها لك ولا تدفعن اليه شيا واتينى فانى غير كتبا

11 لك شيا ادعته على احد منه لم ياتينى منه خيرا وكتب يحى سلا...

12 فى جمادى الاخر سنة ست وثلثين وماية

13 † cὺν θ(εῷ) . α . . πι . . λ . π^υ ⲁⲗⲙⲟⲩⲛ ⲑⲉ . ⲛⲁ . ϣⲉⲛⲥⲍⲓⲁⲗ ⲉϫⲱ ⲡⲣⲏⲥ

14 ⲛϣⲟⲩⲛ ⲧⲡⲟⲗⲓⲥ ⲡϥⲥϩⲁⲓ ⲓⲱⲁⲛ(ⲛⲏ)ⲥ ⲓⲥⲓⲁ.(ⲫⲣⲟⲥ) ⲡⲣⲱⲙⲡⲙⲟⲛⲁⲥⲧⲏⲣⲓ

15 ⲟⲛ ⲛⲁⲡⲁ [ⲁⲡ]ⲟⲗⲗⲱ ϫⲉ ⲛⲁⲓ ⲛⲉ ⲛⲧⲁⲥⲧⲁϩⲟⲕ ⲛⲙⲟⲟⲩ ⲛⲅⲧⲁⲁ[ⲩ]

16 ϩⲁ ⲡⲉⲕⲇⲓⲁ]ⲅ[ⲣⲁϥ]ⲟⲛ ⲛⲡⲕⲁⲛⲱⲛ ἠ ἰνδ(ικτίονος) ἔτ(ο)υ(ς) ρλς ⲉⲧⲉ ⲛⲁⲓ ⲛⲉ νο(μίςματα) β

17 ±3] ⲛⲅⲧⲁⲁⲩ ⲛⲥⲟ ⲕⲁⲧⲁⲃⲟⲩⲗⲏ ⲛⲅⲧⲁⲁⲩ ⲛⲡⲃⲟⲏⲑ(ⲟⲥ) ⲛⲡⲉⲕⲧⲓⲙⲏ

18 ±3] ϫⲓ ⲉⲛⲧⲁⲅⲓⲛ ⲉⲣⲟⲟⲩ ⲉϥⲃⲟⲩⲗⲓⲍⲉ ⲛⲧⲉϥⲃⲟⲩⲗⲁ ϩⲁ ⲟⲩ

19 ±11] ϣⲁϥϣⲱⲡⲉ ϩⲁ ⲟⲩⲣⲱⲙⲉ ⲉϣⲁϥⲙⲟⲩ ⲏⲅⲟⲩⲛ

20 . . . . . ⲅ . ⲟ . ⲁ ⲛ . ⲡⲉⲕⲃⲟⲏⲑ(ⲟⲥ) ⲟⲩⲱϣ ⲛⲧⲓ ⲉⲛⲧⲁⲅⲓⲛ ⲛⲁⲕ ⲁⲙⲟⲩ

21 ⲛⲁⲓ ⲙⲙⲁⲓ . . . ⲉⲩ ⲉⲣⲟⲕ ⲉⲡⲁⲣⲉ ⲡⲉⲕϣⲁⲕϭⲓⲛϥ ⲛⲁⲓ ϩⲙ ⲡ

22 ⲉⲕⲉⲛⲧⲁⲅⲉⲛ ⲧⲁⲣⲉⲕⲉⲓⲙⲉ ⲁⲓ[ⲥ]ⲙⲏⲛ ⲧⲓⲡⲓⲧⲧⲁⲅⲉ ⲛⲁⲕ

10. كتبا: يدفن ان 13. cὺν θ;]π^υ 14. *l.* ⲡⲉ ⲉϥⲥϩⲁⲓ ⲛ̄- ⲓⲱⲁⲛ^ϲ 15. *l.* ⲙ̄ⲙⲟⲟⲩ
16. *l.* ⲙ̄ⲡⲕⲁⲛⲱⲛ; ινδ/ ετ^υ ν° 17. *l.* ⲕⲁⲧⲁⲃⲟⲗⲏ ; ⲙ̄ⲡⲃⲟⲏ^ⲑ *l.* ⲙ̄ⲡⲉⲕⲧⲓⲙⲏ
20, 22. *l.* ⲉⲛⲧⲁⲅⲓⲟⲛ 21. *l.* ⲡⲉϣⲁⲕϭⲛ̄ⲧϥ̄ (?) 22. *l.* ⲥⲙⲛ̄ ⲧⲓⲡⲓⲧⲁⲕⲕⲓⲟⲛ.

1   ... paid (for) indiction

2   In the name of God, the Compassionate, the Merciful.

3   This is a wri[ting] from Hishām son of Z[iyād] the executive [of the] *amīr* ['Ab]d al-Malik
    b. Yazīd over [the Upper Ashmūn?]

4   to Yuḥannis b. Isidūr (*vac.*)

5   of the people of the Monastery of Abū Abūllū in Upper Ashmūn. He has assigned to you as
    your head-tax for the year

6   one hundred and thirty-six two *dīnār*[s in coin. So p]ay it [to] the collector of your village in

7   six instalments. And let him write [for you a receipt] for this, [sealing it?] with his seal and do [not] pa[y] to him

8   anything except this . . .?. And if . . . you should definitely write that he take [. . .] in your villa[ge]

9   with *jizya*, which you sent or someone else. And if he receives from you what he deserves [. . .] to it. [And if] he refuse[s]
10 to write it (the receipt) for you, then do not pay him anything but come to me and I, without . . .
11 for you something else (than what) I claimed from someone who did not come to me from him in a good way. And Yaḥyā wrote it in
12 Jumādā II of the year one hundred and thirty-six.

13 ☨ By God. . . . . Abū? Almūn The.na. b. Ziyād, over the south
14 of Shmoun, the city, writes to Ioannes son of Isidoros of the Monastery
15 of Apa Apollo. This is what has been assigned to you to pay
16 of your *dia*]*g*[*raphon*] over the canon of the 8th *indiction*, year 136 which is *nomismata* 2
17 (imp.)] and pay them in six instalments and pay them to the assistant of your village.
18 And take an *entagion* for them which he seals with his seal for a
19 . . .] it is for a man if he were to die or rather
20 . . .] your assistant wants to give an *entagion* for you. Come
21 to me (if he asks) you for more than the amount you see in
22 your *entagion*. So that you know, I have drawn up this order for payment for you.

1. For similar minutes in Greek before the *basmalla* recording the name of the tax-payer and the amount of tax to be paid in *nomismata*, see *P.Cair.Arab.* III 161.1; 162.1; 163.1 (all 91/709). For ἀν^υ read ἀνυσθέν.

3. *Hādhā kitāb min…li…* is a common opening for legal contracts and is also often used for *entagia*.[61] After *ʿāmil* there is room to fit the name of the governor, Abū ʿAwn ʿAbd al-Malik b. Yazīd and a reference to Hishām b. Ziyād's geographical jurisdiction, i.e. *ʿalā* (*kharāj*) *Aʿlā Ashmūn*.[62] Abū ʿAwn was succeeded as governor of Egypt by ʿAbd al-Malik b. Yazīd on 5 Rabīʿ II 136/8 October 753, some months before our papyrus was written but he did not leave Egypt on a campaign to North-Africa until Shawwāl 136/March-April 754. Abū ʿAwn still appears as the *amīr* on this *entagion*. There is also a pagarch with this name, for whom, see *CPR* XXII 7, where also the Arabic papyri are discussed where this name had been incorrectly associated with the governor rather than a pagarch of the Heracleopolite with this name.

Hishām b. Ziyād. Of the patronymic only the initial *zayn* can be read. This pagarch is not attested in other published documents.

5. *Min ahl al-dayr Abū Abūlū*. The first element of the name of the monastery is not an accurate transliteration of the Coptic.[63] Aʿlā Ashmūn, Upper Ashmūn, remained a separate administrative district until the beginning of the third/ninth century when it was joined with Asfal Ashmūn, Lower Ashmūn, to form *kūrat* Ashmūnayn.[64]

---

[61] See *P.Cair.Arab.* III 161.3-4; 162.3-4; 163.3-4 (all 91/709).
[62] See *CPR* XXI 5.2-4 (182/799); Rāghib 1997: text 3.2-4 (116/734).
[63] See Timm 1984-1992: 643.
[64] Grohmann 1959: 43.

*Annahu aṣābaka min jizyat ra'sika li-sana.*⁶⁵ The term *jizyat ra'sihi* is first attested in a papyrus dated 101/719;⁶⁶ *jizyat ra'sika* first appears in a papyrus dated 113/731-2,⁶⁷ reflecting the fiscal changes that had taken place in the first decades of the eighth century resulting in a separation of the land- and poll-tax.

6. *Sitt wa-thalāthīn wa-mi'a.*⁶⁸ Our document was written in the middle of the *hijra* year 136, demanding the taxes for the whole of the year 136 (July 7, 753-June 26, 754). Another tax demand-note from the monastery of Apa Apollo was similarly issued in the same year that the tax was due.⁶⁹ In his *Kitāb al-kharāj* Abū Yūsuf (d. 182/798) mentions that the poll-tax is due at the end of the year (tr. Ben Shemesh: 86). According to Ibn Ḥawqal (d. > 367/977), cited by Maqrīzī (d. 845/1442), the eighth and final instalment of the agricultural taxes (*kharāj*) was collected in the month of Tybi (December 29-January 26), i.e. one month after our tax demand-note was issued. The poll-tax was most probably collected together with the agricultural and other taxes when tax-payers had enough money to pay. See Sijpesteijn 2004: texts 22, 23 where it is explicitly stated that the *jizya*, in this case probably referring to money taxes in general, should only be paid over harvested goods. It is not clear how the six instalments could be fitted in such a short period.

Dīnār[ayn 'adadan]. The amount of two *dīnār*s falls within the average poll-tax payments recorded in contemporary documents. *Dīnārayn* is restored in accordance with line 16. The *dāl* is written in a very angular way, but compare l. 5 *dayr* and l. 8 *dhālika*. *'Adadan* often follows the amount of taxes in *entagia* making sure the payment was made in coin.⁷⁰

*Qubbāl qaryatika.*⁷¹ These functionaries seem not to have been appointed as professionals, but through some form of liturgy.⁷² He is the same as the *boethos* in lines 17 and 20. *Qubbāl* is written with a defective long *ā*.⁷³

7. *Sittat aṭbāl. Aṭbāl* is written with a defective long *ā*.⁷⁴ The instalments for tax payments in the Islamic period varied between three to eight per year.⁷⁵ The Arabic *ṭabl* in the technical sense of "instalment" is equivalent to the Greek *katabole* which is used in line 17.

7-8. *Wa-in yaktataba [laka barā'a] minhā [khatamahā?] bi-khātami[hi wa-lā tadfa'] ilayhi shay'an sawā dhālika.* Restored on the basis of line 17. A poll-tax demand-note for the year 123/731-2 includes

---

⁶⁵ For this formula see the *entagia P.Cair.Arab.* III 161.5; 162.4-5; 163.5 (all 91/709). For the use of the personal possessive pronoun on the taxes see *min jizyat ra'sika li-sana* Diem 1994: text 7.10 (168/784); *jizyat ra'asika P.Cair.Arab.* III 180 (123/731-2); Grohmann 1934: text 18.6 (196/812).

⁶⁶ Casson 1938: 289; *P.Giss.Arab.* p. 23 n. 5.

⁶⁷ *P.Cair.Arab.* III 180.

⁶⁸ For the numerical composition of dates—first units, then tens, then hundreds—see Hopkins 1984: 119 §102.a.

⁶⁹ See *P.Mon.Apollo* 30 (mid-8th century).

⁷⁰ See *P.Cair.Arab.* III 161-3 (all 91/709).

⁷¹ See *qubbāl qaryatika P.Cair.Arab.* III 169.6 (134/752; Upper Ashmūn) for the *qubbāl*, an administrative functionary active at the village level, see *CPR* XXI, p. 119-20.

⁷² See *P.Heid.Arab.* I 3.25 (91/709).

⁷³ Hopkins 1984: 11 § 10.

⁷⁴ Hopkins 1984: 11 § 10.

⁷⁵ Maqrīzī, *Khiṭaṭ*, I, 734; Gonis 2001b: 227; Morelli 1997: 199-200; Morelli 1998: 165-8; specifically for poll-tax instalments Morimoto 1981: 180.

the payment for a receipt.[76] The recommendation to take receipts at the payment of taxes as a security against having to pay more also appears in Greek and Coptic *entagia* for individual tax-payers.[77] The use of seals on tax-receipts and tax demand-notes is known from early papyri[78] and the use of seals is attested by the many seals of early Muslim *amīr*s and lower officials that are preserved from Egypt.[79] Cf. *CPR* XXII 7, introduction (134/751-2).

10. *Wa-in yakrahu] an yadfaʻahā laka wa-lā tadfaʻanna ilayhi shayʼan wa-atīnī fa-innī* . . . See a tax demand-note from Upper Ashmūn *wa-karaha an yaktubahā lahu fa-lā ta[dfaʻanna] ḥisāb lahu shayʼan P.Cair.Arab.* III 169.9-10 (134/752).[80] In two eighth-century Greek *entagia* for individual tax-payers, the tax-payer is asked to come to the pagarch if he encounters any problems from the tax-collector, such as not receiving a receipt for his payment.[81] Another way to interpret this line is closer in meaning to lines 21-22. *Atīnī* has retained the long final *yāʼ* against Classical Arabic.[82]

11. The sense of this line is not clear to me.

12. Jumādā II 136 = 2-31 December 753.

13. cὺν θ(εῷ) is the standard opening formula for *entagia*.[83] There follow some more words written with Greek letters probably related to the name of the pagarch, but only a few individual letters can be deciphered. The last Greek letters which can be read as π^υ might be restored as ἄπ(ο)υ for Arabic Abū as part of the pagarch's *kunya*. The following letters ⲀⲖⲘⲞⲨⲚ ⲐⲈ . ⲚⲀ̣ . do not seem to fit any known Arabic names.

ⲤⲌⲒⲀⲖ̣. Cζ is occasionally used in Greek papyri to represent Arabic ز (*zayn*).[84] Cζ represents, however, more often Arabic ش (*shīn*).[85] In Coptic papyri ⲍ is usually used for Arabic ز.[86]

---

[76] *P.Cair.Arab.* III 180. See the third/ninth-century tax ledger found in Ahsmūnayn, which contains a column with the charge for drawing up a receipt after each tax-payer's name (Grohmann 1952-3: 161-2). For the recommendation to receive *barāʼāt* at the payment of taxes at the pagarch's granary see Becker 1906: text 10.4-5 (90/709) and at the central treasury *P.Lond.* IV 1335 (709).

[77] *BKU* III 340; 506; Gonis 2004a: text I = *P.Bal.* 130 (723-4?); two texts edited in *P.Bal.* 130 appendix (723-4) *P.Cair.Arab.* III 169. See also the commentary to line 18. For an example of such eighth-century *barāʼāt* for tax payments, see David-Weill 1971: text XVI (156/772) Diem 1984: text 7 (168/784). See too Rāghib 1997: 147 n. 39.

[78] Grohmann 1934: texts 12 (216/832); 13 (237/851-2); 18 (196/812); *CPR* XXII 7 (751/2); *SB* VII 9755 (642).

[79] *CPR* III I/1, p. 78; Allan and Sourdel 1998:1102-5.

[80] Where my readings deviate form the *editio princeps* the original reading is given in brackets.

6 قبال قريتك واكتبن [لك براة ولا تدفعن (واكتنى)]

7 شيا (شتا و) غير ذلك

9 وكره ان يكتبها (تكتبها) له فلا تد[فعن (تد]

10 حساب له شيا . . .]

[81] See *CPR* XXII 7.7-8 (751-2); *SPP* VIII 1195.4-5 (104/723).

[82] Hopkins 1984: 85 § 82.d.

[83] See *CPR* XXII 7.2 commentary.

[84] See e.g. *P.Bal.* 130.1 = Gonis 2004a (723-4?). See also Wessely 1886: 123-124.

[85] See e.g. Cζεριχ *P.Lond.* IV 1335.2, 19; 1336.2, etc.; *CPR* XXII 52.4; Ραζιδ *P.Lond.* IV 1437.10, 15.

[86] See e.g. ⲀⲂⲆⲀⲖⲀⲌⲒⲌ *P.Bal.* 400.1. See also in Greek papyri: Ἀβδελαζιζ *P.Lond.* IV 1412.7; 1431.7, etc.; Ἀβου Ιεζιδ *CPR* XXII 55.11.

13-14. ⲉⲭⲱ ⲡⲣⲏⲥ ⲛ̣ϣ̣ⲙⲟⲩⲛ ⲧⲡ̣ⲟ̣ⲗⲓⲥ. This expression mirrors the Arabic ʿalā Aʿlā Ashmūn, although the addition "the city" is lacking in the Arabic. Correct would have been ⲉⲭⲙ ⲡⲣⲏⲥ ⲧⲡⲟⲗⲓⲥ.[87]

16. ϩⲁ ⲡⲉⲕⲇⲓⲁ]ⲅ̣[ⲣⲁϥ]ⲟⲛ. The Greek equivalent of *jizyat al-raʾas* is διάγραφον or ἀνδρισμός, but the first word seems to fit better at the beginning of this line. There are traces of a letter before *npkanōn* and a slanted line at the top of the line which seems to be part of the letter Γ. Sarah suggested in her notes that some tax like *demosion* or *diagraphon* should be restored at the beginning of the line.

The eighth *indiction* went from May 1 754 until April 30 755, showing an apparent discrepancy of ten months with the *hijra* year 136 (July 7, 753-June 26, 754). Nikolaos Gonis, however, has observed that this does not signal a conflict, but that the *hijra* year was the year in which the *beginning* of the indiction (Pachon 6 = May 1) fell. He has listed the parallels to this phenomenon in a forthcoming article.[88]

ρλσ The scribe seems to have added the ρ after writing λσ, which explains its position under the suprascribed υ of ἔτους.[89] Sarah did not read anything after ⲛⲁⲓ ⲛⲉ.

17. ⲧⲓⲙⲏ. The monastery seems to be referred to here as a village, as is the case in the Arabic. Sarah translated in this line "and you shall pay them in the sixth instalment."

18. ϫⲓ ⲉⲛⲧⲁⲅⲓⲛ ⲉⲣⲟⲟⲩ ⲉϥⲃⲟⲩⲗⲓⲍⲉ ⲛⲧⲉϥⲃⲟⲩⲗⲗⲁ.[90] In the Arabic the recommendation to have the receipt sealed appears in line 7. For the command to take a receipt for tax payments see the commentary to lines 7-8. Sarah did not read anything before ⲉⲣⲟⲟⲩ.

19. ϣⲁϥϣⲱⲡⲉ ϩⲁ ⲟⲩⲣⲱⲙⲉ ⲉϥⲁϥⲙⲟⲩ ⲛ̄ⲅⲟⲩⲛ. It seems unlikely that this unusual phrase refers to the governor ʿAbd Allāh b. Malik's decision that "no dead man should be buried until they had paid the poll-tax for him."[91]

20. At the beginning of this line only a few unrelated letters can be discerned. Sarah did not read anything before ⲡⲉⲕⲃⲟⲏⲑⲟⲥ. She read in this line ⲁⲩⲱ ϣⲛ ⲧⲓⲉⲛⲧⲁⲅⲓⲛ ⲛⲁⲕ which she translated "Ask for your receipt."

20-22. ⲁⲕⲁⲙⲟⲩ ⲛⲁⲓ ⲙ̣ⲙ̣ⲁ̣ⲓ . . . ⲁⲩ ⲉⲣⲟⲕ ⲉⲡⲁⲣⲉ ⲡⲉⲕϣⲁⲕϭⲓⲛϥ ⲛⲁⲓ ϩⲙ ⲡⲉⲕⲉⲛⲧⲁⲅⲉⲛ. See ⲉⲩϣⲁⲛⲙⲁϩⲉ ⲙⲙⲟⲕ ⲡⲁⲣⲁ ⲛⲁⲓ ⲁⲙⲟⲩ ⲛⲁⲓ *P.Mon.Apollo* 29.5-6; 30.6 (both mid-eighth century); *P.Ryl.Copt.* 119.3. Sarah translated in lines 21-2 "you for more than (?) that which you (?) should find for me in your receipt."

22. ⲧ̣ⲁ̣ⲣⲉⲕⲉⲓⲙⲉ ⲁⲓ[ⲥ]ⲙⲏⲛ ⲧⲓⲡⲓⲧⲧⲁⲅⲉ ⲛⲁ̣ⲕ̣. This phrase seems to be related to the expression that appears in official Greek documents from the Islamic period "καὶ πρὸς τῷ δῆλον εἶναι καθυπέγραψο."[92]

---

[87] For the meaning (rule) over, see Crum 1962: 757.

[88] 'Reconsidering Some Fiscal Documents from Early Islamic Egypt III.' I should like to thank Nick Gonis for showing me a draft of this article before publication.

[89] For nº as the abbreviation of *nomismata*, see Gonis 2001a. The two letters are no longer distinguishable, but have merged into one smudge.

[90] For the meaning of "receipt" for *entagion*, see Bell 1945: 531. For ⲃⲟⲩⲗⲗⲁ and ⲃⲟⲩⲗⲓⲍⲉ, see Förster 2002: 141; *KB* 37-8.

[91] *History of the Patriarchs*, 56.

Bibliography

Abbott, N. (1965). "A New Papyrus and a Review of the Administration of 'Ubaid Allāh b. al-Ḥabḥāb," in: Makdisi, G. (ed.) *Arabic and Islamic Studies in Honor of Hamilton A.R. Gibb*, Leiden: Brill. 21-35.

Abū Yūsuf (d. 182/798). *Kitāb al-kharāj*. Ed. al-Bannā, M. I. Cairo. 1981. Tr. Ben Shemesh, A. Leiden: Brill. 1969.

Allan, J. and D. Sourdel (1998). "Khātam," in: van Donzel, E. et al. (eds.) *Encyclopaedia of Islam* (9 vols). 2nd revised edition. Leiden: Brill. IV, 1102-1105.

Becker, C. H. (1906). "Arabische Papyri des Aphroditofundes," *ZAVG* 20, 68-104.

Bell, H. I. (1945). "The Arabic Bilingual Entagion," *ProcPhilSoc* 89, 531-542.

Bierbier, M. L. (1995). *Who Was Who in Egyptology?*, 3rd rev. ed. London: Egypt Exploration Society.

Casson, L. (1938). "Tax-Collection Problems in Early Arab Egypt," *TAPA* 69, 274-291.

Clackson, S. (1993). "The Michaelides Coptic Manuscript Collection in the Cambridge University Library and British Library," in: Johnson, T. W. and Orlandi, T. (eds.) *Acts of the Fifth International Congress of Coptic Studies* (2 vols). Rome: C.I.M. II, 123-138.

Clackson, S. (1994). "The Michaelides Manuscript Collection," *ZPE* 100, 223-226.

Clackson, S. (2008). *It is Our Father Who Writes: Orders from the Monastery of Apollo at Bawit* (= American Studies in Papyrology 43). Oxford: Oxbow 2008.

Diem, W. (1984). "Einige frühe amtliche Urkunden aus der Sammlung Papyrus Erzherzog Rainer (Wien)," *Le Muséon* 97, 109-158.

Gascou, J. and K.A. Worp (1982). "Problèmes de documentation apollinopolite," *ZPE* 49, 83-95.

Gonis, N. (2001a). "Abbreviated Nomismata in Seventh-and Eighth-Century Papyri. Notes on Palaeography and Taxes," *ZPE* 136, 119-122.

Gonis, N. (2001b). "Reconsidering Some Fiscal Documents from Early Islamic Egypt," *ZPE* 137, 225-228.

Gonis, N. (2004a). "Arabs, Monks and Taxes: Notes on Documents from Deir el-Bala'izah," *ZPE* 148, 213-224.

Gonis, N. (2004b). "Another Look at Some Officials in Early 'Abbāsid Egypt," *ZPE* 149, 189-195.

Gonis, N. (forthcoming). "Reconsidering Some Fiscal Documents from Early Islamic Egypt III."

Gonis, N. and F. Morelli (2000). "A Requisition for the 'Commander of the Faithful," *ZPE* 132, 193-195.

---

[92] See *CPR* XXII 2.7 (628/9 or 643/4) and the examples given in the commentary. Perhaps also related to ⲉⲩⲱⲣⲝ ⲛⲁⲕ ⲟⲩⲛ ⲁⲓⲥⲙⲛ ⲧⲓⲁⲡⲟⲗⲉⲓⲝⲓⲥ ⲛⲁⲕ. See *BKU* III 419.5.

Grohmann, A. (1934). "Probleme der arabischen Papyrusforschung II," *ArOr* 6, 125-149; 377-398.

Grohmann, A. (1959). *Studien zur historischen Geographie und Verwaltung des frühmittelalterlichen Ägypten.* (*DÖAWW, Philosophisch-historische Klasse*, 77, Band 2, Abhandlung). Vienna: R.M. Rohrer.

Grohmann, A. (1966). *Handbuch der Orientalistik. I Arabische Chronologie. II Arabische Papyruskunde*, Leiden: Brill.

Guest, R. (1923). "An Arabic Papyrus of the 8th Century," *JAOS* 43, 247-248.

Hopkins, S. (1984). *Studies in the Grammar of Early Arabic.* Oxford: Oxford University Press.

Husselman, E. M. (1951). "Some Coptic Documents Dealing with the Poll-Tax," *Aegyptus* 31, 332-338.

Ibn 'Abd al-Ḥakam (d. 257/871), *Futūḥ Miṣr*, ed. Ch. Torrey, *The History of the Conquests of Egypt, North Africa and Spain*, New Haven 1922: Yale University Press.

Kennedy, H. (1998). "Egypt as a Province in the Islamic Caliphate," in: Petry, C. F. (ed.) *The Cambridge History of Egypt* (2 vols.). Cambridge: Cambridge University Press. I, 62-85.

Kindī (d. 350/961). *Kitāb al-wulāt wa-kitāb al-quḍāt. The Governors and Judges of Egypt.* Ed. Guest, R. Leiden: Brill. 1912.

Maqrīzī (d. 845/1442). *Al-Mawāʿiz wa-l-iʿtibār fī dhikr al-khiṭaṭ wa-l-āthār.* Ed. Sayyid, A. F. London: Al-Furqān Islamic Heritage Foundation. 2002-2003.

Morelli, F. (1997). "Sei καταβολαιν in P.Bodl I 107," *ZPE* 115, 199-200.

Morelli, F. (1998). "Tre registri fiscali del periodo arabo," *Eirene* 34, 159-168.

Morelli, F. (2000). "Agri deserti (mawāt), fuggitivi, fisco, una κλήρωσις in più in SPP VIII 1183," *ZPE* 129, 167-178.

Morimoto, K. (1981). *The Fiscal Administration of Egypt in the Early Islamic Period.* Dohosha: Dohosha Publisher, Inc.

Rāghib, Y. (1997). "Sauf-conduits d'Égypte omeyyade et abbasside," *AnIsl* 31, 143-168.

Rémondon, R. (1952). "Ordre de paiement d'époque arabe pour l'impôt de capitation," *Aegyptus* 32, 257-264.

Robinson, C. F. (2005). "Neck-Sealing in Early Islam," *Journal of the Economic and Social History of the Orient* 48, 401-441.

Sijpesteijn, P. M. (2001). "Profit Following Responsibility. A Leaf from the Records of a Third/Ninth Century Tax-Collecting Agent," *JJP* 31, 91-132.

Sijpesteijn, P. M. (2004). *Shaping a Muslim State. Papyri Related to a Mid-Eighth-Century Egyptian Official.* Ph.D. thesis Princeton.

Sijpesteijn, P. M. (2007a). "New Rule over Old Structures: Egypt after the Muslim Conquest," in: Crawford, H. (ed.) *Régime Change in the Ancient Near East and Egypt. From Sargon of Agade to Saddam Hussein. Proceedings of the British Academy* 136. 183-200.

Sijpesteijn, P. M. (2007b). "The Arab Conquest of Egypt and the Beginning of Muslim Rule," in: Bagnall, R. S. (ed.) *Byzantine Egypt.* 437-459.

Sijpesteijn, P. M. (forthcoming). *Shaping a Muslim State. The World of a Mid-Eighth-Century Egyptian Official.*

Ṭabarī (d. 310/923). *Ta'rīkh al-rusul wa-l-mulūk.* Ed. de Goeje, M. J. et al. Leiden: Brill. 1964-1965.

Timm, S. (1984-92). *Das christlich-koptische Ägypten in arabischer Zeit. Eine Sammlung christlicher Stätten in Ägypten in arabischer Zeit unter Ausschluß von Alexandria, Kairo, des Apa-Mena-Klosters (Der Abu Mina), der Sketis (Wadi n-Natrun) und der Sinai-Region* (6 vols). Wiesbaden: Dr. Ludwig Reichert.

Wessely, K. (1886). "Griechisch cz und š," *Mitteilungen aus der Papyrussammlung Erzherzog Rainer* 1, 123-124.

Appendix

NIKOLAOS GONIS

P.Clackson 46

P.Camb.UL Michael. 807 (B) 26 x 18 cm 10 January 758?
Plate XX

The back of the tax demand (*P.Clackson* 45) was later reused for a tax receipt in Greek. The name of the tax is virtually impossible to read owing to abrasion; the poll-tax, perhaps in combination with something else, is one possibility (see further 1 n).

There is no verb indicating that a payment is made; the preposition διά was thought sufficient for this purpose. For a similar arrangement, cf. the Hermopolite *P.Lond.* V 1746, *SB* VIII 9759, *SPP* III 290-291 (= *SB* XXII 15609-15610) or the Arsinoite *SPP* III 693, 701, VIII 750.

Two further texts of two lines each, both almost entirely washed off, are written further below; one seems to start † Ἰωά(ννης), the other (perhaps) † Βίκτ(ωρ); they are certainly in Greek, and abbreviations are used. It is conceivable that these two texts were more or less of the same kind as the text transcribed below, and we are dealing with a sheet recording successive tax payments by one or two persons; on such documents, see *CPR* XXII 16 introd. (pp. 83-5).

TEXT

1 † μ(ηνὸς) Τυ(βι) ιε, ἰ(ν)δ(ικτίωνος) ια. δ(ιὰ) Ἰωά[ν(νο)]υ Γεωρ[(γίου)] *c*.6 αν *c*.6
2 ἐνδεκ(άτης) ἰ(ν)δ(ικτίωνος) ἀριθ(μίου) νο(μίσματος) ϛ´ κδ μδ ἔκτον εἰκουσι-
τ(έταρτον)
τεσσαρ(ακοστ)όγδ(οον)
3 μό(να) δοθ(έντα) Ἀβρ(ααμίῳ) Γεωρ(γίου). Ζαχαρ(ίας) στοιχ(εῖ).

TRANSLATION

1 In the month of Tybi, (day) 15, indiction 11. Through Ioannes son of Georgios . . .
2 of the eleventh indiction, ¹⁄₆ ¹⁄₂₄ ¹⁄₄₈ of a reckoned solidus, one-sixth one twenty- fourth one forty-eighth
3 only, given to Abraamios son of Georgios. Zacharias agrees (?).

COMMENTARY

1. Τυ(βι) ιε, ἰ(ν)δ(ικτίωνος) ια. The conversion of the date to 10 January 758 relies on the assumption that this indiction 11 belongs to the same cycle as indiction 8 of the tax demand. But a later date should be possible too.

I have not been able to arrive at a satisfactory reading of what is written at the end of the line, which is badly abraded (I have worked from a scan of medium resolution, but I doubt that work on the original would have changed things significantly). After the taxpayer's patronymic, there may have stood an indication of his *origo*, his profession or other description (note that μονάζοντος, whether abbreviated or not, cannot be read), followed by a preposition such as ἀπό or ὑπέρ (probably abbreviated) and the name of the tax(es). The only letters that can be read with certainty, αν, are perhaps preceded by the symbol for ὑπέρ; one may consider reading (ὑπὲρ) ἀνδ(ρισμοῦ), assuming that a high trace after nu is part of a raised delta, but this cannot be confirmed. Then comes what may be a sinusoid such as the abbreviation for καί, possibly followed by διαστ ; yet διαστολή or διασταλμός are not expected in this context.

2. μδ. The fraction is guessed at rather than read.

ἕκτον. The superscript writing may also be read as omega: ἕκτω(ν) (l. ἕκτον).

τεσσαρ(ακοστ)όγδ(οον). Though it is unclear what exactly the scribe intended, I have resolved the most common form in this period; see F. T. Gignac, *A Grammar of the Greek Papyri of the Roman and Byzantine Periods* II (Milan 1981) 208-9. For the abbreviation cf. *SPP* XX 199.5, where read τεσσερακ(οστ)όγδον instead of τεσσαρ(ακοντ)όγδον (correct also *SPP* VIII 1343.3); *SB* VIII 9760.4 has another abbreviated form, to be expanded as δετρακ(οστ)όγδο(ον).

3. δοθ(έντα). The implication is that the payment did not go to the treasury but was transferred to a third party, probably in compensation for services offered to the state or its operands; the payment would have come out of the taxes of the local community rather than the treasury. There are several parallels, mostly in Hermopolite tax receipts of this period (e.g. *P.Lond.* V 1745, 1749. 1752).

στοιχ(εῖ). The reading, originally suggested by Sarah, is largely intuitive, based on an attempt to make sense out of the ink visible after Ζαχαρ( ). But one would normally expect the scribe's name to be preceded by a cross, which we do not have.

P.CLACKSON 47

A FRAGMENT OF A COPTIC DOCUMENT FROM THE MONASTERY OF APA APOLLO

SOFÍA TORALLAS TOVAR

Some time ago, I identified this text in the Roca-Puig collection at the Abbey of Montserrat (Barcelona) as coming from the monastery of Apa Apollo and sent a message to Sarah with a draft transcription of it. She manifested interest immediately. I promised to send her a photo as soon as I had the facilities at the monastery to digitalize the papyri, but when I did, it was sadly too late.

The document is broken and the nature of it cannot be established with certainty. It is a fragment of a document issued by brother Apollo, addressed to the *dikaion* or juridical body of the monastery,[1] through its head, whose name has also disappeared. A quantity of wheat "according to the Athenian *oipe*" and an amount of money in *solidi* are involved, so this might be a document related to a loan, an acknowledgement of a debt. It is clearly the same scribe who wrote *P.Mon.Apoll.* 60, which, as described by Sarah, was written by a professional scribe, a village scribe.[2] It can be dated to the eighth century on paleographical grounds.[3]

P.Clackson 47

P.Monts.Roca inv. 549   13,2 cm x 6,6 cm   VIIIth century
Plate XXI   Hermoupolis

Papyrus Upper and left margin preserved. Five lines of text are visible, written across the fibres, as well as the end of the line on the verso.

↓
1   † ⲁⲛⲟⲕ ⲡⲁⲥⲟⲛ ⲁⲡⲟⲗⲗⲱ ⲡϣⲛ ⲥⲧ[ⲉⲓⲥϩⲁⲓ ⲙⲡⲇⲓⲕⲁⲓⲟⲛ]
2   ⲛⲡⲙⲟⲛⲁ(ⲥⲧⲏⲣⲓⲟⲛ) ⲛⲫⲁⲅⲓⲟⲥ ⲁⲡⲁ ⲁⲡⲟⲗⲗⲱ ϩⲓⲧ[ⲟⲟⲧϥ (name)
     ⲡⲁⲣⲭ(ⲓ)ⲙ(ⲁⲛ)ⲁ(ⲣⲓⲧⲏⲥ)]
3   ⲁⲩⲱ ⲡⲉⲓⲱⲧ ⲛⲡⲧⲟⲡⲟⲥ ϫⲉ ⲉⲡⲓⲇⲏ[   ]
3b   ϩⲁⲣⲟⲓ ⲛⲥⲓⲁⲱ[ⲣⲟⲥ   ]
4   ⲛⲧⲟⲓⲡⲉ ⲛⲧⲁⲑⲉⲛⲏⲥ ⲉⲣⲟⲓ ⲙⲛ ϩⲟⲗⲟⲕ[ⲟⲧ   ]
5   ⲉ̣ⲧ̣ⲁ̣ⲁ̣ⲩ [   ]

→

---

[1] Clackson 2000: 29; Wipszycka 1991; Schmidt 1931: 103-5.
[2] Clackson 2000: 35.
[3] I want to thank Anne Boud'hors and Alain Delattre for helping me to understand this document.

] . (ὑπὲρ) cί(του) ἀρτ(αβῶν) ε ἀθ(ηναίῳ μετρῷ) (καὶ) χρυ(cοῦ νομιcμάτων) ἀρ(ι)θ(μίων) βγ́ +

6. cι αρ^τ, αθ/ ϛ χρ^υ αρ^θ

1   I, Brother Apollo, son of St... [am writing to the *dikaion*]
2   of the monastery of the Holy Apa Apollo, through [N.N. the archimandrite]
3   and the father of the topos, whereas [...
3b   instead of me (the debt is for) Isidor [...
4   of the Athenian *oipe* to me and [two and one third] *holokottinoi* [...
5   giving them [...

6:        ] . . ?? artabes of wheat of the Athenian (measure) and 2 ⅓ gold-solidi.

1. There are a number of monks named Apollo in the *P.Mon.Apoll.* documents. None of them presents a patronym beginning with cт[. It could be Stephanos or Staurakios, etc. Isidor in line 3b does not appear either.

3b. This line has been inserted later by a different hand. It has been written right above єроι, and may refer to the person who shares the debt or has inherited it.

4. The complete formula would be "ογnтaк or ογnтєтn x *artabai* of wheat nтоιπє nтаθєnнc and two ⅓ *solidi* єроι": "I owe you ..." This is one of the few instances of this Athenian *oipe*, a measure of volume used for grain. It appears also among the problematic abbreviations in the orders of transport, *O.Clackson* **1-17**.[4]

5. This would be the closing formula "I am ready to give it to you" or "I shall give these to you."

BIBLIOGRAPHY

Förster, H. (2002). *Wörterbuch der griechischen Wörter in den koptischen dokumentarischen Texten*. Berlin: De Gruyter.
Clarysse, W. (1985). "The Athenian Measure at Hermopolis," *ZPE* 60, 232-236.
Schmidt, C. (1931), "Ein koptischer Werkvertrag," *ZÄS* 67, 102-106.
Wipszycka, E. (1991), "Dikaion," *CE*, vol. 3, 901-902.

---

[4] See the discussion of the abbreviation αθ/^η here in *P.Clackson* **1-17**. On this see Clarysse 1985 and Förster 2001.

P.CLACKSON 48-50

THREE GREEK MONTSERRAT TEXTS RELATED TO THE MONASTERY OF APA APOLLO

SOFÍA TORALLAS TOVAR AND KLAAS A. WORP

Below we publish three Greek texts from the papyrus collection at the Benedictine abbey of Montserrat near Barcelona.[1]

P.Clackson 48
(LIST OF PAYMENTS)

P.Monts.Roca inv. 516   17,5 x 6,5 cm   VIIth-VIIIth century
Plate XXII

P.Clackson **48**r (folded several times vertically) contains a list of anthroponyms followed by amounts of solidi, written in two columns of five lines each across the direction of the fibers. The provenance of the text is probably the Hermopolite nome, cf. Titkois in l. 2. The palaeographical aspects of the handwriting allow us to assign the text to a date in the VII/VIII centuries C.E. The precise purpose of the list is not indicated by way of a heading with a word like γνῶσις or λόγος, but it is connected with payments, e.g. rents or taxes. The individual amounts recorded range between $^{1}/_{12}$ sol. (line 5) and 1 $^{1}/_{6}$ sol. (line 6), while in between columns i and ii mention is made of an amount of 6 $^{11}/_{12}$ sol. Given the variation in payments it does not seem very likely that one is dealing with a register of payments of a single per capita tax like the diagraphon.

→ col. i
1   †Ἰωά(ννης) ἀνυ(τής) τῆς   νο(μ.) ϛ S γ´ ιβ
2   Τιτκώ(εως) (M2) ... (M1)   νο(μ.) α
3   Ἀπολλ( ) πρε(σβυτερ ..)   νο(μ.) β)
4   Ἰωάννου   νο(μ.) α
5   Ἰο[ύ]στου   νο(μ.) ιβ
col. ii
6   Ἰσακ( ) [.]ποσ( )   νο(μ.) α ϛ
7   Μασκοι   νο(μ.) α
8   Γεωργ(ίου)   νο(μ.) γ´
9   Ἀνουφίου   νο(μ.) δ/
10   γί(ν.)   νο(μ.) ιβ γ´ ιβ

1   Johannes, *exactor* of the (village)   6 $^{1}/_{2}$ $^{1}/_{3}$ $^{1}/_{12}$ sol.

---

[1] For this collection see Torallas Tovar and Worp 2007, 1019.

2	of Titkois,	1 sol.
3	Apoll(o), priest	$^2/_3$ sol.
4	of Johannes	1 sol.
5	of Justus	$^1/_{12}$ sol.
6	of Isak, -*pos*( )	1 $^1/_6$ sol.
7	of Maskoi	1 sol.
8	of George	$^1/_3$ sol.
9	of Anouphius	$^1/_4$ sol.
10	in total	12 $^1/_3$ $^1/_{12}$ sol.

It seems certain that one should take ll. 1-2, †'Ιωά(ννης) ἀνυ(τής) τῆς Τιτκώ(εως), together; in other words, we do not think that the amount of 6 $^1/_2$ $^1/_3$ $^1/_{12}$ sol. belongs to John himself, and we assume that this amount refers to a collection of money referred to earlier on. Adding the amounts in lines 2-9 one arrives to the total of 5 $^1/_2$ sol. which sum, augmented with the 6 $^1/_2$ $^1/_3$ $^1/_{12}$ sol., yields in line 10 the total of 12 $^1/_3$ $^1/_{12}$ nom.

1. For the ἀνυτής = exactor, cf. *Just. Nov.* 163 (2).

2. For the village of Titkois in the Hermopolite nome, see Calderini and Daris 2007: 131; Clackson 2000, in the introduction to *P.Mon.Apollo*, pp. 5-9. It is unclear what the function of the letters added by a second (previous?) hand is; their reading is far from certain and we have refrained from proposing any reading at all (should the papyrus be turned by 90 or 180 degrees?)

3. Instead of reading πρε(σβύτερος) one may also consider a reading πρά(κτωρ) or πρα(γματευτής).

6. We do not know how to resolve the abbreviation [.]ποσ( ).

7. A personal name *Maskoi* is not known from Greek or Coptic documentary sources; for the latter see M. Hasitzka's website for Coptic personal names found in such papyri,[2] s.n. We think it conceivable that one should separate the elements μασ(ε) and κο(υ)ι for the former[3] (yielding translations like "young," "young calf/bull;" we observe that μασ(ε) often forms the first element in compounded personal names); for the latter compare κουι = "small."

9. It should be noticed that in other lines the fractions of a solidus (1 sol. = 24 ker.) are given in the order of $^2/_3$ (l. 3), $^1/_3$ (ll. 1, 8), $^1/_6$ (l. 6), $^1/_{12}$ (ll. 1, 5), rather than as $^1/_2$, $^1/_4$, $^1/_8$, $^1/_{16}$, $^1/_{32}$, etc. Only in l. 1 one finds the fraction of ½.

The text on the verso of *P.Clackson* **48** may offer a continuation of the text on the recto. This side holds the remains of four lines also written perpendicular to the direction of the fibres on this side:

↓		
1	† ἐν χρ(ήσει)	νο(μ.) β δ
2	ἄμα Θεοδ(ώρα)	νο(μ.) δ ⟋
3	Ἀπολ( )	νο(μ.) δ
4	παλ..	νο(μ.) α

---

[2] *Namen in koptischen dokumentarischen Texten*, http://www.onb.ac.at/files/kopt_namen.pdf.

[3] See Crum, *Coptic Dictionary*, 185b/186a.

1. Or χρ(υσῷ)
2. Read ἅμα Θεοδ(ώρα) or ἅμα Θεοδ(ώρ...)

Furthermore one finds various traces of an earlier (?), very faded (intentionally erased?) text written perpendicular (i.e. at an angle of 90 degrees) to these lines (and parallel with the fibre direction). Of this text only the words Θελε' Ἀπολλω( ) are still legible.

P.Clackson 49
(Receipt for Loaves of Bread)

P.Monts.Roca inv. 619   15 x 4,9 cm   VIth-VIIth century
Plate XXIII   Provenance unknown

Verso blank. The margins at top, left, and bottom are all less than 1 cm. The writing stands perpendicular to the fibre direction.
Provenance unknown, VI/VII century.

1   † Τῷ εὐλαβ(εστάτῳ) ἀββᾶ Μήτρᾳ μονάζ(οντι) Ἱερακίων·
2   παράσχ(ου) τοῖς ἀγγαρ(ευταῖς) Δωράνης ψωμία δέκα
3   ὀκτώ, γί(ν.) ψωμ(ία) ιη. Μηνὶ Μεσορὴ κδ α ἰνδ(ικτίωνος)

1. ἱερακιων

1   † To the most pious abba Metras the monk, Hierakion.
2   Deliver to the labourers of Dorane (?), eighteen loaves of bread,
3   makes 18 loaves of bread. In the month of Mesoré on the 24th of the first indiction.

1. For the title "abba," see Derda and Wipszycka 1994. The name Μήτρας appears to date in documentary papyri only in *SB* XXII 15365.4 (Oxy., VII cent.).

2. For the word ἀγγαρευτής = "labourer," see *P.Hamb.* III 216 introd.; *P.Oxy.* LVIII 3958.28n.; *CPR* XXII 45.5.

For the personal name Δωράνης, cf. *P.Herm.* 73.2, where Δωρανις (ed.: l. Δωρανίῳ) is written where a dative should be used. We think it not unconceivable that in fact Δωρανις is a iotacistic spelling of Δωρανης and that the latter form is left uninflected. It seems also conceivable that one is dealing with a female personal or geographical name Δωρανη, gen. in -ης; such a name, however, is not yet found in the standard onomastica or in the *DDBDP*. There are names that can be compared to ours: Τωράνιος, *P.Lond.* V 1771.4 (Hermopolite VI cent.), or Τωράννος, *SPP* XX 221.21 (Hermopolite, VI cent.). However, Preisigke, *NB*, s.v. connects these with Τύραννος.

On bread and baking in Graeco-Roman Egypt, see Battaglia 1989; for ψωμία, see esp. ibidem pp. 97-99.

3. For the word μηνί written out in full, cf. the remarks made by Gonis 2000: 154 note to l. 3 and fn. 16 and Gonis 2001: 226 n.12. Our text does not contribute to sharing his preference for μ(ηνός) instead

of μ(ηνί). For the use of the temporal dative in such datings in Byzantine papyri, compare also the many cases of datings of the type Ἐγράφη μηνί [month name], with μηνί written out in full (we have not found any case of Ἐγράφη + μηνός written out in full); E. Mayser discusses the temporal dative in Ptolemaic documents in his *Grammatik* II.2 296-7.

Mesore 24 = 17 viii. there is no way to establish which Julian year was covered by the 1st indiction (in the late VIth century = 552/553, 567/568, 582/583, 597/598; in the early VIIth century = 612/613, 627/628, 642/643, etc.).

P.Clackson 50
(FRAGMENT OF A GREEK DOCUMENT RELATED TO TAX COLLECTION)

P.Monts.Roca inv. 713　　　　　　　10,2 x 3,7 cm　　　　　　　VIIth-VIIIth century
Plates XXIII-XXIV　　　　　　　　　　　　　　　　　　　　　Provenance unknown

Verso blank. This papyrus contains a fragment of a Greek document written across the fibres, which seems to have been cut from a larger document; interestingly, it is provided with a clay seal.

1　(traces)
2　] ..λμων Ἀφοῦ(τος) μοναζοντ( ) ἁγίου Ἀπολλῶ
3　](κεράτια) γ
4　] . μ(ηνὶ) Π(α)ῦ(νι) α ἰ(ν)δ(ικτίωνος) ιγ † (Clay seal covering traces of writing)

In this text one seems to be dealing with a payment of a sum of money (only three carats preserved in line 3, but in the preceding lacuna one or more solidi may have been mentioned). The payment may be related to matters of taxation as also the use of the clay seal seems to suggest (see below). It is of interest that line 2 refers to one or more monks of the monastery of the Holy Apollos. It is true that the word μοναστήριον itself has not been written, but nevertheless we venture to think that a phrasing "monk(s) of the Holy Apollos" cannot be interpreted otherwise. The precise date of the text, given in the text as Pauni 1 of the 13th indiction, cannot be pinpointed any further; the handwriting makes us feel that it probably belongs to the late VIIth or early VIIIth century C.E.

The clay seal has been stamped twice, and is thus a double one. Each side features a round face of about 5 mm in diametre. On the one side we think we can see a cornucopia, and on the other side a human (perhaps female) figure standing, holding a long object in the left arm. It should be kept in mind that clay seals are frequently found in late papyrus documents dealing with taxation, i.e. either receipts for payment or tax demands. See Wassiliou and Harrauer 1999; on the basis of this general finding it may be supposed that also in the case of *P.Clackson* 50 one is dealing with such a document. If this is correct, it may be argued that between a mention of a tax payer (l. 2) and a date (l. 4) one expects in line 3 a tax payment or an imposition to have mentioned, hence our idea to read here (κεράτια) γ. It must be admitted, however, that the reading of the symbol for κεράτια is all but certain and that the name of the tax paid for is now lost. For seals related to the monastery of Apa Apollo, see Delattre 2007, although his seals feature only monograms.

2. The DDBDP, when searched for μοναζ-, produces 185 matches, among which there are some doubles. Another term for "monk/nun" is μοναχός / μοναχή, but it is far less common than μονάζων, μοναζοντ-, μοναζουσα-/ση. On these terms, see for example F.E. Morard, "Monachos, moine. Histoire du terme grec jusqu'au 4e siècle," *Freiburger Zeitschrift für Philosophie und Theologie* 20 (1973), 332-411; A. Guillaumont, "Les *remnuoth* de Saint Jérôme," *Christianisme d'Égypte*, Paris-Louvain, 1995, 87-92. For the rising importance of monkhood in the 4th century see M. Choat, "The development and use of terms for monk in Late Antique Egypt," *JAC* 45 (2002) 5-23.

If -λμων is in fact the end of a personal name in the nominative (something of which we are all but certain), it does not seem attractive to resolve here μονάζοντ(ος) going with a father's name Ἀφοῦ(τος); monks generally do not have children, unless they have entered the monastery after marriage.

Bibliography

Battaglia, E. (1989). *"Artos." Il lessico della panificazione nei papiri greci*, Milano: Vita e Pensiero.

Calderini, A. and Daris, S. (2007). *Dizionario dei nomi geografici e topografici dell'egitto greco-romano*: Suppl. 4. Pisa/Roma: Fabrizio Serra.

Derda, T. and Wipszycka, E. (1994). "L'emploi des titres *abba*, *apa* et *papas* dans l'Egypte byzantine," *JJP* 24, 23-56.

Gonis, N. (2000). "Two Poll-Tax Receipts from Early Islamic Egypt," *ZPE* 131, 150-154.

Gonis, N. (2001). "Reconsidering some Fiscal Documents from Early Islamic Egypt," *ZPE* 137, 225-228.

Torallas Tovar, S. and Worp, K. A. (2007). "New Literary Texts from Montserrat: (1) A Fragment of Johannes Chrysostomos' *De Virginitate*, Ch. 73 and (2) A New Papyrus of the *Comparatio Menandri & Philistionis*," *Proceedings of the 24th International Congress of Papyrology* II, Helsinki, 1-7 August 2004. Helsinki: Societas Scientarum Fennica, 1019-1031.

Vandorpe, K. (1995). *Breaking the Seal of Secrecy. Sealing Practices in Graeco-Roman and Byzantine Egypt Based on Greek, Demotic and Latin Papyrological Evidence*. Leiden (= *Uitgaven vanwege de stichting "Het Leids Papyrologisch Instituut,"* 18).

Wassiliou, A.-K. and Harrauer, H. (1999). *Siegel und Papyri: das Siegelwesen in Ägypten von römischer bis in frühbyzantinischer Zeit*. Vienna: Österreichischen Verlagsgesellschaft.

Property Ownership and Tax Payment in Fourth-Century Monasticism

Malcolm Choat

By the late Byzantine and early Islamic period, the leaders and economic administrators of many monasteries could look through long lists of property owned and worked by their monasteries, and collate receipts for taxes paid on them. Such estates did not spring up overnight, but were the product of centuries of accretion and donation. Here I want to contribute to our knowledge of how these may have developed by investigating their existence, or lack of it, in the earliest period of monasticism, up to the end of the fourth century.

In terms of the theme of this volume, we will want to ask about the extent of monastic estates in the fourth century, and indeed about their existence; put simply, were there monastic estates to administer in the first century of monasticism in Egypt? The documentation as we have it also leads me to ask to what extent land and property owned by monks was under the control of monasteries, rather than the monks themselves, and to what extent the monasteries took collective responsibility for the taxation levied on these lands. Finally, I want to consider to what extent the results we arrive at are a function of the nature of the documentation and how it has come to us, and conversely, to what extent they reflect fourth-century norms and practices.

In terms of the day-to-day supply of food and goods to monasteries, and the sale of their wares, the papyri serve us reasonably well.[1] The letters from Paul to Nepheros[2] show the writer seeking out various wares for the monks in the capital,[3] and selling "bundles" (δεσμίδια) which context suggests are wares from the monastery.[4] Elsewhere, letters such as *P.Iand.* V 100[5] and some of the correspondence in *P.NagHamm.*[6] provide valuable information, but have less context. Here, however, I want to reflect more narrowly on monastic ownership of land and property, and payment of taxes. The evidence for this is, unfortunately, neither extensive nor in many cases explicit. It may be set out as follows:

P.Neph. 48 (Hathor; Heracleopolite, 323?[7]): NN, resident of the ὄρος called Hathor, sells a well-appointed οἰκία to Aurelius Eusebios(?) μοναχός(?)[8] from the same ὄρος.

---

[1] See Schmelz 2002: 162-254; Wipszycka 1972, both drawing on predominantly later evidence. The classic discussion of the legal position of ecclesiastical and monastic property is Steinwenter 1930.

[2] *P.Neph.* 1-9, written from Alexandria to the monastery of Hathor in the Heracleopolite, probably in the first half of the 350's (*BL* 9, 173; cf. *P.Neph.*, Intro., p. 3-5).

[3] E.g. buying and sending oil (*P.Neph.* 3, 4, 6, 8, 9); iron (*P.Neph.* 5, 8); liquid pitch (*P.Neph.* 8).

[4] *P.Neph.* 4, 8. The monastery also seems to be in a position to supply grain and bread to Paul (*P.Neph.* 4, 5, 6); cf. *P.Neph.* 12.18-20.

[5] *P.Iand.* V 100 (?, IV²), 7ff.

[6] *P.NagHamm.* Gr. 67, 68, 72; Copt. 5.

[7] On the date, see *BL* 9, 174 and Bagnall and Worp 2004: App. D, p. 180 s.a. 323.

[8] ll.4-5: Αὐρ[ηλί]ῳ Ε[.].β.[.]ωι | [c.8 -ο]υ μ[ονα]χῷ: other restorations, such as e.g. σ]υμ[μά]χῳ, might also be entertained, but the context seems to favour the editors' text.

P.Herm.Landl. G 505, F 722 (Hermopolis, shortly after 346/347): Makarios ἀποτακτικός owns 16 aroura in the 6th pagus.

P.Oxy. XLVI 3311 (Oxyrhynchus, c. 373-374): Ammonios ἀποτακτικός, who inherited the πράγματα (presumably including any property he owned) of one Gemellos, has passed it onto Ammon, himself perhaps a monk.[9]

SB XXII 15311 (Hermopolite, 367/368?[10]): The ship of the Pachomian community (μοναστήριον Ταβεννησε) and Anoubion the ἀποτακτικός feature in a list of tax payments.

P.Lips. 28 (Hermopolis, 381): Silvanos the ἀποτακτικός takes legal responsibility for the share in the family estate of his ten year-old nephew (whom he formally adopts), including land, property, and various household goods.

PSI VI 698 (Oxyrhynchus, 392): A family notes where their property stood in Oxyrhynchus: "to the south of the public street, to the East (the property) of Annis the μοναχή."

P.Oxy. XLIV 3203 (Oxyrhynchus, 400): Two μοναχαὶ ἀποτακτικαί let out the hall and cellar of their property in the *Hippeon paremboles* quarter.

P.Genova II 69 (?, IV²): Grain loaded onto a ship "in the name of the μονή"(?).[11]

For more explicit, if still slightly confusing testimony, such as the request for information on the taxes of a smith directed to Apa Sabinos the ἀναχωρητής by the *sitologoi* of Alabastrine in *PSI* 1342, we wait until the fifth century.[12]

This is the evidence, such as we have it. I would like to have discussed the land rented by the *Topos Mani*, as recorded in the Kellis Agricultural Account Book.[13] The nature of that establishment is still unclear; whatever it was, it would at least provide a parallel for some institution leasing property, but while its exact status (a Manichaean monastery?[14]) remains unclear, I reluctantly pass over it.

The most suggestive, and most often cited or discussed, is P.Berol. inv. 11860, which has most recently reappeared as *SB* XXII 15311.[15] Even as reinterpreted by Klaas Worp,[16] this is still our best evidence for the landholdings of a monastery in the fourth century. But it is still frustratingly obscure. The crucial lines are as follows:[17]

---

[9] Thus suggested by Bagnall 2001: 15ff, not implausibly.

[10] 382/383 is a less probable alternative, see BL 9, 277.

[11] On the date see BL 10, 279.

[12] The fourth century date advanced by the first editor of this letter has rightly been called into question; several elements make it certain it belongs in the fifth (see BL 4, 91; 6, 186; 9, 231).

[13] *P.Kell.* IV Gr. 96.320, 513.

[14] See *P.Kell.* IV, Intro, pp. 81-82; Gardner 2000.

[15] Ed.pr. Wipszycka 1975= *SB* XIV 11972; *SB* XXII 15311 reprints textual advances made by Worp 1993.

[16] Worp 1993.

[17] Reproduced from the text of Worp; superseded readings from the ed.pr. are not explicitly noted.

(m3)
17   εἰς πλ(οῖον¹⁸) μοναστηρίου Ταβεννησε [ ]¹⁹
     [ ] ρι ηγ( ) Ἀνουβίωνος [   ]
(m1) εἰς πλ(οῖον) μοναστηρίου Ταβεννησε περὶ Τι [ ]
20   [Ἀν]ουβίων Ὡρίωνος ἀποτακτικ[ὸς τοῦ (αὐτοῦ) μονα-   ]
     στηρίου ἀπὸ Ἀλαβαστρίνης τοῦ Ἀντ[ινοΐτου   ]
     οὕτως

The monastery itself is only explicitly mentioned as the owner of the boat on which, presumably, the taxes which are listed following οὕτως were transported. The monastery to which the *apotaktikos* Anoubion son of Horion belongs is obscured in a lacuna; αὐτοῦ is a reasonable restoration, but makes it unlikely that he will be found in Alabastrine, or that he is practicing his asceticism there.[20] He has customarilly been assumed to be responsible for the taxes owed on the lands which are listed in lines 23ff.[21] He is on this interpretation either the tax payer himself,[22] or a representative of the monastery, perhaps because of a previous connection with the properties in question.[23]

If the payments listed in ll. 23ff are those which Anoubion himself owes, it would provide additional support for the suggestion below that monks usually represented themselves before the state in matters of taxation in the fourth century. However, there may be a more cogent explanation of Anoubion's presence in this part of the document.

The information on his Alabastrinian origin might be not unexpected were Anoubion personally responsible for the taxes,[24] but it is also distinctly reminiscent of the way in which ship's captains are quite regularly required to state their origin with an ἀπό-clause identical to that found here.[25] Anoubion's primary supervision, therefore (as already suggested by Worp) may be over the transport of the taxes; that is, over the ship itself.[26] If so, he may have been one of the "brothers who are on the boats" (ⲛⲓⲥⲛⲏⲟⲩ ⲉⲧϩⲓⲡϫⲟⲓ), who appear in the Pachomian texts.[27] While charge of a ship is often

---

[18] So restored by all editors and commentators on this text except Fournet and Gascou (2002: 37), who resolve πλ(οῖον / α) in deference to the varied number apparent in the later documents they deal with; cf. Fournet and Gascou 2002: 30 n.19.

[19] Amounts are lost at the right-hand edge (Bagnall 1993: 290 n.170; Gascou 1976: 183), but nothing may have stood to the right of ll. 19 and 21 (although see below).

[20] Μοναστηρίου Ταβεννησε reads most naturally as referring to the original Pachomian monastery, rather than the Pachomian federation (Bagnall 1993: 290 n.171, contra ed.pr.; cf. Fournet and Gascou 2002: 37 n. 54).

[21] Rousseau 1999: 154; Bagnall 1993: 290; Goehring 1999: 49, 57, 95, 107.

[22] Fournet and Gascou 37 n.53, suggesting the format of the document at this point could make this probable, but struggling to reconcile this with the Pachomian requirement for incoming monks to divest themselves of their property.

[23] Rousseau 1999: 154. Fournet and Gascou 2002: 37 n.53 cite ⲁⲛⲁⲧⲇⲓⲁⲕⲟⲛⲓⲁ ⲛⲁⲡⲟⲧⲁⲕⲧⲓⲕⲟⲥ ϣⲁ ⲉϩⲟⲩⲛ in the Apocalypse of Karour (Lefort 1956: 100:33-34) as a possible clue that *apotaktikos* could have denoted a specific supervisory function, but they nevertheless consider it more likely that Anoubion was a tax payer.

[24] That such information would be superfluous if his role was in some way analogous to the Pachomian *diaconitae* who supervise such transports in later papyri is recognised by Fournet and Gascou 2002: 37 n.53.

[25] See e.g. *P.Vind.Sijp.* 1.5-6 (Hermopolite, 24.12.338); *P.Amh.* II 138.4-5 (Arsinoite, before 1.1.327); *P.Cair.Isid.* 50.2, 18-19, 33-34 (Karanis, 16.5.310).

[26] Worp 1993: 34 (n. to ll. 19, 21), suggesting the verb ἐνεβάλετο might have stood at the end of 19.

[27] *Vita Pachomii*, Bohairic (cited below according to the edition of Lefort 1925 and the chapter divisions of Veilleux 1980, largely those of Lefort 1943) §96, 201; the *nautas* mentioned in Rule § 67 are presumably the same people.

signalled by a ὑπό-clause, something rendered unlikely here by the case of ['Άν]ουβίων,[28] one can imagine the format of the document rendering such syntax unnecessary.

The Pachomian tradition records that the early Federation owned at least two boats, one donated by Petronius,[29] the other by an unnamed "great and pious councillor" (πολιτευόμενος) of Apollonopolis (Kôs).[30] According to the Greek *Life* the monks later built a fleet of boats, one for each community.[31] If the redactors of the Pachomian hagiographical tradition correctly located these events in time—and were not seeking to explain the focus on Nile-borne traffic in their own day[32]—this enabling of river-borne transport throughout the federation had probably occurred by the date of SB XXII 15311, as Theodore—in whose stewardship this boat-building is placed—died in 368.[33] Supplies for the monastery, and the brothers themselves, were ferried down and up the Nile.[34]

Elsewhere in fourth century texts we see the church and its officials transporting grain for which it has no particular taxation responsibility,[35] and the Pachomians were clearly in the same business by the sixth century.[36] While it is important not to read SB XXII 15311 explicitly in light of the well-developed system visible in late Byzantine papyri, the focus of the Pachomian order on the river[37] provides an instructive context in which to consider the present text.

One should thus read the contributions in ll. 23-31 not as taxes paid by a monk, monastery, or monastic federation, but as taxes paid by villages or *epoikia*, which were carried on the ship of the Pachomian monastery. If [εἰς πλ(οῖον) NN] σπεκουλάτο[ρος]—*speculatores* own ships in other documents[38]—began fragment b, Theon son of Dionysios could stand to that ship as Anoubion does to

---

[28] The accusative would be expected in this case, see the documents discussed in Gonis 2003, and a genitive were the monastery's representation by Anoubion signalled by a διά clause (as is the role of the διακονητής in the sixth and seventh century Pachomian papyri [cf. Fournet and Gascou 2002]). An argument for a mistaken case in ['Άν]ουβίων at 20 would have to take into consideration the corrrect case endings observed elsewhere in the text; one might note however Ἀνουβίονος[or Ἀνουβίωνα[, to be read in the damaged (or corrupt and abandoned?) first mention of the "boat of the monastary of Tabennese" in 17-18.

[29] *Vita Pachomii*, Bohairic §56; on Petronius cf. below, n. 51.

[30] Lefort 1933: 145.31ff; S⁵ § 53 in Lefort 1943: 247; and restored from here to be § 53 in the composite Coptic *Life* translated in Veilleux 1980. It is presumably these two boats that are referred to at *Vita Pachomii*, Greek 1 (ed. Halkin 1932) § 113.

[31] *Vita Pachomii*, Greek 1 (ed. Halkin 1932) § 146. But note the misgivings expressed by just this monk about ownership of property (explicitly including boats) both here, and more dramatically in the parallel in Bohairic *Life* §197; on the literary character of both passages Wipszycka 1996: 179ff., Fournet and Gascou 2002:42; cf. the following note.

[32] Fournet and Gascou 2002: 41, in the course of a thorough discussion of the relationship of the Pachomians with boats and the river; see also Villeux 1980: 276, noting the way § 53 interrupts the narrative at this section and looks out of place. SB XXII 15311 at the very least confirms the Pachomians did own at least one ship near the end of Theodore's life.

[33] *Vita Pachomii*, Bohairic (ed. Lefort 1925) §206, with Villeux 1980: 294.

[34] E.g, *Vita Pachomii*, Bohairic (ed. Lefort 1925) § 96, 124, 132; Greek 1 (ed. Halkin 1932) § 113; among the *Rules* see esp. § 118 "About the Boats"; further references and discussion in Fournet and Gascou 2002: 40-42.

[35] *P.Münch.* III 99 (Hermopolis, 390); cf. the ναυταὶ ἐκκλησίας of *P.Hamb.* IV 267 (Oxyrhynchite?, 336-348); *P.Oxy.* XXXIV 2729 (Oxyrhynchus, IV) (δι(ὰ) τοῦ πλοίου Θεοδώρου τοῦ ἐπισκόπου ἡμῶν, 7-8); and of course the boats owned by Hierakapollon the Bishop in *P.Col.* VII 160-61 (Karanis, 345-51).

[36] See now Fournet and Gascou 2002.

[37] The proximity of the majority of the Pachomian settlements to the Nile is noted by Fournet and Gascou 2002: 40.

[38] *P.Oxy.* XLII 3079.6 (IV¹; see Gonis 2003); *SB* XIV 11551.3 (324-337).

the Pachomian ship.³⁹ If this is a document whose primary purpose is to list the taxes transported by ships, we should read it not so much as the forerunner to the documents recording the existence of and taxation on monastic estates, but to those which provide us with evidence for the role of monastic ships (and particularly Pachomian ships) in the transport of taxes.⁴⁰

P.Genova II 69, were it not broken, might prove to be a receipt (ἀποχή) written by Aurelius Hierax, *grammateus*, confirming the payment of grain to the *curator frumenti* for a lost location "in the name of a monastery," [ὑπὲρ?] | ὀνόματος μονη[(3). Acceptable proper names to stand here are rare,⁴¹ but there are other senses of μονή which might give sense.⁴² Thus this is an insecure base on which to build a picture of a fourth-century tax-payments by a monastery itself.

As regards the other documents listed above, it is difficult to use them to discuss monastic estates in the sense of those belonging to monasteries, because in the majority of our fourth-century evidence, we deal with individual monks: they act in their own capacity, as individuals for legal purposes, and no membership of any monastery is expressed (or even implied) for any of them.

Where membership of a monastery is specified, it is nearly always in personal letters, for the addressee or sender, but most commonly for third parties.⁴³ Outside of these, we have *P.Neph*. 48, a contract for the sale of a house, where the buyer, and quite possibly the seller, are μοναχοί on the ὄρος καλούμενος Φαθώρ;⁴⁴ this document is destined to be kept by one or other party. The contract to appoint a deputy in *P.Lond*. VI 1913 is addressed to the overseers of the monastery of Hathor,⁴⁵ and will have stayed there. Finally there is *SB* XXII 15311, already discussed. Of these, only the last is really a 'public' document.

In the other documents listed, the monastic concerned is identified only by name and title. Does this mean that they were not attached to any federation? Both because of their apparent urbanity, and associations argued between the term ἀποτακτικός and communal monasticism,⁴⁶ these monks are often assumed to live in some sort of community. The term ἀποτακτικός, which five of these monks are called, does not guarantee such,⁴⁷ but leaving that aside—since not all these monastics are designated thus—it would be statistically unlikely if all these monks and nuns were true loners. The "house" on the *oros* of Hathor in *P.Neph*. 48 has "neighbours,"⁴⁸ the apotactic nuns in *P.Oxy*. 3203 own a property together, and there is a fair chance that the beneficiary of the arrangements which the

---

³⁹ Were this the case, one should probably restore an ἀπό clause following his name, featuring a village in the Hermopolite, or the polis itself (Ἑρμουπολ( ), b.3).

⁴⁰ Accepted as such in Wipsycka 1996 185-186 with n. 32; on the sixth and seventh century papyri see Fournet and Gascou 2002, Gascou 1976 (esp. 178-184), Rémondon 1971: the evidence concerns specifically the boats of the monastery of Metanoia. For the problem of how the Pachomians resolved this activity with the instructions of the founder and their rules, see Fournet and Gascou 2002: 42-43.

⁴¹ Possibilities at *P.Genova* II 69.3n.

⁴² See e.g. the discussion at *O.Oslo* 22 comm. on the ἐπιμελητὴς μονῆς Ἰσίου who features therein.

⁴³ *P.Neph*. 3, 6, 11, 12; *SB* VIII 9683

⁴⁴ See above, at n. 8. *Oros* is at this stage only in the childhood of its meaning of "monastery" (cf. Copt. ⲧⲟⲟⲩ) as later observed (see Cadell and Rémondon 1967), but should refer here to the location of some form of monastic community.

⁴⁵ τοῖς προεστῶσ[ι] μονῆς μονοχῶν (*l*. μοναχῶν) [καλ]ουμένης Ἄθορ.

⁴⁶ Goehring 1999a.

⁴⁷ Wipszycka 2001; Choat 2002.

⁴⁸ The papyrus unfortunately breaks off before the description of the γείτονες (15).

composers of *P.Oxy.* 3311 object to is a monk;[49] sorts of quasi-federations or communal arrangements at least. But there is no necessity to specify any such arrangement, or certainly for it to have any legal standing in any of these arrangements.

I have eschewed detailed comparison with literary sources because one should not reduce our overview of the papyri to a simple comparison with them. The Pachomian evidence, and that really is what we are talking about,[50] provides a pole at least.[51] But the degree to which monastic property was administered in common cannot be usefully addressed through the papyri. It seems better to follow the direction the latter lead, and ask to what extent monks took full legal responsibility for their own lands in this period while living in some form of federation, by which I mean anything from at least one other monk to a full monastery.

If we look outside the documents discussed above, at letters to and from monks, in *P.Neph.* 12 Sarapion asks Nepheros to exercise oversight (προνοήσῃς, line 18) over a plot of land, presumably Sarapion's, although the reading is slightly obscure.[52] Sarapion is the only person who calls himself μοναχός in the whole archive of Nepheros; his long letter, composed in the best traditions almost entirely of greetings, is our primary source of prosopographical information on the inhabitants of Hathor. It is difficult to believe he was not a resident, because he repeatedly forecast a return home (ἔρχομαι). It is hard to contextualise the request, which goes on to ask that some grain (from Sarapion's land?) be put in the cemetery. We can at least say that if the monastery manages the property brought to it as a collective, administering the estate and providing or arranging workers on behalf of all monks, then Sarapion should not have to make such a request.

Even in the late Byzantine period, despite the evidence for centralised control of monastic property, some monasteries could still be treated as personal property:[53] Abraham of Hermonthis leaves the monastery of Phoibammon and its properties to his successor Victor in his will.[54] Such individual management of property seems to be the case in the fourth century papyri. Literary sources record the acquisition of property by the Pachomian federation, but its exact status is not specified. That a church as an entity could own property was recognised by the government already in the early fourth century,[55] and while this legislation seems to have been understood to cover monastic foundations once

---

[49] See above at n. 9.

[50] Although see hints in other sources, such as the *Apophthegmata* discussed in Bagnall 2001.

[51] Most often cited is Petronius, who joined the federation with his monastery of Thbew (*Vita Pachomii*, Greek 1, ed. Halkin 1932, § 80 and Bohairic, ed. Lefort 1925, § 56); this monastery was on his well-off parents' land, although the testimonies are (intentionally?) vague as to whether he actually gave any land to the Federation, cf. Wipszycka 1996: 187. By the time of Theodore the Pachomians had "acquired many fields" according to *Vita Pachomii*, Greek 1 (ed. Halkin 1932) § 146; cf. Rousseau 1999, 153-154, Wipszycka 1996: 185ff.

[52] τὸ μικρὸν [ ] ον γῆν, l. 18-19. The editors advise reading the genitive γῆς; as the scribe confuses case-endings repeatedly, I wonder if some form of the possessive pronoun was not intended in the lacuna ("my little plot of land"?).

[53] Even to the extent of being disposable (see e.g. the Melitian monastery at Labla, *P.Dubl.* 32-34 [Arsinoïte, 511-513] with Steinwenter 1930: 5-6), much to the displeasure of the Emperor Justinian (*Novella* 7.1). In a later context see the documents recording property transfer between monks at Bawit (BL Or. 6201-6204, 6206 [833-49], text in MacCoull 1994, discussion in Krause 1985:126-128).

[54] *P.Lond.* 1.77.25ff (Thebes, c. 610), trans. L. S. B. Macoull, in Thomas and Constantinides Hero 2000: 55-56. Cf. Steinwenter 1930: 12ff.

[55] Constantine and Licinius were aware of this already in 313 (Lactantius, *de mort. persec.* 48.9); laws in 321 (*CTh* 16.2.4) and 398 (*CTh* 16.5.33) explicity recognise that churches could inherit and own property, cf. Steinwenter 1930: 3-4.

they were sufficiently developed, they are explicitly the subject of legislation in this regard only in the following century.[56] Papyrological evidence to corroborate the apparent testimony of the Pachomian sources is likewise not apparent until later centuries,[57] possibly because the legal impediments to larger transfers[58] meant donations were rare, or perhaps because the internal administration needed for management of such collections of property took some time to develop.

Payment of taxes on the behalf of dependents of the monasteries[59] seems visible in the fifth century, but evidence that monasteries were making a collective response to taxation at this stage[60] is not apparent, and it would follow that individual monks retained personal taxation liability along with the legal title over their lands. An impulse to communal response to taxation was however already present elsewhere in third century society: at least one large estate arranged for the collective payment of taxes and a coordinated response to liturgical obligations for its employees.[61] Such an arrangement would seem logical for monastic communities, but we have no evidence that they adopted anything similar in the early period.

We can see individual monks acquiring and owning property in the fourth-century papyri. The *Vitae Pachomii* assume the same applied for monasteries as well. We may well be dealing here with the way the compilers of the *Lives* remembered earlier events, perhaps casting them in terms with which they were familiar. Even in that case, we should start seeing evidence for similar practices in the papyri near the end of the fourth century. So why do we not? Why do we not find, for instance, receipts for tax made out to monasteries, or monasteries listed as landholders? Papers proving ownership of land, or detailing its acquisition, might also be expected.

I am not inclined to think that this is a true lacuna in the papyri, i.e. that we have lost a whole class of papyri recording monastic tax payers and landholders. But it may also be that such are not explicitly signalled (and are thus unrecognised) in those we do have.

We might elucidate this by considering the nature of our papyri documenting monasticism in the fourth century, and whence they come. One of the useful facts that characterises monastic documentation from the later period is that a lot of it either was, or demonstrably must have been, found *in situ* in the ruins of monasteries; one thinks of Bawit, or the core documentation of some of the Theban monasteries. When we look at the fourth century documentation, we have no such certainty. We cannot, in fact, be certain that any of the fourth century papyri which deal with monasticism were

---

See among the fourth century papyri *SB* VI 9527 (Arsinoïte, 385-412) with Bagnall 1993: 290-291; and perhaps *SB* XVI 13066 (?, IV/V), recording a payment by a priest (? π]ρε(σβυτέρ-) (ὑπέρ) ἰδ(ιωτικῆς) γῆς τῆς ἐκκλησίας).

[56] *CTh* 5.3.1 (434), mandating, *inter alia*, that monasteries shall inherit the property of monks who die intestate.

[57] Explicit evidence of such donations of property to monasteries comes only later, e.g. *P.Cair.Masp.* II 67250 (Antinoopolis?, 565-578); *P.Cair.Masp.* II 67151 (Antinoopolis, 15.11.570); *P.KRU* 106 (Thebes, 735); *O.Brit.Mus.Copt.* I, pl. 66.2 (Thebes, VII-VIII). Evidence indicating monastic administration of property is likewise of late Byzantine date, e.g. *P.Ross.Georg.* III 48 (Antaiopolite, VI), *P.Giss.* I 56 (Hermopolite, VI), *P.Lond.* II 483 (Apollonopolites Heptakomias, 615 or 616). In many cases we are aware of this because of the leasing of the property to others by the monastery; on such arrangements see Gascou 1985: 8ff.

[58] I.e. the necessity of assuming the financial burdens associated with landholding, see Wipszycka 1996: 186-188.

[59] *PSI* 1352, see above, at n. 12; for later evidence, see e.g. *P.Lond.Copt.* I 1049, with Schmelz 2002: 200-201.

[60] For later times see e.g. the many payments listed under the names of Hermopolite monasteries in *P.Sorb.* II 69(618/19 or 633/34), summarised at Gascou 1994: 79ff. The plentiful evidence from the Early Islamic period (e.g. Bawit and Bala'izah; see S. J. Clackson in *P.Mon.Apollo,* Intro., 23-26 and P. Kahle in *P.Bal.* I, 30-45 respectively) of course responds to different historical circumstances.

[61] See the Appianus estate, discussed by Rathbone 1991: 121ff, 133ff, 405ff.

found in monasteries; that is the reasonable presumption, of course, in the case of the large archives of Paieous, Nepheros, and Johannes. But they could have been already discarded in more communal dumps.

By my own count, around 80 papyri dated IV or IV/V document monasticism in some way or another.[62] "Around" encodes a number of variables which could subtract from this number: insecure terminology and Coptic palaeography are only two. Of these papyri, over three quarters are personal letters. Many are to monks, but quite a number are casual mentions; the μοναχοί do not like the cheese in *P.Haun.* II 19, for example.

As I mentioned, it is not unlikely that the well-known archives were found in the ruins of monasteries. But not many of the other texts mentioning monks or monasteries are likely to have been found in such, and the majority of the better known texts were demonstrably not; the find-spot of the Kellis Agricultural Account book is known precisely;[63] statements to officials such as the petitions *P.Oxy.* 3311 and *P.Col.* VII 171 will have remained with their originators if drafts or been in official archives if sent; records such as *P.Herm.Landl.* or *SB* XXII 15311 will have been in the hands of an official somewhere. Beyond that we have lists, declarations, or orders where monks appear incidentally as third parities.[64] The deed of appointment *P.Lond.* VI 1913 must have been with Paieous' papers at Hathor, but aside from this we have only a small group of texts which are at all likely to have been in the possession of monks, or at least a copy of the same text: the adoption document *P.Lips.* 28; the lease *P.Oxy.* XLIV 3203, the sale contract *P.Neph.* 48, perhaps the fragmentary *P.Neph.* 49.

It is notable that the documents most explicitly attesting the monastery of Hathor were not acquired as part of the main purchase of texts in the Nepheros archive, but found their way to Heidelberg separately.[65] Among the first 42 items in *P.Neph.* (the "archive" proper), we have a number of non-epistolary pieces, avowedly from the same source according to the dealers.[66] There are several texts which most easily read as being associated with the monastery or being generated within it: *P.Neph.* 37, on the back of *P.Neph.* 2, for instance. For texts with no obvious connection to the archive (27, 29-34, 38), one can make suggestions—and the editors do—as to how they may have been in the monastery.[67] But other possibilities they raise, such as a communal dump with the nearby village of Nesos, or papyri purchased for reuse, might better explain some of the more random elements.

Excluding the famous archives, then, most of the early documents mentioning monks or monasteries either come through the antiquities market with no secure indication of provenance, or derive from undifferentiated large scale excavation, either provably or probably from dumps.

Of those texts which we can say are most likely to have been found in monasteries, the archives of Paieous, Nepheros, and Johannes, the core documentation seems to be letters. Is it then the case that these were all that were kept in the monasteries at this period? Or that we have found only the private

---

[62] This includes all documents which mention or refer to monks or monasteries (or can be argued to) in any way. Previous treatments (e.g. Barison 1938) require updating.

[63] *P.Kell.* IV, Intro.: 5-11.

[64] *PSI* VI 698 (Oxyrhynchus, 392); *O.Douch* III 190, V 611 (Kysis, IV/V); *P.Würzb.* 16 (Arsinoite 349); *SB* XX 15199 (Oxyrhynchus IV?).

[65] *Viz. P.Neph.* 48 and 49: compare their inventory numbers (1509 and 1353 respectively) with those of the rest of the archive (in the 2140's); cf. *P.Neph.* 129.

[66] See *P.Neph.*, Intro., p. 3.

[67] See *P.Neph.*, Intro., pp. 5-6.

archives of some of these monks, the letters written to the heads of these monasteries? It is possible that these were kept in later generations, and other documents were thrown out? But if they were thrown out, then why have we not found any?

Or is it possible that they were found along with the letters, but not recognised as being associated with them, because they did not mention monks or monasteries? (Non-exhaustive) searches of what else turned up in the British Museum and American collections who were purchasing in collaboration with it in 1923 and 1924 have so far failed to reveal anything else which looks like it may have come from the monastery of Hathor and been found with the letters to Paieous. I have also looked in the John Rylands University Library for documents other than letters which may have been associated with whatever monastery Apa Johannes inhabited. The search has so far proved time-consuming and fruitless, in part because many of texts remain unpublished. One might hope that, in the case of the Paieous archive, Bell (who undertook the initial description of these papyri) would have noticed anything that seemed to be associated with the archive.

We are driven back to the suggestion that monks were not regularly identifying themselves as such in transactions concerning tax and land in the period. Thinking thus we might allow ourselves to see Paphnuthis son of Kollouthos, who pays tax on land he is responsible for in *P.Neph.* 27, as a monk from Hathor.[68] The state had, however, always been prepared to accept an occupation, cult or otherwise, as an identifier, with or without a patronymic, and as μοναχός can be used in public documents by the 320's[69] and ἀποτακτικός the same by the late 340's,[70] this holds some weight, but not much.

We should also consider the possibility that monasteries were already acting through agents, but no fourth century papyrological evidence for the οἰκονόμοι or διοικηταί that we see in later texts[71] is obvious. They might be there, but if so they are operating on behalf of monasteries without giving any explicit signal that this is what they are doing.

In the end, it is best to retain some agnosticism about the question. Our best fourth-century source, *P.Herm.Landl.*, still lists only the landholders for a small percentage of the Hermopolite, and other documentation is scattered. That we do not have evidence for any particular practice cannot be used as proof that it did not occur.

As the evidence stands, however, I would tentatively suggest that even within monastic federations, it remained common in the fourth century for monks to take individual responsibility for their lands and the taxes on them, even if they were worked by other monks. Such cannot be disproved from the contemporary literary record, as the Pachomian material exhibits some vagueness on the exact arrangements as regarded the status of the land brought to the community and how it was represented to the state. While some coyness might be understandable given that the writers and actors were part of a fundamentally renunciatory movement, it is nevertheless notable that there are no detailed

---

[68] Of course, as the editors note, that *P.Neph.* 27 is clearly a copy might indicate it related to a dispute that Nepheros was asked to adjudicate on.

[69] *P.Col.* VII 171.

[70] *P.Herm.Landl.* G 505, F 722.

[71] Schmeltz 2002: 162 ff; such officials were usually monks or clergy themselves, as he makes clear at 163, where a summary of terminology (which extended beyond the two titles cited here) can also be found; see also Wipszycka 1972: 135ff.

instructions in the Pachomian Rules on how to handle taxation, or stories involving encounters with tax collectors in the *Lives*; nor are the *Lives* particularly interested in the details of Petronius' property once he brought it to the *koinonia*.[72] Likelihood, and what "must have happened" are more frequently put forward than actual evidence on these matters. While the Pachomians clearly appropriated "deserted"[73] land in the vicinity of Pbôw,[74] the *Lives* do not dwell on how taxation on this land was accessed or paid.[75] If, as has been suggested, they assisted villagers in meeting their tax-burden, perhaps we are on the way to monasteries asserting a status of their own in a taxation situation. Monastic lands were not tax-exempt,[76] and it is only natural that grain-producing monastic land would attract taxation.[77]

The legal situation regarding corporate ownership of monastic property and its taxation may only have been clarified in later centuries.[78] In these circumstances, individual responsibility for property may have proved easier for the State to comprehend, and simpler for monks and their monasteries to administer. It is only as we move into the fifth and following centuries, when the fame of monasticism had spread and people were familiar with the existence and concept of monasteries, that the monasteries themselves began putting their name to lands they held in their own name, and paying taxes on them as such.

Bibliography

Bagnall, R. S. (1993). *Egypt in Late Antiquity*. Princeton: Princeton University Press.

Bagnall, R. S. (2001). "Monks and Property: Rhetoric, Law and Patronage in the *Apophthegmata Patrum* and the Papyri," *Greek Roman and Byzantine Studies* 42, 7-24.

Bagnall, R. S. and Worp, K. A. (2004). *Chronological Systems of Byzantine Egypt* (2nd edn.). Leiden: Brill.

Barison, P. (1938). "Ricerche sui monasteri dell'Egitto bizantino ed arabo secondo i documenti dei papiri greci," *Aegyptus* 18, 29-148.

Cadell, H. and Rémondon, R. (1967). "Sens et emplois de τὸ ὄρος dans les documents papyrologiques," *Revue des études grecques* 80, 343-349.

Choat, M. (2002). "Terms for 'Monk' in Late Antique Egypt," *Jahrbuch für Antike und Christentum* 45, 5-23.

---

[72] Cf. above, n. 51.

[73] The quotation-marks justified by the attentive reading of Goehring 1999c: 97ff.

[74] Further Goehring 1999c: 95ff.

[75] Goehring 1999c: 99.

[76] Bagnall 1993: 290.

[77] Goehring 1999b: 49-50.

[78] The corporate legal personality was not necessarily a familiar concept in Graeco-Roman law; see Taubenschlag, 1955: 57-65:, esp. 64-65 on Christian institutions.

Fournet, J.-L. and Gascou, J. (2002). "Moines pachômiens et batellerie," in: C. Décobert, (ed) *Alexandrie médiévale 2. = Études alexandrines* 8. Cairo: Institut Français d'Archéologie Orientale.

Gardner, I. (2000). "He has gone to the Monastery," in: Emmerick, R. E., Sundermann, W. and Zieme, P. (eds.) *Studia Manichaica*. Berlin: Akademie Verlag, 247-57.

Gascou, J. (1976). "*P.Fouad* 87: Les monastères pachômiens et l'État byzantin," *BIFAO* 76, 157-184.

Gascou, J. (1985). "Les grands domaines, la cité et l'État en Égypte byzantine," *TravMem* 9, 1-90.

Gascou, J. (1994). *Un codex fiscal hermopolite (P.Sorb. II 69)*. Atlanta: Scholars Press.

Goehring, J. E. (1999). *Ascetics, Society, and the Desert: Studies in Early Egyptian Monasticism*. Harrisburg: Trinity Press International.

Goehring, J. E. (1999a). "Through a Glass Darkly: Diverse Images of the Ἀποτακτικοί(αί) in Early Egyptian Monasticism," in: Goehring 1999, 53-72.

Goehring, J. E. (1999b). "The World Engaged. The Social and Economic World of Early Egyptian Monasticism," in: Goehring 1999, 39-52.

Goehring, J. E. (1999c). "Withdrawing from the Desert: Pachomius and the Development of Village Monasticism in Upper Egypt," in: Goehring 1999, 89-109.

Gonis, N. (2003). "Ship-Owners and Skippers in Fourth-Century Oxyrhynchus," *ZPE* 143, 163-165.

Halkin, F. (ed.) (1932). *S. Pachomii Vitae Graecae*. Brussels: Société des Bollandistes.

Krause, M. (1985). "Zur Möglichkeit von Besitz im apotaktischen Mönchtum Ägyptens," in: Orlandi, T. and Wisse, F. (eds.), *Acts of the Second International Congress of Coptic Studies*. Rome : C.I.M., 121-133.

Lefort, L.-Th. (ed.) (1925). *S. Pachomii Vita Bohairice Scripta*. Paris: E Typographeo Reipublicae.

Lefort, L.-Th. (ed.) (1933). *S. Pachomii Vitae Sahidice Scriptae*. Paris: E Typographeo Reipublicae.

Lefort, L.-Th. (1943). *Les Vies coptes de saint Pachôme et de ses premiers successeurs*. Louvain: Bureaux du Muséon.

Lefort, L.-Th. (ed.) (1956). *Œuvres de S.Pachôme et de ses disciples*. Louvain: L. Durbecq.

MacCoull, L. S. B. (1994). "The Bawit Contracts: Texts and Translations," *BASP* 31, 141-158.

Rathbone, D. (1991). *Economic Rationalism and Rural Society in Third-Century A.D. Egypt: The Heroninos Archive and the Appianus Estate*. Cambridge: Cambridge University Press.

Rémondon, R. (1971). "Le monastère alexandrin de la Métanoia était-il bénéficiaire du fisc ou à son service?" in: *Studi in onore di Edoardo Volterra*. Volume 5. Milan: A. Guiffrè, 769-781.

Rousseau, P. (1999). *Pachomius. The Making of a Community in Fourth-Century Egypt* (2nd edn.). Berkeley: University of California Press.

Schmelz, G. (2002). *Kirchliche Amtsträger im spätantiken Ägypten: nach den Aussagen der griechischen und koptischen Papyri und Ostraka*. Munich/Leipzig: K.G. Saur.

Steinwenter, A. (1930). "Die Rechtsstellung der Kirchen und Kloster nach den Papyri," *Zeitschrift der Savigny-Stiftung für Rechtsgeschite. Kanonistische Abteilung* 50, 1-50.

Taubenschlag, R. (1955). *The Law of Greco-Roman Egypt in the Light of the Papyri, 332 B.C.-640 A.D.* Second Edition, Revised and Enlarged. Warszawa, Panstwowe Wydawnictwo Naukowe.

Thomas, J. and Constantinides Hero A. (eds). (2000). *Byzantine Monastic Foundation Documents: A Complete Translation of the Surviving Founders' Typika and Testaments = Dumbarton Oak Studies* 35. Washington D.C.

Veilleux, A. (1980). *Pachomian Koinonia*, vol. 1. Kalamazoo: Cistercian Publications.

Wipszycka, E. (1972). *Les ressources et les activités économiques des églises en Égypte de IVe au VIIIe siècles*. Bruxelles: Fondation Égyptologique Reine Élisabeth.

Wipszycka, E. (1975). "Les terres de la Congrégation pachômienne dans une liste de payements pour les apora," in: Bingen, J., Cambier, G. and Nachtergael, G. (eds.). *Le monde grec. Pensée, littérature, histoire, documents. Hommages à Claire Préaux*. Bruxelles: Éditions de l'Université, 625-636.

Wipszycka, E. (1996). "Contribution a l'étude de l'économie de la congregation pachomienne," *JJP* 26, 167-210.

Wipszycka, E. (2001). "Ἀναχωρητής, ἐρημίτης, ἔγκλειστος, ἀποτακτικός," *JJP* 31, 147-168.

Worp, K. A. (1993). "*SB* XIV 11972 Fr. A: Eine Neuedition," *APF* 39, 29-34.

Conversion religieuse dans un graffito de Baouit ? Révision de *SB* III 6042

Jean-Luc Fournet

Il est curieux que le graffito dont je vais parler ait aussi peu attiré l'attention des historiens du premier Islam en Égypte. Son contenu est pourtant, d'après l'édition et le commentaire qui en a été fait, exceptionnel. Seule, à ma connaissance, Sarah Clackson s'y était intéressée et nous avions eu tous deux l'occasion d'en parler en 2001, lors d'une visite que j'avais faite à Cambridge.

Il s'agit de l'inscription 222 de J. Maspero (1932), p. 90 (1943, pl. XXV c), passée dans le *Sammelbuch* des papyrologues (III 6042). Elle a été trouvée sur la paroi ouest de la salle 6. Voici le texte tel qu'il est édité, accompagné d'une reproduction de la photographie:

† ⲕⲉ ⲟ ⲑⲉ¹ | ⲓⲥ ⲭⲥ | ⲃⲟⲏⲑ ⲁⲅⲉⲛⲟⲩ | ⲅⲉⲱⲣⲅⲓⲥ ⲓⲉⲟⲥ | ⲥⲉⲣⲅⲓⲟⲩ ⲅⲉⲛⲟⲙⲉⲛⲟⲩ | ⲙⲁⲗⲉⲕ ⲁⲃⲇⲁⲗⲗⲁ | ⲓⲉⲟⲥ ⲁⲙⲣⲟⲩ | ⲙⲟⲁⲅⲉⲣ ⲓⲉⲟⲥ | ⲗⲉⲅⲗⲁⲛ ⲅⲉⲛⲟⲙⲉ|ⲛⲟⲩ ⲁⲡⲟ ⲥⲁⲗⲉⲉⲛ.

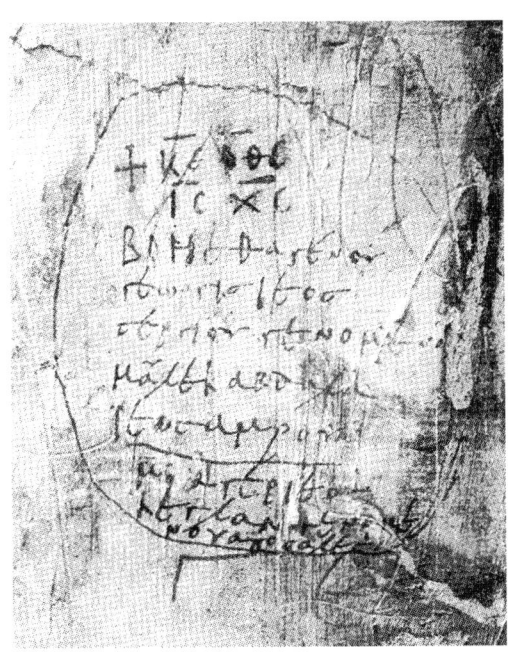

Donné sans traduction, il est néanmoins commenté par son inventeur, J. Maspero, dans l'introduction, p. VIII: "Un autre graffito mérite aussi une mention spéciale. D'après l'écriture, il est sans doute du

---

Je tiens à remercier tout particulièrement Jean-Michel Mouton pour ses suggestions, ses conseils bibliographiques et sa relecture.

¹ "Je lirais plutôt sur la photographie: ⲑⲥ.—E[tienne] D[rioton]."

début du VIIIe siècle. Il est l'œuvre d'un certain Georges, qui croyait écrire en grec, et qui décline ainsi son identité: Γεώργιος ἱεὸς Σεργίου, γενομένου Μᾶλεκ ᾿Αβδαλα ἱεὸς ῎Αμρου, Georges, fils de Sergios, autrefois Mâlek 'Abdallah fils d''Amr. Cette conversion d'un Arabe au christianisme est assez rare pour valoir d'être signalée."

Rare est assurément un euphémisme! Cette conversion, dans les conditions historiques et religieuses de l'islam, serait tout à fait extraordinaire et n'est étayée, à ma connaissance, par aucun parallèle contemporain, au point qu'elle suscite le scepticisme.

Il faut avouer que l'interprétation de J. Maspero n'est pas sans difficulté: que Mâlek 'Abdallah se soit converti au christianisme, ce qui entraîna son changement de nom, est déjà étonnant; mais l'inscription oblige à considérer que son père aussi, 'Amr, s'est converti puisqu'il serait devenu Sergios. Cette conversion sur deux générations serait peu banale.[2] En outre, l'explication de Maspero ne prend pas en considération la fin de l'inscription (ⲙⲟⲁⲅⲉⲣ ⲓⲉⲟⲥ | ⲗⲉⲅⲗⲁⲛ ⲅⲉⲛⲟⲙⲉ|ⲛⲟⲩ ⲁⲡⲟ ⲥⲁⲗⲉⲉⲛ), où, d'après le participe γενομένου, il serait encore question de conversion.

Quoique cette inscription ait été partiellement intégrée dans le *Sammelbuch* des papyrologues,[3] l'exégèse qu'en fait Maspero n'a pas été remise en cause jusqu'à ce que Sarah Clackson (2000, p. 23) en propose une nouvelle interprétation, inverse de la précédente: "A Greek graffito from Bawit (Maspero and Drioton 1932-1943 no. 222, see also p. viii) records the names of two Christian converts to Islam: Geôrgi(o)s son of Sergios, who has become Malek Abdala son of Amros (Malik 'Abd Allāh ibn 'Amr) (Γεωργις ιεος Σεργιου γενομενου Μᾱλεκ Αβδαλα ϊεος Αμρου); and Moager son of Leglan, who has become Abu Saleen (Μοαγερ ιεος Λεγλαν γενομενου Απο Σαλεεν)." Elle en tire ensuite des conséquences sur l'islamisation de l'Égypte.[4]

La conversion de chrétiens à l'islam est cette fois-ci vraisemblable malgré sa précocité et le contexte monastique dans lequel elle est annoncée. Il faut savoir gré à Sarah d'avoir mis fin au contresens de Maspero. Je crois malgré tout que son explication n'est pas sans difficultés. Nous en avions parlé ensemble, je l'ai dit, en 2001; je lui avais exposé mes vues sur cette inscription et elle les avait acceptées. C'est en souvenir de cette stimulante discussion que j'ai décidé de présenter ici ce graffito.

---

[2] J.-M. Mouton attire néanmoins mon attention sur un autre cas possible qu'il a rencontré dans les archives fatimides de Naqlûn, en voie de publication (cf. Mouton 2002): dans un acte d'achat se rencontre un certain "'Alī ibn Aḥmad connu sous le nom de Ḥurūfah ibn Ṣad." L'auteur envisage la possibilité selon laquelle le second nom serait son nom copte de naissance et que le premier soit son nouveau nom musulman. "Le fait que le nom du père change aussi laisserait supposer que la famille entière est passée en même temps à l'islam" (*ibid.*: 454). Notons qu'il s'agit là, comme l'écrit l'auteur, d'un cas "contestable."

[3] *SB* III 6042, qui ne donne que les l. 4-8 (Γεωργις ιεὸς Σεργίου γενομένου Μαλὲκ ᾿Αβδάλα ἱεὸς ᾿Αμροῦ) d'après J. Maspero, *CRAIBL* 1913: 292 (édité avec l'accentuation suivante : Γεωργις ιεὸς Σεργίου γενομένου Μᾶλεκ ᾿Αβδαλα ιεὸς ῎Αμρου.

[4] "The date of this rare declaration of conversion has been estimated as the beginning of the 8th century based on palaeographical grounds. If correctly dated, this graffito is noteworthy for several reasons. Chief of these is why George and Moager decided to convert at this relatively early date, before the major fiscal changes which severely affected native Egyptians were carried out by the Arab government (Frantz-Murphy 1991). Although tax avoidance would have been a major incentive for Christians to convert to Islam, few appear to have taken this step until the 9th century (Gellens 1991). Furthermore, it would be interesting to know what these converts to Islam were doing in the monastery, which was still flourishing as far as we can tell from archaeological evidence and textual sources (§ 1.4.1), and continued to do so at least a century, to judge from mid-9th-century textual evidence from the monastery (§ 2.2.2.)."

La première objection est soulevée par Sarah elle-même: la présence de cette déclaration de conversion à l'islam dans un haut lieu du christianisme égyptien, en pleine prospérité, paraît quelque peu étrange, d'autant plus qu'elle est placée sous la protection du "Seigneur Dieu, Jésus-Christ" (l. 1-2). De plus, là encore, la formulation de l'inscription oblige à conclure à une double conversion du fils et du père, ce qui est peu vraisemblable. Enfin, l'onomastique s'oppose à cette interprétation: Moager, loin d'être chrétien, est un anthroponyme arabe (Muhâǧir). En outre, il est difficile de voir dans ⲀⲠⲞ ⲤⲀⲖⲈⲈⲚ un nom arabe dont le premier élément serait Abû, normalement transcrit en grec Αβου.[5] En revanche, ⲀⲠⲞ ⲤⲀⲖⲈⲈⲚ a tous les caractères d'une *origo* (ἀπὸ Σαλεεν), même si l'identification du toponyme fait encore problème.[6]

Je propose donc de reprendre le graffito ligne à ligne, d'après la photographie du livre de J. Maspero puisqu'il est aujourd'hui détruit.

Je passe sur les deux premières lignes, invocations chrétiennes banales.[7] La l. 3 est éditée par Maspero avec un blanc entre ⲔⲞⲎⲈⲐ et ⲀⲄⲈⲚⲞⲨ comme s'il comprenait "Boêeth fils d'Agenês." Ce graffito comprendrait alors la signature de trois personnages (Boêeth, Geôrgios et Moager). Cette solution se heurte à plusieurs objections: 1) Boêeth est un hapax; 2) Agenê(s) est un nom certes connu, mais dont le génitif, quand il est décliné, est en -οῦς et non en -ου;[8] 3) on est en droit de se demander pourquoi l'auteur du graffito n'a pas sous-tendu le patronyme par υἱός comme il le fait ailleurs; 4) enfin, on constate qu'un trait a été tiré entre les l. 7 et 8 comme pour séparer les noms de Geôrgios et de Moager. Ainsi n'y aurait-il que deux signataires dans cette inscription. En fait la l. 3 continue les invocations des deux lignes précédentes en offrant une forme très corrompue de l'expression βοηθὸς γενοῦ "sois notre secours".[9] Je serais même tenté, pour rendre compte de toutes les lettres, d'y voir l'expression à peu près synonyme βοήθεια γενοῦ (avec chute du ι et interversion des θ et ε), dont je ne connais qu'un seul exemple, provenant de Jordanie, dans un contexte un peu différent.[10] Cette interprétation est confirmée par un autre graffito de Baouît, trouvé dans la même salle 6, le n° 225 du recueil de J. Maspero: on y lit, après une liste de noms, ϤⲞⲎⲐⲒⲀ ⲈⲢⲞⲞⲨ "(sois) leur secours (βοήθεια)." Il est possible que, dans notre inscription, les noms de personnes qui suivent, quoiqu'au nominatif, dépendent de cette séquence: "Sois le secours de ..."

Le reste de l'inscription, rédigé par la même main, donne donc les noms de deux personnes en visite au monastère, séparés par un trait:

– l. 4-7: Γεώργις ἰεὸς Σεργίου γενομένου Μαλεκ Αβδαλα ἰεὸς Αμρου

---

[5] Voir, par exemple, l'index onomastique des *P.Lond.* IV ou des *P.Ness.* III.

[6] J.-M. Mouton, à qui j'ai soumis cette question, me signale que Muḥammad Ramzî mentionne dans son *Al-Qāmūs al-jugrafī li-l-bilād al-Miṣriyya*, IV: 37, un district du Haut Ṣaʿīd (rive est) portant le nom de Sīlīn. Mais, si l'on tient compte de l'origine arabe du personnage en même temps que de la date de cette inscription (voir ci-dessous), on s'attend à ce que Moager vienne, non de l'Égypte encore récemment byzantine, mais d'un pays déjà islamisé.

[7] Je suis la correction d'É. Drioton, qui normalise ce début, malgré la juxtaposition du vocatif et du nominatif: cf. pour se limiter à l'Égypte, *I.Lefebvre* 67, 1; 188, 1; 234, 2; 237, 2; 10; 541, 6; 661, 9.

[8] Cf. van Minnen et Worp 1990: 97, note à 3, 1.

[9] Cf., par exemple, *IGLS* II 542, 1 (350): εἷς θεὸς καὶ Χριστέ, βοηθὸς γενοῦ.

[10] *IGLS* XXI 145 (Madaba, VIIᵉ s.): βοήθεια γίνο[υ τ]ούτοις τε κτλ. (cf. D. Feissel, *Bull. ép.* 1989, n° 987 = Feissel 2006, n° 884). Voir aussi, encore que dans une formule différente, *SEG* XXXVII 1468, 1-3 ('Arraba, Vᵉ/VIᵉ s.): ✝ Θεοῦ δυ|✝|✝|νάμι, Χ(ριστο)ῦ βο|✝|ηθίᾳ, κτλ.

– l. 8-10: Μοαγερ ἰεὸς Λεγλαν γενομένου ἀπὸ Σαλεεν.

La structure est identique: nom, suivi d'un patronyme introduit par υἱός, suivi de γενομένου, terme capital pour comprendre cette inscription et qui est à l'origine du contresens de Maspero. Si j'ai raison de voir dans ἀπὸ Σαλεεν de la seconde séquence onomastique une *origo*, γενομένου ne peut porter que sur le patronyme. On a là en fait l'expression, d'emploi usuel surtout à partir de l'époque byzantine, signifiant "défunt."[11] Ainsi Geôrgios et Moager ont perdu leur père. Que faire de ce qui suit? Pour le second, j'ai déjà proposé d'y voir une *origo*. Mais, pour le premier, on est plus embarrassé. Il serait tentant de voir dans Μαλεκ Αβδαλα ἰεὸς Αμρου un autre personnage. Mais outre que manque le trait séparateur que l'on trouve entre les l. 7 et 8, la séquence onomastique Malik 'Abd Allāh est étrange en arabe. L'examen attentif de l'inscription met fin au malentendu: on n'y lit pas Μαλεκ, mais μαυλεκ ou μαυλεη. L'alpha est surmonté d'une ligne brisée qui est un bon upsilon. Je propose de voir dans ce mot la transcription de l'arabe *mawlā*, désignant le client d'un patron appartenant à la société islamique.[12] Ainsi Geôrgios fils de Sergios serait *mawlā* d''Abd Allāh fils d''Amr. Je reviendrai plus tard sur les implications historiques de cette relation régie par l'institution du *walâ'*. Je voudrais pour l'instant m'arrêter sur la forme du mot. La lettre finale a été lue par Maspero comme un kappa. Si c'est le cas, on aurait une suffixation pronominale erronée: *mawlāk* "ton *mawlā*." On pourrait mettre cette erreur sur le compte d'une méconnaissance de l'arabe de la part de Geôrgios, dont le nom montre qu'on a affaire à un hellénophone ou un coptophone. Pour ma part, je doute du kappa: l'élément oblique supérieur est inexistant d'après la photo et la lettre ressemble plutôt à un êta, de type cursif. C'est, semble-t-il, la même lettre que l'on rencontre peut-être dans le nom qui suit (Αβδηλα)[13] et très clairement au début du nom en tête de la l. 9. Ce nom a été lu Λεγλαν par Maspero. Pourtant le lambda interne du mot, qui est certain, est de forme bien différente; par ailleurs, Leglan est un anthroponyme inconnu. En revanche, on peut rapprocher cette forme de deux noms arabes connus: Haglān ou 'Aglān. L'êta serait peut-être là une façon de noter le 'ayin. Je me suis demandé si l'êta après μαυλε ne devait pas aller avec le nom suivant, 'Abd Allāh, commençant aussi par un 'ayn. Mais ce serait, à ma connaissance, une graphie inconnue de ce nom banal; en outre, l'êta me semble plus près du mot précédent que du mot suivant. Aurait-il pour but de noter la longue de *mawlā*? Signalons, en tout cas, que la transcription de ce mot arabe en grec ou en copte n'est pas uniforme: μαυλε, μαῦλος, voire ⲙⲉⲟⲩⲗⲗ.[14]

---

[11] Sur cet emploi, voir, récemment, H. Buchinger, A. Gehring, P. Patsio et S. Tost 1998: 92, note à 13 (= *SPP* III 1), 1.

[12] Sur le *mawlā*, voir en général Crone 1991, et Onimus 2005 (l'auteur a pu intégrer ma correction de l'inscription de Baouît p. 89).

[13] Maspero avait lu Αβδαλα. Sur la photo, on lirait plutôt Αβδηλα. Notons que, dans les papyrus égyptiens, la forme avec alpha est rarissime (*CPR* III 52, 8 [Ars., 709-714]: Αβδαλλα) alors que la forme courante est avec epsilon (Αβδελλα, *passim*).—Le scripteur du graffito simplifie aussi la géminée -λλ-.

[14] La plus grande fréquence d'occurrences de ce terme est dans les comptabilités des *P.Lond.* IV où, à l'exception de deux occurrences (μαύλων en *P.Lond.* IV 1447, 184 et 1449, 53), la finale du mot est abrégée: μαυ^λ, μαυλ^ε ou μαυλ^ω. L'éditeur en concluait: "The form is not certain. The form μαυλ^ε (**1441**, 61, etc.) in the gen. sing. would suggest μαυλεύς, but the plur. gen. μαυλων (**1447**, 184, **1449**, 53) suggests a nom. plur. μαῦλοι. Possibly there were two forms, μαῦλος and μαυλεύς; but the most likely explanation is that the form is μαυλεύς throughout, and that μαυλων is simply the plur. gen. form which in late Greek supplanted the -εων form (Jannaris, *Hist. Gr. Grammar*, 264, 267)" (*P.Lond.* IV, p. XXIV, n. 3). C'est ainsi que l'éditeur des *CPR* XXII résoud μαυ^λ en μαυλ(εύς) (34, 6; 7; 55, 6; 8 [VIIIe s.]). Je reste sceptique sur le fait

Je propose donc de lire et de comprendre le graffito de la façon suivante:

1   † Κ(ύρι)ε ὁ Θ(εὸ)ς
2   Ἰ(ησοῦ)ς Χ(ριστὸ)ς
3   βοηεθα γενοῦ.
4   Γεώργις ἰεὸς
5   Σεργίου γενομένου,
6   μαυλε Αβδηλα
7   ἰεὸς Αμρου

8   Μοαγερ ἰεὸς
9   Ηεγλαν γενομέ-
10 νου ἀπὸ Σαλεεν.

1. κεοθc ‖ 2. ιc̄χc̄ ‖ 3. l. βοήθεια ‖ 4, 7, 8 l. υἱὸς ‖ 6. μᾶλε : μαυλεκ vel μαυλεη ‖ Αβδηλα vel Λβδαλα; l. Αβδελλα ‖ 7. ἰεοc.

Seigneur Dieu, Jésus-Christ, sois notre secours. Geôrgios fils du défunt Sergios, mawlâ d'Abdêla fils d'Amr, Moager fils du défunt Êeglan, originaire de Saleen.

Ce graffito ne pourra donc plus être utilisé pour illustrer les phénomènes de conversion religieuse dans l'Égypte omeyyade. Il peut à tout le moins être le témoignage plus modeste de ce que des musulmans visitaient aussi les lieux saints chrétiens et, au même titre que les pèlerins chrétiens, pouvaient y laisser leur signature en souvenir. Notons cependant que le premier nom, celui du pèlerin à qui l'on doit très probablement l'inscription, est manifestement porté par un chrétien. Il aura visité le monastère d'Apa Apollo en compagnie d'un camarade d'une autre religion, dont il aura tenu à graver le nom en même temps que le sien.

Quoique ramenée à un contenu *a priori* banal, cette inscription n'en prend pas moins une dimension historique insoupçonnée. Tout d'abord, elle n'est pas sans intérêt sur l'institution du *walā'* qui lie le *mawlā* à son patron (appelé aussi "*mawlā* supérieur"). Cette dernière est avant tout connue sous deux formes: le patronat par affranchissement et celui par conversion à l'islam. Or le *walā'* de Geôrgios n'appartient à aucun des deux: la mention de son patronyme ne permet guère d'y voir un affranchi; son nom et celui de son père ainsi que le fait qu'il se place sous la protection du Dieu des chrétiens interdisent de voir en lui un converti à l'islam. Ce graffito documente donc un type de *walā'* peu

---

que le mot arabe ait été intégré dans une déclinaison qui était, à cette époque, moins usitée. J'aurais tendance à voir dans la graphie μαυλε, malgré la suspension du ε d'après l'édition, la forme indéclinable μαυλε, bien attestée dans le *P.Ness.* III 72, 4 (684 ?) et évidemment en copte, dans le *CPR* XII 32, 29 (VIIe/VIIIe s.)—où il faut comprendre ⲭⲁⲓⲣⲱⲛ ⲙⲁⲩⲗⲉ ⲙⲱⲭ, non pas "Chairon, (Sohn des) Herrn Moch" (éd.), mais "Chairôn, *mawlā* de Môch."—Ce dernier papyrus contient probablement une autre forme de *mawlā* (unique, à ma connaissance) dans la séquence ⲁⲡⲁⲉⲗⲗⲁ ⲙⲉⲟⲩⲗⲁ ⟨ⲗ⟩ⲉⲓ, "'Abd Allāh, *mawlā* de Leï (ou 'Alī)."

attesté: le lien de clientèle entre un musulman et un chrétien libre. Quoique contestée,[15] son existence est confirmée par au moins un autre cas, celui de Sarjūn fils de Mansûr (probablement le père de Jean Damascène, d'une famille noble de chrétiens arabes), *mawlā* du caliphe Muʿāwiya (VIIe s.).[16] Cette forme de clientélisme peut s'expliquer par l'importance sociale ou les qualités du *mawlā* en question et par la politique omeyyade désireuse d'intégrer des conquis appartenant à l'élite et nécessaires au bon fonctionnement d'une nouvelle administration civile et militaire.[17] Devenir *mawlā* était alors avant tout une façon de s'intégrer à une tribu, de s'affilier à une famille, ce qui impliquait de pouvoir bénéficier d'un utile réseau de protection. C'était aussi pour le patron une manière de se concilier une clientèle riche ou puissante dont il pouvait tirer des avantages.[18]

Le second intérêt de cette inscription tient au patron de Geôrgios, ʿAbd Allāh fils d'ʿAmr. Il est tentant d'y voir le fils du conquérant de l'Égypte, ʿAmr b. al-ʿĀṣ. Ce personnage historique est connu pour avoir été le seul à refuser le serment d'allégeance à Yazīd, le fils du calife Muʿāwiya, lorsque ce dernier mourut en 680[19]—serment d'allégeance qui donna naissance au principe dynastique en islam. Il fut aussi gouverneur d'Égypte, il est vrai peu de temps. D'après l'ouvrage sur les gouverneurs d'Égypte (*Kitāb al-Wulāt Miṣr*) d'al-Kindī, auteur qui vécut de 896 (A.H. 283) à 961 (A.H. 350), donc très proche des événements, et qui est réputé pour sa fiabilité, ʿAbd Allāh succéda à son père qui mourut le jour de la rupture du jeûne de l'année 43 de l'Hégire (= 6 janvier 664); il n'en fait pourtant pas le septième gouverneur d'Égypte, titre qu'il attribue à ʿUtba ibn Abī Sufyān qui arrive en Égypte en février 664 (en *dhū l-qaʿda* de la même année). ʿAbd Allāh n'aurait donc assumé les fonctions de gouverneur de l'Égypte qu'un mois, par intérim.[20] D'après la même source, il serait mort en 684/685 (A.H. 65). Maqrīzī, lui, le fait mourir plus tôt en 682/683 (A.H. 63), à l'âge de 72 ans, en Égypte. ʿAbd Allāh aurait donc vécu en Égypte depuis le premier gouvernorat de son père (640-644) jusqu'à sa mort (entre 682 et 685). Si Geôrgios a bien été directement *mawlā* de ʿAbd Allāh (et non par transmission héréditaire du *walāʾ*), notre inscription serait donc antérieure à 685, ce qui paléographiquement est fort possible. Elle offre accessoirement le témoignage le plus ancien de *mawālī* en Égypte. Mais ce qui est plus intéressant, c'est qu'elle documente très probablement une catégorie de fonctionnaires attachés à un grand dignitaire omeyyade par une institution que les nécessités de la conquête et de sa consolidation rendaient encore très souple.

---

[15] Juda 1983: 71-72, fait de tous les *mawālī* non affranchis des convertis. On pourrait aussi penser, dans la mesure où le *walāʾ* peut se transmettre héréditairement, que c'est le père de Geôrgios qui est devenu *mawlā* par affranchissement.

[16] Crone 2003: 237, n. 358. Voir aussi, sur ce personnage, Sourdel et Bosch Vila 1988: 20 (qui renvoient à Sahas 1972: 26).—Les cas de chrétiens *mawālī* sont rares dans la documentation papyrologique. Onimus 2005: 83, n'en recense que quatre; il n'est pas certain qu'il s'agisse, comme il l'écrit, d'affranchis.

[17] Sur les qualités et le milieu social des *mawālī*, je renvoie à l'étude d'Onimus 2005.

[18] La richesse du *mawlā* peut justifier cette forme de clientélisme: en l'absence d'héritier agnatique, le patron héritait des biens de son protégé (cf. C. Onimus 2005: 98).

[19] Il finit par céder sous les menaces de mort du gouverneur d'Égypte de l'époque, Maslama ibn Mukhallad al-Anṣārī. Cf. en dernier lieu Kennedy 1998: 69.

[20] Kennedy 1998 ne le cite même pas comme successeur d'ʿAmr.—Lane-Poole 1925: 45, confirme le témoignage d'al-Kindī en incluant ʿAbd Allāh dans son tableau des gouverneurs pour la seule année 664. Il ajoute en commentaire: 45, n. 1: "Ṭabarī makes ʿAbdallāh succeed his father ʿAmr in 664 and govern Egypt till 667 (A.H. 47), when he was replaced by Moʿāwiya b. Ḥudeyǧ (47-50) who was followed by Maslama in 670 (50): thus ignoring ʿOtba and ʿOḳba; Bilādhurî and Abū-l-Maḥāsin adopt this version. Ṭabarî, however, is singularly defective in his scanty notices of Egyptian governors (…)."

Il est assez inattendu que les murs du monastère chrétien de Baouît nous livrent le seul témoignage non littéraire d'un des grands personnages historiques de la dynastie omeyyade.

BIBLIOGRAPHIE

Buchinger, H., Gehring, A., Patsio, P. et Tost, S. (1998). "Beiträge zu SPP III 1-6," *Eirene* 34, 87-97.

Crone, P. (1991). "*Mawlā*," in: *Encyclopédie de l'Islam*, 2ᵉ éd., VI. Leyde: Brill, 868-874.

Crone, P. (2003). *Slaves on Horses. The Evolution of the Islamic Policy*, 2ᵉ éd. Cambridge: Cambridge University Press.

Feissel, D. (2006). *Chroniques d'épigraphie byzantine 1987-2004*. Paris: Centre d'Histoire et Civilisation de Byzance (Monographies 20).

Frantz-Murphy, G. (1991). "Conversion in Early Islamic Egypt: The Economic Factor," in: Ragib, Y. (ed.), *Documents de l'Islam médiéval: nouvelles perspectives de recherches*. Le Caire: Institut français d'archéologie orientale 1991, 11-17.

Gellens, S. I. (1991). "Egypt, Islamization of," in: Atiya, A. S. (ed.), *The Coptic Encyclopedia*. New York; Macmillan 1991, III, 936-942.

Juda, J. (1983). *Die sozialen und wirtschaftlichen Aspekte der Mawāli in frühislamischer Zeit*. Tübingen.. Dissertation.

Kennedy, H. (1998). "Egypt as a Province in the Islamic Caliphate, 641-68," *The Cambridge History of Egypt. I. Islamic Egypt 640-1517*. Cambridge: Cambridge University Press.

Lane-Poole, S. (1925). *A History of Egypt in the Middle Ages*, 4ᵉ éd. Londres: Cass.

Maspero, J. (1932-1943). *Fouilles exécutées à Baouît*, notes mises en ordre et éditées par É. Drioton, *MIFAO* 59, fasc. 1, Le Caire: Institut français d'archéologie orientale 1932, fasc. 2. Le Caire: Institut français d'archéologie orientale 1943.

Mouton, J.-M. (2002). "Un village copte du Fayyoum au XIᵉ siècle, d'après la découverte d'un lot d'archives," *CRAIBL*, 447-458.

Onimus, C. (2005). "Les *mawālī* en Égypte dans la documentation papyrologique Iᵉʳ-Vᵉ s. H.," *AnIsl* 39, 81-107.

Ramzī, M. (1953-1945). *Al-Qāmūs al-jughrafī li-l-bilād al-miṣriyya*. Le Caire: Maṭbaʻ Dār al-Kutub al-Miṣrīya.

Sahas, D. J. (1972). *John of Damascus on Islam*. Leyde: Brill.

Sourdel, D. et J. Bosch Vila (1988). *Regierung und Verwaltung des Vorderen Orients in islamischer Zeit*, II. Leyde: Brill.

Van Minnen, P. et Worp, K. A. (1990). "A New Edition of Ostraka from Akoris", *Tyche* 5, 95-99.

DIE ANAPHORISCHE INTERZESSION FÜR DIE VERSTORBENEN NACH DEN FRÜHEN ZEUGNISSEN KOPTISCHER LITURGIE

JUTTA HENNER

Über die Vielseitigkeit der koptischen Liturgie, die Schwierigkeiten auch bei der Deutung früher Zeugnisse ist viel gesprochen und geschrieben worden; es sei einmal mehr Quecke, einer der Pioniere der Forschung auf diesem Gebiet, zitiert: "Und was speziell die koptische Liturgie betrifft, so bin auch ich immer wieder beeindruckt von der Fülle von Fakten, die in unserem bruchstückhaften Wissen so isoliert dastehen, daß man daran verzweifeln möchte, sie jemals in den rechten Zusammenhang einzuordnen und deuten zu können."[1] Ein Aspekt sei im Folgenden aus der Fülle der liturgiegeschichtlichen Fragestellungen herausgenommen und in aller Unvollständigkeit und Vorläufigkeit in Grundzügen dargestellt: Die verschiedenen Formen der anaphorischen Interzession für Verstorbene und ihre Entwicklung. Auch in diesem Bereich ist die Quellenlage nicht hinreichend, alle Fragen zu klären, doch lassen sich Leitlinien nachzeichnen.

Aus dem ersten Jahrtausend ist—teilweise nur fragmentarisch—eine Vielzahl von Anaphoren in griechischer oder sahidischer Fassung überliefert; die ältesten Textzeugen gehen dabei zurück bis ins 4. Jahrhundert. Manche Anaphoren sind vollständig überliefert und ihr Name ist bekannt; von anderen ist der Name bekannt, ihr Text jedoch nur unvollständig; von wieder anderen sind lediglich Textreste erhalten. Charakteristisch für die Feier der eucharistischen Liturgie in Ägypten ist offensichtlich das Fehlen jeder Uniformität vor dem 11./12. Jahrhundert: die Vielzahl der überlieferten Anaphoren gibt beredtes Zeugnis davon; Gebete konnten regional und temporär flexibel verwendet werden. Allerdings sollten sich nach und nach drei Hauptanaphoren durchsetzen: Hier ist zunächst die genuin ägyptische, nach dem Evangelisten Markos benannte Markos- oder Kyrillosanaphora zu nennen, die durch einige typisch ägyptisch-alexandrinische Besonderheiten wie die doppelte Epiklese oder die Stellung der Interzessionen noch vor dem Sanctus ausgezeichnet ist.[2] Syrisch-antiochenischen Ursprungs sind dann die beiden anderen wohl im 5. Jahrhundert nach Ägypten importierten Anaphoren, die Gregoriosanaphora,[3] deren Besonderheit ist, dass sich alle Gebete an Christus richten, sowie die Basiliosanaphora,[4] die bis heute das Standardformular des eucharistischen Gottesdienstes der koptischen Kirche bleiben sollte. Die größte Zahl erhaltener sahidischer Eucharistieformulare sollte sich jedoch in einer Handschrift aus dem 10./11. Jahrhundert finden, dem sog. "Großen Euchologion"

---

[1] Vgl. Quecke 1978.

[2] Beschreibung und ausführliche Literaturangaben finden sich bei Henner 2000: 21-24. Neueditionen früher Textzeugen und ihre Zuordnung zur Markosanaphora finden sich bei Hammerstaedt 1999.

[3] Zum griechischen Text vgl. Gerhards 1984. Eine Edition des bohairischen Textes findet sich bei Hammerschmidt 1957. Eine Übersicht über die Forschungsgeschichte findet sich bei Henner 2000: 31-35. Eine Neuedition des ältesten erhaltenen Zeugen, eines sahidischen Fragmentes aus dem späten 6. Jahrhundert, findet sich ebenfalls bei Henner 2000: 36-79.

[4] Eine Edition der griechischen, sahidischen sowie bohairischen Handschriften vom 6. bis ins 20. Jahrhundert mit ausführlichem Kommentar und liturgiehistorischer Würdigung besorgte jüngst Budde 2004.

aus dem Weißen Kloster[5] im Süden Ägyptens.[6] Reste einer ganzen Reihe bekannter, aber auch sonst unbekannter Anaphoren sind hier erhalten; mit Ausnahme der Markos-/Kyrillosanaphora wird auch hier der syrische Einfluß sichtbar.[7] Darüber hinaus sind zahlreiche weitere Anaphorenfragmente in griechischer oder sahidischer Sprache erhalten.[8]

Christen zu allen Zeiten trägt die Hoffnung über den Tod hinaus; die Auferstehung Jesu Christi ist Garant dafür, dass der Weg des Glaubenden mit seinem Tod nicht zu Ende ist. Krankheit, Leid und Sterben können in der Gewißheit der Nähe Gottes mit Gebet und Beistand begleitet werden; eigene christliche Bestattungsriten sollten sich bald herausbilden. Das fürbittende Gebet für Verstorbene, wiewohl im Neuen Testament selbst noch nicht belegt, gehört zur alten christlichen Tradition. Ihm wohnen jeweils auch die Dimensionen des Trostes für die Trauernden sowie der Bewußtmachung der eigenen Vergänglichkeit inne. Dies ist auch in der koptischen Kirche seit ihrer Frühzeit nicht anders.[9] So sind Gebete für Verstorbene zu vielfältigen Anlässen wie dem Begräbnis oder einem Gedenktag selbstverständlich. Nicht nur Märtyrer und Heilige, sondern alle Christen, so die Hoffnung, mögen nach ihrem Tode Gutes erfahren in der Nähe des barmherzigen Gottes. Doch Gebete für Verstorbene haben auch Eingang gefunden in die sog. Kondolenzepistolographie[10] oder finden sich auch wiederholt mit ähnlichen Motiven in Grabinschriften;[11] Gebete ohne besonderen konkreten Anlass nehmen auf das Schicksal der "Entschlafenen," wie es meist heißt, Bezug.[12] Ein traditioneller Ort der Fürbitte für die Verstorbenen—Heilige wie gewöhnliche Christen—ist traditionell der eucharistische Gottesdienst.

---

[5] Zu den Liturgica aus dem Weißen Kloster bemerkt zuletzt H. Brakmann: "Im Vergleich mit den literarischen und biblischen Handschriften des Weißen Klosters werden die Liturgica im engeren Sinn bisher bestenfalls stiefmütterlich behandelt." Vgl. Brakmann 2004b.

[6] Die Edition besorgte Lanne 1958. Vgl. zu diesen Anaphoren Henner 2000: 12-34, ferner Brakmann 2004a, dort S. 127 f. Brakmann verneint dort die Anfrage H. Quecke's, ob diese Anaphoren überhaupt je außerhalb des Weißen Klosters Verwendung gefunden hätten, oder es sich nicht möglicherweise um "Kunstprodukte" gehandelt haben könne.

[7] So begegnen nur in diesem Euchologion eine Anaphora des hl. Matthäus, eine Anaphora des hl. Thomas, eine Anaphora des Johannes von Bosra und eine—allerdings auch in Syrien bekannte—Anaphora des Severos von Antiochien. Ferner finden sich Teile der Jakobosanaphora, der Gregorios- sowie der Kyrillosanaphora. Darüber hinaus sind Teile von mindestens vier (Brakmann) oder fünf (Henner) weiteren Anaphoren, deren Name unbekannt ist, in diesem Euchologion erhalten.

[8] Vgl. die entsprechende Übersicht bei Henner 2000: 4-11, sowie dazu Brakmann 2004a: 123f.

[9] Krause 2003, weist auf S. 34 darauf hin: "Auch der christliche Ägypter glaubte an ein Weiterleben nach dem Tode durch die Auferstehung von den Toten." Krause bezieht die vor- und außerchristlichen Gebräuche rund um Tod und Bestattung in seine Studie ein und kommt zu dem Schluß: "Die ägyptische Kirche versuchte die Totenklage durch Gebete und Psalmensingen zu ersetzen." (S. 36).

[10] Vgl. beispielsweise das Zeugnis aus dem 6./7. Jh, das Papathomas 1998, ediert hat, sowie die dort angeführte Literatur zum Thema. Im Rahmen dieses Textes findet sich das Gebet für den Verstorbenen, dass Gott ihm "Leben in Fülle und unsagbare Freude sowie Frieden und Ruhe für seine Seele in alle Ewigkeit gewähre."

[11] Krause 2003, weist auf S. 42 darauf hin, dass sich auf zahlreichen Grabsteinen eine "Anrede an die Lebenden" finde mit der Aufforderung, ein Gebet für den Toten zu sprechen, dass Gott sich seiner Seele erbarme.

[12] Über den ägyptischen Raum hinaus sei hier exemplarisch *P.Ness.* III 96, ein Papyrusfragment aus dem 7. Jahrhundert erwähnt, wo sich ein byzantinisches Gebet für Verstorbene findet, das offensichtlich zu privater Verwendung abgeschrieben worden war, und von dem es zahlreiche Parallelen auf Inschriften aus Nubien gibt. Vgl. Kraemer 1958: 309 f., bei van Haelst 1976: Nr. 904:

ὁ θεὸς τῶν πνευμάτων καὶ πάσης σαρκός ὁ τὸν θάνατον καταργήσας καὶ τὸν ᾅδην καταπατήσας καὶ ζωὴν τῷ κόσμῳ χαρισάμενος, ἀνάπαυσον τῇ ψυχῇ τοῦ δούλου σου ἐν τόπῳ ἀνα[παύσεως ἔνθα ἀπέδρα] ὀδύνη κ(αὶ) στ[εναγμός.

Schließlich ereignet sich bei der Feier dieses Mysterions eine Vereinigung des irdischen mit dem himmlischen Gottesdienst. Die Feier der Eucharistie, Höhepunkt der liturgischen Feiern, vergegenwärtigt Leiden, Tod und Auferstehung Jesu Christi und rückt so den Tod, besonders aber den Sieg über ihn ins Zentrum. Dass die Gaben der Eucharistie als Wegzehrung auf dem Weg bis zum Ende des eigenen Lebens verstanden wurde und wird, braucht nicht eigens erwähnt zu werden.[13] Allen Fürbitten für Verstorbene ist mit Abweichungen in der Formulierung der Wunsch und die Hoffnung zu eigen, dass der Verstorbene bzw. die Verstorbenen Ruhe, ja Erquickung in der göttlichen Sphäre finden mögen; geradezu paradiesische Schilderungen führen den Zustand der im Glauben Vorangegangen vor Augen.

Im Rahmen der in Ägypten verwendeten Anaphoren finden sich durchwegs—soweit erhalten, ausführliche anaphorische Interzessionen.[14] Schon sehr bald sollte im Rahmen dieser Interzessionsgebete zwischen priesterlichen Gebeten und Gebetsaufforderungen bzw. Einleitungen in die Fürbitten durch den Diakon unterschieden werden. Dem Diakon kommt dann auch die Verlesung der Diptychen,[15] die Liste der Namen der Verstorbenen während des eucharistischen Hochgebetes, zu. Daneben finden sich jedoch seit spätestens dem 6. Jahrhundert zuweilen auch in priesterlichen Gebeten lange Listen verstorbener Heiliger, Märtyrer und Bischöfe. Bezüglich der diakonalen Elemente der Anaphora ist die Tendenz zu beobachten, dass diese Teile der Liturgie länger in der griechischen Sprache tradiert und gebraucht werden, daneben ist das Phänomen der Zweisprachigkeit der diakonalen Gebete zu beobachten.

Bevor die priesterlichen Gebete in den Blick genommen werden, sollen zunächst beispielhaft einige der diakonalen Gebetstexte im Blick auf ihre Überlieferung der Fürbitte für Verstorbene betrachtet werden.[16]

Kürzeste Texte sind die Gebetsaufforderungen. Während die Pergamenthandschrift MS Insinger 30[17] aus dem Weißen Kloster, eine zweisprachige Handschrift, lediglich den kurzen Ruf des Diakons "Sagt die Namen" als Einleitung der Diptychen und infolge die kurze Aufforderung, gleichsam Überschrift, für das folgende priesterliche Gebet "für die Ruhenden"[18] überliefert, sind auch andere

---

[13] Einmal mehr sei auf Ignatius von Antiochien verwiesen (Ep. ad. Eph. 20,2), der die eucharistische Gabe als "Medizin zur Unsterblichkeit" bezeichnete.

[14] Die Stellung der Interzessionen im Hochgebet differiert; so ist bei der Markos- bzw. Kyrillosanaphora das Interzessionsgebet im Anschluß an das Lob- und Dankgebet noch vor dem Sanctus; bei den Anaphoren syrisch-antiochenischen Typs findet sich das Interzessionsgebet im Anschluß an Einsetzungsbericht, Anamnese und Epiklese.

[15] Zu den Diptychen vgl. die Aufstellung bei Henner 2000: 130-135, ergänzende Literatur und Bemerkungen bei Brakmann 2004a: 156 f. Vgl. ferner Taft 1991.

[16] Aus der Betrachtung ausgenommen werden müssen außeranaphorische diakonale Gebete wie sie beispielsweise das zweisprachige Pergamentfragment British Museum, Or. 6954(28) aus dem Weißen Kloster überliefert; zur Edition vgl. Henner 2000: 152-161. Dort findet sich vollständig erhalten die griechische und fragmentarisch erhalten die sahidische Fassung einer Fürbitte für "unsere im Glauben entschlafenen Väter und Brüder, dass der Herr sie nach der Ordnung aufnehme an den Ort der Ruhe im Paradies der Freude, wo Schmerz und Trauer und Seufzen entflohen ist.": ὑπὲρ τῶν ἐν πίστει προσκεκοιμημένων πατέρων ἡμῶν καὶ ἀδελφῶν ὅπως κ(ύριο)ς προσλαβόμενος αὐτὸς κατὰ τάξιν εἰς τόπον ἀναπαύσεως ἐν παραδίσῳ τρυφῆς ὅθεν ἀπέδρα ὀδύνη καὶ λύπη καὶ στεναγμὸς τὸν κ(ύριο)ν παρακαλέσω(μεν) ⲉⲧⲃⲉ ⲧⲡⲓⲥⲧⲓⲥ ⲛⲛⲉⲛⲉⲓⲟⲧⲉ ⲉⲛⲧⲁⲩⲛ̄ⲕⲟⲧⲕ̄ [

[17] Vgl. Pleyte und Boeser 1897: 130-132.

[18] Vgl. dazu ZZ. 10-12 auf dem Recto. εἴπατε τὰ ὀνόματα ... ⲛⲉⲩⲣⲁⲛ: -
περὶ τῶν ἀναπαυσαμένων ϢⲀⲎⲖ ⲉϪⲛ ⲛⲉⲛⲧⲁⲩⲙⲧⲟⲛ ⲙ̄ⲙⲟⲟⲩ·

Formulierungen zu den Gebetsaufforderungen zu den anaphorischen Fürbitten erhalten. So überliefert MS Insinger 31,[19] eine zweisprachige Pergamenthandschrift aus dem Weißen Kloster, nach Gebetsaufforderungen für die Früchte der Erde, für die Armen, Witwen und Waisen, den Herrscher und die Erstlingsgaben die kurze—rein griechische—diakonale Gebetsaufforderung für die Ruhe der Seelen:[20]

περὶ τῆς τελείας ἐν Χ(ριστ)ῷ ἀναπαύσεως τῶν ψυχῶν τῶν μακαρίων ἀδελφῶν ἡμῶν καὶ πάντων τῶν κοιμηθέντων.

Leider nur fragmentarisch erhalten ist dagegen die Textfassung der diakonalen Gebetsaufforderungen der Basiliosanaphora im zweisprachigen Pergamentblatt P.Vindob. K. 9742[21] aus dem Weißen Kloster, wobei die diakonalen Einladungen zu den anaphorischen Interzessionen rein griechisch gehalten sind.

Περ[ὶ] τῶ[ν] πάν[των τῶν ἐν πίστει Χριστοῦ κοι]μηθέντων [[22]

Wohl aus dem 10. Jahrhundert stammen die fünf Pergamentkodexblätter P.Berol. 9755 mit diakonalen Gebeten in griechischer Sprache, lediglich die Überschriften über jeder der Fürbitten sind auf Sahidisch niedergeschrieben worden.[23] Der Fürbitte für die Verstorbenen gehen Bitten um Regen, für die Fische sowie für den König voran. Die Bitte ist bereits sehr ausführlich formuliert:

περὶ τῆς μνήμης τῶν πατέρων ἡμῶν καὶ ἀδελφῶν τῶν μακαριωτάτων κεκοιμημένων ὅπως κατὰ τὸ ἔλεός σου, κύριε, ἀνάπαυσον τὰς ψυχὰς αὐτῶν ἐν κόλποις (τῶν) ἁγίων πατέρων ἡμῶν πατριάρχων Ἀβρααμ καὶ Ἰσαακ καὶ Ἰακώβ ἐν τόπῳ χλόης ἐπὶ ὕδατος ἀναπαύσεως ἐν παραδείσῳ τῆς τρυφῆς καὶ ἀξίωσον αὐτοὺς (τῆς) ἀναστάσεως τῶν δικαίων καὶ πάντας τοὺς ἐν πίστει χριστου κοιμηθέντας.

Bei der Mehrzahl der überlieferten Handschriften handelt es sich jedoch um den Text des priesterlichen anaphorischen Gebetes für die Verstorbenen.[24] Dieses Gebet wurde in späterer Überlieferung bis heute ein stilles Gebet, das parallel zur Verlesung der Diptychen durch den Diakon gebetet wird.

Auf dem Verso des ältesten erhaltenen Zeugen, eines Papyrusfragmentes aus Straßburg, P.Strassb. gr. inv. 254, findet sich in den Zeilen 11-15 ein anaphorisches Interzessionsgebet.[25]

---

[19] Vgl. Pleyte und Boeser 1897: 133-135.

[20] Vgl. dazu ZZ. 6-8 auf dem Verso.

[21] Zur Erstedition des Pergamentblattes aus dem 9./10. Jahrhundert vgl. Wessely 1917, dort Nr. 260. Die Neuedition besorgte Henner 2000: 183-206. Eine Beschreibung des Einzelblattes findet sich ferner bei Budde 2004, 101 f. Ein noch unveröffentlichter Paralleltext aus dem Weißen Kloster ist in Paris erhalten (Paris, BN Copte 129,20 fol. 139-145).

[22] Ebenfalls für eine inhaltliche Würdigung zu fragmentarisch ist der Erhaltungszustand von P.Lond.Copt. 156, einem Pergamentfragment, das die anaphorischen Diakonika der Basiliosanaphora überliefert: Zweisprachig ist die Einleitung zur Verlesung der Diptychen erhalten. Im Anschluß daran sind lesbar die Worte "Ruhe" sowie "der in Christus Entschlafenen." Vgl. P.Lond.Copt.: 44f.

[23] Vgl. Junker und Schubart 1902.

[24] Vgl. allgemein zu dieser Art des priesterlichen Interzessionsgebetes u.a. Winkler 1971, dort S. 339-344, sowie Wagner 1972.

[25] Neuedition bei Hammerstaedt 1999: 22-41. Zur Frage, inwieweit bei diesem Text bereits eine Trennung von diakonalen und priesterlichen Texten zu erkennen ist, vgl. Taft 1991: 36: "Can these texts be taken as showing already a distinction between *anaphoral intercessions* read by the presiding bishop or presbyter, and *diptychs* or names read perhaps

Hammerstaedt rechnet diesen Text als frühesten Zeugen der anaphorischen Interzessionen der Markosanaphora.[26]

> τῶν κεκοιμημένων τὰς ψυχὰς ἀνάπαυσον·
>
> μνήσθητι καὶ ὧν ἐπὶ τῆς σήμερον ἡμέρας τὴν ὑπόμνησιν ποιούμεθα·
>
> καὶ ὧν λέγομεν καὶ ὧν οὐ λέγομεν τὰ ὀνόματα.

P.Ryl. 465, ein Pergamentblatt wohl aus dem 6. Jahrhundert, enthält auf dem Rekto und den ersten Zeilen des Verso Teile einer Anaphora mit Post-Sanctus, Einsetzungsbericht, Anamnese und zweiter Epiklese, die als frühe Form der Markos-/Kyrillosanaphora identifiziert werden kann.[27] Auf dem Verso findet sich in Z. 11-21 von anderer Hand ein Interzessionsgebet für Verstorbene. Dieses Gebet übernimmt in Z. 15-21 Formulierungen des anaphorischen Fürbittgebets der Markosanaphora, ist aber wohl ein eigenständiger Text, dafür spricht die stark erweiterte Gottesanrede, die die Interzession in Z. 11f einleitet.[28]

> δεόμεθα καὶ
>
> πα[ρακαλοῦμέν σε φιλάνθ
>
> ρωπε τῶν κοιμηθέντων [πατέρων καὶ ἀδελφῶν ἐν
>
> πίστει θεοῦ ἀναπαυσαμένω[ν τὰς ψυχὰς ἀνάκλινον
>
> μετὰ τῶν ἁγίων σου συνά[πτων ἔνθα ἀπέδρα ὀδύνη
>
> καὶ λύπη καὶ στεναγμὸς [ἐν τῇ λαμπρότητί σου τῶν
>
> ἁγίων συνανεγείρων. καὶ τὴν σάρκα αὐτῶν ἐν ᾗ
>
> ὥρισας ἡμέρᾳ κατὰ τὰ[ς ἀληθεῖς καὶ ἀψευδεῖς

---

by the deacon, even if the later nomenclature is still absent? Nothing justifies such a conclusion, though we have here, clearly, the embryonic form of what would soon be separated into distinct liturgical units, possibly as a result of the multiplication of the names to be proclaimed. The reasons for such a development should be obvious. Every pastor knows that people wish to hear read aloud in church the names of those for whom they have made an offering and requested prayers. When such lists became so long as to be a nuisance, what better solution than to leave their proclamation to the deacon? It was his job, after all, to give the congregation its orders and announce the intentions it was to pray for."

[26] Die spätere griechische Fassung der Markosanaphora sollte völlig andere Formulierungen und Motive für das priesterliche Gebet im Anschluß an die Verlesung der Diptychen finden: καὶ τούτων καὶ πάντων τὰς ψυχὰς ἀνάπαυσον, Δέσποτα Κύριε, ὁ θεὸς ἡμῶν, ἐν ταῖς τῶν ἁγίων σκηναῖς, ἐν τῇ βασιλείᾳ σου, χαριζόμενος αὐτοῖς κατὰ τῶν ἐπαγγελιῶν σου ἀνεκλάλητα ἀγαθά, ἃ ὀφθαλμὸς οὐκ εἶδεν, καὶ οὓς οὐκ ἤκουσεν, καὶ ἐπὶ καρδίαν ἀνθρώπου οὐκ ἀνέβη, ἃ ἡτοίμασεν ὁ Θεὸς τοῖς ἀγαπῶσι τὸ ὄνομά σου τὸ ἅγιον. αὐτῶν μὲν τὰς ψυχὰς ἀνάπαυσον, Κύριε, καὶ βασιλείας οὐρανῶν καταξίωσον· ἡμῶν δὲ τὰ τέλη τῆς ζωῆς χριστιανὰ καὶ εὐάρεστα καὶ ἀναμάρτητα δώρησαι· καὶ δὸς ἡμῖν μερίδα καὶ κλῆρον ἔχειν μετὰ πάντων τῶν ἁγίων σου. Vgl. Cuming 1990, dort S. 30. Vgl. dazu ferner H. Engberding 1964, dort S. 427 f.

[27] Vgl. *P.Ryl.* III: 25-28; Neuedition bei Hammerstaedt 1999: 76-95.

[28] Auf die Frage, ob eine gemeinsame Vorlage des Gebetes auf *P.Ryl.* 465 und in der koptischen Kyrillosanaphora vorliegt, die bereits im 6. Jahrhundert bei Kosmas Indikopleustes auftaucht, soll hier nicht näher eingegangen werden. Vgl. Hammerstaedt 1999: 94. Der Text bei Kosmas Indikopleustes, *Christliche Topographie* 7,97, SC 197,16, lautet: τὴν ψυχὴν τοῦδε ἀνάπαυσον συνανεγείρων καὶ τὴν σάρκα αὐτοῦ ἐν ᾗ ἂν ἡμέρᾳ ὥρισας κατὰ τὰς ἀληθεῖς καὶ ἀψευδεῖς σου ἐπαγγελίας.

σου ἐπαγγελείας ἀποδι[δοὺς αὐτοῖς ἃ ὀφθαλμὸς

οὐκ εἶδεν καὶ οὓς οὐκ ἤκ[ουσεν καὶ ἐπὶ καρδίαν

ἀνθρώπου ο[ὐ]κ ἀνέβη.

Bereits in erweiterter Form ist die Fürbitte für die Verstorbenen auf dem griechischen Papyrusfragment *P.Cair.* 10395A aus dem 6. Jahrhundert erhalten.[29] Dort finden sich Fürbitten für Heilige und Verstorbene in den Zeilen 17-19. Die Bezugnahme auf die Verlesung der Diptychen legt die Deutung des Fragmentes als Anaphorenfragment nahe.

Bei der griechischen Gregoriosanaphora[30] weist eine Rubrik auf die Verlesung der Diptychen durch den Diakon hin; anschließend ist folgendes priesterliches stilles Gebet angeführt:

Μνήσθητι κύριε τῶν προκεκοιμημένων ἐν τῇ ὀρθοδόξῳ πίστει πατέρων ἡμῶν καὶ ἀδελφῶν, καὶ ἀνάπαυσον τὰς ψυχὰς αὐτῶν μετὰ ὁσίων, μετὰ δικαίων. Ἔκτρεψον, σύναψον εἰς τόπον χλόης, ἐπὶ ὕδατος ἀναπαύσεως, ἐν παραδείσῳ τρυφῆς, καὶ μετὰ τούτων, ὧν εἴπομεν τὰ ὀνόματα αὐτῶν.

Der älteste erhaltene Textzeuge der Basiliosanaphora sind die vier Pergament-Doppelblätter Louvain, Ms. Lefort copt. s.n.[31], deren Text wohl das Überlieferungsstadium dieser Anaphora im 7. Jahrhundert spiegelt:[32]

ⲚⲄ† ⲘⲦⲞⲚ ⲚⲀⲨ ⲌⲚⲔⲞⲨⲞⲨⲚⲞⲨ ⲚⲀⲂⲢⲀⲌⲀⲘ ⲘⲚⲒⲤⲀⲀⲔ ⲘⲚⲒⲀⲔⲰⲂ · ⲌⲚⲞⲨⲘⲀ ⲚⲞⲨ[Ⲟ]ⲦⲞⲨⲈⲦ ⲌⲚⲞⲨⲘⲞⲞⲨ ⲚⲘⲦⲞⲚ... ⲠⲘⲀ ⲚⲦⲀϤⲠⲰⲦ ⲚⲌⲎⲦϤ ⲚϬⲒⲠⲘⲔⲀⲌ ⲚⲌⲎ[Ⲧ] ⲘⲚⲦⲀⲨⲠⲎ ⲘⲚ [Ⲡ]ⲀϢⲈⲌⲞⲘ: -- εἴπατε τὰ ὀνόματα ⲚⲈⲦⲘⲘⲀⲨ †ⲘⲦⲞⲚ ⲚⲀⲨ ⲌⲀⲦⲎⲔ.

Bei den meisten sahidischen wie den griechischen und bohairischen Textzeugen der Basiliosanaphora ist der Verlesung der Diptychen vorangestellt im Anschluß an die Fürbitte für die Stände der Kirche die Fürbitte für die Verstorbenen überliefert. In dieser Fürbitte findet sich das Motiv der Ruhe im Schoß der Patriarchen, der grüne Ort am Wasser der Ruhe, von wo Kummer Leid und Klage flieht.[33]

Bei der Anaphora des Severos von Antiochia, die im "Großen Euchologion" erhalten ist, findet sich ein ausführliches Gedenken "rechtgläubiger Bischöfe, die seit dem Erzbischof und Märtyrer Jakobos entschlafen sind," sodann werden alle kirchlichen Stände aufgezählt. Es folgt der Hinweis auf die Verlesung der Diptychen am Seitenende. Die folgenden Seiten, die wahrscheinlich die Fürbitte für Verstorbene enthielten, sind leider nicht erhalten.[34]

Die sahidische Anaphora des hl. Matthäus überliefert eine kurze allgemeine Einleitung zu den Diptychen, den Hinweis auf "diejenigen, deren Namen der Diakon nennt sowie diejenigen, derer jeder

---

[29] Editio princeps durch Bastianini und Gallazzi 1985. Neuedition durch Hammerstaedt 1999: 161-163.

[30] Vgl. Gerhards 1984: 46 f.

[31] Zur Editio princeps vgl. Doresse und Lanne 1960. Eine Beschreibung der aus vier Pergament-Doppelblättern bestehenden Handschrift findet sich auch bei Budde 2004: 95 f.; Budde verwendet in seiner Edition für diesen Textzeugen die Abkürzung α.

[32] Vgl. dazu Budde 2004: 95f.

[33] Synoptische Übersicht über die griechische, sahidische und bohairische Textfassung bei Budde 2004, S. 190 f., dort Nr. 163-168. Budde macht in seinem Kommentar auf S. 506 darauf aufmerksam, dass einige Textzeugen die Verlesung der Diptychen erst im Anschluß an dieses Gebet vorsehen.

[34] Vgl. S. 108 des Euchologions.

in seinem Herzen gedenkt" sowie daran anschließend eine ausführliche Interzession, die in die Hoffnung mündet, dass Gott keinen von seinem Reich abweisen wird, sondern diejenigen, die auf ihn hoffen, am festgesetzten Tag versammeln wird.[35]

> ⲟⲛⲟⲙⲁⲧⲁ ⲛⲉⲛⲧⲁⲡⲇⲓⲁⲕⲟⲛⲟⲥ ⲧⲁⲩⲉ ⲛⲉⲩⲣⲁⲛ ⲙⲛ ⲛⲉⲧⲉⲣⲉ ⲡⲟⲩⲁ ⲡⲟⲩⲁ
> ⲛⲁⲣⲡⲉⲩⲙⲉⲉⲩⲉ ϩⲙ ⲡⲉⲩϩⲏⲧ ⲁⲣⲓ ⲡⲉⲩⲙⲉⲉⲩⲉ ⲛⲅⲁⲛⲁⲡⲉⲩⲉ ⲙⲙⲟⲟⲩ ϫⲉ ⲛⲧⲟⲕ ⲡⲉ
> ⲡⲉⲩⲉⲓⲛⲉ ⲙⲛ ⲛⲉⲩϩⲃⲏⲩⲉ ⲁⲩⲱ ⲉⲣⲉ ⲛⲉⲩⲡⲣⲁⲝⲓⲥ ϩⲁ ϩⲧⲏⲕ ⲧⲉϣ ⲛⲉⲩⲯⲩⲭⲏ
> ⲉⲛⲧⲟⲡⲟⲥ ⲛⲧⲁⲛⲁⲡⲁⲩⲥⲓⲥ ⲛⲧⲉⲧⲣⲩⲫⲏ ⲉⲧϩⲙ ⲡⲡⲁⲣⲁⲇⲓⲥⲟⲥ ⲉⲕⲟⲩⲛϥ ⲛⲁⲃⲣⲁϩⲁⲙ
> ⲙⲛ ⲓⲥⲁⲁⲕ ⲙⲛ ⲓⲁⲕⲱⲃ ⲛⲅⲧⲙⲛⲉϫ ⲗⲁⲁⲩ ⲙⲙⲟⲛ ⲛⲥⲁⲃⲟⲗ ⲙⲙⲟⲕ ϩⲛ ⲧⲉⲕⲙⲛⲧⲉⲣⲟ
> ⲉⲧϩⲛ ⲙⲡⲏⲩⲉ ⲁⲗⲗⲁ ϩⲙ ⲡⲉϩⲟⲟⲩ ⲉⲧⲕⲛⲁⲧⲛⲛⲟⲟⲩ ⲙⲡⲉⲕⲙⲟⲛⲟⲅⲉⲛⲏⲥ ⲛϣⲏⲣⲉ
> ⲉⲧⲣⲉϥⲥⲱⲟⲩϩ ⲉϩⲟⲩⲛ ⲛⲛⲉⲧϩⲉⲗⲡⲓⲍⲉ ⲉⲣⲟϥ (...)

S. 136 f. des "Großen Euchologion" überliefert aus einer namentlich unbekannten Anaphora die Einleitung zu den Diptychen sowie ein Gedenken der rechtgläubigen geistlichen Stände. Nach dem Hinweis auf die Verlesung der Diptychen folgt das priesterliche Gebet für Verstorbene:

> ⲧⲁ ⲟⲛⲟⲙⲁⲧⲁ - ⲇⲓⲟ ⲡϫⲟⲉⲓⲥ ⲁⲣⲓ ⲡⲉⲕⲛⲁ ⲛⲙⲙⲁⲩ ⲧⲏⲣⲟⲩ ϩⲓ ⲟⲩⲥⲟⲡ ⲡⲛⲟⲩⲧⲉ
> ⲛⲛⲉⲡⲛⲁ ⲙⲛ ⲥⲁⲣⲝ ⲛⲓⲙ ϩⲛ ⲕⲟⲩⲛϥ ⲛⲁⲃⲣⲁϩⲁⲙ ⲙⲛ ⲓⲥⲁⲁⲕ ⲙⲛ ⲓⲁⲕⲱⲃ ⲥⲁⲛⲟⲩⲱⲟⲩ
> ϩⲓϫⲛ ⲟⲩⲙⲁ ⲛⲟⲩⲟⲧⲟⲩⲉⲧ ϩⲓϫⲛ ⲟⲩⲙⲟⲟⲩ ⲛⲙⲧⲟⲛ ⲡⲙⲁ ⲛⲧⲁ ⲡⲙⲕⲁϩ ⲛϩⲏⲧ ⲡⲱⲧ
> ⲛϩⲏⲧϥ ⲙⲛ ⲧⲁⲩⲡⲏ ⲙⲛ ⲧⲁϣⲁϩⲟⲙ ϩⲓⲧⲙ ⲡⲟⲩⲟⲉⲓⲛ ⲛⲛⲉⲕⲡⲉⲧⲟⲩⲁⲁⲃ.

Einen sehr eigenständigen und von den anderen Anaphoren deutlich abweichenden Text bietet die unbekannte Anaphora aus dem "Großen Euchologion," die auf den Seiten 61 und 62 des Euchologions erhalten ist. Auf den Hinweis zur Verlesung der Diptychen folgt dort ein ausführliches Memento der kirchlichen Stände,[36] der Hinweis auf diejenigen, deren Namen der Diakon erwähnt, sowie diejenigen, derer jeder einzelne gedenkt. Es folgt die Bitte um Gottes Erbarmen, der von jedem Gestalt und Wandel kennt, die Bitte um Vergebung aller Sünden der Verstorbenen wie der Anwesenden, die Bitte ihre Seelen ins Land des Lichts zu befehlen, ins Paradies der Freude, in den Schoß der Patriarchen, an den Ort der Ruhe der Väter:

> ... ⲛⲉⲛⲧⲁ ⲡⲇⲓⲁⲕⲟⲛⲟⲥ ⲧⲁⲩⲉ ⲛⲉⲩⲣⲁⲛ ⲙⲛ ⲛⲉⲧⲉ ⲙⲡϥⲧⲁⲩⲟⲟⲩ· ⲙⲛ ⲛⲉⲧⲉⲣⲉ
> ⲡⲟⲩⲁ ⲡⲟⲩⲁ ⲙⲙⲟⲛ ⲉⲓⲣⲉ ⲙⲡⲉⲩⲙⲉⲉⲩⲉ· ⲁⲣⲓ ⲡⲉⲩⲙⲉⲉⲩⲉ ⲧⲏⲣⲟⲩ ϩⲓ ⲟⲩⲥⲟⲡ
> ⲛⲅⲃⲱϣ ⲛⲁⲩ ⲛⲁⲓ ⲉⲧⲕⲥⲟⲟⲩⲛ ⲙⲁⲩⲁⲁⲕ ⲛⲛⲉⲩⲙⲟⲣⲫⲏ ⲙⲛ ⲛⲉⲩⲉⲓⲛⲉ ⲙⲛ
> ⲛⲉⲩⲡⲣⲁⲝⲓⲥ ⲁⲩⲱ ⲛⲅⲛⲁ ⲛⲁⲛ ⲛⲅⲕⲱ ⲛⲁⲛ ⲉⲃⲟⲗ ⲛⲙⲙⲁⲩ ⲛⲛⲉⲛⲛⲟⲃⲉ ⲁⲩⲱ
> ⲛⲅⲧⲉϣ ⲧⲉⲩⲯⲩⲭⲏ ⲉⲧⲉⲭⲱⲣⲁ ⲙⲡⲟⲩⲟⲉⲓⲛ ⲉⲡⲡⲁⲣⲁⲇⲓⲥⲟⲥ ⲛⲧⲉⲧⲣⲩⲫⲏ ⲉⲡⲧⲟⲡ
> ⲛⲁⲃⲣⲁϩⲁⲙ ⲙⲛ ⲓⲥⲁⲁⲕ ⲙⲛ ⲓⲁⲕⲱⲃ ⲡⲙⲁ ⲉⲧⲉⲣⲉ ⲛⲉⲛⲉⲓⲟⲧⲉ ⲙⲧⲟⲛ ⲙⲙⲟⲟⲩ ⲛϩⲏⲧϥ
> ...

Trotz der Vielzahl und Verschiedenheit der Textzeugen des anaphorischen Fürbittgebetes für Verstorbene[37] lassen sich Übereinstimmungen und parallele Motive feststellen. Ganz allgemein wird das Faktum des Todes in allen anaphorischen Interzessionsgebeten euphemistisch umschrieben, wobei

---

[35] Vgl. die Seiten 147 f. des "Großen Euchologions."
[36] Vgl. dazu Foerster 2006.
[37] Vgl. zu einigen der Topoi Botte 1975. Allerdings beleuchtet Botte v.a. die Entwicklung des Gebets für Verstobene im westlichen Ritus und zieht eher beiläufig die koptische Kyrillosanaphora hinzu.

Begriffe aus dem Bereich des "Ruhens" bzw. "Schlafens" verwendet werden.[38] Die Gebete sind getragen von Zuversicht und christlicher Auferstehungshoffnung,[39] wobei die konkreten Vorstellungen und Formulierungen vor allem alttestamentliche Wurzeln—und hier bevorzugt in den Psalmen und Prophetenbüchern—haben.

In der Überleitung von den Diptychen findet sich bei drei Anaphoren aus dem Weißen Kloster, der Matthäusanaphora, der Kyrillosanaphora (Z 100,40) sowie der unbekannten Anaphora (Z 100,61) der Hinweis auf die Nennung der Namen Verstorbener durch den Diakon wie durch das stille innere Gebet der einzelnen Gläubigen.

Im Prinzip alle anaphorischen Interzessionen wie die diakonalen Gebetsaufforderungen dazu enthalten das Motiv der Ruhe, die Gott den Verstorbenen schenken möge.[40] Die Ruhe als eschatologischer Zustand klingt bereits in Ps. 95,11 an und wird in Hebr 3,7-11 aufgenommen. In der Apokalypse findet dieser Begriff ebenfalls Eingang (Apkl 6,11; 14,13). Dieser Begriff wird nach und nach zur spezifisch christlichen Bezeichnung für den Tod und findet sich beispielsweise wiederholt in Grabinschriften.

Das Bild des Ruhens im Schoß der drei Erzväter Abraham, Isaak und Jakob findet sich bei *P.Berol.* 9755, der Basiliosanaphora, den Interzessionsgebeten der beiden unbekannten sahidischen Anaphoren Z. 100,61 f. sowie Z. 100,136 f., der sahidischen Matthäusanaphora sowie der sahidischen Kyrillosanaphora Z. 100,40.[41] Es hat seine Wurzel im Gleichnis vom reichen Mann und armen Lazarus, wobei letzterer nach seinem Tod im Schoß Abrahams zu ruhen kommt (Lk 16,22). Die Zusammenstellung eben der drei Erzväter geht auf früheste alttestamentliche Zeit zurück.[42]

Bei den paradiesischen Vorstellungen des Ortes des Grünens und des Wassers der Ruhe unverkennbar ist der Einfluss des 23. Psalms (LXX 22,2). Dieses paradiesische Motiv findet sich u.a. in *P.Berol.* 9755, in der priesterlichen Fürbitte für Verstorbene der Basiliosanaphora, der griechischen Gregoriosanaphora, der unbekannten Anaphoren in Z. 100,61 f. sowie Z. 100,136 f. Mit der Formulierung vom "Paradies der Freude" klingt die Vorstellung an, nach dem Tode in den paradiesischen Urzustand zurückversetzt zu werden. Nach Gen 2,15 war der Mensch an eben diesen Ort gesetzt, nach Gen 3,23 aus diesem vertrieben worden. Seit Ez 31,9 ist das Paradies ein eschatologischer Ort, vgl. auch Lk 23,43 die Verheißung Jesu an den mit ihm gekreuzigten Schächter und 2. Kor 12,4 die Schilderung des Paulus von seiner Entrückung. Diese Formulierung findet sich in

---

[38] Krause 2003: 43, "Vor allem aber vermeidet der Ägypter zu allen Zeiten das Wort 'sterben' und ersetzt es durch Umschreibungen..."

[39] Botte 1975: 97 f., spricht in diesem Zusammenhang von "images d'espérance" und einer gewissen "sérénité des anciennes prières."

[40] So bereits *P.Stras.* 254, Kosmas Indikopleustes, *P.Cair.* 10.395A, MS Insinger 30 und 31, Vat 109,100, P.Berol. 9755, *P.Lond.Copt.* 156 und natürlich im priesterlichen Gebet der Basiliosanaphora, der Gregoriosanaphora sowie der Matthäusanaphora. Genannt werden könnte hier auch die nicht ägyptische griechische Jakobosanaphora, vgl. Mercier 1974: 220: τούτων πάντων μνήσθητι, κύριε, ὁ θεὸς τῶν πνευμάτων καὶ πάσης σαρκός, ὧν ἐμνήσθημεν καὶ ὧν οὐκ ἐμνήσθημεν ὀρθοδόξων, αὐτὸς ἐκεῖ αὐτοὺς ἀνάπαυσον ἐν χώρᾳ ζώντων, ἐν τῇ βασιλείᾳ σου, ἐν τῇ τρυφῇ τοῦ παραδείσου, ἐν κόλποις Ἀβραὰμ καὶ Ἰσαὰκ καὶ Ἰακώβ, τῶν ἁγίων πατέρων ἡμῶν, ὅθεν ἀπέδρα ὀδύνη, λύπη καὶ στεναγμός, ἔνθα ἐπισκοπεῖ τὸ φῶς τοῦ προσώπου σου καὶ καταλάμπει διὰ παντός. Auffallend ist das Fehlen des Motivs der Ruhe im Gebet der unbekannten Anaphora auf Z. 100,61 f.

[41] Diese Wendung begegnet ebenfalls bei der griechischen Jakobosanaphora, dort mit dem Zusatz "unserer heiligen Väter."

[42] Vgl. nur Ex 3,6 u.ö.—der Gott Israels ist der Gott "Abrahams, Isaaks und Jakobs."

P.Berol. 9755 sowie u.a. in späteren Zeugen der Basiliosanaphora,[43] der griechischen Gregoriosanaphora, in der sahidischen Matthäusanaphora sowie der unbekannten Anaphora auf Z. 100,61 f.[44]

Auch die Vorstellung des Fernseins von Schmerz, Kummer und Seufzen greift auf alttestamentliche Vorstellungen zurück; sie ist wörtlich den eschatologischen Ausblicken des Propheten Jesaja entnommen.[45] In unterschiedlichen Kombinationen finden sich die drei annähernd synonymen Bezeichnungen für Leid auch im Neuen Testament.[46] Dieses Motiv ist weit verbreitet, so findet es sich beispielsweise auch in *P.Ness.* 3.96, im priesterlichen Interzessionsgebet der Basiliosanaphora wie in dem der unbekannten Anaphora in Z. 100, 136f.[47]

Das Bild vom Glanz der Heiligen geht zurück auf Ps 110,3 (LXX 109). Es findet sich in den Interzessionen bei *P.Ryl.* III 465, Kosmas Indikopleustes, in den priesterlichen Gebeten der Basiliosanaphora sowie der Anaphoren von Z. 100, 136 f. sowie Z. 100, 40 f.[48]

Die Bitte um Gottes Erbarmen findet sich ganz zu Beginn der anaphorischen Interzession bei der unbekannten Anaphora von Z. 100,136 f., auch bei der Matthäusanaphora sowie sehr ausführlich in Verbindung mit der Vergebung nicht nur der Sünden der Verstorbenen, sondern auch der eigenen Sünden im Gebet der unbekannten Anaphora in Z. 100,61 f. Dort wird auch darauf Bezug genommen, dass Gott die Gestalt und den Wandel der Verstorbenen kenne und Vergebung schenke.

Wörtlich von der "Auferstehung" ist selten die Rede; in *P.Berol.* 9755 wird der Hoffnung Ausdruck verliehen, "Gott möge die Verstorbenen würdig machen seiner Auferstehung." Das Bild von der "Auferstehung des Fleisches am festgesetzten Tag" findet sich lediglich in *P.Ryl.* 465, bei Kosmas Indikopleustes und Zeugen der Markos-/Kyrillosanaphora.

Die Vielzahl der Textzeugen und Schwierigkeiten bei der Datierung mancher Texte—eine spätere Handschrift überliefert nicht selten ein viel älteres Textstadium—machen die Auswertung des Zusammengetragenen nicht einfach. Sicher ist, dass nach und nach nicht nur bei den Diptychen, sondern auch—wo vorhanden—bei den vorangehenden Kommemorationen von Heiligen, Märtyrern und kirchlichen Ständen eine immer längere Liste wuchs.[49] Parallelen aus anderen Gebeten fanden Eingang. Eine weitere Tendenz ist aber auch, dass der Abstand zwischen dem allmächtigen Gott und seinem Sohn, dem Pantokrator, immer stärker erfahren und zum Ausdruck gebracht wird. Menschen erfahren sich als der Gnade Gottes immer unwürdiger. Während in früheren Texten Bilder vom Paradies, vom Schoß der Patriarchen den Ort beschreiben, an dem der verstorbene Glaubende

---

[43] Vgl. dazu Budde 2004: 512, "Dabei zeigen konkret die Zeugen unseres Textes, dass das Paradies-Motiv erst nachträglich zum grünenden Ort und zum Wasser der Ruhe hinzugefügt wurde; die sahidischen Zeugen kennen es noch nicht."

[44] Auch diese Wendung begegnet bei der griechischen Jakobosanaphora.

[45] Vgl. Jes 35,10 und 51,11. Die beiden letzteren Wendungen finden sich in dieser Kombination in der LXX in Gen 3,16 anläßlich der Vertreibung aus dem Paradies.

[46] So in 1. Tim 6,10, Röm 8,26; 9,2.

[47] Auch diese Wendung ist im anaphorischen Interzessionsgebet für Verstorbene der griechischen Jakobosanaphora bezeugt.

[48] Ein Lichtmotiv, allerdings mit anderen Formulierungen, bietet auch die griechische Jakobosanaphora mit der Wendung: "dort scheint das Licht deines Angesichts und überstrahlt alle Zeit bzw. das All."

[49] Gerhards 1984: 100 f., bemerkt: "Die Tendenz zu einer verstärkten Einbeziehung der Heiligen in die Intercessio ist besonders an der Namensliste abzulesen. Während sich der griechische Text auf fünf Namen beschränkt (Maria, Johannes, Stephanus, Markus und Gregor), weitet die koptische Rezension die Liste auf über zwanzig Namen aus."

unmittelbar nach seinem Tod ankommt, scheint in manchen späteren Texten dies mehr ein vorläufiger "Warteraum" wo die Seele des gläubigen Verstorbenen des letzten Gerichts harrt. Die Parallelität mancher Formulierungen und Vorstellungen nötigt jedoch nicht immer dazu, zeitlich aufeinander folgende Entwicklungsstadien anzunehmen. Die Fürbitte für die Verstorbenen in all ihren Ausformungen spiegelt die Glaubenszuversicht der Christen Ägyptens und die Verwurzelung ihrer liturgischen Sprache in der Bibel, vor allem im Alten Testament.

Im Vorangehenden war es lediglich möglich, einen kurzen Überblick in die Formulierung der anaphorischen Interzession für Verstorbene und Grundlinien ihrer Entwicklung anzureißen. In jedem Fall lohnenswert wäre eine umfassendere Darstellung des erweiterten Themas, wo nicht nur anaphorische Texte, sondern auch vor- und außeranaphorische Fürbittengebete mit einbezogen werden sollten ebenso wie dokumentarische Texte und Inschriften. Eine derartige Studie könnte einmal mehr das Bild der "Einheit in der Vielfalt," das die ägyptische Liturgie und Frömmigkeit bietet, bestärken.

BIBLIOGRAPHIE

Bastianini, G. und Gallazzi, C. (1985). "*P.Cair.* 10935: Frammento liturgico," *ZPE* 58, 99-102 + Abb Tafel Ivc.

Botte, B. (1975). "Les plus anciennes formules de prière pour les morts," in: *La Maladie et la Mort du chrétien dans la Liturgie. Conférences Saint-Serge, XXIe semaine d'études liturgiques, Paris 1er-4 juillet 1974*, Bibliotheca Ephemerides Liturgicae Subsidia 1, Roma: Edizioni Liturgiche, 83-99.

Brakmann, H. (2004a). "Fragmenta Graeco-Copto-Thebaica. Zu Jutta Henners Veröffentlichung alter und neuer Dokumente südägyptischer Liturgie," *OrChr* 88, 117-172.

Brakmann, H. (2004b). "Neue Funde und Forschungen zur Liturgie der Kopten. 1996-2000," in: Immerzeel, M. und Vliet, J. van der (hg.), *Coptic Studies on the threshold of a new millenium. Proceedings of the Seventh International Congress of Coptic Studies, Leiden 27. Aug.-2. Sept. 2000*, Leiden: Brill, 575-606.

Budde, A. (2004). *Die ägyptische Basilios-Anaphora. Text—Kommentar—Geschichte* (= JThF 7). Münster: Aschendorff.

Cuming, G. J. (1990). *The Liturgy of St. Mark* (= OCA 234). Roma: Pontificium Institutum Studiorum Orientalium.

Doresse, J. und Lanne, E. (1960). *Un témoin archaique de la Liturgie Copte de S. Basile. En annexe: Les liturgies "basiliennes" et saint Basile par Dom. B. Capelle* (= BMus 47). Louvain: Publications Universitaires.

Engberding, H. (1964). "Das anaphorische Fürbittgebet der Markus-Liturgie," *OCP* 30, 398-446.

Foerster, H. (2006). "Sich des Gebrauchs der Frauen enthalten. Eine Anfrage an die grammatikalische Struktur einer Interzession für Verstorbene im Großen Euchologion aus dem Weißen Kloster," *ZAC* 9, 584-591.

Gerhards, A. (1984). *Die griechische Gregoriosanaphora. Ein Beitrag zur Geschichte des eucharistischen Hochgebets* (= *LQF* 65). Münster: Aschendorff.

Haelst, J. van (1976). *Catalogue des papyrus littéraires juifs et chrétiens*. Paris: Sorbonne.

Hammerschmidt, E. (1957). *Die koptische Gregoriosanaphora. Syrische und griechische Einflüsse auf eine ägyptische Liturgie* (= *BBA* 8). Berlin: Akademie-Verlag.

Hammerstaedt, J. (1999). *Griechische Anaphorenfragmente aus Ägypten und Nubien* (*Papyrologica Coloniensia* 28). Opladen/Wiesbaden: Westdeutscher Verlag.

Henner, J. (2000). *Fragmenta Liturgica Coptica, Editionen und Kommentar liturgischer Texte der Koptischen Kirche des ersten Jahrtausends* (= *STAC* 5). Tübingen: Mohr Siebeck.

Junker, H. und W. Schubart (1902). "Ein griechisch-koptisches Kirchengebet," *ZÄS* 40, 1-31.

Krause, M. (2003). "Das Totenwesen der Kopten," in: Froschauer, H., Gastgeber, Chr. und Harrauer H. (hg.), *Tod am Nil. Totenkult im antiken Ägypten* (= *Nilus* 8). Wien: Phoibos, 33-44,

Lanne, E. (1958). *Le Grand Euchologe du Monastère Blanc* (= *PO* 28,2). Paris: Firmin-Didot.

Mercier, Dom B.-Ch. (1974). *La liturgie de saint Jacques. Edition critique du texte grec avec traduction latine* (= *PO* 26/2.). Paris: Firmin-Didot.

Papathomas, A. (1998). "Ein neues Zeugnis frühchristlicher griechischer Kondolenzepistolographie," *Tyche* 13, 195-206.

Pleyte, W. und P. A. A. Boeser (hg.) (1897). *Manuscrits coptes du Musée d'Antiquités des Pays-Bas à Leide*. Leiden: Brill.

Quecke, H. (1978). "Zukunftschancen bei der Erforschung der koptischen Liturgie," in: McL.Wilson, R. (hg.), *The Future of Coptic Studies* (= *Coptic Studies* 1). Leiden: Brill, 164-196.

Taft, R. F. (1991). "The diptychs. A History of the Liturgy of St. John Chrysostom IV," *OCP* 238, 79-94.

Wagner, G. (1972). "La commémoration des Saints dans la prière eucharistique," *Ir* 45, 447-456.

Wessely, C. (1917). *Griechische und koptische Texte theologischen Inhalts* V (= *SPP* 18). Leipzig: Avenarus/Haessel.

Winkler, G. (1971). "Die Interzessionen der Chrysostomusanaphora in ihrer geschichtlichen Entwicklung," *OCP* 37, 333-383.

DIE KOPTISCHEN KAUFURKUNDEN VON KLOSTERZELLEN DES APOLLO-KLOSTERS VON BAWIT AUS ABBASIDISCHER ZEIT[1]

MARTIN KRAUSE

Über die Person Apollo, nach dem acht[2] Klöster in Ägypten benannt worden sind, wissen wir vorläufig nichts Endgültiges. Die schriftlichen Quellen, vor allem die arabischen Synaxare, berichten über mehrere Personen namens Apollo[3] und sind bisher nur zum Teil veröffentlicht worden. Zwei Apollo-Klöster liegen südlich von Hermopolis in Bawit und/oder[4] in Titkooh. Auch unsere leider viel zu früh verstorbene Kollegin Sarah Clackson konnte sich nicht entscheiden, ob die in den schriftlichen Quellen genannten beiden Apollo-Klöster südlich von Hermopolis sich auf zwei verschiedene Klöster beziehen, oder ob das in den schriftlichen Quellen als Apollo-Kloster von Titkooh bezeugte Apollo-Kloster, das archäologisch bisher nicht nachgewiesen worden ist, identisch ist mit den Ruinen des Apollo-Kloster von Bawit.[5]

Die von ägyptischen Bauern vor 1900 auf der Suche nach Sebah für ihre Felder in der Wüste zwei km von dem Dorf Bawit entfernt entdeckten Klosterruinen waren zunächst als Grabkapellen eines Friedhofs angesehen worden, bevor erkannt wurde, daß man ein aus vielen kleineren Bauten und Kirchen bestehendes Doppelkloster[6] von etwa 780 m in nordsüdlicher und 720 m in westöstlicher Richtung freilegte, das von einer Mauer umgeben war. Von Ausgrabungen, die heutigen Ansprüchen genügen, kann man erst seit Wiederaufnahme der Ausgrabungen im Jahre 2002 durch das französische Archäologische Institut in Kairo in Zusammenarbeit mit dem Louvre in Paris sprechen. Mit der Veröffentlichung des wissenschaftlichen Nachlasses des ersten Ausgräbers J. Clédat[7] 1999 hatten die französischen Arbeiten in Bawit sowohl einen Abschluß als auch einen viel versprechenden Neubeginn erreicht, zumal in ihm auch mit der Publikation der in der Grabung gefundenen Papyri und Ostraka[8] begonnen wurde. Sie werden hoffentlich helfen bei der Zuweisung der vielen aus dem Antikenhandel stammenden Papyri auf die verschiedenen Apollo-Klöster, um deren Aufspürung in Museen und Sammlungen und Publikation Sarah Clackson sich bleibende Verdienste erworben hat.[9]

Aus dem Antikenhandel stammen auch die fünf großen Kaufurkunden aus dem Apollon-Kloster von Bawit, über die hier berichtet werden soll. Sie wurden 1903 vom British Museum in London angekauft und tragen jetzt die Signaturen BL Or 6201-6204 und 6206. Sie wurden von W. E. Crum teilweise kopiert und von P. E. Kahle in Crums Nachlaß[10] wieder gefunden. Kahles früher Tod

---

[1] Dieser Aufsatz ist eine kurze Zusammenfassung einer im Druck befindlichen überarbeiteten Leipziger Dissertation von 1958, deren Erscheinen durch die Flucht aus der ehemaligen DDR verhindert worden ist.

[2] Krause 2003: 156 ff.

[3] Krause 2003: 160.

[4] Coquin 1977: 435-446.

[5] Clackson 2001: 222 f.

[6] Nach den Inschriften lag das Männerkloster im Norden und das Frauenkloster im Süden.

[7] Clédat 1999. In dieser Publikation ist auf Plan I-IV der neueste Grundriß des Klosters veröffentlicht.

[8] Boud'hors: 1995, 1999 u. 2004.

[9] Clackson 2001 u. 2004.

[10] Group V,5.

verhinderte eine Publikation. 1994 hat L. S. B. MacCoull[11] vier dieser Urkunden publiziert, auf die Publikation der fünften, 6201, aber verzichtet, weil sie der Meinung war, sie sei nur eine Kopie von 6202,[12] was nicht zutreffend ist. Vielmehr enthält diese Urkunde weitere neue und wichtige Aussagen, wie wir noch sehen werden. Vor allem aber gewinnen wir durch die fünf Urkunden neue Quellen für das ägyptische Mönchtum aus abbasidischer Zeit, einer Zeit, in der—wie Wilhelm Hengstenberg[13] formuliert hat—der "Geldkomplex" in das ägyptische Mönchtum eingezogen war, nunmehr aus Bawit, einem großen Kloster, und genauestens datiert aus den Jahren 833-849. Alle fünf Urkunden sind Teil eines Archivs, das von demselben Schreiber, dem Diakon Petrus, dem Sohn des verstorbenen Diakon Hor, in den Jahren zwischen 833 und 849 geschrieben worden ist. Sie sind fast vollständig erhalten. Nur das Ende der Urkunde 6203 mit der Einverständniserklärung der Verkäufer und den Unterschriften der Zeugen fehlt. In 6203,30 ff. wird von dem Verkauf eines kleinen Hofes berichtet, der nördlich der Zellengruppe lag, dessen Urkunde bisher noch nicht gefunden wurde.

Die fünf uns erhaltenen Urkunden beurkunden den Verkauf von zwei verschiedenen Zellengruppen des Apollon-Klosters. Vier von ihnen betreffen eine in der *neuen Werkstatt* gelegene Zellengruppe, die fünfte, die bisher noch nicht publizierte 6201, eine kleine in der *großen Bäckerei* gelegene Zellengruppe. Die Bezeichnungen "neu" bzw. "groß" setzen die Existenz sowohl einer "alten Werkstatt" als auch einer "kleinen Bäckerei" im Kloster voraus, deren präzise Lagen hoffentlich durch die neuen französischen Ausgrabungen festgestellt werden kann, falls diese Zellengruppen nicht von den Sebahin zerstört worden sind.

Bereits in omaijadischer Zeit mußten die Mönche eine Kopfsteuer an den islamischen Staat zahlen, von der sie zuvor befreit waren. Im 8. und 9. Jahrhundert versuchten sie vergeblich durch Aufstände sich von dieser Steuerlast zu befreien.[14] Nachdem die Aufstände niedergeschlagen worden waren, wurden vor allem kleinere und ärmere Klöster verlassen, weil ihre Bewohner die Steuern nicht bezahlen konnten. Andere Klöster suchten einen Weg, wie sie zu Geld kommen und weiterexistieren konnten. Eine Möglichkeit bestand z. B. darin, Klosterbesitz oder sogar Klosterämter[15] zu verkaufen.

Auch im Apollo-Kloster von Bawit wurde nach Ausweis der Urkunden unterschieden zwischen verkäuflichen und unverkäuflichen Teilen des Klosters. Nicht verkäuflich waren offensichtlich die Einrichtungen, die von allen Mönchen genutzt werden konnten. Genannt werden in der von L. S. B. MacCoull nicht edierten Urkunde 6201 ausdrücklich Arbeitsplätze und die Zisterne: "Und der Arbeitsplatz unterhalb davon, den man zu einer Bäckerei machen kann, ist nicht euer, sondern gehört der Diakonia—und alle Brüder backen in ihm—denn man kann ihn nicht verkaufen; und die kleine Dattelpalme gehört euch, weil ihr sie gepflanzt habt."[16] Und kurz vor der zitierten Passage lesen wir in Zeile 66 eine Aussage über eine wohl in der Nähe liegende Zisterne: "Und ihr seid frei und füllt Wasser aus der Zisterne," das heißt, den Käufern einer Zellengruppe wird das Recht auf Mitnutzung der Zisterne eingeräumt. Auch die Zisterne ist somit—ebenso wie der Backplatz—nicht verkäuflich, weil beide von allen Mönchen des Klosters genutzt werden können.

---

[11] MacCoull 1994: 141-158 u. Taf. 36-54. Zu ihrer Edition vgl. die Kritik in der in A. 1 genannten Arbeit. Im Folgenden wird bei Nennungen der 5 Papyri auf BL Or verzichtet.

[12] MacCoull 1994: 156.

[13] Hengstenberg 1935: 359.

[14] Krause 1985: 124 f.

[15] Kahle 1954: I, 30 u. 41.

[16] 6201,70 ff., Krause 1985: 127.

Verkäuflich sind dagegen die Klosterzellen. Die koptisch als ⲙⲁ ⲛ̄ϣⲱⲡⲉ[17] "monk's cell" oder "group of cells" bezeichneten Gebäude werden mit "Zellengruppe" übersetzt, weil sie aus mehreren Räumen, aus Kapelle, Wohnraum, Gewölbe, Treppen und Dächern,[18] bestanden. Wie die bisherigen Freilegungen gezeigt haben, waren diese Klosterzellen nicht große Säle—wie z.B. im Apollo-Kloster von Balaizah—,[19] sondern kleine Gebäude, die innerhalb der Klostermauern über das große Gelände des Klosters verteilt waren. Die Urkunden benennen außerdem die Anrainer dieser Zellengruppe auf allen vier Seiten in der Reihenfolge: Norden, Süden, Osten und Westen. Während z.B. im Süden für die Zeit von 833-849 dieselben Nachbarn, der kleine Hof des Johannes und Houmise,[20] genannt werden, stellen wir in diesem Zeitraum im Osten einen Wechsel der Nachbarn fest. Es werden drei verschiedene Nachbarn als Bewohner der kleinen Zelle im Osten nacheinander genannt: Schenute, Markus und zuletzt der Hof des Markus. Auch den Kaufpreis, dessen Höhe zwischen drei und zwei Solidi schwankt, erfahren wir, und seine Übergabe durch die Käufer an die Verkäufer wird durch die Zeugen, die am Ende der Urkunde unterschreiben, bezeugt.

In den 4 Verkaufsurkunden der in der *neuen Werkstatt* gelegenen Zellengruppe, deren Verkauf in den Jahren 833 bis 849 in dieser zeitlichen Abfolge: 6203, 6204, 6206 und 6202 erfolgte, werden uns sowohl die Namen und Ämter der Verkäufer und der Käufer als auch die Namen der Vorbesitzer genannt, so daß wir eine ununterbrochene Abfolge der Besitzer dieser Gruppe, nicht nur für die Jahre 833 bis 849, sondern auch für einen uns nicht näher bekannten Zeitpunkt vor 833 erhalten, als der Vorbesitzer die Zellengruppe an den Käufer von 6203 verkaufte; und die Verkäufer der letzten erhaltenen Urkunde in 6202 nennen die letzten uns bekannten Käufer. Somit erfahren wir den Wechsel über sechs aufeinander folgende Besitzer dieser Zellengruppe. Ein exaktes Datum für den Beginn der Verkäufe kennen wir leider nicht, denn in der ältesten erhaltenen Urkunde, in 6203, wird zwar als ehemaliger Vorbesitzer des Kaufobjektes der Archimandrit Ammonius genannt, die Verkaufsurkunde ist uns aber bisher nicht erhalten, so daß wir nicht wissen, wann er in ihren Besitz kam, wie lange der Archimandrit Besitzer dieses Klosterteiles war, wer der Vorbesitzer war und vor allem nicht, wann mit dem Verkauf von Klosterteilen im Apollo-Kloster begonnen wurde, zumal auch der Zeitraum, in dem die Zellengruppe nach Ausweis der Urkunden im Besitz ihrer Käufer war, unterschiedlich lang und dabei abnehmend immer kürzer wurde: nämlich nur knapp 10, 7 oder nur noch 2 Jahre war.

Die 5. Urkunde, 6201, beschreibt den Verkauf eines anderen Kaufobjektes, nämlich einer kleineren Zellengruppe in der *großen Bäckerei* südlich eines Gebäudes, das als "Diakonia" bezeichnet wird. Zu ihr gehören eine Treppe, die auf das Dach führt, eine Veranda auf dem Dach und ein kleines Gewölbe. Anrainer —wie in der Zellengruppe der *neuen Werkstatt*—werden nicht genannt. Nur die Urkunde 6201 beurkundet den Verkauf dieser Zellengruppe, der 849, kurz vor dem Verkauf der Zellengruppe in der *neuen Werkstatt*, erfolgt ist. Außerdem fällt auf, daß in den Urkunden 6202 und 6201 dieselben Personen als Verkäufer und Käufer bezeugt sind: in beiden Urkunden verkauft Schenute, der

---

[17] Crum 1939: 580.

[18] 6203, 53 f. u. Par.

[19] Grossmann 1993: 190.

[20] 6203,32 f.; 6204,27f.; 6206, 17; 6202,33 f. In der in A. 1 genannten Arbeit sind Übersichtspläne der beiden Zellengruppen veröffentlicht, in denen auch die Namen der Anrainer der Zellengruppen und die Zeit ihres Wohnens eingezeichnet sind.

Archimandrit des Klosters, in 6202 mit seinen Brüdern, den Mönchen Paulus und Severus, in 6201 mit den jetzt im Amt befindlichen Verwaltern—wohl denselben Personen—, in 6202 an die Mönche Staurus, Susinnius und Phoibammon, in 6201 an dieselben Personen, die nur in anderer Reihenfolge: Susinnius, Phoibammon und Staurus genannt und nun als *apotaktische* Mönche bezeichnet werden. Auch in 6206, 8 f. werden die Käufer der Zellengruppe in der *neuen Werkstatt* als *apotaktische* Mönche bezeichnet. Von den 11 Zeugen bezeugen 7 Personen in beiden Urkunden, in 6201 unterschreiben noch 4 weitere Zeugen. Die Höhe des Kaufpreises ist in beiden Urkunden unterschiedlich,[21] weil es sich um verschieden große Zellengruppen handelt.

Betrachten wir zunächst die Angaben der Urkunden zum Zeitpunkt des Kaufes/Verkaufes, die Namen und Ämter der Verkäufer und Käufer, die Höhe des Kaufpreises und achten dabei vor allem auch auf die Motive für den Kauf und Verkauf, auf die genannte Verwendung des Verkaufserlöses und errechnen den Zeitraum, in dem die Zellengruppe im Besitz der Verkäufer war. Beginnen wir mit den vier Urkunden, in denen der in der *neuen Werkstatt* des Apollo-Kloster gelegene Zellenverband verkauft wird.

Als erster Vorbesitzer wird 6203,21 f. der vor 833 verstorbene Archimandrit Apa Ammonius genannt, der diese Zellengruppe an Joseph verkauft hat. Welchen Rang der Käufer zum Zeitpunkt des Kaufes hatte, wissen wir nicht, ebensowenig, ob auch Josephs Bruder Markus als Käufer in der nicht erhaltenen Urkunde auftrat. Dieser Käufer namens Joseph verkauft nach Ausweis von 6203, 3 ff. am 9.Tybi der 11. Indiktion im 549. Jahr nach Diokletian und dem 217. Jahr der Hidschra, nunmehr als Priester und Archimandrit des Apollo-Klosters mit seinem Bruder, dem Mönch Markus, diese Zellengruppe an Makarius, den Sohn des verstorbenen Pehev Hatre, der um den Kauf gebeten hatte. Mit der Urkunde 6203 ist uns die bisher älteste Verkaufsurkunde erhalten. Nach Nennung der Anrainer auf allen 4 Seiten wird die Höhe des vereinbarten Kaufpreises mit drei Goldsolidi angegeben und ebenso seine Übergabe durch die Käufer an die Verkäufer. Diese haben das Geld überwiesen für die Verwaltung der Diakonia des Klosters.

Die Käufer dieser Zellengruppe, Makarius Pehev und seine Söhne Theodor, Anubion und Merkur, verkaufen in der Urkunde 6204 am 9. Choiak, der 6. Indiktion des 559. Jahres nach Diokletian und dem 227. Jahr der Sarazenen, nach knapp 10 Jahren die von Joseph und Markus gekaufte Zellengruppe weiter an den Priester Paulus und seinen Bruder Petrus. Der Verkauf erfolgte aus Not der Verkäufer und auf Anfrage der Käufer. Der Kaufpreis beträgt wieder drei Goldsolidi. Eine Aussage über die Verwendung des Kaufpreises fehlt zwar, doch kann aus der Aussage ⲁⲧⲉⲣⲭⲣⲓⲁ ϣⲱⲡⲉ "es trat die Notwendigkeit ein"[22] erschlossen werden, daß die Verkäufer das Geld benötigten.

Der Käufer dieser Zellengruppe, der Priester Paulus und Verwalter unseres Vaters Apa Pamun aus Ahnas, verkauft in der Urkunde 6206 am 3. Paophi der 11. Indiktion des 564. Jahres nach Diokletian und dem 233. Jahr der Sarazenen, nach knapp 7 Jahren die von Makarius, dem Sohn des Pehev Hatre gekaufte Zellengruppe weiter an die apotaktischen Mönche Schenute, Severus, Paulus und Timotheus. Der Verkauf erfolgte auf Wunsch des Verkäufers, der den Kaufpreis für sich und das Kloster verwenden wollte. Eine nähere Angabe über das Teilungsverhältnis des Kaufpreises, ob es hälftig oder unterschiedlich geteilt werden soll, wird nicht gemacht. Der Kaufpreis beträgt nur noch zwei Goldsolidi.

---

[21] 2 Solidi in 6202 und 1 1/3 Solidi in 6201.
[22] 6204,19.

Die Käufer dieser Zellengruppe, Schenute, der sich nun als Priester und Archimandrit vorstellt, und seine Brüder, die Mönche Paulus und Severus, verkaufen in der Urkunde 6202 am 15. Thot der 14. Indiktion des 566. Jahres nach Diokletian, also bereits nach knapp zwei Jahren, die von dem Priester und Verwalter des Apa Pamun gekaufte Zellengruppe weiter an die Mönche Staurus, Susinnius und Phoibammon, die Söhne des verstorbenen Apa Hev. Der Verkauf erfolgte auf Anfrage der Käufer. Der Kaufpreis beträgt 2 Goldsolidi, über dessen Verwendung nichts ausgesagt wird.

Für die vier Urkunden, die den Verkauf der in der *neuen Werkstatt* gelegenen Zellengruppe dokumentieren, hat sich also ergeben, daß in 6203 und 6202 jeweils der Klosterabt als Verkäufer auftrat und ebenso schon der in 6203 genannte Vorbesitzer der Zellengruppe ein Abt namens Ammonius war. In 6206 war der Verkäufer Paulus Priester und Verwalter "unseres Apa Pamun" aus Ahnas,[23] der in 6204 zusammen mit seinem Bruder Petrus die Zellengruppe gekauft hatte. In 6202 und auch in 6201 ist dieser Priester Paulus später noch als Zeuge für den Kauf/Verkauf von beiden Zellengruppen tätig.[24] Von den Verkäufern in 6304 fehlen Amtsangaben. Ebenso werden für die Käufer in 6203 keine Ämter genannt, in 6206 sind die Käufer apotaktische Mönche, in 6202 Mönche, nur in 6204 waren ein Priester und sein Bruder die Käufer. In zwei Fällen, 6206 u. 6202, wollen die Käufer, Mönche, ohne Angabe des Grundes Zellengruppen kaufen und zweimal wollen die Besitzer von Zellen verkaufen, entweder, weil sie in Not sind[25] oder weil sie das Geld für sich und das Kloster benötigen.[26] In 6203 will der Klosterabt den Verkaufserlös für die Verwaltung der Diakonia des Klosters verwenden.[27]

Als Fazit ergibt sich, daß in der Mehrheit Klosteräbte als Verkäufer der Zellengruppe auftreten, die Geld für das Kloster und seine Verwaltung benötigen. Bei den Käufern sind überwiegend Mönche und apotaktische Mönche vertreten. Einen Sonderfall stellt der Priester Paulus dar, der in 6204 mit seinem Bruder den in Not geratenen Besitzern die Zellengruppe abkaufte, um sie in 6206 nach 6 Jahren an apotaktische Mönche weiter zu verkaufen und das Geld für sich und das Kloster zu verwenden.

In der Urkunde 6201 wird der Verkauf einer in der *großen Bäckerei* gelegenen kleinen Zellengruppe südlich der Diakonia beurkundet. Sie datiert vom 10. Thot der 14. Indiktion[28] des 566. Jahres nach Diokletian. In ihr verkauft der auch in 6202 bezeugte Priester und Archimandrit Schenute mit den im Amte befindlichen Verwaltern, deren Namen nicht genannt werden, diese kleine Zellengruppe, die sich im Besitz der Diakonia befindet, an die apotaktischen Mönche Susinnius, Phoibammon und Staurus, die auch in 6202 als Käufer einer Zellengruppe in der neuen Werkstatt bezeugt sind. Der Kauf erfolgte auf Anfrage der Käufer. Der Kaufpreis betrug nur 1 Solidus und 1 Trimesion, den Schenute für die Verwaltung der Diakonia des Klosters[29] verwandt hat. Damit haben die Käufer, die apotaktischen Mönche von 6202 und 6201, zwei Zellengruppen gekauft, eine in der *neuen Werkstatt* und eine in der *großen Bäckerei*.

---

[23] zu Apa Pamun aus Ahnas (Herakleopolis Magna), vgl. Timm 1985: Teil 3, 1162 f.

[24] in 6202,90 f. und 6201,91.

[25] 6204,19.

[26] 6206,12.

[27] 6203,49 f.

[28] So 6201,31. 6201,3 ist die Zahl 13 in 14 zu verbessern.

[29] 6201,41 f.

In allen Verträgen ist—wie wir sahen—dieselbe Person als Schreiber tätig: der Diakon Petrus, Sohn des verstorbenen Diakon Hor. Er beurkundet alle Kaufverträge und amtiert zusätzlich noch in zwei Urkunden als Zeuge. Er verwendet für alle Verkäufe dasselbe Formular, offenbar das Verkaufsformular von Hermopolis, das von dem in Oberägypten benutzten, bezeugt durch die Verkaufsurkunden von Djeme, abweicht.[30]

Das Kaufformular enthält eine Reihe von Widersprüchen, von denen hier nur der wichtigste genannt werden soll. Einerseits erhalten der bzw. die Käufer durch die Bezahlung des Kaufpreises, dessen Übergabe die Zeugen bezeugen, alle Rechte eines Eigentümers über den Kaufgegenstand—eine Zellengruppe—zeit ihres Lebens und auf ewige Zeiten und der Kauf soll auch für ihre Erben gültig sein.[31] Und es wird ihnen garantiert, daß weder geistliche noch weltliche Instanzen—genannt werden die Verkäufer[32] noch ihre Amtsnachfolger[33] noch weltliche Behörden[34] die Gültigkeit des Vertrages anfechten können. Andererseits soll nach dem Tode des oder der Käufer[35] kein Verwandter des Käufers Herr über die Zellengruppe werden, vielmehr soll die Diakonia des Klosters[36] Herr über diese Zellengruppe werden, und zwar nach Aussagen von zwei Urkunden (6204,56 und 6206,39 f.)—ⲛⲑⲉ ⲛϣⲟⲣⲡ—das heißt "wie zuerst" oder "wie früher." Eine Übersetzung "wie vorher" ist nicht möglich, denn sie würde die Vorbesitzer der Zellengruppe meinen, die wir namentlich kennen, weil ihre Namen in den Verkaufsurkunden genannt werden:[37] Die Aussage ⲛⲑⲉ ⲛϣⲟⲣⲡ muß demnach mit "wie früher" übersetzt werden, weil es sich nicht—wie wir sahen—auf die jeweiligen Vorbesitzer der Zellengruppe beziehen kann, sondern einen noch früheren, weiter zurückliegenden Zeitpunkt meinen muß. Das dürfte sich auf eine ältere Regelung oder vielleicht sogar auf die Klosterregel beziehen, die bei der Gründung des Klosters oder zu einem späteren Zeitpunkt beschlossen worden war. Diese Regelung mußte offensichtlich der Zeitlage angepaßt werden, als Steuerzahlungen an die islamische Obrigkeit geleistet werden mußten und führte zu einer Änderung der Regel, die als "eine Übereinstimmung in unserer Mitte untereinander"[38] bezeichnet wird. Es muß also eine Zeit gegeben haben, in der alle Teile des Klosters, auch die Klosterzellen, der Diakonia des Klosters gehörten, bevor eine neue Vereinbarung unter den Mönchen einen Kauf der Zellen möglich machte. Wann genau mit dem Verkauf von Zellengruppen im Apollon-Kloster begonnen wurde, wissen wir nicht. Neufunde von Papyri könnten uns weiterhelfen. Dieser Kauf hatte also nur eine eingeschränkte Gültigkeit, weil er nur

---

[30] Vgl. Zum Vergleich mit dem Verkaufsformular von Djeme vgl. die A.1 genannte Arbeit.

[31] 6203, 25-27 u. Parallelen.

[32] 6203, 55-57 u. Parallelen: "der Archimandrit und die jetzt im Amt befindlichen Verwalter."

[33] 6203, 57-59 u. Parallelen: "seien es Priester, Diakone, Vorleser, Klostervorsteher, Mönche oder Laien."

[34] 6203, 59 f. u. Parallelen: "Ämter, Behörden und Richter."

[35] 6203, 75-77 u. Parallelen.

[36] 6203, 78 f.

[37] In 6204, Z.17-18 werden als Vorbesitzer der Zellengruppe der ehemalige Klosterabt Joseph und sein Bruder Markus genannt. Das bestätigt auch die Verkaufsurkunde 6203 selbst in Zeile 15-17: der Priester und Archimandrit des Klosters, Joseph, und sein Bruder, der Mönch Markus, verkaufen die in ihrem Besitz befindliche Zellengruppe, die sie von dem Archimandriten Ammonius gekauft hatten (Z. 20-22), an Pehev Hatre. Für 6206 wird in Zeile 11 als Vorbesitzer Makarios, der Sohn des Pehev Hatre genannt und die Verkaufsurkunde 6204 selbst bestätigt in Zeile 12-14, daß Makarios, der Sohn des Pehev Hatre—zusammen mit seinen Söhnen Theodor, Anubion und Merkur—die Zellengruppe weiterverkauft hat.

[38] 6203, 79 f.

bis zum Tode des Inhabers galt.[39] Die Aussage der *ewigen*[40] Gültigkeit des Kaufes, die im Widerspruch zu der Vereinbarung steht, daß der Besitz nur bis zum Tode des Käufers gilt, dürfte auf die Verwendung des Kaufformulars zurückgehen, das die Klausel der ewigen Gültigkeit des Vertrages enthielt. Die Bestimmung, wonach beim Tod des Besitzers die Zellengruppe an die Diakonia des Klosters zurückfällt, findet sich nur in den vier Urkunden über den Verkauf der in der *neuen Werkstatt* gelegenen Zellengruppe, nicht für die Zellengruppe in der *großen Bäckerei*. Ob diese, in 6201 fehlende Aussage nur als Auslassungsfehler des Schreibers anzusehen ist oder ob sie für diese Zellengruppe keine Gültigkeit hatte, wissen wir nicht.

Der Verkauf gilt also nur bis zum Tod des Käufers. Danach fällt die Zellengruppe an die Diakonia des Klosters zurück, und die Diakonia des Klosters kann sie wieder verkaufen und kommt durch den Wiederverkauf der Zellengruppe erneut zu Geld. Somit ist durch ein generelles Abkommen unter den Mönchen eine Lösung gefunden worden, daß für den Kaufpreis ein lebenslanges Besitzrecht an einer Zellengruppe erworben wird, das auch das Recht des Umbaus, der Zerstörung und des Weiterverkaufs[41] der Zellengruppe einschließt. Vom Recht des Weiterverkaufs wird im Apollon-Klosters, wie die vier Urkunden 6203, 6204, 6206 und 6202 zeigen, die den Verkauf der Zellengruppe in der *neuen Werkstatt* betreffen, reger Gebrauch gemacht: bereits nach knapp 10, 7 bzw. 2 Jahren wird die Zellengruppe von den Besitzern an andere Mönche weiterverkauft, wie wir sahen.

In den vier Urkunden, in denen der Verkauf der Zellengruppe in der *neuen Werkstatt* beurkundet ist, wird noch mehrfach ausgesagt, daß auch Nachbargrundstücke, vor allem Höfe im Norden[42] verkauft wurden. Diese Verkaufsurkunden sind uns aber nicht erhalten. Das spricht dafür, daß die uns bisher bekannten Verkaufsurkunden nur einen kleinen Teil der abgeschlossenen Verkaufsverträge bilden.

In 6201 liegt dieselbe Ausgangssituation eines Verkaufes vor wie beim erstmaligen Verkauf einer Zellengruppe vor, wo eine im Besitze der Diakonia des Klosters befindliche Zellengruppe vom Klosterabt und den im Amte befindlichen Ökonomen, den Verwaltern, an Mönche verkauft wird. Diese Situation wiederholt sich dann immer wieder, wenn der Besitzer einer Zellengruppe stirbt und seine Zellengruppe an die Diakonia des Klosters zurückfällt. Nach diesem erstmaligen Verkauf einer im Besitze der Diakonia befindlichen Zellengruppe an einen Käufer kann der Käufer sie an andere Käufer weiterverkaufen, wie wir das bei der in der "neuen Werkstatt" gelegenen Zellengruppe in den Urkunden gesehen haben.

Erstaunlich an den Urkunden 6206 und 6201 ist, daß die Käufer als ⲀⲠⲞⲦⲀⲔⲦⲒⲔⲞⲤ ⲘⲘⲞⲚⲀⲬⲞⲤ "apotaktische Mönche" bezeichnet werden. In den 5 Urkunden begegnen uns folgende Bezeichnungen für "Mönche" ein koptischer ⲠⲀⲤⲞⲚ, wörtlich "mein Bruder = Mönch" und zwei griechische: μονόζοντ(ος) und μοναχός. Während ⲠⲀⲤⲞⲚ die gängige Bezeichnung für den Mönch ist,[43] begegnet

---

[39] 6204, 24 u. 6206, 15 f. beschränken den "ewigen" Zeitraum durch den Zusatz: "alle Tage eures Lebens."

[40] 6203, 29.

[41] So 6206, 29 f. die ausführlichste Beschreibung: "Wenn ihr bauen wollt, seid ihr dazu berechtigt, wenn ihr einreissen wollt, seid ihr dazu berechtigt, wenn ihr sie (d.h. die Zellengruppe) behalten wollt, wenn ihr sie verkaufen wollt, seid ihr dazu berechtigt." Während die beiden jüngsten Urkunden (6202, 57 u. 6201, 48 f.) eine Kurzfassung bieten, fehlt das Baurecht in den beiden ältesten Urkunden (6203 u. 6204).

[42] 6203, 31 f.; 6204, 25-27.

[43] vgl. die Belege von ⲠⲀⲤⲞⲚ im Index der Textedition.

μονόζοντ(ος) nur einmal in 6204,71. Dort bezeichnet sich der Zeuge Schenute als "geringster Priester (und) Mönch" ϢЄΝΟΥΤЄ ΠЄΙЄΛΑΧ/ ΝΠΡ ΜΟΝΟΖΟΝΤ.

Der Terminus μοναχός begegnet dagegen mehrfach. Er wird verwendet in der βεβαίωσις-Klausel, in der alle Personen und Ämter genannt werden, die als mögliche Anfechter des Vertrages aufgezählt werden. Genannt werden in 6203, 56 ff.: "seien wir es, die wir jetzt Archimandrit und Verwalter sind, seien es die, die nach uns kommen werden, sei es ein Priester, sei es ein Diakon, sei es ein Vorleser, sei es ein Vorsteher, sei es ein Mönch (μοναχός), sei es ein Laie..." Außerdem werden in zwei Urkunden, in 6206,9 und 6201,19, die Käufer der jeweiligen Zellengruppe sowohl als ΠΑϹΟΝ als auch als ΑΠΟΤΑΚΤΙΚΟϹ ΜΜΟΝΑΧ/ angeschrieben mit dem Zusatz, "die mit uns in demselben Kloster sind," also Mitmönche des Apollon-Klosters sind. Wie ist dieser Terminus ΑΠΟΤΑΚΤΙΚΟϹ, den ich nicht übersetzt habe, zu verstehen? Er gehört ursprünglich in das pachomianische Mönchtum.[44] Pachom forderte von den Novizen die Apotaxis, den Verzicht auf die Welt. Ausgangspunkt des Terminus dürfte ein Jesuswort in Lukas 14,33 sein, wo er von jedem, der sein Jünger werden will, fordert, auf allen Besitz zu verzichten. Die Apotaxis bezieht sich im frühen Mönchtum auf die Welt und das, was zu ihr gehört, also auch auf Besitztümer und Geld. Der hier in den Urkunden verwendete Terminus ΑΠΟΤΑΚΤΙΚΟϹ ΜΜΟΝΑΧΟϹ kann nicht mehr dieselbe Bedeutung wie am Anfang des Mönchtums haben. Wenn die apotaktischen Mönche—wie hier bezeugt—noch über Geld verfügen, um Klosterteile zu kaufen, dann kann hier nur ein eingeschränkter Verzicht auf die Welt, ohne Verzicht auf Geld, vorliegen, was für das Mönchtum der späteren Zeit charakteristisch ist. Möglich wäre auch, daß der griechische Terminus im 9. Jh. von den Mönchen nicht mehr verstanden wurde.[45] Ein Mönchtum ohne Geldbesitz ist nicht mehr möglich seitdem Mönche und Klöster an die arabische Obrigkeit Steuern bezahlen müssen. Die apotaktischen Mönche Susinnius, Phoibammon und Staurus begegnen aber nicht nur als Käufer der kleineren Zellengruppe in 6201, sondern werden auch als Käufer der größeren Zellengruppe 6206 genannt. Auch apotaktische Mönche im Apollo-Kloster können also mit Geld nicht nur eine, sondern sogar mehrere Zellengruppen kaufen, die ihnen bis zu ihrem Tod gehören, und bei ihrem Tod an die Diakonia des Klosters zurückfallen, falls sie die Zellengruppen nicht vorher weiterverkaufen. Der Verlauf des Kaufes wird zwar beschrieben und auch der Verwendungszweck des beim Verkauf gezahlten Geldes, aber nicht das Motiv für den Kauf genannt. Warum werden Zellengruppen gekauft, aber schon nach einigen Jahren weiterverkauft, wenn der Käufer sie bis zu seinem Tod besitzen kann?

Hierfür gibt es vorläufig nur Vermutungen: Die Verkäufe finden statt, weil die Verkaufenden Geld benötigen, entweder für sich selbst oder für das Kloster oder für beide. Sie bleiben aber im Kloster wohnen, d. h. sie müssen neben der Zellengruppe, die sie verkaufen, zumindest noch eine weitere besitzen, in der sie gewohnt haben und in der sie weiter wohnen bleiben. Das legt die Vermutung nahe, daß die gekaufte und wieder verkaufte Zellengruppe eine Form von Geldanlage für die Mönche darstellt. Man kauft eine oder mehrere Zellengruppen um sein Geld anzulegen, das im pachomianischen Mönchtum beim Eintritt ins Kloster an das Kloster abgegeben werden mußte. Jetzt erhält man für das Geld Klosterzellen, die man an andere Mönche weiterverkaufen kann, wenn man Geld benötigt wie mehrere Urkunden aussagen, z.B. Geld für Steuern.

---

[44] vgl. Krause 1985: 122 ff.

[45] Man vergleiche die in den 5 Urkunden belegten griechischen Lehnwörter, die oft falsch geschrieben wurden, z.B. in 6203,49 die Schreibung ΤΙΥΓЄΝΗϹ für das griechische διοίκησις.

P. E. Kahle hat in den Urkunden von Balaizah[46] bemerkt, daß ein offensichtlich wohlhabender Mönch des Apollo-Klosters von Balaizah, der seinem Kloster zur Bezahlung seiner Steuern Geld geliehen hatte, in späteren Urkunden als Klosterabt begegnet. Kahle schloß daraus, daß diese finanzielle Hilfe dazu beigetragen haben könnte, daß der Mönch als Entgelt der Steuerzahlung für das Kloster Klosterabt geworden ist. Ein ähnlicher Fall könnte auch für das Apollo-Kloster in den drei Urkunden 6206, 6202 und 6201 vorliegen. In der Urkunde 6206 kauft Schenute mit Severus, Paulus und Timotheus—alle werden als apotaktische Mönche bezeichnet—im Jahre 847 die Zellengruppe in der *neuen Werkstatt* und in 6202 verkauft Schenute im Jahre 849—nunmehr als Archimandrit und Priester—zusammen mit seinen Brüdern Paulus und Severus, lediglich Timotheus wird nicht mehr genannt, diese Zellengruppe wieder, als die Käufer ihn darum bitten. Schenute müßte also zwischen 847 und 849 Klosterabt geworden sein, da er 847 beim Kauf der Zellengruppe in der neuen Werkstatt nur als apotaktischer Mönch bezeichnet worden war, und er drei Jahre später als Klosterabt nicht nur diese Zellengruppe in der *neuen Werkstatt* wieder verkaufte, sondern auch die kleinere Zellengruppe in der *großen Bäckerei*, die sich im Besitz der Diakonia des Klosters befand. Den Verkaufserlös verwandte er nach Aussage der Urkunde 6201 für die Verwaltung der Diakonia des Klosters. Entspricht diese Beobachtung den Realitäten, dann hätten wir für die Urkunde 6206 das Motiv für den Ankauf der Zellengruppe: den Wunsch Klosterabt zu werden, was durch die Urkunden 6202 und 6201 verwirklicht zu sein scheint, aber nicht sicher ist, zumal die in den Urkunden von Bala'izah genannten Geldbeträge höher als in Bawit sind.

Einen Schritt weiter geht eine Urkunde aus dem Apa-Mena-Kloster bei Sbeht,[47] die etwa in dieselbe Zeit gehört. Hier kauft sogar ein Laie unter Auflagen für seine und der Mönche Pflichten und durch Bezahlung von 53 Solidi das Amt des Klosterabtes. Der Endpunkt ist dann erreicht, wenn nur noch Vermögende ins Kloster aufgenommen werden, die sowohl ihre eigenen Steuern als auch die des Klosters bezahlen können.

Die 5 Urkunden vermitteln uns überdies für den Zeitraum von knapp 17 Jahren Einblicke in Teile des Apollo-Klosters in abbasidischer Zeit. Wir lernen Gebäude des Klosters und ihre Umgebung mit ihren Anrainern kennen, erfahren vom Wechsel ihrer Besitzer, Bewohner und ihrer Nachbarn. Die in den Urkunden genannten Personen, die uns als Verkäufer, Käufer, Nachbarn und Zeugen in den datierten Urkunden begegnen, nennen uns ihre Ämter und Berufe. Ihre Namen zeigen uns, wie verbreitet noch lateinische und griechisch- christliche Namen neben ägyptischen oder ägyptisierenden Namensformen waren. Die in den Urkunden genannten Ämter lassen den mönchischen und klerikalen Aufbau der Hierarchie im Kloster erkennen. Selbst die ungefähre Dauer ihrer Funktionen läßt sich zum Teil aus ihrem mehrfachen Auftreten in den datierten Urkunden ablesen. Das Bildungsniveau der Zeugen ist an der Verwendung der griechischen und koptischen Sprache, auch an der Rechtschreibung der Wörter und dem Stil ihrer Schrift ablesbar.[48]

Für das Mönchtum dieser Zeit ist vor allem wichtig, daß offensichtlich durch die Steuerzahlungen an den islamischen Staat und die dadurch verursachte Finanznot des Klosters und der Mönche die ursprüngliche Klosterverfassung, nach der sich die Klosterzellen im Besitz der Diakonia des Klosters

---

[46] *P.Bal.* 149 u. 290, vgl. dazu Kahle 1954: I, 30 u. 41.
[47] BP 11937, vgl. dazu Krause 1985: 125 und Krause 1990: 123-127 (mit Lit.).
[48] Näheres demnächst in der in A. 1 genannten Arbeit.

befanden, geändert wurde und nun im Apollo-Kloster Zellengruppen gekauft und verkauft werden konnten, die aber beim Tod des jeweiligen Besitzers an die Diakonia des Klosters zurückfielen und neu verkauft werden konnten, um dem Kloster neue Einkünfte zu verschaffen und somit die weitere Existenz des Klosters zu sichern. Möglich—aber nicht sicher—ist die Annahme, daß mit dem Kauf mehrerer Zellengruppen auch Klosterämter, vielleicht sogar das Amt des Klosterabtes, erworben werden konnte.

Von der Publikation des Nachlasses von Sarah J. Clackson, vor allem der von ihr zu Bawit gesammelten koptischen und griechischen Papyri, und der Auffindung und Publikation neuer Urkunden aus den neuen Ausgrabungen in Bawit erhoffen wir uns weitere Auskünfte über das Mönchtum in Bawit. Auch die Veröffentlichungen der arabischen zeitgenössischen Quellen und Papyri und die Zusammenarbeit mit den Vertretern der arabischen Papyrologie können hilfreich bei der Lösung der angesprochenen Probleme sein.

BIBLIOGRAPHIE

Boud'hors, A. (1995). "Papyrus de Clédat au Musée du Louvre," in: Fluck, C. et al. (eds.), *Divitiae Aegypti. Koptologische und verwandte Studien zu Ehren von Martin Krause*. Wiesbaden: L. Reichert, 29-35.

Boud'hors, A. (1999). Siehe Clédat (1999): 245-346.

Boud'hors, A (2004). *Ostraca grecs et coptes des fouilles de Jean Maspero à Baouit. O.BawitIFAO 1-67 et O.Nancy*. Le Caire: Insitut français d'archéologie orientale (*BEC* 17).

Clackson, S. J. (2001). "Reconstructing the Archives of the Monastery of Apollo at Bawit," in: Andorlini, I. et al. (eds.), *Atti del XXII congresso internazionale di papirologia 1998*. Istituto papirologico "G. Vitelli," Firenze, I, 219-236.

Clackson, S. J. (2004). "Museum Archaeology and Coptic Papyrology: the Bawit Papyri," in: Immerzeel, M. und Vliet, J. van der (eds.), *Coptic Studies on the Threshold of a New Millennium. Proceedings of the Seventh International Congress of Coptic Studies*, Leiden 2000, I,. Leuven/Paris/Dudley MA: Peeters (*OLA* 133), 477-489.

Clédat, J. (1999). *Le monastère et la nécropole de Baouit*. D. Bénazeth et Rutschowscaya, M.-H. (eds.) avec des contributions de A. Boud'hors, R.-G. Coquin, E. Gaillard. Le Caire (*MIFAO* 111).

Coquin, R.-G (1977). "Apollon de Titkooh ou/et Apollon de Baouît ?," *Orientalia*, N.S. 46, 435-446.

Crum, W. E. (1939). *A Coptic Dictionary*. Oxford: Clarendon Press.

Grossmann, P. (1993). "Ruinen des Klosters Dair al-Balaiza in Oberägypten," *JAC* 36, 171-205. Münster: Aschendorff.

Hengstenberg, W. (1934). "Bemerkungen zur Entwicklungsgeschichte des ägyptischen Mönchtums," in: *Actes du congrès international des études byzantines*. Sofia (*BIAB* 9), 355-362.

Krause, M. (1985). "Zur Möglichkeit von Besitz im apotaktischen Mönchtum Ägypten," in: Orlandi, T. und Wisse, F. (eds.), *Acts of the Second International Congress of Coptic Studies*. Roma: C. I. M., 120-133.

Krause, M. (1990). "Carl Schmidts Beiträge zum ägyptischen Mönchtum auf Grund koptischer Urkunden," in: Nagel, P. (ed.), *Carl-Schmidt-Colloquium an der Martin-Luther-Universität 1988*. Halle (Saale) (*Wissenschaftliche Beiträge* 1990/23), 119-127.

Krause, M.(2003). "Zu den nach Apollo benannten Klöstern in Ägypten," in: Beltz, W. et al. (eds.), *Sprache und Geist. Peter Nagel zum 65. Geburtstag*. Halle (Saale) (*Hallesche Beiträge zur Orientwissenschaft* 35), 149-166.

MacCoull, L. S. B. (1994). "The Bawit Contracts: Texts and Translations," *BASP* 31, 141-158.

Timm, St. (1986). *Das christlich-koptische Ägypten in arabischer Zeit*, Teil 3 (G-L). Wiesbaden: L. Reichert (*Beihefte zum Tübinger Atlas des Vorderen Orients*, Reihe B Nr. 41,3).

THE MONASTIC RULES OF SHENOUTE

BENTLEY LAYTON

One kind of scholarship that especially delighted Sarah Clackson was the publication of new data: either stuff that nobody had ever seen before, or collections of things whose significance was unknown until Sarah collected and explained them. Remembering this wonderful facet of Sarah's scholarship, I would like to describe an extremely interesting new set of data, namely, my collection of nearly five hundred very early monastic commands that I have found in the surviving portions of the *Canons* of Shenoute. My work on this corpus has only just begun, and this is an early progress report. This particular topic will take us, of course, into the earliest history of Christian organized monasticism. The earliest coenobitic monasteries were in Egypt, where the founders and leaders spoke and wrote the Coptic language. Among these, the best documented figure is Shenoute (C.E. ca. 347-465). Shenoute's writings, especially his work called *Canons,* provide a sensationally detailed picture of Christian life in the third generation of monasticism. Shenoute was not the founder of his monastic federation: he was its third leader.[1]

Shenoute wrote the *Canons* over a stretch of eighty years—from C.E. ca. 385-465 (more or less)[2]— while he was the leader of a federation of three religious congregations: two monasteries and a nunnery, together with a cluster of hermits in the adjacent desert. This was in the Nile valley, opposite Achmim. Led by Prof. Emmel, we are in the process of making a first complete edition of the surviving parts of this work.[3] Despite its title, Shenoute's *Canons* is not simply a set of monastic rules. Most of the *Canons* contains not rules but general moralistic diatribe and self-presentation. In the course of this diatribe, Shenoute often cites one or more short, carefully formulated rules of behaviour that specifically apply to the members of his ascetic federation. But my interest here is in the rules themselves, not the literary matrix where they lie embedded. I want to raise two questions: what are they like? And what is the basis of their authority?

The genre of Christian monastic rules had been invented somewhat earlier by Pachomius the Great (C.E. 292-346)—and indeed, not far from Shenoute's neighbourhood. A written corpus of monastic rules circulated up and down the Pachomian federation. As an organization, Shenoute's monastic federation more or less followed the Pachomian model, though it was administratively independent.

My initial working corpus consists of 476 short passages in Shenoute's *Canons* that seem to *be*, or to *cite*, or to *reflect*, a monastic rule. If all of the *Canons* had survived,[4] my corpus would be much, much larger. In order to assemble the initial working corpus of commands, I have cast the net fairly wide. Of course I omitted general moral commands having no reference to monastic life. On the other hand, I did include a variety of rhetorical and grammatical forms, some of them parallel to Pachomius, and others very different. I would now like to describe the two main formal types in my corpus.

---

[1] As demonstrated by Stephen Emmel (Emmel 2004: 9-10).

[2] Emmel apud Layton 2002: 30 note 25.

[3] The edition was organized, under Emmel's leadership, at Yale University in March 2000, through the generous initiative of the Beinecke Rare Book and Manuscript Library and Dr. Robert Babcock.

[4] Although some 1,300 pages of the *Canons* survive, this is only a part of the complete work.

I will start with Shenoutean commands that have the same form as those of Pachomius. What was the Pachomian form? The actual rules of St. Pachomius in Coptic are now incomplete: less than a hundred clauses are published in Lefort's edition.[5] But all are formulated in similar ways, so we can get a good idea of the style. They are simply a list of rules, with no filler. The Pachomian rules are both affirmative and negative. Affirmatives are usually expressed by ϥⲛⲁ- (sometimes ⲉϥⲉ-); negatives, always by ⲛⲛⲉϥ-. In traditional terminology, second or third future affirmative, and third future negative.

Now for some typical examples from Pachomius. Affirmative: (*Pr.* 110) ⲉⲕⲧⲁⲗⲏⲩ ⲇⲉ ⲉⲩⲉⲓⲱ ⲉⲕϣⲁⲛⲡⲱϩ ⲉⲧⲥⲟⲟⲩϩⲥ ⲭⲱⲣⲓⲥⲁⲛⲁⲅⲕⲏ ⲉⲕⲛⲁϭⲱϭⲉ ⲉⲃⲟⲗ ⲉⲕⲥⲱⲕ ϩⲏⲧϥ "When you are riding an ass, when you get to the assembly *you shall*, except in case of emergency (ⲁⲛⲁⲅⲕⲏ), *dismount*, leading it." And negative: (*Pr.* 91) ⲛⲛⲉⲣⲱⲙⲉ ⲙⲟⲟϣⲉ ϩⲛⲧⲥⲟⲟⲩϩⲥ ⲛⲟⲩⲉϣⲛⲣⲁϩⲧⲟⲩ ϩⲓⲧⲟⲗⲟⲙⲱⲛ "*A person shall not go about* in the assembly without goatskin and hood."[6]

Let us now compare the Pachomian form with the somewhat later Shenoutean commands. Out of my corpus of more than 475 Shenoutean commands, about forty per cent are the Pachomian type. Here are some typical Shenoutean examples.

"At meal time, at any time, *they shall pray* without kneeling in that place." ⲡⲛⲁⲩ ⲛⲟⲩⲱⲙ ⲛⲟⲩⲟⲉⲓϣ ⲛⲓⲙ ⲉⲩⲛⲁϣⲗⲏⲗ ⲛⲟⲩⲉϣⲛⲕⲁϫⲡⲁⲧ ⲙⲡⲙⲁ ⲉⲧⲙⲙⲁⲩ.[7]

"*Those who live* in these congregations at any time *shall eat* with one another." ⲉⲣⲉⲛⲉⲧⲟⲩⲏϩ ϩⲛⲛⲉⲓⲥⲩⲛⲁⲅⲱⲅⲏ ⲛⲟⲩⲟⲉⲓϣ ⲛⲓⲙ ⲛⲁⲟⲩⲟⲙⲟⲩ ⲙⲛⲛⲉⲩⲉⲣⲏⲩ.[8]

"At all times in these abodes *there shall be some person*, and whoever he has selected to help him, who gathers the fruit of the orchard and what falls from the date palms." ⲛⲟⲩⲟⲉⲓϣ ⲛⲓⲙ ϩⲣⲁⲓ ϩⲛⲛⲉⲓⲧⲟⲡⲟⲥ ⲉⲣⲉⲟⲩⲣⲱⲙⲉ ⲛⲁϣⲱⲡⲉ ⲁⲩⲱ ⲡⲉⲧϥⲛⲁϫⲓⲧϥ ⲉⲣⲟϥ ⲉⲧⲣⲉϥⲕⲱⲧϥ ⲛⲛⲕⲁⲣⲡⲟⲥ ⲛⲛϣⲏⲛ ⲁⲩⲱ ⲛⲉⲧϩⲉ ⲉϩⲣⲁⲓ ϩⲓⲛⲃⲛⲛⲉ.[9]

And next, examples of the negative command in Shenoute, always expressed by ⲛⲛⲉϥ-.[10]

"*No person shall be timid* as he preaches from the pulpit (? *literally*, meditates upon the column). And *no person shall draw it out* beyond the limit as he preaches from the pulpit." ⲛⲛⲉⲣⲱ[ⲙⲉ ⲣ]ϩⲏⲧ ϣⲏⲙ ⲉ[ϥⲙ]ⲉⲗⲉⲧⲁ ϩⲓⲡⲉⲥⲧⲩⲗⲗⲟⲥ. ⲟⲩⲇⲉ ⲛⲛⲉⲣⲱⲙⲉ ⲱⲥⲕ ⲡⲁⲣⲁⲡϣⲓ ⲉϥⲙⲉⲗⲉⲧⲁ ϩⲓⲡⲉⲥⲧⲩⲗⲗⲟⲥ.[11]

---

[5] Lefort 1956: 30-35. Jerome's Latin version preserves a more extensive text.

[6] Very rarely, Pachomius combines ⲛⲛⲉϥ- with ⲉϣ- "be able to" in the sense of "be permitted to": (*Pr.* 118) ⲟⲩⲧⲉ ⲛⲛⲉⲩⲉϣⲧⲁⲗⲉⲕⲟⲥⲙⲓⲕⲟⲛ ⲛⲙⲙⲁⲩ ⲉⲛⲕⲟⲧⲕ ϩⲓⲡϫⲟⲓ "And they shall not be empowered to bring a secular person to sleep together with them in the boat."

[7] *Canons*, book 9, YX57-58 = Amélineau 1895: 282. For references to the *Canons*, I give book number, codex siglum and ancient pagination (thus "YX57-58"), and edition or else a manuscript reference. I use the standard codex sigla following Emmel 2004.

[8] *Canons*, book 9, FM92 = Leipoldt 1913: 87.

[9] *Canons*, book 9, DF 176-77 = Leipoldt 1913: 97-98.

[10] Like the Pachomian rules, Shenoute's commands include a few examples of negative ⲛⲛⲉϥ- combined with ⲉϣ- "not be empowered to." Both the Pachomian rules and this group of Shenoutean commands also use affirmative ⲉϥⲉ- to express commands, though less frequently than ⲉϥⲛⲁ-.

[11] *Canons*, book 5, XL fragment 3 recto = Vienna Nationalbibliothek ms. K9593 recto.

"If a little bit (of food) is left over to the next day, *none* from it *shall be taken* to the gate house." ⲉⲣϣⲁⲛⲟⲩⲕⲟⲩⲓ ⲇⲉ ⲥⲉⲉⲡⲉ ⲉⲡϥⲣⲁⲥⲧⲉ ⲛⲛⲉⲩϫⲓ ⲉⲡⲙⲁ ⲙⲡⲣⲟ ⲛ2ⲏⲧϥ.[12]

"*No outside priest and deacon shall enter* the congregation of the men's division to bury a woman who has died excepting only the priests of the village at the women's division and the deacons and a reader that they may bring with them to read." ⲛⲛⲉⲗⲁⲁⲩ ⲙⲡⲣⲉⲥⲃⲩⲧⲉⲣⲟⲥ ⲛϣⲙⲙⲟ ⲏ ⲇⲓⲁⲕⲟⲛⲟⲥ ⲉⲓ ⲉ2ⲟⲩⲛ ⲉⲧⲥⲩⲛⲁⲅⲱⲅⲏ 2ⲁ2ⲧⲏⲛ ⲉⲕⲱⲥ ⲛⲧⲛⲧⲁⲥⲙⲟⲩ ⲉⲓⲙⲏⲧⲓ ⲙⲡⲣⲉⲥⲃⲩⲧⲉⲣⲟⲥ ⲙⲙⲁⲧⲉ ⲙⲡ†ⲙⲉ 2ⲁ2ⲧⲏⲧⲛ ⲙⲛⲛⲇⲓⲁⲕⲟⲛⲟⲥ ⲏ ⲟⲩⲁⲛⲁⲅⲛⲱⲥⲧⲏⲥ ⲉⲁⲩⲛⲧϥ ⲛⲙⲙⲁⲩ ϫⲉⲉϥⲉⲱϣ.[13]

Apart from formal conditionals, there are a great many casuistic elements in the Shenoutean commands: *at any given time, anyone in this congregation, anyone in this congregation whether male or female, except with permission of such-and-such an officer, except in case of emergency or of sickness*, etc. These only reinforce the impression that we have to do with actual administrative rules that were to be applied in daily practice. A special problem for Shenoute was the fact that his commands addressed both monks and nuns.[14]

How closely were these Shenoutean commands modeled on those of Pachomius? Are there significant similarities, or noteworthy contradictions, in their content or attitude?

I will point out that Shenoute knows about Pachomius—and how could he not?—and mentions him by name in the *Canons*; he also knows about the tradition that Pachomius received his rules from the hand of an angel.[15] Yet Shenoute seems unwilling to claim the authority of Pachomius for any of his own commands. For example, he once refers to what we can recognize as one of the surviving Pachomian rules,[16] but vaguely attributes it to "those who have said."[17] Nonetheless, Shenoute several times calls his monastic federation a Koinonia,[18] favourite jargon of the Pachomians. Furthermore, the two surviving manuscript fragments of Pachomius' own Coptic rules both belonged to the library of Shenoute's monastery (according to Orlandi[19]) and date from the early middle ages. Thus Shenoute may have owned and studied a (now lost) complete copy of Pachomius' rules, which was the archetype of our existing Pachomian manuscripts. A detailed comparison of Shenoute's rules with those of Pachomius and his later imitators is an important part of my continuing research. At the same time I am studying the rules to reconstruct the structure and daily operations of the monastic federation.

I turn now to a second important form of Shenoutean commands, one that has no parallel in early monastic rules. These are in the form of curses. Eighty-five surviving Shenoutean commands are curses. Half of them begin with a curse expressed as ϥⲥ2ⲟⲩⲟⲣⲧ ⲛϭⲓ-: "cursed be any who does so-

---

[12] *Canons*, book 5, XS320 = Leipoldt 1913: 54.

[13] *Canons*, book 5, XS356 = Leipoldt 1913: 62.

[14] Studied in Krawiec 2002.

[15] *Canons*, book 4, BZ10 = Leipoldt 1908: 120.

[16] Pachomius, *Pr.* 95, "You shall leave a cubit between yourself and him (your fellow monk) whether sitting, standing, or walking;" text in Lefort 1956: 31.

[17] *Canons*, book 9, DF145-46 = Leipoldt 1913: 95, speaking of "those [i.e. Pachomius] who have said, You shall leave a cubit between yourselves and them."

[18] *Canons*, book 1, YW78 = Paris Bibliotheque nationale de France ms. copte 1302 f. 78 verso; book 3, YA313 = Leipoldt 1913: 122; book 9, FM96 = Leipoldt 1913: 89, and BV283 = Leipoldt 1913: 172.

[19] Orlandi 2004, Clavis patrum copticorum, s.n. Pacomio. The manuscript sigla are MONB.BC and MONB.BF.

and-so." Another third have the curse at the end, almost always expressed as ⲉϥⲉϣⲱⲡⲉ ⲉϥⲥϩⲟⲩⲣⲧ: "anyone who does so-and-so shall be under a curse."

Now for examples of the Shenoutean curse prohibition:

"*Cursed be* any boy who removes a thorn from the foot of a boy without being commanded and in a place alone." ϥⲥϩⲟⲩⲟⲣⲧ ⲛϭⲓⲟⲩϣⲏⲣⲉ ϣⲏⲙ ⲉϥⲛⲁⲛⲟⲩⲥⲟⲩⲣⲉ ⲉⲃⲟⲗ ϩⲛⲣⲁⲧϥ ⲛⲟⲩϣⲏⲣⲉ ϣⲏⲙ ⲉϫⲛ(i.e. ⲁϫⲛ)ⲧⲣⲉⲩⲧⲟϣϥ ⲏ ⲛⲥⲁⲟⲩⲥⲁ ⲙⲁⲩⲁⲁϥ.[20]

Or:

"Any who stare with desirous feeling at their own nakedness *shall be under a curse*." ⲛⲉⲧⲛⲁϭⲱϣⲧ ⲇⲉ ⲟⲛ ϩⲛⲟⲩⲡⲁⲑⲟⲥ ⲛⲉⲡⲓⲑⲩⲙⲓⲁ ⲉϩⲣⲁⲓ ⲉϫⲙⲡⲉⲩϭⲱⲗⲡ ⲉⲃⲟⲗ ⲙⲙⲓⲛⲙⲙⲟⲟⲩ ⲉⲩⲉϣⲱⲡⲉ ⲉⲩⲥϩⲟⲩⲟⲣⲧ.[21]

There are so many commands formulated in this way, that they really cry out for explanation. The Shenoutean curses are not generally paired with blessings, as we sometimes find in early Christian rhetoric; so they are not exactly a known rhetorical form for issuing injunctions. I have found one Biblical parallel, in the legislation of Deuteronomy chapter 27, which describes Israel's reaffirmation of the Ten Commandments by acclamation. Here a series of curses are formulated ϥⲥϩⲟⲩⲟⲣⲧ ⲛϭⲓⲡⲉⲧⲛⲁ ... with a constant refrain, ⲁⲩⲱ ⲉⲣⲉⲡⲗⲁⲟⲥ ⲧⲏⲣϥ ϫⲟⲟⲥ ϫⲉⲉϥⲉϣⲱⲡⲉ. "Cursed be any who does so-and-so, and all the people shall say, So be it."[22]

Of course, Shenoute's curse formula might be nothing more than a personal tool of rhetoric. However, the problem is made more complicated by Emmel's discovery that there are no less than three manuscripts of Shenoute's *Canons* in which the curse rules were numbered sequentially in the margins. All three manuscripts are fragmentary. The surviving curse numbers in Codex GI range from 6 to 11 (and presumably beyond),[23] the surviving ones in Codex YA run from 56 to 204 (with many lacunas),[24] and the sole surviving number in Codex YD is 5.[25] Each manuscript is copied by a different copyist. Since the three surviving numberings do not overlap, they may well attest to a single sequence of numbers. It is a curious fact that the numbering series from 6 to 11 occurs in *Canons* book 4, while the series 56 to 204 occurs in book 3.

Marginal curse no. 5	in book 2
Marginal curse nos. 6-11	in book 4
Marginal curse nos. 56-204	in book 3

If these three number sequences belong to the same numbering, this would seem to suggest that the sequence of curse numbers was completely independent of the volume numbering of Shenoute's *Canons*. However, precisely because the three sequences never overlap, one cannot prove that any two

---

[20] *Canons*, book 1, XC7-8 = Vienna Nationalbibliothek ms. K9101 recto and verso.

[21] *Canons*, book 3, YA258 = Paris Bibliotheque nationale de France ms. copte 1301 f. 37 verso.

[22] Deuteronomy 17:14-26; text in the photographic facsimile edition of Pierpont Morgan Library, Hyvernat 1922: ms. M566 f. 139 verso column b-140 recto column b.

[23] Emmel 2004: 162.

[24] Emmel 2004: 147-48.

[25] YD frag. 2 verso = Cairo Institut français d'archéologie orientale ms. copte inv. 2349A; Emmel *per litt.* 26.VIII.2004.

scribes had access to the same system of numbering. The three number sequences might also (as Wolf-Peter Funk has reminded me) be unrelated, free marginalia, each from a different numbering system.

Furthermore, the numbered curses can be interrupted by other types of material. In other words, when Shenoute utters commands in *other* forms, they do *not* have numbers, even when these interrupt a series of numbered curses. This, too, might suggest that the curse prohibitions had an independent existence.[26] These arguments are open to doubt; but if true, they might suggest that Shenoute used a separate rule book in the form of numbered curse prohibitions, which he occasionally quoted to add authority to what he was saying. Perhaps he—or his scribe[27]—even wrote the appropriate curse numbers in the margin of his text as a mark of authority.

Let us now consider the content of the numbered curse prohibitions, looking for clues about their particular social context or authorship. Table 1 is a list of the topics of all the numbered curses. This range of cursed monastic sins is similar to the overall range of punishable deeds in my entire corpus of Shenoutean commands, and thus in terms of its content it can be called typically Shenoutean. Furthermore, the organizational structure seems compatible with the structure of Shenoute's federation.[28]

TABLE 1: TOPICS OF THE NUMBERED CURSES

No.	Topic	No.	Topic
5	Metaphor: Wolves preying upon holy sheep (corruption of children)	128	Hermit priest celebrating Mass alone
6	Biblical history: Cain was "cursed"	129	Illicitly being ordained by irregular bishop
7	Sex	130	Hermit monk or nun who retains possessions
8	Sex	131	Seeking to undo one's renunciation of property
9	Refusal to inform on sinners	132	Secret business transaction
10	Insulting an administrator	133	Stealing to give to relatives
11	Gossip	134	Stealing to give to fellow monk or nun
56	Refusal to confess a sin	135	Illicit shaving by monk or nun
57	Pretending not to be a penitent	136	Illicit thorn removal
58	Sex	137	Sex
59	Sex	138	Sex (sleeping too close together)
60	Sex	139	Sex (sitting too close together)
116	Pampering one's body	192	Illicit use of pot for defecation
117	Coveting a beautiful garment	193	Slander
118	Favoritism to relatives	194	Slander
119	Stealing food	195	Lying
		204	Lying

---

[26] For the record, most manuscripts of the *Canons* did not contain marginal numbering, and this kind of evidence is no more than suggestive.

[27] "I am weeping as I speak these words: just as I did many a time before today, so also now, with God as my witness; and our little brother who is writing down these words is also a witness . . ." from *Canons,* book 2, XC226-27 = Kuhn 1956: 120.

[28] Described in Layton 2002: 28-29.

Who wrote these curse prohibitions? One of the numbered curses speaks in the voice of the head of the entire federation—that is, Shenoute or one of his predecessors: "[Number] 11. Cursed in all their works shall be any of us, whether males or females, who see any mortally sinful deed and speak of it to certain people, who speak to others, and they to many in the congregation, and the whole congregation becomes full of disturbance and meddlesomeness, and they have not even informed *me* so that *I* might know."[29]

On the other hand, a very different possibility is also suggested by the corpus, looking now at all types of commands. In twenty commands, Shenoute speaks of "us," thus including himself, as having *inherited* the commands from predecessors. He refers to the "canons" or "tradition" or "commands" or "commandments" or "laws" that a group called "our fathers" either "established" or "laid down" or "wrote" or "commanded to us," or "that we have"; or something similar.[30] These examples include both the Pachomian type and the curse prohibition, and are spread out over all the books of Shenoute's *Canons* where commands occur.[31] Already in book 1, the earliest book, we find a reference to annual rituals of scrutinizing monks.[32] Since Shenoute speaks of "the commands written for us"[33] and curses "in the book written for us,"[34] as well as speaking of "our written regulations,"[35] he at least creates the impression of a prior, written source of rules. Furthermore, once when enunciating a certain economic policy, he remarks, "This is obvious, and the rule about it is written for us elsewhere."[36]

What does Shenoute mean by "elsewhere"? Where could that book, or those written regulations, be? What are the "canons that were laid down for us"? Who was their author, or their authors? As a curiosity, I will call attention to one of Shenoute's commands, in which he, at the end of his career[37] speaks of the author of one of his policies in the singular number, as "our father." Four weeks per year—he says—the (weeks) that *our father* (in the singular) established for us, everyone in the

---

[29] *Canons*, book 4, GI117 = Leipoldt 1908: 156.

[30] Thus (all from *Canons*, book 3): "Let us not forget what is asked of us by the canons that our fathers established for us"; "they have caused great anger to the word of God, just as the tradition of our fathers commanded them not show favoritism "; "the commands that our fathers laid down for us"; "the commandments that our fathers commanded to us"; "not by God's will or the command of the laws of our fathers"; etc.

[31] No commands occur in the surviving text of *Canons*, book 7.

[32] "If they happen to read them (the aforementioned books) in the Houses, nothing stands in the way. And also if they happen to read from them, whenever they want to, on days when all are gathered in the assembly, scrutinizing their words and their deeds according to our canons, nothing stands in the way. However—on these four yearly occasions they shall all be read without fail, even if there is someone who hates to hear them because he hates his very soul": *Canons*, book 1, YW210 = Munier 1916: 117, as recollated by Stephen Emmel (per litt. IX.2004).

[33] *Canons*, book 9, FM187 = Leipoldt 1913: 161.

[34] "Cursed along with all their works in the book written for us," *Canons*, book 8, XO288 = Cairo Institut français d'archéologie orientale ms. copte 2.

[35] ⲛⲉⲧⲥⲏϩ ⲛⲁⲛ "Our written regulations," *Canons*, book 9, DF187 = Leipoldt 1913: 106; so also, "(Our physicians) shall consider what is bound to happen and what ought to be done, according to our written regulations" ⲕⲁⲧⲁⲛⲉⲧⲥⲏϩ ⲛⲁⲛ, book 9, FM186 = Leipoldt 1913: 161.

[36] ⲡϩⲱⲃ ⲟⲩⲟⲛϩ ⲉⲃⲟⲗ ⲁⲩⲱ ⲡⲉϥⲧⲱϣ ⲥⲏϩ ⲛⲁⲛ ϩⲛϩⲉⲛⲕⲉⲙⲁ, *Canons*, book 9, YX53 = Amélineau 1895: 278.

[37] In *Canons*, book 3, which is probably the latest book of the work. I follow Emmel's chronology apud Layton 2002: 30 note 23.

federation shall gather.[38] Now, he cites this command immediately after some talk about a person called "our father Apa Pshoi,"[39] perhaps implying that "our father" mentioned as the source of the policy means Apa Pshoi, an early monastic leader who seems to have headed, or even founded, the small men's monastery of Shenoute's federation, in the time of Shenoute's youth.[40]

In conclusion, Shenoute gives the impression of using, quoting, elaborating, and referring to external, earlier bodies of rules, curses, and regulations in various rhetorical forms, both Pachomian and non-Pachomian. He cites these authorities as he directs the temporal and spiritual life of his monks and nuns, and makes them his own.

---

[38] "Four weeks per year, the ones that our father established for us, also everyone who dwells in the desert in our territory shall assemble with the monastics and come together," *Canons,* book 3, YA310 = Leipoldt 1913: 120; see also in note 32 above.

39 "Any who contentiously celebrates mass anywhere within our territory ... except within our congregations where all the brethren assemble, and in the *topos* of our Father, where the church is, in the desert, shall be under a curse. Our territory is from the valley north of the village of Triphiou northwards to the edge of the valley south of the building (i.e. *topos*? Coptic ⲎⲒ) of our venerable father Apa Pshoi, where he originally lived in the desert," *Canons,* book 3, YA309 = Leipoldt 1913: 120. The crucial adverb "northwards" is erroneously omitted in my translation of this passage in Layton 2002: 27 note 9.

[40] Of course, this passage may merely refer to a noteworthy policy of Pshoi, not a written rule collection.

Bibliography

Amélineau, É. (ed.) (1895). *Monuments pour servir à l'histoire de l'égypte chrétienne aux ive, ve vie et viie siècles* (*MMAF* IV). Paris: Leroux.

Emmel, S. (2004). *Shenoute's Literary Corpus*. 2 vols. Louvain: Peeters.

Hyvernat, H. (ed.) (1922). *Bybliothecae Pierpont Morgan codices coptici photographice expressi*. Vol. 1. Rome.

Krawiec, R. (2002). *Shenoute and the Women of the White Monastery: Egyptian Monasticism in Late Antiquity*. New York: Oxford University Press.

Kuhn, K. H. (ed.) (1956). *Letters and Sermons of Besa*. Louvain: Imprimerie orientaliste.

Layton, B. (2002). "Social Structure and Food Consumption in an Early Christian Monastery: The Evidence of Shenoute's *Canons* and the White Monastery Federation A.D. 385-465," *Le Muséon* 115, 25-55.

Lefort, L. Th. (ed.) (1956). *Œuvres de s. Pachôme et de ses disciples*. Louvain: Imprimerie Orientaliste.

Leipoldt, J. (ed.) (1908). *Sinuthii archimandritae Vita et opera omnia*. Vol. 3. Paris: Imprimerie Nationale.

Leipoldt, J. (ed.) (1913). *Sinuthii archimandritae Vita et opera omnia*. Vol. 4. Paris: Imprimerie Nationale.

Munier, H. (1916). *Catalogue général des antiquités égyptiennes du Musée du Caire nos. 9201-9304, Manuscrits coptes*. Cairo: Imprimerie de l'Institut français d'archéologie orientale.

Orlandi, T. (2004). *Corpus dei manoscritti copti letterari*. Electronic media online by subscription (29.XII.2004) at http://rmcisadu.let.uniroma1.it/cmcl/ammini/entrata.html.

THE CHURCH, CLERICS, MONKS AND CREDIT IN THE PAPYRI

Tomasz Markiewicz

Among the documents concerning the Hermopolite monastery of Apa Apollo, texts relating to loans given (and, much less frequently, taken) by its monks form a substantial group. Such documents are also not infrequent in other monastic dossiers, e.g. among *P.Bal.* or *P.Mon.Epiph.* This led Sarah Clackson to the conclusion that "monasteries performed a public service by providing what appear to have been interest-free 'banking' facilities for laypeople."[1] I was struck by this statement and decided to take a closer look at monks' and clerics' involvement in lending and borrowing in the papyri.[2]

The fact that Egyptian clerics and monks disposed of considerable personal and institutional wealth and frequently conducted transactions involving credit is a well-known one, but has received relatively little attention up to now, the notable exception being the recent book of Georg Schmelz, in which some relevant sources are quoted.[3] In fact, these sources refer to two phenomena: the role of credit in the financial dealings of various Church institutions, represented by members of their clergy, and credit in private financial dealings of monks and clerics. The two cannot always be separated from each other, e.g. the extant evidence suggests that monasteries frequently borrowed money from (or lent to) their own monks. On the other hand, sometimes it is not entirely clear whether a clergyman appearing in a contract acted on his own behalf or that of a Church institution.[4]

The purpose of the present paper is therefore twofold: to analyze the role of credit in internal dealings of Church institutions and in private affairs of the clergy (and monks). The latter can tell us—potentially—a lot about the financial and economic standing of this social group. Roger Rémondon cited the evidence of loan contracts as proof for the Egyptian clergy's wealth, stating: "in nine cases out of ten clergymen would appear as creditors, not debtors."[5] Although I hope to be able to show that this proportion is far from true, the loan contracts can be revealing in this respect.

Finally, I shall try to answer the question whether the Church—through financial activities of its institutions and staff—was really an important source of credit for the lay population, providing the "banking" facilities, as Sarah Clackson put it. And if it did, whether it was indeed interest-free credit, in keeping with ecclesiastical views on usury.

---

[1] Clackson 2000: 26.

[2] The present study is not limited to papyri from Egypt, since one important piece of evidence comes from Palestine (*P.Ness.* III) and there are no reasons for leaving it out.

[3] Schmelz 2002: 195-197 (on credit in the economy of Church institutions) and 247-249 (on private transactions of monks and clerics).

[4] The ambiguity is in some cases due to the imperfect state of preservation, but one text gives us doubts about whether we can take even the well-preserved ones at face-value. *P.Lond.Copt.* 1031 has on the *recto* what appears to be a loan of wine and corn contracted by a *presbyteros* with a monastery (through its *pronoetes*). The priest seems to be acting in his own name. However, on the *verso* we find a receipt issued by the same *pronoetes* to a church in Hermopolis, stating that the debt of wine has been paid. If we are to believe Crum's description, the original loan was taken out in the name of a church, even though the text on the *recto* does not mention this fact. Unfortunately this interesting papyrus has not been properly published.

[5] Rémondon 1972: 259: "Les clers ont souvent une fortune personelle: neuf fois sur dix, ils apparaissent dans les textes comme créanciers et non débiteurs, propriétaires de terres ou de maisons et non locataires."

Before turning to documentary sources, I shall briefly discuss some normative and literary evidence for credit and usury in Late Antiquity. In the Greco-Roman world short-term loans of cash or in kind were always one of the preferred ways of making use of accumulated capital. In the classical Roman law period the maximum allowed rate of interest was not to exceed the traditional rate of 12 per cent per year (*hekatostiaios tokos, centesimae usurae*) for loans of money for everybody except senators who were prohibited from demanding more than 6 per cent (C.Th. 2.33.4). This rate was slightly increased as a result of Constantine the Great's currency reform, to 12.5% and 6.25% respectively. For loans in kind the traditional rate was 50% irrespective of the duration of the loan (*hemiolion*) (C.Th. 2.33.1).

Influenced perhaps by the Christian views on usury (which I discuss below), Justinian reduced these rates in C.E. 528 to 6% (6.25%) for lower classes and 4% (4.2%) for the *viri illustres* respectively (CI 4.32.26). However, people involved in trade and banking were allowed to charge 8% (8.33%), while for the naval loan the maximum was set at 12% (12.5%)—previously it had been unrestricted. In several novels of C.E. 535 Nov. 32, 34) the same emperor modified these rates, including special regulations for loans to poor farmers: 4% (4.2%) for loans in cash and 12% for loans in kind. Another special exception was established by Novel 120 of C.E. 544, which set a maximum of 3% for loans to churches and charitable foundations.[6]

These regulations remained in force in the Byzantine Empire into the 9th century, or at least we do not know of any attempts to alter them. We can safely assume that in Egypt this was the law on interest for the remainder of the Byzantine period and probably even longer. It can be noted here that in Middle Ages the attitude towards interest in Byzantium was more relaxed than in the Latin West: despite several attempts on the part of some emperors usury was never completely abolished.[7]

However, there is another factor which influenced credit and interest: Christian ideology. The Church Fathers condemned any interest received on loans, continuing the disapproval of usury found in several passages of the Old Testament (Ex. 22, 24; Lev. 25, 36; Psalm 15 (14), 5; Ezekiel 18, 8) and allowed only in transactions with foreigners (Deut. 23, 20-21). A considerable number of treatises and sermons on this subject survive: among those critical of interest we may mention Basil of Caesarea, Gregory of Nyssa and John Chrysostom in the East, and Ambrose, Jerome and Pope Leo the Great in the West. Their moral condemnation extended to any form of interest, including those in kind.

This thinking quickly found its way into Church legislation. As early as C.E. 305 the Council of Elvira in Spain (Can. 20) threatened to depose clerics employing usury; laymen who refused to give up usury were to be excluded from the Church. The Council of Arles in Gaul (C.E. 314) was only concerned with usury amongst clergy (usurious priests were to be excommunicated; Can. 12), as was

---

[6] Some scholars have expressed views that despite Justinian's efforts the usual interest rate remained in practice at 12%, cf. Preissner 1954: 61-62. To his list of documents with 12% interest after C.E. 528 we should probably add *P.Mich.* XIII 669 (D56). This text is dated to the 8th indiction and its editor, P. J. Sijpestijn, opted for C.E. 529 or 514 as the possible dates. J. Gascou (*CdÉ* 52 (1977), 365) held C.E. 514 for very improbable and argued in favor of C.E. 544. He did not comment on the fact that the interest charged here was 12.5%, which would have been theoretically illegal after C.E. 528 (CI 4.32.26). In my view there are two possibilities: either Gascou is right in dating the document to C.E. 544 (then we have here another example of the old interest rate being used despite Imperial legislation); or we should date *P.Mich.* XIII 669 to C.E. 12/13.09.529. The interest charged on this loan would have been already illegal, but it would probably take some time before this was realized in Aphrodito.

[7] Gofas 2002.

the Ecumenical Council of Nice (C.E. 325). Its Canon 17 was the most important prohibition of usury: clergymen violating this rule were liable to be deposed.

Similar bans were frequently repeated, e.g. in the Canons of the council of Laodicea (C.E. 325/381; Can. 4); the council of Hippona (C.E. 393; Can. 22); the third council of Carthage (C.E. 397; Can. 16); in the Apostolic Canons (Can. ap. VIII 47, 44) and in the Canons of Pseudo-Basilios (Can. Bas. 58). All these provisions concern ordained priests—laymen, including unordained monks, were subject to the regulations of the Civil law.[8]

Even if we had no documentary sources at our disposal, the frequency with which such prohibitions were issued alone attests that they were to some extent futile. Various Church institutions—churches, chapels, monasteries and charitable foundations—were also business enterprises, in so far as they had incomes and expenditures; sometimes they left them with surplus capital that could be (and was, as we shall see) lent at interest, sometimes they were forced to borrow money to meet their obligations.[9]

On the other hand we also find numerous monks and clerics involved in the process of moneylending on both sides, as private creditors or debtors. The Church did not provide for the daily needs of all its clerics (or monks for that matter), so that they had to earn their living exercising mundane professions—including sometimes moneylending.[10] Personal poverty and asceticism of clerics and monks was an ideal that was often advocated, but not a condition *sine qua non*, as in some Roman Catholic orders. Wealthy people entering the ranks of clergy or becoming a monk retained their personal property, even though a Novel of Justinian (Nov. 5, 5 of C.E. 535) required of people entering monasteries to dispose of their wealth (here again a need to prohibit is a proof of a practice to the contrary). Even a poor monk could accumulate some wealth through selling products of his handiwork, as one anecdote told by Jerome about the monks of Nitria attests. That is, a monk died at the Mount of Nitria, leaving a small hoard of money which he had earned by weaving flax. After some deliberation the monks decided to bury the coins with their owner, quoting Saint Peter, "Thy money perish with thee" (Acts 8, 20).[11] Such wealth could—and was, as numerous sources attest—be used as source of credit. But let us first look at the dealings of the Church institutions.

1. CHURCH INSTITUTIONS AS CREDITORS

The list of documents featuring Church institutions as creditors is not a very long one[12] (see Table A), but such texts are numerous enough to show that the Church could and did practice moneylending. To be exact, not all of these contracts record loans; debts could result from other transactions, e.g. in *P.Köln* III 153 (A1) a farmers acknowledges to a monastery his debt resulting from unpaid rent on monastic land that he had leased. Similarly, we can imagine that other agreements that we classify as "loans" had some other sort of transaction behind them; the documents seldom inform us about the

---

[8] On the Canonic legislation against usury, see Bianchi 1984a and 1984b.

[9] Schmelz 2002: 162-202, on moneylending esp. 195-197.

[10] Schmelz 2002: 203-254, on moneylending esp. 247-249.

[11] Jerome, *Ep.* 22.33.

[12] 18 texts, several of which record "doubtful" cases, e.g. *P.Oxy.* XVI 1890 (A2) records a loan for operation of a milling-bakery belonging to a monastery. The monastery itself, however, appears to be private property of a Oxyrhynchite landowner Serena, who grants the loan. I am not sure whom to regard as the creditor in this case.

circumstances in which they were drawn. For that reason we are usually unable to answer the most interesting question: why would some people turn to a church or a monastery for a loan and why would it be granted in some cases. Most probably personal contacts with Church officials were decisive, especially in case of the monasteries lending money to—or borrowing from—their own monks, which was quite common (see below). We also find several cases of priests running up debts with ecclesiastical institutions, e.g. *O.Crum* 194 (A6); *P.Lond.Copt.* 1031 (A16), possibly also *O.Crum* 311 (A13).

In several agreements Church institutions obviously try to secure some future services in exchange for loans: e.g. in *O.Brit.Mus.Copt.* II 12 (A7) a debt of one *solidus* owed to the Theban monastery of Apa Phoibammon is to be repaid with work: the debtor undertakes to cultivate one *aroura* of the monastery's land.[13] *P.Harrauer* 54 (A4) records a loan advanced by the church of St. Victor in Arsinoiton polis to a leather-cutter. The loan (2 *solidi* less 15 ½ carats) was apparently to be repaid by the artisan with work, i.e. making of some object for the altar of the church. Unfortunately this interesting text breaks off at this crucial point, but it seems that we are dealing here with some kind of commission with advance payment.[14] Such commercial credit would have been advantageous for both parties, providing the artisan with means for buying materials and ensuring the creditor that the work will be really carried out, so it is no wonder that also Church officials would have resorted to it.[15]

Similar ways of thinking were concealed behind the agreement of *P.Ryl.Copt.* 196 (A11) in which a *dikaion* (of a monastery?) advanced a payment of 12 ⅛ *solidi* to a certain Theodore of Hermopolis against a promise of delivery of 60 *artabai* of corn in Epeiph, i.e. just after the harvest. Here an ecclesiastical institution uses the instrument of "sale on delivery" to secure future supply.

The most notable single text featuring a Church institution acting as a creditor and lending substantial sums of money is preserved in *P.Oxy.* LXIII 4397 (A3). This settlement of claims of C.E. 545 recounts a complicated story of financial dealings involving a little known Oxyrhynchite monastery of Abbas Hierax, an Oxyrhynchite landowner Diogenes and the Apiones family. What interests us here is the fact that Diogenes, while staying in Constantinople, had borrowed from an agent of the monastery eighty solidi of gold at 6% interest (the maximum amount allowed by law at this period). He secured the loan with an antichretic pledge of a piece of land in the Oxyrhynchite. Some time afterwards he contracted with the same monastery another loan of fifty *solidi* pledging his entire property (*hypotheca generalis*). This was only the beginning of a lengthy affair (the debts proved difficult to be recovered), but here two points need to be stressed. Firstly, a little known provincial monastery was wealthy enough to send a business agent as far as to Constantinople with substantial sums of money: at least 130 *solidi*, but possibly even more. The exact purpose of his mission to the capital remains unfortunately unknown, it was most probably not moneylending as the moneys could have been also invested in Egypt—the eventual debtor was after all an Oxyrhynchite landowner. Apparently the agent had much freedom as to how to invest this capital. The sum, 130 *solidi*, gives us an idea about the volume of capital that a monastery had at its disposal and could invest in loans, even

---

[13] On debts repaid with work see *P.Heid.* V, chapt. 7, 271 ff.

[14] *Werklieferungvertrag*, see *P.Heid.* V: 332-341. On the nature of the agreement of this particular case see the editor's commentary to *P.Harrauer* 54, 192-194.

[15] Perhaps a similar arrangement was concealed behind *P.Rein.* II 107 (A8), in which Abba Iakob, *hegoumenos* of a monastery in the Coptite nome, advances 1 *solidus* to a coppersmith. However, since we are not told how the debt is to be repaid, the transaction may have been a regular loan, or any other sort of agreement.

though in this particular case it was probably an eventual acquisition of land and not the profit from interest that was the motif behind the transaction.

Secondly, we can see that despite all condemnation of usury on the part of Church fathers and Canon law, a monastery could and did draw profit from lending on interest: we hear of 6% interest on the loan of 80 *solidi* and of an unspecified interest from 72 *solidi* deposited with a *zygostates* of Oxyrhynchus when the original debt was partially recovered—this too would enrich the monastery until the monks decided to purchase a suitable piece of land with the money.

The sums appearing in other contracts are much lower: we have medium-size loans of 12 *solidi* in *P.Oxy.* XVI 1890 (A2) and *P.Ryl.Copt.* 196 (A11) and 11 *solidi* of *P.Iand.* 44 (A9) and petty loans ranging from 1 *trimesion* (*CPR* IV 78—A12) to 2 *solidi* (*P.Harrauer* 54—A4). The latter type seems to have been the most popular one, just as it was among private individuals.

2. CHURCH INSTITUTIONS AS DEBTORS

Church institutions could and did borrow money themselves. Even if we had not had any papyrological evidence at hand, it would have been evident from normative sources: the above-mentioned Novel 120 of Justinian (C.E. 544) allowed Church officials to pledge Church property and to indebt Church institutions when in financial need, especially one caused by fiscal obligations. The maximum allowed interest rate on such loans was 3%.[16]

Documentary evidence for such practice is unfortunately rather scarce and it is difficult to state whether the limit of 3% was observed. The only possible example of such interest rate known to me can be found in *P.Baden* VI 173 (B18). This document mentions a substantial loan of 48 *solidi* contracted by a clergyman acting on behalf of a *xenon*[17] with an official of the Imperial estate (ὑποβοηθὸς τοῦ θείου δεσποτικοῦ οἴκου). The sum was apparently used for purchase of grain needed for the ἐμβολή. The capital, together with interest of 2 *solidi*, was secured by pledge of 500 *artabai* of lentils. Unfortunately we are not sure as to the duration of the loan; if it was one year, then the interest rate was slightly above 4%, i.e. close to the 3% permitted by Justinian's Novel 120. If it was four months (Mesore to Hathyr), as the document seems to suggest, then the interest rate was over 12% and would be illegal after C.E. 528. This could be the *terminus ante quem* for this undated document.[18]

Among the documents from the Apollonopolite monastery of Apa Apollo (*P.Bal.*) we find two instances of the monastery's *dikaion* (represented by the *proestos*) borrowing money from its own

---

[16] Nov. 120,6: "Si vero contigerit aliquam praedictarum venerabilium domorum nomine fiscalium tributorum aut alterius cuiuslibet supervenientis necessitatis venerabili domui pecuniis egere, liceat eius ordinatoribus immobilem rem [aut] supponere et dare in speciale pignus, ut creditor possideat eandem rem et eius fructus colligat et reputet sibi tam in his creditis pecuniis quam in usuris, non autem maioribus quam quarta parte centesimae. Si vero persolverint debitum praepositi eiusdem venerabilis domus aut ex fructibus adimpleatur creditum, redeat iterum res ad venerabilem domum ex qua data est."

[17] Ξενῶνες were hospices run by the clergy; together with other ecclesiastical charitable institutions they belonged to the *venerabiles domus* (εὐαγεῖς οἶκοι) subject to Nov. 120.6 quoted above. Cf. Hagemann 1956. On charitable institutions in Egypt, see Wipszycka 1972: 115-119.

[18] Cf. the editor's remarks, *P.Baden* VI 13, 15 and 17.

monks.[19] In *P.Bal.* 102 (E101) the *proestos* Apa Kyre borrows from one of the monks 8 *solidi* that are to be repaid with commodities (6 *solidi* with lentils, 2 *solidi* with either honey or lentils). In *P.Bal.* 103 (E102) another *proestos* Apa Psha borrows 1 *solidus* from Apa Ammone; this debt is to be settled later with 10 *artabai* of wheat. In both cases we are told that the money is needed for the payment of the *demosion*-tax of the monastery. It is notable that the monastery is borrowing money to pay its land tax, which is exactly the situation foreseen by the provision of Justinian's Novel 120—only that we are most probably in the Arab period now.

These documents are complemented by the interesting (if somewhat obscure) text of *P.Bal.* 293 (E109). It appears to be a financial account with two kinds of entries: personal name(s) followed by a note "for his/their poll-tax (*andrismos*)" and a sum of money; personal name with a note "for the debt (*chreos*) of the monastery," followed with a sum of money. The sums are rather modest, usually ⅓ of a *solidus*, only in one case the "debt" is more substantial: 4⅔ *solidi*. What I find difficult to establish here is the direction in which money flows: either this is an account of the monastery's incomes,[20] or expenditures.[21] The question is perhaps not that important, in either case we have more evidence for the monastery borrowing money in connection with taxes (this time it is the poll-tax).[22] The creditors seem to be again monks (most of them bear the honorific title of "Apa," though this is not decisive); in one case we find a shoemaker—but he may have been a monk as well.

The sums are relatively modest and we can presume that they represent but a fraction of sums that the monastery had to borrow at times to meet its financial obligations. In the absence of any "banking facilities" the *proestos* had to assemble money from many short-term loans, to be repaid from the monastery's expected income after harvest. His own monks, those of some means at least, would have been the obvious choice as the source of credit.[23] We do not hear of any interest, but in sales on delivery it could have been easily hidden in the price of the commodity.

An interesting question is whether borrowing money to pay the taxes is indeed a sign of financial hardship.[24] Lack of coined money may be a sign of undermonetized economy, but not necessarily of financial distress. The monastery would have drawn the majority of its income from its lands, and it may choose either to sell the crops from the *last* harvest and to keep money to pay the taxes, or to sell the crops from the *future* harvest in advance when the need to raise money for the taxes arose. The

---

[19] The third example, *P.Bal.* 115 (E107), is doubtful as the beginning of the text is lost, and we are not certain as to who borrowed from whom and for what purpose. But here as well the debtor was probably the *dikaion* of the monastery, since the *proestos* Isaac assents to the document, just as in *P.Bal.* 102 (E101) and 103 (E102) (the creditors do not assent). The object of debt were 4 *solidi* 8½ carats, to be repaid "from the harvest of the fifth indiction." In interpreting this document I differ from Wipszycka 2001: 172-173, who regarded the *dikaion* to be the creditor here.

[20] The "debts" being loans contracted by the monastery with various individuals; the *andrismos*-entries—revenues from the poll-tax which the monastery had paid to the Arab authorities for the whole community and the payment of which it is now demanding from its members (cf. *P.Bal.*, p. 43).

[21] In this case the *andrismos*-entries record what the monastery pays as poll tax for its individual members; the *chreos*-entries record payments to the creditors of the monastery. The document is dated to the 14th of Mecheir, i.e. just before the grain harvest. I would expect such payments to occur after the harvest, when the rent from monastic estates had been collected. But perhaps the Bala'izah monastery derived its income from other sources.

[22] On the poll-tax paid by monasteries in the Arab period, see Kahle, *P.Bal.*, p. 43 and Clackson 2008, § I 7.

[23] Unsurprisingly this mechanism worked both ways; among the papyri from Apa Apollo monastery at Bawit we find one instance of a reverse situation: in *P.Mon.Apollo* 38 (E96) the *dikaion* of the monastery is lending 2 *solidi* to one of the monks.

[24] So Kahle, *P.Bal.*, pp. 41-42.

instrument of "advance sale" could have been advantageous to both parties and not necessarily a sign that the monastery was unable to meet its fiscal obligations and had to borrow cash at usurious rates.[25] I do not wish to imply that the monastery was definitely not in financial distress, but borrowing money to pay the taxes is in my view not enough of a proof for that. We simply do not have enough information on the situation behind the transactions of this particular monastery.

A good example of problems arising from a debt incurred by a monastery can be found in *SB* VIII 9683 (B17).[26] We find here a petition written by a monk Timotheus, who complains that a soldier Paulus had seized an anchor belonging to a monastery in Ankyron polis. Apparently he did so as a reprisal for an unsettled debt of the deacon Horus. We do not know for sure whether Horus had borrowed money on behalf of the monastery, but the context suggest so: the author of the petition does not protest the debtor's trying to satisfy his claims from the property of the monastery. He merely states that the anchor was worth much more than the 2400 myriads constituting the original debt. The involvement of another cleric, the *presbyteros* Apa Aiantinos from the same monastery, who made a public statement about the debt, also suggests that it was the monastic community that was regarded as responsible for the debt by both parties.[27]

3. CLERICS AND MONKS AS CREDITORS

The *Heidelberger Gesamtverzeichnis der griechischen Papyrusurkunden Ägyptens*[28] lists ca. 350 Greek documents labeled as "loans" and "sales on delivery" for the period C.E. 300-900. To these we

---

[25] There is a vast bibliography on "sales with deferred delivery," *cf.* Jakab 1999, and the literature quoted there, esp. n. 1. There has been some controversy among papyrologists and historians of law whether these common transactions constituted real sales with payment in advance or rather loans of money to be repaid later in kind (*datio in solutum*). It is not necessary to dwell on the legal nature of these transactions here; suffice it to say that they do represent a sort of agricultural credit giving the farmer financial means to proceed with cultivation of his fields in winter in exchange for his crop delivered at the time of harvest. The advantages of this arrangement are discussed by Bagnall 1977: "For the lender there was the security of the crop, a good rate of interest, and the repayment in a non-depreciating commodity. For the borrower there was at least relatively easy access to cash which would be inaccessible at 12 per cent and illegal at a higher rate [in 4th cent.—TM]" (p. 95). He stressed the role of advance sales in concealing usury, since it was legal to exact 50% interest in loans in kind, compared to 12% in money loans (and the difference is even bigger compared to Justinian's 6% or 3% allowed for loans to Church institutions). However, Bagnall did not take into account the fluctuations of commodity prices within the year: such loans would normally have been contracted in winter, when their prices were higher, and repaid after harvest when they were much lower, *cf.* Tenger (1993), 33. The effective interest may have been much lower than the nominal 50%. The problem requires further study.

[26] First published and discussed by Zilliacus 1954.

[27] Zilliacus 1954: 206, note to l. 11 f., says "This seems to indicate that the monastery was the actual debtor whereas Apa Horus only acted as an intermediary agent or, rather, that the *proestos* was responsible for the debts made by the monks." I am not sure how to understand this statement. If Zilliacus meant by "the monks" the whole monastic community, i.e. the monastery as an institution, then he is right in so far as it was indeed the *proestos* who represented the monastery in business dealings with the outside world. If he, however, means to say that the *proestos* was responsible for private debts incurred by individual monks, then this conclusion seems to be far-fetched. Steinwenter 1930: 41, whom Zilliacus quotes here, only asserts that in the provincial legal practice of Byzantine Egypt monasteries were often regarded as the private patrimony of the abbots despite the prescriptions of the Imperial law. This does not mean that abbots were responsible for obligations of their monks. See also p. 192 on the bad debt problem in Nepheros' correspondence.

[28] http://www.rzuser.uni-heidelberg.de/~gv0/gvz.html.

should add some 400 Coptic texts similarly identified in the *Brussels Coptic Database*.²⁹ Together they make up some 750 known documents relating to the debts from the Byzantine and Early Arab periods.³⁰ Among these I was able to identify *ca.* 80 documents³¹ featuring monks and members of the clergy (presbyters and deacons) as private debtors and/or creditors (Tables C, D and E), i.e. roughly 10%. Admittedly, such "statistics" must be treated with caution—the sample is fairly small and publication of a single new monastic *dossier* could change the proportion—but we can safely state that this particular social group played a not insignificant part in the process of lending and borrowing.³² On the other hand, lending and borrowing was relatively widely practiced and acceptable economic activity for monks and clerics.

Among these documents we find monks and clergymen appearing as creditors in ca. 55 cases and as debtors in ca. 35 cases.³³ The 10:1 ratio given by Rémondon (see above, n. 5) is far from accurate; 2:1 is more correct for the material available at present.³⁴ But in my view the sample is too small to draw far-fetched conclusions; the flow of new publications can easily change the proportion. The slight prevalence of ecclesiastical creditors over debtors is not a strong argument in the discussion on the wealth in the churchmen's hands.

What is potentially more fruitful is the analysis of the sums changing hands in such transactions. A glance at the contracts featuring monks and clerics as private creditors (TABLES C and E) shows that these sums were usually relatively modest. Most of them stay just above the borderline, below which loans went unrecorded.³⁵ So among money debts we find several sums smaller that 1 *solidus*;³⁶ the most common debts are those of 1 *solidus*,³⁷ 2 *solidi*³⁸ or 3 *solidi*.³⁹ More substantial debts are less

---

²⁹ http://dev.ulb.ac.be/~amartin/copte/baseuk.php?page=accueiluk.php (English version).

³⁰ In this number there are not only debt acknowledgements, but also other documents mentioning debts, e.g. letters, receipts, petitions, etc.

³¹ Here and elsewhere I prefer to give the approximate—rather than exact—figure, since in some documents (especially if the beginning is lost) the status of one (or both) parties is a mere guess and can be questioned.

³² 10% is several times more than the clergy's share in the total population. On the other hand, the papyri record only transactions involving larger sums. The majority of petty loans probably went unrecorded, so we can take into consideration only the transactions of the "middle class."

³³ These figures add up to 90 because there are 10 cases of monks/clerics appearing on each side of the transaction; such documents are counted twice.

³⁴ We have to bear in mind that the evidence may be biased by the survival pattern of the documents: debt acknowledgements remained in the hands of the creditor at least until the debt was repaid and the texts kept by monks in their monasteries at the fringe of the desert were more likely to be preserved than papyri stored in towns and villages within the cultivation zone.

³⁵ It would require a thorough analysis of all preserved debt acknowledgements to see where this bottom line was, but my guess for the Byzantine period is that it was around 1 *trimesion*, smaller debts appearing only rarely (but see e.g. *O. Crum* 165 (C53) or *CPR* IV 54 (C46)).

³⁶ *O.Brit.Mus.Copt.* I 73,1 (C37); *O.IFAO* sn (C39); *SPP* III 190 (C43); *CPR* IV 54 (C46); *O.Crum* 165 (C53); *P.Mon.Apollo* 40 (E100) and 42 (E92).

³⁷ *O.Crum* 158 (C26); *P.Ness.* III 44 (C28); *CPR* IV 72 (C35); *O.Brit.Mus.Copt.* I 76,1 (C38); perhaps *CPR* IV 55 (C47); *P.Athen.Xyla* 5 (E77), 17 (E80) and 12 (E82); *P.Mon.Apollo* 34 (E91); perhaps P.Duke inv. 811 (E93); *P.Bal.* 114 (E106).

³⁸ *P.Ryl.Copt.* 332 (C27) and 192 (C36); *O.Vind.Copt.* 23 (C40); *P.KRU* 58 (C44); *BKU* III 364 (C45); *CPR* IV 54 (C46); *P.Mon.Apollo* 38 (E96).

³⁹ *P.Princ.* II 87 (C31); perhaps *P.Mich.* XIII 669 (D56); *P.Mon.Apollo* 39 (E89).

frequent[40] and do not exceed 9 *solidi* (with the possible exception of *P.Dubl.* 28 (C32), but the reading of the sum—50 *solidi*—is very doubtful and I find it quite improbable in a transaction among villagers).

Besides money debts we also find some debts in kind, usually wine and corn.[41] The most intriguing of them is recorded in *P.Ryl.Copt.* 209 (C42). It is a loan (probably a true loan, not a sale on delivery) of "1800 jars of wine." If the reading is correct, we have here evidence for a very impressive transaction—it would be interesting to know the monetary value of that large amount of wine. We can compare it with the sale on delivery of *SB* XX 14712 (C22) in which the creditor is a woman bearing the titles οὐράνιος ἡ καὶ ζωοποιός normally reserved for members of the clergy,[42] perhaps a nun (she is represented by a *presbyteros*). The debtor is to deliver 2400 wine barrels—another possible example of the clergy's involvement in the wine trade. Unfortunately in both cases we are not entirely sure of the status of the creditors.

Our documents seldom shed light on the motives behind the deal. In most cases we are unable to tell whether a particular papyrus records a casual friendly—possibly interest-free—loan between acquaintances or a business transaction aiming at profit. Such information could be gained from studying archives, but unfortunately we have only one archive of money-lending priests and it comes from outside of Egypt: from Nessana in Palestine. Among the papyri found in the monastery church of SS. Sergius and Bacchus there are two archives that can be associated with one family, which kept the post of the abbot (*hegoumenos*) for about one hundred years in the 7th century. One member of this family, Patrick son of Sergius (died C.E. 628) appears three times as creditor in the archive, in *P.Ness.* III 44 (C28), 46 (C29) and 147 (C30).[43] In the first of these Patrick acknowledges that he has received the receipt of the borrower. The sum is relatively small and the deal appears to have been rather informal,[44] especially when compared with the full-blown notary contract of *P.Ness.* III 46. In this text Patrick lends to one Abraham the much more considerable sum of 9 *solidi*, 6 of which were subject to 6% interest (and the remaining 3 interest free). It seems that we are dealing here with two sorts of transactions: a rather informal "friendly" loan with no interest and a regular business transaction.

Some eighty years later Patrick's son George, himself also a *hegoumenos*, appears as the borrower in two contracts drawn in Gaza. In *P.Ness.* III 55 (C33) the lender is actually Sergius son of George, who later succeeded his father as the Abbot of SS. Sergius and Bacchus. While in Gaza he lent 4⅓ *solidi* belonging to his father to a certain Sergius son of Menas for the latter's land tax (*demosion*). The money was handed over directly to tax collectors. We do not hear of any interest and it could not have been hidden in the sum due, since the document served as debt acknowledgement and tax receipt at the

---

[40] 4 *solidi*: *P.Bal.* 112 (E105); 5 *solidi*: *P.Mon.Apollo* 41 (E90), *P.YaleCopt.* 18 (E94), *P.Bal.* 115 (E107); 6 *solidi*: *P.Athen.Xyla* 18 (E73); 7 *solidi*: *CPR* XIX 10 (C24), *P.Warr.* 10 (C25), *P.Athen.Xyla* 10 (E79); 8 *solidi*: *P.Bal.* 102 (E101); 9 *solidi*: *P.Ness.* III 46 (C29), perhaps *BKU* III 365 (C49).

[41] But see also the debt concerning 80 boxes of unguent in a transaction between a *presbyteros* and an oil-manufacturer, *BKU* III 421 (C50).

[42] Sijpesteijn 1991.

[43] *P.Ness.* III 147 is too fragmentary to reveal any significant information. It is unknown who was the creditor in *P.Ness.* III 48 from the same archive.

[44] *P.Ness.* III: 133, "It would appear that part or all of this transaction was carried out by messenger, i.e. that Patrick sent the solidus (or a draft from the money) to the borrower Stephan, who sent back the note, receipt of which is hereby acknowledged."

same time. A similar situation is recorded in *P.Ness.* III 59 (C34), in which George advances 6 (?) *solidi* for the payment of the land tax of another Sergius (it cannot be definitely stated whether this is the same person as in *P.Ness.* III 55). It seems that the Abbot George, himself a large landowner and a wealthy man,[45] was helping other landowners (or at least one) who found themselves short of cash. We cannot be sure if this was selfless help—his father Patrick did lend money at interest at least once even though as a *presbyteros* he was forbidden to do that by Canon law.

This brings us to the question of the clergy practicing usury. If the Church ban of lending money at interest had been effective, all loans issued by clerics could be regarded as interest-free (in the case of unordained monks lending at interest would have been "merely" a moral transgression, but still a serious one in view of the Church's radical opinion on usury). But—as we all know—the more often a legal norm was repeated by the lawgivers, the less effective it must have been. We have seen one example of this among the Nessana papyri; the evidence from Egypt also confirms this occasionally.

In the Coptic ostracon *O.Crum* 29 we see three newly ordained (or about to be ordained) deacons commit themselves in the face of bishop Apa Abraham of Hermonthis:

> Since we have requested your paternity that you would ordain us deacons, we are ready to observe the commands and canons and to obey those above us and be obedient to the superiors and to watch our beds on the days of communion and to master the Gospel according to John and to learn it by heart by the end of the Pentecost; and if we do not so but keep it by us and recite it, we shall not have ordination. And we will not trade nor take usury (ϩⲓ ⲙⲏⲥⲉ—'take interest') nor will we go abroad without asking (leave).

Other such undertakings by would-be deacons or priests are known (e.g. *O.Crum* 30-35), but only the one quoted above explicitly mentions trading and money lending as forbidden to the clerics, perhaps because it was self-evident that such bans belonged to the set of rules (*entolai*; *kanones*) binding members of the clergy. Nonetheless, *O.Crum* 29 gives evidence for the bishop Abraham taking extra precaution that his men do not practice trades unfit for members of the clergy.

Another text, *P.Mon.Epiph.* 157, reports how someone went to the town of Djeme and found someone "taking interest." Unfortunately the text is very fragmentary, but the context suggests that the author— probably a bishop—enumerates the transgressions made by local clergy.[46] Even if not entirely certain, we have here a proof that despite all bans and prohibitions clergymen were tempted to increase their wealth by means of lending at interest, and that it was the bishop's duty to check on them.

Scarce as it is, there is also some direct evidence that clergymen and monastics did practice usury. Beside *P.Ness.* III 46 (C29), we find mentions of interest in: *P.Warr.* 10 (C25); *CPR* IV 72 (C35) and *P.Ryl.Copt.* 192 (C36), possibly also *P.Mich.* XIII 669 (D56). In *P.Köln* III 151 (C21) the sum of 2 *solidi* borrowed from a monk is said to start bringing yearly punitive interest (480 *myriades* per *solidus*) if the debt is not repaid on the agreed date.

---

[45] In *P.Ness.* III 58 he pays a rather large tax—37½ *solidi*—on land that had been assigned to him by the Arab governor; it seems likely that this was not the only land in his possession.

[46] He also complains that they were using a baptismal font, which had not been consecrated by him. Consecrating a baptismal font would have been probably a bishop's duty.

The interesting question is, whether all other loans, not mentioning interest explicitly, were really interest-free. As the old list of loans compiled by Mickwitz shows, Byzantine loan contracts rarely mention interest, in general more rarely than the earlier Roman loans.[47] But interest could well have been hidden in the principal stipulated by the contract, the actual amount lent being smaller than the one recorded. Such a practice is already attested among demotic and Greek loan contracts of the Ptolemaic period. It has been plausibly argued by Pestman that the frequent expression *atokos daneion* (or *chresis*) does not indicate an interest-free loan, but merely that no additional interest was required, it being most probably hidden in the principal in most cases.[48] Interest could also have been stipulated in a separate document, seemingly unconnected with the principal loan agreement. A very convenient instrument for practicing usury may have been the common contracts of sale on delivery: depending on fluctuations of commodity prices the profit of the lender could have in some cases exceeded the customary 50% permitted by law (*hemiolion*). In many cases such contracts do not state how much has been actually advanced to the debtor.

In sum, many loans appearing to us as interest-free may have actually borne interest, but interest was not mentioned either because the parties feared possible consequences or because it was not customary to mention this in general.[49] However, it would be useless to speculate about the extent of such practice. We can only state that, in the light of the evidence, some clerics and monks did practice usury at times and that Church authorities occasionally tried to see that they did not do so.

4. CLERICS AS DEBTORS

As has been noted above, texts featuring clerics and monks as borrowers are somewhat less frequent, though by no means rare. They give a similar impression: they record mostly petty transactions of the provincial "middle class." The sums are rather modest (1, 2 or 3 *solidi*); in *CPR* IV 63 (D65) the more substantial sum of 12 *solidi* has to be divided by two, since the debt is the joint obligation of a *presbyteros* and another person.

Interesting evidence for provincial clergy conducting various business transactions with members of the local gentry can be found among the papers of Dioscorus of Aphrodito.[50] Dioscorus' family included a priest (his cousin Victor was a *presbyteros*) and his father Apollos died as a monk in a monastery he had founded. Priests appear quite often in the archive conducting all sorts of business with Dioscorus and his relatives.[51] In *P.Mich.* XIII 699 (D56; on the date of this document see above, n. 6) Apollos, his son Senuthes and his nephew Victor son of Besarion borrow 3 *solidi* at 12.5% interest from a woman bearing the title of *eulabestate*, possibly a nun.

---

[47] Mickwitz 1932.

[48] Pestman 1971.

[49] Note that reverse situation, i.e. of laics lending money at interest to clerics, is also quite rare, and the only examples known to me are *P.Rain.Cent.* 86 (D55) and the exceptional case of *P.Cair.Masp.* 67126 (D57).

[50] Conveniently summarized by MacCoull 1988: 9-14. Note that in *P.Cair.Masp.* II 67162 (D63) the deacon Iohannes is the borrower, not the lender as MacCoull writes on p. 12.

[51] *E.g.* we see priests leasing land from Dioscorus in *P.Cair.Masp.* I 67108 and *P.Cair.Masp.* II 67128 or ceding land to him in *P.Cair.Masp.* I 67118 and *P.Cair.Masp.* I 67088.

We have seen how an Oxyrhynchite landowner borrowed money from an agent of an Egyptian monastery in Constantinople (*P.Oxy.* LXIII 4397, A3, discussed above). Another interesting example of Egyptian churchmen contracting a loan in the Imperial capital, this time in their own name, can be found in the papers of the well-known Dioscorus of Aphrodito (*P.Cair.Masp.* II 67126, D57). In the early 540s Apollos of Aphrodito, the father of Dioscorus undertook a journey to Constantinople in the company of his nephew Victor, son of Besarion. By that time Apollos might have already been a monk (*cf. PSI* VIII 933)[52] and Victor is styled as *presbyteros* (*P.Cair.Masp.* II 67126, ll. 1 and 43). On 7th of January 541 they borrowed a not insubstantial sum of 20 *solidi* from a Constantinopolitan banker (*argyroprates*) Flavius Anastasius. The loan was to be repaid four months later in Alexandria, where the bank apparently had another branch. The interest was set at two-thirds of the legal maximum (*dimoiraios tokos*), most probably 8%, which the bankers were allowed to charge under Justinian's legislation (C. 4.32.26.1 and Nov. 136.4).[53] We can only speculate as to the purpose of Apollos and Victor's journey to Constantinople, but apparently they found themselves short of cash (for bribes? for personal expenditures?), and borrowed money, which they hoped to be able to repay back in Egypt.[54]

Not all debts result from loans and we have to be aware that some contracts appearing to be loans may have concealed different types of transactions. *P.Cair.Masp.* II 67128 (D58), 67129 (D59) and possibly also 67130 (D61) have priests featuring as debtors in agreements being, despite some external features of debt acknowledgements,[55] actually land leases.

5. Lending and Borrowing in the Monasteries

Monks involved in lending and borrowing are best attested among the papyri associated with the Hermopolite monastery of Apa Apollo. There are 21 known Coptic and Greek loan agreements that can be safely connected with this monastery and several more doubtful ones.[56] The texts date from the 5th to the 8th century, we have among them 9 (?) loans of money and 9 loans of commodities (in several cases the object of debt remains unknown). In the second category, only one text *SB* XVI 12267 (E78) records a true (from the legal point of view) loan of wine. One contract is probably a sale with deferred

---

[52] So Keenan 1984 and MacCoull 1993 and 1988: 29. Whether Apollos was indeed a monk while still occupying the post of *protokometes* is questioned by Derda and Wipszycka 1994: 44.

[53] For a different view on the interest rate in this papyrus see Preissner 1954: 63.

[54] Keenan 1984: 958-959.

[55] The phrase ὁμολογῶ διὰ ταύτης μου τῆς ἐγγράφου ἀσφαλείας ὀφείλειν καὶ χρεωστεῖν (*P.Cair.Masp.* II 67128, 11-13; *P.Cair.Masp.* II 67129, 7-9) can appear in debt acknowledgements resulting from various transactions, *cf.* Kühnert 1965: 146.

[56] Either because the state of preservation leaves doubts as to the nature of the agreement or we are not sure if at least one of the parties was a monk. The latter is often the case, especially in case of creditors, since their names would have been mentioned at the beginning of a document, now often missing. But there are reasons to believe that if a document can be safely connected with a monastery, at least one of the parties was a monk. The full up-to-date list of these agreements can be found in Delattre 2004. Among the documents listed there, *P.Athen.Xyla* 6, 12, 17 and *P.YaleCopt.* 18 can be attributed to the Bawit monastery on various grounds, as Alain Delattre has shown (*P.Brux.Bawit*). I am grateful to him for this information and for providing me with his transcription and translation of *P.YaleCopt* 18. I have decided not to include P.Duke inv. 469, although there are some (feeble) indications that it might have been another loan agreement from Bawit, see Markiewicz 2002.

payment: *P.Mon.Apollo* 44 (E98), an unknown amount of wine to be paid with more than 1 *solidus*. The rest are sales with deferred delivery (the price is paid in advance): [6 cases ?]. The sums appearing in money loans vary between 15 *folles* and nearly 6 *solidi* of gold, perhaps some 2 *solidi* on the average—if we can speak of any "statistics" in case of such a meager sample. This would have been a rather substantial sum of money from an ordinary person's point of view: two *solidi* could represent a worker's yearly wages in 6th century (*P.Dubl.* I 47), but not great wealth either.

In almost all cases in which it can be determined, the creditors were individual monks disposing most probably of their personal wealth. In two cases—*P.Amst.* I 47 (E75) and 48 (E76)—money is lent by the abbots, but they seem to be acting on their own behalf. Only one loan *P.Mon.Apollo* 38 (E96) is said to be given by the monastery as an institution: the dikaion of the monastery represented by its head, Apa Theodoros. Lending and borrowing in Apa Apollo seems to have been principally a private affair.

Among debtors we also find monks, who seem to have had the liberty of conducting all sorts of transactions with their fellow brothers (8 cases in the dossier of the Apa Apollo monastery). However, most of the debtors seem to have been people from the neighbouring villages. Their social status is rarely known. In *SB* XVI 12267 (E78) the debtor is a *protokometes* of Senthryphis, but many seem to have been people of some means at least, inspiring hope that they would repay their debts.

A good example of a bad debt incurred by a monk is known from the Nepheros archive.[57] In seven out of nine letters sent to Nepheros by Paulus (*P.Neph.* 1, 2, 4, 5, 6, 7 and 8), a trader and possibly the agent of Nepheros' monastery in Alexandria, we find repeated mentions of a debt of 16 *artabai* of wheat owed to Paulus by a certain Papnuthis son of Horion, a monk of the same monastery. The debt resulted from an interest-bearing loan, if we are to believe Paulus (*P.Neph.* 7, 4-8). Nepheros, who is a *presbyteros* and clearly a personage of high rank within the monastery (perhaps even the *proestos*), is expected to exact pressure on the stubborn debtor and recover the wheat, then have it sent in the form of bread to Paulos in Alexandria. He fails to do so for reasons that escape us, for we do not have Nepheros' letters to Paulus. Presumably Papnuthis simply denied his debt in front of Nepheros, a filthy lie unworthy of a monk in Paulus' eyes (*P.Neph.* 7, 5). The unfortunate creditor then suggests Papnuthis be made to swear an oath and become excluded from the participation in the Holy Mass if he commits perjury, i.e. denies his debt again (*P.Neph.* 8, 30-31).

As we can see, Paulus does not resort to civil procedure to recover the loan;[58] instead he hopes to succeed through the authority of Nepheros, Papnuthis' superior within the monastery. He expects Nepheros to persuade his opponent, ordering him to pay up or even imposing an ecclesiastical sanction against him.[59] He does not, however, expects the debt to paid off by Nepheros as the *proestos*. Clearly Papnuthis conducts his business affairs in his own name and the monastic community is not responsible for them.

In sum, credit seems to have played some role both in the economic activities of Church institutions and in the private dealings of clergy and monks. The economic importance of this is difficult to estimate, for the available material is unfortunately not too abundant. Churches and monasteries can be

---

[57] *P.Neph.*: 24-5 and 29-30.

[58] The debtor does not even threaten going to court, even though it would have been perfectly possible, since the *episcopalis audientia* was introduced for cases involving monks only in C.E. 539 (Nov. 79).

[59] *P.Neph.*: 29-30.

seen taking loans, especially when cash for payment of taxes was needed, but at times these institutions would also appear as creditors, investing surplus funds for profit or advancing payments for future services or deliveries. With one exception the sums appearing in such transactions are modest and the documents show us that moneylending was limited in scale and conducted only locally—in the absence of any "banking" facilities monasteries had to borrow small sums of money from many individuals.

As far as the papyri can give us insight into the private affairs of the clergy, they convey a similar picture. Priests and monks appearing in our documents seem to belong to the provincial "middle class"; they conduct their rather modest affairs with their peers, not infrequently with other monks or clerics. Contrary to Rémondon's impression, there does not seem to be a particular concentration of wealth in their hands, or at least debt acknowledgements are not a proof for that. There is a noticeable prevalence of ecclesiastical creditors over debtors, but the data sample is too meager to draw far-fetched conclusions.

We cannot answer with too much certainty the interesting question, whether the credit offered by members of clergy was really interest-free in keeping with the Canon law. The documents rarely mention interest, but this is not decisive—they seldom do so in general, even if the creditor is not an ordained priest. A certain number of loans may have been indeed interest-free, but the ultimate purpose of all this lending and borrowing, leasing and trading, was profit, not charity. The poorer clergymen had to earn their living and the wealthier (like the Abbot Patrick of Nessana) had nothing against increasing their wealth.

What is interesting to observe is that a monastery like the monastery of Apa Apollo at Bawit could—through economic activities of its monks—play an active role in the system of agricultural credit, providing the local farmers with working capital, not unlike the provincial *metropoleis* did for their hinterland.[60] In that sense Sarah Clackson was right in stating that monasteries provided 'banking' facilities for laypeople. But I doubt whether the credit offered there was really interest-free.

6. TABLES

Note: The following tables contain all the texts known to me which record, or allude to, debts owed to, or by, clergymen, monks or Church institutions. In compiling them I used the *Heidelberger Gesamtverzeichnis der griechischen Papyrusurkunden Ägyptens* and the *Brussels Coptic Database*.

The asterisk (*) indicates "doubtful" texts: the state of preservation leaves some doubts either to the nature of the transaction or to the status of the parties (in other words we are not quite sure whether the papyrus in question does indeed record a loan or/and whether at least one of the parties was a either a monk or a clergyman).

Some dates could be only tentatively assigned to texts by their editors on the criterion of paleography and are therefore subject to challenge; this goes especially for Coptic agreements.

---

[60] On this system see Foraboschi and Gara 1982; Bagnall 1993: 73-8.

A. Church Institutions as Creditors

No.	Text	Date and provenance	Creditor	Debtor	Object of debt
1.	P.Köln III 153 (Greek)	5th-6th cent. Antinoupolis	the *dikaion* of the "Monastery on the Northern Rock," through *presbyteros* Kolluthos, the *proestos*	Aurelius Pheus, a farmer	unknown amount of *solidi*, resulting from unpaid rent
2.	*P.Oxy. XVI 1890 (Greek)	C.E. 508 Oxyrhynchus	the monastery of Abbas Kopreous, through its owner Serena	Aurelius Apphouas and his son Abraham, bakers and millers from Oxyrhynchus	12 *solidi* as a loan for operation of the milling-bakery in the monastery
3.	P.Oxy. LXIII 4397 (Greek)	C.E. 545 Oxyrhynchus	the monastery of Abbas Hierax in the Oxyrhynchite, through its agent in Constantinople, Theophilus	Diogenes, an Oxhyrhynchite landowner	80 *solidi* at 6% interest per year 50 *solidi* (interest unknown, none?)
4.	P.Harrauer 54 (Greek)	C.E. 579 Arsinoiton polis	the church of St. Victor in Arsinoe, through Kometes, a deacon or *oikonomos*	Aurelius Pusis, a leather-cutter	2 *solidi* less 15½ *keratia*, to be repaid with work (?) (some object for the altar of the church ?)
5.	SBKopt. I 922 (Coptic)	ca. C.E. 600 Thebes	"brothers of the monastery of Apa Phoibammon," probably acting on behalf of the monastery	Patape, son of Pus, "writing in the name of my brothers"	1 *solidus*
6.	O.Crum 194 (Coptic)	ca. C.E. 600 Thebes Deir el-Bahari	"the clergy of Tamuhite" acting on behalf of a church institution (?)	Papnute, a *presbyteros*	½ *solidus*
7.	O.Brit.Mus. Copt. II, 12 (Coptic)	C.E. 622 or 637 Thebes, Deir el-Bahri	the monastery of Apa Phoibammon, through Apa Victor, a *presbyteros* "and the brothers"	Surus	1 *solidus*, to be repaid with work (cultivation of one *aroura* of land belonging to the monastery)
8.	P.Rein. II 107 (Greek)	6th-7th cent. Coptites	the monastery of Apa Samuel of Phel in the Coptite, through Abba Iakob, *presbyteros* and *hegoumenos*	Aurelius Allamonos, a smith from Syene	1 *solidus*

No.	Text	Date and provenance	Creditor	Debtor	Object of debt
9.	P.Iand. 44 (Greek)	6th-7th cent. provenance unknown	NN, a *presbyteros*, acting on behalf of a church	NN	11 *solidi*
10.	CPR IV 93 (Coptic)	7th cent. Hermopolites	the *dikaion* of the monastery of St. Theodore of Shteh, through its clergy (*klerikoi*)	Theodore from Hermopolis	120 *artabai* of wheat, resulting from an unidentified agreement
11.	P.Ryl.Copt. 196 (Coptic)	beginning of 8th cent. Hermopolites	a *dikaion* (of a monastery ?)	Theodore, son of Leontius, from Hermopolis	12⅛ *solidi*, to be repaid with 60 *artabai* of corn in Epeiph (sale on delivery)
12.	CPR IV 78 (Coptic)	8th cent. Heracleopolites	Apa Theodore, a *presbyteros* acting on behalf of an *eukterion* of St. John	NN, a man from Hermopolis magna	1 *trimesion* against a pledge
13.	*O.Crum 311 (Coptic)	date unknown Thebais	Victor, a bishop (acting on behalf of an institution?)	Moises, a *presbyteros*	unknown
14.	P.Lond.Copt. 1028 (Coptic)	date unknown Hermopolites	a *dikaion* (of a monastery)	Heronodj	unknown, possibly corn
15.	P.Lond.Copt. 1046 (Coptic)	date unknown Hermopolites	a *dikaion* (of a monastery)	Kolthe, an *archigeron*	money
16.	*P.Lond.Copt. 1031 (Coptic)	date unknown Hermopolites	a monastery, through its *pronoetes*	a *presbyteros* (acting on behalf of a church in Hermopolis ?)	corn and wine
see also *P.Mon.Apollo* 38; *P.Bal.* 108.					

B. CHURCH INSTITUTIONS AS DEBTORS

No.	Text	Date and provenance	Creditor	Debtor	Object of debt
17.	SB VIII 9683 (Greek)	end of 4th cent. Heracleopolites	Paulus, a soldier	Apa Horus, a deacon in the monastery of Ankyronites (acting on behalf of the monastery ?)	2400 *myriades* of denars
18.	P.Bad. VI 173 (Greek)	before C.E. 528? provenance unknown	the administration of the Imperial estate, through Georgios, a *hypoboethos*	a *xenon*, through Gregorios, an *anagnostes* and *dioiketes*	48 *solidi* + 2 *solidi* of interest, against security of 500 *artabai* of lentils

| 19. | P.Ryl.Copt. 201 (Coptic) | 7th-8th cent. provenance unknown | NN, a woman | the *dikaion* of (the monastery ?) of Apa Th[…] | money (gold), to be repaid in kind(?)from the crop of the harvest of the 14th indiction |

See also *P.Bal.* 102; *P.Bal.* 103; *P.Bal.* 293; **P.Bal.* 115.

C. CLERICS AND MONKS AS PRIVATE CREDITORS

No.	Text	Date and provenance	Creditor	Debtor	Object of debt
20.	*SB* XXII 15728 (Greek)	C.E. 347 Arsinoites	Aurelius Petros, a deacon of the *katholike ekklesia*	Aurelii Neilos and Apollon from Euhemeria	the price of two *artabai* of wheat and two *artabai* of vegetable seed (sale on delivery)
21.	*P.Köln* III 151 (Greek)	C.E. 423 Kynopolites	Aurelius Pasalymios, a monk from Terythis	Aurelius Lukios from Terythis	2 *solidi* to be repaid in two instalments: 1 *solidus* with cash; 1 *solidus* with tow at the time of olive harvest
22.	*SB XX 14712 (Greek)	C.E. 498 Hermopolites	Kyria *vel* Photine, a nun (?), through NN, a *presbyteros* and *oikonomos*	Aurelius Kolluthos, a potter from Phby	the price of 2400 wine barrels (sale on delivery)
23.	*P.Oxy.* LXVIII 4702 (Greek)	C.E. 520 Oxyrhynchus	Phoibammon, a *presbyteros* of the holy church in Oxyrhynchus	Aurelii Philoxenos and Ioannes, full brothers from the village of Neophytou Antiochou	unknown
24.	*CPR* XIX 10 (Greek)	C.E. 521(?) Hermopolites	Apa Nokis, a *presbyteros* from a church in Hermopolis	NN	7 *solidi* less 42 *keratia*, to be repaid with work?
25.	*P.Warr.* 10 (Greek)	C.E. 591/592 Oxyrhynchus	Georgius, a *presbyteros*	Aurelii Iakob and Victor	7 *solidi*, against interest of 64 bundles of grass, upon security of 1.5 *aroura*
26.	*O.Crum* 158 (Coptic)	ca. C.E. 600 Thebais	NN, *theophilestatos* monk and *oikonomos* of the monastery of Apa Phiobammon	NN	1 *solidus*, to be repaid with corn (sale on delivery ?)

27.	*P.Ryl.Copt. 332 (Coptic)	ca. C.E. 600 provenance unknown	NN, "saintly lord father" (a monk? a cleric?)	Kolluthus	2 *solidi*
28.	*P.Ness.* 44 (Greek)	C.E. 598 Nessana	Patrick (styled later as *anagnostes* and *hegoumenos* of the monastery of Sergius and Bacchus in Nessana)	Stephanus	1 *solidus*
29.	*P.Ness.* 46 (Greek)	C.E. 605 Nessana	Patrick, *anagnostes* and *hegoumenos* of the monastery of Sergius and Bacchus in Nessana	Abraham, son of Procopius, from Nessana	9 *solidi* less 9 *keratia* (6 *solidi* at 6% interest and 3 *solidi* interest-free)
30.	*P.Ness.* 147 (Greek)	early 7th cent. Nessana	Patrick, *anagnostes* and *hegoumenos* of the monastery of Sergius and Bacchus in Nessana	NN	unknown
31.	*P.Princ.* II 87 (Greek)	C.E. 612 Oxyrhynchus	Aurelius Phib, doorman at the church of St. Theodoros in Oxyrhynchus	Aurelius Georgius	3 *solidi*
32.	*P.Dubl.* 28 (Greek)	C.E. 611/612(?) Heracleopolites	Heracleides, a *presbyteros* from the village of Leukogion	NN and NN, full brothers from the village of Leukogion	50 *solidi* ???
33.	*P.Ness.* 55 (Greek)	C.E. 682(?) Nessana	George son of Patrick, *hegoumenos* of the monastery of Segius and Bacchus at Nessana, through his son Sergius, a *presbyteros* (and later also *hegoumenos*)	Sergius son of Menas	4⅓ *solidi* for the payment of the borrower's *demosion*-tax, handed over directly to tax-officials at Gaza
34.	*P.Ness.* 59 (Greek)	C.E. 684(?) Nessana	George son of Patrick, *hegoumenos* of the monastery of Segius and Bacchus at Nessana	Sergius (the same as in *P.Ness.* 55?)	6 (?) *solidi* for the payment of the borrower's *demosion*-tax, handed over directly to tax-officials at Gaza
35.	*CPR* IV 72 (Coptic)	7th cent. Hermopolites	Apa Phiobammon, a deacon from Hermopolis	Paulos, a man from Hermopolis	1 *solidus*, to be repaid after 1 month "with its interest"

36.	*P.Ryl.Copt.* 192 (Coptic)	7th cent. Hermopolis	Ama Ei[...], a nun	NN, a woman	2 *solidi* less 6 *keratia* with interest of ⅛ [...]
37.	*O.Brit.Mus.Copt.* I, 73, 1 (Coptic)	7th-8th cent. Thebes	Apa Shenute, a monk from the mountain of [Djeme?]	Isak from Hermonthis	1 *trimesion*
38.	*O.Brit.Mus.Copt.* I 76, 1 (Coptic)	7th-8th cent. Thebais	Apa Philoteos, a monk	Ionas	1 *solidus*, repaid with a camel (as the debtor is insolvent)
39.	*O.IFAO s.n.*[61] (Coptic)	7th-8th cent. Assiout	Apa Iohannes, "father of the hospital," a monk	Apa Victor from Apouhot	3 *keratia*, to be repaid with honey (sale on delivery)
40.	*O.Vind.Copt.* 23 (Coptic)	7th-8th cent. Thebais	Harau, a monk from the monastery of Apa Iohannes	Marcos, *lashane* from Pseparios	2 *solidi*
41.	**O.Vind. Copt.* 45 (Coptic)	7th-8th cent. Thebais	*pater* Marcos, a priest (?)	Timotheos, son of Helessevus	unknown
42.	**P.Ryl. Copt.* 209 (Coptic)	7th-8th cent. Hermopolis	NN, a deacon (?)	Theodore	1800 jars of wine, to be repaid at harvest
43.	*SPP* III 190 (Greek)	C.E. 710 Arsinoites or Heracleopolites	Elias, a deacon	Cosmas, a weaver	½ *solidus*
44.	*P.KRU* 58 (Coptic)	C.E. 765(?) Djeme	Shenute, a *presbyteros*	Petrus	2 *solidi* upon security of a house
45.	*BKU* III 364 (Coptic)	C.E. 783/784 Heracleopolis magna	Apa NN, (a priest ?) of the church of St. John	Paseth, a man from Heracleopolis	2 *solidi*, to be repaid with wine from the crop of the next harvest (sale on delivery)
46.	*CPR* IV 54 (Coptic)	8th cent. Hermopolites	Apa Daniel, *oikonomos* of the monastery of Pachear in Hermopolis	Ioseph, son of Mena	2¼ *keratia*
47.	*CPR* IV 55 (Coptic)	8th cent. Fayoum	Phausthe, a deacon and *collectarius*	Moises, a deacon and *lebposhen* (= *leitourgos*)	1(?) *solidus*
48.	**BKU* I 67 (Coptic)	date unknown Thebes	Apa Isak, a priest (?)	NN	unknown
49.	**BKU* III 365 (Coptic)	date unknown Hermopolites	Apa Herwodj, a *hegoumenos* (?) from Hermopolis	Basile	unknown (9 *solidi*?)
50.	**BKU* III 421 (Coptic)	date unknown Hermopolites	Apa Damiane, a *presbyteros* from Hermopolis	Kamoul, oil-manufacturer (*elaiourgos*)	80 boxes (?) of unguent (*smema*) (sale on delivery?)

---

[61] Published in Bacot 2002.

No.	Text	Date and provenance	Creditor	Debtor	Object of debt
51.	*BKU* III 422 (Coptic)	date unknown Hermopolites	Apa Damiane, a *presbyteros* (the creditor of BKU III 421)	NN	unknown (sale on delivery)
52.	**BKU* III 424 (Coptic)	date unknown Hermopolites	Apa Kerkorie and NN	Kapai and NN	unknown (money)
53.	*O.Crum* 165 (Coptic)	date unknown Thebais, Djeme	Apa Hello, a monk	Ioseph, son of Iakob	½ *trimesion*, to be repaid with wheat? (sale on delivery?)
54.	*P.Lond.Copt.* 1039 (Coptic)	date unknown Hermopolites	Theodosius, a deacon	Athanasius	20 jars of wine

D. Clerics and Monks as Private Debtors

No.	Text	Date and provenance	Creditor	Debtor	Object of debt
55.	*P.Rain.Cent.* 86 (Greek)	C.E. 381 Heracleopolites	Aurelius Leontius	Aurelius Kephalon, a deacon of the *katholike ekklesia* from the village Tamoro	5 *solidi* "with interest," to be repaid with flax, against pledge (sale on delivery? *datio in solutum*?)
56.	*P.Mich.* XIII 669 (Greek)	C.E. 526 or 544 Aphrodito	NN, a woman bearing the title *eulabestate* (an abbess?)	Victor son of Besarion, a *presbyteros*; Apollos, son of Dioscorus; Senuthes, son of Apollos	3 *solidi* at 12.5%
57.	*P.Cair.Masp.* II 67126 (Greek)	C.E. 541 Aphrodito (Constantinople)	Flavius Anastasius, a banker (*argyroprates*) in Constantinople	Flavius Apollos and Flavius Victor, a *presbyteros* of the church of Aphrodito	20 *solidi* at 8% interest, to be returned after 4 months
58.	*P.Cair. Masp.* II 67128 (Greek)	C.E. 547 Aphrodito	Dioscorus, *protokometes* of Aphrodito	Psais, a deacon from Aphrodito	1 *solidus* less 2 *keratia*, resulting from a lease agreement disguised as a debt acknowledgement
59.	*P.Cair. Masp.* II 67129 (Greek)	C.E. 549 Aphrodito	Dioscorus, *protokometes* of Aphrodito	Psais, a *presbyteros* from Aphrodito (the debtor of *P.Cair.Masp.* II 67128)	2 *solidi* less 4 *keratia*, resulting from a lease agreement disguised as a debt acknowledgement

60.	*P.Cair. Masp.* II 67251 (Greek)	C.E. 549 Aphrodito	Dioscorus, *protokometes* of Aphrodito	Iakubis, a *presbyteros*	1 *solidus* less 2 *keratia*, resulting from a lease agreement
61.	*P.Cair. Masp.* II 67130 (Greek)	C.E. 557 Aphrodito	Dioscorus, *protokometes* of Aphrodito	Mousaios, a deacon from Aphrodito	unknown (arrangement similar to *P.Cair.Masp.* II 67128 and 67129?)
62.	*P.Oxy.* XVI 1972 (Greek)	C.E. 560 Oxyrhynchus	Apphous	Anoup, a *presbyteros* (with his brother acting as surety)	unknown
63.	*P.Cair.Masp.* II 67162 (Greek)	C.E. 568 Antinoe	Flavius Christophorus, a landowner from Antinoe	Iohannes, a deacon from the monastery of Apa Victor in Pindaros in the Antinoite	2 *solidi* less 10 *keratia*, to be repaid after 2 months, *atokos*
64.	*P.Oxy.* XVI 1892 (Greek)	C.E. 581 Oxyrhynchus	Epimachos, overseer (*epikeimenos*) of the imperial estate	Hareotes, a *presbyteros* of the Holy (episcopal?) church	3 *solidi*, to be repaid in three installments over three years, against security of a half *aroura*
65.	*CPR* IV 63 (Coptic)	7th cent. Hermopolites	NN and Polideuke from Tsesio and NN from Hermopolis	NN and Kolluthe, a *presbyteros*	12 *solidi*
66.	*CPR* IV 75 (Coptic)	7th cent. Hermopolites	Apa Isak from Hermopolis?	Victor, a deacon from Hermopolis?	1 *solidus*
67.	*CPR* IV 85 (Coptic)	7th-8th cent. Hermopolites	Apa Phiobammon from Hermopolis	Shenuti, a deacon	money? to be repaid partially with commodities?
68.	*O.Medin.HabuCopt.* 131 (Coptic)	7th-8th cent. Thebes, Djeme	Euha	David, a deacon	1 *ho* of wheat, "without interest until Pauni"
69.	*O.Vind.Copt.* 287 (Coptic)	7th-8th cent. Thebais	Eusebius	Apa Iohannes, a *presbyteros*	1 *solidus*
70.	**CPR* IV 29 (Coptic)	8th cent. Heracleopolis	Christodothe, a woman from Heracleopolis	Georgi, creditor's brother, a deacon	money (doubtful if a real debt, probably division of inheritance)
71.	*CPR* IV 64 (Coptic)	8th cent. Arsinoites	Theodoros, son of Papa Hamai	Theophilos and Shenuti, a *presbyteros*	1 *solidus* 1 *keration* for the payment of the *demosion*-tax
72.	*O.Brit.Mus.Copt.* II, 10 (Coptic)	8th cent.? Thebes, Deir el-Bahri	Hiob from the *kastron* of Djeme	Victor, a *presbyteros*	4 *trimesia*
See also *CPR* IV 55; *O.Crum* 194, **O.Crum* 311.					

E. Lending and Borrowing within Monasteries

Note: These texts could be, in theory, distributed among TABLES A, B, C, and D, according to whether they feature particular monks or monasteries as creditors or debtors. However, since they can be connected to several better-known monasteries, they are better studied together as groups and not separately. I assume that in texts with established monastic provenance at least one of the parties was a monk, even if a particular document does not mention this (anymore).

All monks come from the monastery named in the respective heading, unless stated otherwise.

No.	Text	Date and provenance	Creditor	Debtor	Object of debt
		Heracleopolite monastery of Hathor			
	P.Neph. 1, 2, 4, 5, 6, 7, 8	mid 4th cent.	Paulos, an agent (?) of the monastery in Alexandria	Papnuthis, a monk	16 *artabai* of wheat
		Hermopolite monastery of Apa Apollo			
73.	P.Athen.Xyla 18 (Greek)	C.E. 487/488	a monk (?)	Aurelius Victor	6 *solidi* less 15 *keratia*
74.	SB XXII 15322 (Greek)	C.E. 535	Aurelius NN, a camel-driver (and a monk?)	Aurelius Abraham from Magdolon Mega in the Hermopolite	money (?)
75.	P.Amst. I 47 (Greek)	C.E. 537	Serenos, *archimandrites* of the monastery	Aurelius NN from a village in the Hermopolite	unknown amount of money, to be repaid with new wine (sale on delivery)
76.	P.Amst. I 48 (Greek)	6th cent.	Serenos, *archimandrites* of the monastery of Apa Apollo	NN, a villager from the Hermopolite	unknown amount of money, to be repaid with 450 *knidia* of wine (sale on delivery)
77.	P.Athen.Xyla 5 (Greek)	C.E. 539	Apa Anouphis, a monk	Aurelius Mathias from Moirai in the Coussite	1 *solidus*
78.	SB XVI 12267 (Greek)	C.E. 540	Aurelius Apollos, a monk	Aurelius NN, *protokometes* of Senthrypis in the Hermopolite	Unknown amount of wine (not a sale on delivery)
79.	P.Athen.Xyla 10 (Greek)	C.E. 543	Apa Phibis, a monk and chief manufacurer of oil in the monastery of Apa Apollo	Aurelius Phoibammon from Demetriou in the Hermopolite	7 *solidi* less 42 *keratia*

80.	*P.Athen.Xyla 17 (Greek)	C.E. 548/549?	NN, a monk (?)	Aurelius Phoibammon	1 *solidus* less 6 *keratia*, to be repaid in kind from the next crop (sale on delivery ?)
81.	P.Athen.Xyla 6 (Greek)	6th cent.	NN, a monk (?)	NN from Demetriou in the Hermopolite	unknown amount of money, to be repaid with 150 *metra* of wine (sale on delivery)
82.	P.Athen.Xyla 12 (Greek)	6th cent. ?	Apa Andreas, a monk (?)	Aurelius Anoup	1 *solidus* less 6 *keratia*
83.	P.PalauRib. 243a (Greek)	6th cent.	NN, a monk	NN	unknown (sale on delivery ?)
84.	SB XX 15596 (Greek)	6th cent.	Abba Phoibammon, a monk (?)	Aurelius Matheias from Tanemois in the Hermopolite	unknown amount of money, to be repaid with 3⅓ *artabai* of wheat (sale on delivery)
85.	P.Mon.Apollo 36 (Coptic)	6th cent. ?	Apa Enoch, a monk	Victor from Esou in the Hermopolite	30 *sextarii* of oil, to be repaid after the olive harvest (sale on delivery ?)
86.	SB XX 15595 (Greek)	6th-7th cent.	Abba Apollos, a monk	Aurelius Anouphis from Tanemios in the Hermopolite	unknown amount of money, to be repaid with 150 *metra* of wine (sale on delivery)
87.	P.Mon.Apollo 37 (Coptic)	6th-7th cent.	Paule, a monk	Ieremias, a monk of the *topos* of […]ammon	unknown, secured by pledges
88.	SBKopt. II 923 (Coptic)	6th-7th cent.	Apa Ienoch, a monk	Pia, a woman from Tahrouj in the Hermopolite	unknown
89.	P.Mon.Apollo 39 (Coptic)	7th cent.	NN, a monk	Pesoou, a monk	3 *solidi* less […] *keratia*
90.	P.Mon.Apollo 41 (Coptic)	7th cent.	Hor, a monk	Enoch, a monk	5 *solidi*
91.	P.Mon.Apollo 34 (Coptic)	7th-8th cent.	Kosma, a monk	Anoup and Kolthe, headmen of Migdol of the Four Villages in the Hermopolite	1 *solidus* to be repaid with 13 ounces of oil and 10 *artabai* of wheat (sale on delivery ?)
92.	P.Mon.Apollo 42 (Coptic)	7th-8th cent.	Shoi, a monk	Paule, a monk (of the same monastery ?)	½ *solidus*
93.	*P.Duke inv. 811 (Coptic)	7th-8th cent.	NN	NN, a monk (?)	1 (?) *solidus*

94.	*P.YaleCopt.* 18 (Coptic)	7th-8th cent.	NN and Victor, brothers and monks from the monastery of Apa Ma[.]ltes (?)	brother Cosma, a monk	5 *solidi* and 1 *trimesion*, to be repaid at the harvest time
95.	*P.Mon.Apollo* 35 (Coptic)	8th cent.	NN, a monk ?	NN	unknown commodity, 'worth forty…'
96.	*P.Mon.Apollo* 38 (Coptic)	8th cent.	the *dikaion* of the monastery, through its head Apa Theodoros	NN, a monk	2 *solidi*
97.	**P.Mon.Apollo* 43 (Coptic)	8th cent.	Constantine, a monk	Paule, a monk	unknown
98.	**P.Mon.Apollo* 44 (Coptic)	8th cent.	a monk	a monk (?)	unknown amount of wine to be repaid with money, more than 1 *solidus* (?) (sale on payment ?)
99.	**P.Mich.Copt.* 21 (Coptic)	10th cent. ?	Apa Ioannes, a monk (?)	Pyew, from […] in the Hermopolite	20 (?) *sextarii* of wine (*not* a sale on delivery)
100.	*P.Mon.Apollo* 40 (Coptic)	unknown	NN	Loukas, a monk	15 *folles* of gold
	Apollonopolite monastery of Apa Apollo (Bala'izah)				
101.	*P.Bal.* 102 (Coptic)	7th-8th cent.	Apa Amorou, monk and *shaliou* (= *pistikos*)	the *dikaion* of the monastery, through Apa Kyre, the *proestos*	8 *solidi* for the payment of the *demosion*, to be repaid with commodities (6 *solidi* with lentils, 2 *solidi* with honey or lentils)
102.	*P.Bal.* 103 (Coptic)	7th-8th cent.	Apa Ammone, a monk	the *dikaion* of the monastery, through Apa Psha, the *proestos*	1 *solidus* for the payment of the *demosion*, to be repaid with 10 *artabai* of wheat
103.	*P.Bal.* 108 (Coptic)	7th-8th cent.	the *dikaion* of the monastery of Apa Apollo (?)	NN	unknown
104.	**P.Bal.* 111 (Coptic)	7th-8th cent.	the *dikaion* of the monastery of Apa Apollo (?)	NN	unknown
105.	*P.Bal.* 112 (Coptic)	7th-8th cent.	NN, a monk (?)	NN	4 *solidi*

106.	P.Bal. 114 (Coptic)	7th-8th cent.	Lampou, monk and deacon	Iakob and George from Pnom[..]ets in the Antinoopolites, monks (of the monastery of Apollo?)	1 *solidus*, to be repaid with wine (sale on delivery)
107.	*P.Bal. 115 (Coptic)	7th-8th cent.	Iohannes, a monk (?)	unknown, possibly the *dikaion* of the monastery through Isaac, its *proestos*, who assents to the document	4 *solidi* 8½ *keratia* to be repaid "from the harvest of the 5th indiction" (sale on delivery? *datio in solutum*?)
108.	*P.Bal. 116 (Coptic)	7th-8th cent.	NN	NN, possibly *presbyteros* A[…], who assents to the document	unknown number of *solidi*, to be repaid with 7 jars of wine "from the harvest of the 14th indiction" (sale on delivery?)
109.	P.Bal. 293 (Coptic)	7th-8th cent.	deacon Severos: ⅓ *solidus* Apa Diometes: 4⅔ *solidi* Apa Iohannes from Lahmef: ⅓ *solidus* Apa Isaac and Theodoros: ⅔ *solidus* Apa Kyri and Zacharias: 1 *solidus* Ioseph the shoemaker: ⅓ *solidus*	monastery of Apa Apollo	

Theban monastery of Apa Epiphanius

110.	O.Mon.Epiph. 90 (Coptic)	7th cent.	NN	a *presbyteros* (?) of the *topos* of Apa (Epiphanius?)	unknown amount of money, to be repaid with 50 jars (*aggen*) of wine from the next harvest (sale on delivery)
111.	O.Mon.Epiph. 91 (Coptic)	7th cent.	Enoch	Zekaiel, a *presbyteros*	3 *artabai* of wheat to be repaid in Pauni
112.	O.Mon.Epiph. 92 (Coptic)	7th cent.	Iohannes and Abraham, traders	Hello, a monk (?)	7 *solidi*
113.	O.Mon.Epiph. 94 (Coptic)	7th cent.	NN	Isaac and Elias, monks	some commodity

Bibliography

Bacot, S. (2002). "Une nouvelle attestation de 'la petra d'Apa Mèna' ou sud d'Assiout," *BIFAO* 102, 1-16.

Bagnall, R. (1977). "Price in 'Sales on Delivery'," *GRBS* 18 (1977), 85-96 (= R. Bagnall, *Later Roman Egypt: Society, Religion, Economy and Administration*, Aldershot: Ashgate, 2003, XV).

Bagnall, R. (1993). *Egypt in Late Antiquity*, Princeton: Princeton University Press.

Bianchi, E. (1984a). "In tema d'usuria. Canoni conciliari e legislazione imperiale del IV secolo. I," *Atheneum* 61, 321-342.

Bianchi, E. (1984b). "In tema d'usuria. Canoni conciliari e legislazione imperiale del IV secolo. II," *Atheneum* 62, 136-153.

Clackson, S. (2008). *It is Our Father Who Writes: Orders from the Monastery of Apollo at Bawit* (= *American Studies in Papyrology* 43). Oxford: Oxbow 2008.

Delattre, A. (2004). "Un contrat de prêt copte du monastère de Baouît," *CdÉ* 79, 385-389.

Derda, T. and Wipszycka, E. (1994). "L'emploi des titres *abba, apa* et *papas* dans l'Égypte byzantine," *JJP* 24, 23-56.

Foraboschi, D. and Gara, A. (1982). "L'economia dei crediti in natura (Egitto)," *Athenaeum* 60, 69-83.

Gofas, D. (2002). "Byzantine Law of Interest," in: Laiou, A. (ed.), *The Economic History of Byzantium*, Dumbarton Oaks, vol. 3, 1095-1104.

Hagemann, H. R. (1956). "Die rechtliche Stellung der christlichen Wohltätigkeitsanstalten in der östlichen Reichshälfte," *RIDA* 3, 265-283.

Jakab, É. (1999). "Guarantee and Jars in Sales of Wine on Delivery," *JJP* 29, 33-44.

Keenan, J. G. (1984). "Aurelius Apollos and the Aphrodite Village Élite," *Atti del XVII Congresso Internazionale di Papirologia, III*, Napoli: Centro internazionale per lo studio dei papiri ercolanesi, 957-963.

Kramer B., Shelton, J. C. and Browne, G. M. (1987). *Das Archiv des Nepheros und verwandte Texte*, Mainz a. Rhein, 24-25 and 29-30.

Kühnert, H. (1965). *Zum Kreditgeschäft in den hellenistischen Papyri Ägyptens bis Diokletian*, Ph.D. thesis Freiburg.

MacCoull, L. S. B. (1988). *Dioscorus of Aphrodito. His Work and His World*, Berkeley/Los Angeles/London: University of California Press.

MacCoull, L. S. B. (1993). "The Apa Apollos Monastery of Pharoou (Aphrodito) and its Papyrus Archive," *Le Muséon* 106, 21-63.

Markiewicz, T. (2002). "P.Duke inv. 469: A Papyrus Illustrating *sacramentum corporaliter praestitum* in Coptic Egypt," in: Derda, T., Urbanik, J. and Wecowski, M. (eds.), *Studies Presented to Benedetto Bravo and Ewa Wipszycka by Their Disciples*, Warsaw, 193-200.

Mickwitz, G. (1932). *Geld und Wirtschaft im römischen Reich des 4. Jahrhunderts n. Chr.*, Helsinki: Akademische Buchhandlung, 207-225.

Pestman, P. W. (1971). "Loans Bearing No Interest?," *JJP* 16, 7-30.

Preissner, H. (1954). *Das verzinsliche und das zinslose Darlehen in den byzantinischen Papyri des 6./7. Jahrhunderts*, Ph.D. thesis Erlangen.

Rémondon, R. (1972). "L'Église dans la société égyptienne à l'époque byzantine," *CdÉ* 47, 254-277.

Schmelz, G. (2002). *Kirchliche Amtsträger im spätantiken Ägypten nach den Aussagen der griechischen und koptischen Papyri und Ostraka*, Leipzig : K.G. Saur.

Sijpestijn, P. J. (1991). "οὐράνιος ἡ καὶ ζωοποιὸς μονάζουσα. Kauf von Fässern gegen Vorauszählung," *Tyche* 6, 197-199.

Steinwenter, A. (1930). "Die Rechtsstellung der Kirchen und Klöster nach den Papyri," *Zeitschrift der Savigny-Stiftung*, Kan. Abt., 19, 1-50.

Tenger, B. (1993), *Die Verschuldung im römischen Ägypten (1.-2. Jh. n. Chr.)*, St. Katherinen: Scripta Mercaturae Verlag.

Wipszycka, E. (1972). *Les resources et les activités économiques des églises en Égypte du IVe au VIIIe siècle*, Bruxelles: Fondation Égyptologique Reine Élisabeth.

Wipszycka, E. (2001). "Le fonctionnement interne des monastères et des laures en Égypte du point de vue économique," *JJP* 31, 169-186.

Zilliacus, H. (1954). "The Stolen Anchor," *Arctos* 1, 199-208.

THE CULTIVATION OF MONASTIC ESTATES IN LATE ANTIQUE AND EARLY ISLAMIC EGYPT: SOME EVIDENCE FROM COPTIC LAND LEASES AND RELATED DOCUMENTS[*]

TONIO SEBASTIAN RICHTER

INTRODUCTION

The following survey on cultivation of monastic estates according to the evidence from Coptic leases is in three parts. First, I sketch out the evidence, particularly as it relates to the occurrence of monks and monasteries in Coptic lease documents. Next, I deal with two documents from the dossier worked on by Sarah Clackson, the Coptic papyri from the Hermopolite monastery of Apa Apollo. In an analysis of *P.Mon.Apollo* 26, a text which is called *misthôsis*, although it differs conspicuously from all other Coptic *misthôsis* documents, I will argue that this text, which attests to two monks taking possession of land belonging to the monastery's estate, has a functional counterpart in *P.Mon.Apollo* 25, which records a monk's renunciation of land from his monastery's estate. Finally, I will reconsider a crucial issue connected with the *P.Mon.Apollo* dossier, the *aparchê* collection, and I will try to show how *P.Mon.Apollo* 25 and 26 could have been related to the *aparchê* collection documents.

1. COPTIC LEASE DOCUMENTS AND THE EGYPTIAN MONASTERIES

1.1 *General Remarks*

Unlike the Greek,[1] Demotic[2] and Arabic[3] land-leasing dossiers which have been assembled and thoroughly investigated over the last century, the Coptic lease documents—a collection of more then 100 items—are scattered over several editions, some of which are still provisional, and they have scarcely been analyzed or interpreted.[4] Apart from occasional, but significant, references to lessors, lessees, and leases in private and business letters and in literary texts, Coptic evidence of land-leasing

---

[*] I should like to express my gratitude to Petra Sijpesteijn and James Clackson, the organizers of the Oxford conference *The Administration of Monastic Estates in Late Antique and Early Islamic Egypt*, for giving me opportunity to pay a small tribute to the memory of Sarah Clackson.

[1] Fundamental studies by Waszynski 1905, Comfort 1933 and 1937, Herrmann 1958, Hennig 1967, Hengstl 1972 and *P.Heid.* V; cf. also the abundant literature on particular issues based on those works, such as Banaji 1999 and 2001, Jördens 1999, Oates 1963, Rathbone 1990 and 1991, Rowlandson 1994, 1996 and 1999, Ruffing 1999 and Schnebel 1925, to give only some outstanding examples.

[2] Cf. Hughes 1952; Seidl 1973; Eyre 1997; Felber 1997; Manning 1999; Mrsich 2003.

[3] Cf. Grohman 1935-; Frantz-Murphy 1986, 1994, 1999 and 2001.

[4] I try to fill this gap by my habilitation thesis "Pacht nach koptischen Quellen. Beiträge zur Rechts-, Wirtschafts- und Sozialgeschichte des byzantinischen und früharabischen Ägypten," to be published in the *Papyrologica Vindobonensia*.

comes from two legal formulae in particular: lease contracts (better termed lease declarations, since they are usually unilateral in style), and rent receipts confirming the annual payments for leasehold property. Coptic lease documents fall into three groups with regard to provenance: Fayyumic, Hermupolite and Theban. As a fourth provenance, Aphrodito is attested by the 6th or 7th century Coptic lease document P.BL inv. 2849, but this important text is still unpublished. The small *Fayyum* dossier, although interesting, may be left out of consideration here.[5] The Hermupolite and Antinooupolite area is a major source of byzantine Greek documents, and it also yields the bulk of Coptic lease documents. The overall formal similarity between Coptic and Greek documents of this provenance is striking. Leases on limited time, called ⲙⲓⲥⲑⲱⲥⲓⲥ,[6] as well as long-term agreements, called ⲉⲙⲫⲩⲧⲉⲩⲥⲓⲥ, ⲉⲙⲫⲩⲧⲉⲩⲧⲓⲕⲏ ϩⲟⲙⲟⲗⲟⲅⲓⲁ, etc.,[7] are clearly modelled on the respective Greek forms. Both types of agreements are also attested in rent receipts, issued to acknowledge payments of *phoros* and *pakton*.[8] The latest attested lease document drawn up in the Coptic language, dated in 900 C.E., comes from Ashmunein.[9] From the *Theban area* in the Byzantine and early Arabic period, for which there are scarcely any Greek documents attested, we have two Coptic *misthôsis* texts[10] and some twenty so-called *epitropê* documents,[11] all of which are written on potsherds or limestone pieces. According to the *epitropê* formula, the issuer/owner authorizes somebody to sow a plot of his or her estate.[12] To the

---

[5] *CPR* IV 120; 126-127; 129a = *CPR* II 131. One of four relevant documents, *CPR* IV 120, has been issued by a tenant bearing the title ⲡⲁⲡⲁ to a lessor in the rank of a diacon.

[6] I know of some forty *misthôsis* documents: *BKU* III 347; 348; *CPR* IV 117-119; 121-124; 129c-f; *CPR* II 139 (= *CPR* IV 129b); P.Heid. inv. Kopt. 38; P.Heid. inv. Kopt. 276; *P.Laur.Copt.* 193; *P.Lond.Copt.* I 1016; 1019; 1021-1022; 1067; 1073; *P.Mon.Apollo* 26 (=*P.HermitageCopt.* 3); *P.Ryl.Copt.* 158-159; 161-164; 166-168; 170; 173, and a number of fragments from the Beinecke library which I am about to reedit.

[7] I know of seven *emphyteusis* documents: *CPR* IV 128; *P.Lond.Copt.* I 1013-1015; *P.Ryl.Copt.* 174-176.

[8] I know of thirty rent receipts, eleven of them mentioning *phoros* (corresponding to *misthôsis*) and nineteen mentioning *pakton* (corresponding to *emphyteusis*): Phoros: *CPR* IV 134-141; P.Heid. inv. Kopt. 45; *P.HermitageCopt.* 4; *P.Ryl.Copt.* 181. Pakton: BL Or 6201 A 22a; 6201 A 22b; 6201 A 23; 6201 A 66; 6201 A 68; 6201 A 103; *CPR* IV 146-153; P.Beatty Copt. inv. 2177.7; *P.Lond.Copt.* I 1027; 1056; *P.Ryl.Copt.* 179-180. On terminologal issues, cf. Richter 2002a.

[9] *P.Lond.Copt.* I 487, reedited by Richter 2003. This text is no longer influenced by Greek legal language, but employs Arabic terms and concepts. It deals with a *qabāla bi-lā misāḥa* 'tenancy without survey' (cf. Frantz-Murphy 2001).

[10] *BKU* I 82; *O.CrumVC* 33.

[11] *BKU* I 40; 48; 64; 75; 79; 95; *O.Brit.Mus.Copt.* I 35/4; *O.Crum* 138-139; 206; 307; 482; *O.Crum Ad.* 26; *O.CrumST* 38-39; *O.CrumVC* 28; *O.Engelbach* 3; *O.Medin.HabuCopt.* 81; *O.Theb.* 6; *O.Vind.Copt.* 42 (= *O.CrumST* 37).

[12] See here the form of an *epitropê* with fixed rent (*pakton*) in money (e.g. *BKU* I 79):

+ ⲁⲛⲟⲕ (landowner) ⲉⲧ-ⲥϩⲁⲓ ⲛ-(tenant) ϫⲉ	It is I, *A*, who writes to *B*:
ϯ-ⲉⲡⲓⲧⲣⲉⲡⲉ ⲛⲁ⸗ⲕ ⲉ-ⲧⲣⲉ⸗ⲕ-ϫⲟ (object)	I admit you, that you shall sow …
ϩⲙ-ⲡ-ϫⲟ ⲉϩⲣⲁⲓ ⲛ-ϯ-ⲣⲟⲙⲡⲉ (ind.-year *x*)	in the sowing of this year *x*,
ⲛⲅ-ϯ-ⲡⲉⲩ-ⲡⲁⲕⲧⲟⲛ ⲛⲁ⸗ⲓ ⲉⲧⲉ-(amount)	and you shall give me their *pakton*, being …
ⲛⲧⲁ-ⲣⲟⲉⲓⲥ ⲡ⸗ⲕ-ⲁϭⲏⲙⲓⲟⲥ ϩⲛ-ϩⲱⲃ ⲛⲓⲙ	and I shall keep you free from penalty in every respect.
ⲉ-ⲩ-ⲱⲣϫ ⲛⲁ⸗ⲕ ⲁ⸗ⲓ-ⲥⲙⲛ ϯ-ⲉⲡⲓⲧⲣⲟⲡⲏ	For your security, I have drawn up this *epitropê*,
ⲉ⸗ⲥ-ⲟⲣϫ ⲉ⸗ⲥ-ϭⲛϭⲟⲙ ϩⲙ-ⲙⲁ ⲛⲓⲙ	it is sure and valid at every place.
ⲁⲛⲟⲕ (landowner) ϯ-ⲥⲧⲟⲓⲭ/	I, *A*, I agree.

best of my knowledge, only four Greek documents of this type are hitherto known.[13] The conspicuous use of the term *epitrepein* in these texts may be considered a semantic calque on the Demotic verb *shn* "to lease," literally, "to command, to confide."[14] There are also a few Theban rent receipts.[15]

The economic activities of monasteries and churches with respect to their estates have been much discussed,[16] but only a few scholars, Sarah Clackson among them, have made use of the rich Coptic evidence.[17] In all the types of Coptic lease documents so far mentioned, there is evidence for monks and monasteries acting in several different ways. In the following I want to discuss just a number of more conspicious cases.

1.2 *Monasteries as Owners of Leasehold Property*

Monasteries often occur as lessors of land, acting through their *dikaion* and represented by an *oikonomos*, *phrontistês* or *pronoêtês*. This is the case in Coptic *misthôsis* documents[18] as well as in *emphyteusis* documents[19] and rent receipts[20] of the Hermopolite group.[21] While *misthôsis* documents

---

Apart from documents with fixed rent amounts in money or kinds, there is a second *epitropê* type containing a sharecropping clause (e.g. *O.Vind.Copt.* 42).

[13] *O.Wilcken* 1224, *PSI* III 279, *SB* XX 14353, and *O.Qurnat* Mar^{c}y inv. 249. I owe my knowledge of the latter to Jean-Luc Fournet.

[14] The meaning of the Demotic verb *shn* lies somewhere in the semantic area of "beauftragen" (Erichsen, Dem. Glossar 446), "überlassen, anvertrauen" (Felber 1997: 116-119), "confier" (Pestman, Recueil II 102), "to hand over to a persons care" (Pestman, *P.Survey*, 150, Anm. c), while the Greek word *epitrepein* means "auftragen, anbefehlen, gestatten, zulassen, erlauben" (Preisigke, Wb. I 582/3) "to commit, to entrust to, to rely upon, to leave to, to yield up, to permit, to command" (*LSJ* 667/8). I imagine the Theban Coptic term ⲉⲡⲓⲧⲣⲉⲡⲉ ⲛⲁ⸗ acquired its legal meaning from the Demotic expression *shn n≠*, both expressions literally meaning "to commit to somebody, to authorize somebody." The designation ⲉⲡⲓⲧⲣⲟⲡⲏ of these documents may have likewise been shaped semantically by the Demotic noun *shn* "lease document."

[15] *BKU* I 65; *O.Brit.Mus.Copt.* I 87/1; *O.Crum* 169; *O.CrumST* 70. The Theban term usually designating lease rent is *pakton*, see Richter 2002a.

[16] Cf. e.g. de Zulueta 1909; Gascou 1985; Hardy 1931.

[17] Such as Artur Steinwenter 1958, the doyen of Coptic juristic papyrology, in his study *Kirchliches Vermögensrecht der Papyri*, Éwa Wipszycka 1972 in her fundamental study *Ressources et activités économiques des églises en Égypte du IVe au VIIIe siècle*, or Georg Schmelz 2002 in his work on church officials in late antique Egypt.

[18] E.g. *CPR* IV 117 (land owner is the "*dikaion* of S. Theodor"); *P.Ryl.Copt.* 163 (land owner is a "holy monastery"); 164 (owner is the "*dikaion* of the monastery of St. Severos"); 166 (land owner is the "*dikaion* of the holy Topos of [...]").

[19] E.g. *CPR* IV 128: (owner is the "*dikaion* of the holy chapel of [...]"); *P.Lond.Copt.* I 1013 (issued by the *patêrion* of a *philoponeion*); *P.Ryl.Copt.* 174 (owner is the "holy *dikaion* of [...]").

[20] *Phoros* receipts: e.g. *CPR* IV 140 (issued by the Proestôs of a mosastery), *P.Ryl.Copt.* 181 (issued by the "*dikaion* of the holy altar of St. George"). *Pakton* receipts: e.g. *CPR* IV 147 (issued by the "*dikaion* of the holy altar of St. Herwoj"); 153 (issued by the oikonomos of the "holy topos of [...]"); BL Or 6201 A66, A 22a, A 103; P.Beatty Copt. inv. 2177.7 (from the archive of Lulu, issued by the dikaion of "St. Kollouthos at the gateway"); BL Or 6201 A22b, A23 and A 68 (from the same archive, issued by the monastery of Gabriel); *CPR* IV 146 (issued by the *dikaion* of the "holy monastery of Apa Jeremias in the south of the City Antinou"); *P.Lond.Copt.* I 1027 (issued by the *patêrion* of a *philoponeion*); *CPR* IV 151 (issued by the "*dikaion* of our lords, the apostles"); *P.Lond.Copt.* I 1055a/b (issued by the "*dikaion* of the holy monastery of Phoibammon").

[21] Altogether, nearly 50% of the lessors attested in Coptic *misthôsis* documents and *phoros* receipts from the Hermupolite dossier bear ecclesiastic titles and epithets, although not all of them are explicitly said to be representatives of ecclesiastical institutions such as churches, monasteries and *philoponeia*. In fourteen of twenty-three cases of *emphyteusis*

were styled as the tenant's acknowledgement of the lessor's conditions, Coptic emphyteutic (hereditary) leases were issued in bilateral subjective or even objective style, just like the Greek ones, and were drawn up in two copies, one for each party, lessor and tenant. As is well-known, long-term leasing was a typical strategy used by ecclesiastical institutions in order to earn money from their estates.[22] This custom is also confirmed by the Coptic evidence, only one of seven Coptic emphyteutic contracts does not involve such an institution.[23] However, the Theban dossier appears quite different with regard to the participation of monasteries and churches. There is only one single *epitropê* document where a *dikaion* is mentioned,[24] and few ecclesiastic or monastic titles occur. But it is possible that local monasteries like the one of St. Phoibammôn could have acted through representatives who were not explicitly identified in the documents.[25]

1.3 *Monks and Clergymen Privately Involved in Leases*

At first glance, the case of monks and clergymen privately acting in leases is quite different from the occurrence of monasteries as owners of leasehold property.[26] Unfortunately, it is not easy, if at all possible, to distinguish monks from clergymen, nor is it easy to define the nature of their property and its relationship to the estates of their monasteries or churches. Sometimes, however, we actually meet expressions clearly pointing to a closer kind of relationship. *O.Crum* 138 and 482 were issued by a certain Viktor from the (monastery) of the holy Apa John. *O.Crum* 482 was drawn up, as is said, in the presence of Apa Viktôr the priest from the monastery of Apa Phoibammon, who might be the well-known successor of Bishop Abraham. In *O.Crum* 138, the better preserved document, the issuer does not speak about "my fields" as usual, but he uses the non-possessive expression "*the* fields." This could be a reference to the fact that he was not himself the owner of the plots which he was to let. Another *epitropê* document, *O.CrumST* 37, was drawn up by a diacon called Eustathios. The leasehold property dealt with in the text are "two plots of clay-land under the sloping ground, from the district of Tribu southward up to the end of my district, which (*namely* the first-mentioned two plots) belong to

---

(attested by the contracts and *pakton* receipts), ecclesiastical institutions take part as lessors. However, unless it is indicated, it is difficult to decide what kind of institution it is, whether a church or a monastery. There is a tendency of scholars to consider all institutions called "*dikaion* of St. So-and-so" as monasteries, but some of them can be shown rather to have been churches. E.g. the "holy *thysiasterion* of St. Herwôj" is listed as a monastery by Timm 1984-: 205f. and the "*dikaion* of St. Kollouthos at the gateway" is called a monastery by MacCoull 1986: 200 and Krause 1992: 99, but they were probably churches. The latter occurs in the church list *P.Lond.Copt.* I, 1077, its designation "at the gateway" might have served to distinguish it from another church of St. Kollouthos at that town (*P.Lond.Copt.* I 1100).

[22] See Mitteis 1901; de Zulueta 1909; Gascou 1985; Hardy 1931; Taubenschlag 1938.

[23] *P.Lond.Copt.* I 1014, where a *koinon*, a village community, acts as owner.

[24] *O.Medin.HabuCopt.* 81. The name of the monastery is lost in a gap, but St. Phoibammôn would seem a reasonable candidate (as the monastery is called "in the *jebel* of Jême," but there are some other monasteries located there, e.g. those of the Apa Psate: *P.KRU* 54,34-4; of Apa Pesynthios: *P.KRU* 73,45, etc.).

[25] Theben *epitropê* documents used to be awfully terse in conveying personal datas, in many cases only the parties' Christian names are given. Since the population of Jême was so much smaller than that of, say, Ashmunein, and the kind of business recorded by *epitropê* documents lasted one season only, there was obviously little need of caution as to the identity of persons well known to each other.

[26] Cf. e.g. from *Ashmunein*: *BKU* III 347; *CPR* IV 148; 149; 152; P.Heid. inv. Kopt. 45; *P.HermitageCopt.* 4; *P.Lond.* I 1056; 1073; from the *Theban area*: *BKU* I 48; 79; 95; *O.Crum* 138; 139; 206; 307; 482; *O.CrumST* 37; *O.CrumVC* 28; 30.

(the monastery of) St. Philotheos." This detailed description is of some significance, as two degrees of ownership are indicated. The actual landlord was St. Philotheos, i.e. his monastery, but obviously the issuer holds certain limited rights permitting him to claim a plot as ⲡⲁⲧⲟϣ "my district" (quite an unusual expression) and to authorize a tenant in his own name to cultivate crops on this plot and another one. All this happens without participation of the legal department of the monastery. This observation leads me to the second section.

2. A Monastery Leasing Land to Its Monks

In *P.Mon.Apollo* 26, a document designates itself as a *misthôsis* which varies considerably from all other Coptic *misthôsis* documents with regard to both formulae and content. The document is issued by two monks of the Hermupolite monastery of Apa Apollo and is addressed to the *dikaion* of the same monastery, represented by Apa Georgios, the abbot (*archimandritês*). The fairly well-preserved business clauses (lines 5-10) read as follows:

> You have given us more or less eight waterless artabas in the fields of the little irrigated field, which you have (formerly) exchanged with the inhabitants of Senesla, so that we shall possess them (ⲁⲙⲁϩⲉ ⲉⲣⲟⲟⲩ) and cultivate them with our own hands (ⲁⲩⲧⲟⲩⲣⲅⲉⲓ ⲉⲣⲟⲟⲩ) under (ϩⲁⲣⲁⲧϥ) the Topos and your Fatherhood, from the coming crop of the—with God's will!—eighth indiction, which we are charged with, and ... (*gap*) ... all days of our life.

The last words before the papyrus breaks off, "thus we, the first-mentioned brother Enoch and brother B..., are ready," might indicate the beginning of a clause dealing with the rent payment. The docket, preserved on the *verso*, indicates that the rent was two *nomismata* a year, a considerable amount. There are many oddities in this so-called *misthôsis*. The Coptic verb ⲁⲙⲁϩⲉ, meaning "possession," would fit an emphyteutic context at best, but sounds strange in a *misthôsis* implying much more limited leaseholder rights. There is reason to believe that this expression was chosen in order to make the lessees liable for the land-tax payment, which the lessor would have been charged with otherwise. Also the Greek loan-word ⲁⲩⲧⲟⲩⲣⲅⲉⲓ "execute of oneself, work with one's own hands" is unexpected. According to Hans Förster's dictionary,[27] *P.Mon.Apollo* 26 yields the only instance of the word within the entire corpus of Coptic documentary texts. And even here, its occurrence is remarkable. It was surely the purpose of any lease to excuse the lessors from the burden of fieldwork, and the natural duty of tenants to do the job with their own hands, so why emphasize this fact? Indeed, there is another possible interpretation which cannot be explicitly excluded. In the Greek papyri from Egypt, ⲁⲩⲧⲟⲩⲣⲅⲉⲓ has a special semantic value: according to Preisigke, "to work with one's own hands" may also mean "not to let out on lease."[28] The wording of *P.Mon.Apollo* 26 might thus have been intended to *exclude subletting* of the tenancy by the tenants. If so, this would be a clear difference to cases such as *O.CrumST* 37, where monks apparently had been *permitted to sublet* leasehold property owned by their monastery. A further unique feature of the *misthôsis P.Mon.Apollo* 26 is its term of

---

[27] Förster 2002, s.v., p. 125.
[28] Preisigke 1925-, vol. I: 243.

validity: unlike usual terms of *misthôsis* agreements which run from one year to ten or twelve years (in a few cases), this agreement was practically unlimited, lasting "all the days" of the tenants' life. Another document from the *P.Mon.Apollo* dossier, number 25, seems to be closely connected with the strange *misthôsis* document *P.Mon.Apollo* 26:[29] a monk claims himself unable to make further payments of land-tax for a plot of swampy ground which is "upon" him (ϩⲓϫⲱ=ⲓ)[30] as he says, and he formally renounces every right to—and any liability for—this plot. His renunciation is addressed to the *dikaion* of the monastery, represented by its abbot Apa Daniêl, who is said to have previously granted his permission to this transaction. Thus *P.Mon.Apollo* 25 bears evidence for the reversal of the procedure attested by *P.Mon.Apollo* 26.

3. THE RIDDLE OF THE APARCHÊ COLLECTION

Anybody acquainted with Sarah Clackson's *magnum opus* knows the most intriguing issue connected with a certain type of documents in the *P.Mon.Apollo* dossier: what was the function and setting of the undertaking called *aparchê* (literally, "first-fruit") collection? Comprising twenty-three items in *P.Mon.Apollo*, it is by far the best attested business transaction carried out and recorded by the monks,[31] yet the institution is still far from clear to us. There are two main formulae, rediscovered and reconstructed by Sarah: The better preserved formula, which she called "Tithe collection guarantee,"[32] works as follows.[33] A monk issues a document styled as an acknowledgement of debt (and even named as such, *asphaleia*) to a fellow monk, acknowledging the *receipt* of (one or more) *villages* (instead of a loan in money or in kind, as it were). In these villages, a so-called "*aparchê* for Apa Apollo" is to be

---

[29] *P.Mon.Apollo* 25,3-6: "As two places were upon me, poverty befell me (and) I was no longer able to manage (*dioikein*) both of them. I requested some trustworthy brethren from the monastery and they requested your Fatherhood on my behalf. Your mercy met me, you took one of them (i.e. the two places) from me, that makes the half of the swampy ground, and you seized the brother Jeremias and loaded it onto him, so that he shall be liable for its taxes (*dêmosia*). Now I renounce my plot from the swampy ground."

[30] The precise meaning of this expression has been debated by Krause 1985: 147 *contra* Brunsch 1981: 97. I have suggested elsewhere that the legal meaning of ϩⲓϫⲱ= "being upon somebody" implies *liability* for something rather than possession, cf. Richter 2004: 177.

[31] *P.Mon.Apollo* 1-23, see Clackson 2000: 47-76.

[32] Clackson 2000: 47-57, *P.Mon.Apollo* 1-7.

[33] See here the form of the "Tithe collection guarantee" (*P.Mon.Apollo* 1-7, ed. Clackson 2000):

ⲁⲛⲟⲕ ⲡⲁⲥⲟⲛ … ⲉⲓⲥϩⲁⲓ ⲛ(ⲡⲁⲥⲟⲛ) …	I, the brother NN, am writing to (the brother) NN.
ϫⲉ ⲉⲡⲉⲓⲇⲏ ⲁⲕ(ⲥⲉⲙ)ⲡⲉⲓⲑⲉ ⲛⲙⲙⲁⲓ	After you have agreed with me,
ⲁⲕϯ ⲛⲁⲓ ⲛ-(place name)	you have given me the (village[s]) A(, B, C)
ⲉⲧⲣⲁⲥⲱⲕ ⲧⲉ=ϥ/ⲥ/ⲩ-ⲁⲡⲁⲣⲭⲏ ϩⲁ ⲁⲡⲁ ⲁⲡⲟⲗⲗⲟ	so that I collect its/their *aparchê* for Apa Apollo
ϩⲙⲡⲕⲁⲣⲡⲟⲥ ⲛⲧⲣⲟⲙⲡⲉ ⲧⲁⲓ … ⲓⲛⲁ./	in the crop of the *x*th year of indiction
ϩⲁⲡⲉ=ϥ/ⲥ/ⲩ-ⲇⲏⲙⲟⲥⲓⲟⲛ/ⲡⲁⲕⲧⲟⲛ ⲉⲧⲉⲡⲁⲓ ⲡⲉ …	for its/their *dêmosion* (or: *pakton*), makes (amount).
ⲧⲉⲛⲟⲩ ⲟⲩⲛ ϩⲙⲟⲩⲱϣ ⲙⲡⲛⲟⲩⲧⲉ ϯⲟ ⲛϩⲉⲧⲟⲓⲙⲟⲥ	Now, with god's will, I am ready,
ⲧⲁⲧⲁⲁ= ⲛⲁⲧϩⲁⲡ ⲛⲁⲧⲛⲟⲙⲟⲥ ⲛⲁⲧⲁⲁⲁⲩ ⲛⲁⲙϥⲓⲃⲟⲗⲓⲁ	that I will give it without judgement, without law, without any trouble at all.

collected. Certain amounts of either *dêmosion* or *pakton* or both are mentioned, specifying or explaining the content of this *aparchê*. Besides this formula, there is another called "Tithe collection contract" by Sarah,[34] which forms a straight counterpart to the "guarantee" type: whenever the "guarantee" has "I," the "contract" says "You," and *vice versa*.

According to Sarah Clackson's interpretation,[35] the setting, or *Sitz im Leben*, of these *aparchê* collection documents was the collection of rent and tax payments to be paid by tenants of the monastery: "In the texts, monks are allocated areas for tithe collection which probably corresponded to monastic estates,"[36] and elsewhere: "This interpretation is the most appropriate for the texts in this edition because they specify that tithe is then paid out as a tax-rent designated pactum or dêmosion."[37] This view has been challenged by Ewa Wipszycka, who claimed estates owned by a monastery could neither be leased out nor could their rents be collected without participation of the monastery's legal entity, the *dikaion*. Instead, Ewa Wipszycka suggested another interpretation of the procedure: "Je pense que dans les textes publiés par S. J. Clackson, le mot aparche désigne ce qu'il désigne normalement, à savoir les prémices, et que ces textes attestent l'existence, en Égypte, d'une coutume que nous ignorions jusqu'à présent et qui consiste en ce que les moines collectent eux-mêmes les prémices, probablement en faisant du porte-à-porte. ... Ce qu'un moine recevait ... au cours de la collecte, devait lui servir pour payer ses impôts (demosion ou pakton). Dès le moment où la répartition des localités entre les moines était faite, c'étaient les moines eux-mêmes qui devaient verser l'argent au percepteur des impôts; le *dikaion* du monastère n'en était pas responsable."[38]

Yet there is a terminological argument speaking against this explanation and in favour of that given by Sarah Clackson. Admittedly, *dêmosion*, although meaning "land tax" in particular, is more often used to designate "taxes" in general. However, to the best of my knowledge, *pakton* in Coptic documents always means rent to be paid by tenants for their leasehold property.[39] In a Fayyumic *misthôsis* document[40] and in all Theban records concerned with leasehold affairs,[41] *pakton* generally means the rent to be paid for one-year leases. In Hermupolite documents, it always designates the rent for emphyteutic leasehold property, in contrast to *phoros*, the term used to designate rent of short-term leases in the *misthôsis* documents from that area.[42]

Is there a way out of that dilemma? Perhaps our observations concerning monks privately involved in leases and monks being tenants of their own monastery could indicate a solution. If it could be confirmed that monasteries let out their property to individual members of their communities, permitting them to sublease, monks would have been entitled to act as private lessors, letting out their small plots without direct participation of the actual land owner, the *dikaion*. The income collected from the tenants or rather, sub-tenants, could have been solemnly claimed "first-fruits" for the holy landlord Apa Apollo, in keeping with Sarah Clackson's interpretation. However, the question to be

---

[34] Clackson 2000: 58-66, *P.Mon.Apollo* 8-14.

[35] Clackson 2000: 17-23.

[36] Clackson 2000: 19.

[37] Clackson 2000: 18.

[38] Wipszycka 2001: 185.

[39] Cf. Richter 2002a; cf. also Papaconstantinou 2002: 102-105.

[40] *CPR* IV 120.

[41] In particular, the *misthôsis* and *epitropê* documents, cf. above, n. 10 and 11.

[42] Cf. above, n. 8, cf. also Richter 2002a and 2002b: 116f.

asked is, what advantage would such a complicated arrangement have brought to the monastery. In *P.Mon.Apollo* 25 we met a monk liable to pay land tax for two plots from his monastery's estates, who had obviously not succeeded in earning money from their cultivation. But since *he* was the possessor, at least with regard to tax liability, he was the one who became indebted to the state, while the *dikaion* remained free from debt. Could this have been the intended strategy, invented under the continued tax pressure upon monasteries following the legislation of Abd el-Malik ibn Marwân? On the other hand, by leasing land from their monastery, monks also became creditors to its *dikaion*, such as the monk Enoch and his brother in *P.Mon.Apollo* 26 who engaged themselves to pay two *nomismata* a year. Seen from this angle, Ewa Wispzycka may be right in her idea of monks begging in villages in order to raise money or produce to be paid for their leasehold property as land tax to the state and as rent to the monastery. But why did they not grow cash-crops on their fields? Whatever the outcome, any resolution of the *aparchê* question has economic implications which will have to be reconciled with other papyrological and broader historical evidence.

Bibliography

Banaji, J. (1999). "Agrarian History and the Labour Organisation of Byzantine Large Estates," in: Bowman and Rogan 1999 193-216.

Banaji, J. (2001). *Agrarian Change in Late Antiquity: Gold, Labour, and Aristocratic Dominance*. Oxford: Oxford University Press.

Bowman, A. K. and Rogan, E. (eds.) (1999). *Agriculture in Egypt from Pharaonic to Modern Times*. (*PBA* 96). Oxford: Oxford University Press.

Brunsch, W. (1981). "*P.Würzburg* 43—eine koptische Verzichterklärung," *ZÄS* 108, 93-105.

Comfort, H. (1933). "Prolegomena to a Study of late Byzantine Land-Leases," *Aegyptus* 13, 589-609.

Comfort, H. (1937). "Emphyteusis among the Papyri," *Aegyptus* 17, 3-24.

Eyre, Ch. (1997). "Peasants and 'Modern' Leasing Strategies in Ancient Egypt," *JESHO* 40, 367-390.

Felber, H. (1997). *Demotische Ackerpachtverträge der Ptolemäerzeit. Untersuchungen zu Aufbau, Entwicklung und inhaltlichen Aspekten einer Gruppe von demotischen Urkunden.* (*ÄgAbh* 58). Wiesbaden: Harrassowitz.

Förster, H. (2002). *Wörterbuch der griechischen Wörter in den koptischen dokumentarischen Texten*. Berlin/New York: De Gruyter.

Frantz-Murphy, G. (1986). *The Agrarian Administration of Egypt from the Arab Conquest to the Ottomans*. Cairo: Insititut français d'archéologie orientale.

Frantz-Murphy, G. (1994). "Papyrus Agricultural Contracts in the Oriental Institute Museum from Third/Ninth Century Egypt," in: *Itinéraires d'Orient. Hommages à Claude Cahen*. (*Res Orientales* 6). Paris, 119-131.

Frantz-Murphy, G. (1999). "Land-Tenure in Egypt in the First Five Centuries of Islamic Rule (Seventh-Twelfth centuries A.D.)," in: Bowman and Rogan 1999, 237-266.

Gascou, J. (1985). "Les grands domaines, la cité et l'état en Égypte byzantine (recherches d'histoire agraire, fiscale et administrative)," *TravMem* 9, 1-90.

Hardy, E. R. (1931). *The Large Estates of Byzantine Egypt*. New York: Columbia University Press.

Hughes, G. R. (1952). *Saite Demotic Land Leases*. (*SAOC* 28). Chicago: University of Chicago Press.

Hengstl, J. (1972). *Private Arbeitsverhältnisse freier Personen in den hellenistischen Papyri bis Diokletian*. Ph.D. thesis Bonn.

Hennig, D. (1967). *Untersuchungen zur Bodenpacht im ptolemäisch-römischen Ägypten*. Ph.D. thesis Munich.

Herrmann, J. (1958). *Studien zur Bodenpacht im Recht der graeco-aegyptischen Papyri*. (*Münchener Beiträge zur Papyrusforschung und antiken Rechtsgeschichte* 41). München: Beck.

Jördens, A. (1999). "Die Agrarverhältnisse im spätantiken Ägypten," *Laverna* 10, 114-152.

Krause, M. (1985). "Zur Edition koptischer nichtliterarischer Texte. *P.Würzburg* 43 neu bearbeitet," *ZÄS* 112, 143-153.

Krause, M. (1992). "Publikationen koptischer nichtliterarischer Texte der Jahre 1984-1988," in: Rassart-Debergh, M. and Ries, J. (eds.), *Actes du IVe congrès Copte, Lovain-la-Neuve, 5-10 septembre 1988*, vol. II. Louvain: Université catholique de Louvain, Institut orientaliste, 89-103.

MacCoull L. S. B. (1986). "Coptic Documentary Papyri from Aphrodito in the Chester Beatty Library," *BASP* 22, 197-203.

Manning, J. G. (1999). "The Land-Tenure Regime in Ptolemaic Upper Egpyt," in: Bowman and Rogan 1999, 83-105.

Mitteis, L. (1901). *Zur Geschichte der Erbpacht im Alterthum*. (*ASGW* Bd. XX, Abh. IV). Leipzig: B. G. Teubner.

Mrsich, T. Q. (2003). *Rechtsgeschichtliches zur Ackerverpachtung auf Tempelland nach demotischem Formular*. (*Österreichische Akademie der Wissenschaften, Sitzungsberichte der phil.-hist. Kl. 703 = Veröffentlichungen der Kommission für antike Rechtsgeschichte* 10). Wien: Verlag der Österreichischen Akademie der Wissenschaften.

Oates, J. F. (1963). "Chronological Aspects of Ptolemaic Land Leases," *BASP* 1, 47-62.

Papaconstantinou, A. (2002). "Notes sur les actes de donation d'enfant au monastère thébain de Saint-Phoibammon," *JJP* 32, 83-105.

Preisigke, F. (1925-1931). *Wörterbuch der griechischen Papyrusurkunden*. 3 vols. Berlin: Selbstverlag der Erben.

Rathbone, D. (1990). "Villages, Land and Population in Graeco-Roman Egypt," *Cambridge Philosophical Society* 216, 103-142.

Rathbone, D. (1991). *Economic Rationalism and Rural Society in Third-Century A.D. Egypt: The Heroninos Archive and the Appianus Estate*. Cambridge: Cambridge University Press.

Richter, T. S. (2002a). "Alte Isoglossen im Rechtswortschatz koptischer Urkunden," *LingAeg* 10, 389-399.

Richter, T. S. (2002b). "Koptische Mietverträge über Gebäude und Teile von Gebäuden," *JJP* 32, 113-168.

Richter, T. S. (2003). "Spätkoptische Rechtsurkunden neu bearbeitet (III): *P.Lond.Copt.* I 487— Arabische Pacht in koptischem Gewand," *JJP* 33, 213-230.

Richter, T. S. (2004). "Review on S. J. Clackson, *Coptic and Greek Texts Relating to the Hermopolite Monastery of Apa Apollo*," *OLZ* 99, 168-180.

Rowlandson, J. (1994). "Crop Rotation and Rent Payment in Oxyrhynchite Land Leases: Social and Economic Interpretations," in: Bülow-Jacobsen, A. (ed.) (1994). *Proceedings of the 20th International Congress of Papyrologists, Copenhagen 23-29 August 1992*. Copenhagen: Museum Tusculanum Press, University of Copenhagen, 495-499.

Rowlandson, J. (1996). *Landowners and Tenants in Roman Egypt: The Social Relations of Agriculture in the Oxyrhynchite Nome*. Oxford: Clarendon Press.

Rowlandson, J. (1999). "Agricultural Tenancy and Village Society in Roman Egypt," in: Bowman and Rogan 1999, 139-158.

Ruffing, K. (1999). *Weinbau im römischen Ägypten*. St. Katharinen: Scripta Mercaturae Verlag.

Schmelz, G. (2002). *Kirchliche Amtsträger im spätantiken Ägypten nach den Aussagen der griechischen und koptischen Papyri und Ostraka*. (*Archiv für Papyrusforschung Beiheft* 13). München/Leipzig: K.G. Saur.

Schnebel, M. (1925). *Die Landwirtschaft im hellenistischen Ägypten*. (*Münchener Beiträge zur Papyrusforschung und antiken Rechtsgeschichte* 7). Munich: Beck.

Seidl, E. (1973). *Bodennutzung und Bodenpacht nach den demotischen Texten der Ptolemäerzeit. Österreichische Akademie der Wissenschaften, Sitzungsberichte der phil.-hist. Kl.* 291. Vienna: Österr. Akad. d. Wiss.

Steinwenter, A. (1955). *Das Recht der koptischen Urkunden*. (*Handbuch der Altertumswissenschaft, Rechtsgeschichte des Altertums*, 4. Teil: *Das Recht der Papyri*, 2. Bd.), Munich: Beck.

Steinwenter, A. (1958). "Aus dem kirchlichen Vermögensrechte der Papyri," *Savigny-Zeitschrift für Rechtsgeschichte, Kan. Abtg.* 33, 1-34.

Taubenschlag, R. (1938). "Le bail à long terme dans le droit gréco-égyptien," *Recueil de la Société J. Bodin*, vol. III, 59-65.

Thür, G. (2000). "Misthosis," in: *Der neue Pauly*, vol. 8, 271-275.

Timm, S. (1984-1992). *Das christlich-koptische Ägypten in arabischer Zeit*. 6 vols. (*TAVO*, Beihefte B41/1-6). Wiesbaden: L. Reichert.

Waszynski, S. (1905). *Die Bodenpacht. Agrargeschichtliche Papyrusstudien*, 1: *Die Privatpacht*. Leipzig/Berlin: B. G. Teubner.

Wilfong, T. H. (1999). "Agriculture among the Christian Population of Early Islamic Egypt: Practice and Theory," in: Bowman and Rogan 1999, 217-235.

Wipszycka, E. (1972). *Les ressources et activités économiques des églises en Égypte du IVe au VIIIe siècle*. (*PapBrux* 10). Brussels: Fondation Égyptologique Reine Élisabeth.

Wipszycka, E. (1992). "Fonctionnement de l'église égyptienne aux IVe-VIIIe siècles (sur quelques aspects)," in: Décobert, Chr. (ed.), *Itinéraires d'Égypte. Mélanges offerts au père Maurice Martin s.j.* (*BiEtud* 107). Cairo: Institut français d'archéologie orientale, 116-145.

Wipszycka, E. (2001). "Le fonctionnement interne des monastères et des laures en Égypte du point de vue économique. À propos d'une publication récente de textes coptes de Bawit," *JJP* 31, 169-186.

De Zulueta, F. (1909). *De Patrociniis Vicorum. Oxford Studies in Social and Legal History* I/2. Oxford.

Das Archiv des Archimandriten Apa Georgios.
Texte aus *P.Fay.Copt.* und *P.Lond.Copt.*

Georg Schmelz

Das am Ostrand des Fayyum, rund 8 km nördlich des Dorfes Lahun, gelegene Kloster Deir el-Hammam hat bisher nur wenig Aufmerksamkeit von Reisenden und Forschern erfahren. Johann Georg besuchte es auf seinen "Streifzügen" und möchte seine Anfänge ins 6. Jh. datieren,[1] Otto Meinardus, für den es "by far the most picturesque monastery in the Fayyum" ist, denkt eher an das 8. Jh.[2] Flinders Petrie kam während seinen Arbeiten in Maidum 1889 nach Deir el-Hammam und brachte von dort koptische Papyri mit, die W.E. Crum 1893 publizierte.[3] Sie—und weitere in *P.Lond.Copt.*[4] edierte Texte—sind zur Zeit die einzigen verfügbaren Quellen über das Kloster in spätantiker und frühmittelalterlicher Zeit.

Über Petries Tätigkeiten in Deir el-Hammam gibt es keinen Bericht, nur einen Brief an Crum, aus dem dieser im Vorwort seiner Edition zitiert: "'The Deir has been rebuilt a few centuries ago, but there are outlines of a much larger Deir showing on the ground. Outside the older Deir are rubbish-mounds. Here we found plenty of scraps of papyrus,' which the natives brought and sold to me in scrap lots. I never had any occasion to suspect any outside admixture."[5] Demnach wurde noch nie eine systematische Ausgrabung oder auch nur eine Survey-Aufnahme durchgeführt,[6] obwohl Petrie und Meinardus Strukturen und Keramik-Funden auf der Oberfläche erwähnen. Eine archäologische Untersuchung der Stätte würde zweifellos weitere Informationen über das Kloster ergeben, vielleicht auch neue Papyri ans Licht bringen.

Die von Einheimischen gefundenen Stücke hat Crum wohl direkt von Petrie erhalten; sie befinden sich heute in der British Library. Einige von ihnen sind in *P.Lond.Copt.* neu ediert oder beschrieben, außerdem sind dort auch sieben weitere Texte abgedruckt, die zu den Papyri von Deir el-Hammam gehören.[7] Die Inventarnummern zeigen, dass diese weiteren Texte auf anderem Wege und wohl früher in die British Library kamen; möglicherweise gibt es auch noch inedita. Crum publizierte in *P.Fay.Copt.* 56 Texte, von denen vier aus Hawara stammen[8] und einer in Sohag gekauft wurde, doch zeigen auch diese durch Personen- und Ortsnamen eine große Nähe zu den Deir el-Hammam-Papyri.

---

[1] Johann Georg 1930: 19 f. mit Taf. 44-46.

[2] Meinardus 1977: 457 f. Eine Photo des Klosters findet sich bei Capuani 2002: 128 Abb. 47.

[3] *P.Fay.Copt.* = *Coptic Manuscripts brought from the Fayyum by W.M. Flinders Petrie ... edited with commentaries and indices by W. E. Crum*, London 1893.

[4] *P.Lond.Copt.* I = *Catalogue of the Coptic Manuscripts in the British Museum* by W. E. Crum, London 1905.

[5] *P.Fay.Copt.*, S. v. Der Brief befindt sich im Griffith Institute (Oxford), Crum klebte ihn in sein Exemplar der *P.Fay.Copt.* Mrs. Miles, Mrs. Bergman and Mr. Ganley sei herzlich gedankt für die Suche nach dem Brief und für gescannte images davon. Im Petrie Museum des University College London werden die Notizbücher Petries aufbewahrt, darunter auch eines von 1889, doch enthält es keine Informationen über Petries Aufenthalt in Deir el-Hammam.

[6] Die Fayyum-Survey unter der Leitung von Dominic Rathbone und Cornelia Römer konzentriert sich auf das westliche Fayum und v.a. auf die römische Epoche; vgl. Rathbone 2001: 1109-1117.

[7] *P.Lond.Copt.* I 529; 539; 546; 588; 589; 632; 637.

[8] Zu Hawara, vgl. Uytterhoeven 2001.

Kleinere Stücke, die ihm nicht publikationswert erschienen, ließ Crum weg,[9] unediert sind außerdem einige arabische und syrische Papiere[10] und die arabischen Rückseiten von *P.Fay.Copt.* 15; 19; 22 und 37. In den Editionen *P.Fay.Copt.* und *P.Lond.Copt.* liegen damit 63 Texte vor, die in Deir el-Hammam gefunden wurden oder die zu dieser Gruppe gehören. Ihr Ertrag für die historische Beschreibung des Klosters soll im folgenden dargestellt werden.

Es handelt sich bei diesen Texten zum überwiegenden Teil um Briefe, dreizehn Listen stammen aus dem wirtschaftlichen Leben und dem Steuerwesen, zehn Papyri und Pergamente enthalten biblische, patristische und liturgische Texte. Keiner der Texte enthält ein fixes Datum, und nur in neun Fällen macht Crum Angaben auf paläographischer Grundlage. Abgesehen von *P.Fay.Copt.* 2, Fragmenten des Jakobus- und Judasbriefes aus dem Neuen Testament, die Crum auf 300-350 n.Chr. datiert, setzt er die Texte alle ins 10./11. Jh. Die auf den der Edition beigegebenen Tafeln abgebildeten Papyri scheinen mir jedoch eher aus dem 8./9. Jh. zu stammen.[11] Bei Überlegungen zum Beschreibstoff kommt Crum zu einer ähnlichen Einschätzung: "There is so little paper in the collection, that we may suppose it not to reach much beyond the end of the ninth century; while the comparative frequency of Arabic names, etc., point to about the beginning of the eighth century as a probable *terminus a quo*."[12]

Die Hauptperson in dieser Gruppe von Texten, an die viele Briefe gerichtet sind, die selbst viele Briefe geschrieben hat, und die in verschiedenen Texten erwähnt wird, ist der Archimandrit Apa Georgios. Nur in zweien der dreizehn Texte, in denen er begegnet[13], wird er als Archimandrit bezeichnet,[14] viermal nennt man ihn Apa Georgios.[15] Die Briefe, die er selbst verfaßt, unterschreibt er einfach mit ⲅⲉⲱⲣⲅⲓⲟⲥ,[16] manchmal fügt er ⲡⲓⲉⲗⲁⲭⲓⲥⲧⲟⲥ[17] hinzu. Zweimal trägt er den Titel Diakon,[18] einmal sogar mit der Herkunftsbezeichnung ⲡⲁⲧⲁⲛϣⲉⲉⲓ.[19] Georgios kann als "heiliger Vater"[20] und als ⲡⲣⲟⲥⲧⲁⲧⲏⲥ ⲛⲓⲱⲧ[21] angeredet werden, er ist aber nicht die ranghöchste Person im Kloster. Er selbst schreibt einmal an einen "geliebten heiligen Vater,"[22] und neben ihm wird einmal ein

---

[9] Vgl. *P.Fay.Copt.*, S. v.vi.

[10] Vgl. *P.Fay.Copt.* 15 Einl.

[11] Vgl. Stegemann 1936: 11 und MacCoull 1994: 141-158 pl. 36-54 (Herzlichen Dank an Sebastian Richter [Leipzig] für sein paläographisches Urteil und für diese Hinweise).

[12] *P.Fay.Copt.*, S. vi. Der Brief *P.Fay.Copt.* 19 hat arabische Schriftspuren auf dem verso, die Karabacek für Crum datierte und ins 9. Jh. setzte.

[13] *P.Fay.Copt.* 11 v; 13,2; 14 v; 20 v; 22,5; 24 v; 25 v; *P.Lond.Copt.* I 529; 539; 546; 588; 589 v; 632. Ob es sich bei den Georgii in *P.Fay.Copt.* 36,2 und 37,3 um den Archimandriten handelt, lässt sich nicht entscheiden. Der Töpfer und der Ziegenhirt in *P.Fay.Copt.* ap r 31 und v 6 dürften andere Personen gewesen sein, bei dem Diakon und Schreiner in *P.Fay.Copt.* 45 r a 16; r b 11; v a 9 ist das unsicher.

[14] *P.Fay.Copt.* 25v; *P.Lond.Copt.* I 588.

[15] *P.Fay.Copt.* 20v; *P.Lond.Copt.* I 539; 546; 589v.

[16] *P.Fay.Copt.* 14v; 24v; *P.Lond.Copt.* I 637.

[17] *P.Fay.Copt.* 11v; *P.Lond.Copt.* I 529v.

[18] *P.Fay.Copt.* 13,2; 22,5. Ob er es bis zum Archipresbyter gebracht hat, ist fraglich: die Abgrenzung in P.Fay.Copt. 24 v ist unklar.

[19] *P.Fay.Copt.* 22,5. Zu diesem Ort vgl. Timm 1992: 2506 f.

[20] *P.Lond.Copt.* I 539.

[21] *P.Fay.Copt.* 25v.

[22] *P.Fay.Copt.* 14v.

ἡγούμενος des Klosters erwähnt.[23] Georgios scheint v.a. für die praktischen Dinge im Kloster zuständig gewesen zu sein—zumindest ist er vorwiegend so dokumentiert: in einem Brief geht es darum, dass er die Trauben geerntet hat,[24] in einem anderen beschwert sich ein Arbeiter bei ihm, er habe zu wenig Lohn erhalten.[25] Eine nächtliche Aktion, bei der Esel heimlich an den Ort Tmuiubesti gebracht werden, wird von ihm organisiert.[26] In einem Brief geht es um Wein und um zwei Bücher, die ans Kloster geschickt werden sollen,[27] in einem anderen um einen größeren Konflikt mit Bauern und auch mit verschiedenen Mönchen, der bis zum Bischof gebracht wurde.[28]

In den Texten, die Georgios betreffen, begegnen auch andere Personen, die ebenso in weiteren Texten vorkommen, in denen Georgios nicht erwähnt wird. Auch diese Texte gehören zum "Archiv des Archimandriten Apa Georgios."[29] In ihnen begegnen wiederum weitere Personen, so dass insgesamt eine recht große Zahl von Klosterangehörigen und Menschen, die im weiteren Sinne mit dem Kloster zu tun hatten, dokumentiert ist.

Häufiger erwähnt werden die Mönche Philotheos, Phoibammon und Kosma—vielleicht hatten sie eine etwas wichtigere Stellung im Kloster. Philotheos schreibt den Brief *P.Fay.Copt.* 13, in dem sehr viele Mönche gegrüßt werden.[30] Zusammen mit Chael wendet er sich mit dem Brief *P.Fay.Copt.* 20 an Georgios, es geht dabei um die Traubenernte. Eventuell war er ein Archidiakon, wie *P.Fay.Copt.* 24 v nahelegt. An der heimlichen Aktion mit den Eseln war er beteiligt. Den Brief *P.Lond.Copt.* 529, mit dem diese Aktion geplant wird, richtet Georgios allerdings an Phoibammon. Er war ein Archidiakon,[31] vielleicht ist er auch gemeint, wenn ein Diakon Phoibammon erwähnt wird.[32] Von Kosma stammen zwei Briefe an Georgios, *P.Lond.Copt.* 588 betreffs Weines und zweier Bücher und *P.Fay.Copt.* 25, in dem ein καμάσιον (ein Hemd, vielleicht ein liturgisches Kleidungsstück)[33] erwähnt wird.[34]

Eine wichtige Person im Kloster war auch Pihew (ⲡⲓϩⲏⲩ), der in dem Brief *P.Fay.Copt.* 12,1f. als κύριος und ενδ/ αρχ/ angeredet wird. Crum wägt ab, ob diese Abkürzungen als ἐνδοξότατος ἄρχων oder als ἐνδοξότατος ἀρχιμανδρίτης aufzulösen ist. Er entscheidet sich für ersteres, weil seiner Ansicht nach ἐνδοξότατος eher mit weltlichen Titel vorkommt. Allerdings ist es—nach Aussage der Duke Data Bank—auch mit solchen Titeln seltener als erwartet; der Inhalt des Briefes (die Lieferung von saurem Wein durch verschiedene Kleriker und Mönche an einen Mann namens Gabriel) und der klösterliche Kontext legen eher die zweite Auflösung als ἐνδοξότατος ἀρχιμανδρίτης nahe. Damit

---

[23] *P.Lond.Copt.* I 632.

[24] *P.Fay.Copt.* 20.

[25] *P.Lond.Copt.* I 589.

[26] *P.Lond.Copt.* I 529.

[27] *P.Lond.Copt.* I 588.

[28] *P.Fay.Copt.* 11; s.u.

[29] Die übrigen Texten in *P.Fay.Copt.* sind meist zu schlecht erhalten und lassen von ihrem Wortlaut keine Beziehung zum Kloster erkennen. Da sie aber aus derselben Fundmasse stammen, werden auch sie zu dieser Textgruppe und in den Zusammenhang des Klosters gehören.

[30] Er selbst wird in *P.Fay.Copt.* 22,3 gegrüßt.

[31] *P.Lond.Copt.* I 529v; 588,14.

[32] *P.Lond.Copt.* I 632; *P.Fay.Copt.* ap v 47 (?).

[33] Vgl. Schmelz 2002: 118 f.

[34] Ob sich die Nennungen in 45 r b 8.27; v a 3.27; b 21; 50, r 2.10; v 3—in 45 v a 3 mit der Herkunftsangabe ⲡⲁϣⲏⲛⲁⲣⲱ—auf ihn beziehen, läßt sich nicht feststellen.

wäre neben Georgios ein zweiter Archimandrit bezeugt. Rückschlüsse auf die Art des Mönchtums bzw. auf die Klosterverfassung lassen sich aus dem Begriff ἀρχιμανδρίτης nicht ziehen, da er mehr ein Ehrentitel und keine Funktionsbezeichnung war.[35] Auch die Frage, ob es immer nur einen Archimandriten im Kloster geben konnte, ob Pihew also vor oder nach Georgios anzusetzen ist, oder ob sie eventuell zur gleichen Zeit existierten, muss offen bleiben.[36]

Mehrere Angehörige des Klosters waren Diakone, zweimal sind Priester bezeugt. Öfters begegnet der Name Petros, und aus *P.Fay.Copt.* 13,3f. wird deutlich, dass es sich um mindestens drei verschiedene Personen handeln muss. Eine von ihnen war Diakon,[37] eine andere Priester.[38] Ein weiterer Priester ist Onnophrios,[39] weitere Diakone sind Apa Juli,[40] Chael,[41] Damianos,[42] Gabriel,[43] Kyros,[44] Menas,[45] Mone,[46] Pisynthios,[47] Remiel,[48] Schenute[49] und Thomas.[50] Als Laienmönche begegnen Apa Hol,[51] Apa Jakob,[52] Apa Marine,[53] Apa Mela,[54] Apa Merkurios,[55] Apa Pischai,[56] Apa Poimen,[57] Apa Viktor,[58] Athanasios,[59] Hathre,[60] Isaak,[61] Johannes,[62] Kamul,[63] Kyprianos,[64]

---

[35] Vgl. Wipszycka 1991: 192-194.

[36] Neben Georgios ist auch ein ἡγούμενος bezeugt: *P.Lond.Copt.* I 632.

[37] *P.Fay.Copt.* 13,3.

[38] *P.Fay.Copt.* 17v. Ob Petro und Kosma, die gelegentlich gemeinsam (*P.Fay.Copt.* 45r b 8; v a 27) vorkommen, die beiden Mönche sind, ist unsicher; andere Träger dieses Namens—ein Kameltreiber (*P.Fay.Copt.* 45r b 21), ein Gärtner (*P.Fay.Copt.* 45v a 13), ein Matrose (*P.Fay.Copt.* ap r 20), ein Ziegenhirte (*P.Fay.Copt.* ap v 25)—sind wohl nicht mit dem Mönch identisch.

[39] *P.Fay.Copt.* 27v.

[40] *P.Fay.Copt.* 45r b 13; 46,12.

[41] *P.Fay.Copt.* 42,1f. zeigt, dass es mindestens zwei Personen im Kloster mit Namen Chael gab: einen Diakon und einen anderen; s. auch *P.Fay.Copt.* 13,11 und 20v.

[42] *P.Fay.Copt.* 14,9;—vielleicht dieselbe Person wie in *P.Fay.Copt.* 13,2.

[43] *P.Fay.Copt.* 24,24.

[44] *P.Fay.Copt.* 12,12.

[45] *P.Fay.Copt.* ap v 5.22; ein—wohl älterer—Mönch begegnet auch in *P.Fay.Copt.* 17v, ein Apa Menas in *P.Lond.Copt.* I 529v.

[46] *P.Fay.Copt.* 13,2.

[47] *P.Fay.Copt.* 12,17f.

[48] *P.Fay.Copt.* 15,4.

[49] *P.Fay.Copt.* 27v; eventuell identisch mit dem in 22v genannten.

[50] *P.Fay.Copt.* 13,3; ap v9.

[51] *P.Lond.Copt.* I 632.

[52] *P.Fay.Copt.* 12,16f.

[53] *P.Lond.Copt.* I 632.

[54] *P.Fay.Copt.* 29,18.

[55] *P.Fay.Copt.* 15,2.

[56] *P.Lond.Copt.* I 529v.

[57] *P.Fay.Copt.* 13,4; 22,4.

[58] *P.Fay.Copt.* 13,2; 14,2; ap v 7 (?).

[59] *P.Fay.Copt.* 13,3; 29,21.

[60] *P.Fay.Copt.* 27,4; 28,3.4.

[61] *P.Fay.Copt.* 16 v; 37,6; 51,14; *P.Lond.Copt.* I 529,13.

[62] *P.Fay.Copt.* 13,2; 15,2; 17,3 (?).

Eustathios,⁶⁵ Lukas,⁶⁶ Simeon,⁶⁷ Stephanos⁶⁸ und Theodoros.⁶⁹ Möglicherweise war auch Kolluthos ein Mönch: aus dem Brief *P.Lond.Copt.* 546 geht nur hervor, dass er sich in Babylon aufhält und durch den Schiffer Kyriakos etwas gebracht bekommen soll.

Eine Episode aus dem Klosterleben, die Licht auf verschiedene Bereiche wirft, lässt sich andeutungsweise aus dem Brief *P.Fay.Copt.* 11 erfahren: Georgios schreibt an ihm untergeordnete Mönche (seine "Söhne"), die im Streit mit ihm liegen. Es geht darum, wie man mit Bauern umgeht, mit denen es Schwierigkeiten mit der Ernte gibt, und besonders mit einem jungen Mann, Mustharion. Er hätte vor das ἱλαστήριον (den Altar bzw. das *sanctuarium* in der Kirche) gestellt werden sollen, hat sich aber wohl durch Flucht entzogen. Georgios rät, nun seine Frau vor das ἱλαστήριον zu bringen. Im übrigen bemerkt er, dass seine Briefpartner die Sache vor den Bischof gebracht hatten.

Auch wenn sich der Streitpunkt nicht mehr völlig aufklären läßt, wird doch deutlich, dass es sich um einen Konflikt größerer Ordnung handelt. Mustharion sollte in der Kirche zur Rechenschaft gezogen werden, die Mönche, die den Fall hätten regeln sollen, konnten ihn aber nicht finden und wandten sich deshalb an den Bischof. Zweierlei liegt nahe zu vermuten: Die Bauern sollten wohl dem Kloster Abgaben bringen. Georgios fühlt sich übergangen, weil mit dem Bischof gleich die übergeordnete kirchenrechtliche Instanz herangezogen wurde. Bemerkenswert ist, dass eine Verhandlung offenbar im Kirchenraum, vor dem Altar, üblich war, und nicht wie in *P.Lips.* I 43,1f. im Vorhof (ἐν τῷ πυλῶνι) der Kirche oder wie in *P.Münch.* I 14 ganz außerhalb. Ein Bischof wird nicht nur in *P.Fay.Copt.* 11, sondern auch in den Briefen *P.Fay.Copt.* 22 und 23 erwähnt; in 23,10f. hat er den Namen Abbi. Man wird in ihm einen Bischof aus Medinet el-Fayyum sehen wollen, doch ist dieser Name in den Listen von Munier,⁷⁰ Fedalto⁷¹ und Worp⁷² nicht verzeichnet.

Über die wirtschaftlichen Verhältnisse des Klosters gibt es nur wenige Andeutungen: neben dem Konflikt mit den Bauern in *P.Fay.Copt.* 11 werden in einem Brief Datteln,⁷³ in einem anderen Vieh⁷⁴ erwähnt. Eine Liste, *P.Fay.Copt.* 55, verzeichnet Gefäße (τήγανον,⁷⁵ ϭⲓⲥⲗⲁⲕ,⁷⁶ ⲉⲗⲕⲟⲩ⁷⁷) und Werkzeuge (ϭⲟⲣⲧⲉ,⁷⁸ σουβλίον,⁷⁹ ⲧⲣⲁⲡ,⁸⁰ ⲙⲉⲥⲱⲕⲓ⁸¹) und stammt wohl aus einer Werkstatt. Die

---

⁶³ *P.Lond.Copt.* I 529v; 588,15.
⁶⁴ *P.Fay.Copt.* 23,4.
⁶⁵ *P.Fay.Copt.* 13,9.
⁶⁶ *P.Fay.Copt.* 15,7.
⁶⁷ *P.Fay.Copt.* 27v.
⁶⁸ *P.Fay.Copt.* 14,9.
⁶⁹ *P.Fay.Copt.* 14,9.
⁷⁰ Munier 1943.
⁷¹ Fedalto 1988.
⁷² Worp 1994.
⁷³ *P.Lond.Copt.* I 637.
⁷⁴ *P.Fay.Copt.* 17.
⁷⁵ *P.Fay.Copt.* 55,6.
⁷⁶ *P.Fay.Copt.* 55,8.
⁷⁷ *P.Fay.Copt.* 55,9.
⁷⁸ *P.Fay.Copt.* 55,11.
⁷⁹ *P.Fay.Copt.* 55,7.
⁸⁰ *P.Fay.Copt.* 55,13.

beiden Ahlen (σουβλίον, ⲧⲣⲁⲡ) und die Nadel (ⲙⲉⲥⲱⲃⲓ) deuten auf Lederverarbeitung o.ä. hin. Der Bezug dieser Liste zum Kloster ist allerdings nur durch den Fundkontext der Papyri gegeben. Weiterhin gibt es verschiedene Listen, die sich auf Weinverkauf[82] beziehen, deren genauer Zusammenhang mit dem Kloster aber nicht klar ist, sowie eine Liste, die eventuell aus dem Steuerwesen[83] stammt.

Auf das geistliche Leben im Kloster bezieht sich die Liste *P.Fay.Copt.* 47, ein Verzeichnis gottesdienstlicher Gewänder und Textilien. Es ist auf ein bereits gebrauchtes Papyrusblatt geschrieben[84] und wurde wohl zu einem informellen Zweck erstellt. Vielleicht verschaffte sich der Verfasser einen Überblick über die liturgischen Kleidungsstücke und Tücher. Verschiedene Schultertücher von Geistlichen (πάλλιον,[85] ἐπωμίς[86]) werden erwähnt, Gewänder (ϩⲁⲩⲛⲉ[87])—eines davon wohl mit Kapuze (ⲁⲗⲙⲉϣⲙⲉⲗⲁⲓ[88]), eines rot (ϣⲧⲏⲛ ⲛⲅⲱⲕⲅⲟⲥ[89])—und ein Mantel mit einem Kreuz (ⲉⲣϣⲱⲛ ⲉϥⲭⲓⲥⲧⲁⲩⲣⲟⲥ[90]). Zweimal werden Tücher für die Abendmahlsgeräte genannt (ⲙⲁⲡⲡⲁ[91]), dann ein Altarvorhang (καταπέτασμα[92]) und eine Decke mit einem Kreuz darauf (ϩⲱⲃⲥ ⲉϥⲭⲓⲥⲧⲁⲩⲣⲟⲥ[93]).

Eine Liste besonderer Art ist *P.Fay.Copt.* 44, ein Bücherverzeichnis, das wohl zur Klosterbibliothek gehörte. Die aufgeführten Werke stammen fast alle aus dem Neuen Testament, summarisch sind auch 32 alte und 12 neue Bücher auf Pergament sowie 66 (?) und 15 alte auf Papyrus genannt. Insgesamt kommt man auf deutlich über 100 Bücher, wobei *P.Fay.Copt.* 44 an vielen Stellen nicht sicher gelesen werden kann—die Klosterbibliothek umfaßte also mehr Bücher. Darauf deutet auch die Überschrift der Liste hin: ⲡⲗⲟⲅⲟⲥ ⲛⲉⲛϫⲱⲱⲙⲓ ⲛⲁⲧⲁⲛⲥϯⲥⲓ ⲙⲙⲁⲩ (Liste der Bücher, die wir markiert [στίζειν] haben). Mit welcher Art von Markierungen oder diakritischen Zeichen die Bücher versehen wurden, wird nicht deutlich, doch zeigt die Überschrift an, dass ein Teil der Klosterbibliothek auf diese Weise bearbeitet wurde. Dies deutet auf eine Art Schreiberwerkstatt hin, in der man solche Arbeiten ausführte. Die große Zahl der Bücher legt nahe, dass das Kloster wohlhabend war. *P.Fay.Copt.* 2, die Fragmente des Jakobus- und Judasbriefes, die Crum auf 300-350 n.Chr. datiert, waren wohl Teil dieser Bibliothek.

---

[81] *P.Fay.Copt.* 55,14.

[82] *P.Fay.Copt.* 45; 48; 54.

[83] *P.Fay.Copt.* 54,10ff.

[84] Oberhalb der Liste steht *P.Fay.Copt.* 21, ein Anfang oder Entwurf eines Briefes; vgl. Schmelz 2002: 97 sowie zum folgenden 113-120.

[85] *P.Fay.Copt.* 47,7.10.

[86] *P.Fay.Copt.* 47,11.

[87] *P.Fay.Copt.* 47,1.

[88] *P.Fay.Copt.* 47,2; vgl. Graf 1954, s.v. شملة Humerale mit Kapuze.

[89] *P.Fay.Copt.* 47,6.

[90] *P.Fay.Copt.* 47,4.

[91] *P.Fay.Copt.* 47,5.8.

[92] *P.Fay.Copt.* 47,9.

[93] *P.Fay.Copt.* 47,3.

Anhang: Texte und Personen des Georgios-Archivs

	Briefe von Georgios
	Erwähnte Personen
P.Fay.Copt. 11 = P.Lond.Copt. 554 Inv. Nr.: BL Or. 5300 (8)	Georgios (v)
P.Fay.Copt. 14 = P.Lond.Copt. 555 Inv. Nr.: BL Or. 5300 (9)	Diakon Damianos (9), Viktor (2), Georgios (v), Stephanos (9), Theodoros (9)
P.Fay.Copt. 24 = P.Lond.Copt. 551(1) Inv. Nr.: BL Or. 5300 (5)	Philotheos (v), Diakon Gabriel (24), Georgios (v), Horapollon, Simeon (5.10.14), Severos (14)
P.Lond.Copt. 529 Inv. Nr.: BL Or. 4720 (1)	Chamoul (v), Isaak (13), Philotheos, Pishai (v), Georgios (v), Menas (v), Phoibammon (v)
P.Lond.Copt. 637 Inv. Nr.: BL Or. 4720 (78)	Georgios
	Briefe an Georgios
P.Fay.Copt. 20 = P.Lond.Copt. 558 Inv. Nr.: BL Or. 5300 (12)	Chael (v), Philotheos (v), Georgios (v)
P.Fay.Copt. 25 = P.Lond.Copt. 557 Inv. Nr.: BL Or. 5300 (11)	Georgios (v), Kosma (v)
P.Lond.Copt. 539 Inv. Nr.: BL Or. 5300 (2)	
P.Lond.Copt. 546 (2) Inv. Nr.: BL Or. 4720 (14)	Cyriacus (5.7), Georgios, Kolluthos (7)
P.Lond.Copt. 588 Inv. Nr.: BL Or. 4720 (29)	Chamoul (15), Georgios (v), Kosma (v), Phoibammon (14)
P.Lond.Copt. 589 Inv. Nr.: BL Or. 4720 (30)	Georgios (v)
P.Lond.Copt. 632 Inv. Nr.: BL Or. 4720 (73)	Apa Hol, Marine, Georgios, Phoibammon
	Texte, in denen Georgios erwähnt ist
P.Fay.Copt. 13	Apa Athanasios (3), Chael (11), Damianos (2f.), Eustathios (9), Diakon Georgios (2), Apa Johannes (2), Diakon Mone (2), Petros (Apa 3 und ein anderer 4; Diakon 3), Apa Philotheos (v), Apa Poimen (4), Diakon Thomas (3), Viktor (2).
P.Fay.Copt. 22	Apa Philotheos (3), Apa Poimen (4), Diakon Georgios (5), Samuel (v), Schenute?
	Texte mit Personen, die in Georgios-Texten erwähnt sind
P.Fay.Copt. 12	Apa Jakob (16f.), Diakon Apa Kyros (12), Gabriel (1), Pihew (1), Diakon Pisynthios (17f.)
P.Fay.Copt. 15	Apa Chael (1), Johannes (2), Apa Mercurios (2), Lukas (7), Diakon Remiel (5)
P.Fay.Copt. 16	Isaak (v)
P.Fay.Copt. 17	Johannes (3), Mena (v), Petros (v)
P.Fay.Copt. 19	Petros (v)
P.Fay.Copt. 23	Cyprianos (4), Diakon Celestius (7), Kosma (8.13), Petros (8), Bischof Abbi (10.11.v)
P.Fay.Copt. 27	Hathre (4), Onnophrios (v), Schenute (v), Simeon (v)
P.Fay.Copt. 28	Hathre (3.4)

P.Fay.Copt. 29	Abraham (6), Apa Mela (18), Athanasios (21)
P.Fay.Copt. 42	Chael (1.2)
P.Fay.Copt. 45	Abraham (v a 1), Chael (r b 5.24; v b 16 Töpfer), Johannes (r b 29), Diakon Georgios (r a 16 Schreiner; r b 11; v a 9.19; b 5), Kosma (r b 8.27; v a 3.27; b 21), Apa Makarius (r a 12), Onnophrios (v a 11), Apa Petros (r b 3.8.21 Kameltreiber; v a 13 Gärtner; 27), Shenoute (r b 6), Theodoros (v a 10 Walker), Diakon Apa Juli (r b 13; v b 18)
P.Fay.Copt. 46	Abraham (1.20), Viktor (19), Hathre (26.30), Mena (25), Onnophrios (A 2), Petros (3), Diakon Apa Juli (12), Papnute (31), Apa Makarius (31f.)
P.Fay.Copt. 51	Kamul (A 2), Isaak (14)
P.Fay.Copt. Appendix	Abraham (r 25.33), Athanasios (r 40), Chael (r 13; v 40), Georgios (r 26 aus Tansheii; 31 Töpfer; v 6 Ziegenhirt), Isaak (r 33; v 21), Jakob (v 1), Johannes (r 15.16; v 23.33.34), Menas (v 5.22 Diakon), Onnophrios (v 4.17), Petros (r 20; v 25), Philotheos (r 32), Phoibammon (r 42, v 47), Pisynthios (r 17), Samuel (r 28.34), Schenute (r 37), Theodoros (r 14.18.32), Thomas (v 9 Diakon), Viktor (v 7)

Auch die übrigen Texte aus *P.Fay.Copt.* gehören im weiteren Sinne zum Georgios-Archiv dazu, da sie aus demselben Fundzusammenhang stammen.

Bibliographie

Capuani, M. (2002). *Christian Egypt. Coptic Art and Monuments through Two Millennia*. Minnesota: Liturgical Press.

Fedalto, G. (1988). *Hierarchia Ecclesiastica Orientalis, II: Patriarchatus Alexandriae, Antiochiae, Hierosolymitanae*. Padua: Messagero.

Graf, G. (Hg.) (1954). *Verzeichnis arabischer kirchlicher Termini*. (*CSCO* 147 Sub. 8 [2. Auflage]). Löwen: Peeters.

Johann Georg (1930). *Neue Streifzüge durch die Kirchen und Klöster Ägyptens*. Leipzig: Hinrichs.

MacCoull, L. S. B. (1994). "The Bawit Contracts: Texts and Translations," *BASP* 31, 141-158 pl. 36-54.

Meinardus, O. F. A. (1977). *Christian Egypt. Ancient and Modern*. Kairo: AUC Press.

Munier, H. (1943). *Recueil des listes épiscopales de l'Église Copte*. Kairo: Société d'Archéologie Copte.

Rathbone, D. (2001). "Mapping the South-West Fayyum: Sites and Texts," in: Andorlini, I. u.a. (Hgg.), *Atti del XXII Congresso Internazionale di Papirologia* II. Florenz: Istituto G. Vitelli, 1109-1117.

Schmelz, G. (2002). *Kirchliche Amtsträger im spätantiken Ägypten*. Leipzig: Saur.

Stegemann, V. (1936). *Koptische Paläographie* II. Heidelberg: Selbstverlag Bilabel.

Timm, S. (1992). *Das christlich-koptische Ägypten in arabischer Zeit* VI. Wiesbaden: Reichert.

Uytterhoeven, I. (2001). "Hawara (Fayum): Tombs and Houses on the Surface. A Preliminary Report of the K.U. Leuven Site Survey," *Ricerche di Egittologia e di Antichità Copte* 3, 45-83.

Wipszycka, E. (1991). Art. "Archimandrite," *CE* I, 192-194.

Worp, K. A. (1994). "A Checklist of Bishops in Byzantine Egypt," *ZPE* 100, 283-318.

P. Oxy. LXIII 4397: The Monastery Comes First or Pious Reasons before Earthly Securities[*]

Jakub Urbanik

The deed which is the object of the present study, one of the longest documentary texts preserved on a papyrus, tells us of a certain risky financial business entered into by the 'well-sanctified' monastery of Apa Hierax. The whole account covers quite a time span and all the original *dramatis personae* had probably been dead long before the final act was concluded. The story finally resulted in the present settlement of claims in which the monastery of Apa Hierax confirms having received its money back from none less than the actual head of the house of the Apiones: Flavius Apion II.[1] This document raises a number of questions concerning the legal status of monasteries and their representatives in conducting financial and legal transactions and especially about the relation between legal theory and practice in late Antique Egypt. It is also one of the most important pieces of evidence of the late Antique popularity of a practice nowadays commonly referred to as 'alternative dispute resolution.' In the present paper I shall try to examine the legal content of the deed and to provide an answer why this conflict solving form was chosen by the counterparts.

The parties to the deed were, on the one side, Flavius Apion II, represented by his slave Menas, who in the absence of his master received a stipulation guaranteeing the execution of the settlement, and, on the other, the priest Ioseph and Theodoros, prior and steward respectively of the monastery of Apa Hierax, who in turn submitted that they acted with the approval and on behalf of all their confriars. They both declared to be illiterate—at first sight a curious thing for a priest and a steward. It most probably meant that neither Ioseph nor Theodoros could read and write Greek, but that they were literate in Coptic.[2] The document is subscribed on their behalf by Pamouthios son of Philoxenos.

The present agreement was preceded by a long legal dispute. Some years before the year 545 when this final settlement of claims was made, a certain Diogenes, *vir illustrissimus* originating from Oxyrhynchos, while in the capital city, found himself in need of financial support. Luckily, he met there his kinsman, Theophilos, acting on behalf of the monastery of Apa Hierax. This spiritual foundation, whose exact location remains a mystery, is only known from yet another papyrus, *P.Oxy.* LI 3640 (C.E. 533). The latter text informs us that the monks of Apa Hierax produced ropes (interestingly the other party in the document is again closely connected to the Apiones and it must have been preserved in the Apiones' dossier as well). Theophilos lent to Diogenes eighty *solidi* belonging to his

---

[*] I would like to thank Ewa Wipszycka (Warsaw), who has read the draft of this article, for her comments and explanations, and Derek Scally (Berlin) for having corrected my English. I have also discussed this paper with José Luis Alonso (San Sebastián) and benefited from his remarks for which I am very grateful. Finally, but not the least, I am indebted to Petra Sijpesteijn (Paris) to whose careful reading and important comments the final version owes a lot.

[1] Most recently on the Apions see a very useful book by Roberta Mazza (Mazza 2001), on *P.Oxy.* LXIII 4397: 134-135; on Fl. Strategios II and Fl. Apion II who appear in our document see esp. pp. 53-68 and the extensive literature therein cited; see also my review thereof (Urbanik 2004). Cf. too, the classical study by Jean Gascou (Gascou 1985).

[2] Cf. a similar situation in Apa Abraham's will, *P.Lond.* I 77: 231-236) with *BL* I 241, ll. 80-81. (English translation in MacCoull 2000) where Ioseph, a priest of Hermonthis subscribes for Abraham who "does not know letters." As Leslie MacCoull rightly points out, we know, however, that Abraham was perfectly literate in Coptic.

monastery with an annual interest of six per cent. The debt was duly secured by a mortgage of an irrigated plot of land measuring sixteen and one-half arouras that Diogenes owned in the village of Ophis. Some time afterwards Diogenes, still much in financial troubles as it seems, borrowed another fifty *solidi* from the monastery, again through the agency of Theophilos. This time, a *hypotheca generalis* (a mortgage of all the present and future property of the debtor, securing the creditor's claims) was created in favour of the monastery to guarantee repayment of the full debt with the accumulated interest.

At this point we already spot a few curiosities. Firstly, one may ask how it was possible that a relatively unknown monastery had provided its representative with such an impressive sum of money (which basically means that the holy institution must have disposed of much greater funds)? The editor of *P.Oxy.* LI 3640 supposed Apa Hierax to be a very humble monastery: not only the amount of ropes was not impressive but also its prior was only a deacon. But neither of these facts seems decisive in determining the wealth and importance of the monastery. The quantity of merchandise recorded in the papyrus depended on the order and the ecclesiastical rank of the prior may have nothing to do with the real size of his religious establishment. This conclusion only shows how pieces of information drawn from a singular document may be misleading, our document indicates in any case that the monastery could freely dispose of great sums of money.

Tomasz Markiewicz shows in his article in this book that monks not only frequently took part in the credit turn-out, but also apparently disposed of rather large sums of ready money. They—notwithstanding the imperial regulations and canonical norms[3]—did have their private resources, which they used and multiplied sometimes even accumulating apparently considerable wealth).[4] In addition, various legal regulations indicate that monasteries took part in financial transactions as important moneylenders and borrowers. We may recall, for instance, the *Novella* 46 of C.E. 537, which—in cases when a church lacked money to pay its debts—granted an exception to the general ban on the alienation of ecclesiastical real estates introduced by the *Novella* 7 of C.E. 535. In such situations monks would obviously be the natural proxies of their own spiritual houses investing common wealth. We have to recall here however, that sometimes it is actually difficult to discern whether a monk or a nun acted in his or her own name,[5] or on behalf of their monastic community.

In our case, however, it is absolutely certain that the money was lent on behalf of the whole monastic community: it is a party to the settlement (cf. ll. 8-9), and to its favour the mortgage was instituted and the deeds were executed (cf. ll. 27-45). A lawyer spots here immediately a crucial issue:

---

[3] Cf. on this subject see a recent exhaustive study of G. Barone Adesi (Barone Adesi 1988); and an older text of R. Orestano, (Orestano 1956). From the ecclesiastical norms see, for example *Can.* 3 of the Council of Chalcedon forbidding bishops, clergymen, and monks to hire possessions, or engage in business, or occupy themselves privately in worldly engagements, its existence proves only that the reality was exactly opposite.

[4] A particularly illustrative example of the private possession of a large sum of money by a religious person, moreover a woman, is *P.Lond.* V 1731 (= Porter 1996 D42, Syene C.E. 585). By this deed Aurelia Tsone, a nun, ends an ongoing dispute with her own mother, Aurelia Tapia, issuing a receipt for 4 *solidi*. This money had been left for the little girl's upbringing by her father upon his divorce from Aurelia Tapia. The mother, however, never took care of Tsone, who grew up with the father, and instead kept the money for herself.

[5] One curious document, *SB* XX 14712, illustrates it well: the papyrus concerns a sale of two thousand four hundred wine jars on defer of payment to a woman described by the epithets οὐράνιος ἡ καὶ ζωοποιός, and represented by a presbyter, which could indicate she was a member of the clergy (cf. Sijpesteijn 1991: 197-199). Nothing in the text alludes to whether the purchase was made for her own use or on behalf of her monastic community.

the problem of the legal personality of the ecclesiastical entities. As this topic concerns my theme only marginally, I shall limit myself to a very brief statement on it. Suffice to say, that there has been an ongoing debate about the existence of the legal person as such in Roman law. There is no doubt, however, that if there was anything approaching the notion of a legal personality, it was indeed in the case of, as we shall call them, 'church persons,' such as bishoprics, monasteries, orphanages, hospices for the old and poor, and infirmaries. They are often characterised by the legal transactions (such as donations, inheritances, trusts, etc.) made to them *super piis causis* or εἰς εὐσεβεῖς αἰτίας, and therefore one tends to call them generically—albeit not very technically—*piae causae*.[6] There is a number of imperial regulations pertaining to them and usually identifying them jointly (cf. for instance, the formulation used in the *Novella 7 praef.* of 535: *existimavimus oportere legislationem imponere omnibus sanctissi sanctissmarum ecclesarium <et> xenodochiorum et nosocomiorum et monasteriorum et brephotrophiorum et gerontocomiorum et totius sacrati collegii rebus...*, repeated later in the same law, or the similar formulation in the *Novella* 120 of C.E. 544 which to some extent derogated the provisions of the ban on alienation found in the *Novella* 7).

What is extremely important for the proper juridical collocation of our document is the question of the legal representation of such *quasi*-legal persons. Interestingly, the only general legal provision on the matter deals merely vaguely with the problem. Chapter 5 of the *Novella* 133 (C.E. 539)—a sort of a digest of norms concerning monks (*quodmodo oportet monachos vivere*)—orders that a monastery should be placed under the care of an abbot and *apocrisiari*, who, being elderly and experienced monks, should be charged with the management of affairs and interests of the house. As soon as we read the following part of the norm regarding female convents, we immediately notice how imprecise and non-technical this regulation is, mixing the mundane with the celestial affairs. The statute commands by the very same clause that three *apocrisiari*—either eunuchs, or men advanced in years and distinguished by their chastity—would have to conduct litigation on behalf of the nuns and administer the holy communion to them; they also—for the sake of chastity—would act as intermediaries between the reverend mothers and their business agents.[7]

More particulars may be deducted from the specific regulations concerning *piae causae*. The monasteries were to be normally represented by the abbot/prior and/or steward, and the other religious institutions by their stewards or governors (*rectores*).[8] This seems to be somewhat, *mutatis mutandis*,

---

[6] See C. 1.2.19 (C.E. 528) regulating the problem of illegally-made donations to *sancta ecclesia, xenodochium, nosocomium, orphanotrophium, ptochotrophium*, the poor or cities because of holy reasons and C. 1.3.45 (46).1a [C.E. 530] on trusts and bequests made to the holy institutions respectively. On the problem, see the general overview in Kaser 1975, § 214 V and the literature quoted in the footnotes therein. See also the classical study on legal persons: Orestano 1968, *passim*, but above all, pp. 79-90 as well as, more specifically on *piae causae*, a paper of G. Barone Adesi, (Barone Adesi 1993).

[7] Seeing that this statute does not nullify the provisions of the *Novella* 7 which introduced personal liability of an abbess for an illegal transaction on behalf of a monastery (see *infra*, ft. 8), I suppose that this norm presented rather wishful thinking of the legislator than a practical solution. Furthermore, we may see how well Aurelia Tsone managed her affairs without any intermediaries—of course we cannot be certain, if there had been any formal litigation between herself and her mother before the settlement documented in *P.Lond.* V 1731 (however the ll. 18-20 may allude to it, cf. *supra* ft. 3).

[8] Just to illustrate this: *Novella* 7 C.E. 535), ch. 3 vests the power of making of an emphyteutic contract on behalf of the monastery in its steward (*oeconomus* = οἰκονόμος) (provided that they have received a sworn opinion from two mechanics or architects—if the place in question had only one expert, his single opinion would suffice). The same statute in chapter 1 addresses abbots and abbesses generally, prohibiting alienation of monastic property. It is obvious therefore that the

corroborated by the disposition of the *Canons* attributed to Athanasius. *Can.* 61b states that no economic activity on behalf of a church should be conducted by the bishop or steward alone, they always should act jointly. In the case of a monastery we might expect that it would be the abbot who was required to act jointly with the steward.[9] These powers of attorney are contrasted by personal liability of the persons in charge—with no gender discrimination[10]—for the illegal transactions conducted on behalf of a religious institution: the agreements shall be void, but the parties thereof may sue the abbot, steward or abbess.[11] Curiously, there is no trace in the normative texts of the important administrative and economic role of the *dikaion/diakonia*, which become obvious—albeit the particulars remain obscure—even after a very superfluous examination of various monastic papyrological *corpora* (one may consult both volumes of Sarah Clackson's Apa Apollo papyri).[12]

It is also very likely that the cases of the private monasteries differed: their representation was very likely vested with their owners,[13] founders or the guardians appointed by them.[14] This all calls for a fresh thorough examination of the papyri—as new important material has become known since the publication of Artur Steintwenter's classical studies—to confront the legal theory with the practice. At any rate, seeing the formulations in *P.Oxy.* LXIII 4397, it is obvious, that only the prior and the *oeconomus* acting jointly validly represented Apa Hierax.

Now how is it possible that Theophilos, who may have been one of the brethren of Apa Hierax—the document, referring to him as already dead styles him as τῆς εὐλαβοῦς μνήμης—but did not in fact need to have been a monk at all, contracted legally binding actions on behalf of the monastery operating with certainly more than petty sums of money? In the later course of events he may have

---

legislator saw the heads of the monastic houses vested with powers to dispose of their belongings. The *Novella* 54.2 (C.E. 537), which levies the general ban on the alienation of ecclesiastical property, authorised the heads of the religious houses (*praesules* = προεστῶτες) to exchange property on their behalf but only between two religious institutions. The abbots and *apocrisarii* may also represent singular monks. The *Novella* 79.1 of C.E. 539 establishing rules concerning the summons of the monks, nuns and clerics, ordered them to appear in court either in person or through representation of their abbots, *apocrisiarii* or other persons (*sive oportet per abbates, sive per responsales sive per alios quoslibet hoc fieri* = εἴτε δέοι διὰ τῶν ἡγουμένων εἴτε διὰ τῶν ἀποκρισιαρίων εἴτε δι' ἑτέρων τινῶν παραγίνεσθαι).

[9] Ed. Crum and Riedel 1904: 40. On the authorship of the canons, which may actually be rightly attributed to Athanasius, see pp. XX-XXVI. Similar provisions may be found, *e.g.* in *Can.* 26 of the *Council of Chalcedon*.

[10] A mention of an abbess in Ch. 5 and 6 of the *Novella* 7 (C.E. 535) shows that, in legal practice, nuns were by no means deprived of the capacity to engage in legal transactions, see also, *supra*, ft. 6

[11] And so the *Novella* 7 provided in chapter 5 that a contract of sale of ecclesiastical property was void, but that the purchase price might be demanded from the steward (*oeconomus* = οἰκονομός), abbot or abbess (*abba, abbatissa* = ἡγουμένος, ἡγουμένη), or head of the religious institutions. Similarly, chapter 6 introduced personal liability of the persons in charge of a religious institution for an illegally made pledge of particular objects belonging to it (in case of a monastery it is *praesulis* = ἡγουμένος). Finally, chapter 12 of the same *Novella* encumbers the abbot, steward and head of the religious house with all the expenses resulting from acquiring by whatever means a sterile field.

[12] On *dikaion* and *diakonia* with examples, see Steinwenter 1930 at 30-34, 39-40 and Steinwenter 1958 at 26-27.

[13] Just as the clauses of Apa Abraham's will show: his heir, Victor obtained unhindered powers to do anything he wished with the monastery as it became his sole property (see ft. 2 above and *P.Lond.* I 77 (pp. 231-236), ll. 25-40, especially 35-45, where the contents of the full property rights are described). See also, Steinwenter 1932, pp. 55-64, and Steinwenter 1930 at pp. 8-19.

[14] As in the case of the monastery founded by Apollos of which Dioskoros was to become *curator* and *phrontistes* "by the order of his father": cf. *P.Cair.Masp.* i 67096 (C.E. 573/4) where he co-represents the house together with its *oeconomus* Enoch. On this establishment, see MacCoull 1993: 21-63. Cf. also Steinwenter 1930: 21-23 and Steinwenter 1958: 28-29.

become the steward of the monastery—the text describes him as οἰκονομούμενος in the l. 96—but at the beginning he is significantly not titled at all.

Another question goes beyond the legal stratum of the text: what was he actually doing in Constantinople with such a handsome amount? What made the pious monastery send its envoy to the capital? The original purpose of the journey cannot have been lending money to Diogenes (he could have transferred the funds back home). A hint on this issue may be given by the fact that Theophilos was at least twice in the Capital: first when he lent Diogenes his money and a second time to negotiate with Fl. Strategios the monastery's claims to the mortgaged plot of land (cf. ll. 66-75), once the feebleness of Diogenes' securities had been discovered. This may mean that Theophilos was a regular envoy of Apa Hierax, who would travel to the Bosphorus, whenever there was a need to put in a petition at the imperial courts. He might have thus been the ordinary procurator of the monastery, a figure described in another digest concerning church persons, the *Novella* 123 (C.E. 546)—*de sanctissimis et deo amabilibus et reverentissimis episcopis et clericis et monachis*. Chapter 27 of this law foresees that whenever a monk or a nun, or a monastery is summoned to court *pro qualibet pecuniaria causa sive publica sive privata* (i.e. the house) he or she shall be represented by an attorney, either the general procurator of the monastery or his/her own.[15] If Theophilos was indeed an ἐντολεὺς τὰς τοῦ μοναστηρίου, he was probably empowered to use the wealth he was carrying. Such a supposition may also explain well why he had this enormous sum of money with him. Veering into speculations, we might imagine that the gold might have been intended to influence gently decision-making process in the Capital, perhaps to push forward any possible petitions he was carrying for the imperial justice. In this instance one immediately recollects the gifts advocating the cause and supplications of the Alexandrian patriarch Cyril at the Capital. A scrupulous list of the presents distributed by his envoys among the courtiers of the pious empress Pulcheria less then a century before our settlement sheds light on the ways of imperial justice.[16]

Returning to the original contract that gave rise to the later settlement, we encounter the issue of the interest. The parties agreed on six per cent per year, the highest amount legally executable at this time, since Justinian set the admissible level of interest at 4% for *illustres*, at 8% for professional bankers, and at 6% for all others in 528 (*CI* 4.32.26.2).[17] We are used to looking for abnormalities in the papyri rather than for confirmation of the imperial legal norms, as presented by our document. The correct 6% may, however, have been due to the execution of the original loan documents in Constantinople. It is still interesting, as Tomasz Markiewicz's research has shown, that loans given in the ecclesiastical milieu only rarely stipulate for interest. Obviously, one cannot exclude the possibility that the interest, even higher than the admissible one, was hidden in the initial loan capital (just as it most probably

---

[15] There is an interesting difference between the Greek and the Latin version of the constitution. The Latin allows a monk to *per se sive per procuratorem monasteris causam agere*. The Greek adds to this a personal attorney of the monk: δι' ἑαυτῶν εἴτε δι' τῶν ἐντολέων τὰς ἰδίας ἢ τὰς τοῦ μοναστηρίου πράττειν.

[16] See Batiffol 1911: 247-264. The list was contained in the letter sent by Epiphanios, archdeacon and syncellos of Cyril to Maximianus, archbishop of Constantinople. The epistle, which purpose was to stimulate actions of the persons who had received gifts, but apparently wanted even more, makes part of *Synodicon adversus tragoediam Irenaei*, and was probably translated from Greek into Latin by its anonymous 6th-century compiler (*ibidem*: 248 and the ft. 2). Batiffol estimated the value of the presents as exceeding one million francs of the time (256).

[17] See also Bonini 1968: 259-263.

happened in the case of loans documented in the *Tabulae Pompeianae Sulpiciorum*).[18] In any case: the general lack of interest is not without reason: already at the time of the Council of Nicea, the church law was very negative about *usura*. The seventeenth canon of this assembly openly prohibited the clergy to lend money for profit.[19] One might argue that canon seventeen did not specifically address monks or monasteries, but its wording is on the other hand rather general. Moreover, among the brethren of Apa Hierax there must also have been ordained clerics (like Ioseph the prior). The repeated prohibition for clergy of usury—both on the canonical sources and the pastoral writings—of lending money at interest by clergy clearly shows that the practice was far from the gospel example found in *Luke* 6.34-35.[20]

This striking contradiction between the canonical norms and the loans granted by Apa Hierax might be mitigated by the fact that the interest was to be paid from the annual revenue and fruits of the irrigated land pledged by Diogenes and not in money. The parties may have styled their pledge as antichretical in order to circumvent the obvious prohibition, and perhaps they did not see it as contrary to the ecclesiastical norm. Which leads to another problem. Let us firstly recall that in this very late period the classical terminological distinction between *hypotheca* (mortgage, conventional pledge, or to use the German legal terminology for obvious reasons closer to the Roman one: *Hypotheke*), and *pignus* (corporal pledge, *Besitzpfand*) had disappeared in legal practice: the documents use these terms synonymously.[21] Now, the construction of *antichresis* (a pledge with the right to use the pledged thing vested with the pledgee) must obviously involve a transfer of possession of the thing pledged to the creditor.[22] And in fact our papyrus uses in l. 20 the verb λαμβάνω, by which we should understand that the plot of land was really handed over to the monastery. But apparently it was not, because we learn from the continuation of the story that the plot later entered the property of Diogenes' other creditor, Fl. Strategios II.

This circumstance brings about the issue of the effectiveness of the securities in the original loan deeds between the Monastery and its debtor, and, more generally, guarantees attested in the papyri, particular pledges and *hypothecae generales*. Given the commonness of the latter (it is, for instance, a standard burden introduced in marriage documents on the husband's part to secure the rights of the wife to her dowry, it also normally appears as a security in settlements of claims), one may strongly doubt its real efficacy. We also realise how widespread general mortgage on all property was through the fact that Fl. Strategios made several of these with Diogenes (l. 50). This feeling is not altered even by the fact that in the actual case of Fl. Strategios this clause really worked at the end of the day (see below). Reading the legislative sources lends credence to this sensation: the provision of chapter 6 of

---

[18] See Camodeca 1999: introduction; Camodeca 1992: 176; Gröschler 1997: 156-177; A useful overview of the problem may be found at Verboven 2003: 7-28.

An indirect proof of such practices in Byzantine times may be found in the Justinianic constitution imposing limits on interests., See Cl. 4.32.26.4, where the legislator states that any illegally extracted interest should be counted as already repaid capital.

[19] Cf. as well, *Const. Apol.* 44. On this topic, see: Gaudemet 1958, chap. III 'Économie et societé', passim, but above all sec. II 'La Morale économique' and § 3 'Le commerce et l'usure' (577-581) with the sources therein cited.

[20] Of the same opinion is, *e.g.* Gaudemet 1958: 581.

[21] Cf. Kaser 1975: § 250 I-III.

[22] On the rules concerning *antichresis* see Kupiszewski 1974: 229-235, Kupiszewski 1986: 133-149. Cf. also D. 20.1.13.1 (Marcianus, lib. sing. *ad formulam hypothecariam*) for a very clear example showing that *antichresis* always meant transfer of possession of the thing pledged.

the *Novella* 7 wherein a corporal pledge of church property is prohibited and—if attempted—declared void, but a *hypotheca generalis* is still admitted. Seeing that the scope of the norm was protection of the ecclesiastical and monastic property, we observe that the legislator himself seems to have associated little risk with this kind of security, at the same time recognizing the efficacy of the corporal pledge.

Returning to the monastery's loans, we arrive at the point at which, upon Diogenes' death, the debts were still not repaid (ll. 45-66). At that moment the monks learnt that their debtor was not only insolvent, but that he also had other creditors whose rights were secured by prior mortgages. Apparently the most eminent was Fl. Strategios II, who started legal actions wishing to sue Diogenes' heirs in order to get his money back.

Once the presumptive *ab intestato* heirs of Diogenes, his brother Apphaus and sister Klematia, had renounced the succession, Fl. Strategios had to find other ways to get his obligation fulfilled. Lines 58-59 describe how he did it: in absence of the heirs, he had to petition to obtain the ownership of Diogenes' inheritance by the right of the mortgages (ἀπορίᾳ κληρονόμου αἰτῆσαι τὴν δεσποτίαν λαβεῖν τῷ δικαίῳ ὑποθηκῶν). It seems that Strategios applied a mixture of two legal procedures. Firstly, as there were no heirs of his debtor, he probably asked for *missio in possessionem* of the deceased debtor's estate.[23] Having obtained it, he should have tried to sell it (*venditio bonorum*) and get satisfaction from the price obtained. This, however, did not happen—either he did not attempt it at all, or he was not successful, as the papyrus tells us that he was compelled to "petition for ownership." It is very likely that what is meant here is the procedure known as *impetratio domini*.[24] This kind of pledge execution was reformed by Justinian by CI. 8.33.3 (C.E. 530): the creditor—unless the original loan contract secured by pledge foresaw a different way of its execution—having obtained the possession of the pledge was supposed to try to sell it for a period of two years, in case no possible purchaser could be found, he could petition the emperor to obtain ownership. And so the imperial privilege, even more likely to have been granted considering the social position of Strategios, made him the rightful owner of all of Diogenes' property, included of course the plot of irrigated land pledged to the monastery.

Apparently the monastery was seeking its own right at the same time. The monks must have realised quite quickly the successful efforts of Fl. Strategios, and so they sent Theophilos again to Constantinople in order to sue Strategios for (at least) the irrigated land. The monastery's envoy may have started a judicial proceeding—the formulation of the renunciation clause, that the monks had "learnt from accurate laws they had no right or action on mortgage" seems to allude to a failed trial, cf. ll. 170-172. And his claims were refused (ll. 66-82): a simple and ancient rule of law concerning pledges was applied: *prior tempore, potior iure*. Later security cedes before the earlier one (ll. 82-86). Theophilos at that point changed his strategy abandoning the legal way (useless as he well knew—he realised that monastery had no claim—οὐδεμία δικαιολογία—to the plot) and setting to appeal to Strategios' religious and pious consciousness. Curiously, the consular did not want to hand the contestable plot of land over to Apa Hierax, he rather preferred paying off Diogenes' debts in money. We may only speculate to the reason—perhaps the value of the field was much higher than the original

---

[23] The procedure was originally described in the rubric *cui heres non extabit* of *Edictum perpetuum* (Lenel 1927, § 207), cf. D. 40.5.2.4. D. 42.6.6 and G. 3.78.

[24] See Kaser 1975: § 252 1c.

debts that it secured. And so Strategios ordered people managing his estates to return the money to the monastery. They were, however, only ready to pay one pound (72 solidi) of gold. Interestingly, they did not give it to the monastery but deposited it with the Oxyrhinchite zygotastes, Serenos, apparently creating a *depositum irregulare*: the money was to be lent at profit to provide income for the monastery until a suitable plot of land was found, once it was found it was to be bought and transferred to the monastery. Just to complicate the story further: both Serenos and Strategios II died (the latter before 543)[25] and the remaining fifty-eight *solidi* were repaid before any suitable estate was found.

The monastery managed to get seventy-two *solidi* from Seronos' heirs and again sent an envoy to the capital to ask the present head of the house, Fl. Apion II, for the rest of the debt. He, acting together with his mother Leontia as curator, ordered his people to return the remaining part of the money. A small note on Leontia's role in the document may now be appropriate. Contrary to what the editor of the document says, her son was already a major, as every other Roman male *sui iuris* from the age of fourteen. The presence of the curator and her approval for the act was due to the ancient rules introduced by the *Lex Laetoria* which allowed Romans younger than twenty-five (*minores vigintiquinque annos*) to evade the effects of their legal actions should they turn out to have been concluded to their detriment.[26] The application of *Lex Laetoria* means that a curator had to approve only of dispositive transactions of his or her ward. A ratified dispositive act of a *minor viginti quinque annos* got full legal efficacy. On the contrary, no authorisation was needed for any acquisitive acts—as long as the person in question was older than 7. No conclusion may therefore be drawn concerning the age of Fl. Apion II from the fact that in *P.Oxy.* XVI 1985, of 9th October 543 he acted alone.[27] This document is a simple receipt addressed to him in which someone confirms having received various tools. There was no danger that Apion would ever think of evading the legal results of this act.

Back to the Apa Hierax debt. So, finally the monks got their money back, and moreover in ready coin and not, as Strategios originally wanted, in a kind of a trust to buy a new plot of land. Theodoros and Ioseph stressed that they were receiving money back only because of the piously-disposed will of young Apion and his mother, and before them of Strategios, who had all acted εὐσεβείας χάριν. What follows, is basically the clause of the final renunciation of any claims to the plot of land presently belonging Fl. Apion's estate. Its format is typical: the clause excludes any possibility of any further controversy conducted both in court and out of it. It further states that the parties abandoned the right to petition the emperor and would not try to seek justice in the holy church (ll. 168-169).[28] This clause is strengthened by a penal stipulation (l. 180), and its fulfillment secured by a general mortgage on the monastery's property (ll. 183-185). All the parties involved clearly stated that earthly securities ceded before pious reasons. Still, the settlement of claims was made, probably to prevent any future legal (even if not very well founded) claims on the part of the monastery.

A final and conclusive point that has to be briefly considered here is the legal form of the present deed. In terms of legal anthropology this conflict was resolved through a negotiation, as—it seems at least—the parties, unlike many other late Antique settlements, were not aided by intermediaries.[29] This

---

[25] See Mazza 2001: 59.

[26] Various studies have been conducted on the topic, but see from the most recent works Francesco Musumeci, (Musumeci 2001; Musumeci 2004) and the literature therein cited.

[27] See also my review of Mazza 2001: Urbanik 2004: 273.

[28] Cf. a very similar formulation in Apa Abraham's will: *P.Lond.* I 77, ll. 45-47.

[29] Cf. Rouland 1992: 298-299; Hobson 1993: 199-120; Gagos and van Minnen 1994: 30-32; Allam 1992: 3.

was probably due to the great discrepancy between their positions, and the factual feebleness of Apa Hierax's argumentation. The monks were only petitioners from the moment they had realised they had no legal claim to the mortgaged land.

Settlements of claims or *transactiones* become extremely common in the late Antique papyri as a way of conflict resolution., At the same time we have very few testimonies of the application of civil judicial procedure[30]. Scholarship has formulated various hypotheses explaining this phenomenon. The most extreme opinion, postulating that civil courts ceased to exist in the course of the sixth century C.E., has justly been proven to be too far-fetched.[31] It is much more likely that the rise of transactions was due to a mixture of circumstances: settlements may have seemed to the contestants quicker, easier and more durable, and above all cheaper than civil judgments. Many settlements were reached within families (especially in litigations resulting from hereditary disputes),[32] and a few involve people connected to the church.[33] In both of these contexts an out-of-court conflict resolution may have been chosen because of its more discreet character. Finally, a settlement was the only way to achieve results in discordance with the statutory law. This was precisely the case of Apa Hierax's conflict with the *domus gloriosa* of Apiones, where pious inclination prevailed over earthly guarantees.

BIBLIOGRAPHY:

Allam, S. (1992). "Observations on Civil Jurisdiction in Late Byzantine and Early Arabic Egypt," in: Johnson, J. H. (ed.), *Life in the Mutli-Cultural Society: Egypt from Cambyses to Constantine and Beyond*. Chicago: University of Chicago Oriental Institute (= *Studies in Ancient Oriental Civilization* 51), 1-9.

Barone Adesi, G. (1988). "Il sistema giustinianeo delle proprietà eccesiastiche," in: Cortese, E. (ed.), *La proprietà e le proprietà*. Milan: Giuffré, 75120.

Barone Adesi, G. (1993). "Dal dibattito cristiano sulla destinazione dei beni economici alla configurazione in termini di persona delle *venerabiles domus* destinate *piis causis*," in: *Atti dell'Accademia Romanistica Costantiniana. IX Convegno Internazionale*, Perugia, 231-326.

Batiffol, P. (1911). "Les présents de Saint Cyrille a la cour de Constantinople," *Bulletin d'ancienne littérature et d'archéologie chrétiennes*, 247-264.

Bonini, R. (1968). *Ricerche di diritto giustinianeo*. Milano: Giuffré, 259-263.

Camodeca, G. (1992). *L'Archivio puteolaneo dei Sulpicii* I. Napoli: Jovene

---

[30] Cf. Gagos and van Minnen 199: in part. 30-46; I have dealt with the problem in Urbanik 2007: 377-400 with the literature cited therein.

[31] Schiller 1971: 469-502; for the first criticisms see: Simon 1971: 624 ss. Cf. as well Urbanik 2007: 395-398.

[32] See for example settlements from the Archive of Pathermouthis and Kako, *P.Münch.* I 1, 6, 7 and 14; a tiny Coptic family dossier concerning inheritance, *P.KRU* 34-36 or *P.Mich.Aphrod.* (ca. 537). For other examples see Urbanik 2007: fts. 29-30.

[33] Apart from our document, cf. *SBKopt.* I 36 and other texts documenting the same controversy: *SB* VI 8987 and 8988 (Apollinopolis, C.E. 647), *P.Princ.* II 82 + *SB* III 7033, Lykopolis—481 and *P.Lond.* V 1731, Syene, 20.09.585.

Camodeca, G. (1999). *Tabulae Pompeianae Sulpiciorum. Edizione critica dell'archivio puteolano dei Sulpicii* (*Vetera. Ricerche di storia epigrafia ed antichità* 12). Roma: Edizioni Quasar

Crum, W. E. and Riedel, W. (1904). *The Canons of Athanasius of Alexandria—The Arabic and Coptic Versions*. Oxford.

Gagos, T. and van Minnen, P. (1994). *Settling a Dispute. Toward a Legal Anthropology of Late Antique Egypt*. Ann Arbor: University of Michigan Press (*New Texts from Ancient Cultures* 1) (= *P.Mich. Aphr.*)

Gascou, J. (1985). "Les grands domaines, la cité et l'État en Égypte byzantine," *TravMem* 9, 4-90.

Gaudemet, J. (1958). *L'Église dans l'Empire romain (IVe-Ve siècles)*. Paris: Sirey

Gröschler, P. (1997). *Die tabellae-Urkunden aus den pompejanischen und herkulanensischen Urkundenfunden (= Freiburger Rechtsgeschichtliche Abhandlungen, Neue Folge—Bd* 26). Berlin: Duncker & Humblot.

Hobson, D. W. (1993). "The Impact of Law on Village Life in Roman Egypt," in: Halpern, B. and Hobson, D. W., *Law Politics and Society in the Ancient Mediterranean World*. Sheffield: Sheffield Academic Press, 193-219.

Kaser, M. (1975). *Römisches Privatrecht*. II. *Nachklassische Entwicklungen*. Munich: C. H. Beck (*Handbuch der Altertumswissenschaft* X.3.3.2).

Kupiszewski, H. (1974). "Quelques remarques sur les vocabula ἀντιχρέσις, ἄρρα, παραφέρνα dans le Digeste", *JJP* 18, 227-238 (= *Scritti Minori*, Napoli 2000, 267-278).

Kupiszewski, H. (1986), "Antichrese und Nutzpfand in den Papyri" in *Iuris Professio. Festgabe M. Kaser zum 80. Geburtstag*. Vienna-Cologne-Graz, 133-149 (= *Scritti minori*, Napoli 2000, 473-489).

Lenel, O. (1927). *Das Edictum Perpetuum*. Leipzig: B. Tauchnitz [3 ed.].

MacCoull, L. S. B. (1993), "The Apa Apollos Monastery of Pharoou (Aphrodito) and its Papyrus Archive," *Le Muséon* 106, 21-63.

MacCoull, L. S. B (2000), "Translation and Commentary of *P.Lond.* I 77 (pp. 231-236)," in: Thomas, J. and Constantinides Hero, A. (eds.), *Byzantine Monastic Foundation Documents: A Complete Translation of the Surviving Founders' Typika and Testaments*. Washington (*Dumbarton Oaks Studies* 35), 51-58, online version: www.doaks.org/etexts.html).

Mazza, R. (2001), *L'archivio degli Apioni. Terra, lavoro e proprietà senatoria nell'Egitto tardoantico*. Bari: Edipuglia.

Musumeci, F. (2001). "Editto sui minori di 25 anni e ius controversum nell'età dei Severi," in: *Iuris vincula. Studi in onore di Mario Talamanca*. Napoli, vol. 6, 33-72.

Musumeci, F. (2004), "Pretore, giudice e protezione dei minori di venticinque anni," *Labeo* 50, 64-83.

Orestano R. (1956). "Beni dei monaci e monastery nella legislazione giustinianea," in: *Studi in onore di Pietro de Francisci* III. Milano: Giuffré, 563-593 (= *Scritti*, III, no. 29, 1245-1275).

Orestano, R. (1998). *Il "problema delle persone giuridiche' in diritto romano*. Torino: Giappichelli.

Porter, B. (1996). The Elephantine Papyri in English: Three Millennia of Cross-Cultural Continuity and Change. Leiden/New York: Brill.

Rouland, N. (1992). *Antropologia giuridica*. Milano: Giuffré.

Schiller, A. A. (1971). "The Courts Are No More" in *Studi Volterra*, vol. I. Milano: Pubblicazioni della Facolta di giurisprudenza dell'Università di Roma, 469-502.

Sijpesteijn, P. J. (1991). "Οὐράνιος ἡ καὶ ζωοποιὸς μοναζοῦσα. Kauf von Fässern gegen Vorauszählung," *Tyche* 6, 197-199.

Simon, D. (1971). "Zur Zivilgerichtsbarkeit im spätbyzantinischen Ägypten," *Revue Internationale de Droit de l'Antiquité* 18, 629-657.

Steinwenter, A. (1932). "Byzantinische Mönchstestamente," *Aegyptus* 12, 55-64

Steinwenter. A. (1930), "Die Rechtsstellung der Kirchen und Klöster nach den Papyri, " *Zeitschrift der Savigny Stiftung für Rechtsgeschichte. Kanonistische Abteilung* 19, 1-50.

Steinwenter. A. (1958). "Aus dem kirchlichen Vermögensrechte der Papyri," *Zeitschrift der Savigny Stiftung für Rechtsgeschichte. Kanonistische Abteilung* 44, 1-34.

Urbanik, J. (2004). review of Mazza 2001, *JJP* 34, 271-274.

Urbanik, J. (2007). "Compromesso o processo? Alternativa risoluzione dei conflitti e tutela dei diritti nella prassi della tarda antichità" in E. Cantarella, J. Mélèze Modrzejewski and G. Thür (Hrsgg.), *Symposion 2005. Vorträge zur griechischen und hellenistischen Rechtsgeschichte*. Vienna: Verlag der österreichischen Akademie der Wissenschaften, 377-400.

Verboven, K. (2003). "The Sulpicii from Puteoli and Usury," *Tijdschrift voor Rechtsgechiedenis* 71, 7-28.

MONKS AND MONASTIC DWELLINGS.
P.DUBL. 32-34, *P.KRU* 105 AND BL MS.OR. 6201-6206 REVISITED

EWA WIPSZYCKA

1. DID MONKS NEED TO SECURE THEIR RIGHT OF OWNERSHIP ON DESERT LAND?[1]

The question may reasonably surprise you. Many literary texts belonging to our monastic dossier show us monks settling in the desert—from Antony who simply took possession of a Pharaonic tomb, through Makarios who gave origin to Sketis, up to Samuel who created, at the beginning of the seventh century, an important monastic centre at Kalamun: nowhere is there any hint at any legal problem.

However, reality was much more complex. Complications might arise when monks wanted to settle not in the "great desert," where there was place enough for anybody, but on the *gabal*, that is on the fringes of the desert, where they could find a home in ancient tombs cut out from the rock or in abandoned quarries. Here competitors could turn up, therefore monks who were going to spend money to adapt ancient tombs or quarries for their needs wanted to be sure that they would have the right to dispose of the given area of the *gabal*. It is easy to understand why literary texts do not mention such worries: the technical and material aspects of the rise of monastic centres did not interest them.

The oldest piece of evidence showing that acting on a ground situated on the border of the desert was not always free to anybody is the document Chrest.Wilk. 373 of the year 276-277, from Philadelphia in the Fayum. A certain Aurelios Iason delivers to his brother a receipt by which he acknowledges having got his part of the paternal heritage "except for the part that falls to me of the *oros* of the aforesaid village" (χωρὶς τοῦ ἐπιβάλλοντός μοι μέρος ὄρους τῆς προκειμένης). Iason belonged to the category of the *allophyloi*. This word, as Jean Gascou has shown, is one of the terms denoting gravediggers, people working and in many cases dwelling in the cemeteries.[2] The *oros*, a part of which Iason was entitled to, could obviously be used for some practical purposes. We do not know how one could become owner of a part of the *gabal*, nor what fiscal consequences derived from being its owner.

---

[1] Any discussion about monastic institutions of Late Antiquity in Egypt is bound to come up against terminological difficulties. The terms used in our sources—in particular μοναστήριον—denote different realities in different contexts. In my paper I shall use the terms "monastery," "*koinobion*" or "cenobitic community," "hermitage," and "*laura*," as follows:
  – "monastery": any monastic community;
  – "*koinobion*" or "cenobitic community": a monastic community whose members work, eat and pray together and accept to submit to the authority of a prior;
  – "hermitage": a dwelling which is usually inhabited either by a single monk or by a monk and his servant, but which is sometimes inhabited by two or three monks (the teacher and his disciples, or the monk who owns it and one or two monks who have no hermitage of their own); a hermitage can be a dwelling dug in the rock, or adapted from a quarry or from a Pharaonic tomb, or built like the houses of the peasants, with sun dried bricks;
  – "*laura*": a monastic centre consisting of hermitages and whose members usually eat separately, while the common meals take place on Sundays, after the mass; the role of the prior depends on his personality: if he has the qualities of a charismatic leader, he leads his community effectively; if he has no such qualities, his role in the life of the monks is very limited.

[2] Gascou 1997: 285-294.

Monks too could be owners of parts of the *gabal*. It was in the *gabal* that most of them built their homes and settled. Those who did so might foresee that other monks would be interested in finding in the same area a convenient place for practising asceticism.

Among the papyrological texts of our monastic dossier the clearest piece of evidence showing that monks needed to secure their right of ownership on the area of the *gabal* on which they lived, is *P.KRU* 105 (end of the sixth century), relating to the monastery of Apa Phoibammon, situated in Western Thebes, among the ruins of the temple of Deir el Bahari.[3]

W. C. Till described this document as being an "Anerkennung des Eigentumsrechtes des Phoibammon-Klosters." The village whose name must have been given in the lost first lines of the document, is certainly Jême, for the persons and churches appearing here as guarantors also appear in other documents from Jême. The representatives of the village, i.e. the presbyters and deacons here named and the *lashane*, confirm the right of the prior (his name has disappeared in the lost part of the document) to dispose of the *topos* of Apa Phoibammon: he has the right to live in the *topos*, to build and to pull down anything in it, to admit monks to it, to transmit it to his successor. If anybody dares to question the prior's right, they will not only incur divine chastisement, but also pay a fine of six ounces of gold. The prior, to whom the document is addressed, is the monk who founded the monastery on a ground that had formerly been desert. The document will be recognized as valid by any authority. There follows the formula: "We, the whole village, represented by the εὐλαβέστατοι presbyters and by Papnute, the τιμιώτατος *lashane*, agree with this deed." The number of the witnesses—both clerics and laymen—is considerable.

At first sight the document might seem strange: is the village really entitled to take decisions in matters concerning the monastery? Commenting on this text, A. Steinwenter was concerned to notice the intervention of a lay authority and the fact that there is no mention of a decision taken by the bishop, who according to him was the only authority entitled to consent to the foundation of a monastery. (Steinwenter did not cite any legal rule, but had doubtless in mind Canon 4 of the council of Chalcedon). W. Godlewski, who discussed *P.KRU* 105 in his study on the monastery of Apa Phoibammon,[4] maintained that there was no reason to be concerned about this: the monastery of Apa

---

[3] *P.KRU*. Cf. Steinwenter 1935: 377-385; Till 1964: 188-190. Let me quote Till's translation: "… die nach Gottes und eurem Willen nach euch kommen werden, wie es sich gehört, weil ihr Herr des ganzen τόπος des Apa Phoibammon seid, daß ihr darin wohnt, aufbaut oder niederreißt, Leute zu euch hinein nehmt von allen, die einen gottesfürchtigen Lebenswandel führen, für die ganze Dauer eures Lebens und (des Lebens dessen), den ihr nach euch in den τόπος einsetzt, daß er die Angelegenheit des Almosens der Armen verwalte. Niemandem soll es möglich sein [-(*10 letters*)-] der gewagt hat, es zu tun, [macht sich schuldig] des Gerichtes Gottes. Sie sollen das Strafgeld zahlen, das unsere Herren, die christusliebenden Könige, mit 6 Unzen Gold festgesetzt haben. Nach (der Zahlung) des Strafgeldes soll er herkommen und alles anerkennen, was in dieser Urkunde steht, denn wir finden, daß ihr es warest, die sich vom Anfang an um den τόπος bemüht haben. Ihr habt ihn errichtet, als er wüst war. Deswegen soll derjenige, den ihr nach eurem Scheiden aus dem Leibe in den τόπος einsetzen werdet, über den Ort herrschen, wie wir schon oben geschrieben haben.

"Niemand soll ihm den Prozeß machen können bei Gericht oder vor den Rechtsprechstellen, denn es schien uns so richtig und gefiel uns. Wir haben diese Urkunde ausgestellt, die sicher, garantiert und gültig sein wird, wo immer sie bei einer Obrigkeit oder einer Behörde vorgezeigt werden wird. Wir sind gefragt worden und haben (uns dazu) bekannt.

"Wir, das ganze Dorf, (vertreten) durch die εὐλαβέστατοι Priester und Papnute, den τιμιώτατος Laschanen, wir stimmen dieser Urkunde zu."

There follow the signatures of one *archipresbyteros*, of six *presbyteroi* and of four *diakonoi*, and then the signatures of the witnesses.

[4] Godlewski 1988: 63-65.

Apollo at Deir el Bahari—he argued—is likely to have been a continuation of a small monastery of the same name, which had existed in a desert *wadi* and had been abandoned, probably because of the danger of falling stones;[5] if this was the case, the foundation of this monastic community had already been accepted before by the bishop. I am convinced that both Steinwenter and Godlewski were wrong in thinking that Egyptian monks felt obliged to comply with the rule formulated by the aforesaid canon and later repeated by Justinian's legislation. The fact that a canon was voted by a council of bishops or that a constitution was promulgated by an emperor does not mean that the given rule came immediately into force in the whole empire. Canon law (as a set of rules valid in the whole Church) did not yet exist. There was no authority that could force upon the whole Church compliance with rules formulated by councils or emperors. There still remained something of the diversity and institutional liberty that had characterised the old Church up to the fourth century. The ecclesiastical hierarchy could ignore them and keep the local custom, if such custom did not give rise to conflicts. Egyptian monks, who lived in various and loose structures, do not seem to have bothered very much about legal rules. Local custom in Egypt did not give to bishops many opportunities of interfering with internal matters of the monastic communities: if no scandalous conflict arose, even the choice of a prior did not necessitate an official pronouncement of the bishop. Of course, the monks talked with the bishop when they wanted to found a new community as well as when they had to choose a new prior; however, they did so in an informal manner and this gave them the possibility of doing as they liked, if the bishop was not enthusiastic about their project, but had no reason for opposing it by a formal prohibition.

The village gave to the monastic community an area of the desert that was, thanks to the ruins of the temple, particularly convenient for building a monastery. It was the village, not the bishop, who decided to give the land. The decision was taken at the beginning of the existence of the monastic community. (I quite agree with W. Godlewski that *P.KRU* 105 must be dated to the end of the sixth century, a time when the area was ἔρημος). The village's consent given to the founder of the monastery, together with his own financial contribution towards the building of it, was the basis of his right of ownership on the area.

It was probably about the same time that the semi-anachoretic community that we call the *laura* of Epiphanios (though Epiphanios was not its founder: he inherited it from a monk who had previously been its chief) was allowed to occupy a plot of ground in the *gabal*. This community settled on the western slope of the rocky amphitheatre closed on the North by the ruins of the temple of Deir el Bahari. The nucleus of the *laura* was in the Pharaonic tomb of Daǧa.

We fortunately possess a substantial dossier concerning this *laura* and consisting of documents, private letters, lists of payments, etc. From my point of view the most interesting piece is *P.KRU* 75, a will made about the middle of the seventh century by two monks, Jacob and Elias, the owners of the *laura*. The document mentions the former owners and their decisions. Elias had received the monastery from Psan, a disciple of Epiphanios (Epiphanios himself had been the second chief of the monastery; we know that he had inherited it). Psan had destined the monastery to Jacob, but later on he had drawn up a second document which took account not only of Jacob, but also of a new member of the community, Elias. Elias had the right to stay in the monastery up to the end of his life. In *P.KRU* 75 Jacob and Elias appear jointly as owners. They bequeath the monastery to a monk named Stephen. Stephen will inherit not only the dwelling-places with all their effects, but also a surprisingly vast area

---

[5] Bachatly 1982; Krause 1981: 155-160.

of desert land surrounding the dwellings. The property bequeathed is not defined by the name of the *laura*, nor by a description of its buildings, but by a description of the boundaries of the area. This is so precise that H. E. Winlock was able to draw the boundaries on a map.

The foundation of the *laura* must have been preceded by an agreement with the authorities of Jême as to the extent of the slope that had to be destined to the *laura*. On that area nobody would have the right to build a hermitage without the permission of the monk leading the monastic community. The chief of this community acted as if that area were his private property.[6]

2. Deeds of Sale of Monastic Dwellings

I am now going to deal with two sets of documents, *P.Dubl.* 32-34 and five Coptic documents from the British Library.[7] Others have commented on them before me. However, I think I can contribute something new towards their interpretation.

The three documents *P.Dubl.* 32-34[8] were found together near the Hawara pyramid, we do not know exactly where—among the ruins of a building of the Byzantine period? or in a small church? or in a room adjacent to it?—but in any case at the very place where somebody, who obviously was interested in them, had hidden them at the beginning of the sixth century. They were contained in a jar buried in the soil; each of them was carefully rolled up, and the whole was wrapped up with belts of reed and protected with a piece of linen and finally with a piece of woollen cloth. These details are important, for they witness that the three documents go together and form a whole, at least in that sense that the monk who hid them did not possess any other document relating to the same matter. It is unfortunate that Flinders Petrie did not give information about the archaeological context of the finding.[9] I inspected the surroundings of the Hawara pyramid, but I was not able to find out anything useful in this respect.

The problem of the localization of Labla deserves some attention. One is naturally inclined to think that Labla should be identified with the ruins of a small *laura* found at the foot of the Hawara pyramid. This is what J. Gascou[10] and others (including myself) have thought. However, this is not quite sure, for we do not know exactly where the papyri were found. If we assume that they were buried inside one of the hermitages, the identification of Labla with Hawara goes without saying. If we assume that they were buried inside the church, the situation is not so simple, for everybody had access to the church. Anyway, if Labla is not to be identified with Hawara, it was situated very near Hawara, in the

---

[6] The problem of who is entitled to dispose of a *laura* was not confined to monastic communities in Egypt. In the Life of saint Sabas by Cyril of Skythopolis there appear worries (chapter 19) analogous to those which we have observed in *P.KRU* 105: to what extent has the founder of a *laura* the right of deciding about it, and what are the rights of the other monks? For this text, see Flusin 2007.

[7] I leave aside a document which might or might not be connected with the sale of a monastic dwelling: BL Ms. Or. 4917(15) of the year 986/987, first published by Crum (*P.KRU* 673), reedited by Richter (1999: 85-89).

[8] *P.Dubl.* 32 and 33, first published by Sayce, were reprinted in *SB* I 5174 and 5175; they have been (and still are) often cited by reference to this reprint. B. C. M. McGing identified a third document as belonging to the same dossier; he published the three documents together in McGing 1990: 67-94. McGing's paper contains an extensive commentary, which has not been repeated in *P.Dubl.*; it must therefore be read together with the text of the new edition.

[9] Flinders Petrie 1889: 21, pl. VIII, 1.

[10] Gascou 1990.

"monastic desert." From the point of view of my argument this does not matter very much.[11] Why were our papyri buried? I have no idea.

It is clear from these texts that the monks appearing in a deed of sale and in a ὁμολογία διαλύσεως live (or used to live) in a very loosely structured monastic ensemble (or in a gathering of independent hermitages) called Labla and situated in the *proastion* of Arsinoe in the Fayum. *Proastion* means "suburb," but a place designated by this word was not necessarily very near to a town.

Let us look first at the deeds of sale *P.Dubl.* 32 of 7 September 512 and *P.Dubl.* 33 of 9 July 513. One and the same person, the monk Eulogios son of Joseph, sells twice one and the same hermitage, i.e. one and the same monastic dwelling (the description of the boundaries does not allow any doubts). He lives at the time in another hermitage, in the community of Mikrou Psyon, which must have been not far away, being situated in the *proastion* of Arsinoe.[12] The purchasers are, in the deed *P.Dubl.* 32, Pousi son of A[...], living at Labla, and in the deed *P.Dubl.* 33, Paphnoutios son of Isaac and Ioulios son of Aranthios, who also live at Labla. The deeds state the rights of the purchasers according to notarial standards, without any qualification. The price is 8 *solidi* in the case of *P.Dubl.* 32, 10 *solidi* in that of *P.Dubl.* 33. B. C. M. McGing thinks that in both deeds the sale is a legal fiction, performing the function of guaranty of a loan, for there is no evidence that in the interval between 7 September 512 and 9 July 513 Eulogios bought back the hermitage. We must ask: since Eulogios, at the time when the first deed was written, did not live any longer in this hermitage, who lived in it? Of course, the fictitious sale did not mean that the purchasers, who had their own hermitages in Labla, moved into the hermitage; on the other hand, it is unlikely that a dwelling worth 8 *solidi* was empty. The question cannot be answered.

The third document contained in the jar, *P.Dubl.* 34, is one year older than *P.Dubl.* 32: it bears the date 24 August 511. It is an agreement between two monks living in a hermitage at Labla; nothing is said of the location of the hermitage, which is unfortunate, for such a piece of information would have been for us the best means of establishing whether this is the same hermitage as that of the other two documents. The owner of the hermitage, Aioulios son of Aranthios, promises to Eulogios son of Pousi that after his death the hermitage will become Eulogios' property; he also declares that he annuls his former written decision by which he had destined it to Isaac son of Sabinos. Moreover, the document contains the following clauses: Aioulios will not have the right of introducing into the hermitage any other monk or any man "of the world" (we do not know what sort of man is meant: a disciple wishing to become a monk? or a servant?) without Eulogios' consent; if he does introduce somebody, Eulogios will immediately become the owner of the hermitage. This will also happen if Aioulios leaves the hermitage (nothing is said of the possible reasons of such a decision). Eulogios commits himself to not expelling Aioulios as long as he lives. The last clause is curious: after all Aioulios was the owner!

---

[11] Willy Clarysse has communicated to me a passage of the unpublished doctoral dissertation of Inge Uytterhoeven, *Hawara in the Graeco-Roman Periods. Life and Death in a Fayum Village* (Catholic University of Leuven, 2003). I take the liberty of quoting it: "In the 6th cent. the toponym Nabla had changed into Labla. In the Eulogios archive discovered by Petrie in the church at Hawara the monk Eulogios sold his cell at Labla (*P.Dubl.* 32-34). The find place of this small archive confirms the identification of Labla with Graeco-Roman Nabla near (or even at) Hawara. The description of Labla as τὸ ὄρος τὸ καλούμενον Λάβλα (*P.Dubl.* 32), located in the district of Arsinoe or in the outskirts of Arsinoe (*P.Dubl.* 33), indicates that Labla was situated in the desert area. It was apparently a zone of monasteries, a kind of laura, with independent cells that were part of a larger monastic organisation, but could be privately owned and administered."

[12] I do not know why B. C. M. McGing considers Mikrou Psyon to be the name of a hermitage or of a group of hermitages neighbouring with the one that is the object of the present discussion. This does not result from the text.

The name of Aioulios' father, Aranthios, is very rare. This makes it likely that this Aioulios is identic with the Ioulios of *P.Dubl.* 33 (Aioulios and Ioulios are not two names, but one name under two forms). This in turn suggests that the Eulogios to whom Aioulios/Ioulios wants to pass on his hermitage is identical with the Eulogios of the other two documents (though Eulogios is a frequent name), and that the three documents refer to one hermitage. The trouble is that in *P.Dubl.* 34 Eulogios is said to be son of Pousi, not of Joseph, as in the two deeds of sale *P.Dubl.* 32 and 33. This is a strong argument against the identification. However, if we assume that this Eulogios is another person, the fact that *P.Dubl.* 34 was packed up together with *P.Dubl.* 32 and 33 becomes unintelligible. We need a hypothesis accounting for each of the three documents and for their having been put together.

I think that in all three documents we have to do with one and the same Eulogios. It is possible that the scribe made a mistake in writing the name of Eulogios' father, but it is more likely that Eulogios' father had two names, Joseph and Pousi: analogous cases occur frequently in papyri. If Eulogios is the same monk, the hermitage is also one and the same monastic dwelling. Under circumstances unknown to us Eulogios must have got the ownership of the hermitage from Ioulios, though the latter was still alive. Ioulios might perhaps have decided—for reasons escaping our knowledge—to leave his hermitage, turning it over to Eulogios. In any case he stayed in Labla. On the other hand Eulogios left Labla between August 511 and September 512 and settled at Mikrou Psyon, after which he performed a fictitious sale (to Pousi, for 8 *solidi*) of the hermitage in Labla in which he was no longer living. In July 513 he sold the same hermitage, this time really, not fictitiously, to Ioulios son of Aranthios and to Papnouthios son of Isaac for 10 *solidi*. It was Ioulios, I think, who wrapped up, put into a jar and buried the three documents. At least one document was lacking when he did so, namely a document attesting that the ownership of the hermitage had passed from Ioulios to Eulogios; why it was lacking, we cannot guess.

The hypothesis I propose seems to me to have the merit of explaining why *P.Dubl.* 34 was put together with the two deeds of sale—a fact that McGing could not explain.

P.Dubl. 33 and 34 prove that monks who were more or less equal in respect of their monastic status could live in one and the same hermitage. When studying the results of the excavations of the monastic centres of Kellia, Esna or Naqlun, we take it for granted that each hermitage was usually inhabited by a monk (the "teacher," "the old man") and his disciple or disciples. However, the documents under discussion show that a hermitage could be inhabited by two monks of equal status. Of course, one of the two might have stood higher on the ladder of monastic prestige (he might have been practising asceticism for a longer time; he might have built or furnished the hermitage and be its exclusive owner, etc.), but the relationships between the two were founded on a substantial equality.

If we now turn to the literary dossier of Egyptian monasticism having in mind the lesson of *P.Dubl.* 33 and 34, we shall easily find confirmation of this. A passage of the Arabic Life of John of Sketis (from the eighties of the seventh century) is marvellously clear:[13]

"Il nous disait encore: 'Vous savez, mes enfants, que je n'ai jamais fait souffrir un frère qui se trouvait dans ma cellule, ni ne l'ai mis dehors, alors même que je n'avais aucun besoin de lui: je n'ai jamais commis cette faute devant le Seigneur. Pour votre part, faites de même. Si vous êtes nombreux, habitez dans une seule cellule et n'attristez pas une âme égarée (et) persécutée, comme le font ceux qui rejettent (les autres), qui ont des pensées terrestres et qui prétextent la solitude'."

---

[13] "La Vie de saint Jean, higoumène de Scété au VIIe siècle", in Zanetti 1996. I quote Zanetti's translation, p. 354.

It is worthwhile to quote a passage belonging to the collection of apophthegms of Daniel.[14]

"Abba Daniel again narrated: 'When Abba Arsenios was at Sketis, there was there a monk who was in the habit of stealing things belonging to the elders. And Abba Arsenios took him to his own cell in order to gain him and to procure peace to the elders. And he told him: If you want something, I shall give it to you, but do not steal'." (The story then tells that Arsenios' generous action did not have effect: the monk who was in the habit of stealing went on stealing, so that it was necessary to expel him from "the desert"). From this apophthegm it appears that a hermitage—normally, of course, of a monk who was well-to-do—could be spacious enough for its owner to be able to introduce into it another monk who would pray and work without disturbing him.

Monks whom the monastic tradition did not compel to absolute obedience and who lived together in one hermitage needed a high degree of self-discipline and tact to avoid small conflicts that might make life miserable for them. In the *Logoi* of Isaiah there are plenty of instructions on this subject. They arouse our admiration by their subtlety.[15]

A group of five Coptic texts found in Bawit and dated more than two hundred years later than the *P.Dubl.* I have just discussed, furnishes unambiguous evidence of the phenomenon I am discussing— the sale of monastic dwellings.[16] These texts are deeds of sale of a hermitage. Judging by the description of its location, they all refer to one and the same dwelling house, situated inside the monastic village which was, as we all know, a cenobitic monastery.

In the year 833 Joseph, the archimandrite of the monastery of Apa Apollo, and his brother Mark sell a hermitage to Makare and his sons at the price of 3 *solidi* (n° 6203). This sum is to be paid not to the sellers, but to the *diakonia*, i.e. to the service of the monastery managing its economic affairs. In spite of this we can be sure that the archimandrite does not act as a representative of the monastery, but as the owner of the dwelling, for we learn that he bought it some time before from a monk who is no longer alive. A clause states that if the purchasers die, the hermitage will return to the *diakonia*. However, nine years later Makare and his sons sell it at the price of 3 *solidi* to Paul and his brother Peter (n° 6204). In this deed there is no clause concerning the *diakonia*'s rights in the case of the death of the purchasers, but the omission is certainly fortuitous, for in the following deed, written five years later and by which a group of monks buy the hermitage for 2 *solidi* (n° 6205), the clause is there. These monks sell it two years later at the same price (n° 6202).

This set of documents is rather curious. It is surprising to see that during seventeen years the hermitage changed hands four times, though there is no mention of an owner having died. I am inclined to think that the successive purchasers appearing in these deeds bought the hermitage not in order to live in it, but in order to let it to new monks of the monastery. This does not seem unlikely, since we have to do with a big monastery, where there was probably a considerable movement going on.

---

[14] *Apophtegmes* 2003: 28-29, n° 23 = Dan. 6 (156 B).

[15] Abbé Isaïe, *Recueil ascétique* (1985).

[16] The documents were first used by M. Krause in his unpublished doctoral dissertation *Das Apa-Apollo-Kloster zu Bawit*, Theologische Dissertation Leipzig 1958; they were published by L. McCoull 1994: 141-158, with plates (the commentary is scanty). The dossier preserved in the British Library consists of five pieces, but two of them—BL Ms. Or. 6201 and 6202—are identical, though one of the two was written five days after the other. Of these two pieces L. McCoull published only the younger one.

In all these documents there appear monks who are related to each other: brothers or father and sons. This is also curious, though not without parallel. Analogous situations are attested elsewhere, mostly in literary texts, rarely in documents. It is a pity that nobody has ever studied this aspect of Egyptian monasticism. What is surprising is the fact that two or more monks related to each other live in one and the same monastery, in spite of the rule according to which a man wanting to abandon "the world" and practise asceticism ought to cut all ties with his family.

This dossier from Bawit proves that monastic dwellings were goods that could be sold and bought, though they were not an object of free trade, since they could not be acquired by people not belonging to the monastery. It witnesses moreover that atmosphere of formalistic pedantry which we have already observed: the monks' concern about the possibility of complications that would cause them to forfeit a hermitage in which they have invested money, the monks' need of gathering evidence that might be useful in case of complications. It is not enough for them to make a contract in the presence of the prior and/or of witnesses: they want to have a notarial document. Other texts from Bawit, published by Sarah Clackson, show an analogous phenomenon: the regulation of relationships inside a monastery by means of documents.[17]

M. Krause maintained that the selling and buying of monastic dwellings was a consequence of economic difficulties due to the fiscal pressure exerted by the Arabs. However, in the years 511-513, when our *P.Dubl.* were written, the monastic movement was flourishing (single communities might have had difficulties from time to time, but monks as a social category enjoyed prestige and had a privileged position when it came to calculating the fiscal burdens). The phenomenon asks for a different explanation, outside of economy.

---

[17] I studied this phenomenon in Wipszycka 2001.

Bibliography

Apophtegmes (2003). *Les Apophtegmes des pères. Collection systématique*, vol. II, *Chapitres X-XVI*. Introduction, texte critique, traduction par J.-C. Guy, s.j. (*SC* 74). Paris : Editions du Cerf.

Bachatly, C. (1982). *Le monastère de Phoebammon dans la Thébaïde*. Cairo: Publications de la Société d'archéologie copte.

Flinders Petrie, P. (1889). *Hawara, Biahmu and Arsinoe*, London.

Flusin, B. (2007). "Sain Sabas ; un leader monastique à l'autorité contestée," in: Camplani, A. and Filoramo, G., *Foundations of Power and Conflicts of Authority in Late-Antique Monasticism*. Louvain: Peeters, 195-216.

Gascou, J. (1990). "Nabla/Labla," *CdE* 65, 111-115.

Gascou, J. (1997). "Les ἀλλόφυλοι," *REG* 110, 285-294.

Godlewski, W. (1988). *Le monastère de St. Phoibammon*. Warsaw, 63-65.

Isaïe, *Recueil ascétique* (1985). Abbé Isaïe, *Recueil ascétique*. Introduction par Dom L. Regnault osb. et traduction française par Dom H. de Broc, osb. Troisième édition revue et augmentée. Abbaye de Bellefontaine.

Krause, M. (1981). "Zwei Phoibammon-Klöster in Theben-West," *MDAIK* 37, 155-160.

McCoull, L. (1994). "The Bawit Contracts: Texts and Translations," *BASP* 31, 141-158.

McGing, B.C.M. (1990). "Melitian Monks at Labla," *Tyche* 5, 67-94.

Richter, T.S. (1999). "Spätkoptische Rechtsurkunden neu bearbeitet: BM OR 4917(15) und P.Med. Copto inv. 69.69," *JJP* 29, 85-89.

Steinwenter, A. (1935). "Zur Edition der koptischen Rechtsurkunden aus Djême," *Orientalia* N.s. 4, 377-385.

Till, W. C. (1964). *Die koptischen Rechtsurkunden aus Theben*. Wien.

Wipszycka, E. (2001). "Le fonctionnement interne des monastères et des laures en Égypte du point de vue économique," *JJP* 31, 169-186.

Zanetti, U. (1996). "La Vie de saint Jean, higoumène de Scété au VIIe siècle," *AnBoll* 114, 273-405.

INDICES TO COPTIC, GREEK, AND ARABIC TEXTS

INDICES

This consolidated index covers only the Greek, Coptic and Arabic (in transliteration) terms appearing in the text editions, arranged according to the Greek/Coptic alphabet. *P.Clackson* **35** has been omitted as this is an alphabetical list of Coptic words.

1. Personal Names

ʻAbd al-Malik	**45**.3	ⲕⲩⲣⲁⲕⲁⲗⲏ	**44**.18
Ἀβραάμιος	**46**.3	Κῦρος	**4**.7
ⲁⲃⲣⲁϩⲁⲙ	**40**.2	ⲙⲁⲕⲁⲣⲉ	**41**.5?
Ἀνούφιος	**48**.9	Μασκοι	**48**.7
Ἀπα Κῖρε	**11**.1/2; **12**.2; **13**.1	Μηνᾶ	**39**.5
Ἀπολλῶ	**48**.3; **48v**.3	ⲙⲏⲛⲁ	**40**.7
ⲁⲡⲟⲗⲗⲱ	**7**.5; **47**.1	Μήτρας	**49**.1
Ἀφοῦς	**50**.2	Μουσαῖος	**38**.2; **39**.3
Βίκτωρ	**14**.1; **36**.4; **37**.4; **39**.4	ⲡⲉⲧⲣⲟⲥ	**5**.3
Γεώργιος	**46**.1, 3; **48**.8	ⲡⲉⲧⲣⲉ	**6**.5
Γεωργε	**37**.1	ⲡⲓⲕ	**40**.5
Δωράνης	**49**.2	Πινουτίων	**36**.3
ⲉⲛⲱⲭ/ Ἐνωχ	**1**.4; **8**.3; **15**.1	ⲡⲣⲱⲟⲩ	**40**.11
Ζαχαρίας	**46**.3	Σαιας	**36**.1
Ηεγλαν	**Fournet**.9	ⲥⲉⲩⲏⲣⲟⲥ (ⲁⲡⲁ)	**44**.15
Θεοδώρα	**48v**.2	ⲥϩⲓⲗⲁ	**45**.13
Ἱερακίων	**49**.1	ⲥⲧ[	**47**.1
ⲓⲥⲓⲁⲱ[ⲣⲟⲥ	**45**.14; **47**.3b	Ταυρῖνε	**16**.2
Ἰοῦστος	**48**.5	Φῖβ	**37**.3
Ἰσακ( )	**48**.6	Yaḥyā	**45**.11
Isidūr	**45**.3	Yazīd	**45**.3
Ἰωάννης	**36**.5; **46**.1; **48**.1,4	Yuḥannis	**45**.4
ⲓⲱⲁⲛⲏⲥ	**10**.6	Ziyād	**45**.3
ⲓⲱⲁⲛ(ⲛⲏ)ⲥ	**45**.14		
Hishām	**45**.3		

2. Place Names

Aʻlā Ashmūn	**45**.5	ⲙⲁ ⲛⲁⲣⲓⲱⲛ	**33**.2
Dayr Abū Abūlū	**45**.5	ⲙⲁ ⲛⲛⲉⲡⲏⲣⲅⲟⲥ	**26**.1, **27**.2, **28**.2, **29**.2
ⲙⲁ ⲛⲁⲡⲟⲗⲱⲛ	**19**.2, **20**.2, **21**.3, **22**.2/3(?), **23**.2, **24**.3, **25**.3	ⲙⲁ ⲛⲡⲁⲃⲓⲛⲉⲟⲥ	**30**.2, **31**.1, **32**.1
		ⲡⲙⲁ ⲛ̄ⲁⲡⲁⲭⲱⲓ̈	**5**.2; **6**.3
		ⲡⲙⲁ ⲛⲃⲓϫ	**1**.2

[ⲡ]ⲙⲁ ⲛ̄ⲕⲩⲣⲓⲥ	3.4	τόπος νοταρίου	16.1
ⲡⲙⲟⲛⲁⲥ(ⲧⲏⲣⲓⲟⲛ) ⲛ̄ⲫⲁⲅⲓⲟⲥ ⲁⲡⲁ ⲁⲡⲟⲗⲗⲱ	47.2	ϥⲟⲓ ⲛ̄ⲕⲗⲁⲩⲇⲉ	8.2
		ϥⲟⲓ ⲛ̄ⲙⲁⲕⲁⲣⲉ	10.3
ⲡⲙⲟⲛⲁⲥⲧⲏⲣⲓⲟⲛ ⲛ̄ⲁⲡⲁ ⲁⲡⲟⲗⲗⲱ	45.14/15	ϥⲟⲓⲡⲁⲧⲁⲡⲉ	7.4/5
		ϥⲟⲓ[	4.5
Ἁγίου Ἀπολλῶ	50.2	ϣⲙⲟⲩⲛ	45.14
ⲡⲟϩⲉ	3.2	…]ⲗⲟ	9.4
Τιτκῶις	48.1	…]ⲛⲉⲙⲟⲛⲧ	4.4

3. ABSOLUTE DATES

December 753	**45**	10 January 758?	**46**

4. PROFESSIONS AND TITLES

ἀββᾶ	**49**.1	μαυλε	**Fournet**.6
ἀγγαρευτής	**49**.2	μονάζων	**36**.1; **37**.2; **38**.1; **48**.1; **50**.2
ἄμα	**48v**.2		
ʿāmil	**45**.3	ⲛⲟⲧ(ⲁⲣⲓⲟⲥ)?	**40**.3
amīr	**45**.3	ὁσιώτατος	
ἀνυτής	**48**.1	ϩⲟⲥⲓⲱⲧ(ⲁⲧⲟⲥ)	**43**.5
ⲁⲣⲭ(ⲓ)ⲙ(ⲁⲛ)ⲁ(ⲣⲓⲧⲏⲥ)	**41**.5; **47**.2	ⲟⲩⲟⲉⲓⲉ	**40**.10
ⲃⲟⲏⲑⲟⲥ	**45**.17	ⲟⲩⲟⲉⲓⲉⲙⲁⲥⲉ	**1**.4; **4**.4/5 (?)
ⲉⲓⲱⲧ ⲙ̄ⲡⲧⲟⲡⲟⲥ	**47**.3	ⲡⲁⲥⲟⲛ	**47**.1
εὐλαβέστατος	**49**.1	πιστικός	**5**.4; **10**.6
ⲕⲁⲑⲏⲅⲏⲧⲏⲥ	**36**.5	πρεσβύτερος	**48**.3
καμηλίτης	**15**.2	qubbāl (qaryatika)	**45**.6
ⲙⲁⲛⲉⲁⲙⲟⲩⲗ	**7**.5/6	ⲥⲉϣⲧ	**40**.8
ⲙⲛ̄ⲧⲣⲉ	**42**.2,3		

5. MEASURES AND CONTAINERS

ἀθηναῖον (μέτρον)		θαλλίον	**1**.5; **4**.8; **5**.4; **6**.6; **7**.6; **8**.4; **10**.7; **11**.3; **12**.3; **13**.3; **14**.2; **15**.2
ⲁⲑⲉ/	**1**.3; **2**.5,8; **47**.6		
ἀρτάβη	**1**.5; **2**.3,7; **4**.6; **5**.4; **7**.4,7; **10**.4; **13**.3; **47**.6		
		καμήλιον	**11**.2; **12**.2; **13**.2; **14**.2
		μγ	**16**.3
διακονία		οⲓⲡⲉ	
ⲇⲓⲁⲕⲟⲛⲓⲁ	**43**.2	ⲕⲟⲩⲓ ⲛ̄[ⲟⲓⲡⲉ?	**4**.6
		ⲟⲓⲡⲉ ⲛ̄ⲧⲁⲑⲉⲛⲏⲥ	**47**.4
		σάκκος	

ⲥⲁⲕⲕ	18.3		28.4, 29.4, 30.3, 31.2, 32.2, 33.3
ⲥⲁⲕ	19.3, 20.3, 21.4, 22.4, 23.3, 24.4, 25.4, 26.3, 27.4,	ⲥⲟⲟⲩⲛⲉ	1.1; 2.2,4; 3.1; 5.1; 6.2; 7.2; 8.1; 9.2; 10.2

6. Wares

(ἄραξ)			19.4, 20.4; 21.5;
ⲁⲣⲁⲕⲉ	2.5		22.5; 23.4; 24.5;
κριθή	2.6,8		25.5; 26.4; 27.6;
[λ]ⲁ̣ⲯ̇ⲁⲛⲉ	17.4		28.6; 29.6; 30.4;
ⲛ̣ⲉ︤ϩ︥	44.13		31.3; 32.4; 33.4; 47.6
οἶνος παλαιός	16.3	ⲥⲟⲩⲟ	1.2; 2.3; 4.3; 5.2; 6.3;
σῖτος	1.3,5; 2.3,7; 4.6; 5.3; 6.4,6; 7.4,6,7; 8.4; 10.4; 15.2; 18.3 ;	ψωμίον	7.3; 9.2; 10.2 49.2,3
		ϩⲙ︤ϫ︥	44.26

7. Taxes

ἀνδρισμός	36.2; 37.2	jizyat ra'sika	45.5
ⲇⲓⲁⲅⲣⲁⲫⲟⲛ	45.16		
jizya	45.9		

8. Coinage

ἀρίθμιον	36.3; 37.3; 39.2; 46.2; 47.6	νόμισμα	36.2; 45.16; 46.2; 48.1-10 ; 48v.1-4
dīnārayn	45.6	χρυ(σοῦ νόμισμα)	47.6
(κεράτιον)	50.3	ϩⲟⲗⲟⲕ[	47.4

9. Various (Technical) Terms or Forms

ⲁⲅⲁⲑⲟⲛ	44.7		27.4, 28.4, 29.4,
ahl	45.5		30.3, 31.2, 32.2, 33.3
(ἅμαξα)		aṣāba (aṣābaka)	45.5
ⲁⲙⲁ︤ϩ︥	18.3, 19.3, 20.3, 21.4, 22.4, 23.3, 24.4, 25.4, 26.2,	ⲁϭⲟⲗⲧⲉ 'atā	18.4
		wa-'tīnī (!)	45.10
		ya'tīnī	45.11

βοήθεια γενοῦ	**Fournet**.3	μόνα	46.3
βούλλα		(μυλών)	
ⲃⲟⲩⲗⲗⲁ	45.18	ⲙⲟⲩⲗⲟⲛ	18.2, **19**.5, **20**.5,
(βουλλίζειν)			21.6, **22**.6, **23**.5,
ⲃⲟⲩⲗⲓⲍⲉ	45.18		24.6, **25**.6, **28**.7,
dafaʿa			30.5, **31**.4, **32**.5, **33**.5
fa-dfaʿ	45.6	(παρὰ μέρος)	
lā tadfaʿ	45.7	ⲡⲁⲣⲁⲙⲉⲣⲟⲥ	18.5/6
an yadfaʿahā	45.10	(πιττάκιον)	
lā tadfaʿanna	45.10	ⲡⲓⲧⲧⲁⲕⲓⲟⲛ	45.22
ἐγράφη	3.5	ⲡⲗⲏⲛ	44.3
ἔγραψα	4.7; **36**.3; **37**.3; **38**.2;	(πρώτη)	
	39.3	ⲡⲣⲱᵀ	10.5
		qarya	45.6; 8
(ἐντάγιον)		στοιχεῖν	**36**.4; **36**.5 (στηχεῖ);
ⲉⲛⲧⲁⲅⲓⲛ	45.18,20		**37**.3; **37**.4 (στηχε);
ⲉⲛⲧⲁⲅⲉⲛ	45.22		**38**.3; **39**.4,5; **46**.3
εὐχαριστεῖν		ṭabl (aṭbāl)	45.7
ⲉⲩⲭⲁⲣⲓⲥⲧⲁ	44.8	τρίας	
iktataba (yaktatiba)	45.7	ⲧⲣⲓⲁⲥ	44.22
(κανών)		φορά	1.7; **5**.4; **6**.8; **7**.8; **8**.5;
ⲕⲁⲛⲱⲛ	45.16		10.5 (ϕⲱ); **11**.1;
(καταβολή)			12.1; **13**.1; **14**.1;
ⲕⲁⲧⲁⲃⲟⲩⲗⲏ	45.17		15.1; **16**.5
khātam	45.7		
kitāb	45.3		

10. Symbols

⸗ (artabe)	1.3,5; **5**.3; **6**.4,6; **18**.3, **19**.4, **20**.4, **21**.5, **22**.5, **23**.4, **24**.5, **25**.5, **26**.4, **27**.6,
	28.6, **29**.6, **30**.4, **31**.3, **32**.4, **33**.4
ϛ (καί)	1.5; **2**.3,8; **47**.6

PLATES

Plate I

1
SBKopt. I 226 = Ägyptologisches Institut Heidelberg inv. 993

2
SBKopt. I 234 = Ägyptologisches Institut Heidelberg inv. 998

Plate II

3

SBKopt. I 233 = Ägyptologisches Institut Heidelberg inv. 994

4

SBKopt. I 230 = Ägyptologisches Institut Heidelberg inv. 987

PLATE III

5
SBKopt. I 227 = Ägyptologisches Institut Heidelberg inv. 996

6
SBKopt. I 228 = Ägyptologisches Institut Heidelberg inv. 980

PLATE IV

7
SBKopt. I 229 = Ägyptologisches Institut Heidelberg inv. 979

8
SBKopt. I 231 = Ägyptologisches Institut Heidelberg inv. 986

PLATE V

9
SBKopt. I 232 = Ägyptologisches Institut Heidelberg inv. 981

10
Ägyptologisches Institut Heidelberg inv. 995

PLATE VI

11
SB XVIII 13563 = Ägyptologisches Institut Heidelberg inv. 984

12
SB XVIII 13564 = Ägyptologisches Institut Heidelberg inv. 992

PLATE VII

13
Ägyptologisches Institut Heidelberg inv. 988

14
Ägyptologisches Institut Heidelberg inv. 991

PLATE VIII

15
Ägyptologisches Institut Heidelberg inv. 990

16
Ägyptologisches Institut Heidelberg inv. 983

PLATE IX

17
Ägyptologisches Institut Heidelberg inv. 997

Crédits photographiques: Ägyptologisches Institut Heidelberg

PLATE X

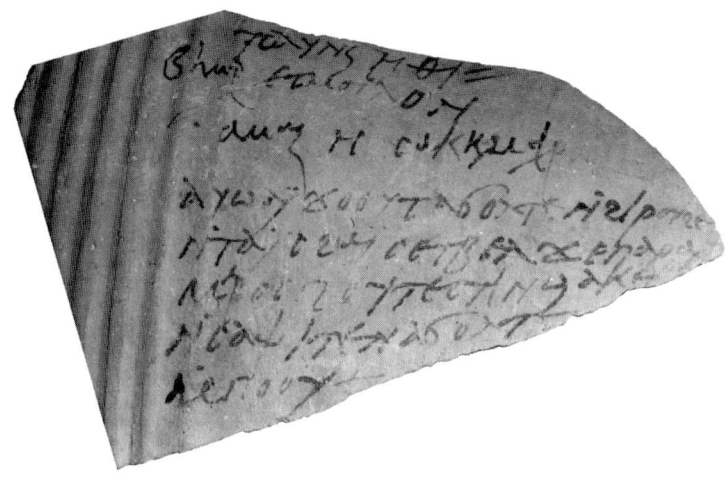

18
O.Brit.Mus. inv. GR 1999.6-29.1
(Photo: Charles Ede, Ltd.)

19
O.Berol. inv. 14705
Ägyptisches Museum u. Papyrussammlung SMB
(Photo: Margarete Büsing)

PLATE XI

25
SBKopt. I 151 = Kelsey Mus. inv. 25009
Courtesy of the Kelsey Museum of Archaeology

26
O.Berol. inv. 14706
Ägyptisches Museum u. Papyrussammlung SMB
(Photo: Margarete Büsing)

PLATE XII

29
SBKopt. I 167 = Kelsey Mus. inv. 25028
Courtesy of the Kelsey Museum of Archaeology

31
O.Berol. inv. 14713
Ägyptisches Museum u. Papyrussammlung SMB
(Photo: Margarete Büsing)

PLATE XIII

32
SBKopt. I 185 = Kelsey Mus. inv. 25041
Courtesy of the Kelsey Museum of Archaeology

33
O.IFAO
Reproduit avec l'autorisation de l'IFAO

PLATE XIV

34
Kelsey Mus. inv. 25124
Courtesy of the Kelsey Museum of Archaeology

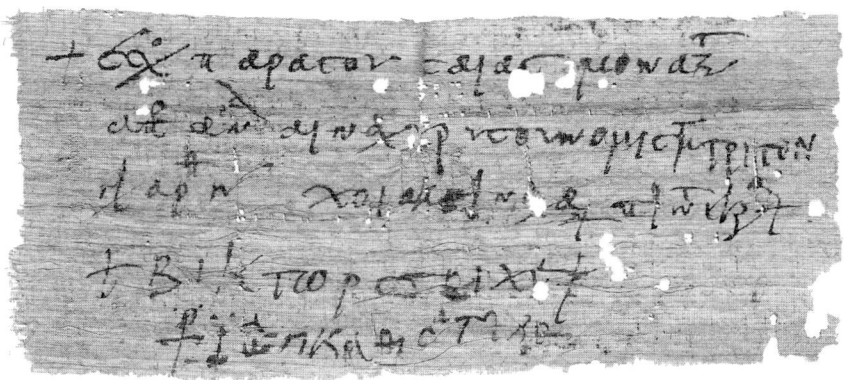

36
P. Heid. inv. K. 308 v.

37
P. CtYBR inv. 1841 v.

38
P. Brux. inv. E. 9483 v.

PLATE XVI

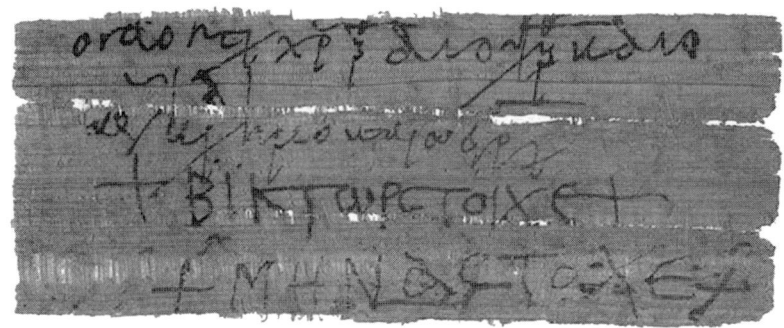

39
P.CtYBR inv. 1843 v.

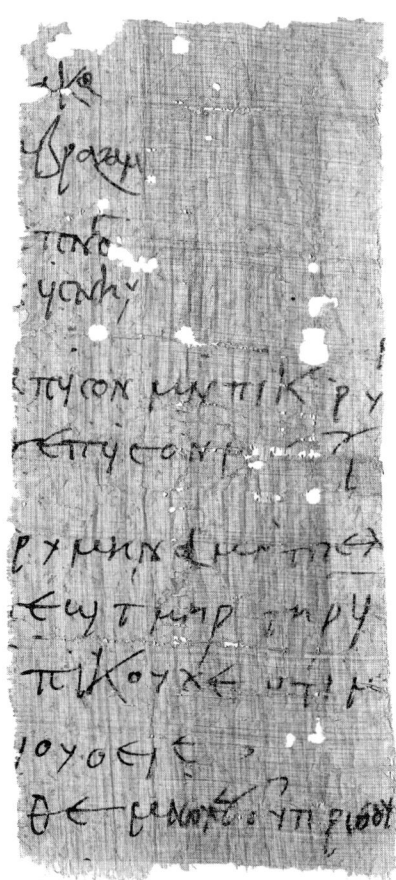

40
P.Heid. inv. K. 308 r.

PLATE XVII

41
P.CtYBR inv. 1841 r.

42
P.Brux. inv. E. 9483 r.

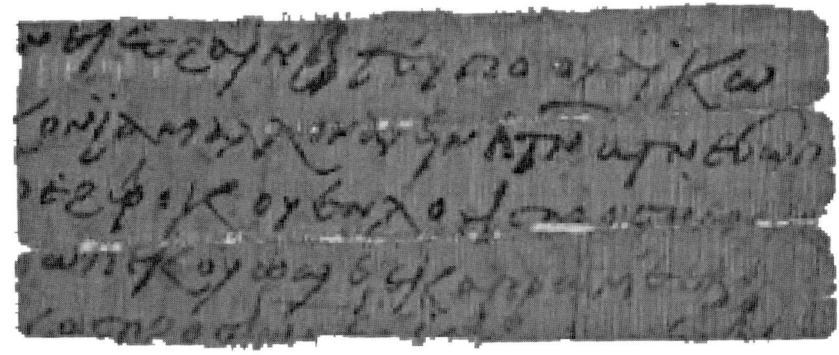

43
P.CtYBR inv. 1843 r.

PLATE XVIII

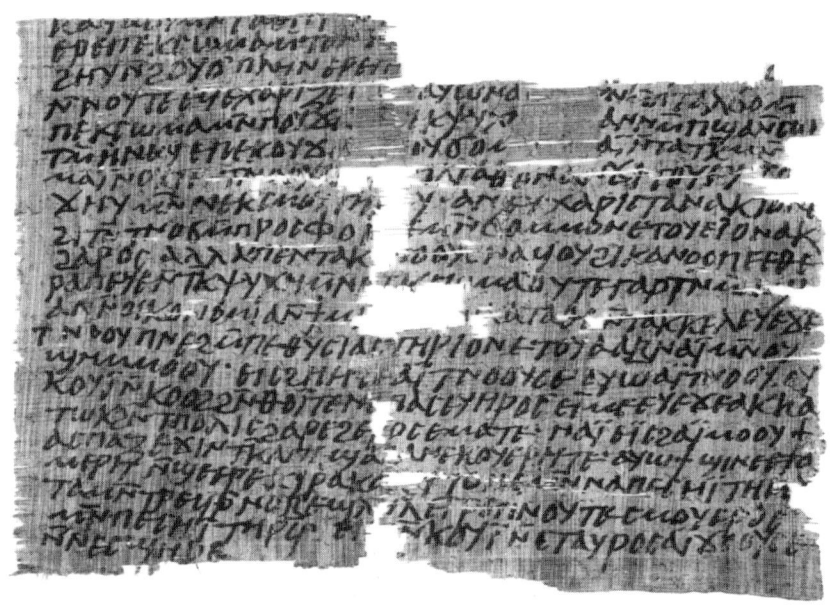

44
P.Vindob. K. 4725 v.

44
P.Vindob. K. 4725 r.

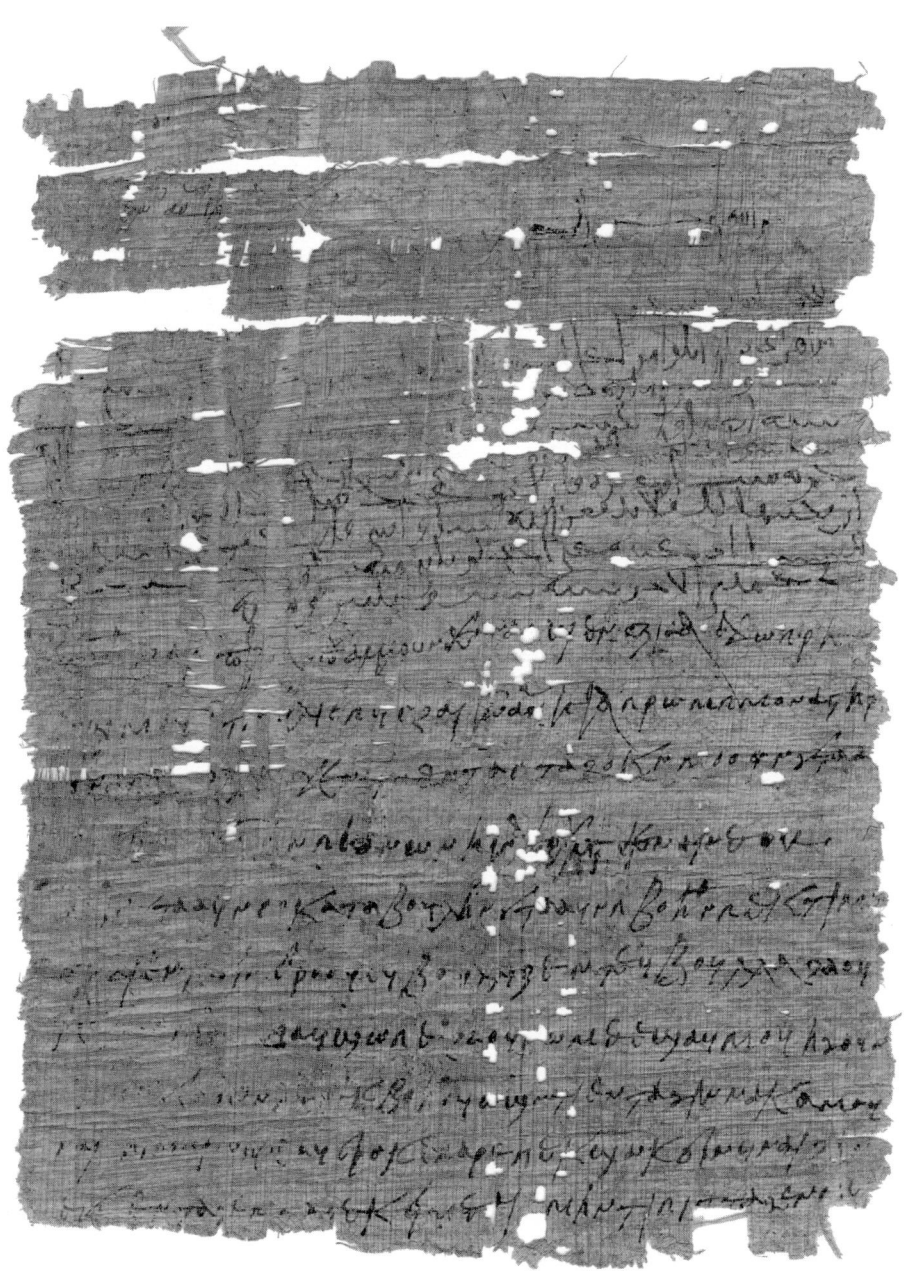

45
P.Camb.UL Michael. 807 r.

46
P.Camb.UL Michael. 807 v.

Plate XXI

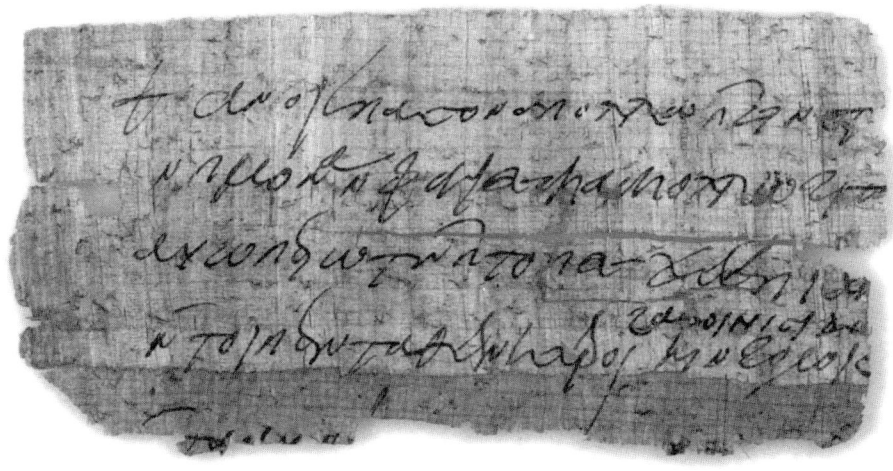

47
P.Monts.Roca inv. 549 v.

47
P.Monts.Roca inv. 549 r.

PLATE XXII

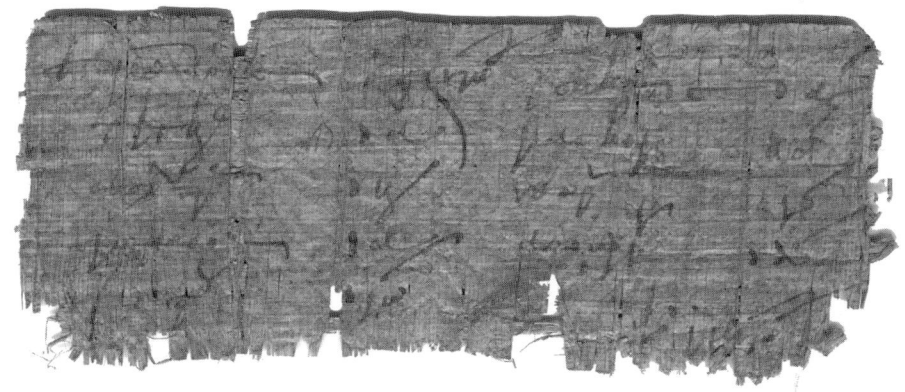

48
P.Monts.Roca inv. 516 r.

48
P.Monts.Roca inv. 516 v.

PLATE XXIII

49
P.Monts.Roca inv. 619

50
P.Monts.Roca inv. 713

PLATE XXIV

50
P.Monts.Roca inv. 713, seal [1]

50
P.Monts.Roca inv. 713, seal [2]